**From Classical to Quantum Coding**

**IEEE Press**
445 Hoes Lane
Piscataway, NJ 08854

# From Classical to Quantum Coding

*Zunaira Babar*
*University of Southampton*
*UK*

*Daryus Chandra*
*University of Southampton*
*UK*

*Soon Xin Ng*
*University of Southampton*
*UK*

*Lajos Hanzo*
*University of Southampton*
*UK*

IEEE Press
WILEY

Published by John Wiley & Sons, Inc., Hoboken, New Jersey.



For general information on our other products and services or for technical support, please contact our Customer Care Department within the United States at (800) 762-2974, outside the United States at (317) 572-3993 or fax (317) 572-4002.

Wiley also publishes its books in a variety of electronic formats. Some content that appears in print may not be available in electronic formats. For more information about Wiley products, visit our web site at www.wiley.com.

***Library of Congress Cataloging-in-Publication Data has been applied for:***

Print ISBN: 9781394331932
ePDF ISBN: 9781394331956
ePub ISBN: 9781394331949
oBook ISBN: 9781394331963

Cover Design: Wiley
Cover Image: © tosha_genije/Getty Images

*We dedicate this book to the numerous contributors of the field, whose work has been cited.*

## Other Wiley/IEEE Press Books by the Authors

- R. Steele and L. Hanzo (Ed), *Mobile Radio Communications: Second and Third Generation Cellular and WATM Systems*. John Wiley and IEEE Press, 2nd edition, 1999, ISBN 07 273-1406-8, 1064 pages.
- L. Hanzo, T. H. Liew, and B. L. Yeap, *Turbo Coding, Turbo Equalisation and Space-time Coding*. John Wiley and IEEE Press, 2002, 751 pages.
- L. Hanzo, C. H. Wong, and M. S. Yee, *Adaptive Wireless Transceivers: Turbo-coded, Turbo-equalised and Space-time Coded TDMA, CDMA and OFDM Systems*. John Wiley and IEEE Press, 2002, 737 pages.
- L. Hanzo, L.-L. Yang, E.-L. Kuan, and K. Yen, *Single-and Multi-carrier CDMA: Multi-user Detection, Space-time Spreading, Synchronisation, Networking and Standards*. John Wiley and IEEE Press, June 2003, 1060 pages.
- L. Hanzo, M. Münster, T. Keller, and B.-J. Choi, *OFDM and MC-CDMA for Broadband Multi-user Communications, WLANs and Broadcasting*. John Wiley and IEEE Press, 2003, 978 pages.
- L. Hanzo, S.-X. Ng, T. Keller, and W. T. Webb, *Quadrature Amplitude Modulation: From Basics to Adaptive Trellis-coded, Turbo-equalised and Space-time Coded OFDM, CDMA and MC-CDMA Systems*. John Wiley and IEEE Press, 2004, 1105 pages.
- L. Hanzo and T. Keller, *An OFDM and MC-CDMA Primer*. John Wiley and IEEE Press, 2006, 430 pages.
- L. Hanzo, F. C. A. Somerville, and J. P. Woodard, *Voice and Audio Compression for Wireless Communications*, John Wiley and IEEE Press, 2007, 858 pages.
- L. Hanzo, P. J. Cherriman, and J. Streit, *Video Compression and Communications: H.261, H.263, H.264, MPEG4 and HSDPA-style Adaptive Turbo-transceivers*. John Wiley and IEEE Press, 2007, 680 pages.
- L. Hanzo, J. S. Blogh, and S. Ni, *3G, HSDPA, HSUPA and FDD Versus TDD Networking: Smart Antennas and Adaptive Modulation*. John Wiley and IEEE Press, 2008, 564 pages.
- L. Hanzo, O. Alamri, M. El-Hajjar, and N. Wu, *Near-capacity Multi-functional MIMO Systems: Sphere-packing, Iterative Detection and Cooperation*. IEEE Press and John Wiley, 2009.
- L. Hanzo, J. Akhtman, M. Jiang, and L. Wang, *MIMO-OFDM for LTE, WIFI and WIMAX: Coherent versus Non-Coherent and Cooperative Turbo-transceivers*. John Wiley and IEEE Press, 2010, 608 pages.
- L. Hanzo, R. G. Maunder, J. Wang, and L.-L. Yang, *Near-capacity Variable-length Coding*. John Wiley and IEEE Press, 2010, 608 pages, 2011, 494 pages.

1 For detailed contents and sample chapters please refer to http://www-mobile.ecs.soton.ac.uk

# Contents

## About the Authors

**Zunaira Babar** received B.Eng. degree from the National University of Science and Technology (NUST), Pakistan, in 2008, and the MSc (Hons) and PhD degrees from the University of Southampton, UK, in 2011 and 2015, respectively. Currently, she is a staff research scientist at VIAVI Marconi Labs, UK. She published numerous journal papers on quantum communications.

**Daryus Chandra** received the BEng and MEng degrees from Universitas Gadjah Mada (UGM), Indonesia, in 2013 and 2014, respectively, and the PhD degree from the University of Southampton, UK, in 2020. Currently, he is a senior quantum error correction researcher at Photonic Inc., Canada. He has published widely on quantum communications.

**Soon Xin Ng** (S'99-M'03-SM'08) received the BEng degree (First class) in electronic engineering and the PhD degree in telecommunications from the University of Southampton, UK, in 1999 and 2002, respectively. He is currently a professor of Next Generation Communications at the University of Southampton. He has published widely in classical and quantum communications. He is a senior member of the IEEE, a Chartered Engineer, a Fellow of the Higher Education Academy in the UK, and a Fellow of IET.

**Lajos Hanzo** (FIEEE'04, fellow of the Royal Academy of Engineering (FREng), of the IET and of EURASIP) received Honorary Doctorates from the Technical University of Budapest (2009) and Edinburgh University (2015). He is a foreign member of the Hungarian Academy of Sciences, fellow of the Royal Academy of Engineering (FREng), IET, and EURASIP, and holds the IEEE Eric Sumner Technical Field Award.

## List of Acronyms

| | |
|---|---|
| BCH | Bose–Chaudhuri–Hocquenghem |
| BER | Bit Error Rate |
| CNOT | Controlled-NOT |
| CSS | Calderbank–Shor–Steane |
| DFS | Decoherence-free Subspace |
| EA | Entanglement-assisted |
| EXIT | EXtrinsic Information Transfer |
| GV | Gilbert–Varshamov |
| LDPC | Low-density Parity-check |
| LUT | Look-up Table |
| MDS | Maximum Separable Distance |
| MRRW | McEliece–Rodemich–Rumsey–Welch |
| PCM | Parity-check Matrix |
| QBCH | Quantum Bose–Chaudhuri–Hocquenghem |
| QBER | QuBit Error Ratio |
| QCC | Quantum Convolutional Code |
| QECC | Quantum Error Correction Code |
| QEDC | Quantum Error Detection Code |
| QIrCC | Quantum Irregular Convolutional Code |
| QLDPC | Quantum Low-density Parity-check |
| QPC | Quantum Polar Code |
| QRM | Quantum Reed–Muller |
| QRS | Quantum Reed–Solomon |
| QSBC | Quantum Short-block Code |
| QSC | Quantum Stabilizer Code |
| QTC | Quantum Turbo Code |
| QTECC | Quantum Topological Error Correction Code |

| | |
|---|---|
| QURC | Quantum Unity-rate Code |
| RS | Reed–Solomon |
| SBC | Short-block Code |
| SPC | Single Parity-check |
| TECC | Topological Error Correction Code |

## Preface

*Many thanks for your interest in this book, valued Colleague!*

*Naturally, our intention with the book is multifold, but primarily to pave the way for the classical coding community to enter the field of quantum coding.*

Quantum error correction codes are expected to play a pivotal role in terms of mitigating the deleterious effects of quantum decoherence, which limits the performance of both quantum computers and quantum-secured communications systems. Indeed, error correction codes are ubiquitous even in less susceptible classical communications and storage systems. Explicitly, all digital wireless systems conceived over the past five decades heavily relied on the potent signal-decontamination capability of classical error correction codes. They are also capable of estimating the system's operating status by monitoring the prevalent error rate and exploit this for the near-instantaneous reconfiguration of the system. Similar benefits may be anticipated also for quantum systems upon harnessing quantum codes, because quantum systems are significantly more susceptible to corruption by the surrounding electromagnetic environment.

A complex-valued qubit may be exposed to a bit-flip, a phase-flip or to a simultaneous bit- and phase-flip. Hence, the first ever 1/9-rate quantum code was conceived by Peter Shor by simply exploiting the fact that a 1/3-rate repetition code can separately be applied for guarding against bit- and phase-flips. Calderbank, Steane and Shor later defined the specific conditions under which this appealingly simple principle may be extended to the employment of more sophisticated near-capacity classical codes for conceiving powerful quantum codes. Hence, in this self-contained monograph, we portray this evolutionary process from the first principles all the way to the design of adaptive-rate near-hashing-bound codes.

Part I provides a gentle introduction to the rudimentary principles, paving the way for readers familiar with classical coding to quantum coding, including the associated quantum and classical coding basics. Part II is dedicated to the family of near-term quantum codes, which do not require a high number of qubits and, hence, are suitable for near-term intermediate scale (NISC) quantum computers, for example. Finally, Part III elaborates on the design of a suite of sophisticated long-term quantum coding solutions, when having a relatively high number of qubits becomes realistic, as quantum technology matures. A range of adaptive-rate quantum codes are also conceived for practical scenarios of time-variant depolarizing probability.

*Wishing you intellectual stimulation, valued Colleague!*

# Acknowledgments

We are indebted to our many colleagues who have enhanced our understanding of the subject. These colleagues and valued friends, too numerous to be mentioned individually, have influenced our views concerning the subject of the book. We thank them for the enlightenment gained from our collaborations on various projects, papers, and books. We are particularly grateful to our academic colleagues Professors Sheng Chen, Mohammed El-Hajjar, Rob Maunder, Lie-Liang Yang, and Dr. Chao Xu. We would also like to express our gratitude to our former colleagues and collaborators, Drs. Dimitrios Alanis, Panagiotis Botsinis, Jing-Jing Cui, Balint Koczor, Hung Viet Nguyen, Yifeng Xiong, Prof. Dan Browne, and Thomas Melham.

Finally, Lajos Hanzo would like to gratefully acknowledge the financial support of the following research projects: the Beam-Me-Up and QuantCom Advanced Fellow Grants of the European Research Council (ERC); the Platform for Driving Ultimate Connectivity (TITAN) funded by the Engineering and Physical Sciences Research Council (EPSRC), UK; and Robust and Reliable Quantum Computing (RoaRQ) of the EPSRC.

*Zunaira Babar, Daryus Chandra, Soon Xin Ng, and Lajos Hanzo*
*School of Electronics and Computer Science*
*University of Southampton, UK*

# Part I

# From Classical to Quantum Codes

# 1

# Introduction

## 1.1 Motivation

In 1935, Erwin Schrödinger, an Austrian physicist, proposed a thought experiment to illustrate the interpretation of uncertainty in quantum mechanics. This thought experiment later acquired the fond connotation of the "Schrödinger's Cat" experiment [1, 2]. In this treatise, we will refer to another thought experiment, namely the "Black Box Experiment." Let us assume that we have a black box with a coin spinning in it. It does not have to be a fair coin. Inside the box, we then start spinning the coin. We do not have any prior knowledge about the coin, namely whether the coin is fair or biased and we do not know whether it landed on the face or the tail side when it finally stopped spinning. At this moment, we may say that the coin inside the box is within a *superposition* of two states and has a certain probability for each of the two states. Let us continue the experiment by using several boxes. We may proceed by using two, three, or even an arbitrary number of $N \in \mathbb{N}$ boxes for this experiment. Similarly, we spin all the $N$ coins simultaneously and close the boxes. This situation may be viewed as having $2^N$ states, suggesting that we can increase the computational power exponentially in line with $2^N$ if we can exploit the above-mentioned superposition. Let us now continue the experiment with the following step. Up to this moment, all of the boxes are completely sealed and we have secured the $2^N$ states of the coins simultaneously. Now, we decide to open all of the boxes at once and observe all the coins. After observing the state of each coin in each box, we are now in the position to observe a single specific state from the full set of $2^N$ possible states. This illustrates that after lifting the lid of the boxes the quantum states suddenly collapse into a single deterministic classical state due to the action of "observation," which is also often termed in parlance as a "measurement." This property is exploited by quantum computers, which will create a powerful computational tool that is potentially capable of breaking conventional cryptography.

Consequently, while an $N$-bit classical register can store only a single $N$-bit value, an $N$-qubit quantum register can store all the $2^N$ states concurrently. This allows the parallel evaluation of certain functions with regular global structure at a complexity cost that is equivalent to a single classical evaluation [3, 4], as illustrated in Figure 1.1. Therefore, as exemplified by Shor's factorization algorithm [5] and Grover's search algorithm [6], quantum-based computation is capable of solving certain complex problems at a substantially lower complexity than classical computing.

In 1965, Gordon E. Moore released the general rule of thumb projecting the number of transistors on a single integrated circuit chip used in the semiconductor industry. This notable rule of thumb was later termed "Moore's Law," which dictates that the number of the transistors on an integrated circuit chip will be doubled every 18 months or two years [9]. This law has maintained its validity over the past few decades, as illustrated in Figure 1.2, but it has been hypothesized that the trend is expected to slow down [10]. As the transistor's size is reduced, we encounter new physical phenomena as we enter the nanoscale world, which can only be described using the postulates of quantum mechanics [11]. We encounter both pros and cons as we embark on this journey into the unknown. First, the ability to create the above-mentioned simultaneous states at any instant lends itself to high-power parallel computing by exploiting the quantum-domain superposition. Second, the collapse of quantum superposition into a classical state upon observation potentially allows us to conceive unbreachable communication schemes and detect eavesdropping, which is the main advantage of quantum communication.

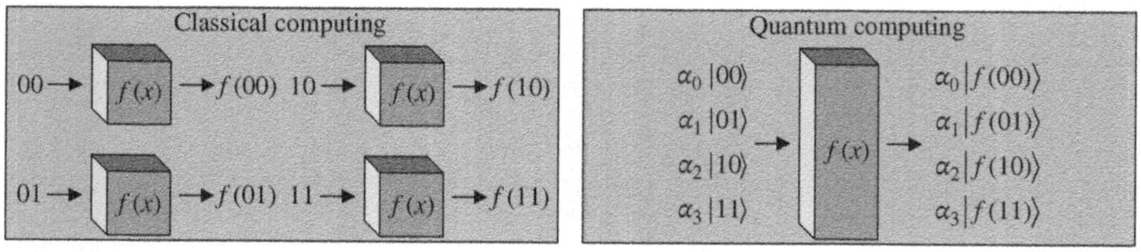


**Figure 1.1** Quantum Parallelism: Given a function $f(x)$, which has a regular global structure such that $f(x) : \{0, 1\}^2 \to \{0, 1\}^2$, a classical system requires four evaluations to compute $f(x)$ for all possible $x \in \{00, 01, 10, 11\}$. By contrast, a two-qubit quantum register can be in a superposition of all the four possible states concurrently. This may be written as $|\psi\rangle = \alpha_0\,|00\rangle + \alpha_1\,|01\rangle + \alpha_2\,|10\rangle + \alpha_3\,|11\rangle$, where the operation $|\ \rangle$ distinguishes the quantum states. Therefore, quantum computing requires only a single classical evaluation/observation to yield the outcome, which is also in a superposition of all the four possibilities, i.e. $\alpha_0\,|f(00)\rangle + \alpha_1\,|f(01)\rangle + \alpha_2\,|f(10)\rangle + \alpha_3\,|f(11)\rangle$. However, it is not possible to read all the four states, because the quantum register collapses to one of the four superimposed states upon measurement. Nevertheless, we may manipulate the resultant superposition of the four possible states before observing the quantum register for the sake of determining a desired property of the function. *Source*: Adapted from [5–8].

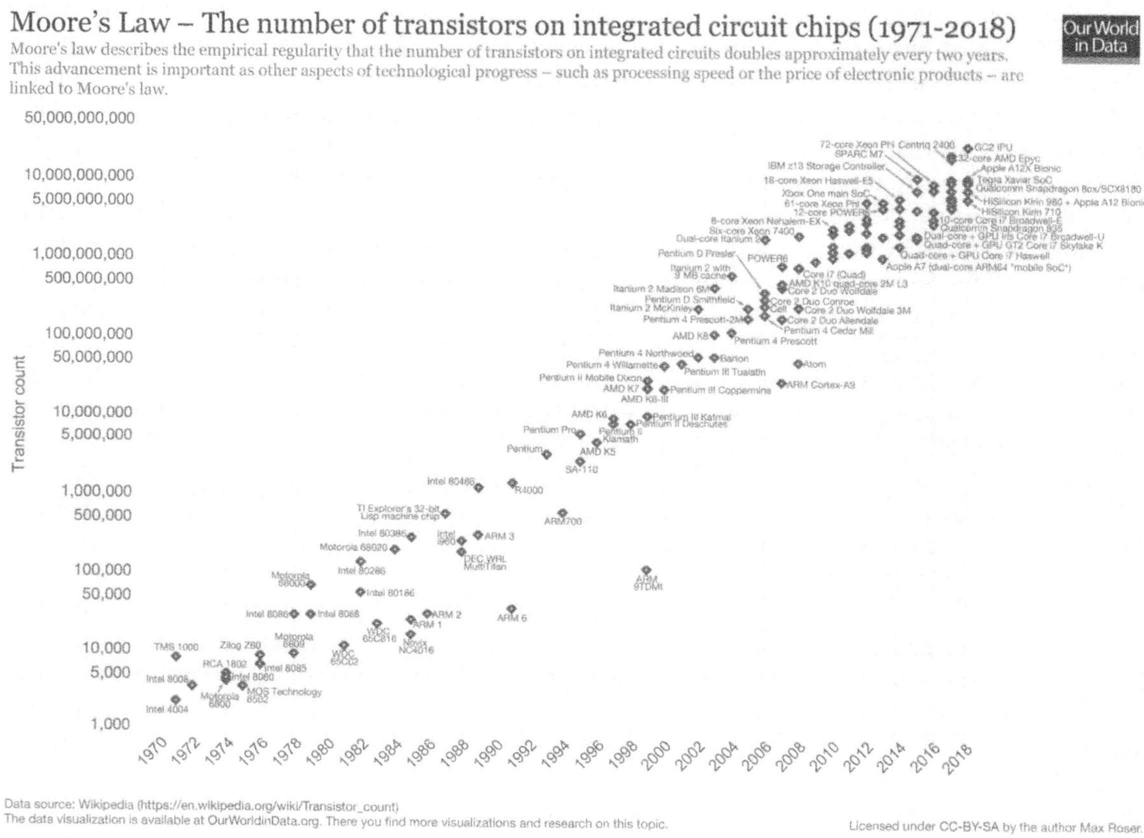


**Figure 1.2** The number of transistors on an integrated circuit has doubled every two years since 1971. *Source*: [12]/Our World in Data/CC BY 4.0.

The field of theoretical quantum computing was established five decades after the Schrödinger Cat experiment by the renowned physicist Richard Feynman, who suggested how to simulate quantum phenomena using quantum computers [13]. Since then, diverse quantum-domain algorithms have been invented and indeed have shown that the laws of quantum mechanics can help us to speed up computations in some applications [4–7, 14–26]. In parallel to the quantum computing developments, attractive quantum-based solutions capable of providing absolute security have also been conceived [27–36].

Despite the above-mentioned advances, the physical implementation of quantum computers is still far from perfection. Substantial efforts have been invested in building a scalable and reliable quantum computer relying on different solutions. For instance, by using spin electron-based techniques [37, 38], photonic chips [39–41], superconducting qubits [42–44], and recently also by using silicon [45, 46] as well as microwave trapped-ion techniques have been conceived [47, 48]. In order to arrive at the best architecture for quantum computers, the physical implementations of quantum computation must satisfy the so-called "DiVincenzo's Criteria" [49] described below:

a. **A scalable physical system with well-characterized qubits**
The elementary unit of information in classical computers is represented by *binary digits* or *bits*. Each bit can hold only a logical value of "0" or "1" at any instant, but not both. By contrast, the elementary unit of information in quantum computers is represented by a *quantum bit* or *qubit*. In quantum mechanics, the states of "0" and "1" are commonly represented using the Dirac notation, i.e. $|0\rangle$ for state "0" and $|1\rangle$ for state "1" [50]. Each qubit can hold a value of $|0\rangle$, $|1\rangle$, or the superposition of both states. The physical realization of a qubit should reliably distinguish the state $|0\rangle$ and $|1\rangle$ as well as the superposition of both states. For instance, we can have a two-level quantum system using the up/down spin states of a particle, or the ground and excited states of an atom, or the vertical and horizontal polarization of a single photon.
b. **The ability to initialize the state of the qubits to a simple fiducial state**
One of the essential requirements in classical computing is to know the initial state of a register before starting the computations. Similar requirements are also applicable in the quantum domain. For instance, to initialize the process of quantum search and quantum factoring algorithms, the quantum registers must supply a certain number of fresh auxiliary qubits in the state $|0\rangle$. Similarly, operations such as quantum teleportation, quantum superdense coding, and quantum key distribution (QKD) also require the quantum registers to provide a continuous supply of fresh qubits in a certain superposition state.
c. **Sufficiently long decoherence times, much longer than the gates' operation time**
In quantum computers, the qubits will be involved in a series of quantum-domain operations to carry out certain quantum computation or quantum communication tasks. Ideally, a quantum computing algorithm and similarly a quantum communication scheme should be designed by ensuring that the computational process or transmission finishes before the qubits are corrupted by the decoherence phenomenon caused by their undesired coupling with the surrounding environment. However, a long decoherence time does not necessarily mean that the qubits are more reliable. We primarily care about the number of operations that can be completed before the qubits decohere. Hence, we should take into account the gate operation time. The maximal number of reliable operations in quantum computers is defined by the ratio of the qubits' decoherence time to the per-gate operation duration. A quantum solution with a higher maximal number of reliable operations may be more preferable, because as we scale up the quantum computers, the number of gate operations will increase.
d. **A universal set of quantum gates**
The power of quantum computers in speeding up some computations hinges on the availability of a universal set of quantum gates. More specifically, a universal set of quantum gates primarily entails the family of gates that can be simulated by classical probabilistic computers in polynomial time – namely, the so-called Clifford group defined in [51]. Additionally, there are non-Clifford gates, which impose higher simulation complexity. Hence, in order to develop fully functioning quantum computers achieving a beneficial quantum speed-up, a set of quantum gates outside the Clifford group also have to be realized.
e. **A qubit-specific measurement capability**
Eventually, the results from a series of quantum operations carrying out certain computational tasks have to be read out. For this reason, quantum computers require so-called measurement operators, which have to be reliable and capable of operating in various measurement bases.

As for quantum communications, there are two additional criteria, as described below:

a. **The ability to convert stationary qubits to "flying" qubits and vice versa**
Numerous applications of quantum computers require the transmission of qubits to different locations. Hence, the capability of converting the stationary qubits to flying qubits is essential.
b. **The capability of reliably transmit flying qubits between specific locations**
To guarantee that the state of the qubits remains intact after their displacement to a different location, their protection against quantum decoherence is required, since we cannot completely isolate the interaction of the qubits with the surrounding environment, even when high-grade electromagnetic shielding and near-absolute-zero temperatures are used.

Quantum computers face the same problem as their classical counterparts, namely decoherence. The aforementioned criteria for developing scalable and reliable quantum computers may not be accomplishable if the deleterious effects of quantum decoherence cannot be mitigated. Therefore, it is a challenge to ensure the reliability of quantum computers in the face of ubiquitous quantum decoherence. Quantum error correction codes (QECCs) constitute one of the most popular techniques for tackling the deleterious effects of quantum decoherence. The employment of QECCs may enable quantum computers to achieve high-reliability, reproducible operations, in line with the DiVincenzo's Criteria [52]. Therefore, it might be surmised that one of the key ingredients in realizing reliable quantum computers is the employment of QECCs.

## 1.2 Historical Overview

### 1.2.1 Quantum Stabilizer Codes

The concept of protecting the quantum information from decoherence is similar to that of its classical counterpart by attaching redundancy to the information [53], which is then invoked later for error correction. The quest for finding good QECCs was inspired by Shor, who conceived a 9-qubit code, which is judiciously often referred to as Shor's code [54]. Shor's code encodes a single information qubit, which is also referred to as the "logical qubit," into nine encoded qubits or "physical qubits." Shor's 9-qubit code is capable of protecting the nine physical qubits from any type of single-qubit error. Following the discovery of Shor's code, another QECC scheme—namely, Steane's code—was proposed in [55]. The latter is capable of protecting the physical qubits from any single-qubit error by encoding a single logical qubit into seven physical qubits, instead of nine qubits. The question concerning the minimum number of physical qubits required to protect them from any type of single-qubit error was answered by Laflamme *et al.*, who proposed the 5-qubit quantum code having a quantum coding rate of 1/5 [56]. This 5-qubit code may also be referred to as Laflamme's "perfect code" since the code construction achieves the quantum Hamming bound and the quantum Singleton bound of binary codes. This is the upper bound of the achievable quantum coding rate when aiming to correct a single qubit [57, 58]. To elaborate briefly, each of the five complex-valued qubits may have a bit-flip, a phase-flip as well as a joint bit-flip and phase-flip error. The bit-flip and phase-flip errors are shown in the stylized illustration of Figure 1.3.

Hence, in Laflamme's code, we have $3 \cdot 5 = 15$ legitimate error events plus the error-free scenario. Hence, we have to attach four redundant qubits to the original logical qubit for distinguishing the above-mentioned 16 possible error scenarios. In exchange for this undesirably low code rate we have a powerful error correction capability, since an arbitrary error can be eliminated in a set of five qubits, i.e. when the error rate imposed by decoherence is as high as 20%. Suffice it to say in closing that it is perfectly feasible to create high-rate codes, which would, however, correct a lower error rate, as it will transpire throughout the rest of this monograph.

The field of QECCs entered its golden age following the invention of quantum stabilizer codes (QSCs) [59, 60]. The QSC paradigm allows us to transform classical error correction codes into their quantum counterparts. QSCs must be constructed to circumvent the problem of estimating both the number and the position of quantum-domain errors imposed by quantum decoherence without observing the actual quantum states, since observing the quantum states would collapse the qubits into classical bits. This extremely beneficial error estimation technique

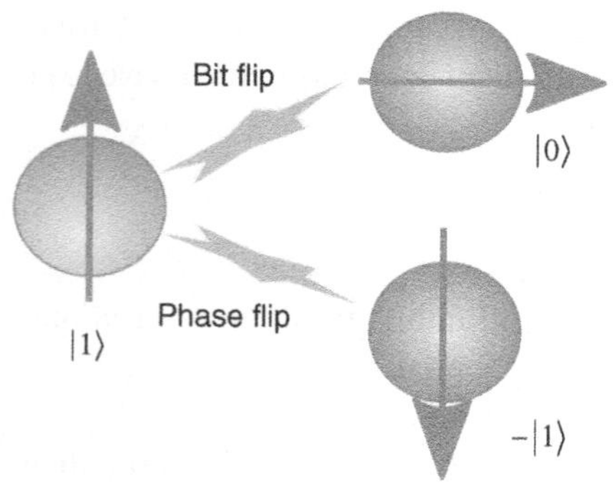


**Figure 1.3** Quantum decoherence characterized by bit-flips and phase-flips. The vertical polarization represents the state $|1\rangle$, while the horizontal polarization represents the state $|0\rangle$.

was achieved by introducing the syndrome-measurement-based approach [59, 60]. In classical error correction codes, the syndrome-measurement-based approach has been widely exploited as a popular error detection and correction procedure. Therefore, the formulation of QSCs expanded the search space for good QECCs to a broader horizon. This new paradigm of incorporating the classical-to-quantum isomorphisms led to the transformation of classical codes into their quantum domain dual pairs, such as quantum Bose–Chaudhuri–Hocquenghem (QBCH) codes [61, 62], quantum Reed–Solomon (QRS) codes [63], quantum Reed–Muller (QRM) codes [64], quantum convolutional codes (QCCs) [65, 66], quantum low-density parity-check (QLDPC) codes [67], quantum turbo codes (QTCs) [68], and quantum polar codes (QPCs) [69]. A timeline that portrays the milestones of QSCs at a glance is depicted in Figure 1.4. Although the QSC formulation creates an important class of QECCs, we note that there are also other classes of QECCs beside QSCs, such as the class of decoherence-free subspace (DFS) codes [70–72]. DFS codes can be viewed as a family of passive QECCs, while QSCs constitute a specific example of the active ones. To elaborate a little further, DFS codes constitute a highly degenerate class of QECCs, which rely on the fact that

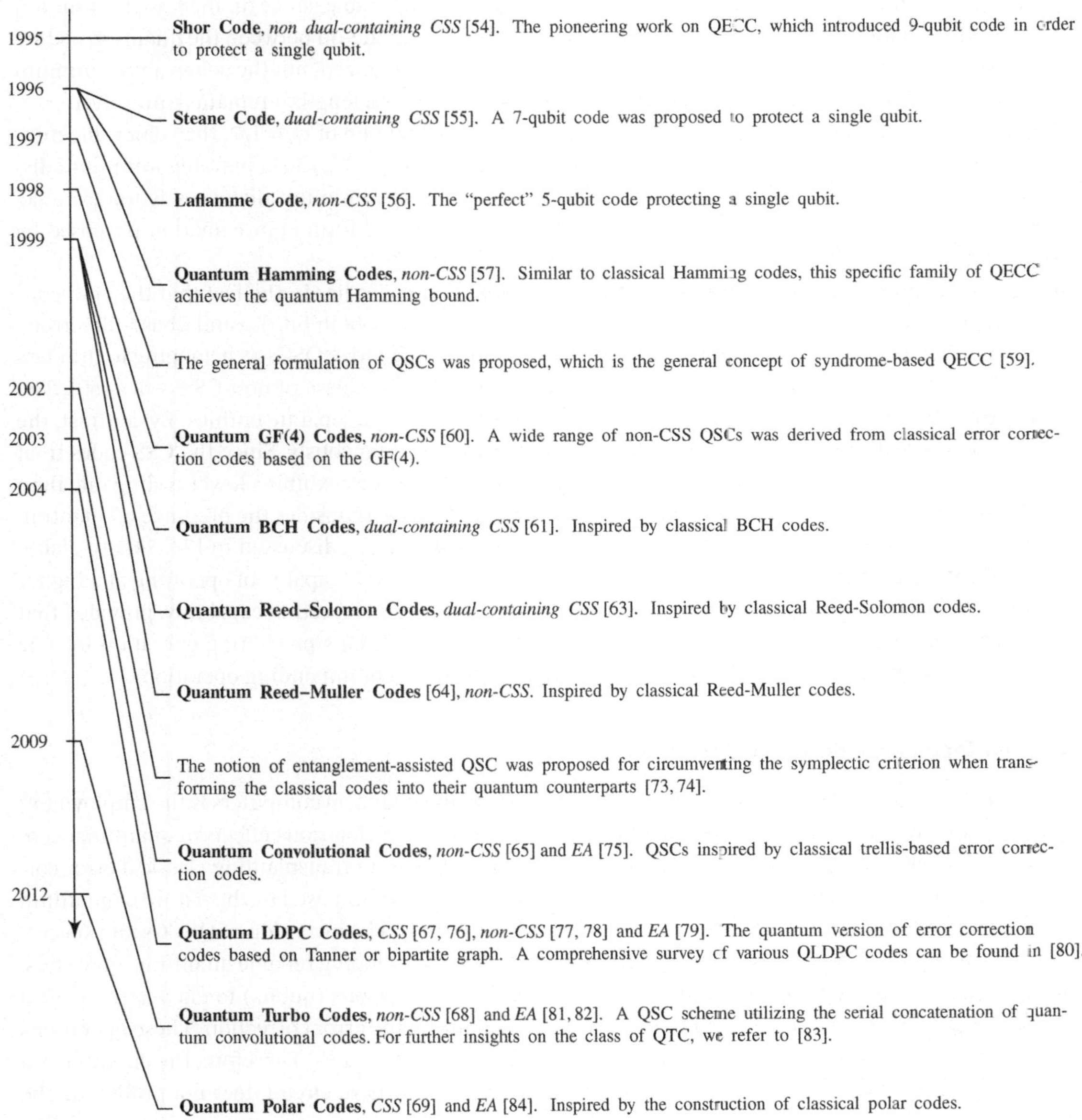


**Figure 1.4** Timeline of important milestones in the QECC field, specifically in the development of QSCs. The code construction is highlighted in **bold** font, while the associated code type is printed in *italics*.

the error patterns may preserve the state of physical qubits and therefore they do not necessarily require a recovery procedure. Due to their strong reliance on the degeneracy property exhibited by the set of QECCs that do not have a classical counterpart, the class of DFS codes bears no resemblance to any classical error correction codes. Therefore, in this treatise, we focus our discussion purely on QSCs, which exhibit strong analogies with classical error correction codes.

Even though intensive research efforts have been invested in exploring the field of QSCs, one of its mysteries remains unresolved. Since the development of the first QSC, one of the open problems has been how to determine the realistically achievable size of the codebook $|\mathcal{C}| = 2^k$, given the number of physical qubits $n$, the minimum distance $d$, and the quantum coding rate of $r_Q = k/n$, where $k$ denotes the number of logical qubits. The minimum distance $d$ of the legitimate codewords is the parameter that defines the error correction capability of the corresponding code. The complete formulation of the realistically achievable minimum distance $d$, given the number of physical qubits $n$ and the quantum coding rate $r_Q$ is unknown at the time of writing, but several theoretical lower and upper bounds can be found in the literature [58, 85, 86]. Naturally, finding code constructions associated with growing minimum distances upon reducing the coding rate is desirable, since an increased minimum distance improves the reliability of quantum computation [52, 87–90]. The trade-off between the quantum coding rate and the minimum distance as well as the codeword length is widely recognized, but the achievable minimum distance $d$ of a quantum code given the quantum coding rate $r_Q$ and codeword length $n$ remains unresolved.

For example, for a given codeword length of $n = 128$ and quantum coding rate of $r_Q = 1/2$, the achievable minimum distance is loosely bounded by $11 < d < 22$, while for $n = 1024$ and $r_Q = 1/2$, the achievable minimum distance is bounded by $78 < d < 157$. Naturally, having such a wide range of minimum distances is undesirable. For binary classical codes, this problem has been circumvented by the closed-form approximation proposed by Akhtman *et al.* [91].

The challenge of creating the quantum counterpart of error correction codes lies in the fact that the QSC constructions have to mitigate not only bit-flip errors but also phase-flip errors or both bit-flip and phase-flip errors. Based on how we mitigate those different types of errors, we can simply categorize QSCs as belonging to the class of Calderbank–Shor–Steane (CSS) codes [55, 86, 92] or to the complementary class of non-CSS codes [60]. The CSS codes handle qubit errors by treating bit-flip errors and phase-flip errors as separate entities. By contrast, the class of non-CSS codes treats both bit-flip errors and phase-flip errors simultaneously. Since the CSS codes treat the bit-flip and phase-flip error correction procedures separately, in general, they exhibit a lower coding rate than their non-CSS counterparts having the same code rate. Furthermore, if we also consider the presence of quantum entanglement, we may conceive more powerful quantum code constructions as discussed in [73, 74]. To elaborate, the family of entanglement-assisted quantum stabilizer codes (EA-QSCs) is capable of operating at a higher quantum coding rate than the unassisted QSC constructions at the same error correction capability, provided that error-free maximally entangled qubits have already been preshared [73, 74]. This presharing operation may be carried out when the circuits are not actively harnessed for carrying out urgent impending operations.

### 1.2.2 Quantum Topological Error Correction Codes

We have established that one of the essential prerequisites of constructing quantum computers is the employment of QECCs for ensuring that the computers operate reliably by mitigating the deleterious effects of quantum decoherence [49, 52, 93]. However, the laws of quantum mechanics prevent us from transplanting classical error correction codes directly into the quantum domain. To circumvent the constraints imposed by the nature of quantum physics, the notion of quantum stabilizer codes (QSCs) emerged [59, 60, 94]. The invention of QECCs and specifically QSC formalism did not immediately eradicate all of the obstacles of developing reliable quantum computers. Employing the QSCs requires redundancy in the form of *auxiliary* quantum bits (qubits) to encode the logical qubits into physical qubits. The redundant qubits are then exploited during the error correction. These operations rely on the quantum encoder and decoder circuits constructed from quantum gates. Therefore, the circuit-based implementation of a QSC itself has to be fault-tolerant to guarantee that the QSC circuit does not proliferate the existing errors.

The notion of the QSC triggered numerous discoveries in the domain of QECCs, which are inspired by classical error correction codes. Essentially, QSCs represent the quantum-domain version of the classical syndrome-decoding-based error correction codes. Since the concept of utilizing the syndrome values for error correction is widely exploited in the classical domain, diverse classical error correction codes can be conveniently "quantumized." Consequently, we can find in the literature the quantum version of error correction codes based on algebraic formalisms such as those of the Bose–Chaudhuri–Hocquenghem (BCH) codes [61] and of Reed–Solomon (RS) codes [63], quantum codes based on a conventional trellis structure such as convolutional codes [65] and turbo codes [68, 83], quantum codes based on bipartite graphs, such as low-density parity-check (LDPC) codes [67, 76–78, 80], as well as quantum codes based on channel polarization, such as polar codes [69, 84].

Apart from exploiting the above isomorphism, there are also significant contributions on directly developing code constructions solely based on the pure quantum topology and homology, as exemplified by the family of so-called toric codes [95–97], surface codes [98, 99], color codes [100], cubic codes [101], hyperbolic surface codes [102, 103], hyperbolic color codes [104], hypergraph product codes [105–107] and homological product codes [108]. Unfortunately, this concept has not been widely explored in the classical domain. By contrast, in the quantum domain, having a code construction relying on the physical configuration of qubits is highly desirable for the conception of low-complexity, high-reliability quantum computers.

For instance, this strategy has been deployed for developing IBM's superconducting quantum computers, as shown in Figure 1.5. From this figure, we can see the qubit arrangement of the three prototypes of IBM's quantum computer—which can be viewed online—namely the ibmqx2, ibmqx4, and ibmqx5 configurations [109]. The first two quantum computers are the 5-qubit quantum computers, while the third one is a 16-qubit quantum computer. The circles in Figure 1.5 represent the qubits, while the arrows represent all their two-qubit interactions. It can be seen that the existing architectures impose a limitation, namely the two-qubit interactions can only be performed between the neighboring qubits. Even though this particular limitation potentially imposes additional challenges, when it comes to QSCs deployment, the stabilizer effect can still be achieved by the corresponding qubit arrangement by invoking the family of QTECCs. A timeline that portrays the milestones in the evolution of QTECCs is portrayed at a glance in Figure 1.6.

Again, Shor's 9-qubit code protects 9 physical qubits from any type of single-qubit error, namely bit-flip (**X**), phase-flip (**Z**), as well as from simultaneous bit and phase-flip (**Y**). Furthermore, as alluded to above, not long after the discovery of the first QECCs, Steane invented the 7-qubit code, which was followed by Laflamme's perfect 5-qubit code [55, 56]. However, the construction of these codes does not naturally exhibit inherent fault-tolerance. Briefly, a QSC is said to be fault-tolerant if the circuit-based implementation of the QSC does not introduce more errors than the error correction capability of the QSC, when the quantum gates required for implementing the QSC are imperfect. The quantum circuit-based implementation of these pioneering QSCs always involves a high number of qubit interactions within the codeword of physical qubits. As a consequence, an error caused by an imperfect gate potentially propagates to other qubits, and instead of being eliminated, the deleterious effects of quantum decoherence are further aggravated.

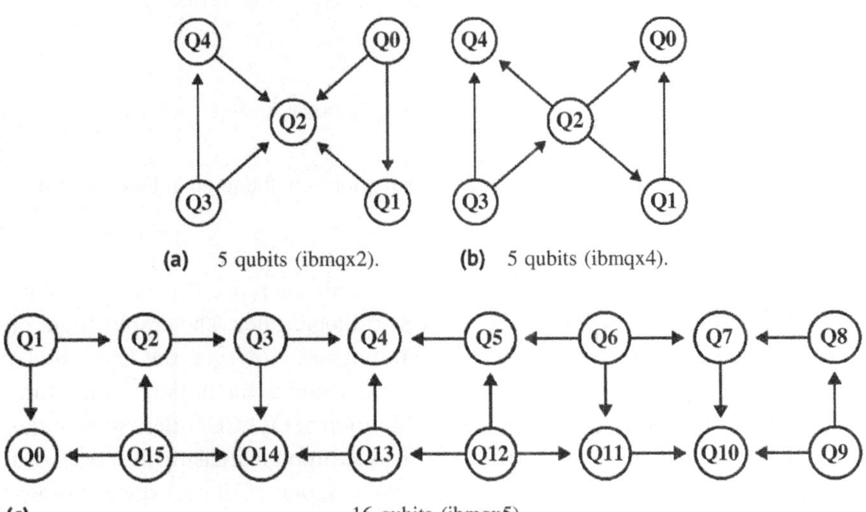


**Figure 1.5** The qubit arrangement of IBM's superconducting quantum computers. The circles represent the qubits, while the arrows represent the possible qubit interactions within the computers. *Source*: Adapted from [109].

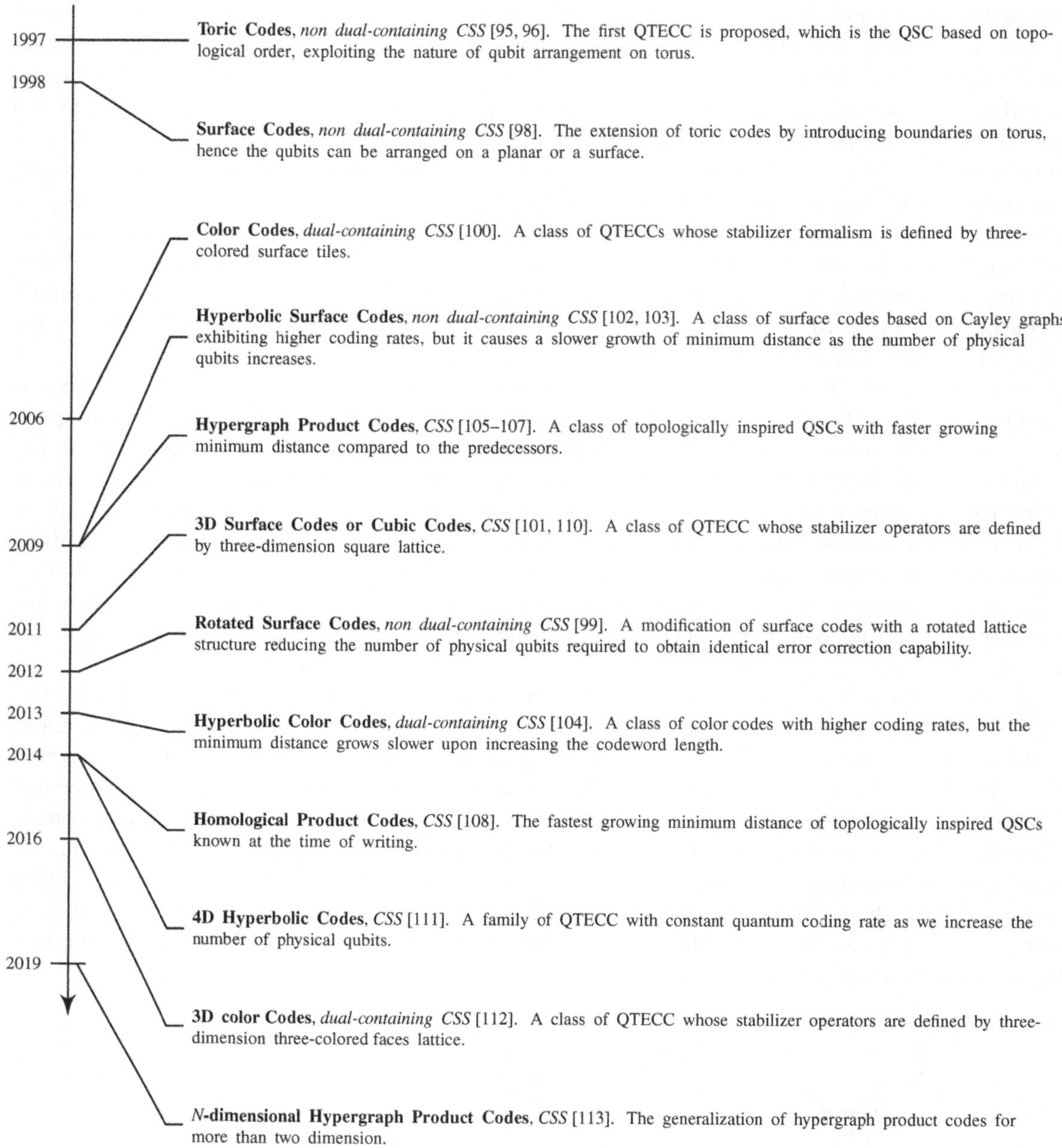


**Figure 1.6** Timeline of important milestones in the area of QTECCs. The code construction is highlighted in **bold** while the associated code type is marked in *italics*.

At the current development stage of quantum computers, a QSC exhibiting fault-tolerance is more favorable, since the reliability of quantum gates is substantially lower than that of classical logic gates. The employment of QSCs is expected to mitigate the deleterious effects of the imperfect quantum gates. However, the QSC circuit itself is prone to decoherence. For the sake of constructing a fault-tolerant QSC scheme, the notion of quantum topological error correction codes (QTECCs) was proposed [95, 96]. The formulation of QTECCs offers substantial fault-tolerance improvements because they exhibit an increased minimum distance upon increasing the codeword length. Furthermore, they rely on localized stabilizer measurements. Nonetheless, one of the substantial drawbacks of QTECCs is their low quantum coding rate. More specifically, the quantum coding rate of QTECCs tends to zero for an asymptotically long codeword.

Another class of codes that are considered to be fault-tolerant QSCs is constituted by the family of QLDPC codes. The QLDPC codes inherit the property of fault-tolerance due to having a sparse parity-check matrix, which

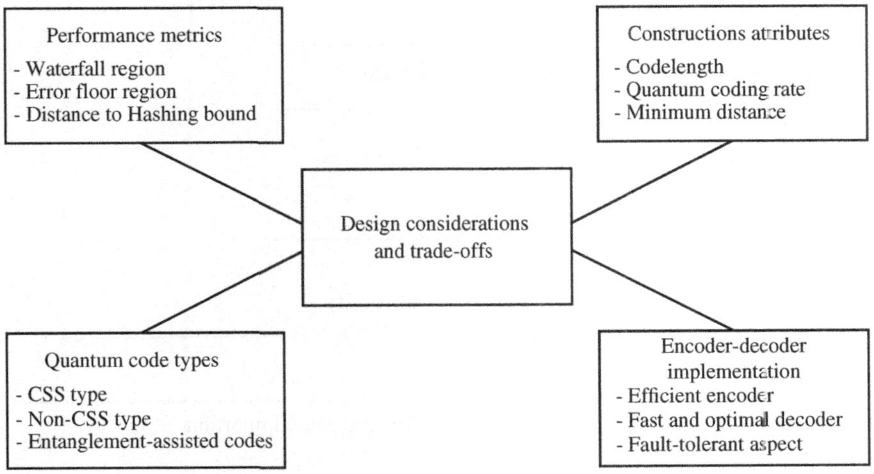


**Figure 1.7** The conflicting design factors related to QECC code design.

guarantees the limited interaction of the qubits within the same block of codewords. Even though QLDPC codes can achieve good performance at a relatively high quantum coding rate, the construction of QLDPC has a bounded minimum distance [67, 107] and they tend to perform best for long codeword. Even though intensive research efforts have been invested in exploring the QECC field, the fundamental trade-off between the quantum coding rate and the minimum distance remains unresolved. Having a high minimum distance is important for guaranteeing a low error floor and robust fault-tolerance. However, it is infeasible to construct a QSC exhibiting high minimum distance without unduly reducing the quantum coding rate or increasing the number of physical qubits. Indeed, this is only a specific example of the quantum coding rate versus minimum distance trade-off. Furthermore, the quantum coding rate versus minimum distance trade-off is not the only one involved in designing QSCs, as seen in Figure 1.7. The discussion of these intricately interlinked aspects will pervade the rest of the book.

### 1.2.3 Quantum Convolutional Codes

The inception of QCCs dates back to 1998. Inspired by the higher coding efficiencies of classical convolutional codes (CCCs) as compared to the comparable block codes and the low latency associated with the online encoding and decoding of CCCs [114], Chau conceived the first QCC in [66]. He also generalized the classical Viterbi decoding algorithm for the class of quantum codes in [115], but he overlooked some crucial encoding and decoding aspects. Later, Ollivier *et al.* [65, 116] revisited the class of stabilizer-based convolutional codes. Similar to the classical Viterbi decoding philosophy, they also conceived a look-up table (LUT) based quantum Viterbi algorithm for the maximum likelihood decoding of QCCs, whose complexity increases linearly with the number of encoded qubits. Ollivier *et al.* also derived the corresponding online encoding and decoding circuits having a complexity that increased linearly with the number of encoded qubits. Unfortunately, their proposed rate-1/5 single-error-correcting QCC did not provide any performance or decoding complexity gain over the rate-1/5 single-error correcting block code of [56]. Pursuing this line of research, Almeida *et al.* [117] constructed a rate-1/4 single-error correcting Shor-type concatenated QCC from a CCC(2, 1, 2) and invoked the classical syndrome-based trellis decoding for the quantum domain. Hence, the proposed QCC had a higher coding rate than the QCC of [65, 116]. However, this coding efficiency was achieved at the cost of a relatively high encoding complexity associated with the concatenated trellis structure. It must be pointed out here that the pair of independent trellises used for decoding the bit-flips and phase-flips imposes a lower complexity than a large joint trellis would. Finally, Forney *et al.* [118, 119] designed rate-$(n-2)/n$ QCCs comparable to their classical counterparts, thus providing higher coding efficiencies than the comparable block codes. Forney *et al.* [118, 119] achieved this by invoking arbitrary classical self-orthogonal rate-$1/n$ $\mathbb{F}_4$-linear and $\mathbb{F}_2$-linear convolutional codes for constructing unrestricted and CSS-type QCCs, respectively. Forney *et al.* [118, 119] also conceived a simple decoding algorithm for single-error-correcting codes. Both the coding efficiency and the decoding complexity of the aforementioned QCC structures are compared in Table 1.1.

**Table 1.1** Comparison of the quantum convolutional code (QCC) structures.

| Author(s) | Coding efficiency | Decoding complexity |
|---|---|---|
| Ollivier and Tillich [65, 116] | Low | Moderate |
| Almeida and Palazzo [117] | Moderate | Moderate |
| Forney *et al.* [118, 119] | High | Low |

**Table 1.2** Major contributions to the development of quantum convolutional codes (QCCs).

| Year | Author(s) | Contribution |
|---|---|---|
| 1998 | Chau [66] | The first QCCs were developed. Unfortunately, some important encoding/decoding aspects were ignored. |
| 1999 | Chau [115] | Classical Viterbi decoding algorithm was generalized to the quantum domain. However, similar to [66], some crucial encoding/decoding aspects were overlooked. |
| 2003 | Ollivier and Tillich [65, 116] | Stabilizer-based convolutional codes and their maximum likelihood decoding using the Viterbi algorithm were revisited to overcome the deficiencies of [66, 116]. Failed to provide better performance or decoding complexity than the comparable block codes. |
| 2004 | Almeida and Palazzo [117] | Shor-type concatenated QCC was conceived and classical syndrome trellis was invoked for decoding. A high coding efficiency was achieved at the cost of a relatively high encoding complexity. |
| 2005 | Forney *et al.* [118, 119] | Unrestricted and CSS-type QCCs were derived from arbitrary classical self-orthogonal $\mathbb{F}_4$ and $\mathbb{F}_2$ CCCs, respectively, yielding a higher coding efficiency as well as a lower decoding complexity than the comparable block codes. |
| 2005 | Grassl and Rotteler [120, 121] | Conceived a new construction for QCCs from the classical self-orthogonal product codes. |
| 2007 | Aly *et al.* [122] | Algebraic QCCs derived from BCH codes. |
| 2008 | Aly *et al.* [123] | Algebraic QCCs constructed from Reed–Solomon and Reed–Muller codes. |
| 2013 | Pelchat and Poulin [124] | Degenerate Viterbi decoding was conceived, which runs the MAP algorithm over the equivalent classes of degenerate errors, thereby improving performance. |

Furthermore, in the spirit of finding new constructions for QCCs, Grassl *et al.* [120, 121] constructed QCCs using the classical self-orthogonal product codes, while Aly *et al.* explored various algebraic constructions in [122, 123]. Particularly, the QCCs of [122] were derived from classical BCH codes, while the QCCs of [123] were constructed from the classical Reed–Solomon and Reed–Muller codes. Recently, Pelchat and Poulin made a major contribution to the decoding of QCCs by proposing degenerate Viterbi decoding [124], which runs the Maximum *A Posteriori* (MAP) algorithm [125] over the equivalent classes of degenerate errors, thereby improving the attainable performance. The major contributions to the development of QCCs are summarized in Table 1.2.

### 1.2.4 Quantum Low Density Parity Check Codes

Although convolutional codes provide somewhat better performance than the comparable block codes, yet they are not powerful enough to yield a capacity approaching performance, when used on their own. Consequently, the desire to operate close to the achievable capacity at an affordable decoding complexity further motivated researchers to design beneficial quantum counterparts of the classical LDPC codes [126], which achieve information rates close to the Shannonian capacity limit with the aid of iterative decoding schemes. Furthermore, the sparseness of the LDPC matrix is of particular interest in the quantum domain, because it requires only a small number of interactions per qubit during the error correction procedure, thus facilitating fault-tolerant decoding. Moreover, this sparse nature also makes QLDPC codes highly degenerate.

Postol [76] conceived the first example of a non-dual-containing CSS-based QLDPC code from a finite-geometry-based classical LDPC in 2001. Later, MacKay *et al.* [67] proposed various code structures (e.g. bicycle codes and unicycle codes) for constructing QLDPC codes from the family of classical dual-containing LDPC codes. Additionally, MacKay *et al.* also proposed the class of Cayley graph-based dual-containing codes in [127], which were further investigated by Couvreur *et al.* in [103, 128].

Aly *et al.* contributed to these developments by constructing dual-containing QLDPC codes from finite geometries in [129], while Djordjevic exploited the balanced incomplete block designs (BIBDs) in [130], albeit neither of these provided any gain over MacKay's bicycle codes. Lou *et al.* [131, 132] invoked the non-dual-containing CSS structure by using both the generator and the PCM of classical low-density generator matrix (LDGM)-based codes. Hagiwara *et al.* [133] conceived Quasi-Cyclic (QC) QLDPC codes, whereby the constituent PCMs of non-dual-containing CSS-type QLDPCs were constructed from a pair of QC-LDPC codes found using algebraic combinatorics. Hagiwara's design of [133] was extended to non-binary QLDPC codes in [134, 135], which operate closer to the Hashing limit than MacKay's bicycle codes. The concept of QC-QLDPC codes was further extended to the class of spatially-coupled QC codes in [136]. While all the aforementioned QLDPC constructions were CSS-based, Camara *et al.* [78] were the first authors to conceive non-CSS QLDPC codes. Later, Tan *et al.* [137] proposed several systematic constructions for non-CSS QLDPC codes, four of which were based on classical binary QC-LDPC codes, while one was derived from classical binary LDPC-convolutional codes. Since most of the above-listed QLDPC constructions exhibit an upper-bounded minimum distance, topological QLDPCs[1] were derived from Kitaev's construction in [104, 107, 138]. Amidst these activities, which focused on the construction of QLDPC codes, Poulin *et al.* were the first scientists to address the decoding issues of QLDPC codes [139], which were further improved in [140]. The major contributions made in the context of QLDPC codes are summarized in Table 1.3, while the most promising QLDPC construction methods are compared in Table 1.4[2].

**Table 1.3** Major contributions to the development of iterative quantum codes. The code types "dual-containing CSS" and "non-dual-containing CSS" are abbreviated as "dual" and "non-dual," respectively.

| Year | Author(s) | Code Type | Contribution |
|---|---|---|---|
| 2001 | Postol [76] | Non-dual | The first example of QLDPC code constructed from a finite geometry-based classical code. A generalized formalism for constructing QLDPC codes from the corresponding classical codes was not developed. |
| 2004 | MacKay *et al.* [67] | Dual | Various code structures, e.g. bicycle codes and unicycle codes, were conceived for constructing QLDPC codes from classical dual-containing LDPC codes. Performance impairment due to the presence of unavoidable length-4 cycles was first pointed out in this work. Minimum distance of the resulting codes was upper bounded by the row weight. |
| 2005 | Lou *et al.* [131, 132] | Non-dual | The generator and PCM of classical LDGM codes were exploited for constructing CSS codes. An increased decoding complexity was imposed and the codes had an upper bounded minimum distance. |
| 2007 | MacKay [127] | Dual | Cayley graph-based QLDPC codes were proposed, which had numerous length-4 cycles. |
| 2007 | Camara *et al.* [78] | Non-CSS | QLDPC codes derived from classical self-orthogonal quaternary LDPC codes were conceived, which failed to outperform MacKay's bicycle codes. |
| 2007 | Hagiwara *et al.* [133] | Non-dual | Quasi-cyclic QLDPC codes were constructed using a pair of quasi-cyclic LDPC codes, which were found using algebraic combinatorics. The resultant codes had at least a girth of 6, but they failed to outperform MacKay's constructions given in [67]. |
| 2008 | Aly *et al.* [129] | Dual | QLDPC codes were constructed from finite geometries, which failed to outperform MacKay's bicycle codes. |

(*Continued*)

1 Topological code structures are beyond the scope of this book.

2 All QLDPC codes must have short cycles in the quaternary formalism, which will be discussed in Chapter 14. The second column only indicates "short cycles" in the binary formalism.

**Table 1.3** (Continued)

| Year | Author(s) | Code Type | Contribution |
|---|---|---|---|
| 2008 | Djordjevic [130] | Dual | BIBDs were exploited to design QLDPC codes, which failed to outperform MacKay's bicycle codes. |
| 2010 | Tan *et al.* [137] | Non-CSS | Several systematic constructions for non-CSS QLDPC codes were proposed, four of which were based on classical binary quasi-cyclic LDPC codes, while one was derived from classical binary LDPC-convolutional codes. These code designs failed to outperform MacKay's bicycle codes. |
| 2011 | Couvreur *et al.* [103, 128] | Dual | Cayley graph-based QLDPC codes of [127] were further investigated. The lower bound on the minimum distance of the resulting QLDPC was logarithmic in the code length, but this was achieved at the cost of an increased decoding complexity. |
| 2011 | Kasai [134, 135] | Non-dual | Quasi-cyclic QLDPC codes of [133] were extended to non-binary constructions, which outperformed MacKay's bicycle codes at the cost of an increased decoding complexity. Performance was still not at par with the classical LDPC codes and minimum distance was upper bounded. |
| 2011 | Hagiwara *et al.* [136] | Non-dual | Spatially-coupled QC-QLDPC codes were developed, which outperformed the "non-coupled" design of [133] at the cost of a small coding rate loss. Performance was similar to that of [134, 135], but larger block lengths were required. |
| 2008 | Poulin *et al.* [139] | | Heuristic methods were developed to alleviate the performance degradation caused by unavoidable length-4 cycles and symmetric degeneracy error. |
| 2012 | Wang *et al.* [140] | | Feedback mechanism was introduced in the context of the heuristic methods of [139] to further improve the performance. |
| 2008 | Poulin *et al.* [68, 141] | Non-CSS | QTCs were conceived based on the interleaved serial concatenation of QCCs. QTCs are free from the decoding issue associated with the length-4 cycles and they offer a wider range of code parameters. Degenerate iterative decoding algorithm was also proposed. Unfortunately, QTCs have an upper bounded minimum distance. |
| 2014 | Wilde *et al.* [82] | | The iterative decoding algorithm of [68, 141] failed to yield performance similar to the classical turbo codes. The decoding algorithm was improved by iteratively exchanging the *extrinsic* rather than the *a posteriori* information. |

**Table 1.4** Comparison of the quantum low-density parity check (QLDPC) code structures.

| Code construction | Short cycles | Minimum distance | Delay | Decoding complexity |
|---|---|---|---|---|
| Bicycle codes [67] | Yes | Upper-bounded | Standard | Standard |
| Cayley-graph based codes [103, 127, 128] | Yes | Increases with the code length | Standard | Increases with the code length |
| LDGM-based codes [131, 132] | Yes | Upper-bounded | Standard | High |
| Non-binary quasi-cyclic codes [134, 135] | No | Upper-bounded | Standard | High |
| Spatially-coupled quasi-cyclic codes [136] | No | Upper-bounded | High | High |

### 1.2.5 Quantum Turbo Codes

Pursuing further the direction of iterative code structures, Poulin *et al.* conceived QTCs in [68, 141], based on the interleaved serial concatenation of QCCs. Unlike QLDPC codes, QTCs offer a complete freedom in choosing the code parameters, such as the frame length, coding rate, constraint length and interleaver type. Moreover, their decoding is not impaired by the presence of length-4 cycles associated with the symplectic criterion. Furthermore, in contrast to QLDPC codes, the iterative decoding invoked for QTCs takes into account the inherent degeneracy associated with quantum codes. However, it was found in [68, 141, 142] that the constituent QCCs cannot be simultaneously both recursive and noncatastrophic. Since the recursive nature of the inner code is essential for ensuring an unbounded minimum distance, whereas the noncatastrophic nature is a necessary condition to be satisfied for achieving decoding convergence to a vanishingly low error rate, the QTCs designed in [68, 141] had a bounded minimum distance. The QBER performance curves of the QTCs conceived in [68, 141] also failed to match the classical turbo codes. This issue was dealt with in [82], where the quantum turbo decoding algorithm of [68] was improved by iteratively exchanging the *extrinsic* rather than the *a posteriori* information. The major contributions made in the domain of QTCs are summarized in Table 1.3.

### 1.2.6 Entanglement-assisted Quantum Codes

Some of the well-known classical codes cannot be imported into the quantum domain by invoking the aforementioned stabilizer-based code constructions because the stabilizer codes have to satisfy the stringent symplectic product criterion. This limitation was overcome in [73, 74, 143, 144] with the notion of EA quantum codes, which exploit pre-shared entanglement between the transmitter and receiver. Later, this concept was extended to numerous other code structures, e.g. EA-QLDPC codes [79], EA-QCC [75], EA-QTC [81, 82] and EA-polar codes [84]. In [81, 82], it was also found that EA-QCCs may be simultaneously both recursive and non-catastrophic. Therefore, the issue of bounded minimum distance of QTCs was resolved with the notion of entanglement. Furthermore, EA-QLDPC codes are free from length-4 cycles in the binary formalism, which in turn results in an impressive performance similar to that of the corresponding classical LDPC codes. Hence, the concept of the entanglement-assisted regime resulted in a major breakthrough in terms of constructing quantum codes, whose behavior is similar to that of the corresponding classical codes. The major milestones achieved in the history of entanglement-assisted quantum error correction codes are chronologically arranged in Figure 1.8.

### 1.2.7 Protecting Quantum Gates

Although the field of QECCs benefited from a rapid pace of development, because under certain conditions we can transform various classes of powerful classical error correction codes into their quantum counterparts, several challenges remain, hindering the immediate employment of these powerful QSCs in quantum computers.

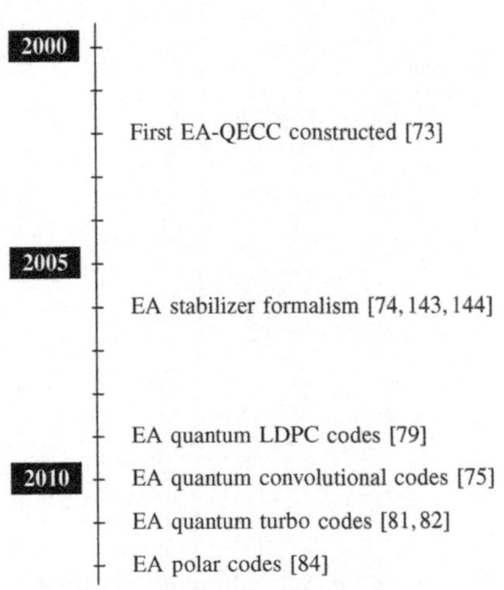


**Figure 1.8** Major milestones achieved in the history of entanglement-assisted quantum error correction codes.

First, the reliability of the state-of-the-art quantum gates is still significantly lower compared to classical gates. For example, the reliability of a two-qubit quantum gate is between 90.00% and 99.90% across the various technology platforms, such as spin electronics, photonics, superconducting, trapped-ion, and silicon solutions [37–40, 42, 44–46, 145]. Similar to the classical domain, invoking an error correction code within a quantum computer requires additional components. However, adding components for error correction also implies that we unavoidably introduce an additional source of decoherence into quantum computers, since the encoder and decoder of QSCs are also composed of quantum gates.

Second, the powerful QSCs such as QTCs, QPCs, and QLDPC codes require long codewords in order to operate close to the quantum Hashing bound. In other words, they require a very high number of physical quantum bits (qubits) to correct numerous errors. Additionally, the qubits have a relatively short coherence time [146], and hence, the error correction procedure has to be completed before the ensemble of qubits starts decohering. Consequently, utilizing QSCs having a high number of qubits for correcting many errors has the potential threat of encountering an avalanche of more erroneous qubits before the error correction procedure is even completed. Third, the state-of-the-art architecture of quantum computers imposes an additional challenge, where the interactions among the qubits are ideally limited to the nearest neighbor qubits, which can be arranged by introducing a lattice-based topological architecture. However, the aforementioned challenges impose limitations on creating a fault-tolerant error correction architecture.

The quest for creating fault-tolerant gates was inspired when the notion of transversal configuration was introduced for quantum gates [52, 89]. Briefly, the concept of transversal gates relies on a parallel set of identical quantum gates invoked for carrying out the operation of a single quantum gate, as illustrated in Figure. 1.9. At the right of the figure we can see a controlled NOT (CNOT) gate. This gate does not affect the target qubit if the control bit is 0 otherwise it flips the target qubit. By contrast, the subfigure on the left is a stylized portrayal of this CNOT gate, where the multiple control and target qubits represent protected operands.

The fact that transversal quantum Clifford gates are suitable for combination with the stabilizer formalism creates an opportunity for employing a wide range of QSCs for protecting transversal quantum gates. However, the challenges we have described earlier suggest that the less populous family of QTECCs is the most suitable candidate for protecting the transversal quantum gates. Again, the motivation behind combining the QTECCs with the transversal configuration of quantum gates is that their benefits conveniently complement each other. More explicitly, the QTECCs provide localized stabilizer measurements, which consequently have the benefit of a constant number of qubit interactions, as we increase the number of physical qubits harnessed. Thus, the benefits provided by the topologically inspired stabilizer formalism will not be affected by the transversal implementation

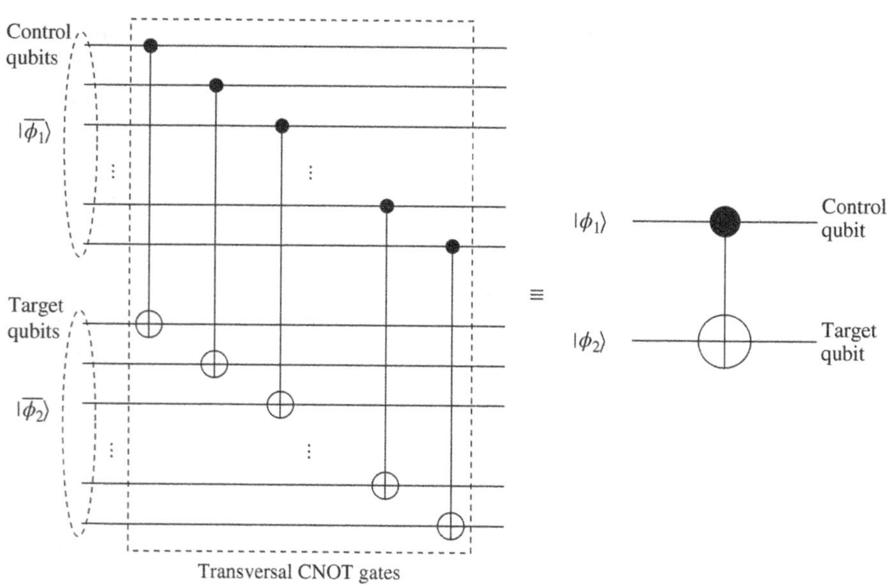


**Figure 1.9** Under a certain formulation, a set of less-reliable identical quantum gates in a transversal configuration can be used for conceiving a more reliable quantum gate.

of quantum gates. Hence, the localized action of stabilizer operators among the adjacent qubits—which offers fault-tolerance—is still preserved even after the desired quantum operation has been carried out by the transversal quantum gates.

But again, the amalgamation of the QSCs and the transversal quantum gates can only be implemented for quantum Clifford gates, rather than for the entire wider family of universal quantum gates. To achieve the universality of quantum computation, a set of fault-tolerant non-Clifford quantum gates is also required. Fortunately, this wider set may also be created by using QSCs by harnessing a method referred to as magic state distillation [147], which is however beyond the scope of this work. However, protecting Clifford gates is of significant importance, since the development of large-scale quantum computers relies heavily on improving their fidelity.

The threshold theorem defined in [148] was introduced for demonstrating that a quantum computation task subject to a vanishingly low qubit error ratio (QBER) can be carried out with the aid of QECCs even when relying on realistic error-prone quantum gates, provided that the error rate imposed by the quantum gates is below a certain threshold. Since the error-prone quantum gates may also provide error-prone stabilizer measurements, typically repeated stabilizer measurements are required for reliably concluding the error correction procedure. The number of stabilizer measurements required for making a high-fidelity observation tends to grow as we increase the number of physical qubits utilized for QECCs. This specific problem has led to the emergence of the so-called "single-shot" QSCs [149–152]. Assuming that the syndrome values acquired from the syndrome measurements are not reliable, we can still achieve a vanishingly low QBER for a specific quantum computation task, given that we only perform a single stabilizer measurement for each stabilizer operator. However, beneficial QSC constructions have to exhibit a commensurately increased minimum distance as a function of the number of physical qubits. Unfortunately, the quantum coding rate of the two-dimensional QTECCs tends to zero as the codeword length increases [153–155]. We have to mention that reliably observing the values from the stabilizer measurements is also of current research interest, which is highly relevant for the study of single-shot QSCs [156–159]. Therefore, we can ask a judicious question: "Can we still utilize the two-dimensional QTECCs for fault-tolerant quantum computation, when relying only on a single stabilizer measurement for each of the stabilizer operators?" Arguably, the answer is yes, although certain conditions should be fulfilled before we can guarantee that the QSCs can offer substantial reliability improvements.

## 1.3 Outline of the Book

**Part I of the book is constituted by Chapters 1–5** and it is dedicated to paving the way **from classical to quantum coding**. This part is organized as follows.

a. **Chapter 2: Preliminaries on Quantum Information**
In **Chapter 2**, we will provide a rudimentary introduction to quantum information processing. We commence with the definition of the fundamental unit of quantum information constituted by the quantum bit (qubit) in Section 2.2. This is followed by a brief introduction to quantum information processing, including the reversible unitary transformations and the irreversible quantum measurement operation in Section 2.3. The various quantum decoherence models used are elaborated on in Section 2.4. In Section 2.5, we present the *no-cloning theorem*, while in Section 2.6, we highlight the concept of *quantum entanglement*.

b. **Chapter 3: From Classical to Quantum Coding**
We continue in this chapter by presenting the duality of classical and quantum error correction codes with the aid of QSC constructions. Our objective is to highlight the similarities between the classical and quantum domains as well as to demonstrate how to transplant the well-known syndrome-based classical decoding concept into quantum error correction codes. We commence with a brief review of classical syndrome-based decoding in Section 3.2. In Section 3.3, we present the similarities between the classical syndrome-based decoding and the quantum stabilizer codes (QSCs). Finally, in Section 3.4, we provide detailed examples of the QSC constructions protecting a single qubit, namely a 1/3-rate quantum repetition code, Shor's 9-qubit code, Steane's 7-qubit code, and the Laflamme's perfect 5-qubit code.

c. **Chapter 4: Revisiting Classical Syndrome Decoding**
In this chapter, we discuss the popular classical syndrome decoding techniques designed for classical channels. We commence our discussion with the conceptually simplest LUT-based syndrome decoding in

Section 4.2, while Section 4.3 details the construction of the syndrome-based error trellis constructed for linear block codes and convolutional codes. Finally, in Section 4.4, we detail a block syndrome decoding (BSD) technique designed for reducing the decoding complexity. In particular, we conceive a syndrome-based block decoder for classical turbo trellis-coded modulation (TTCM) schemes.

**d. Chapter 5: Near-capacity Code Designs for Entanglement-assisted Classical Communication**
In this chapter, we invoke EXtrinsic Information Transfer (EXIT) chart-aided near-capacity classical code designs conceived for reliable transmission of classical bits over quantum communication channels. More specifically, we focus our attention on the entanglement-assisted transmission of classical information over quantum channels[3], which is achieved with the aid of the SuperDense (SD) coding protocol. We commence by reviewing the SD protocol in Section 5.2, which is in essence the "Bit → Qubit Mapper." We next characterize the associated capacity in Section 5.3. In Section 5.4, we conceive a bit-based scheme, which exploits classical channel coding by serially concatenating a classical Irregular Convolutional Code (IRCC) and a classical Unity Rate Code (URC) with a quantum-based SD encoder, hence refer to it as an IRCC-URC-SD system. We present our EXIT-chart aided near-capacity design criterion in Section 5.5, where the IRCC is optimized for achieving a near-capacity performance. Our bit-based code structure of Section 5.4 incurs a capacity loss due to the symbol-to-bit conversion. To overcome this capacity loss, we propose a symbol-based code design in Section 5.7, which employs a single-component Convolutional Code (CC) and a symbol interleaver in contrast to the IRCC and bit interleaver of Section 5.7.

**Part II of the book is represented by Chapters 6–9,** and it is focused on relatively low-complexity quantum codes requiring a limited number of qubits. Hence, these codes may be viewed as **near-term coding** solutions. This part of the book is organized as follows.

**a. Chapter 6: Quantum Coding Bounds**
In this chapter, we investigate the trade-off between the quantum coding rate and the minimum distance of QSCs. We commence with a survey of the existing quantum coding bounds in the literature. This is followed by our proposal of a simple and invertible closed-form approximation for determining the realistically achievable minimum distance, given the quantum coding rate of both idealized infinite-length and practical finite-length codewords. Specifically, in Section 6.2, we survey the existing quantum coding bounds and derive some bounds by exploiting the classical-to-quantum isomorphism. These discussions are followed by our proposed closed-form approximation for the idealized asymptotic limit of having an infinite-length codeword in Section 6.3. Since the asymptotic limit has little relevance for practical implementations, we also proposed an approximate formula for finite-length codewords. In order to unify our quantum coding bound formulation for both the entanglement-assisted QSCs and the unassisted QSCs dispensing with entanglement, we derive a closed-form approximation for arbitrarily entangled QSCs in Section 6.5.

**b. Chapter 7: Quantum Topological Error Correction Codes**
In this chapter, we continue our discussions by the detailed construction of classical topological error correction codes (TECCs) and their quantum-domain dual pairs, namely of the family of quantum topological error correction codes (QTECCs). We carry out a detailed parametric study and derive the QBER upper bound expression. Explicitly, in Section 7.2, we commence with design examples of classical TECCs to pave the way for delving into the quantum domain, while in Section 7.3 we detail the corresponding QSC design examples of QTECCs. We continue by characterizing the performance of QTECCs in the context of the popular quantum depolarizing channel in terms of their QBER, their distance from Hashing bound, and their fidelity in Section 7.4.

**c. Chapter 8: Protecting Quantum Gates Using Quantum Topological Error Correction Codes**
We then concentrate our attention on the general framework of protecting quantum gates using QSCs. Here, we consider the amalgamation of the transversal configuration of quantum Clifford gates and the QTECCs. This combination has been opted for because it retains the desirable properties of resulting in fault-tolerant QECCs, as a joint benefit of stabilizer preservation and localized stabilizer measurements. First, we proceed

3 A quantum channel can be used for modeling imperfections in quantum hardware, namely, faults resulting from quantum decoherence and quantum gates. Furthermore, a quantum channel can also model quantum-state flips imposed by the transmission medium, including free-space wireless channels and optical fiber links, when qubits are transmitted across these media.

with the formulation of our framework in Section 8.2. This is followed by the design examples of QSC-protected Hadamard and CNOT gates in Section 8.3, where we invoke a simple quantum repetition code. In order to evaluate the performance of our proposed framework, in Section 8.4, we present the decoherence model utilized in our simulations. Then, in Section 8.5, we quantify the performance of QTECC-protected transversal Hadamard gates and CNOT gates both in terms of their QBER and fidelity along with the derivation of the upper and lower bound of the attainable analytical QBER performance in the face of quantum depolarizing channel.

d. **Chapter 9: Universal Decoding of Quantum BCH and Polar Codes via Classical Guesswork**
In this chapter, a universal decoding scheme is conceived for quantum stabilizer codes (QSCs) by appropriately adapting the "guessing random additive noise decoding" (GRAND) philosophy of classical domain codes. In the spirit of universality, we demonstrate that the generalized quantum decoder conceived is eminently suitable for different QSC decoding paradigms, namely for both stabilizer-measurement-based as well as the inverse-encoder-based decoding of diverse codes. We then harness the resultant decoder for both quantum Bose–Chaudhuri–Hocquenghem (BCH) codes and quantum polar codes and quantify both their quantum block error rate (QBLER) and QBLER per logical qubit as well as their decoding complexity. Furthermore, we provide a parametric study of the associated design trade-offs and offer design guidelines for the implementation of GRAND-based QSC decoders.

Finally, **Part III of the book – namely Chapters 10–14** – delves into the design of more **advanced quantum coding** solutions of the future, when a high number of qubits becomes available. This part is outlined as follows.

a. **Chapter 10: Revisiting the Classical to Quantum Coding Evolution**
As our discussions deepen, in this chapter, we revisit the classical to quantum isomorphism in more detail. In Section 10.2, we review the family of classical linear block codes. We next discuss the class of QSCs in Section 10.3, which are derived from the classical linear block codes of Section 10.2. In particular, we highlight the underlying quantum to classical isomorphism, which forms the basis for morphing arbitrary classical codes into the quantum domain. We then extend our discussions to the construction of QCCs from the CCCs in Section 10.4, while Section 10.5 presents EA-QSCs, which facilitate the design of quantum codes from arbitrary classical codes without imposing any stringent requirements.

b. **Chapter 11: Near-hashing-bound Concatenated Quantum Codes**
Pursuing further the design of QECCs, in this chapter we will construct near-Hashing-bound QECCs. We will commence our discourse by laying out the design objectives in Section 11.2. Section 11.3 then details the circuit-based representation of QCCs, which facilitates the degenerate iterative decoding of concatenated quantum codes. We next present our system model and the associated degenerate iterative decoding in Section 11.4. Finally, in Section 11.5, we extend the application of classical nonbinary EXIT charts to the circuit-based syndrome decoder of QTCs for approaching the Hashing bound[4]. For the sake of further facilitating the Hashing bound approaching code design, we propose the general structure of Quantum Irregular convolutional code (QIRCC) in Section 11.7, which constitutes the outer component of a concatenated quantum code.

c. **Chapter 12: Near-hashing-bound Quantum Turbo Short-block Codes**
In this chapter, we set out to conceive the concept of near-hashing bound quantum turbo short-block codes relying on different-rate quantum encoders for combatting diverse quantum depolarizing probabilities. More explicitly, this multiple-rate scheme was conceived by concatenating quantum short-block codes (QSBCs) as the outer codes with a quantum unity-rate code (QURC) as the inner code, which we refer to as the QSBC-QURC construction. In contrast to two-dimensional QTECCs, whose quantum coding rate tends to zero for long codewords, the resultant QSBC-QURC scheme exhibits a relatively high quantum coding rate. Explicitly, in Section 12.2, we present the general formulation of QSBCs in terms of their code construction, quantum encoder, and stabilizer measurement. This is followed by Section 12.3, where we propose a novel family of serially-concatenated QTCs by utilizing QSBCs as the outer codes and a QURC as the inner code, which we refer to as the QSBC-QURC scheme. We analyze the convergence behavior of our iterative-decoding-aided QSBC-QURC scheme using extrinsic information transfer (EXIT) charts and evaluate its QBER and goodput in Section 12.4.

---

4 The Hashing bound sets the lower limit on the achievable capacity.

**d. Chapter 13: EXIT-chart Aided Design of Irregular Multiple-rate Quantum Turbo Block Codes**
This chapter is dedicated to the EXIT-chart aided design of so-called irregular quantum turbo short-block codes, which rely on multiple-rate quantum short-block codes (MR-QSBCs) as the outer codes and a quantum unity-rate code (QURC) as the inner code. The proposed design is denoted as MR-QSBC-QURC. More specifically, the proposed design exhibits multiple quantum coding rates despite relying only on a single quantum encoder. The benefit of having multiple rates is that this scheme is capable of activating that specific code-rate/throughput combination, which meets the specific fidelity requirement. Moreover, the flexibility offered by the single-encoder MR-QSBCs enables us to leverage extrinsic information transfer (EXIT)-chart based heuristic optimization for determining the optimal weighting of each specific code-rate to be used in the MR-QSBCs scheme. Our simulation results show that the MR-QSBC-QURC scheme conceived performs relatively close to the ultimate limit of the quantum hashing bound. Specifically, when considering the target quantum coding rates of $r_Q = \{0.3, 0.4, 0.5, 0.6, 0.7\}$, the MR-QSBC-QURC operates at a distance of $D = \{0.042, 0.029, 0.030, 0.024, 0.017\}$ from the quantum hashing bound, respectively, at a quantum bit error ratio (QBER) of $10^{-3}$.

**e. Chapter 14: Quantum Low-density Parity Check Codes**
Pursuing further the design of iterative code structures, we focus our efforts on QLDPC codes, which may be constructed from the classical binary as well as quaternary codes. In this context, Section 14.2 reviews the various QLDPC construction methods, while the QLDPC decoding methods and the associated challenges are discussed in Section 14.3. In Section 14.4, we propose a formalism for constructing high-rate row-circulant QC-QLDPC codes from arbitrary row-circulant classical LDPC matrices. In Section 14.6, we conceive a modified non-binary decoding algorithm for homogeneous CSS-type QLDPC codes, for the sake of alleviating the problems imposed by unavoidable length-4 cycles. Finally, Section 14.7 details the reweighted BP algorithm, which is known to alleviate the structural flaw of short cycles in classical LDPC codes.

**f.** Finally, in **Chapter 15** we summarize our findings along with a range of promising future research directions.

# 2

# Preliminaries on Quantum Information

## 2.1 Introduction

Following the easy-to-read historical introduction to the family of quantum error correction codes in Chapter 1, in this chapter we will highlight the concepts of quantum information processing required to pave the way from classical to quantum information theory. The rest of this chapter is organized as follows. We commence with an introduction to quantum information in Section 2.2, followed by a brief tour of quantum information processing in Section 2.3. The quantum channel models used in this treatise are elaborated on in Section 2.4. In Section 2.5, we present the *no-cloning theorem*, followed by *quantum entanglement* in Section 2.6. Finally, we conclude in Section 2.8.

## 2.2 A Brief Review of Quantum Information

We live in a world where information is transmitted and computed in binary form. Therefore, the fundamental unit of information in the classical domain is the *binary digit* or referred to as a *bit*, which can be defined as follows:

$$c = \{0, 1\}. \tag{2.1}$$

Consequently, in the classical domain, each of the classical bits can only carry the value of 0 or 1, not both. By contrast, in the quantum domain, the fundamental unit of information is represented by a *quantum bit* or *qubit*. The state of a qubit can be described as a linear combination of 0 and 1, which can be described in form of their superposition. However, this superposition of the two states will collapse to the corresponding classical state 0 or 1 upon observation or measurement. More specifically, the quantum state of a single qubit $|\psi\rangle$ can be formally expressed as

$$|\psi\rangle = \alpha_0|0\rangle + \alpha_1|1\rangle, \ \alpha_0, \alpha_1 \in \mathbb{C}, \tag{2.2}$$

where the probability of obtaining the classical state 0 and 1 upon measurement is given by $|\alpha_0|^2$ and $|\alpha_1|^2$, respectively. Since the values of $\alpha_0$ and $\alpha_1$ are associated with probability values, the unitary constraint of $|\alpha_0|^2 + |\alpha_1|^2 = 1$ is satisfied. A single-qubit system can also be viewed as a two-dimensional Hilbert space, where the computational basis vectors $|0\rangle$ and $|1\rangle$ are defined as follows:

$$|0\rangle = \begin{pmatrix} 1 \\ 0 \end{pmatrix}, \ |1\rangle = \begin{pmatrix} 0 \\ 1 \end{pmatrix}. \tag{2.3}$$

Consequently, the quantum state of a single qubit given in Eq. (2.2), can also be represented by a two-dimensional complex vector as follows:

$$|\psi\rangle = \alpha_0|0\rangle + \alpha_1|1\rangle = \alpha_0 \begin{pmatrix} 1 \\ 0 \end{pmatrix} + \alpha_1 \begin{pmatrix} 0 \\ 1 \end{pmatrix} = \begin{pmatrix} \alpha_0 \\ \alpha_1 \end{pmatrix}, \ \alpha_0, \alpha_1 \in \mathbb{C}. \tag{2.4}$$

The representation of the basis vector of "0" using the notation $|0\rangle$ and the basis vector "1" using the notation $|1\rangle$ is referred to as the *ket* notation. The terminology *ket* comes from the *bra-ket* notation [50], where the *bra* notation refers to $\langle\psi|$, while the *ket* notation is used for $|\psi\rangle$. The relationship between $|\psi\rangle$ and $\langle\psi|$ is defined as follows:

$$\langle\psi| = |\psi\rangle^{\dagger}, \tag{2.5}$$

where the notation $|\psi\rangle^{\dagger}$ indicates the conjugate transpose of $|\psi\rangle$. Explicitly, based on the vector representation of Eq. (2.4) and the definition of Eq. (2.5), we have

$$\langle\psi| = \begin{pmatrix}\alpha_0^* & \alpha_1^*\end{pmatrix}, \tag{2.6}$$

where $\alpha^*$ denotes the complex conjugate of $\alpha$. Therefore, the following equality holds:

$$\langle\psi|\psi\rangle \equiv \langle\psi| \cdot |\psi\rangle = 1. \tag{2.7}$$

Since the coefficients $\alpha_0$ and $\alpha_1$ are complex numbers, without loss of generality, the state of a qubit can be more explicitly written as follows:

$$|\psi\rangle = e^{i\gamma}\left(\cos\frac{\theta}{2}|0\rangle + e^{i\varphi}\sin\frac{\theta}{2}|1\rangle\right). \tag{2.8}$$

Furthermore, since the coefficient of $e^{i\gamma}$ has no observable effect, i.e. $e^{i\gamma}|\psi\rangle$ and $|\psi\rangle$ provide us with identical output probabilities upon measurement, the state of the qubit in Eq. (2.8) can be simplified to the following:

$$|\psi\rangle = \cos\frac{\theta}{2}|0\rangle + e^{i\varphi}\sin\frac{\theta}{2}|1\rangle. \tag{2.9}$$

Therefore, the quantum state of a qubit can be represented as a point on the surface of a unit-radius sphere, which is referred to as the Bloch sphere [160]. The point can be anywhere on the sphere and can be characterized by two phase variables $\theta$ and $\varphi$. More explicitly, the 3D representation of a quantum state using the Bloch sphere is depicted in Figure 2.1.

In general, a pair of vectors can be used as the basis vectors as long as both of them are orthonormal, i.e. both normalized and mutually orthogonal. For example, apart from the computational basis of $|0\rangle$ and $|1\rangle$ in the field of QECCs, the following Hadamard basis is also widely used:

$$|+\rangle = \frac{1}{\sqrt{2}}\begin{pmatrix}1\\1\end{pmatrix},\ |-\rangle = \frac{1}{\sqrt{2}}\begin{pmatrix}1\\-1\end{pmatrix}. \tag{2.10}$$

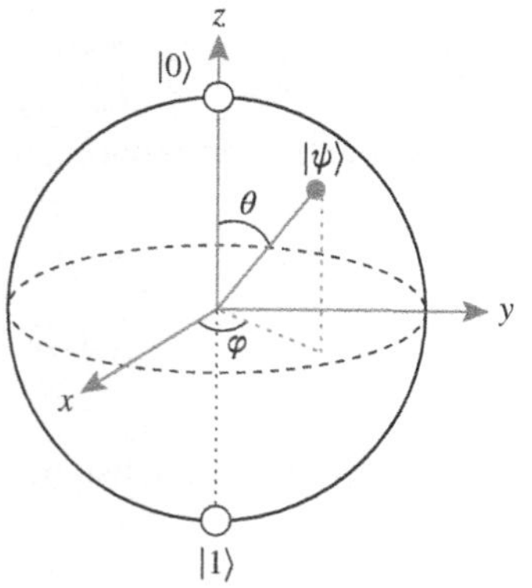


**Figure 2.1** The Bloch sphere is the 3D representation of two-dimensional complex vector space, which is parameterized by the variables $\theta$ and $\varphi$. A pure quantum state is represented by a point on the surface of a unit-radius. The computational basis of $|0\rangle$ corresponds to the north pole of the sphere, while the basis of $|1\rangle$ corresponds to the south pole.

More explicitly, the Hadamard basis can be viewed as the equal-weight superposition of the computational basis $|0\rangle$ and $|1\rangle$ according to the following definition:

$$|+\rangle = \frac{|0\rangle + |1\rangle}{\sqrt{2}}, \ |-\rangle = \frac{|0\rangle - |1\rangle}{\sqrt{2}}, \tag{2.11}$$

and vice versa, the computational basis $|0\rangle$ and $|1\rangle$ can be expressed as an equal-weight superposition of the vectors from the Hadamard basis:

$$|0\rangle = \frac{|+\rangle + |-\rangle}{\sqrt{2}}, \ |1\rangle = \frac{|+\rangle - |-\rangle}{\sqrt{2}}. \tag{2.12}$$

In order to extend the concept of quantum information to multi-qubit systems, we have to introduce the Kronecker tensor product or simply tensor product. Explicitly, for a pair of matrices $\mathbf{P}$ and $\mathbf{Q}$ having $(a \times b)$ elements and $(x \times y)$ elements, respectively, the resultant tensor product is a matrix having $(ax \times by)$ elements formulated by

$$\mathbf{P} \otimes \mathbf{Q} = \begin{pmatrix} p_{11}\mathbf{Q} & \cdots & p_{1(b-1)}\mathbf{Q} & p_{1b}\mathbf{Q} \\ p_{21}\mathbf{Q} & \cdots & p_{2(b-1)}\mathbf{Q} & p_{2b}\mathbf{Q} \\ \vdots & \ddots & \vdots & \vdots \\ p_{(a-1)1}\mathbf{Q} & \cdots & p_{(a-1)(b-1)}\mathbf{Q} & p_{(a-1)b}\mathbf{Q} \\ p_{a1}\mathbf{Q} & \cdots & p_{a(b-1)}\mathbf{Q} & p_{ab}\mathbf{Q} \end{pmatrix}. \tag{2.13}$$

For instance, a 2-qubit system is represented by the tensor product between a pair of two-element vectors given in Eq. (2.4). More explicitly, let us consider two qubits having the state of $|\psi_1\rangle = \alpha_0|0\rangle + \alpha_1|1\rangle$ and $|\psi_2\rangle = \beta_0|0\rangle + \beta_1|1\rangle$. The superimposed state can be described as follows:

$$\begin{aligned} |\psi\rangle = |\psi_1\rangle \otimes |\psi_2\rangle = \begin{pmatrix} \alpha_0 \\ \alpha_1 \end{pmatrix} \otimes \begin{pmatrix} \beta_0 \\ \beta_1 \end{pmatrix} = \begin{pmatrix} \alpha_0\beta_0 \\ \alpha_0\beta_1 \\ \alpha_1\beta_0 \\ \alpha_1\beta_1 \end{pmatrix} \\ \equiv \alpha_0\beta_0|00\rangle + \alpha_0\beta_1|01\rangle + \alpha_1\beta_0|10\rangle + \alpha_1\beta_1|11\rangle, \end{aligned} \tag{2.14}$$

where $\alpha_0, \alpha_1, \beta_0, \beta_1 \in \mathbb{C}$. It can be observed that a 2-qubit state is a superposition of all four possible states that can be generated by two classical bits i.e. 00, 01, 10, and 11. Additionally, the unitary constraint $|\alpha_0\beta_0|^2 + |\alpha_0\beta_1|^2 + |\alpha_1\beta_0|^2 + |\alpha_1\beta_1|^2 = 1$ still holds. The tensor product of a pair of two-element vectors yields a vector consisting of $2^2$ elements. Hence, the $N$-qubit system produces all of the $2^N$ possible states that can be generated by an $N$-bit sequence. If $i$ is the decimal representation of an $N$-bit sequence, the $N$-qubit superposition state can be expressed by the Dirac notation as follows:

$$|\psi\rangle = \sum_{i=0}^{2^N-1} \alpha_i|i\rangle \text{ where } \alpha_i \in \mathbb{C} \text{ and } \sum_{i=0}^{2^N-1} |\alpha_i|^2 = 1. \tag{2.15}$$

As an instance of a very special case, where we have $N$ qubits all having $|+\rangle$ state, provides us with the equal-weight superposition of $2^N$ possible states generated by all possible combination of $N$-bit sequences as follows:

$$|+\rangle^{\otimes N} \equiv |+\rangle_1 \otimes |+\rangle_2 \otimes \cdots \otimes |+\rangle_N = \frac{1}{\sqrt{2^N}} \sum_{i=0}^{2^N-1} |i\rangle, \tag{2.16}$$

where the superscript $\otimes N$ of $|+\rangle$ represents the $N$-fold tensor product. It can be observed that the probability of obtaining each of the $2^N$ quantum states upon their observation in the computational basis is equal to $\frac{1}{2^N}$. This particular state is often used as the initialized quantum state for various quantum computing algorithms, such as Shor's quantum factoring algorithm [5, 14] and Grover's quantum search algorithm [6, 17] as well as for quantum error correction codes.

## 2.3 Quantum Information Processing

So far we have described the quantum state of a qubit. Similar to the classical domain, the qubit can be manipulated to carry out a specific quantum computation or communication task. The evolution of quantum states can be classified into two categories: reversible and irreversible evolution. A reversible evolution is constituted by a unitary transformation, while an irreversible evolution is due to the measurement or observation of our quantum states, which involves an interaction with the so-called *observer*.

### 2.3.1 Unitary Transformation

For quantum computation and communication, the desired unitary transformations are carried out by components termed as quantum gates. In classical computers, the circuits rely on logical gates such as AND, OR, and XOR gates. Similar to the classical computer, a quantum computer relies on quantum gates, which can be mathematically represented by unitary transformation satisfying the following properties:

**a.** Quantum gates, which are denoted by $U$, act linearly on the superposition of quantum states, which is defined as

$$U(\alpha_0|0\rangle + \alpha_1|1\rangle) = \alpha_0 U(|0\rangle) + \alpha_1 U(|1\rangle). \tag{2.17}$$

**b.** The quantum gate $U$ is characterized by a unitary matrix to ensure that the final probability of all possible quantum states after the transformation is equal to 1. The unitary nature of quantum gates is described as

$$UU^\dagger = \mathbf{I}, \tag{2.18}$$

where $U^\dagger$ is the Hermitian conjugate of $U$ and $\mathbf{I}$ is an identity matrix.

Some of the basic quantum gates used in quantum computation and communication will be discussed in the following subsections.

#### 2.3.1.1 Pauli Gates

First, we would like to introduce the quantum gates acting on a single qubit. Pauli gates or Pauli operators are the most common single-qubit quantum gates used for manipulating the quantum state of a single-qubit. Pauli gates are defined by Pauli matrices as follows:

$$\mathbf{I} = \begin{pmatrix} 1 & 0 \\ 0 & 1 \end{pmatrix}, \mathbf{X} = \begin{pmatrix} 0 & 1 \\ 1 & 0 \end{pmatrix}, \mathbf{Y} = \begin{pmatrix} 0 & -i \\ i & 0 \end{pmatrix}, \mathbf{Z} = \begin{pmatrix} 1 & 0 \\ 0 & -1 \end{pmatrix}. \tag{2.19}$$

Let us assume that we have a single qubit having a quantum state of $|\psi\rangle = \alpha_0|0\rangle + \alpha_1|1\rangle$. The Pauli matrix $\mathbf{X}$ transforms the quantum state of a single qubit into $|\psi'\rangle$ as follows:

$$\begin{aligned} |\psi'\rangle = \mathbf{X}|\psi\rangle &= \begin{pmatrix} 0 & 1 \\ 1 & 0 \end{pmatrix}\begin{pmatrix} \alpha_0 \\ \alpha_1 \end{pmatrix} = \begin{pmatrix} \alpha_1 \\ \alpha_0 \end{pmatrix} \\ &\equiv \alpha_1|0\rangle + \alpha_0|1\rangle. \end{aligned} \tag{2.20}$$

The transformation due to the Pauli matrix $\mathbf{Z}$ is given by

$$\begin{aligned} |\psi'\rangle = \mathbf{Z}|\psi\rangle &= \begin{pmatrix} 1 & 0 \\ 0 & -1 \end{pmatrix}\begin{pmatrix} \alpha_0 \\ \alpha_1 \end{pmatrix} = \begin{pmatrix} \alpha_0 \\ -\alpha_1 \end{pmatrix} \\ &\equiv \alpha_0|0\rangle - \alpha_1|1\rangle, \end{aligned} \tag{2.21}$$

while the Pauli matrix **Y** transforms a single qubit $|\psi\rangle$ as follows:

$$|\psi'\rangle = \mathbf{Y}|\psi\rangle = \begin{pmatrix} 0 & -i \\ i & 0 \end{pmatrix} \begin{pmatrix} \alpha_0 \\ \alpha_1 \end{pmatrix} = \begin{pmatrix} i\alpha_1 \\ -i\alpha_0 \end{pmatrix} \equiv i\alpha_1|0\rangle - i\alpha_0|1\rangle. \tag{2.22}$$

Normally, we use unitary transformations for activating the desired quantum-domain evolution of the quantum states of qubits. However, due to the interaction with the environment, or due to the imperfection of quantum gates themselves, some undesired unitary transformations may also take place. In this case, each of the Pauli matrices may also be used to reflect the discrete set of errors that may occur in a single-qubit system, such as a bit-flip error (**X**), a phase-flip error (**Z**), as well as both bit-flip and phase-flip error ($i\mathbf{XZ}=\mathbf{Y}$). Finally, the Pauli matrix **I** represents the identity operator. More details concerning this issue will be presented in Section 2.4.

#### 2.3.1.2 Hadamard Gate

The Hadamard gate maps the pure states of $|0\rangle$ and $|1\rangle$ into an equiprobable superposition of both states. The transformations mapping the pure states by Hadamard gates are described as follows:

$$\mathbf{H}|0\rangle = \frac{1}{\sqrt{2}}(|0\rangle + |1\rangle) \equiv |+\rangle, \tag{2.23}$$

$$\mathbf{H}|1\rangle = \frac{1}{\sqrt{2}}(|0\rangle - |1\rangle) \equiv |-\rangle. \tag{2.24}$$

The Hadamard gates may be represented using a $2 \times 2$ matrix as

$$\mathbf{H} = \frac{1}{\sqrt{2}} \begin{pmatrix} 1 & 1 \\ -1 & 1 \end{pmatrix}. \tag{2.25}$$

The Hadamard gates can be used for transforming the computational basis of $|0\rangle$ and $|1\rangle$ into the Hadamard basis of $|+\rangle$ and $|-\rangle$, which will be shown later to be very useful for handling different types of quantum errors imposed by quantum decoherence. The interesting property of this transformation is that a Pauli matrix **X** in the computational basis $\{|0\rangle, |1\rangle\}$ behaves similarly to a Pauli matrix **Z** in the Hadamard basis $\{|+\rangle, |-\rangle\}$. More explicitly, let us assume that we have a single qubit having a quantum state of $|\psi\rangle = \alpha_0|0\rangle + \alpha_1|1\rangle$. This specific qubit can also be rewritten in the Hadamard basis as $|\psi\rangle = \beta_0|0\rangle + \beta_1|1\rangle$, where we have $\beta_0 = \frac{\alpha_0+\alpha_1}{\sqrt{2}}$ and $\beta_1 = \frac{\alpha_0-\alpha_1}{\sqrt{2}}$. The action of the Pauli matrix **X** in the computational basis $|0\rangle$ and $|1\rangle$ can be described as follows:

$$|\psi'\rangle = \mathbf{X}|\psi\rangle = \alpha_1|0\rangle + \alpha_0|1\rangle. \tag{2.26}$$

Now, the action of the Pauli matrix **Z** in the Hadamard basis is as follows:

$$|\psi'\rangle = \mathbf{Z}|\psi\rangle = \beta_1|+\rangle + \beta_0|-\rangle. \tag{2.27}$$

It can be observed from Eqs. (2.26) and (2.27) that the effect of swapping the complex-valued coefficient between the basis vector in computational basis $|0\rangle$ and $|1\rangle$ is due to the Pauli matrix **X**, but in Hadamard basis, this effect is the result of the Pauli matrix **Z**. Similarly, let us observe the effect of the Pauli matrix **Z** on the quantum state of a single qubit in the computational basis, which can be expressed as follows:

$$|\psi'\rangle = \mathbf{Z}|\psi\rangle = \alpha_0|0\rangle - \alpha_1|1\rangle. \tag{2.28}$$

By contrast, the effect of the Pauli matrix **X** on a single-qubit quantum state in the Hadamard basis can be written as

$$|\psi'\rangle = \mathbf{X}|\psi\rangle = \beta_0|0\rangle - \beta_1|1\rangle. \tag{2.29}$$

From Eqs. (2.28) and (2.29), we can observe that the Pauli matrix **Z** flips the sign of the complex-valued coefficient of the basis vector $|1\rangle$. However, the sign of the complex-valued coefficient of the basis vector $|-\rangle$ is changed by the operation of the Pauli matrix **X** in Hadamard basis. This specific property will be beneficially exploited in the construction of QSCs, specifically when we are dealing with different types of errors imposed by quantum decoherence, as it will be detailed in Chapter 3.

#### 2.3.1.3 Phase Gate

A phase gate **S** or equivalently $i$-phase shift gate transforms the quantum state of a single qubit by shifting the phase of state $|1\rangle$ by a factor of $i$, while the state of $|0\rangle$ remains intact. More specifically, the phase gate **S** is defined by a $2 \times 2$ matrix as follows:

$$\mathbf{S} = \begin{pmatrix} 1 & 0 \\ 0 & i \end{pmatrix}. \tag{2.30}$$

The relationship between the phase gate **S** and Pauli gate **Z** is formulated as follows:

$$\mathbf{S} = \sqrt{\mathbf{Z}}, \tag{2.31}$$

$$\mathbf{S}^2 = \mathbf{Z}. \tag{2.32}$$

#### 2.3.1.4 Controlled-NOT Gate

A controlled-NOT or CNOT gate acts similarly to the XOR logic gate of a classical computer. To elaborate, the inputs of the CNOT gate are labeled as a control qubit $|c\rangle$ and a target qubit $|x\rangle$. When the control qubit $|c\rangle$ is in the state of $|1\rangle$, the target qubit $|x\rangle$ undergoes the NOT operation, or equivalently it is subjected to a Pauli matrix **X** imposing a bit-flip. Otherwise, the state of the target qubit $|x\rangle$ is left unchanged. Therefore, the transformation performed by a CNOT gate can be defined as

$$\mathbf{CNOT}(|c, x\rangle) \equiv |c, (c \oplus x)\rangle. \tag{2.33}$$

The CNOT gate can also be viewed as a controlled Pauli **X** gate, and the corresponding matrix describing the CNOT gate operation is defined as follows:

$$\mathbf{CNOT} = \mathbf{CX} = \begin{pmatrix} 1 & 0 & 0 & 0 \\ 0 & 1 & 0 & 0 \\ 0 & 0 & 0 & 1 \\ 0 & 0 & 1 & 0 \end{pmatrix} = \begin{pmatrix} \mathbf{I} & 0 \\ 0 & \mathbf{X} \end{pmatrix}. \tag{2.34}$$

The quantum circuit representation of a CNOT gate is portrayed in Figure 2.2.

The CNOT gate together with the Pauli gates, the Hadamard gate, and the phase gate create a special class of quantum gates called the Clifford group [161]. A special property of the Clifford group is that it can be efficiently simulated using classical computers. Consequently, a quantum circuit purely relying on quantum Clifford gates can be simulated efficiently on classical computer and hence is not capable of offering any substantial quantum advantage in terms of computational speedup. By contrast, a more general class of quantum computers capable of achieving computational advantages has to be capable of carrying out unitary transformations including the so-called non-Clifford quantum gates.

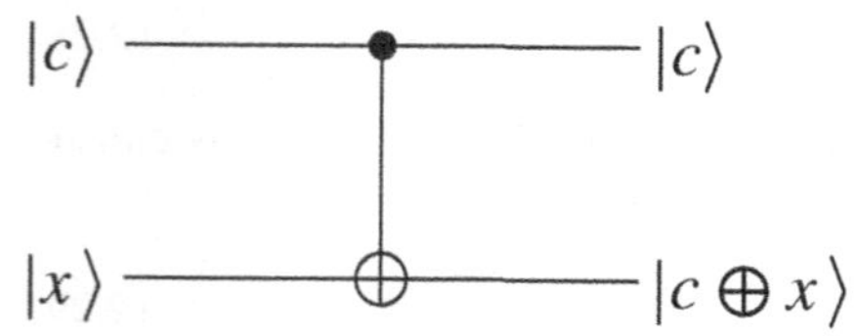


**Figure 2.2** The quantum circuit of the CNOT gate, where $|c\rangle$ is the control qubit and $|x\rangle$ is the target qubit.

#### 2.3.1.5 Toffoli Gate

A very popular example of non-Clifford quantum gates is constituted by Toffoli gate [162], which acts as a controlled-CNOT gate. However, the main difference that it has one target qubit $|x\rangle$ and two control qubits $|c_1\rangle$ and $|c_2\rangle$. The target qubit $|x\rangle$ undergoes a bit flip ($\mathbf{X}$) only when both of the control qubits $|c_1\rangle$ and $|c_2\rangle$ are in the state of $|1\rangle$. Otherwise, the state of the target qubit $|x\rangle$ remains intact. The Toffoli gate processes the quantum state of three qubits, hence its matrix representation reflects the unitary transformation of $2^3$ Hilbert space vectors. Explicitly, the unitary matrix of a Toffoli gate is defined as

$$\mathbf{CCNOT} = \mathbf{CCX} = \begin{pmatrix} 1 & 0 & 0 & 0 & 0 & 0 & 0 & 0 \\ 0 & 1 & 0 & 0 & 0 & 0 & 0 & 0 \\ 0 & 0 & 1 & 0 & 0 & 0 & 0 & 0 \\ 0 & 0 & 0 & 1 & 0 & 0 & 0 & 0 \\ 0 & 0 & 0 & 0 & 1 & 0 & 0 & 0 \\ 0 & 0 & 0 & 0 & 0 & 1 & 0 & 0 \\ 0 & 0 & 0 & 0 & 0 & 0 & 0 & 1 \\ 0 & 0 & 0 & 0 & 0 & 0 & 1 & 0 \end{pmatrix}. \tag{2.35}$$

The quantum circuit representation of a Toffoli gate is portrayed in Figure 2.3. Furthermore, the generalized version of Toffoli gates is required for executing Grover's quantum search algorithm, which has been proven to offer a beneficial quantum computation advantage [26, 163]. The generalized version of Toffoli gate, namely the $(n-1)$-controlled-NOT gate [164], which is denoted by $\mathbf{C^{\otimes(n-1)}NOT}$, transforms a vector of $2^n$ dimensions in Hilbert space. This can be represented by a $(2^n \times 2^n)$-element unitary matrix as follows:

$$\mathbf{C^{\otimes(n-1)}NOT} = \begin{pmatrix} \mathbf{I}^{2^n-2} & \mathbf{0} \\ \mathbf{0} & \mathbf{X} \end{pmatrix}, \tag{2.36}$$

where $\mathbf{I}^{2^n-2}$ is an identity matrix of dimension $(2^n - 2)$, $\mathbf{X}$ is the Pauli matrix, and the rest of the elements of the matrix are equal to zero. According to the unitary transformation of Eq. (2.36), the Pauli matrix $\mathbf{X}$ will be applied to the target qubit $|x\rangle$, if all the $(n-1)$ quantum states of the control qubits sequence are equal to $|1\rangle$. This is a conceptually simple yet powerful unitary transformation carried out by a quantum gate, but it cannot be simulated efficiently using classical computers.

### 2.3.2 Quantum Measurement

We have briefly described the reversible evolution of quantum information, which is mathematically represented by unitary transformations, and it is physically realized by quantum gates. Here, we continue by briefly describing the irreversible evolution of quantum information, namely quantum measurement. The final values of a specific quantum computation or quantum communication task have to be read out at the end. Hence, we need the so-called quantum measurement operators. Quantum measurement is described by a collection of measurement

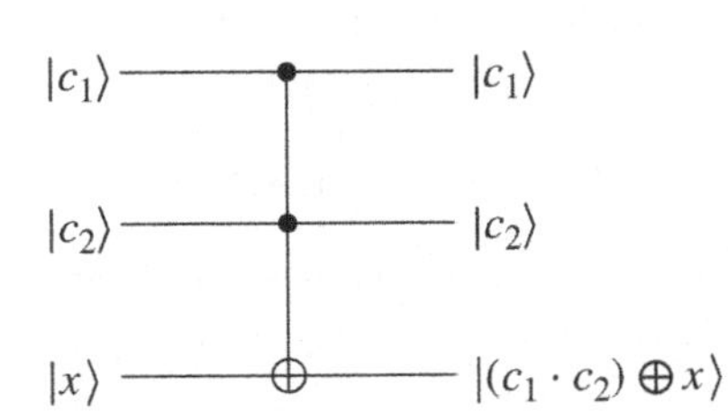


**Figure 2.3** The quantum circuit for Toffoli gate.

operators $\{M_i\}$, where $i$ denotes the measurement outcome that may occur after observations. If a quantum system is in the state of $|\psi\rangle$ before measurement, the probability of the result $i$ may be expressed as

$$p(i) = \langle\psi|M_i^\dagger M_i|\psi\rangle. \tag{2.37}$$

Consequently, the resultant state after measurement is given by

$$|\psi'\rangle = \frac{M_i|\psi\rangle}{\sqrt{\langle\psi|M_i^\dagger M_i|\psi\rangle}} = \frac{M_i|\psi\rangle}{\sqrt{p(i)}}. \tag{2.38}$$

The set of measurement operators has to satisfy the so-called completeness criteria, which are defined as

$$\sum_i M_i^\dagger M_i = \mathbf{I}, \tag{2.39}$$

$$\sum_i p(i) = \sum_i \langle\psi|M_i^\dagger M_i|\psi\rangle = 1. \tag{2.40}$$

For example, for a pair of computational basis states $|0\rangle$ and $|1\rangle$, we have two measurement operators $M_0 = |0\rangle\langle 0|$ and $M_1 = |1\rangle\langle 1|$. For an arbitrary qubit having a quantum state of $|\psi\rangle = \alpha_0|0\rangle + \alpha_1|1\rangle$, the probability of obtaining each state is formulated by

$$p(0) = |\psi\rangle M_0^\dagger M_0\langle\psi| = |\alpha_0|^2, \tag{2.41}$$

$$p(1) = |\psi\rangle M_1^\dagger M_1\langle\psi| = |\alpha_1|^2. \tag{2.42}$$

Hence, the qubit state after measurement may be expressed as

$$|\psi'\rangle_{m=0} = \frac{M_0|\psi\rangle}{|\alpha_0|} = \frac{\alpha_0|0\rangle}{|\alpha_0|}, \tag{2.43}$$

$$|\psi'\rangle_{m=1} = \frac{M_1|\psi\rangle}{|\alpha_1|} = \frac{\alpha_1|1\rangle}{|\alpha_1|}. \tag{2.44}$$

Equations (2.43) and (2.44) explicitly reflect that a qubit will collapse into a classical bit after measurement. The quantum measurement is an irreversible process, because once we obtain our measurement results in the form of classical states, it is impossible to learn the values of the complex coefficients of each of the basis vectors. Therefore, we cannot reconstruct the original quantum state from a single measurement result. Having said that, the quantum state can nonetheless be approximated with a specific level of certainty, as long as we can provide a reasonably large number of qubits prepared in an identical quantum state using a method called quantum state tomography [165, 166].

## 2.4 Quantum Decoherence

Quantum computers are composed of numerous quantum gates, which are prone to environmental impairments resulting in a short coherence time. Consequently, due to the deleterious effects of quantum decoherence, the resultant quantum state at the output may not be the desired outcome of the quantum computation. In this treatise, the terminology quantum channels will be used for encapsulating all the aforementioned imperfections caused by the quantum decoherence. A quantum channel inflicting a single qubit error can be represented by the Pauli group $\mathcal{P}_1$, which defines the discrete set of possible unitary transformations imposed on a single qubit. Explicitly, the Pauli group $\mathcal{P}_1$ is defined as

$$\mathcal{P}_1 = \{eP : P \in \{\mathbf{I}, \mathbf{X}, \mathbf{Y}, \mathbf{Z}\}, e \in \{\pm 1, \pm i\}\}, \tag{2.45}$$

which is closed under multiplication. The unitary matrices **X** and **Z** represent the bit-flip and the phase-flip, respectively, while the matrix **Y** represents a simultaneous bit-flip and phase-flip. Finally, the identity unitary matrix **I** denotes the absence of error. These Pauli matrices have been defined in Eq. (2.19). Since the qubits whose quantum states only differ in their global phase can be deemed to be equivalent, the reduced Pauli group $\mathcal{P}_1$ denoted by $\mathcal{P}_1^*$ is often used for the sake of simulating the quantum errors by exploiting the Pauli-to-binary isomorphism [160], which is defined as

$$\mathcal{P}_1^* = \{\mathbf{I}, \mathbf{X}, \mathbf{Y}, \mathbf{Z}\}. \tag{2.46}$$

From a different perspective, we can also investigate the quantum channel affecting on quantum information by describing the error effects as a unitary transformation $U(\Delta\theta.\Delta\varphi)$, which maps a point on the surface of the Bloch sphere into a different coordinate. Explicitly, using Eq. (2.9), we can define the quantum error imposed by the quantum channel as follows:

$$U(\Delta\theta, \Delta\varphi)|\psi\rangle = \cos\left(\frac{\theta + \Delta\theta}{2}\right)|0\rangle + e^{(i\varphi+\Delta\varphi)}\sin\left(\frac{\theta + \Delta\theta}{2}\right)|1\rangle, \tag{2.47}$$

where $(\theta + \Delta\theta)$ and $(\varphi + \Delta\varphi)$ are the new variables defining the resultant quantum state. By expanding the quantum state in Eq. (2.47), we can rewrite the unitary transformation of $U(\Delta\theta, \Delta\varphi)$ as follows [167]:

$$U(\Delta\theta, \Delta\varphi)|\psi\rangle = \alpha_{\mathbf{I}}\mathbf{I}|\psi\rangle + \alpha_{\mathbf{X}}\mathbf{X}|\psi\rangle + \alpha_{\mathbf{Z}}\mathbf{Z}|\psi\rangle + \alpha_{\mathbf{Y}}\mathbf{Y}|\psi\rangle, \tag{2.48}$$

where $\alpha_{\mathbf{I}}$, $\alpha_{\mathbf{X}}$, $\alpha_{\mathbf{Z}}$, and $\alpha_{\mathbf{Y}}$ are the resultant expansion coefficients. Here, we want to highlight that although the nature of quantum errors is continuous, the unitary transformation can be expressed as a linear combination of Pauli matrices **I**, **X**, **Z**, and **Y**. Furthermore, noting that apart from a phase difference, the Pauli matrix **Y** is equivalent to the product of the Pauli matrices **X** and **Z**, i.e we have $i\mathbf{XZ} = \mathbf{Y}$, the expression given in Eq. (2.48) can be further simplified into the following:

$$U(\Delta\theta, \Delta\varphi)|\psi\rangle = \alpha_{\mathbf{I}}\mathbf{I}|\psi\rangle + \alpha_{\mathbf{X}}\mathbf{X}|\psi\rangle + \alpha_{\mathbf{Z}}\mathbf{Z}|\psi\rangle + \alpha_{\mathbf{XZ}}\mathbf{XZ}|\psi\rangle, \tag{2.49}$$

where now the quantum error can be described as a linear combination of the Pauli matrices **I**, **X**, **Z**, and **XZ**. At the end of the quantum computation or communication task, the continuous nature of quantum errors will be projected into one of the following possibilities the absence of error (**I**), a bit-flip error **X**, a phase-flip error **Z**, or both bit-flip and phase-flip errors **XZ**. This concept is known as the discretization of quantum errors, which is a very useful tool when it comes to designing the associated QECCs for mitigating these error effects.

Now, let us consider the more general concept of quantum channels affecting an $N$-qubit system. When considering the quantum state of an $N$-qubit system, the quantum channel may be described by the Pauli group $\mathcal{P}_n$, which is represented by an $n$-fold tensor product of $\mathcal{P}_1$ as defined in the following:

$$\mathcal{P}_n = \{P_1 \otimes P_2 \cdots \otimes P_n | P_j \in \mathcal{P}_1\}, \tag{2.50}$$

where the index $j$ represents the $j$th qubit of a system having $n$ physical qubits. An operator $P \in \mathcal{P}_n$ transforms the legitimate quantum state $|\psi\rangle$ into an impaired quantum state $|\hat{\psi}\rangle$, as formally described in the following:

$$|\hat{\psi}\rangle = P|\psi\rangle. \tag{2.51}$$

The quantum channel inflicts an error $P \in \mathcal{P}_n$ on an $N$-qubit string, where each qubit may independently experience either a bit-flip error (**X**), a phase-flip error (**Z**), or both bit-flip and phase-flip errors ($i\mathbf{XZ} = \mathbf{Y}$). The effect of each Pauli matrix has been described earlier in Subsection 2.3.1.1. Let us now proceed by applying the unitary transformations to the multi-qubit state of Eq. (2.14), which can also be represented as a four-element complex vector as follows:

$$|\psi\rangle = \begin{pmatrix} \alpha_{00} \\ \alpha_{01} \\ \alpha_{10} \\ \alpha_{11} \end{pmatrix}. \tag{2.52}$$

For instance, let us assume that the quantum channel inflicts a 2-qubit unitary transformation of $(\mathbf{X} \otimes \mathbf{I})$[1] upon a 2-qubit state. The evolution of the quantum state can be described as follows:

$$
\begin{aligned}
|\psi'\rangle &= (\mathbf{X} \otimes \mathbf{I})\,|\psi\rangle \\
&= \left( \begin{pmatrix} 0 & 1 \\ 1 & 0 \end{pmatrix} \otimes \begin{pmatrix} 1 & 0 \\ 0 & 1 \end{pmatrix} \right) \cdot \begin{pmatrix} \alpha_{00} \\ \alpha_{01} \\ \alpha_{10} \\ \alpha_{11} \end{pmatrix} \\
&= \begin{pmatrix} 0 & \begin{pmatrix} 1 & 0 \\ 0 & 1 \end{pmatrix} \\ \begin{pmatrix} 1 & 0 \\ 0 & 1 \end{pmatrix} & 0 \end{pmatrix} \cdot \begin{pmatrix} \alpha_{00} \\ \alpha_{01} \\ \alpha_{10} \\ \alpha_{11} \end{pmatrix} \\
&= \begin{pmatrix} 0 & 0 & 1 & 0 \\ 0 & 0 & 0 & 1 \\ 1 & 0 & 0 & 0 \\ 0 & 1 & 0 & 0 \end{pmatrix} \cdot \begin{pmatrix} \alpha_{00} \\ \alpha_{01} \\ \alpha_{10} \\ \alpha_{11} \end{pmatrix} = \begin{pmatrix} \alpha_{10} \\ \alpha_{11} \\ \alpha_{00} \\ \alpha_{01} \end{pmatrix} \\
&\equiv \alpha_{10}|00\rangle + \alpha_{11}|01\rangle + \alpha_{00}|10\rangle + \alpha_{01}|11\rangle.
\end{aligned}
\tag{2.53}
$$

The final state of Eq. (2.53) can also be obtained without expanding the tensor product of the unitary transformation by flipping the state of the first qubit, since the unitary transformation of **XI** represents a bit-flip error of the first qubit owing to the bit-flip (**X**), while the second qubit does not experience any impairment owing to the effect of identity (**I**). More explicitly, due to the unitary transformation **XI**, the state of $|00\rangle$ is changed to the state of $|10\rangle$. The same transformation is also applied to the states of $|01\rangle$, $|10\rangle$, and $|11\rangle$, where they are transformed to the states of $|11\rangle$, $|00\rangle$, $|01\rangle$, respectively. Hence, the magnitude associated with the state of $|00\rangle$ is no longer $\alpha_{00}$—it becomes $\alpha_{10}$. Therefore, the coefficients associated with the states of $|01\rangle$, $|10\rangle$, and $|11\rangle$ are now $\alpha_{11}$, $\alpha_{00}$, and $\alpha_{01}$, respectively.

In this treatise, we focus our discussions on the family of QSCs, which can be derived from their classical counterparts. Even though most of the well-known QSCs are derived on the basis of the classical-to-quantum isomorphism, there is a certain property of the QSCs, which can only be found in the quantum domain, i.e. it has no classical counterpart. This is the so-called degeneracy property. More explicitly, a degeneracy property implies that a set of different error patterns of $P \in \mathcal{P}_n$ may yield an identical corrupted state and consequently we only need a single error recovery operator for reinstating the original quantum state. For example, let us consider a 2-qubit system having the following quantum state:

$$|\psi\rangle = \frac{1}{\sqrt{2}}(|00\rangle + |11\rangle), \tag{2.54}$$

1 For the sake of simplifying the notation, a set of Pauli matrices for defining a multi-qubit unitary transformation usually does not include the "⊗" operator. For example, a unitary transformation $(\mathbf{X} \otimes \mathbf{Z} \otimes \mathbf{X} \otimes \mathbf{I})$ acting upon a 4-qubit operand can simply be rewritten as **XZXI**. In the rest of Part I, the latter representation will be used for stabilizer operators, unless it is stated otherwise.

and let us consider two different error patterns, which can be described as a pair of 2-qubit unitary transformations given by $P_1 = \mathbf{IZ}$ and $P_2 = \mathbf{ZI}$. The resultant state after the error pattern $P_1$ is imposed on the 2-qubit system can be described as follows:

$$\begin{aligned} |\psi_1'\rangle &= \mathbf{IZ}|\psi\rangle \\ &= \begin{pmatrix} 1 & 0 & 0 & 0 \\ 0 & -1 & 0 & 0 \\ 0 & 0 & 1 & 0 \\ 0 & 0 & 0 & -1 \end{pmatrix} \cdot \begin{pmatrix} \frac{1}{\sqrt{2}} \\ 0 \\ 0 \\ \frac{1}{\sqrt{2}} \end{pmatrix} = \begin{pmatrix} \frac{1}{\sqrt{2}} \\ 0 \\ 0 \\ -\frac{1}{\sqrt{2}} \end{pmatrix} \\ &\equiv \frac{1}{\sqrt{2}}(|00\rangle - |11\rangle), \end{aligned} \tag{2.55}$$

while applying $P_2$ to the state of $|\psi\rangle$ will result in the following quantum state:

$$\begin{aligned} |\psi_2'\rangle &= \mathbf{ZI}|\psi\rangle \\ &= \begin{pmatrix} 1 & 0 & 0 & 0 \\ 0 & 1 & 0 & 0 \\ 0 & 0 & -1 & 0 \\ 0 & 0 & 0 & -1 \end{pmatrix} \cdot \begin{pmatrix} \frac{1}{\sqrt{2}} \\ 0 \\ 0 \\ \frac{1}{\sqrt{2}} \end{pmatrix} = \begin{pmatrix} \frac{1}{\sqrt{2}} \\ 0 \\ 0 \\ -\frac{1}{\sqrt{2}} \end{pmatrix} \\ &\equiv \frac{1}{\sqrt{2}}(|00\rangle - |11\rangle). \end{aligned} \tag{2.56}$$

Since the error patterns $P_1 = \mathbf{IZ}$ and $P_2 = \mathbf{ZI}$ yield identical corrupted states $|\psi_1'\rangle = |\psi_2'\rangle$, they undoubtedly require an identical recovery procedure. Indeed, exploiting the degeneracy property may potentially increase the error correction capability of QSCs. However, the question as to whether there exist degenerate QSCs that are capable of operating beyond the quantum Hamming bound—which is only applicable to nondegenerate QSCs—remains unresolved at the time of writing. Having said that, some research on finding the bounds of degenerate quantum codes can be found in [57, 168, 169].

The terminology of quantum channel incorporates numerous physical phenomena, including the imperfect quantum gates or quantum memories. In either of these cases, the qubits undergo a state change, which can be a linear combination of two types of quantum errors, as described in the following:

- Amplitude error or bit-flip which turns the state $|0\rangle$ into $|1\rangle$, or state $|1\rangle$ into $|0\rangle$. We also encounter this type of error in classical settings.
- Phase error or phase-flip which has no impact on the state $|0\rangle$, but it turns the state $|1\rangle$ into $-|1\rangle$. This type of error distinguishes a quantum system from classical systems.

The quantum channel may inflict an individual bit-flip ($\mathbf{X}$), a phase-flip ($\mathbf{Z}$), as well as a simultaneous bit-flip and phase-flip ($\mathbf{Y}$) error with a probability of $p_\mathbf{X}$, $p_\mathbf{Z}$, and $p_\mathbf{Y}$, respectively. These deleterious effects may be inflicted upon each of the qubits within the $N$-qubit block. For the sake of accommodating three different types of errors, the following are the common quantum channel models widely used for simulation.

### 2.4.1 Symmetric Quantum Depolarizing Channel

The *symmetric depolarizing channel* is characterized by the depolarizing probability $p$. It creates an $N$-tuple of Pauli matrices $P \in \mathcal{P}_n$ for an $N$-qubit system, where the $i$-th qubit undergoes either a bit-flip ($\mathbf{X}$) error, a phase-flip ($\mathbf{Z}$)

error, or simultaneous bit-flip and phase-flip (**Y**) errors with an equal probability of $p_e = p/3$, where $p$ denotes the overall depolarizing probability [80, 83, 170]. Hence the probability of error-free transmission is simply given by

$$p_{\mathrm{I}} = 1 - 3p_e = 1 - p. \tag{2.57}$$

In the realms of practical physical implementations, it has been observed that the probability of bit-flip errors ($p_{\mathrm{X}}$) is not equal to the probability of phase-flip errors ($p_{\mathrm{Z}}$) [171–175]. More specifically, popular materials invoked for producing quantum gates often exhibit an asymmetric behavior, where the phase-flip errors are several orders of magnitude more likely to occur than the bit-flip errors.

### 2.4.2 Asymmetric Quantum Depolarizing Channel

The more realistic quantum channel model that relies on this assumption is referred to as an *asymmetric quantum depolarizing channel* [176]. In the asymmetric case, an extra parameter referred to as the channel's asymmetry ratio $\alpha$ is introduced to portray the ratio of the phase-flip probability $p_{\mathrm{Z}}$ and the bit-flip probability $p_{\mathrm{X}}$ as follows:

$$\alpha = \frac{p_{\mathrm{Z}}}{p_{\mathrm{X}}}. \tag{2.58}$$

In practice, the channel's asymmetry ratio has popular values of $\alpha = 10^2, 10^4, 10^6$ [171–175]. Again, since the probability of phase-flip errors ($p_{\mathrm{Z}}$) is several orders of magnitude higher than that of bit-flip errors ($p_{\mathrm{X}}$), the probability of both phase and bit-flip errors ($p_{\mathrm{Y}}$) is assumed to be close to $p_{\mathrm{X}}$, which can be written as

$$p_{\mathrm{Y}} \approx p_{\mathrm{X}}. \tag{2.59}$$

Consequently, we can directly describe the parameters of the asymmetric depolarizing channel model using the depolarizing probability ($p$) and the channel's asymmetry ratio ($\alpha$) as follows:

$$p_{\mathrm{I}} = 1 - p, \tag{2.60}$$

$$p_{\mathrm{X}} = \left(\frac{1}{\alpha + 2}\right) p, \tag{2.61}$$

$$p_{\mathrm{Y}} = \left(\frac{1}{\alpha + 2}\right) p, \tag{2.62}$$

$$p_{\mathrm{Z}} = \left(\frac{\alpha}{\alpha + 2}\right) p. \tag{2.63}$$

### 2.4.3 Independent Binary-symmetric Channel

By contrast, the *independent binary-symmetric channel* model assumes that each qubit may experience bit-flip errors (**X**) and phase-flip errors (**Z**) independently. This model is equivalent to the combination of two independent binary symmetric channels, where one channel inflicts only bit-flip (**X**) errors and the other channel only inflicts phase flip (**Z**) errors. Therefore, the parameters describing the independent binary-symmetric channel model are

$$p_{\mathrm{I}} = 1 - p_{\mathrm{X}} - p_{\mathrm{Y}} - p_{\mathrm{Z}}, \tag{2.64}$$

$$p_{\mathrm{X}} = p_e^x (1 - p_e^z), \tag{2.65}$$

$$p_{\mathrm{Y}} = p_e^x p_e^z, \tag{2.66}$$

$$p_{\mathrm{Z}} = p_e^z (1 - p_e^x), \tag{2.67}$$

where $p_e^x$ denotes the crossover or flip probability in the channel **X** and $p_e^z$ denotes the crossover or flip probability in the channel **Z**. For the sake of approximating the symmetric quantum depolarizing channel, the crossover probability for each channel is assumed to be equal to $2p/3$, which can be written as

$$p_e^x = p_e^z = \frac{2p}{3}. \tag{2.68}$$

Therefore, the final parameters defining the independent binary-symmetric channel in Eq. (2.67), can be rewritten as follows:

$$p_{\mathrm{I}} = 1 - \left(\frac{4p}{3} - \frac{4p^2}{9}\right), \tag{2.69}$$

$$p_{\mathrm{X}} = \frac{2p}{3} - \frac{4p^2}{9}, \tag{2.70}$$

$$p_{\mathrm{Y}} = \frac{4p^2}{9}, \tag{2.71}$$

$$p_{\mathrm{Z}} = \frac{2p}{3} - \frac{4p^2}{9}. \tag{2.72}$$

Additionally, the independent binary-symmetric channel model can be extended directly to its the asymmetric version, which has $p_e^x \neq p_e^z$. It is important to note that most of our simulations in this treatise rely on the independent binary-symmetric channel model, while most of the analytical results are derived using the assumption of having a symmetric quantum depolarizing channel.

## 2.5 No-cloning Theorem

The concept of copying or cloning the information to protect it is widely used in classical communication and information theory. Unfortunately, the same concept is no longer valid due to the *no-cloning theorem*, as we enter into the quantum domain. Explicitly, the *no-cloning theorem* states that no unitary transformation can copy an arbitrary superposition of quantum states from one qubit to another qubit.

*Proof.* Let us assume that we have two orthogonal basis vector of $|\psi_1\rangle$ and $|\psi_2\rangle$. Let us consider a single-qubit system having a quantum state of $|\psi_1\rangle$, which acts as the data qubit, and another single-qubit system having a quantum state of $|\psi_t\rangle$, which acts as the target qubit for copying the quantum state from data qubit. Thus, the initial value before activating the copying mechanism is given by

$$|\psi'\rangle = |\psi_1\rangle \otimes |\psi_t\rangle. \tag{2.73}$$

Let us assume furthermore that there exists a unitary transformation $U$ having a copying mechanism. Then ideally the final joint quantum state after copying is formulated as

$$U(|\psi_1\rangle \otimes |\psi_t\rangle) = |\psi_1\rangle \otimes |\psi_1\rangle. \tag{2.74}$$

Upon assuming that this copying mechanism is applied to the second data qubit having a quantum state of $|\psi_2\rangle$, the copying procedure yields

$$U(|\psi_2\rangle \otimes |\psi_t\rangle) = |\psi_2\rangle \otimes |\psi_2\rangle. \tag{2.75}$$

Let us now proceed with the cloning of a superimposed quantum state, i.e. $|\lambda\rangle = \alpha_1|\psi_1\rangle + \alpha_2|\psi_2\rangle$, where $\alpha_1, \alpha_2 \in \mathbb{C}$. The copying mechanism can be formulated as

$$U(|\lambda\rangle \otimes |\psi_t\rangle) = |\lambda\rangle \otimes |\lambda\rangle. \tag{2.76}$$

Expanding the left-hand side of Eq. (2.76) yields

$$\begin{aligned} U(|\lambda\rangle \otimes |\psi_t\rangle) &= U[(\alpha_1|\psi_1\rangle + \alpha_2|\psi_2\rangle) \otimes |\psi_t\rangle] \\ &= U(\alpha_1|\psi_1\rangle \otimes |\psi_t\rangle) + U(\alpha_2|\psi_2\rangle \otimes |\psi_t\rangle) \\ &= \alpha_1|\psi_1\rangle \otimes |\psi_1\rangle + \alpha_2|\psi_2\rangle \otimes |\psi_2\rangle \\ &\equiv \alpha_1|\psi_1, \psi_1\rangle + \alpha_2|\psi_2, \psi_2\rangle. \end{aligned} \tag{2.77}$$

Upon simplifying the right-hand side of Eq. (2.76), we obtain

$$\begin{aligned}|\lambda\rangle \otimes |\lambda\rangle &= (\alpha_1|\psi_1\rangle + \alpha_2|\psi_2\rangle)(\alpha_1|\psi_1\rangle + \alpha_2|\psi_2\rangle) \\ &= \alpha_1^2|\psi_1\rangle|\psi_1\rangle + \alpha_1\alpha_2|\psi_1\rangle|\psi_2\rangle + \alpha_1\alpha_2|\psi_2\rangle|\psi_1\rangle + \alpha_2^2|\psi_2\rangle|\psi_2\rangle \\ &\equiv \alpha_1^2|\psi_1,\psi_1\rangle + \alpha_1\alpha_2|\psi_1,\psi_2\rangle + \alpha_1\alpha_2|\psi_2,\psi_1\rangle + \alpha_2^2|\psi_2,\psi_2\rangle.\end{aligned} \tag{2.78}$$

Equating Eqs. (2.77) and (2.78) yields

$$\alpha_1(\alpha_1 - 1)|\psi_1,\psi_1\rangle + \alpha_1\alpha_2|\psi_1,\psi_2\rangle + \alpha_1\alpha_2|\psi_2,\psi_1\rangle + \alpha_2(\alpha_2 - 1)|\psi_2,\psi_2\rangle = 0. \tag{2.79}$$

Equation (2.79) implies that the solution of the equation is given by $\alpha_1, \alpha_2 = \{0, 1\}$, which results in the quantum state $|\psi_1\rangle$ or $|\psi_2\rangle$ itself. We arrive at the conclusion that a quantum-domain copying operation is only capable of cloning the basis states $|\psi_1\rangle$ and $|\psi_2\rangle$, but fails to clone the superposition of the two states $|\lambda\rangle = \alpha_1|\psi_1\rangle + \alpha_2|\psi_2\rangle$.

## 2.6 Quantum Entanglement

Quantum entanglement is a unique property that only exists in the quantum domain, but it has no counterparts in classical systems. It may be described as a phenomenon where a pair or a group of qubits is generated in such way that the quantum state of the constituent qubits cannot be described independently. For instance, let us consider a 2-qubit quantum system having a quantum state of $|\psi\rangle$. The quantum state of $|\psi\rangle$ is said to be separable if it can be expressed as a tensor product of two independent quantum states as follows:

$$|\psi\rangle = |\psi_1\rangle \otimes |\psi_2\rangle. \tag{2.80}$$

Otherwise, the quantum state $|\psi\rangle$ is said to be entangled. More explicitly, to provide a clearer picture about quantum entanglement, let us consider an arbitrary 2-qubit state as follows:

$$|\psi\rangle = \alpha_{00}|00\rangle + \alpha_{11}|11\rangle, \tag{2.81}$$

where $\alpha_{00}, \alpha_{11} \neq 0$. Let us now consider a quantum state constituted by the superposition of two individual qubits, which may be described as follows:

$$\begin{aligned}|\psi\rangle &= (\alpha_0|0\rangle + \alpha_1|1\rangle) \otimes (\beta_0|0\rangle + \beta_1|1\rangle) \\ &= \alpha_0\beta_0|00\rangle + \alpha_0\beta_1|01\rangle + \alpha_1\beta_0|10\rangle + \alpha_1\beta_1|11\rangle.\end{aligned} \tag{2.82}$$

By equating Eqs. (2.81) and (2.82), we arrive at

$$\alpha_{00}|00\rangle + \alpha_{11}|11\rangle = \alpha_0\beta_0|00\rangle + \alpha_0\beta_1|01\rangle + \alpha_1\beta_0|10\rangle + \alpha_1\beta_1|11\rangle. \tag{2.83}$$

Since the non-zero solution for $\alpha_{00}, \alpha_{11}, \alpha_0, \alpha_1, \beta_0$, and $\beta_1$ does not exist for Eq. (2.83), it is impossible to decompose the state of the qubits in Eq. (2.81) into two individual qubit states as in Eq. (2.82).

To elaborate a little further, let us now consider a very specific quantum state defined as follows:

$$|\Phi^+\rangle = \frac{1}{\sqrt{2}}(|00\rangle + |11\rangle). \tag{2.84}$$

In this case, if we perform a quantum measurement on the first qubit in Eq. (2.84), we can determine the value of the second qubit immediately with absolute certainty. If the measurement result of the first qubit is 0, the result of measuring the second qubit will also be 0. Similarly, if the measurement result of the first qubit is 1, the result of observing the second qubit will also be 1. Consequently, this inherent correlation between the two qubits with a quantum state of $|\Phi^+\rangle$ is established even if they are separated in space. This interesting phenomenon was given the fond connotation of "spooky action at a distance" by Einstein.

Quantum entanglement enables a pair or a group of qubits to interact over a distance simultaneously, even if they are at the opposite sides of the universe. However, this intriguing fact does not mean that we can communicate faster than the speed of light. Although there is a connection between the entangled qubits, we still do not know what information is going to be transmitted, since we cannot observe the state of entangled qubits before their measurement. Hence, this connection cannot be used for information transmission. This condition is further elaborated on by the *no communication theorem*, which is a specific theorem of quantum information theory. However, the ability of creating entanglement may be exploited for beneficial applications such as QECCs [73, 74], quantum key distribution [28], quantum superdense coding [29], quantum teleportation [30], and quantum secure-direct communication [31].

## 2.7 Quantum Channels

Again, quantum decoherence is a major impediment in the way of realizing practical quantum computation and communication systems. Decoherence may be viewed as the unwanted entanglement of the qubit with the environment, which perturbs its coherent quantum state. Let us consider the decoherence process for the basis states $|0\rangle$ and $|1\rangle$, which can be encapsulated as [54]:

$$\begin{aligned}|e_0\rangle|0\rangle &\rightarrow |a_0\rangle|0\rangle + |a_1\rangle|1\rangle,\\ |e_0\rangle|1\rangle &\rightarrow |a_2\rangle|0\rangle + |a_3\rangle|1\rangle,\end{aligned} \tag{2.85}$$

where $|e_0\rangle$ is the state of the environment before interaction, while $|a_i\rangle$ denotes the $i$th post-decoherence state of the environment (not necessarily orthogonal or normalized), which ensures that the overall evolution of Eq. (2.85) is unitary. Consequently, a qubit in the state $|\psi\rangle = \alpha|0\rangle + \beta|1\rangle$ decoheres as:

$$|e_0\rangle|\psi\rangle \rightarrow \alpha(|a_0\rangle|0\rangle + |a_1\rangle|1\rangle) + \beta(|a_2\rangle|0\rangle + |a_3\rangle|1\rangle). \tag{2.86}$$

Equation (2.86) can be rearranged as:

$$\begin{aligned}|e_0\rangle|\psi\rangle \rightarrow\ &\frac{1}{2}(|a_0\rangle + |a_3\rangle)(\alpha|0\rangle + \beta|1\rangle) + \frac{1}{2}(|a_0\rangle - |a_3\rangle)(\alpha|0\rangle - \beta|1\rangle) +\\ &\frac{1}{2}(|a_1\rangle + |a_2\rangle)(\alpha|1\rangle + \beta|0\rangle) + \frac{1}{2}(|a_1\rangle - |a_2\rangle)(\alpha|1\rangle - \beta|0\rangle),\end{aligned} \tag{2.87}$$

which is equivalent to:

$$\begin{aligned}|e_0\rangle|\psi\rangle \rightarrow\ &\frac{1}{2}(|a_0\rangle + |a_3\rangle)\mathbf{I}|\psi\rangle + \frac{1}{2}(|a_0\rangle - |a_3\rangle)\mathbf{Z}|\psi\rangle +\\ &\frac{1}{2}(|a_1\rangle + |a_2\rangle)\mathbf{X}|\psi\rangle + \frac{-i}{2}(|a_1\rangle - |a_2\rangle)\mathbf{Y}|\psi\rangle.\end{aligned} \tag{2.88}$$

Hence, as we may observe in Eq. (2.87), the state $\psi$ is mapped onto a linear combination of the original state (Pauli-**I** operation), phase-flipped state (Pauli-**Z** operation), bit-flipped state (Pauli-**X** operation), and both phase- and bit-flipped state (Pauli-**Y** operation). In the process of the quantum error correction, the superimposed state of Eq. (2.87) collapses to one of these four possibilities upon measurement. Therefore, the overall decoherence process can be visualized as inflicting bit errors or phase errors or possibly both errors on the qubit, which were also depicted in Figure 1.3. Alternatively, we may intuitively argue that since any arbitrary unitary operator can be expressed as a linear combination of the Pauli-**I**, Pauli-**Z**, Pauli-**X**, and Pauli-**Y** operators, decoherence can also be described in terms of these Pauli operators. Hence, quantum channel models are defined on the basis of the set of Pauli operators.

A quantum channel can be used for modeling imperfections in quantum hardware, namely, faults resulting from quantum decoherence and quantum gates. Furthermore, a quantum channel can also model quantum-state flips imposed by the transmission medium, including free-space wireless channels and optical fiber links, when qubits are transmitted across these media. Some of the commonly used quantum channel models are discussed in the following [160]:

- **Bit-flip Channel:** Analogous to a classical binary symmetric channel, a bit-flip channel, characterized by the probability $p$ maps the basis state $|0\rangle \rightarrow |1\rangle$ and $|1\rangle \rightarrow |0\rangle$ with a probability of $p$. The associated set of operators are defined as:

$$\mathbf{E}_0 = \sqrt{1-p}\,\mathbf{I} = \sqrt{1-p}\begin{pmatrix} 1 & 0 \\ 0 & 1 \end{pmatrix}, \quad \mathbf{E}_1 = \sqrt{p}\,\mathbf{X} = \sqrt{p}\begin{pmatrix} 0 & 1 \\ 1 & 0 \end{pmatrix}, \tag{2.89}$$

  where $\mathbf{E}_j$ is the $j$th operator, which maps a given channel input onto the corresponding output.
- **Phase-flip Channel:** A phase-flip channel characterized by the probability $p$ inflicts a Pauli-**Z** error on the transmitted qubit with a probability of $p$, which can be encapsulated as:

$$\mathbf{E}_0 = \sqrt{1-p}\,\mathbf{I} = \sqrt{1-p}\begin{pmatrix} 1 & 0 \\ 0 & 1 \end{pmatrix}, \quad \mathbf{E}_1 = \sqrt{p}\,\mathbf{Z} = \sqrt{p}\begin{pmatrix} 1 & 0 \\ 0 & -1 \end{pmatrix}. \tag{2.90}$$

- **Bit-phase-flip Channel:** A bit-phase-flip channel characterized by the probability $p$ inflicts a Pauli-**Y** error on the transmitted qubit with a probability of $p$, which can be defined as:

$$\mathbf{E}_0 = \sqrt{1-p}\,\mathbf{I} = \sqrt{1-p}\begin{pmatrix} 1 & 0 \\ 0 & 1 \end{pmatrix}, \quad \mathbf{E}_1 = \sqrt{p}\,\mathbf{Y} = \sqrt{p}\begin{pmatrix} 0 & -i \\ i & 0 \end{pmatrix}. \tag{2.91}$$

- **Depolarizing Channel:** A depolarizing channel characterized by the probability $p$ inflicts a bit-error (Pauli-**X**) or a phase-error (Pauli-**Z**) or both bit and phase errors (Pauli-**Y**) with a probability of $p/3$ each, which can be expressed as:

$$\begin{aligned} \mathbf{E}_0 &= \sqrt{1-p}\,\mathbf{I} = \sqrt{1-p}\begin{pmatrix} 1 & 0 \\ 0 & 1 \end{pmatrix}, \quad \mathbf{E}_1 = \sqrt{\frac{p}{3}}\,\mathbf{X} = \sqrt{\frac{p}{3}}\begin{pmatrix} 0 & 1 \\ 1 & 0 \end{pmatrix}, \\ \mathbf{E}_2 &= \sqrt{\frac{p}{3}}\,\mathbf{Z} = \sqrt{\frac{p}{3}}\begin{pmatrix} 1 & 0 \\ 0 & -1 \end{pmatrix}, \quad \mathbf{E}_3 = \sqrt{\frac{p}{3}}\,\mathbf{Y} = \sqrt{\frac{p}{3}}\begin{pmatrix} 0 & -i \\ i & 0 \end{pmatrix}. \end{aligned} \tag{2.92}$$

  The depolarizing channel of Eq. (2.92) may be referred to as a symmetric channel, since the three types of errors occur with equal probabilities. By contrast, if the Pauli-**X**, Pauli-**Z** and Pauli-**Y** errors occur with different probabilities, the channel is termed as being asymmetric [176, 177].
- **Amplitude Damping Channel:** Amplitude damping channel models the loss of energy from a quantum system. An amplitude damping channel characterized by the damping probability $\gamma$, or more specifically the probability of losing a photon, is modeled as:

$$\mathbf{E}_0 = \begin{pmatrix} 1 & 0 \\ 0 & \sqrt{1-\gamma} \end{pmatrix}, \quad \mathbf{E}_1 = \begin{pmatrix} 0 & \sqrt{\gamma} \\ 0 & 0 \end{pmatrix}. \tag{2.93}$$

  According to Eq. (2.93), the operator $\mathbf{E}_1$ changes the state $|1\rangle$ to $|0\rangle$ depicting that energy is lost to the environment, while the operator $\mathbf{E}_0$ reduces the amplitude of the state $|1\rangle$ because energy is dissipated, which makes it less likely to encounter the state $|1\rangle$.
- **Phase Damping Channel:** Phase damping characterizes the loss of quantum information without the loss of energy. It may include for example the scattering of photons, or perturbation of electronic states caused by the stray electrical charges. Phase damping channel can be described as follows:

$$\mathbf{E}_0 = \begin{pmatrix} 1 & 0 \\ 0 & \sqrt{1-\lambda} \end{pmatrix}, \quad \mathbf{E}_1 = \begin{pmatrix} 0 & 0 \\ 0 & \sqrt{\lambda} \end{pmatrix}, \tag{2.94}$$

where $\lambda$ is the probability of scattering of a photon (without loss of energy). Similar to the amplitude damping channel, $\mathbf{E}_0$ reduces the amplitude of state $|1\rangle$. On the other hand, the operator $\mathbf{E}_1$ destroys the state $|0\rangle$, while reduces the amplitude of state $|1\rangle$.

In this treatise, we will only consider the widely used symmetric depolarizing channel model of Eq. (2.92) [67, 86, 139, 178], and we will focus our attention on the depolarizing channel model. A compact summary of this section is provided at a glance in Tables 2.1 and 2.2.

**Table 2.1** Summary of the quantum unitary operators of Section 2.1.

| Gate | Symbol | Operation | Matrix |
|---|---|---|---|
| Pauli-I | **I** | Identity operation. | $\begin{pmatrix} 1 & 0 \\ 0 & 1 \end{pmatrix}$ |
| Pauli-**X** | **X** | Bit flip. | $\begin{pmatrix} 0 & 1 \\ 1 & 0 \end{pmatrix}$ |
| Pauli-**Z** | **Z** | Phase flip. | $\begin{pmatrix} 1 & 0 \\ 0 & -1 \end{pmatrix}$ |
| Pauli-**Y** | **Y** | Bit and phase flip. | $\begin{pmatrix} 0 & -i \\ i & 0 \end{pmatrix}$ |
| Hadamard | **H** | Maps a pure state $|0\rangle$ or $|1\rangle$ onto a superposition of the basis states. | $\frac{1}{\sqrt{2}}\begin{pmatrix} 1 & 1 \\ -1 & 1 \end{pmatrix}$ |
| Phase | **S** | Changes the phase of the basis state $|1\rangle$ by $\pi/2$, while leaving $|0\rangle$ intact. | $\begin{pmatrix} 1 & 0 \\ 0 & i \end{pmatrix}$ |
| Contr.-NOT | CNOT | A 2-qubit gate, which flips the target qubit when the control qubit is in the state $|1\rangle$. | $\begin{pmatrix} 1 & 0 & 0 & 0 \\ 0 & 1 & 0 & 0 \\ 0 & 0 & 0 & 1 \\ 0 & 0 & 1 & 0 \end{pmatrix}$ |

**Table 2.2** Summary of the quantum channel models of Section 2.7.

| Channel | Definition |
|---|---|
| Bit-flip | Inflicts a Pauli-**X** error with a probability of $p$. |
| Phase-flip | Inflicts a Pauli-**Z** error with a probability of $p$. |
| Bit-phase-flip | Inflicts a Pauli-**Y** error with a probability of $p$. |
| Depolarizing | Inflicts a Pauli-**X**, **Z**, or **Y** error with a probability of $p/3$ each. |
| Amplitude damping | Models the energy dissipation from a quantum system with a damping probability $\gamma$. |
| Phase damping | Models the loss of quantum information without any energy dissipation, which is characterized by the scattering probability $\lambda$. |

## 2.8 Summary and Conclusions

This chapter provides a brief introduction to fundamental quantum information processing. We have highlighted the basic properties of the qubits along with the quantum evolutions acting on single-qubit and multi-qubit systems. We have categorized the quantum evolution into reversible evolution represented by the unitary transformations and the irreversible evolution constituted by quantum measurements. We have also introduced several quantum gates widely utilized in the development of this treatise. Additionally, we have presented various quantum channel models used for simulating the quantum decoherence imposed on the quantum information. We have presented one of the fundamental limitations in the quantum domain, namely the no-cloning theorem, which states that we cannot replicate the quantum state of a qubit in an arbitrary superposition state. Finally, we have described one of the distinctive features of quantum information, namely, the ability to create quantum entanglement. The rest of Part I will be developed based on the knowledge presented in this chapter.

# 3

# From Classical to Quantum Coding

## 3.1 Introduction

In Chapter 2, we have discussed some of the basic quantum signal processing gates and stated that quantum information suffers from qubit errors. In the classical domain, the deleterious effects of errors imposed by the channel can be mitigated using error correction codes by attaching redundancy to the information part. However, the laws of quantum mechanics prevent us from directly transplanting the classical error correction codes into the quantum domain owing to the following obstacles:

a. **No-cloning Theorem**. In the classical domain, the simplest technique of protecting the information bits is based on repetition coding, copying the same information bits several times and then using majority decisions for finding the most likely transmitted codeword. By contrast, in the quantum domain, this simple approach cannot be implemented, since no unitary quantum transformation is capable of performing this specific task. Formally, this is stated by the no-cloning theorem.
b. **The quantum bit collapses into the corresponding classical bit upon measurement**. In the classical domain, the error correction decoders are typically fed by the bits received at the output of the demodulator. In the quantum domain, measuring the qubits represented by the superposition of the classical states will collapse the superposition into a single classical post-measurement state and consequently, we lose the original quantum information.
c. **QECCs have to handle not only bit-flip errors but also phase-flip errors, as well as the simultaneous bit-flip and phase-flip errors**. By contrast, in the classical domain, we deal with a single type of error, which is the bit-flip error. In the quantum domain, the nature of quantum decoherence is continuous and it can be modeled as a linear combination of bit-flip errors ($\mathbf{X}$), phase-flip errors ($\mathbf{Z}$), or both bit-flip and phase-flip errors ($i\mathbf{XZ} = \mathbf{Y}$). However, thanks to the beneficial effect of the stabilizer measurement, the continuous nature of quantum decoherence can be treated as a discrete set of independent errors imposed on the physical qubits.

Albeit all of the aforementioned obstacles hinder the development of QECC schemes, the invention of QSC formulation succeeded in circumventing these problems.

In this chapter, we present the classical-to-quantum isomorphism of the QSCs, demonstrating the duality between the classical and quantum domains. We will also show how to transplant the well-known syndrome-based decoding of classical codes into quantum codes. The rest of this chapter is organized as follows. We commence with a brief review of classical syndrome-based decoding in Section 3.2. This is followed by Section 3.3, where we present the similarities between classical syndrome-based decoding and the QSCs. In Section 3.4, we provide the examples for the QSC constructions protecting a single qubit using 1/3-rate quantum repetition code, Shor's code, Steane's code, and the perfect 5-qubit code. Finally, we conclude this chapter in Section 3.5.

## 3.2 A Brief Review of Classical Syndrome-based Decoding

As mentioned earlier, the problems revolving around the QECCs are effectively circumvented by QSCs, which essentially constitute the syndrome-based decoding version of QECCs. Hence, for the sake of shedding some light onto the parallelism between the classical and quantum regime, we proceed with the classical syndrome-based decoding first.

In the classical domain a $\mathcal{C}(n,k)$ code maps $k$ information bits into $n$ coded bits, where $k<n$. The objective of attaching $(n-k)$ redundant bits is to facilitate error detection or even error correction. Let us refer to Figure 3.1 and consider the classical $\mathcal{C}(7,4)$ Hamming code, which maps 4 information bits into 7 coded bits and hence becomes capable of correcting a single error. In general, the mapping of the $k$ information bits is performed by multiplying the information row vector $\mathbf{x}$ consisting of $k$ elements by the generator matrix $\mathbf{G}$ having $(k\times n)$ elements. Explicitly, the mapping can be formulated as

$$\mathbf{y}=\mathbf{x}*\mathbf{G}, \tag{3.1}$$

where the resultant codeword $\mathbf{y}$ is a row vector having $n$ elements, while the notation of $*$ represents the matrix multiplication over modulo 2. For instance, the generator matrix of the $\mathcal{C}(7,4)$ Hamming code is defined by

$$\mathbf{G}_{\text{Hamming}}=\begin{pmatrix}1&0&0&0&1&1&0\\0&1&0&0&1&0&1\\0&0&1&0&0&1&1\\0&0&0&1&1&1&1\end{pmatrix}. \tag{3.2}$$

From Eqs. (3.1) and (3.2) we can generate the code space mapping shown in Table 3.1, where $\mathbf{x}_i$ denotes all the possible combinations of the information bits and $\mathbf{y}_i$ represents the associated legitimate codeword bits.

The generator matrix $\mathbf{G}$ can be arranged into a systematic form as

$$\mathbf{G}=(\mathbf{I}_k|\mathbf{P}), \tag{3.3}$$

where $\mathbf{I}_k$ is a $(k\times k)$ identity matrix and $\mathbf{P}$ is a matrix having $k\times(n-k)$ elements. The form given in Eq. (3.3) generates a systematic codeword $\mathbf{y}$ consisting of the $k$-bit information word $\mathbf{x}$ followed by $(n-k)$ parity bits.

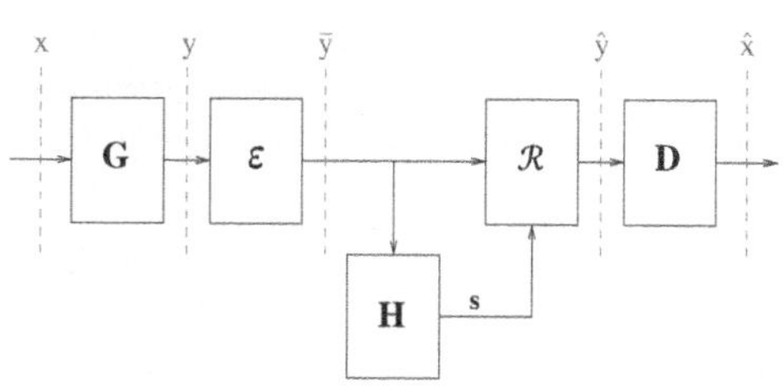


**Figure 3.1** The basic model of classical error correction codes invoking syndrome-based decoding. The $\mathbf{G}$ denotes the generator matrix, which maps the $k$ information bits $\mathbf{x}$ to the $n$ coded bits $\mathbf{y}$. The channel $\mathcal{E}$ inflicts an error vector $\mathbf{e}\in\{0,1\}^n$ to the codeword $\mathbf{y}$ resulting the corrupted received bits $\bar{\mathbf{y}}$. The receiver calculates the syndrome vector $\mathbf{s}$ based on the PCM $\mathbf{H}$ and received bits $\bar{\mathbf{y}}$ to predict the number and the position of errors contained in the received bits $\bar{\mathbf{y}}$. The error recovery $\mathcal{R}$ generates the error recovery vector $\mathbf{r}$, which is applied to the received bits $\bar{\mathbf{y}}$. It collapses the received bits $\bar{\mathbf{y}}$ to one of the legitimate codedword $\mathbf{y}$ yielding the predicted codeword $\hat{\mathbf{y}}$. Finally, we can readily determine the predicted information bits $\hat{\mathbf{x}}$ from the predicted codeword $\hat{\mathbf{y}}$. *Source*: [174]/IEEE/CC BY 4.0.

**Table 3.1** The code space mapping of the $\mathcal{C}(7,4)$ classical Hamming code.

| $i$ | $\mathbf{x}_i$ | $\mathbf{y}_i$ |
|---|---|---|
| 1 | 0000 | 0000000 |
| 2 | 0001 | 0001111 |
| 3 | 0010 | 0010011 |
| 4 | 0011 | 0011100 |
| 5 | 0100 | 0100101 |
| 6 | 0101 | 0101010 |
| 7 | 0110 | 0110110 |
| 8 | 0111 | 0111001 |
| 9 | 1000 | 1000110 |
| 10 | 1001 | 1001001 |
| 11 | 1010 | 1010101 |
| 12 | 1011 | 1011010 |
| 13 | 1100 | 1100011 |
| 14 | 1101 | 1101100 |
| 15 | 1110 | 1110000 |
| 16 | 1111 | 1111111 |

As an example, the encoder has to carry out the following operations for the 4-bit original information segment for generating the 7-bit encoded codeword:

$$\mathbf{y} = \mathbf{x} \cdot \mathbf{G} = [0001] \cdot \begin{pmatrix} 1 & 0 & 0 & 0 & | & 1 & 1 & 0 \\ 0 & 1 & 0 & 0 & | & 1 & 0 & 1 \\ 0 & 0 & 1 & 0 & | & 0 & 1 & 1 \\ 0 & 0 & 0 & 1 & | & 1 & 1 & 1 \end{pmatrix}. \tag{3.4}$$

Explicitly, we write down the element-wise product as a sum and then take the mod 2, as detailed here:

- $0+0+0+0 \pmod 2 = 0$
- $0+0+0+0 \pmod 2 = 0$
- $0+0+0+0 \pmod 2 = 0$
- $0+0+0+1 \pmod 2 = 1$
- $0+0+0+1 \pmod 2 = 1$
- $0+0+0+1 \pmod 2 = 1$
- $0+0+0+1 \pmod 2 = 1$

A generator matrix $\mathbf{G}$ is associated with an $(n-k) \times n$-element parity-check matrix (PCM) $\mathbf{H}$, which is defined as

$$\mathbf{H} = (\mathbf{P}^T | \mathbf{I}_{n-k}). \tag{3.5}$$

As an example, the generator matrix of the classical $\mathcal{C}(7,4)$ Hamming code of Eq. (3.2) is associated with the following PCM:

$$\mathbf{H}_{\text{Hamming}} = \begin{pmatrix} 1 & 1 & 0 & 1 & 1 & 0 & 0 \\ 1 & 0 & 1 & 1 & 0 & 1 & 0 \\ 0 & 1 & 1 & 1 & 0 & 0 & 1 \end{pmatrix}. \tag{3.6}$$

The PCM of $\mathbf{H}$ is constructed for ensuring that a valid codeword $\mathbf{y}$ satisfies the following requirement:

$$\mathbf{y} * \mathbf{H}^T = \mathbf{0}. \tag{3.7}$$

A received word $\overline{\mathbf{y}}$ may be contaminated by an error vector $\mathbf{e} \in \{0,1\}^n$ due to channel impairments, which is denoted by $\mathcal{E}$ in Figure 3.1. More explicitly, the resultant received words corrupted by the additive noise $\mathcal{E}$ can be formulated as

$$\overline{\mathbf{y}} = \mathbf{y} + \mathbf{e}. \tag{3.8}$$

The error syndrome $\mathbf{s}$ is a row vector having $(n-k)$ elements obtained by the following calculation:

$$\begin{aligned} \mathbf{s} = \overline{\mathbf{y}} * \mathbf{H}^T &= (\mathbf{y} + \mathbf{e}) * \mathbf{H}^T \\ &= \mathbf{y} * \mathbf{H}^T + \mathbf{e} * \mathbf{H}^T \\ &= \mathbf{0} + \mathbf{e} * \mathbf{H}^T \\ &= \mathbf{e} * \mathbf{H}^T. \end{aligned} \tag{3.9}$$

The syndrome vector $\mathbf{s}$ contains the information related to the error pattern imposed by the channel. To elaborate, we have $2^k$ legitimate codewords generated by all the possible combinations of the $k$ information bits, $2^n$ possible received bit patterns of $\hat{\mathbf{y}}$ and $2^{(n-k)}$ syndromes $\mathbf{s}$, each unambiguously identifying one of the $2^{(n-k)}$ error patterns, including the error-free scenario.

Hence, for the classical $\mathcal{C}(7,4)$ Hamming code, the syndrome vector $\mathbf{s}_i$ can uniquely and unambiguously detect and correct one of the seven single-bit error patterns, plus the error-free scenario, as specified in Table 3.2.

For example, for the error pattern of $e^T = [0000001]$ the syndrome decoder carries out the following operations:

$$\mathbf{s} = \mathbf{e} \cdot \mathbf{H}^T = [0000001] \cdot \begin{pmatrix} 1 & 1 & 0 \\ 1 & 0 & 1 \\ 0 & 1 & 1 \\ 1 & 1 & 1 \\ 1 & 0 & 0 \\ 0 & 1 & 0 \\ 0 & 0 & 1 \end{pmatrix} = [001]. \tag{3.10}$$

The error recovery $\mathbf{r}_i$ is determined based on the most likely error pattern. After obtaining the syndrome vector, the recovery vector $\mathbf{r}_i$ is applied to the received words to obtain the predicted codeword $\hat{\mathbf{y}} = \overline{\mathbf{y}} + \mathbf{r}$, as depicted in Figure 3.1. The application of the recovery operator to the received word always collapses it into one of the legitimate codewords $\mathbf{y}$, hence the predicted codeword $\hat{\mathbf{y}}$ can be finally demapped in order to obtain the predicted information bits $\hat{\mathbf{x}}$ using Table 3.1, as illustrated in Figure 3.1. For linear systematic codes, this process can be simply performed by chopping the last $(n-k)$ bits, namely the redundant bits.

**Table 3.2** The look-up table to determine the most likely error pattern $\mathbf{e}_i \in \mathcal{E}$ that corresponds to the syndrome value $\mathbf{s}_i$, which is created based on Eqs. (3.6) and (3.9).

| $i$ | $\mathbf{s}_i$ | $\mathbf{e}_i$ |
|---|---|---|
| 1 | 0 0 0 | 0 0 0 0 0 0 0 |
| 2 | 0 0 1 | 0 0 0 0 0 0 1 |
| 3 | 0 1 0 | 0 0 0 0 0 1 0 |
| 4 | 0 1 1 | 0 0 1 0 0 0 0 |
| 5 | 1 0 0 | 0 0 0 0 1 0 0 |
| 6 | 1 0 1 | 0 1 0 0 0 0 0 |
| 7 | 1 1 0 | 1 0 0 0 0 0 0 |
| 8 | 1 1 1 | 0 0 0 1 0 0 0 |

For another detailed example let us consider $k$ information bits of $\mathbf{x} = (1\,1\,0\,1)$. The information bits are encoded using the classical $\mathcal{C}(7,4)$ Hamming code employing the generator matrix of Eq. (3.1), yielding the coded bits of $\mathbf{y} = (1\,1\,0\,1\,1\,0\,0)$. Let us assume that the channel corrupts the legitimate codeword $\mathbf{y}$ by imposing an error pattern of $\mathbf{e} = (1\,0\,0\,0\,0\,0\,0)$ resulting in the received word of $\overline{\mathbf{y}} = (0\,1\,0\,1\,1\,0\,0)$. Next, the received word is fed to the syndrome calculation block, which contains the PCM of Eq. (3.6). Based on Eq. (3.9), the received word $\overline{\mathbf{y}} = (0\,1\,0\,1\,1\,0\,0)$ generates the syndrome vector of $\mathbf{s} = (1\,1\,0)$. Utilizing the look-up table of Table 3.2, the error recovery vector becomes $\mathbf{r} = (1\,0\,0\,0\,0\,0\,0)$. Upon applying the error recovery vector, the received word $\overline{\mathbf{y}}$ is collapsed to one of the legitimate codewords $\mathbf{y}$ in Table 3.1, which is $\hat{\mathbf{y}} = (1\,1\,0\,1\,1\,0\,0)$. Assuming that the predicted codeword $\hat{\mathbf{y}}$ is valid, the demapper decides to translate the predicted codeword $\hat{\mathbf{y}} = (1\,1\,0\,1\,1\,0\,0)$ to the predicted information bits as $\hat{\mathbf{x}} = (1\,1\,0\,1)$. Hence, the original information is successfully recovered. The whole process of syndrome calculation, error recovery and demapping jointly forms the *decoding* process. It is important to note that in practice, the syndrome calculation, recovery operator and demapper are amalgamated into a single *decoder* block.

Let us now assume that the channel imposes an error pattern beyond the error correction capability of the classical $\mathcal{C}(7,4)$ Hamming code. For example, assume that we send the identical $k$ information bits of $\mathbf{x} = (1\,1\,0\,1)$ while the channel inflicts an error pattern of $\mathbf{e} = (1\,1\,0\,0\,0\,0\,0)$. As a result, we have the received codeword bits of $\overline{\mathbf{y}} = (0\,0\,0\,1\,1\,0\,0)$. Based on the received codeword, we have the syndrome vector of $\mathbf{s} = (0\,1\,1)$. Based on the syndrome vector, the error recovery of $\mathbf{r} = (0\,0\,1\,0\,0\,0\,0)$ is chosen. Consequently, the error recovery vector collapses the received word to the incorrect legitimate codeword, which is $\hat{\mathbf{y}} = (0\,0\,1\,1\,1\,0\,0)$, instead of the correct codeword of $\mathbf{y} = (1\,1\,0\,1\,1\,0\,0)$. Since the demapper assumes that the error recovery completes the task perfectly, the demapper decides that the predicted information bits are $\mathbf{x} = (0\,0\,1\,1)$. As a result of this erroneous decoding action we end up having three, rather than two errors. This example demonstrates that the classical $\mathcal{C}(7,4)$ Hamming code is unable to operate flawlessly beyond its error correction capability.

## 3.3 A Brief Review of Quantum Stabilizer Codes

The formulation of QSCs is capable of detecting both the number and the position of errors without actually observing the state of physical qubits, which is vitally important, since otherwise the quantum state will collapse to classical bits upon measurement. This was achieved by amalgamating the classical syndrome-based decoding with the QECCs. Similar to classical error correction codes, QSCs also rely on attaching redundant qubits to the information qubits for invoking error correction. The basic model of QSCs is depicted in Figure 3.2, which will be contrasted to its classical pair in Figure 3.1. To generate the code space $\mathcal{C}$, the redundancy is constituted by $(n-k)$ auxiliary qubits. Next, a unitary transformation $\mathcal{V}$ transforms the $k$ qubits in the state of $|\psi\rangle$ and the $(n-k)$ auxiliary qubits into $n$ qubits in the state of $|\overline{\psi}\rangle$. The unitary transformation of $\mathcal{V}$ represents the action of the

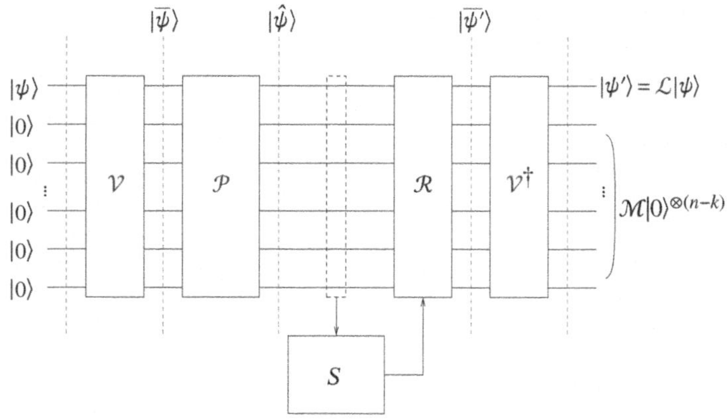


**Figure 3.2** The basic model of QSCs implementation over the quantum depolarizing channel. The $k$ logical qubits is mapped into $n$ physical qubits with the aid of $(n-k)$ redundant/auxiliary qubits (*ancillas*) to provide protection from the quantum decoherence. It is similar to the classical error correction model where $(n-k)$ redundant bits are added to $k$ information bits in order to provide error correction. The quantum encoder $\mathcal{V}$ serves the same purpose with **G** of classical error correction codes in Figure 3.1. The quantum encoder $\mathcal{V}$ transforms the state of $k$ logical qubits $|\psi\rangle$ into the state of $n$ physical qubits $|\overline{\psi}\rangle$ with the aid of $(n-k)$ ancillas. The quantum depolarizing channel imposes vector represented by $n$-tuple Pauli operator $\mathcal{P} \in \mathcal{P}_n$. The syndrome operators $S_i \in \mathcal{S}$ generate eigenvalues of $\pm 1$, which are analogue to the value 0 and 1 of classical syndrome vector, which is provided by the PCM **H** in Figure 3.1. The error recovery $\mathcal{R}$ applies the correction according to the syndrome values provided by the syndrome measurements. Finally, the quantum inverse encoder $\mathcal{V}^\dagger$ transforms the predicted state of physical qubits $|\overline{\psi}'\rangle$ back to the predicted state of logical qubits $|\psi'\rangle$, which bears the same responsibility as the demapper **D** in classical syndrome-based decoding of Figure 3.1. *Source*: [174]/IEEE/CC BY 4.0.

*quantum encoder*. Explicitly, the mapping of the *logical qubits* constituting the state of $|\psi\rangle \in \mathbb{C}^{2^k}$ to the *physical qubits* forming the state of $|\overline{\psi}\rangle \in \mathbb{C}^{2^n}$ by the encoder $\mathcal{V}$ of Figure 3.2 can be mathematically formulated as follows:

$$\mathcal{C} = \{|\overline{\psi}\rangle = \mathcal{V}(|\psi\rangle \otimes |0\rangle^{\otimes(n-k)})\}. \tag{3.11}$$

The QSCs rely on the stabilizer operators $S_i \in \mathcal{S}$ for identifying the type, the number and also the position of the qubit errors. A stabilizer operator $S_i$ is an $n$-tuple Pauli operator, which preserves the state of physical qubits as defined here:

$$S_i|\overline{\psi}\rangle = |\overline{\psi}\rangle. \tag{3.12}$$

The quantum channel inflicts errors represented by $n$-tuple Pauli operators $P \in \mathcal{P}_n$, which transforms the encoded physical qubits that were originally in the state of $|\overline{\psi}\rangle$ to the potentially corrupted physical qubits in the state of $|\widehat{\psi}\rangle$, as seen in Figure 3.2. More explicitly, this process can be described as follows:

$$|\widehat{\psi}\rangle = P|\overline{\psi}\rangle. \tag{3.13}$$

The stabilizer operators act similarly to the syndrome calculations routinely used in classical error correction codes. To elaborate a little further, a stabilizer operator will return an eigenvalue of $+1$, when an error operator $P$ commutes with the stabilizer operator, while we arrive at the eigenvalue of $-1$, if it anti-commutes. The eigenvalues of $+1$ and $-1$ are analogous to the classic syndrome bit of 0 and 1, respectively, which can be defined as follows:

$$S_i|\widehat{\psi}\rangle = \begin{cases} |\widehat{\psi}\rangle, & S_iP = PS_i \\ -|\widehat{\psi}\rangle, & S_iP = -PS_i. \end{cases} \tag{3.14}$$

Therefore, the stabilizer operators naturally have to inherit the commutative property. Consequently, the product between the stabilizer operators $S_i$ yields another legitimate stabilizer operator. Furthermore, the commutativity property implies that

$$S_i|\overline{\psi}\rangle = S_j|\overline{\psi}\rangle = S_iS_j|\overline{\psi}\rangle = |\overline{\psi}\rangle, \forall S_{i,j} \in \mathcal{S}, \tag{3.15}$$

suggesting that the stabilizer group $\mathcal{S}$ is closed under multiplication.

Based on the syndrome measurement by the stabilizer operators $S_i$, a recovery operator constituted by the $n$-tuple Pauli operator of $\mathcal{R} \in \mathcal{P}_n$ seen in Figure 3.2 is applied to the corrupted physical qubit state $|\widehat{\psi}\rangle$, yielding the predicted state of the original encoded logical qubit $|\overline{\psi'}\rangle$, which is formulated as

$$|\overline{\psi'}\rangle = \mathcal{R}|\widehat{\psi}\rangle. \tag{3.16}$$

Finally, the inverse encoder $\mathcal{V}^\dagger$ of Figure 3.2 performs the following transformation[1]:

$$\begin{aligned} \mathcal{V}^\dagger|\overline{\psi'}\rangle &= \mathcal{V}^\dagger\mathcal{R}|\widehat{\psi}\rangle \\ &= \mathcal{V}^\dagger\mathcal{R}\mathcal{P}|\overline{\psi}\rangle \\ &= \mathcal{V}^\dagger\mathcal{R}\mathcal{P}\mathcal{V}(|\psi\rangle \otimes |0\rangle^{\otimes(n-k)}) \\ &= (\mathcal{L}|\psi\rangle) \otimes (\mathcal{M}|0\rangle^{\otimes(n-k)}), \end{aligned} \tag{3.17}$$

where we have $\mathcal{V}^\dagger\mathcal{R}\mathcal{P}\mathcal{V} \equiv \mathcal{L} \otimes \mathcal{M}$ and $\mathcal{L} \in \mathcal{P}_k$ represents the error inflicted on the logical qubits according to $|\psi'\rangle = \mathcal{L}|\psi\rangle$, while $\mathcal{M} \in \mathcal{P}_{n-k}$ represents the residual errors that remained in the $(n-k)$ auxiliary qubits after the error correction procedure. In the case of $\mathcal{R} = \mathcal{P}$, we arrive at $\mathcal{R}\mathcal{P} = \mathbf{I}^{\otimes n}$, where $\mathbf{I}^{\otimes n}$ denotes an $n$-fold tensor product Pauli-I matrix. Another possibility is to arrive at $\mathcal{R}\mathcal{P} = S_i$. In either of these cases, the state of the physical qubits is not altered, since we have $\mathcal{R}\mathcal{P}|\overline{\psi}\rangle = |\overline{\psi}\rangle$. Therefore, the decoding procedure of Figure 3.2 successfully recovers the original quantum state constituted by the logical qubits, yielding $|\psi'\rangle = |\psi\rangle$.

The stabilizer operators can be translated into the classical PCM $\mathbf{H}$ by mapping the Pauli matrices $\mathbf{I}$, $\mathbf{X}$, $\mathbf{Y}$, and $\mathbf{Z}$ onto $(\mathbb{F}_2)^2$ as follows:

$$\begin{aligned} \mathbf{I} &\rightarrow (0 \mid 0), \\ \mathbf{X} &\rightarrow (0 \mid 1), \\ \mathbf{Y} &\rightarrow (1 \mid 1), \\ \mathbf{Z} &\rightarrow (1 \mid 0). \end{aligned} \tag{3.18}$$

This concept is also known as the *Pauli-to-binary isomorphism*. By exploiting the Pauli-to-binary isomorphism, the stabilizer operators of any QSC can be represented as a pair of PCMs $\mathbf{H}_z$ and $\mathbf{H}_z$, where $\mathbf{H}_z$ is invoked for handling the phase-flip ($\mathbf{Z}$) errors and $\mathbf{H}_x$ for handling the bit-flip ($\mathbf{X}$) errors. Explicitly, the classical PCM representation of the QSC stabilizer operators may be written as follows:

$$\mathbf{H} = (\mathbf{H}_z|\mathbf{H}_x). \tag{3.19}$$

The classical representation of the stabilizer operators gives the advantage of predicting and evaluating the performances of QSCs by treating them similarly to classical error correction codes. Additionally, it allows us to transform a pair of classical PCMs into the corresponding quantum counterpart. However, to ensure that the commutative property is preserved in the quantum domain, a pair of classical PCMs have to satisfy the so-called *symplectic criterion* [60] given by

$$\mathbf{H}_z \cdot \mathbf{H}_x^T + \mathbf{H}_x \cdot \mathbf{H}_z^T = 0. \tag{3.20}$$

A special class of QSCs, namely the family of Calderbank–Shore–Steane (CSS) codes, treats the phase-flip ($\mathbf{Z}$) and bit-flip ($\mathbf{X}$) errors as two separate entities. More specifically, this can be interpreted as having the PCMs of

1 The inverse encoder $\mathcal{V}^\dagger$ is the Hermitian transpose of encoder $\mathcal{V}$. It is referred to as the *inverse*, since it satisfies the unitary requirement of $\mathcal{V}^\dagger\mathcal{V} = \mathbf{I}$, as the inverse of the matrix does.

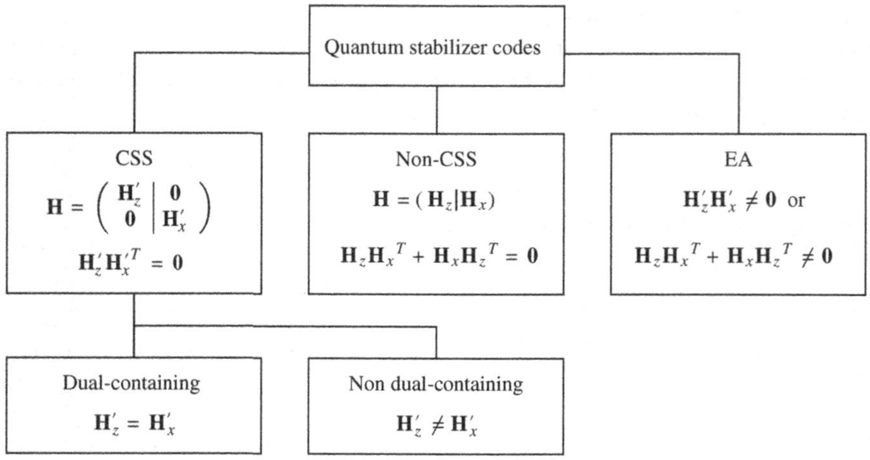


**Figure 3.3** The classification and characterization of QSCs, where CSS stands for *Calderbank–Shor–Steane* and EA for *entanglement-assisted*. *Source*: [204]/IEEE/CC BY 4.0.

$\mathbf{H}_z$ and $\mathbf{H}_x$ in Eq. (3.19) formulated as $\mathbf{H}_z = \begin{pmatrix} \mathbf{H}'_z \\ 0 \end{pmatrix}$ and $\mathbf{H}_x = \begin{pmatrix} 0 \\ \mathbf{H}'_x \end{pmatrix}$, respectively. Therefore, the binary PCM $\mathbf{H}$ can be expressed as follows:

$$\mathbf{H} = \left(\begin{array}{c|c} \mathbf{H}'_z & \mathbf{0} \\ \mathbf{0} & \mathbf{H}'_x \end{array}\right). \tag{3.21}$$

Consequently, the symplectic criterion given in Eq. (3.20) can be reduced to the following criterion:

$$\mathbf{H}'_z \cdot \mathbf{H}'^T_x = 0. \tag{3.22}$$

Furthermore, we can formulate a CSS code by using a PCM of $\mathbf{H}'_z = \mathbf{H}'_x$ and the resultant quantum code may be referred to as a dual-containing quantum CSS code or self-orthogonal quantum CSS code. For dual-containing CSS codes, the symplectic criterion can be further simplified to $\mathbf{H}'_z\mathbf{H}'^T_z = 0$.

Again, the classical code constructions can be readily transformed into their quantum version provided that they satisfy the symplectic criterion of Eq. (3.20). In other words, unless the symplectic condition is satisfied by them, some of the popular classical codes cannot be 'transplanted' into the quantum domain. However, fortunately, this limitation can be relaxed by utilizing the family of EA-QSCs [73, 74]. To elaborate a little further, transforming a classical codes into a QSC does not come without cost. Invoking the above mentioned EA-QSC construction requires so-called preshared maximally entangled qubits before the encoding procedure, as detailed in [74]. However, the mechanism of presharing the maximally entangled qubits allows us to transform a set of non-symplectic QSCs into their symplectic counterpart. In closing this section we note that the classification of QSCs is summarized at a glance in Figure 3.3.

## 3.4 Protecting a Single Qubit: Design Examples

In Chapter 1, we have already mentioned the three pioneering contributions on QSCs, which are only capable of handling a single qubit error, while in Section 3.3, we briefly highlighted the different types of QSC constructions. In this section, we will link up both ideas in a more concrete context.

### 3.4.1 Classical and Quantum 1/3-rate Repetition Codes

Before we delve deeper into the aforementioned QSCs, let us commence with a simple 1/3-rate classical repetition codes, which maps a binary digit of "0" or "1" into a vector that contains three replicas of each binary digit as

$$\begin{aligned} 0 &\xrightarrow{\mathbf{G}} \begin{pmatrix} 0 & 0 & 0 \end{pmatrix}, \\ 1 &\xrightarrow{\mathbf{G}} \begin{pmatrix} 1 & 1 & 1 \end{pmatrix}. \end{aligned} \tag{3.23}$$

To elaborate briefly, we have created two legitimate codewords, which have a Hamming distance of three. Given the 3-bit codewords, we can have eight different received words. Two of these are legitimate error-free codewords and six of them are erroneous. However, even if one of the bits is corrupted, majority logic allows us to correct it. By contrast, if two bits are corrupted, the majority logic decision would opt for the wrong legitimate codeword, because more errors were imposed by the channel than the error correction capability of code. This situation is often referred to as the code being overloaded by an excessive number of errors.

Let us now briefly portray the task of the decoder from a syndrome decoding – rather than majority logic – perspective. If the first and second bit are different, we know that one of them is corrupted, bit it is not clear at this stage, which one. So this is the first symptom of having an error. This simple calculation provides us with the first syndrome bit, which is a logical one. Similarly, if the first and third bit are different, it is not clear, which of these two bits is corrupted, but we have a second syndrome bit. Simple logic dictates that this is only possible, if the first bit was corrupted. This can hence be inverted for correcting this 3-bit codeword. But again, if there are two or three errors, this 1/3-rate code having a minimum distance of three between the legitimate codewords become overwhelmed. The aforementioned pair of syndrome bits allow us to distinguish four possible scenarios, namely an error-free one and having a single error in any of the three positions.

Hence, from the brief description of the basic classical codes given in Section 3.2, the mapping in Eq. (3.23) can be encapsulated into a generator matrix **G** as given here:

$$\mathbf{G} = \begin{pmatrix} 1 & 1 & 1 \end{pmatrix}. \tag{3.24}$$

From the generator matrix **G** given in Eq. (3.24) and the PCM formulation given in Eq. (3.3), we obtain the PCM **H** for a 1/3-rate classical repetition code encapsulated by

$$\mathbf{H} = \begin{pmatrix} 1 & 1 & 0 \\ 1 & 0 & 1 \end{pmatrix}, \tag{3.25}$$

where the first row returns the first bit of the 2-bit syndrome and accordingly the second row evaluates the second bit. Thus, it can be easily checked by using the syndrome computation of Eq. (3.9) that the syndrome value of (0 0) is obtained if the received word $\hat{\mathbf{y}}$ is equal to the valid codeword, either (0 0 0) or (1 1 1). The syndrome computation yields a syndrome vector with $(n-k)$-element and in this case for a 1/3-rate classical repetition code, it generates a syndrome vector with two elements. Therefore, again, there are four possible outcomes from the syndrome computation and one of them indicates the error-free received word, which is the (0 0) syndrome. Since a 1/3-rate classical repetition code may be viewed as a short block code, the syndrome computation and the associated error pattern is readily checked using a look-up table, namely Table 3.3.

Next, we proceed with a simple 1/3-rate quantum repetition code that is capable of recovering a single bit-flip, but no phase-flip. Let us assume that we have a quantum state $|\psi\rangle = \alpha_0|0\rangle + \alpha_1|1\rangle$. As a consequence of the *no-cloning theorem* of quantum mechanics, there is no unitary transformation $U$ capable of mapping an *arbitrary*

**Table 3.3** Syndrome computation and the associated error pattern for a 1/3-rate classical repetition code.

| Syndrome (s) | Error pattern (e) | Index of corrupted bit |
|---|---|---|
| (0 0) | (0 0 0) | - |
| (0 1) | (0 0 1) | 3 |
| (1 0) | (0 1 0) | 2 |
| (1 1) | (1 0 0) | 1 |

quantum state $|\psi\rangle$ onto a state of $|\overline{\psi}\rangle = |\psi\rangle^{\otimes 3}$. However, we are still allowed to make a copy of the *orthogonal* states. Hence, the mapping of the *orthogonal* quantum states $|0\rangle$ and $|1\rangle$ may be carried out by a unitary transformation $U$ as follows:

$$\begin{aligned} |0\rangle_L &= U(|0\rangle \otimes |0\rangle^{\otimes 2}) = |000\rangle, \\ |1\rangle_L &= U(|1\rangle \otimes |0\rangle^{\otimes 2}) = |111\rangle. \end{aligned} \tag{3.26}$$

In a more general scenario, the mapping of a single logical qubit to $n$ physical qubits is arranged by a unitary transformation carried out by a quantum encoder $\mathcal{V}$, which can be formulated as follows:

$$|\overline{\psi}\rangle = \mathcal{V}\left(|\psi\rangle \otimes |0\rangle^{\otimes(n-1)}\right) = \alpha_0|0\rangle_L + \alpha_1|1\rangle_L, \tag{3.27}$$

where $|0\rangle_L$ denotes the encoded state of the logical qubit $|0\rangle$, $|1\rangle_L$ denotes the encoded state of the logical qubit $|1\rangle$, while $|0\rangle^{\otimes n-1}$ represents the auxiliary or redundant qubits (*also referred to as ancillas*), and the superscript of $\otimes(n-1)$ represents $(n-1)$-fold tensor products. Hence, for 1/3-rate quantum repetition codes, the state of the logical qubit $|\psi\rangle$ corresponds to the state of the physical qubit $|\overline{\psi}\rangle$ as given by

$$|\overline{\psi}\rangle = \mathcal{V}\left((\alpha_0|0\rangle + \alpha_1|1\rangle) \otimes |0\rangle^{\otimes 2}\right) = \alpha_0|000\rangle + \alpha_1|111\rangle, \tag{3.28}$$

where the string $|000\rangle$ defines the encoded logical qubit $|0\rangle_L$ and $|111\rangle$ defines $|1\rangle_L$. Again, it is important to bear in mind that the state of $|\overline{\psi}\rangle = \alpha_0|000\rangle + \alpha_1|111\rangle$ is not equal to $|\overline{\psi}\rangle = |\psi\rangle^{\otimes 3}$. More explicitly, this relationship can also be expressed as $|\overline{\psi}\rangle = \alpha_0|000\rangle + \alpha_1|111\rangle \neq |\psi\rangle^{\otimes 3}$. The state of the physical qubits of the 1/3-rate quantum repetition code is stabilized, or synonymously "parity-checked" by the pair of stabilizer operators $S_1 = \mathbf{ZZI}$ and $S_2 = \mathbf{ZIZ}$. A valid codeword or a valid encoded state, which is not affected by the stabilizer operators $S_1$ and $S_2$, has an input state of $|\overline{\psi}\rangle$ and returns the state of $|\overline{\psi}\rangle$, hence it yields the so-called eigenvalues of $+1$, and more explicitly, it is described as follows:

$$\begin{aligned} S_1|\overline{\psi}\rangle &= \alpha_0|000\rangle + \alpha_1|111\rangle \equiv |\overline{\psi}\rangle, \\ S_2|\overline{\psi}\rangle &= \alpha_0|000\rangle + \alpha_1|111\rangle \equiv |\overline{\psi}\rangle. \end{aligned} \tag{3.29}$$

By contrast, if the stabilizer operators $g_1$ and $g_2$ are applied to the corrupted states $|\widehat{\psi}\rangle$, they both yield eigenvalues that are not in the all-one state. For instance, let us assume that we received a corrupted state having a bit-flip error imposed on the first qubit of $|\overline{\psi}\rangle$ yielding $|\widehat{\psi}\rangle = \alpha_0|100\rangle + \alpha_1|011\rangle$. Then, upon applying the stabilizer operators $S_1 = \mathbf{ZZI}$ and $S_2 = \mathbf{ZIZ}$ to the state of $|\widehat{\psi}\rangle$, it may be readily shown after few steps that we arrive at the following eigenvalues:

$$\begin{aligned} S_1|\widehat{\psi}\rangle &= \mathbf{ZZI}(\alpha_0|100\rangle + \alpha_1|011\rangle) \\ &= \begin{pmatrix} 1 & 0 & 0 & 0 & 0 & 0 & 0 & 0 \\ 0 & 1 & 0 & 0 & 0 & 0 & 0 & 0 \\ 0 & 0 & -1 & 0 & 0 & 0 & 0 & 0 \\ 0 & 0 & 0 & -1 & 0 & 0 & 0 & 0 \\ 0 & 0 & 0 & 0 & -1 & 0 & 0 & 0 \\ 0 & 0 & 0 & 0 & 0 & -1 & 0 & 0 \\ 0 & 0 & 0 & 0 & 0 & 0 & 1 & 0 \\ 0 & 0 & 0 & 0 & 0 & 0 & 0 & 1 \end{pmatrix} \cdot \begin{pmatrix} 0 \\ 0 \\ 0 \\ \alpha_1 \\ \alpha_0 \\ 0 \\ 0 \\ 0 \end{pmatrix} = \begin{pmatrix} 0 \\ 0 \\ 0 \\ -\alpha_1 \\ -\alpha_0 \\ 0 \\ 0 \\ 0 \end{pmatrix} \\ &\equiv -\alpha_0|100\rangle - \alpha_1|011\rangle \equiv -|\widehat{\psi}\rangle, \end{aligned} \tag{3.30}$$

$$S_2|\hat{\psi}\rangle = \mathbf{ZIZ}(\alpha_0|100\rangle + \alpha_1|011\rangle)$$
$$= \begin{pmatrix} 1 & 0 & 0 & 0 & 0 & 0 & 0 & 0 \\ 0 & -1 & 0 & 0 & 0 & 0 & 0 & 0 \\ 0 & 0 & 1 & 0 & 0 & 0 & 0 & 0 \\ 0 & 0 & 0 & -1 & 0 & 0 & 0 & 0 \\ 0 & 0 & 0 & 0 & -1 & 0 & 0 & 0 \\ 0 & 0 & 0 & 0 & 0 & 1 & 0 & 0 \\ 0 & 0 & 0 & 0 & 0 & 0 & -1 & 0 \\ 0 & 0 & 0 & 0 & 0 & 0 & 0 & 1 \end{pmatrix} \cdot \begin{pmatrix} 0 \\ 0 \\ 0 \\ \alpha_1 \\ \alpha_0 \\ 0 \\ 0 \\ 0 \end{pmatrix} = \begin{pmatrix} 0 \\ 0 \\ 0 \\ -\alpha_1 \\ -\alpha_0 \\ 0 \\ 0 \\ 0 \end{pmatrix} \tag{3.31}$$
$$\equiv -\alpha_0|100\rangle - \alpha_1|011\rangle \equiv -|\hat{\psi}\rangle.$$

The resultant eigenvalues of $\pm 1$ act similarly to the syndrome vector of classical codes, where the eigenvalue $+1$ is associated with the classical syndrome value 0 and the eigenvalue $-1$ with the classical syndrome value 1. More explicitly, the single-qubit error patterns imposed on the 1/3-rate quantum repetition codes and the associated eigenvalues are portrayed in Table 3.4. However, this specific construction is only capable of detecting and correcting a single bit-flip error imposed by the Pauli channel on the physical qubits, but no phase-flips.

Since the physical qubits may experience not only bit-flip errors, but also phase-flip errors as well as both bit-flip and phase-flip errors, a different mapping is necessitated to protect the physical qubits from phase-flip error. In order to protect the physical qubits from a phase-flip error, we may require a different basis but we can still invoke a similar approach. To elaborate further, the Hadamard transformation (**H**) maps the computational basis of $\{|0\rangle, |1\rangle\}$ onto the Hadamard basis of $\{|+\rangle, |-\rangle\}$, where the states of $|+\rangle$ and $|-\rangle$ are defined as

$$|+\rangle \equiv \mathbf{H}|0\rangle = \frac{1}{\sqrt{2}}(|0\rangle + |1\rangle), \tag{3.32}$$

$$|-\rangle \equiv \mathbf{H}|1\rangle = \frac{1}{\sqrt{2}}(|0\rangle - |1\rangle), \tag{3.33}$$

and the unitary Hadamard transformation **H**, which acts on a single qubit state, is given by

$$\mathbf{H} = \frac{1}{\sqrt{2}}\begin{pmatrix} 1 & 1 \\ 1 & -1 \end{pmatrix}. \tag{3.34}$$

**Table 3.4** Single qubit bit-flip errors along with the associated eigenvalues n 1/3-rate quantum repetition where the eigenvalues act similarly with the syndrome values in classical linear block codes.

| Received states $\lvert\hat{\psi}\rangle$ | Eigenvalue $g_1\lvert\hat{\psi}\rangle$ | Eigenvalue $g_2\lvert\hat{\psi}\rangle$ | Syndrome (s) | Index of corrupted qubit |
|---|---|---|---|---|
| $\alpha_0\lvert 000\rangle + \alpha_1\lvert 111\rangle$ | $+1$ | $+1$ | (0 0) | - |
| $\alpha_0\lvert 001\rangle + \alpha_1\lvert 110\rangle$ | $+1$ | $-1$ | (0 1) | 3 |
| $\alpha_0\lvert 010\rangle + \alpha_1\lvert 101\rangle$ | $-1$ | $+1$ | (1 0) | 2 |
| $\alpha_0\lvert 100\rangle + \alpha_1\lvert 011\rangle$ | $-1$ | $-1$ | (1 1) | 1 |

A phase-flip error defined over the Hadamard basis of $\{|+\rangle, |-\rangle\}$ acts similarly to the bit-flip error defined over the computational basis of $\{|0\rangle, |1\rangle\}$. Hence, for the handling of a single phase-flip error, the encoder of the 1/3-rate quantum repetition code protecting against phase-flips carries out:

$$\begin{aligned} |0\rangle_L &= \mathcal{U}\left(|0\rangle \otimes |0\rangle^{\otimes 2}\right) = |+++\rangle, \\ |1\rangle_L &= \mathcal{U}\left(|1\rangle \otimes |0\rangle^{\otimes 2}\right) = |---\rangle. \end{aligned} \tag{3.35}$$

Therefore, the logical qubit of $|\psi\rangle$ corresponding to the physical qubits $|\overline{\psi}\rangle$ is given by

$$|\overline{\psi}\rangle = \mathcal{V}\left((\alpha_0|0\rangle + \alpha_1|1\rangle) \otimes |0\rangle^{\otimes 2}\right) = \alpha_0|+++\rangle + \alpha_1|---\rangle. \tag{3.36}$$

The state of physical qubits given in Eq. (3.36) can be stabilized by the operators $S_1 = \mathbf{XXI}$ and $S_2 = \mathbf{XIX}$. The detection and correction of a phase flip error can be carried out in analogy with the 1/3-rate quantum repetition code for handling the bit-flip error. The stabilizer operators can be derived from the classical PCM $\mathbf{H}$ by mapping the Pauli matrices $\mathbf{I}$, $\mathbf{X}$, $\mathbf{Y}$, and $\mathbf{Z}$ onto $(\mathbb{F}_2)^2$ using one of the Pauli mappings given in Eq. 3.18. Each row of $\mathbf{H}$ is associated with a stabilizer operator $S_i \in \mathcal{S}$, where the $i$-th column of both $\mathbf{H}_z$ and $\mathbf{H}_x$ corresponds to the $i$-th qubit and the binary 1 locations represent the $\mathbf{Z}$ and $\mathbf{X}$ positions in the PCMs $\mathbf{H}_z$ and $\mathbf{H}_x$, respectively. For instance, for the 1/3-rate quantum repetition code, which is stabilized by the operators $S_1 = \mathbf{ZZI}$ and $S_2 = \mathbf{ZIZ}$, the PCM $\mathbf{H}$ is given as follows:

$$\mathbf{H} = \left(\begin{array}{ccc|ccc} 1 & 1 & 0 & 0 & 0 & 0 \\ 1 & 0 & 1 & 0 & 0 & 0 \end{array}\right). \tag{3.37}$$

Since the 1/3-rate quantum repetition code in this example can only correct a bit-flip ($\mathbf{X}$) error, which is stabilized by the $\mathbf{Z}$ operators, the PCM $\mathbf{H}_x$ contains only zero elements. The same goes for a 1/3-rate quantum repetition code conceived for handling a phase-flip ($\mathbf{Z}$) error, which is stabilized by the operators $S_1 = \mathbf{XXI}$ and $S_2 = \mathbf{XIX}$. The PCM $\mathbf{H}$ corresponding to this particular QSC is defined as follows:

$$\mathbf{H} = \left(\begin{array}{ccc|ccc} 0 & 0 & 0 & 1 & 1 & 0 \\ 0 & 0 & 0 & 1 & 0 & 1 \end{array}\right). \tag{3.38}$$

It is clearly shown in Eqs. (3.37) and (3.38) that the PCM of a 1/3-rate quantum repetition code is similar to that of the 1/3-rate classical repetition code given in Eq. (3.25).

In order to encode the logical qubits into physical qubits, we require the unitary transformation $\mathcal{V}$ acting as the quantum encoder. To represent the quantum encoding circuit, one of the essential components is the controlled-NOT (CNOT) quantum gate, which has been described in subsection 2.3.1.4. A logical qubit in the superimposed state of $|\psi\rangle = \alpha_0|0\rangle + \alpha_1|1\rangle$ and a qubit in the pure state of $|0\rangle$ are manipulated by the quantum CNOT gate into following state:

$$\begin{aligned} \mathbf{CNOT}(|\psi\rangle, |0\rangle) &= \mathbf{CNOT}(\alpha_0|0\rangle + \alpha_1|1\rangle, |0\rangle) \\ &= \mathbf{CNOT}(\alpha_0|00\rangle + \alpha_1|10\rangle) \\ &= \begin{pmatrix} 1 & 0 & 0 & 0 \\ 0 & 1 & 0 & 0 \\ 0 & 0 & 0 & 1 \\ 0 & 0 & 1 & 0 \end{pmatrix} \cdot \begin{pmatrix} \alpha_{00} \\ 0 \\ \alpha_{10} \\ 0 \end{pmatrix} = \begin{pmatrix} \alpha_0 \\ 0 \\ 0 \\ \alpha_1 \end{pmatrix} \\ &\equiv \alpha_0|00\rangle + \alpha_1|11\rangle. \end{aligned} \tag{3.39}$$

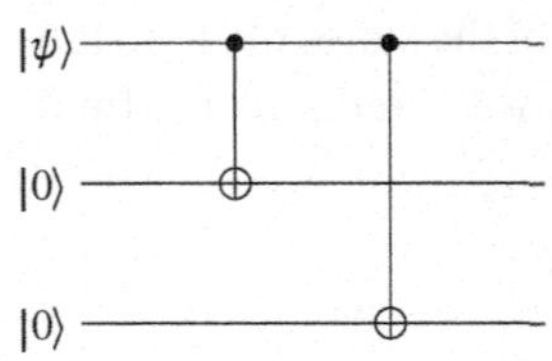


**Figure 3.4** The encoding circuit of the 1/3-rate quantum repetition code protecting the physical qubits from a bit-flip error.

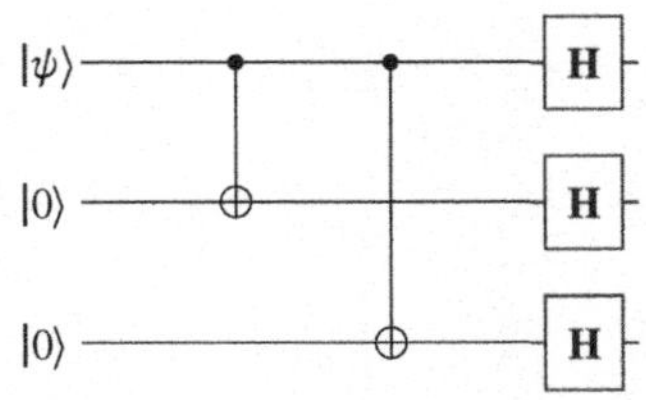


**Figure 3.5** The encoding circuit of the 1/3-rate quantum repetition code protecting the physical qubits from a phase-flip error.

Similarly, we may also use the CNOT definition given in Eq. (2.33) to determine the resultant state as described here:

$$\begin{aligned}\mathbf{CNOT}(|\psi\rangle, |0\rangle) &= \mathbf{CNOT}(\alpha_0|0\rangle + \alpha_1|1\rangle, |0\rangle)\\ &= \mathbf{CNOT}(\alpha_0|00\rangle + \alpha_1|10\rangle)\\ &= \alpha_0|0, (0 \oplus 0)\rangle + \alpha_1|1, (1 \oplus 0)\rangle\\ &= \alpha_0|00\rangle + \alpha_1|11\rangle.\end{aligned} \tag{3.40}$$

For the sake of creating the encoded state of a 1/3-rate quantum repetition code, we require a single logical qubit and two ancillas prepared in the pure state of $|0\rangle$, as described in Eq. (3.28). In the first step, the CNOT unitary transformation is performed between the logical qubit and the first ancilla, in which the logical qubit acts as the control qubit and the ancilla as the target qubit. The same step is repeated during the second stage between the logical qubit and the second ancilla, where the second ancilla is also preserved as the target qubit. Therefore, the encoding circuit of the 1/3-rate quantum repetition code can be represented as in Figure 3.4, which was designed for protecting the physical qubits from a single bit-flip error, as also seen in the mapping given in Eq. (3.26).

For its 1/3-rate quantum repetition code counterpart protecting the physical qubits from a phase-flip error, we require the Hadamard transformation to obtain the mapping given in Eq. (3.35). The Hadamard transformation is required for changing the base of quantum repetition codes from the computational basis $\{|0\rangle, |1\rangle\}$ to the Hadamard basis $\{|+\rangle, |-\rangle\}$. Hence, we can readily create the encoding circuit for a 1/3-rate quantum repetition code for protecting the physical qubits from a phase-flip error by placing the Hadamard gates after the second stage as portrayed in Figure 3.5.

### 3.4.2 Shor's 9-qubit Code

Since we have elaborated briefly on the construction of QSCs along with the Pauli to binary isomorphism, we may now proceed with the corresponding examples of different QSC constructions conceived for protecting the physical qubits from any type of a single qubit error. First, we commence with Shor's code [54]. In order to protect the qubits from any type of single qubit error, a logical qubit is mapped onto 9 physical qubits. This code may also be viewed as a concatenated version of two 1/3-rate quantum repetition codes, where the first stage is dedicated to the protection of the physical qubits from phase-flip errors, while the second stage is invoked for handling the bit-flip errors. To elaborate further, at the first stage of Shor's code, the state of a logical qubit is encoded by using the following mapping: $|0\rangle \rightarrow |+++\rangle$, $|1\rangle \rightarrow |---\rangle$. At the second stage, we encode each of the states of $|+\rangle$ to the state of $(|000\rangle + |111\rangle)/\sqrt{2}$, while the state of $|-\rangle$ is mapped to the state of $(|000\rangle - |111\rangle)/\sqrt{2}$. Therefore, the final state of the encoded logical qubits $|0\rangle_L$ and $|1\rangle_L$ as follows:

$$
\begin{aligned}
|0\rangle_L &= \frac{1}{\sqrt{2}}(|000\rangle + |111\rangle) \otimes \frac{1}{\sqrt{2}}(|000\rangle + |111\rangle) \otimes \frac{1}{\sqrt{2}}(|000\rangle + |111\rangle) \\
&= \frac{1}{2\sqrt{2}}(|000000000\rangle + |000000111\rangle + |000111000\rangle + |000111111\rangle \\
&\quad + |111000000\rangle + |111000111\rangle + |111111000\rangle + |111111111\rangle),
\end{aligned} \tag{3.41}
$$

$$
\begin{aligned}
|1\rangle_L &= \frac{1}{\sqrt{2}}(|000\rangle - |111\rangle) \otimes \frac{1}{\sqrt{2}}(|000\rangle - |111\rangle) \otimes \frac{1}{\sqrt{2}}(|000\rangle - |111\rangle) \\
&= \frac{1}{2\sqrt{2}}(|000000000\rangle - |000000111\rangle - |000111000\rangle + |000111111\rangle \\
&\quad - |111000000\rangle + |111000111\rangle + |111111000\rangle - |111111111\rangle).
\end{aligned} \tag{3.42}
$$

Based on the preceding description, the encoding circuit of Shor's code is portrayed in Figure 3.6. The state determined by the nine physical qubits of Shor's code, where the latter are defined in Eqs. (3.41) and (3.42), is stabilized by the eight stabilizer operators which are listed in Table 3.5.

To elaborate a little further, Shor's code is a member of the class of non-dual-containing CSS codes. Explicitly, it belongs to the class of CSS codes because the stabilizer formalism of Shor's code implies that the code handles the **Z** error and the **X** error separately, while it is a non-dual-containing code because the PCMs $\mathbf{H}_z$ and $\mathbf{H}_x$ are

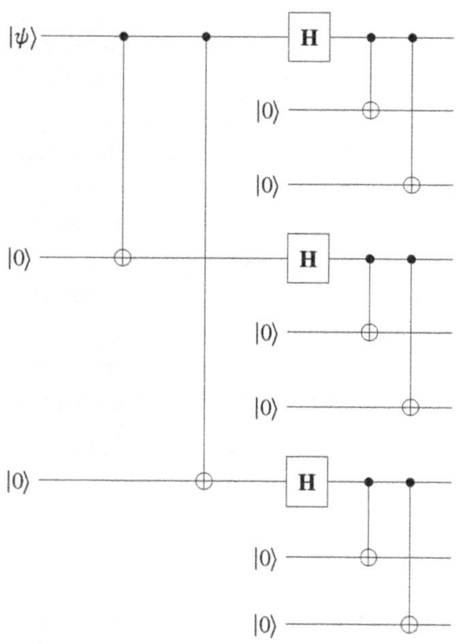


**Figure 3.6** The encoding circuit $\mathcal{V}$ of Shor's 9-qubit code.

**Table 3.5** The eight stabilizer operators of Shor's 9-qubit code, which stabilizes a single logical qubit with the aid of 8 auxiliary qubits.

| $S_i$ | Stabilizer operator |
|---|---|
| $S_1$ | ZZIIIIIII |
| $S_2$ | IZZIIIIII |
| $S_3$ | IIIZZIIII |
| $S_4$ | IIIIZZIII |
| $S_5$ | IIIIIIZZI |
| $S_6$ | IIIIIIIZZ |
| $S_7$ | XXXXXXIII |
| $S_8$ | IIIXXXXXX |

not identical. Based on the list of stabilizer operators given in Table 3.5, the PCM **H** of Shor's code is given in Eq. (3.43), where each row of the PCM corresponds to each of the stabilizer operators listed in Table 3.5.

$$\mathbf{H}_{\text{Shor}} = \left(\begin{array}{ccccccccc|ccccccccc} 1&1&0&0&0&0&0&0&0&0&0&0&0&0&0&0&0&0\\ 0&1&1&0&0&0&0&0&0&0&0&0&0&0&0&0&0&0\\ 0&0&0&1&1&0&0&0&0&0&0&0&0&0&0&0&0&0\\ 0&0&0&0&1&1&0&0&0&0&0&0&0&0&0&0&0&0\\ 0&0&0&0&0&0&1&1&0&0&0&0&0&0&0&0&0&0\\ 0&0&0&0&0&0&0&1&1&0&0&0&0&0&0&0&0&0\\ 0&0&0&0&0&0&0&0&0&1&1&1&1&1&1&0&0&0\\ 0&0&0&0&0&0&0&0&0&0&0&0&1&1&1&1&1&1 \end{array}\right). \tag{3.43}$$

The quantum coding rate ($r_Q$) of a quantum code $\mathcal{C}[n, k]$ is defined by the ratio of the number of logical qubits $k$ to the number of physical qubits $n$, which can be formulated as

$$r_Q = \frac{k}{n}. \tag{3.44}$$

Hence again, for Shor's 9-qubit code the quantum coding rate is $r_Q = 1/9$.

### 3.4.3 Steane's 7-qubit Code

Steane's code was proposed for protecting a single qubit from any type of error by mapping a logical qubit onto 7 physical qubits, instead of 9 qubits. In contrast to Shor's code, Steane's code is a dual-containing CSS code, since the PCMs $\mathbf{H}_z$ and $\mathbf{H}_x$ are based on that of the classical Hamming code $\mathbf{H}_{\text{Ham}}$, which is repeated here for convenience:

$$\mathbf{H}_{\text{Ham}} = \begin{pmatrix} 1&1&0&1&1&0&0\\ 1&0&1&1&0&1&0\\ 0&1&1&1&0&0&1 \end{pmatrix}. \tag{3.45}$$

It can be confirmed that the classical Hamming code is a dual-containing code, because it satisfies the condition $\mathbf{H}_{\text{Ham}}.\mathbf{H}_{\text{Ham}}^T = 0$. Therefore, the PCM $\mathbf{H}$ of Steane's code is defined as:

$$\mathbf{H}_{\text{Steane}} = \left(\begin{array}{c|c} \mathbf{H}_{\text{Ham}} & \mathbf{0} \\ \mathbf{0} & \mathbf{H}_{\text{Ham}} \end{array}\right) = \left(\begin{array}{ccccccc|ccccccc} 1 & 1 & 0 & 1 & 1 & 0 & 0 & 0 & 0 & 0 & 0 & 0 & 0 & 0 \\ 1 & 0 & 1 & 1 & 0 & 1 & 0 & 0 & 0 & 0 & 0 & 0 & 0 & 0 \\ 0 & 1 & 1 & 1 & 0 & 0 & 1 & 0 & 0 & 0 & 0 & 0 & 0 & 0 \\ 0 & 0 & 0 & 0 & 0 & 0 & 0 & 1 & 1 & 0 & 1 & 1 & 0 & 0 \\ 0 & 0 & 0 & 0 & 0 & 0 & 0 & 1 & 0 & 1 & 1 & 0 & 1 & 0 \\ 0 & 0 & 0 & 0 & 0 & 0 & 0 & 0 & 1 & 1 & 1 & 0 & 0 & 1 \end{array}\right). \tag{3.46}$$

Since Steane's code is a member of the dual-containing CSS codes, the encoded state of the logical qubit $|0\rangle_L$ and $|1\rangle_L$ may be determined from its classical code counterpart. Let $\mathcal{C}_1(7,4)$ be the Hamming code and $\mathcal{C}_2(7,3)$ be its dual. Both of the codes are capable of correcting a single bit error. Hence, the resultant CSS quantum code derived from these codes, namely the $\mathcal{C}[n, k_1 - k_2] = \mathcal{C}[7,1]$, is also capable of correcting a single qubit error. For Steane's code the states of the encoded logical qubit of $|0\rangle_L$ and $|1\rangle_L$ are defined as follows:

$$|0\rangle_L = \frac{1}{\sqrt{|\mathcal{C}_2|}} \sum_{x \in \mathcal{C}_1, \mathcal{C}_2} |x\rangle, \tag{3.47}$$

$$|1\rangle_L = \frac{1}{\sqrt{|\mathcal{C}_2|}} \sum_{x \in \mathcal{C}_1, x \notin \mathcal{C}_2} |x\rangle. \tag{3.48}$$

Since $\mathcal{C}_2$ is the dual of $\mathcal{C}_1$, the PCM of $\mathcal{C}_2$, denoted by $\mathbf{H}(\mathcal{C}_2)$ is by definition the generator matrix of $\mathcal{C}_1$, which is denoted by $\mathbf{G}(\mathcal{C}_1)$. Hence, the parity-check matrix of $\mathcal{C}_2$ can be written as

$$\mathbf{H}(\mathcal{C}_2) = \mathbf{G}(\mathcal{C}_1) = \begin{pmatrix} 1 & 0 & 0 & 0 & 1 & 1 & 0 \\ 0 & 1 & 0 & 0 & 1 & 0 & 1 \\ 0 & 0 & 1 & 0 & 0 & 1 & 1 \\ 0 & 0 & 0 & 1 & 1 & 1 & 1 \end{pmatrix}. \tag{3.49}$$

**Table 3.6** The code space of $\mathcal{C}_1$ and $\mathcal{C}_2$ for determining the encoded state of Steane's code.

| $x \in \mathscr{C}_1, \mathscr{C}_2$ | $x \in \mathscr{C}_1, x \notin \mathscr{C}_2$ |
|---|---|
| 0000000 | 1111111 |
| 0111001 | 1000110 |
| 1011010 | 0100101 |
| 1100011 | 0011100 |
| 1101100 | 0010011 |
| 1010101 | 0101010 |
| 0110110 | 1001001 |
| 0001111 | 1110000 |

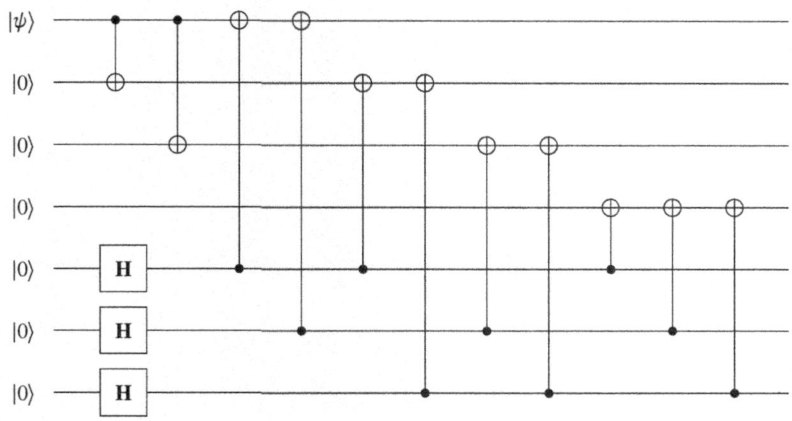


**Figure 3.7** The encoding circuit $\mathcal{V}$ of Steane's 7-qubit code.

Based on the PCM given in Eqs. (3.45) and (3.49), we can define the code space of $\mathcal{C}_1$ and $\mathcal{C}_2$, which is described in Table 3.6. Finally, upon using Eqs. (3.47) and (3.48), and also the code space given in Table 3.6, the encoded states of the logical qubit $|0\rangle_L$ and $|1\rangle_L$ of Steane's code may be formulated as:

$$\begin{aligned}|0\rangle_L = &\frac{1}{2\sqrt{2}}(|0000000\rangle + |0111001\rangle + |1011010\rangle + |1100011\rangle \\ &+ |1101100\rangle + |1010101\rangle + |0110110\rangle + |0001111\rangle),\end{aligned} \tag{3.50}$$

$$\begin{aligned}|1\rangle_L = &\frac{1}{2\sqrt{2}}(|1111111\rangle + |1000110\rangle + |0100101\rangle + |0011100\rangle \\ &+ |0010011\rangle + |0101010\rangle + |1001001\rangle + |1110000\rangle).\end{aligned} \tag{3.51}$$

Again, it can be readily seen that the quantum coding rate of Steane's 7-qubit code is 1/7. Its encoding circuit is portrayed in Figure. 3.7, while the corresponding set of stabilizers is listed in Table 3.7. Observe in the table that in the positions of the logical ones seen in Eq. 3.45 we have either $Z$ or $X$, while the logical zeros correspond to $I$. Furthermore, the first three rows in the table are mirrored by the bottom three rows upon replacing $Z$ by $x$. Steane's code is clearly more efficient than Shor's code, because it requires seven – rather than nine – qubits for protecting a single one. However, the separate treatment of bit-flips and phase-flips is still associated with some extra redundancy, as it becomes explicit by listing the number of possible erroneous scenarios. Explicitly, each of the seven qubits might be corrupted in three possible ways by $X$, $Z$ and $Y$ errors, which results in 21 possibilities plus we have an error-free scenario. Therefore we would require five stabilizers, which would allow us to differentiate up to 32 situations. But given the six stabilizers of Table 3.6 we could potentially distinguish as many as 64 scenarios. Therefore we summarize that there exists a more efficient code. Following the same logic, let us consider a 5-qubit code, where again, each qubit may be corrupted in three different ways, yielding a total of 15 possible cases, plus an error-free scenario. These 16 cases would require four stabilizers for uniquely and unambiguously distinguishing and eventually correcting all single-qubit errors. This is why Laflamme's 1/5-rate code has the fond connotation of being a "perfect" code, which will be discussed in the next section.

### 3.4.4 Laflamme's 5-qubit Code – The Perfect Code

Again, Laflamme's code maps a single logical qubit onto 5 physical qubits, which is also referred to as the "perfect code," because as alluded to in the previous sections, in order to protect a logical qubit, the lowest number of physical qubits required is five [57, 58]. This 5-qubit scheme is a non-CSS code, since the stabilizer formalism is designed to handle the **Z** errors and **X** errors simultaneously. There are several existing designs related to the

**Table 3.7** The stabilizer operators of Steane's 7-qubit code.

| $S_i$ | Stabilizer operator |
|---|---|
| $S_1$ | ZZIZZII |
| $S_2$ | ZIZZIZI |
| $S_3$ | IZZZIIZ |
| $S_4$ | XXIXXII |
| $S_5$ | XIXXIXI |
| $S_6$ | IXXXIIX |

**Table 3.8** The stabilizer formalism of the perfect 5-qubit code.

| $S_i$ | Stabilizer operator |
|---|---|
| $S_1$ | XZZXI |
| $S_2$ | IXZZX |
| $S_3$ | XIXZZ |
| $S_4$ | ZXIXZ |

perfect 5-qubit code [56, 160] and in this treatise, we use the PCM formulation given in [160]. Explicitly, its non-CSS characteristics can be readily observed from the PCM $\mathbf{H}_{\text{perfect}}$, which is specified as follows:

$$\mathbf{H}_{\text{perfect}} = \left(\begin{array}{ccccc|ccccc} 0 & 1 & 1 & 0 & 0 & 1 & 0 & 0 & 1 & 0 \\ 0 & 0 & 1 & 1 & 0 & 0 & 1 & 0 & 0 & 1 \\ 0 & 0 & 0 & 1 & 1 & 1 & 0 & 1 & 0 & 0 \\ 1 & 0 & 0 & 0 & 1 & 0 & 1 & 0 & 1 & 0 \end{array}\right). \tag{3.52}$$

Hence, the stabilizer operators of the 5-qubit code may be explicitly formulated as in Table 3.8.

In general, the encoded state of a QSC which encodes a single-logical qubit into $n$ physical qubits can be defined as follows [167]:

$$|0\rangle_L = \prod_{S_i \in \mathcal{S}} \frac{1}{\sqrt{N}} (\mathbf{I}^{\otimes n} + S_i)\, |0\rangle^{\otimes N}, \tag{3.53}$$

$$|1\rangle_L = \prod_{S_i \in \mathcal{S}} \frac{1}{\sqrt{N}} (\mathbf{I}^{\otimes n} + S_i)\, |1\rangle^{\otimes N}, \tag{3.54}$$

where the factor $N$ is introduced to preserve the unitary constraint. Therefore, based on the stabilizer operators as well as on Eqs. (3.53) and (3.54), the encoded state of Laflamme's 5-qubit code can be defined as follows:

$$\begin{aligned} |0\rangle_L = &\frac{1}{\sqrt{N}} (\mathbf{I}^{\otimes 5} + \mathbf{XZZXI})(\mathbf{I}^{\otimes 5} + \mathbf{XZZXI})(\mathbf{I}^{\otimes 5} + \mathbf{XZZXI}) \\ &(\mathbf{I}^{\otimes 5} + \mathbf{XZZXI})(\mathbf{I}^{\otimes 5} + \mathbf{XZZXI})\, |0\rangle^{\otimes 5}, \end{aligned} \tag{3.55}$$

$$\begin{aligned} |1\rangle_L = &\frac{1}{\sqrt{N}} (\mathbf{I}^{\otimes 5} + \mathbf{XZZXI})(\mathbf{I}^{\otimes 5} + \mathbf{XZZXI})(\mathbf{I}^{\otimes 5} + \mathbf{XZZXI}) \\ &(\mathbf{I}^{\otimes 5} + \mathbf{XZZXI})(\mathbf{I}^{\otimes 5} + \mathbf{XZZXI})\, |1\rangle^{\otimes 5}. \end{aligned} \tag{3.56}$$

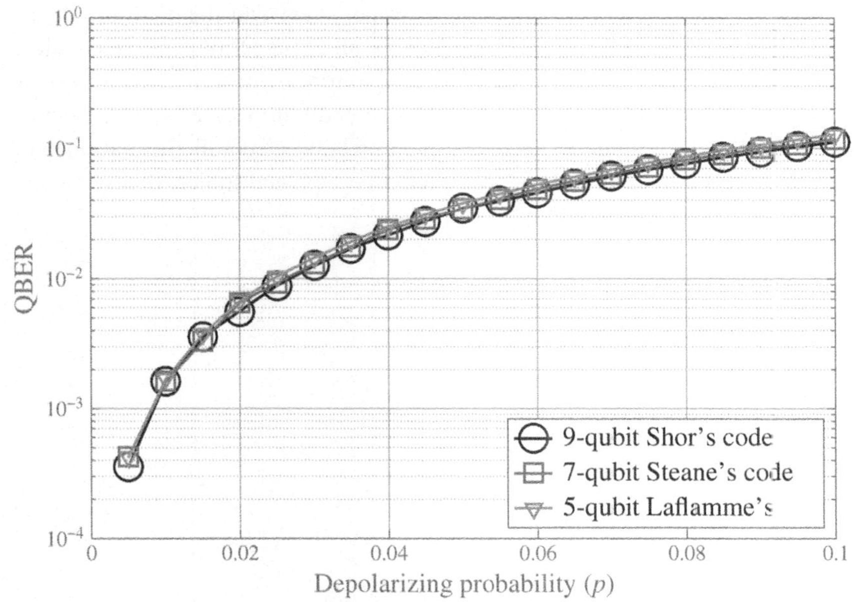


**Figure 3.8** QBER performance of the QSCs protecting a single qubit, namely Shor's 9-qubit code, Steane's 7-qubit code, and the perfect 5-qubit code, recorded for the quantum depolarizing channel. The similarity of performances is because all of the QSCs rely on hard-decision syndrome decoding and they all have the same error correction capabilities.

Finally, after a few further steps we arrive at:

$$|0\rangle_L = \frac{1}{4}(|00000\rangle - |00011\rangle + |00101\rangle - |00110\rangle + |01001\rangle + |01010\rangle - |01100\rangle - |01111\rangle$$
$$- |10001\rangle + |10010\rangle + |10100\rangle - |10111\rangle - |11000\rangle - |11011\rangle - |11101\rangle - |11110\rangle), \tag{3.57}$$
$$|1\rangle_L = \frac{1}{4}(|11111\rangle - |11100\rangle + |11010\rangle - |11001\rangle + |10110\rangle + |10101\rangle - |10011\rangle - |10000\rangle$$
$$- |01110\rangle + |01101\rangle + |01011\rangle - |01000\rangle - |00111\rangle - |00100\rangle - |00010\rangle - |00001\rangle). \tag{3.58}$$

The same method can be utilized for determining the encoded state of a logical qubit for Shor's code and Steane's code. However, both Shor's code and Steane's code offer a more simplistic approach for determining their corresponding encoded states. The design of an efficient encoding circuit $\mathcal{V}$ conceived for the 1/5-rate code of Laflamme can be found in [56, 180, 181].

Based on the aforementioned constructions, we evaluated the performance of the three QSCs by simulation in the context of quantum depolarizing channels. The performance of the 9-qubit Shor-code, 7-qubit Steane-code, and 5-qubit Laflamme-code is portrayed in Figure 3.8 in terms of the qubit error rate (QBER) vs. the depolarizing probability ($p$). It was observed that the performances of all three QSCs are quite similar, which is not unexpected, as they are all capable of correcting a single-qubit error.

## 3.5 Summary and Conclusions

The purpose of this chapter is to provide the similarities between the classical and quantum error correction codes. More specifically, the QSCs can be viewed as the syndrome-based version of QECCs, as exemplified by the 1/3-rate quantum repetition code. By using the classical-to-quantum Pauli isomorphism, we can observe that a QSC can be treated as a syndrome-based classical error-correction code, whose PCM can be separated into two independent PCMs, one for dealing with bit-flip (**X**) errors, which is the PCM $\mathbf{H}_x$, and one for handling the phase-flip (**Z**) errors, which is the PCM $\mathbf{H}_z$. Based on how to mitigate the **X** and the **Z** errors, a QSC can be classified either as a CSS code or a non-CSS code. The main difference between the two is the CSS codes handle the **X** and the **Z** errors independently, as exemplified by the PCMs of Shor's code and Steane's code, while the non-CSS codes treat them simultaneously, as exemplified by the PCM of the Laflamme's code.

We have simulated the QBER performance for Shor's, Steane's, and Laflamme's code over the quantum depolarizing channel. The simulation results show a similar QBER performance for all of the aforementioned codes. The main reason is all of Shor's, Steane's, and Laflamme's code exhibit the same minimum distance ($d = 3$), which translates directly to the error correction capability of the code ($t = 1$) despite of their differences in code type, codeword length and and quantum coding rate. Therefore, we believe that the trade-off between conflicting parameters in QSCs such as minimum distance, quantum coding rate, and codeword length is a pivotal subject to investigate. This specific line of investigation will be carried out in Chapter 6.

# 4

# Revisiting Classical Syndrome Decoding

## 4.1 Introduction

In Chapter 3 we kept the level of treatment relatively simple for readers who are exposed to the quantum coding concepts for the first time, including the syndrome decoding basics relying on the $C(7, 4)$ Hamming code. A rudimentary introduction to quantum stabilizer codes was also provided.

In Chapters 7 and 10, we then offered somewhat deeper insights into the construction of stabilizer codes from the known classical codes based on the underlying quantum-to-classical isomorphism. Let us recall that since a quantum stabilizer code (QSC) can be mapped onto an equivalent classical binary or quaternary parity check matrix (PCM), classical PCM-based syndrome decoding may be invoked during the quantum decoding process. More explicitly, the "syndrome processing" block of Figure 10.1 may be expanded, as shown in Figure 4.1. The process begins with the computation of the syndrome of the received sequence $|\hat{\psi}\rangle$ using the stabilizer generators, which collapse to a binary 0 or 1 upon measurement. For estimating the equivalent channel error $\tilde{P}$ (or $\tilde{\bar{P}}$ in quaternary domain), the binary syndrome sequence $s$ is fed to a classical PCM-based syndrome decoder, which operates over the equivalent classical PCM associated with the QSC. Finally, the estimated binary (or quaternary) error is mapped onto the equivalent Pauli error $\tilde{\mathcal{P}}$ using the binary-to-Pauli mapping of Eq. (10.29) (or quaternary-to-Pauli mapping of Eq. [10.39]). The classical syndrome decoder component used in the middle of Figure 4.1 bears some similarity to that of a conventional classical code, but it also exhibits some differences:

- **(a)** In contrast to the syndrome of a classical code, which is computed as the product of the PCM and the transpose of the channel error vector ($HP^T$), the syndrome of a quantum code is computed using the symplectic product of Eq. (10.37) (or the trace inner product of Eq. [10.45]).
- **(b)** The conventional classical decoding aims for finding the most likely error vector, given the syndrome observed, while quantum decoding aims for finding the most likely error coset, which takes into account the degenerate nature of quantum codes, as discussed in Section 10.3.3.

In this chapter, we will focus our attention on the classical syndrome decoding techniques conceived for conventional classical codes transmitted over a classical channel, thereby ignoring the abovementioned pair of differences. The concepts developed in this chapter together with those of Chapter 10 will be subsequently used in the later chapters in the context of quantum codes. We have also conceived a reduced-complexity syndrome-based decoder in this chapter.

Again, in contrast to conventional codeword decoding, which finds the most likely codeword, having the minimum Hamming distance, syndrome decoding finds the most likely error having the minimum Hamming weight. The notion of syndrome decoding stems from the look-up table (LUT) based decoding of linear block codes, whereby the syndrome of the received sequence characterizes the errors by harnessing a pre-computed LUT [182]. An LUT-based syndrome decoder is in essence a minimum-distance decoder, which finds the error vector having the minimum Hamming weight. By contrast, the soft-decision maximum likelihood (ML) codeword decoding of a linear block code requires a brute force attempt for computing the conditional probability for all possible codewords $\bar{x}$, given the received sequence $y$ $\mathrm{P}(\bar{x}|y)$ (or the probability of all possible errors $e$ given the observed syndrome $s$ for syndrome decoding $\mathrm{P}(e|s)$). To circumvent this tedious task, Bahl *et al.* [183] were the first to conceive the

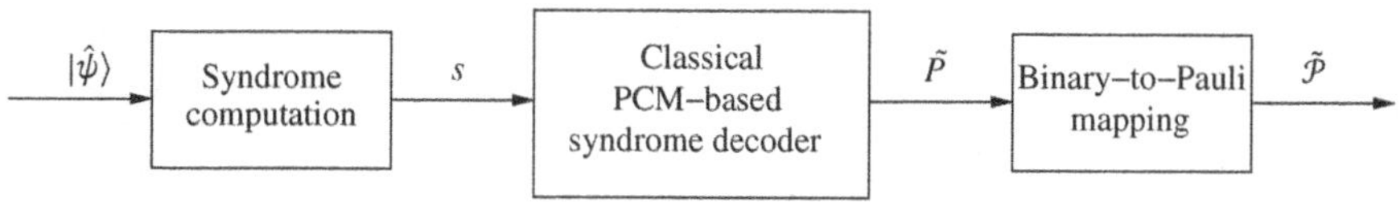


**Figure 4.1** Syndrome processing block seen in Figure 10.1.

syndrome-based[1] code trellis[2] for linear block codes. However, they did not provide a detailed construction. This gap was filled by Wolf in [184], whereby the method of constructing the syndrome-based code trellis for linear block codes was presented. Wolf [184] also proved that in contrast to a brute force ML decoding of a linear block code $C(n, k)$ over GF($q$), which would require $q^k$ evaluations, a code trellis requires only $q^{\min\{k,n-k\}}$ states. The ideas presented in [183, 184] for the trellis-based ML codeword decoding of linear block codes are readily applicable to the trellis-based ML syndrome decoding, which relies on the corresponding syndrome-based error trellis. Parallel to these developments, Schalkwijk and Vinck in [185–187] conceived the idea of a syndrome-based error trellis for convolutional codes. They exploited the inherent symmetries of the trellis structure for reducing the complexity of the decoding hardware required for the hard-decision syndrome decoding of convolutional codes. Later, soft-decision syndrome decoding approaches were presented in [188, 189], which were based on the error trellis and code trellis, respectively. This concept was further extended to the family of high-rate turbo codes in [190].

The error trellis-based syndrome decoding is of particular significance, because the state probabilities of an error trellis are a function of the channel errors rather than of the coded sequence. Consequently, at high signal-to-noise ratios (SNRs), the syndrome decoder is more likely to encounter a zero-state due to the predominant error-free transmissions. This underlying property of syndrome decoding has been exploited in [191, 192] for developing a block syndrome decoder (BSD) for convolutional codes, which divides the received sequence into erroneous and error-free parts based on the syndrome. More specifically, the BSD only decodes the erroneous blocks, with the initial and final states of the trellis initialized to zero. Therefore, the decoding complexity is substantially reduced at higher SNRs. It also offers a potential for parallelization [193]. The concept of BSD was further extended to turbo codes in [194], where a pre-correction sequence[3] was also computed at each iteration to correct the errors. Consequently, the Hamming weight of the syndrome sequence decreases with ongoing iterations. Thus, the decoding complexity was reduced not only at higher SNRs, but also for the higher-indexed iterations. Furthermore, a syndrome-based maximum *a-posteriori* (MAP) decoder was proposed in [195] for designing an adaptive low-complexity decoding approach for turbo equalization. Some other applications of BSD are dealt with in [196–198].

Inspired by the significant decoding complexity reductions reported for BSD, our novel contribution in this chapter is that we have extended the application of the syndrome-based MAP decoder of [195] together with the BSD of [194] to turbo trellis coded modulation (TTCM) for the sake of reducing its decoding complexity [199]. The resultant scheme is referred to as BSD-TTCM. We have investigated the performance of our proposed BSD-TTCM for transmission over the additive white gaussian noise (AWGN) channel as well as over an uncorrelated Rayleigh fading channel in this chapter.

The rest of this chapter is organized as follows. In Section 4.2, we detail the LUT-based syndrome decoding method, which forms the basis of the syndrome decoding concept. This is followed by a discussion on the trellis-based syndrome decoding in Section 4.3. More particularly, Section 4.3.1 focuses on the construction of the syndrome-based trellis of linear block codes, while in Section 4.3.2 we extend this syndrome-based trellis formalism to convolutional codes. Section 4.4 deals with the BSD. More specifically, in Section 4.4.1, we lay out the general BSD formalism, while our proposed block-based syndrome decoder designed for TTCM is presented in Section 4.4.2. We then evaluate the performance of our proposed decoder in Section 4.5. Finally, we summarize the chapter in Section 4.6.

---

1 We call this trellis syndrome-based because it is constructed from the PCM of the linear block code, while the classic trellis of a convolutional code is constructed using the code generators.

2 Each path of a code trellis is a valid codeword, while each path of an error trellis is a possible channel error, which would yield a given syndrome sequence. Therefore, a code trellis is used for codeword decoding, while an error trellis is used for syndrome decoding.

3 Pre-correction sequence is an estimated/predicted error sequence, which is used to correct errors in the received information.

## 4.2 Look-up Table-based Syndrome Decoding

The PCM-based syndrome decoding technique discussed in Section 10.2 is in fact the LUT-based syndrome-based decoder, which is based on Table 10.1. In this section, we will detail the construction of the LUT.

The LUT-based syndrome decoding derives its philosophy from the standard array-based decoding. For a binary linear block code $C(n,k)$, standard array is a $2^{n-k} \times 2^k$ array, which distributes all the possible $2^n$ $n$-tuple vectors into $2^k$ disjoint subsets of size $2^{n-k}$, such that each subset contains only one valid codeword. More specifically, a standard array is constructed as follows:

- Let $\{\bar{x}_1, \bar{x}_2, \ldots, \bar{x}_{2^k}\}$ be the set of valid codewords ($n$-bit each) of $C(n,k)$. Place all these $2^k$ codewords of $C$ in the first row of the standard array, commencing from the all-zero codeword.
- Select any minimum-weight vector $e_2$ from the pool of $2^n$ $n$-bit vectors, which is not contained in the first row. List the coset $(e_2 + C)$ in the second row for ensuring that $e_2 + \bar{x}_i$ is in the $i$th column, where $\bar{x}_i$ is the $i$th valid codeword.
- Select another minimum-weight vector $e_3$ from the remaining pool, i.e. excluding the vectors contained in the first two rows, and list the coset $(e_3 + C)$ in the third row.
- Continue the process for all $2^{n-k}$ cosets.

The resultant standard array may be formulated as:

$$\begin{pmatrix} \bar{x}_1 = 0 & \bar{x}_2 & \cdots & \bar{x}_i & \cdots & \bar{x}_{2^k} \\ e_2 & e_2 + \bar{x}_2 & \cdots & e_2 + \bar{x}_i & \cdots & e_2 + \bar{x}_{2^k} \\ e_3 & e_3 + \bar{x}_2 & \cdots & e_3 + \bar{x}_i & \cdots & e_3 + \bar{x}_{2^k} \\ \vdots & & & & & \vdots \\ e_{2^{n-k}} & e_{2^{n-k}} + \bar{x}_2 & \cdots & e_{2^{n-k}} + \bar{x}_i & \cdots & e_{2^{n-k}} + \bar{x}_{2^k} \end{pmatrix}, \tag{4.1}$$

where $\{e_1 = 0, e_2, \ldots, e_{2^{n-k}}\}$ constitutes the set of possible minimum-weight errors, which may be identified using the code $C(n,k)$. More explicitly, each row of Eq. (4.1) is a unique coset, whose coset leader is the minimum weight vector given in the first column. We may notice in Eq. (4.1) that adding (modulo 2) the coset leader to any element of the same coset yields the corresponding valid codeword. For example, if we add $e_3$ to the second element of the third coset according to $e_3 + \bar{x}_2$, we get $\bar{x}_2$. Hence, the coset leader identifies the most likely (having the minimum Hamming weight) error for its coset.

Since the PCM-based syndrome decoding approach discussed in Section 10.2 LUT-based syndrome decoder, let us construct the associated standard array. Recall from Section 10.2 that a 3-bit repetition code $C(3,1)$ has two valid codewords, i.e. $\bar{x}_1 = [000]$ and $\bar{x}_2 = [111]$. Using Eq. (4.1) and this set of valid codewords, we get the following standard array:

$$\begin{pmatrix} \bar{x}_1 & \bar{x}_2 \\ e_2 & e_2 + \bar{x}_2 \\ e_3 & e_3 + \bar{x}_2 \\ e_4 & e_4 + \bar{x}_2 \end{pmatrix} = \begin{pmatrix} 000 & 111 \\ 001 & 110 \\ 010 & 101 \\ 100 & 011 \end{pmatrix}. \tag{4.2}$$

Let us assume furthermore that the received vector $y = [011]$ lies in the fourth coset. Consequently, the estimated error is $[100]$ and the corresponding estimated codeword is $[011] + [100] = [111]$, which is the first element of the subset (column) to which $y$ belongs.

Since the standard array is a $(2^{n-k} \times 2^k)$-element array, it imposes huge storage requirements for large linear block codes. This may be alleviated by using the LUT-based syndrome decoding. Let us consider the $i$th element of the $j$th coset of the standard array in Eq. (4.1). Its syndrome may be formulated as:

$$s = (e_j + \bar{x}_i)H^T = e_jH^T + \bar{x}_iH^T = e_jH^T. \tag{4.3}$$

Hence, each coset is identified by a unique syndrome. Consequently, rather than storing all the $2^k$ elements of the coset, we can construct an LUT, which only stores the coset leader and the corresponding syndrome, i.e. we have:

$$\begin{pmatrix} e_1 = 0 & 0 \\ e_2 & e_2 H^T \\ e_3 & e_3 H^T \\ e_4 & e_4 H^T \end{pmatrix} = \begin{pmatrix} 000 & 00 \\ 001 & 01 \\ 010 & 10 \\ 100 & 11 \end{pmatrix}. \tag{4.4}$$

This is equivalent to the LUT given in Table 10.1, which also has two columns and $2^{n-k} = 4$ rows.

## 4.3 Trellis-based Syndrome Decoding

Trellis-based syndrome decoding operates over a syndrome-based error trellis. More specifically, each path of an error trellis characterizes a unique channel error for a given syndrome. Consequently, the set of paths of the error trellis for a particular syndrome is the same as the coset of the standard array (Eq. [4.1]) corresponding to that syndrome. When the syndrome is zero, which is equivalent to the first coset of Eq. (4.1), i.e. to set of all valid codewords, the error trellis collapses to a code trellis. The trellis-based syndrome decoding therefore invokes either the classic Viterbi algorithm [200] or the Bahl–Cocke–Jelinek–Raviv (BCJR) decoding (also called MAP decoding) [183] for estimating the most likely channel error for a given syndrome. In this context, let us now have a look at the construction of the syndrome-based error trellis for linear block codes and convolutional codes in Sections 4.3.1 and 4.3.2, respectively. Finally, the MAP algorithm will be presented later in Section 4.4.2.2.

### 4.3.1 Linear Block Codes

Consider a linear block code $C(n, k)$ constituted over GF($q$) having an $(n-k) \times n$ PCM $H$, whose $i$th column is represented by $h_i$ for $i = \{1, 2, \ldots, n\}$. The syndrome-based trellis of this code is defined by a set of states interconnected by unidirectional edges, where a state is basically represented by an $(n-k)$-bit syndrome. Analogously to a conventional trellis, the edges are drawn between the trellis-states at depth $t$ and those at depth $(t-1)$, for $t = \{0, 1, \ldots, n\}$, with the direction of the edge emerging from the state at depth $(t-1)$ and arriving at the state at depth $t$. At any trellis-depth $t$, there are at most $q^{n-k}$ nodes and the $l$th trellis-state at depth $t$ is denoted as $s_l(t)$. Based on this notation, let us now construct the syndrome-based trellis of Figure 4.2 for a binary code $C(5, 3)$, whose PCM is given by,

$$H = \begin{pmatrix} 1 & 1 & 0 & 1 & 0 \\ 1 & 0 & 1 & 0 & 1 \end{pmatrix} = \begin{pmatrix} h_1 & h_2 & h_3 & h_4 & h_5 \end{pmatrix}. \tag{4.5}$$

The trellis of Figure 4.2 can be constructed as follows:

**(a)** The trellis emerges from the trellis-state $(0, 0)$ at $t = 0$, i.e. we have $s_0(0) = (0, 0)$.

**(b)** We next determine the set of trellis-states for $t = \{1, \ldots, 5\}$ as follows:

  **(a)** We compute the edges emerging from the trellis-state $s_0(0)$ at trellis-depth $t = 0$ to the states at depth $t = 1$ using the relationship:

$$s_l(t) = s_i(t-1) + \alpha_j h_t, \quad \text{for } j = 0, 1, \ldots, (q-1), \tag{4.6}$$

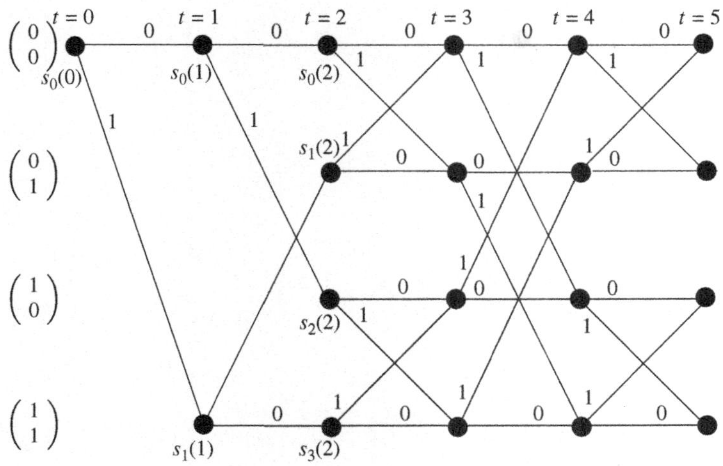


**Figure 4.2** Syndrome-based trellis for a linear block code C(5, 3) constructed over GF(2).

where $s_l(t)$ is the $l$th state at depth $t$, $s_i(t-1)$ is the $i$th state at depth $(t-1)$ and $\alpha_j$ is an element of GF($q$). Since we are using a binary code, there are only two possible values of $\alpha_j$ in Eq. (4.6) i.e. $\alpha_0 = 0$ and $\alpha_1 = 1$. Substituting these values of $\alpha_j$ into Eq. (4.6) at $t = 1$ yields:

$$s_0(1) = s_0(0) + \alpha_0 h_1 = \begin{pmatrix} 0 \\ 0 \end{pmatrix} + 0.\begin{pmatrix} 1 \\ 1 \end{pmatrix} = \begin{pmatrix} 0 \\ 0 \end{pmatrix}, \tag{4.7}$$

$$s_1(1) = s_0(0) + \alpha_1 h_1 = \begin{pmatrix} 0 \\ 0 \end{pmatrix} + 1.\begin{pmatrix} 1 \\ 1 \end{pmatrix} = \begin{pmatrix} 1 \\ 1 \end{pmatrix}. \tag{4.8}$$

Consequently, the trellis-state $s_0(0) = (0, 0)$ at $t = 0$ is connected to the states $s_0(1) = (0, 0)$ and $s_1(1) = (1, 1)$ at $t = 1$, as seen in the trellis of Figure 4.6. The corresponding edges are labeled by 0 and 1 for $\alpha_0 = 0$ and $\alpha_1 = 1$, respectively.

Equations (4.7) and (4.8) may also be computed using an alternate approach. We know that for a received vector $y$ and the PCM $H$, the syndrome vector $s$ is given by,

$$s = yH^T. \tag{4.9}$$

At $t = 1$, we receive only the first element of $y$ i.e. $y = [y_1 0000]^T$. Therefore, Eqs. (4.7) and (4.8) can also be formulated as:

$$s_l(1) = \begin{pmatrix} 1 & 1 & 0 & 1 & 0 \\ 1 & 0 & 1 & 0 & 1 \end{pmatrix} . \begin{pmatrix} y_1 \\ 0 \\ 0 \\ 0 \\ 0 \end{pmatrix} \quad \text{where } y_1 \in \{\alpha_0, \alpha_1\}. \tag{4.10}$$

**(b)** The process is similarly repeated for $t = 2$, where we have:

$$s_l(2) = s_0(1) + \alpha_j h_2 \tag{4.11}$$
$$s_l(2) = s_1(1) + \alpha_j h_2,$$

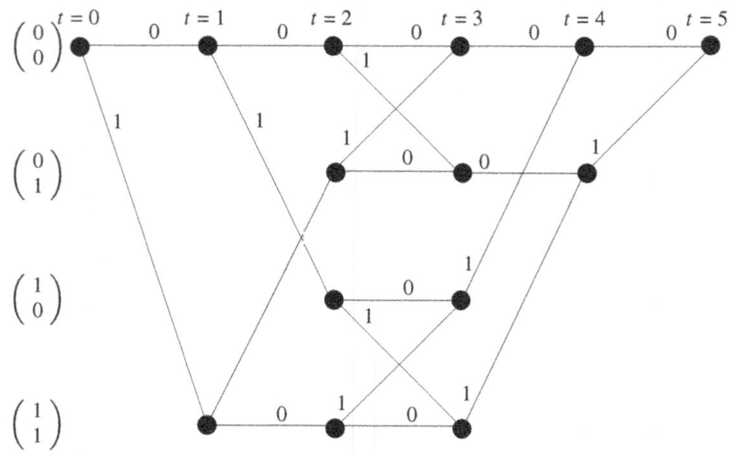


**Figure 4.3** Expurgated syndrome-based code trellis for the binary code $C(5, 3)$.

for $j = \{0, 1\}$. If the alternate approach of Eq. (4.10) is adopted, Eq. (4.11) may be written as:

$$s_l(2) = \begin{pmatrix} 1 & 1 & 0 & 1 & 0 \\ 1 & 0 & 1 & 0 & 1 \end{pmatrix} \cdot \begin{pmatrix} y_1 \\ y_2 \\ 0 \\ 0 \\ 0 \end{pmatrix}, \quad \text{where } y_1, y_2 \in \{\alpha_0, \alpha_1\}, \tag{4.12}$$

since we have two received bits $y_1$ and $y_2$ at $t = 2$.

**(c)** This process is repeated until we reach the end of the PCM, i.e $t = 5$.

**(c)** Finally, any paths that do not terminate at the all-zero syndrome can be removed, hence resulting in the expurgated code trellis, which is shown in Figure 4.3. Since only the paths terminating at the all-zero syndrome are considered, these paths correspond to the valid codewords. For generating the error trellis, we discard all paths, which do not terminate at the syndrome of the received vector $y$. Consequently, each path of the expurgated error trellis defines a possible error sequence. In other words, the error trellis collapses to a code trellis, when the syndrome observed is zero.

The above mentioned process for constructing a syndrome-based trellis of a linear block code may be generalized as follows:

**(a)** The trellis starts from an all-zero state, i.e. there is a single state at $t = 0$ denoted by $s_0(0)$, which is equivalent to an all-zero vector of length $(n - k)$.

**(b)** For each $t = \{1, 2, \dots, n\}$, the trellis-states at depth $t$ are obtained from the set of states at depth $(t - 1)$ using Eq. (4.6). Edges are drawn between the state $s_i(t - 1)$ at trellis-depth $t - 1$ and the $q$ states $s_l(t - 1)$ at depth $t$, which are labeled by the corresponding value of $\alpha_j$.

**(c)** For a code trellis, the constructed trellis is expurgated by removing those paths, which do not lead to an all-zero state at depth $n$. Consequently, each of the $q^k$ paths in the resultant trellis defines a valid codeword. By contrast, for the error trellis, the constructed trellis is expurgated by discarding those paths, which do not terminate at the syndrome observed, i.e. at the syndrome of the received vector $y$.

### 4.3.2 Convolutional Codes

The conventional code trellis of a convolutional code is derived from the generator matrix $G$. By contrast, an error trellis is constructed using the corresponding PCM, which is known as the syndrome former $H^T$ for convolutional codes. Let us review the example given in [201] for illustrating the trellis construction procedure. We use a rate-2/3 convolutional code, whose generator $G(D)$ is given by:

$$G(D) = \begin{pmatrix} 1+D & D & 1+D \\ D & 1 & 1 \end{pmatrix}. \tag{4.13}$$

The corresponding syndrome former is as follows:

$$H^T(D) = \begin{pmatrix} 1 \\ 1+D^2 \\ 1+D+D^2 \end{pmatrix}. \tag{4.14}$$

The circuit of $G(D)$ for $CC(n,k)$ is realized in Figure 4.4a, whereby the input information sequence $u_t = (u_t^{(1)}, \ldots, u_t^{(k)})$ at time instant $t$ is encoded by the generator $G(D)$, yielding the output code sequence of $v_t = (v_t^{(1)}, \ldots, v_t^{(n)})$. Let $e_t = (e_t^{(1)}, \ldots, e_t^{(n)})$ be the channel error experienced during transmission. The received sequence $y_t = (y_t^{(1)}, \ldots, y_t^{(n)})$ is therefore given by:

$$y_t^j = v_t^j \oplus e_t^j. \tag{4.15}$$

Analogously to the linear block codes, we may define the resultant syndrome sequence $s$ using the syndrome former $H^T$ as follows[4]:

$$s = yH^T = (v+e)H^T = eH^T. \tag{4.16}$$

This realization of the syndrome former is shown in Figure 4.4b, which employs the error sequence $e_t = (e_t^{(1)}, \ldots, e_t^{(n)})$ as its input for computing the corresponding syndrome $s_t$ at time instant $t$ using the syndrome former of Eq. (4.14). Consequently, we may construct the trellis for the syndrome former of Figure 4.4b as we conventionally do using the encoder $G$. Furthermore, since the syndrome $s_t$ can either have a value of 0 or 1, we divide the resultant trellis into two sub-trellis modules corresponding to $s_t = 0$ and $s_t = 1$, as shown in Figure 4.5. Here,

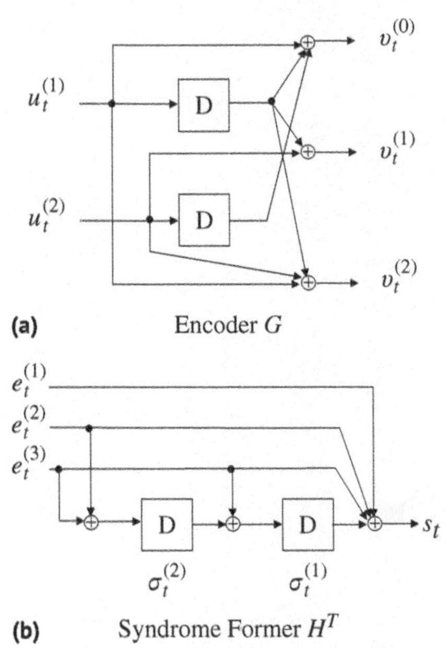


**Figure 4.4** Realization of the encoder and syndrome former given in Eqs. (4.13) and (4.14), respectively.

4 Recall from Section 10.4 that the PCM of a convolutional code is a semi-infinite matrix. The semi-infinite binary matrix $H^T$ corresponding to $H^T(D)$ of Eq. (4.14) is defined later in Eq. (4.20).

the state at time $t$ is defined as $\sigma_t = (\sigma_t^{(1)} \sigma_t^{(2)})$ and each branch leading from $\sigma_{t-1}$ to $\sigma_t$ is labeled with the error $e_t = (e_t^{(1)}, e_t^{(2)}, e_t^{(3)})$.

Let us assume that the received sequence is:

$$\{y_t\}_{t=1}^{3} = \{011 \;\; 011 \;\; 111\}. \tag{4.17}$$

Since the received sequence $y_t$ and the inflicted channel error $e_t$ yield the same syndrome according to Eq. (4.16), we feed $y_t$ into the circuit of Figure 4.4b for computing the syndrome. Consequently, using the syndrome former of Figure 4.4b, whose registers are initialized to the zero state, we get $\{s_t\}_{t=1}^{3} = \{0, 1, 0\}$, while the resultant states are $\sigma_1 = (10)$, $\sigma_2 = (10)$ and $\sigma_3 = (10)$, respectively. The corresponding trellis can be constructed by starting from the state $\sigma_0 = (00)$ and concatenating the sub-trellises of Figure 4.5 based on the value of $s_t$. More specifically, for the syndrome values of $\{s_t\}_{t=1}^{3} = \{0, 1, 0\}$, we concatenate the sub-trellis for $s_t = 0$ to that for the state $s_t = 1$, followed by another sub-trellis for the $s_t = 0$. This yields the trellis of Figure 4.6 for the received sequence of Eq. (4.17), which is initialized to the state $\sigma_0 = (00)$ and terminates at $\sigma_3 = (10)$.

The error trellis of Figure 4.6 is equivalent to the conventional code trellis generated using the generator $G$, which is shown in Figure 4.7. Here the state at time $t$ is $(u_t^{(1)}, u_t^{(2)})$ and each branch is labeled with the coded bits $(v_t^{(1)}, v_t^{(2)}, v_t^{(3)})$. Furthermore, the trellis emerges from and it is terminated at the all-zero states.[5] Each path of Figure 4.6 corresponds to a path of Figure 4.7 and this correspondence is a one-to-one relationship [201].

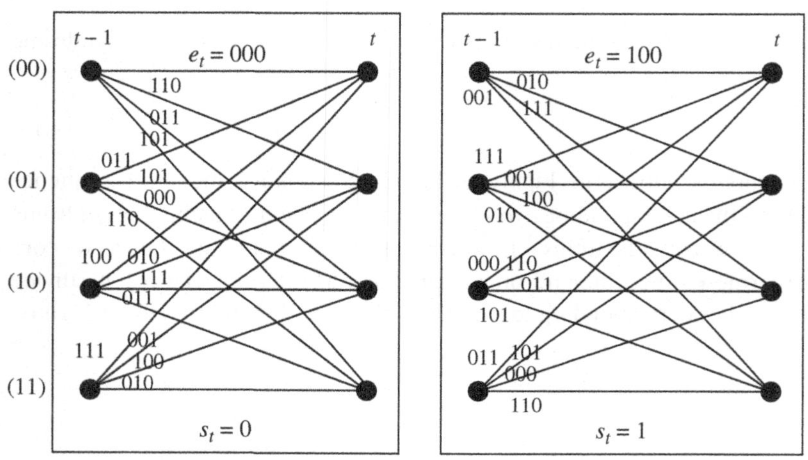


**Figure 4.5** Syndrome-based error sub-trellises for $H^T$ corresponding to $s_t = 0$ and $s_t = 1$.

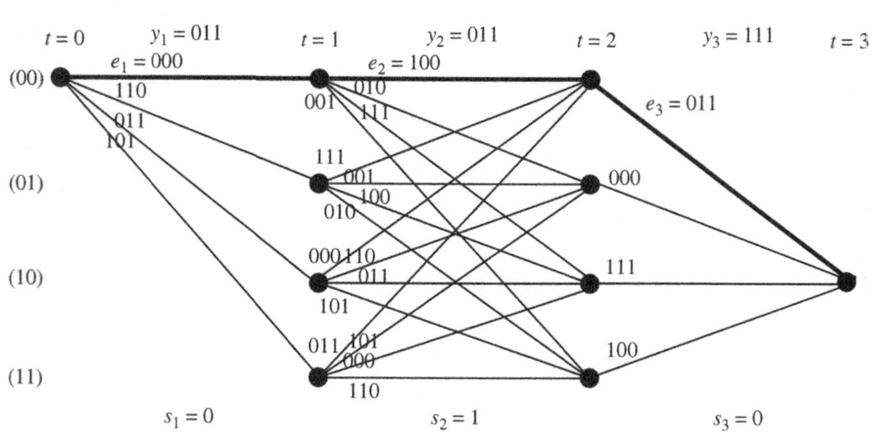


**Figure 4.6** Syndrome-based error trellis for $H^T$ corresponding to the received sequence of Eq. (4.17), which is constructed by concatenating the sub-trellises of Figure 4.5.

5 It is assumed that termination bits are used.

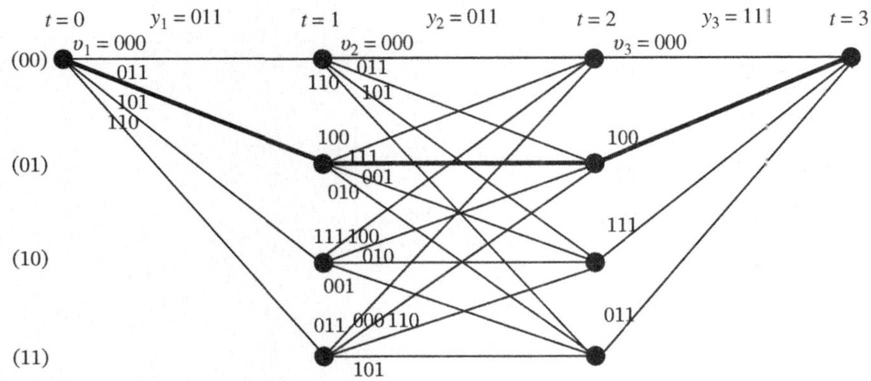


**Figure 4.7** Conventional code trellis, generated using the encoder $G$ of Figure 4.4a, corresponding to Figure 4.6. Each path of Figure 4.6 can be mapped onto a path of the code trellis using Eq. (4.18).

Consider an arbitrary path $\tilde{e} = \{000 \quad 100 \quad 011\}$ of Figure 4.6 (marked with a thick line). Since the received sequence is $y = \{011 \quad 011 \quad 111\}$, the estimated transmitted code sequence $\tilde{v}$ is computed as:

$$\tilde{v}_t^{(j)} = \tilde{e}_t^{(j)} \oplus y_t^{(j)}. \tag{4.18}$$

Hence, we have $\tilde{v} = \{011 \quad 111 \quad 100\}$, which is a path of the trellis seen in Figure 4.7 (marked with a thick line). We may, therefore, conclude that for every error path in the error trellis, there is a corresponding unique path in the conventional code trellis. Either the Viterbi or the MAP algorithm can then be used for determining the most likely error $\tilde{e}$ for the received sequence. The estimated error sequence is then added (bit-wise modulo 2) to the received sequence $y$ as in Eq. (4.18), yielding the most likely transmitted code sequence $\tilde{v}$. It is then passed through the inverse encoder $G^{-1}$ for estimating the most likely information sequence $\tilde{u}$ as follows:

$$\tilde{u} = \tilde{v}G^{-1}. \tag{4.19}$$

The syndrome-based error trellis of Figure 4.6 has the same complexity as the conventional code trellis of Figure 4.7 for soft-decision decoding, which is $\sim nq^k q^m$ for CC$(n, k, m)$ and grows exponentially upon increasing the value of $k$ (increasing the coding rate $R$). By contrast, Sidorenko *et al.* [189] proposed a syndrome-based trellis, which has a lower complexity[6] than the conventional trellis for both hard-decision and soft-decision decoding. This construction is derived from the Wolf trellis of [184] conceived for linear block codes, which was discussed in Section 4.3.1. The complexity of the resultant trellis is $\sim nq^{\min(k,n-k)}q^m$, which decreases upon increasing $R$ for $R > \frac{1}{2}$ and it is approximately equivalent to that of the conventional trellis for $R < \frac{1}{2}$. More explicitly, Sidorenko's method [189] of constructing the syndrome-based trellis divides each branch of Figure 4.6 into $n$ stages.

Let us now continue the same example as in Eq. (4.14). Recall from Section 10.4 that a convolutional code is equivalent to a semi-infinite linear block code. For the syndrome former of Eq. (4.14), the associated semi-infinite parity check matrix can be constructed as:

$$H = \begin{pmatrix} 111 & & & \\ 001 & 111 & & \\ 011 & 001 & 111 & \\ & 011 & 001 & 111 \\ & \ddots & & \ddots \end{pmatrix}, \tag{4.20}$$

6 The complexity of a code trellis is the number of operations (selections and additions) required to decode a block [189].

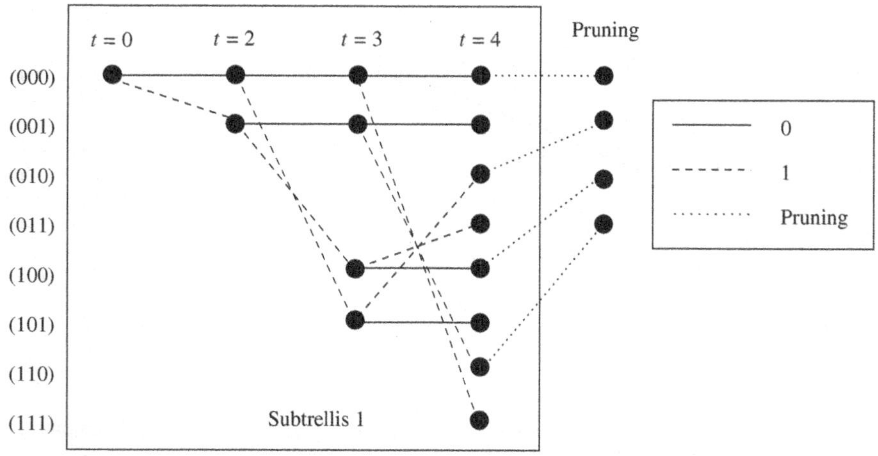


**Figure 4.8** Syndrome-based code trellis for the PCM of Eq. (4.20).

which is composed of the time-shifted versions of the basic PCM $H_b$ given by:

$$H_b = \begin{pmatrix} 111 \\ 001 \\ 011 \end{pmatrix}. \tag{4.21}$$

Consequently, we can construct its syndrome-based trellis by interconnecting a series of sub-trellises formed using the basic PCM $H_b$, where the number of interconnected sub-trellises is equal to the length of the received bit stream.

Figure 4.8 shows the first sub-trellis of the syndrome-based code trellis for the PCM $H$ of Eq. (4.20), which has $(2^3 = 8)$ states, since the associated $H_b$ has three rows (syndromes). The trellis of Figure 4.8 is constructed as follows:

**(a)** The trellis emerges from an all-zero state i.e from $(0, 0, 0)$ at $t = 0$.

**(b)** The first sub-trellis is constructed using Eq. (4.21). Here each state is labeled by three syndromes, namely $s_3s_2s_1$,[7] where $s_1$, $s_2$ and $s_3$ correspond to the first, second and third row of $H_b$. The states at depth $t$ are obtained from the set of states at depth $(t-1)$ using the relationship:

$$s_l(t) = s_i(t-1) + \alpha_j h_t, \quad \text{for } j = 0, 1, \ldots, (q-1). \tag{4.22}$$

Here, $s_l(t)$ is the $l$th node at depth $t$, $s_i(t-1)$ is the $i$th node at depth $(t-1)$, $\alpha_j$ is the element of $\mathbb{F}_q$ and $h_t$ is the $t$th column of $H_b$. Connecting lines are drawn between the node $s_i(t-1)$ and the two nodes at depth $t$ and each line is labeled by the corresponding value of $\alpha_j$. $s_l(t)$ from $s_i(t-1)$. At $t = 1$, we have:

$$s_0(1) = s_0(0) + \alpha_0 h_1 = \begin{pmatrix} 0 \\ 0 \\ 0 \end{pmatrix} + 0.\begin{pmatrix} 1 \\ 0 \\ 0 \end{pmatrix} = \begin{pmatrix} 0 \\ 0 \\ 0 \end{pmatrix}, \tag{4.23}$$

$$s_1(1) = s_0(0) + \alpha_1 h_1 = \begin{pmatrix} 0 \\ 0 \\ 0 \end{pmatrix} + 1.\begin{pmatrix} 1 \\ 0 \\ 0 \end{pmatrix} = \begin{pmatrix} 1 \\ 0 \\ 0 \end{pmatrix}. \tag{4.24}$$

7 In Section 4.3.1, state was represented by $s_1s_2s_3$. Both representations are equivalent.

Consequently, the state (000) at $t = 0$ is connected to states (000) and (001) at $t = 1$ via bits 0 and 1, respectively. At $t = 2$, we have:

$$s_0(2) = s_0(1) + \alpha_0 h_2 = \begin{pmatrix} 0 \\ 0 \\ 0 \end{pmatrix} + 0. \begin{pmatrix} 1 \\ 0 \\ 1 \end{pmatrix} = \begin{pmatrix} 0 \\ 0 \\ 0 \end{pmatrix}, \tag{4.25}$$

$$s_1(2) = s_0(1) + \alpha_1 h_2 = \begin{pmatrix} 0 \\ 0 \\ 0 \end{pmatrix} + 1. \begin{pmatrix} 1 \\ 0 \\ 1 \end{pmatrix} = \begin{pmatrix} 1 \\ 0 \\ 1 \end{pmatrix}. \tag{4.26}$$

$$s_2(2) = s_1(1) + \alpha_0 h_2 = \begin{pmatrix} 1 \\ 0 \\ 0 \end{pmatrix} + 0. \begin{pmatrix} 1 \\ 0 \\ 1 \end{pmatrix} = \begin{pmatrix} 1 \\ 0 \\ 0 \end{pmatrix}, \tag{4.27}$$

$$s_3(2) = s_1(1) + \alpha_1 h_2 = \begin{pmatrix} 1 \\ 0 \\ 0 \end{pmatrix} + 1. \begin{pmatrix} 1 \\ 0 \\ 1 \end{pmatrix} = \begin{pmatrix} 0 \\ 0 \\ 1 \end{pmatrix}. \tag{4.28}$$

Consequently, the state (000) at $t = 1$ is connected to states (000) and (101) at $t = 2$ via bits 0 and 1, respectively, while the state (001) at $t = 1$ is connected to states (001) and (100) at $t = 2$ via bits 0 and 1, respectively. This process is repeated for $t = 3$.

**(c)** Recall that if $y$ is the received bit stream, then the syndrome vector $s$ of a linear block code is formulated as:

$$s = yH^T. \tag{4.29}$$

Since in Eq. (4.20) only the first three ($n = 3$) elements of the first row are non zero, the first element of $s$ in Eq. (4.29), i.e. $s_1$, is therefore only affected by the first three received bits. Consequently, at $t = 3$, which marks the end of the first sub-trellis, only those paths are retained for which the first bit of the syndrome is 0. This implies that the specific paths terminating at states (000), (010), (100), and (110) are retained, while those ending at (001), (011), (101), and (111) are discarded. Moreover, since the first element $s_1$ of the syndrome $s$ (least significant bit of the state) is completely defined at this point, we no longer have to represent this bit in the trellis. This syndrome bit is discarded, making room for the fourth syndrome bit, which is set to 0 initially. This process of removing the least significant bit is referred to as pruning in [202]. Therefore, the trellis states are now represented by $s_4 s_3 s_2$ and the valid states at $t = 3$, i.e. (000), (010), (100), and (110), are mapped onto (000), (001), (010), and (011).

**(d)** Step 2 is repeated in order to construct the second sub-trellis starting from the valid states obtained after pruning in Step 3. The process of generating the sub-trellis and pruning for the sake of interconnecting them is repeated until the length of trellis becomes equivalent to that of the received bit stream.

**(e)** The resultant trellis represents all the valid codewords. The most likely valid codeword is determined by finding the specific path having the minimum Hamming distance from the received sequence.

This approach can also be adapted for reducing the complexity of the syndrome-based error trellis [203]. For the error trellis, the pruning is carried out on the basis of the syndrome of the received sequence, rather than the zero syndrome.

## 4.4 Block Syndrome Decoding

### 4.4.1 General Formalism

The syndrome associated with a received sequence depends on the specific channel conditions. More explicitly, the syndrome is a function of the channel error sequence $e$ encountered during transmission. Consequently, we are more likely to have zero-valued syndromes at higher SNRs, when the channel error sequence $e$ has longer strings of zeros. If these error-free segments are successfully detected, then the decoding complexity can be substantially reduced by decoding only the erroneous portions. More explicitly, the decoder is switched off, when the transmission is assumed to be error-free, leading to the BSD concept of [191, 192].

A critical design parameter for the BSD is the minimum number of consecutive zero syndromes ($L_{min}$) after which the sub-block is deemed to be error-free. This must be long enough to ensure that the performance of BSD approaches that of a full-complexity decoder. A lower value of $L_{min}$ will result in more error-free blocks, thereby reducing the complexity imposed. However, this will increase the likelihood of false detection, thereby degrading the BER performance of the system. On the other hand, a higher value of $L_{min}$ will give a better BER performance, but at the expense of an increased decoding complexity. Hence, the choice of $L_{min}$ hast to strike a trade-off between the BER performance attained and the complexity imposed. The minimum number of consecutive zero syndromes $L_{min}$ can be further split into the parameters $L_{off}$ and $L_{on}$, where we have $L_{min} = (L_{off} + L_{on} + 1)$ [191], as shown in Figure 4.9. Here, $L_{off}$ denotes the number of consecutive zero syndromes after which the decoder can be safely switched off. Therefore this defines the end of the previous erroneous sub-block. By contrast, $L_{on}$ denotes the number of stages before the first non zero syndrome, when the decoder has to be switched on again. Therefore, the start of the next erroneous sub-block is defined by $L_{on}$. More specifically, if $L_0$ is the length of the sub-block having at least $L_{min}$ consecutive zero syndromes, then the initial $L_{off}$ symbols of this sub-block are appended to the previous erroneous block and the last $L_{on}$ symbols are appended to the following erroneous block. Only the remaining $(L_0 - L_{min} + 1)$ symbols are considered to be error-free. This ensures that the trellis of the erroneous sub-blocks starts from and terminates at the all-zero state.

### 4.4.2 Block Syndrome Decoder for TTCM

Turbo trellis-coded modulation (TTCM) [204] constitutes a bandwidth-efficient near-capacity joint modulation/coding solution, which relies on the classic turbo coding architecture, but involves the bandwidth-efficient trellis-coded modulation (TCM) [205] instead of the constituent convolutional codes. More explicitly, the constituent TCM codes, which can be optimally designed using extrinsic information transfer (EXIT) charts [206], are concatenated in a parallel fashion and iterative decoding is invoked at the receiver for exchanging *extrinsic* information between the pair of TCM decoders. In order to reduce its decoding complexity, we propose to reduce the effective number of decoding iterations by appropriately adapting the syndrome-based block decoding approach of [191, 194] for TTCM.

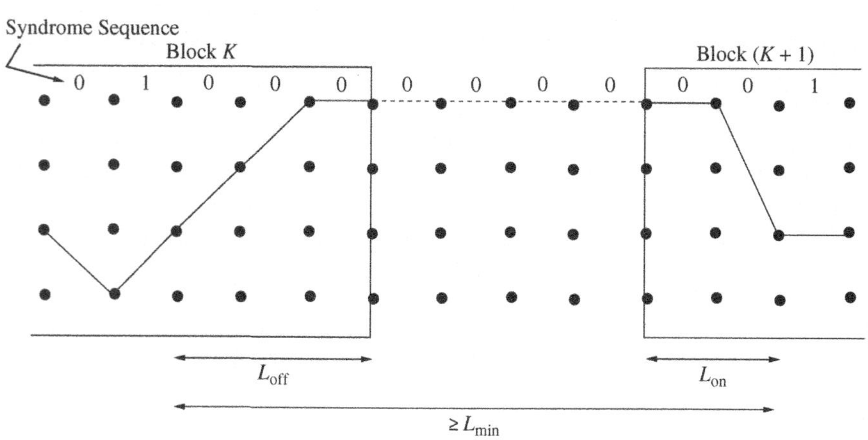


**Figure 4.9** Design parameters of BSD. *Source*: [216]/IEEE.

#### 4.4.2.1 System Model

Figure 4.10 shows the schematic of one of the two constituent decoders of the BSD conceived for TTCM, which we refer to as BSD-TTCM. The received symbol sequence $y_t$ is demapped onto the nearest point $x_i$ in the corresponding $2^n$-ary constellation diagram, yielding the hard-demapped symbols $\tilde{y}_t$, i.e. we have:

$$\tilde{y}_t = \arg\min_i (y_t - h_t x_i), \tag{4.30}$$

for $i \in \{0, \ldots, 2^n - 1\}$ and,

$$y_t = h_t x_t + n_t. \tag{4.31}$$

Here, $x_t$ is the complex-valued phasor corresponding to the $n$-bit transmitted codeword $c_t$, which is obtained using the $2^n$-PSK bit-to-symbol mapper $\mu$ as follows:

$$x_t = \mu(c_t), \tag{4.32}$$

while $h_t$ is the uncorrelated Rayleigh-distributed fading amplitude and $n_t$ is the noise experienced by the $t$th symbol.

Recall that in TTCM, the odd and even symbols are punctured for the upper and lower TCM encoders, respectively [204]. Consequently, the parity bits of the corresponding hard-demapped punctured symbols are set to zero [204] in the "Hard Demapper" block of Figure 4.10. Then, a so-called pre-correction sequence $\tilde{e}_t$, which is predicted by the error estimation module, is used for correcting any predicted errors in the hard-demapped output. This sequence is initialized to zero for the first iteration. The syndrome $s$ is computed for the corrected symbol stream $r$ using the syndrome former matrix $H^T$ as follows:

$$s = rH^T, \tag{4.33}$$

where, the $j$th bit of $r_t$ is related to that of $\tilde{y}_t$ and $\tilde{e}_t$, for $j \in \{0, \ldots, n-1\}$, as follows:

$$r_t^{(j)} = \tilde{y}_t^{(j)} \oplus \tilde{e}_t^{(j)}, \tag{4.34}$$

$$r_t = \left(r_t^{(0)}, \ldots, r_t^{(j)}, \ldots, r_n^{(n-1)}\right),\ \tilde{y}_t = \left(\tilde{y}_t^{(0)}, \ldots, \tilde{y}_t^{(j)}, \ldots, \tilde{y}_t^{(n-1)}\right),\ \tilde{e}_t = \left(\tilde{e}_t^{(0)}, \ldots, \tilde{e}_t^{(j)}, \ldots, \tilde{e}_t^{(n-1)}\right).$$

Then the syndrome is analyzed for the sake of dividing the received block into error-free and erroneous sub-blocks. The error-free sub-blocks are then subjected to a hard-decision and only the erroneous sub-blocks are passed to the MAP decoder. Like in the conventional TTCM decoder, both constituent decoders have a similar structure and iterative decoding is invoked for exchanging *extrinsic* information between the two.

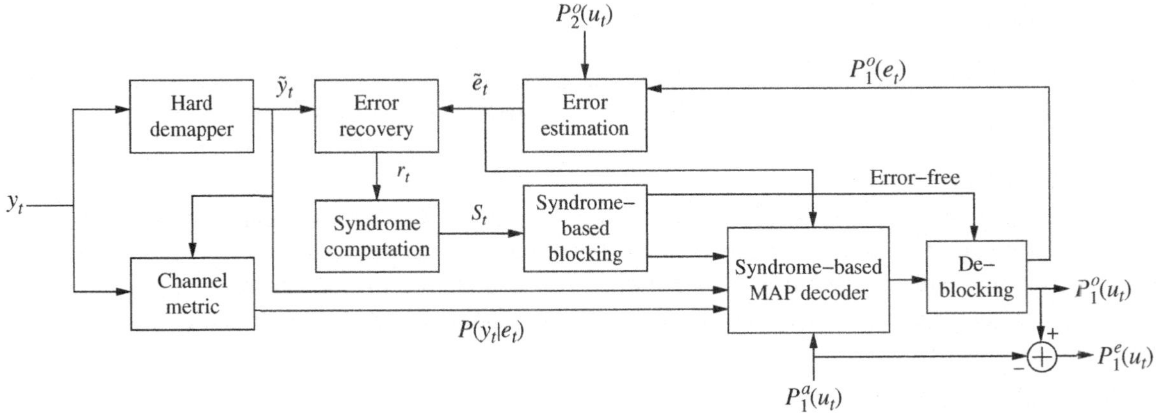


**Figure 4.10** Schematic of the proposed BSD-TTCM Decoder. Only one constituent decoder is shown here. $P_i^a[.]$, $P_i^e[.]$, and $P_i^o[.]$ are the *a-priori, extrinsic,* and *a-posteriori* probabilities related to the *ith* decoder; $e_t$ *is* the channel error on the transmitted symbol and $u_t$ is the information part of the $t$th channel error $e_t$. *Source:* [224]/IEEE.

#### 4.4.2.2 Syndrome-based MAP Decoder

We have invoked the syndrome-based MAP decoder of [195] in the BSD-TTCM of Figure 4.10. In contrast to the conventional MAP decoder, which operates on the basis of the code trellis, its syndrome-based MAP counterpart relies on the error trellis constructed using the syndrome former $H^T$ [185, 201]. More explicitly, each trellis path of a code trellis represents a legitimate codeword. By contrast, each path of an error trellis specifies the hypothetical error sequence causing a departure from a specific legitimate code trellis path. Furthermore, both trellises have the same complexity and every error path in the error trellis uniquely corresponds to a codeword path in the code trellis [201]. The classic MAP algorithm [183] computes the *a-posteriori* probability (APP) $\mathrm{P}^o(u_t)$ for every $M$-ary transmitted information symbol $u_t$ given by $\mathrm{P}^o(u_t) = \mathrm{P}(u_t = m|y_t)$ for $m \in \{0, 1, \dots, M-1\}$, where $M = 2^{n-1}$, $(n-1)$ is the number of bits in an information symbol and $R = \frac{n-1}{n}$ is the coding rate. However, the syndrome-based MAP computes the APP for every $M$-ary channel error experienced by the information symbol. In other words, $u_t$ is the transmitted information symbol in the code trellis, whereas, in the error trellis, $u_t$ denotes the $M$-ary channel error experienced by the information symbol. Therefore, the channel information $\mathrm{P}(y_t|x_t)$ related to the transmitted codeword $x_t$, is modified to $\mathrm{P}(y_t|e_t)$ for the channel error $e_t$, which is formulated as:

$$\mathrm{P}(y_t|e_t) = \frac{1}{2\pi\sigma^2} \cdot e^{-\frac{|y_t - h_t\tilde{x}_t|^2}{2\sigma^2}}, \tag{4.35}$$

where $\sigma^2$ is the noise variance per dimension and $\tilde{x}_t$ is given by:

$$\tilde{x}_t = \mu(\tilde{c}_t), \tag{4.36}$$

for,

$$\tilde{c}_t^{(j)} = \tilde{y}_t^{(j)} \oplus e_t^{(j)}. \tag{4.37}$$

Here, we have $\tilde{c}_t = \left(\tilde{c}_t^{(0)}, \dots, \tilde{c}_t^{(j)}, \dots, \tilde{c}_t^{(n)}\right)$ and $e_t = \left(e_t^{(0)}, \dots, e_t^{(j)}, \dots, e_t^{(n)}\right)$. The APP of $u_t$ can be calculated in terms of the forward–backward recursive coefficients $\alpha_t$ and $\beta_t$ as follows:

$$\mathrm{P}^o(u_t) = \sum_{\substack{(\acute{\tau},\tau)\Rightarrow \\ u_t = m}} \gamma_t(\acute{\tau},\tau) \,.\, \alpha_{t-1}(\acute{\tau}) \,.\, \beta_t(\tau), \tag{4.38}$$

where the summation implies adding all the probabilities associated with those transitions (from state $\acute{\tau}$ to $\tau$) of the error trellis for which $u_t = m$. Furthermore, we have:

$$\begin{aligned} \gamma_t(\acute{\tau},\tau) &= \mathrm{P}^a(u_t) \,.\, \mathrm{P}(y_t|e_t), \\ \alpha_t(\tau) &= \sum_{\text{all } \acute{\tau}} \gamma_t(\acute{\tau},\tau) \,.\, \alpha_{t-1}(\acute{\tau}), \\ \beta_{t-1}(\acute{\tau}) &= \sum_{\text{all } \tau} \gamma_t(\acute{\tau},\tau) \,.\, \beta_t(\tau), \end{aligned} \tag{4.39}$$

where $\mathrm{P}^a(u_t)$ is the *a-priori* probability of the information part of the error $e_t$, i.e. $u_t$. At the first iteration, no *a-priori* information is available; hence, it is initialized to be equiprobable, i.e. $\mathrm{P}^a(u_t) = 1/M$.

#### 4.4.2.3 Error Estimation

Similar to the bit-wise pre-correction sequence proposed in [194] for turbo codes, we make an estimate of the $2^n$-ary symbol error in each iteration to ensure that the Hamming weight of the syndrome decreases throughout the ongoing iterations. While the *extrinsic* information was used in [194] for the estimating the pre-correction sequence, we have improved the estimation by using the APP instead of the *extrinsic* information. This proceeds as follows:

- The information part of the pre-correction sequence $\tilde{e}_t$ is set to the hard decision of the APP of the information symbol ($\mathrm{P}^o(u_t)$) computed by the other decoder.
- The parity part of $\tilde{e}_t$ is set to the hard decision value of the APP of the codeword ($\mathrm{P}^o(e_t)$) gleaned from the previous iteration of the same decoder, which yields the same information symbol as that computed in the first step.

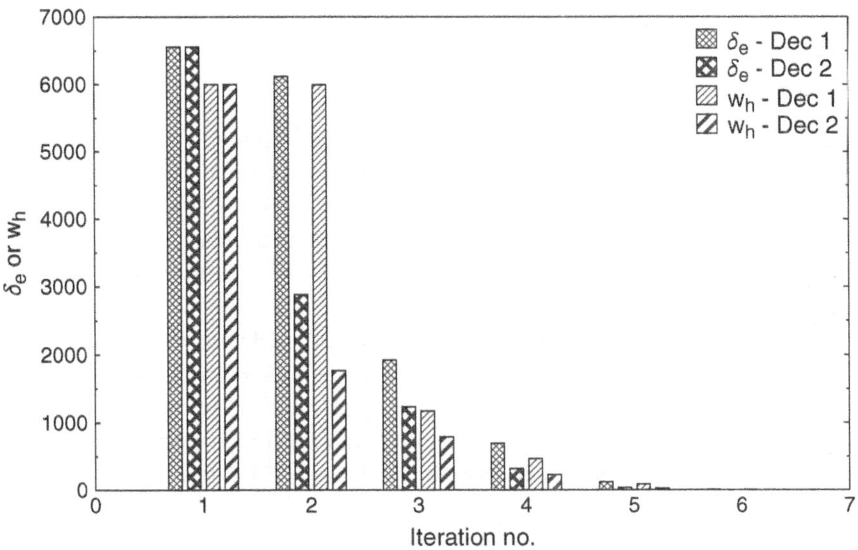


**Figure 4.11** Variation in the number of differences ($\delta_e$) between the actual and estimated error and Hamming weight ($w_h$) of the syndrome with increasing iterations at $E_b/N_0 = 3.8$ dB. *Source*: [224]/IEEE.

Figure 4.11 verifies the accuracy of our pre-correction sequence. Here the average number of differences $\delta_e$ between the actual and estimated error is plotted against the number of iterations at an SNR per bit of $E_b/N_0 = 3.8$ dB, for 1000 frames of 12,000 TTCM-8PSK symbols transmitted over an AWGN channel. Both constituent decoders are characterized separately, which are referred to as *Dec 1* and *Dec 2* in Figure 4.11. Observe that the differences decrease at each successive iteration, eventually approaching zero at the sixth iteration. Furthermore, the Hamming weight $w_h$ of the syndrome closely follows the same trend.

#### 4.4.2.4 Syndrome-based Blocking

The Hamming weight of the syndrome sequence of Eq. (4.33) tends to decrease upon increasing the SNR, since only a few errors are encountered. It also decreases with each successive iteration. This is because the errors are estimated at each iteration and the corresponding correction is applied to the received symbols. In other words, upon increasing either the number of iterations or the SNR, the syndrome tends to exhibit longer sequences of zeros, which indicates near-error-free transmission. This fact can be exploited to partition the received blocks into error-free and error-infested segments, as proposed in [191, 194]. This is achieved by heuristically choosing a design parameter, $L_{\text{min}} = (L_{\text{start}} + L_{\text{end}} + 1)$, which is the minimum number of consecutive zero syndromes after which the sub-block may be deemed error-free. Furthermore, $L_{\text{start}}$ and $L_{\text{end}}$ define the start and end of the next and previous sub-blocks, respectively. If $L_0$ is the length of the sub-block having at least $L_{\text{min}}$ consecutive zero syndromes, then the initial $L_{\text{end}} = (L_{\text{min}} - 1)/2$ symbols of this sub-block are appended to the previous erroneous block and the last $L_{\text{start}} = (L_{\text{min}} - 1)/2$ symbols are appended to the following erroneous block [191, 194]. Only the remaining $(L_0 - L_{\text{min}} + 1)$ symbols are considered error-free. This ensures that the trellis of the erroneous sub-blocks starts from and terminates at the zero state. The hypothetical error-free blocks do not undergo further decoding and the corresponding APPs of the error-free trellis segment are set to 1. On the other hand, the erroneous blocks are fed to a MAP decoder with the initial and final states of the decoding trellis set to zero.

Please bear in mind in this context that the design parameter $L_{\text{min}}$ must be chosen by striking a trade-off between the BER performance attained and the complexity imposed. A lower value of $L_{\text{min}}$ will result in more error-free blocks, thereby reducing the complexity imposed. However, it will degrade the BER performance of the system. On the other hand, a higher value of $L_{\text{min}}$ will give a better BER performance, albeit at the expense of an increased decoding complexity.

## 4.5 Results and Discussion

### 4.5.1 Performance of BSD-TTCM over AWGN Channel

In order to quantify the decoding complexity reduction achieved by the BSD-TTCM scheme, we have analyzed the performance of TTCM in the context of an AWGN channel using the parameters of Table 4.1. Furthermore, we have heuristically optimized the design parameter $L_{\min}$ while ensuring that the BSD-TTCM attains a similar BER to the conventional TTCM decoder. Since the Hamming weight of the syndrome decreases with the SNR, the optimum $L_{\min}$ has to increase with the SNR to ensure that the performance is not compromised. We have particularly focused our attention on the high-SNR region (i.e. $E_b/N_0 \geq 3.5$) and the $L_{\min}$ value was appropriately optimized for every 0.1 dB increment in $E_b/N_0$, as listed in Table 4.2. It must be mentioned here that the optimum $L_{\min}$ for a particular value of $E_b/N_0$ depends on the code parameters of Table 4.1 as well as on the channel type. The BER performance of our BSD-TTCM based on the design parameter $L_{\min}$ of Table 4.2 is compared to that of the conventional TTCM decoder in Figure 4.12. Both decoding schemes exhibit a similar performance. The corresponding reduction in the decoding complexity is quantified in Figures 4.13 and 4.14 in terms of:

- **Percentage of No-decoding**: This quantifies the total number of symbols in the error-free sub-blocks as a percentage of the frame length (i.e. 12,000).
- **Equivalent Number of Iterations**: Each iteration is weighted by the percentage of the symbols that had to be decoded, which quantified the equivalent (or effective) number of iterations.

Observe in Figure 4.13 that as $E_b/N_0$ is increased from 3.0 to 3.5 dB for $L_{\min} = 51$, the percentage of non-decoded symbols increases for each iteration, reaching a maximum of 45% for the 6th iteration at 3.5 dB. When we further increase $L_{\min}$ to 111 at 3.6 dB, the percentage of non-decoded symbols in iterations 2–5 decreases, while that in the 6th increases. This is because at this point there are two counter-acting forces:

**(a)** An increased $L_{\min}$ would reduce the number of error-free blocks.
**(b)** An increased $E_b/N_0$ would decrease the Hamming weight of the syndrome sequence and, therefore, increase the number of error-free blocks.

A similar trend is observed, when $E_b/N_0$ is increased further. Explicitly, at high SNRs, at least a 20% complexity reduction is achieved for the fifth iteration and 45% for the 6th iteration.

**Table 4.1** TTCM parameters.

| | |
|---|---|
| Coding rate | 2/3 |
| Modulation | PSK |
| Interleaver length | 12,000 |
| Iterations | 6 |

**Table 4.2** Optimum $L_{\min}$ for the TTCM of Table 4.1 operating over an AWGN channel.

| SNR range | $L_{\min}$ |
|---|---|
| $E_b/N_0 \leq 3.5$ dB | 51 |
| $3.5 < E_b/N_0 \leq 3.6$ dB | 111 |
| $3.6 < E_b/N_0 \leq 3.7$ dB | 401 |
| $3.7 < E_b/N_0 \leq 3.8$ dB | 3001 |
| $3.8 < E_b/N_0 \leq 3.9$ dB | 5001 |

*Source*: Adapted from [224].

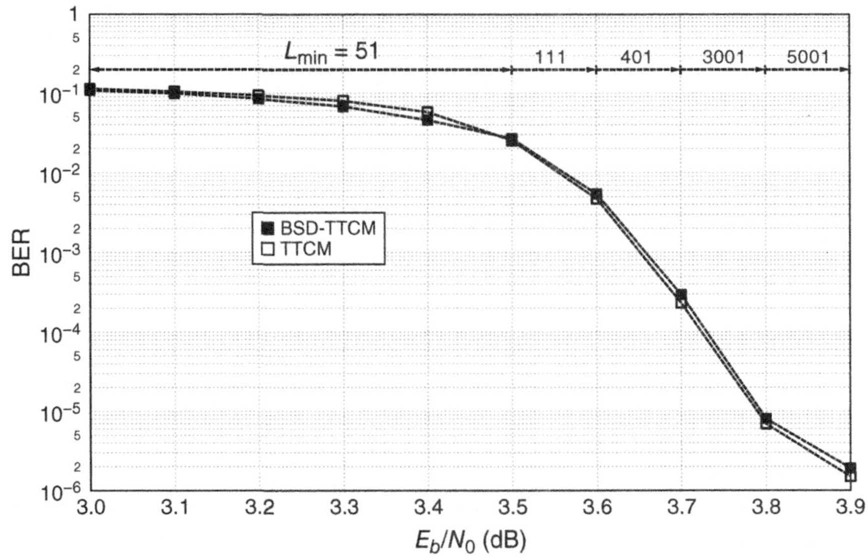


**Figure 4.12** Comparison of the BER performance curve of BSD-TTCM with the conventional TTCM decoding over an AWGN channel. The corresponding TTCM parameters are summarized in Table 4.1, while the optimized $L_{min}$ are listed in Table 4.2. *Source*: [224]/IEEE.

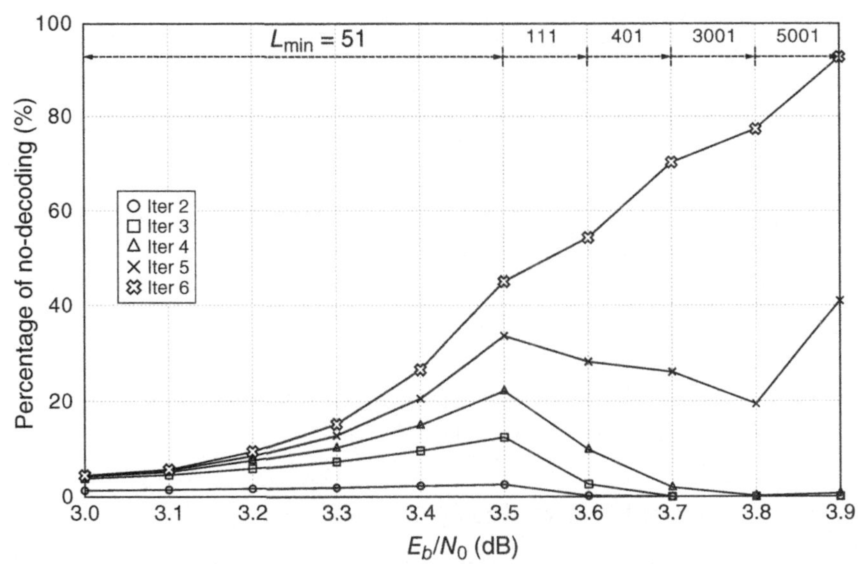


**Figure 4.13** Reduction in decoding complexity of the BSD-TTCM of Figure 4.12, quantified in terms of the "percentage of no-decoding." *Source*: [224]/IEEE.

Figure 4.14 quantifies the decoding complexity in terms of the equivalent number of decoding iterations. We may observe in Figure 4.14 that increasing the $E_b/N_0$ from 3.0 to 3.5 dB for $L_{min} = 51$, reduces the number of effective iterations to a minimum of 4.8 at 3.5 dB. This is equivalent to a $(100 \times (6 - 4.8)/6) = 20\%$ reduction in the number of decoding iterations. Then, when $L_{min}$ is increased to 111 at 3.6 dB, the number of equivalent iterations increases to five. This corresponds to a reduction of $(100 \times (6 - 5)/6) \approx 17\%$ compared to the maximum of six iterations and it is therefore still significant. On average our proposed scheme reduces the effective number of iterations by at least one, i.e. by 17%, for high SNRs. We have also benchmarked the performance of our proposed BSD-TTCM decoder against the conventional hard-decision aided high-SNR early termination (ET) criterion of [194] in Figure 4.14.

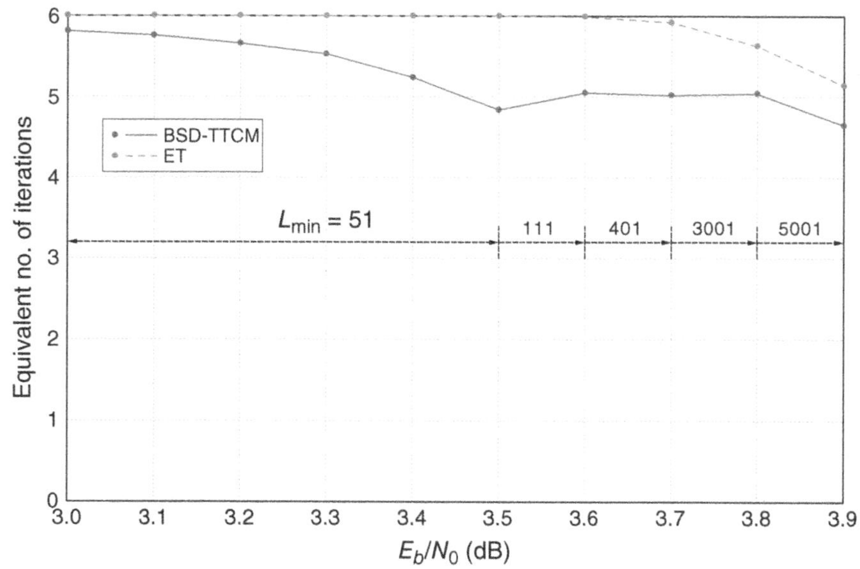


**Figure 4.14** Reduction in decoding complexity of the BSD-TTCM of Figure 4.12, quantified in terms of the "equivalent number of iterations." *Source*: [199]/IEEE.

**Table 4.3** Optimum $L_{min}$ for the TTCM of Table 4.1 operating over an uncorrelated Rayleigh fading channel.

| SNR range | $L_{min}$ |
|---|---|
| $E_b/N_0 \leq 6.2$ dB | 61 |
| $6.2 < E_b/N_0 \leq 6.6$ dB | 101 |
| $6.6 < E_b/N_0 \leq 7.0$ dB | 301 |
| $7.0 < E_b/N_0 \leq 7.4$ dB | 1201 |
| $7.4 < E_b/N_0 \leq 7.8$ dB | 4001 |

The scheme considered outperforms ET by at high SNRs. The complexity may be further reduced by increasing $L_{min}$. However, as discussed before, this will incur a BER performance degradation.

### 4.5.2 Performance of BSD-TTCM over Uncorrelated Rayleigh Fading Channel

We have further investigated the performance of BSD-TTCM in the event of uncorrelated Rayleigh fading channel for the code parameters of Table 4.1. The corresponding optimum design parameter $L_{min}$ for increasing the SNR in the high-SNR region (i.e. for $E_b/N_0 \geq 6.2$) are listed in Table 4.3. Figure 4.15 compares the resultant BER performance of the proposed BSD-TTCM to that of the conventional TTCM. As seen from Figure 4.15, syndrome-based blocking does not incur any significant BER degradation and that both decoding schemes exhibit a similar BER performance. The corresponding reduction in the decoding complexity is quantified in Figures 4.16 and 4.17 in terms of the "percentage of no-decoding" and "equivalent number of iterations," respectively.

In Figure 4.16, as $E_b/N_0$ is increased from 5.0 to 6.2 dB for $L_{min} = 61$, the percentage of non-decoded symbols for each iteration increases, reaching about 30% for the sixth iteration at 6.2 dB. As $E_b/N_0$ is increased further, the percentage of non-decoded symbols decreases during the iterations spanning from 2 to 4, while it increases during the iterations five and six. This behavior is similar to that observed in Figure 4.13. We may also notice in Figure 4.16 that in the high-SNR region at least a 20% complexity reduction is achieved for the fifth iteration and 30% for the sixth. By contrast, at least 20% and 45% complexity reduction was achieved for the fifth and the sixth iteration for transmission in the context of an AWGN channel in Figure 4.13.

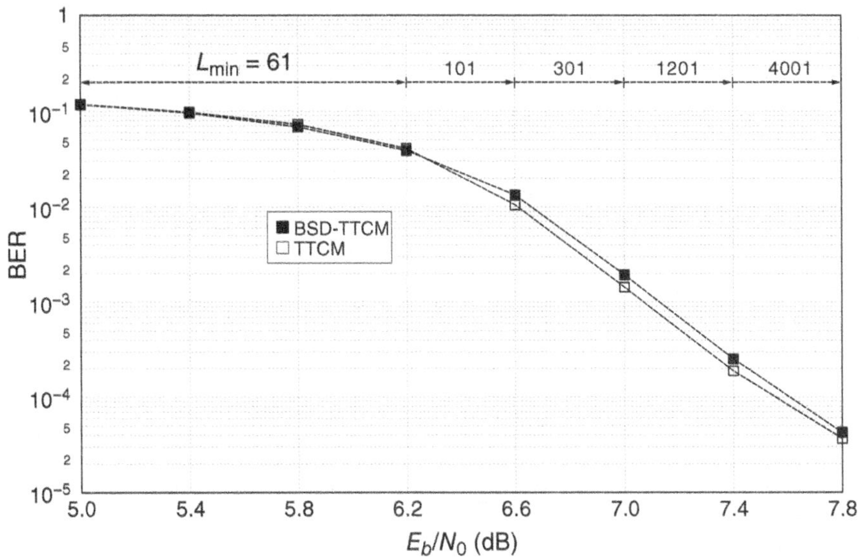


**Figure 4.15** Comparison of the BER performance curve of BSD-TTCM with the conventional TTCM decoding over an uncorrelated Rayleigh fading channel. The corresponding TTCM parameters are summarized in Table 4.1, while the optimized $L_{min}$ are listed in Table 4.3.

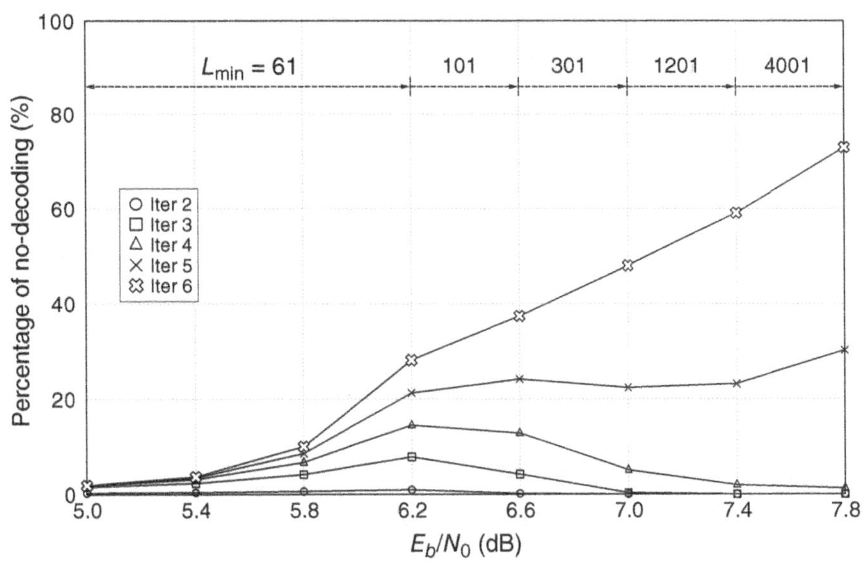


**Figure 4.16** Reduction in decoding complexity of the BSD-TTCM of Figure 4.15, quantified in terms of the "percentage of no-decoding."

Figure 4.17 plots the corresponding decoding complexity in terms of the effective number of iterations. Increasing $E_b/N_0$ from 5.0 to 6.2 dB for $L_{min} = 61$ reduces the number of effective iterations to a minimum of 5.27 at 6.2 dB. This is equivalent to a $(100 \times (6 - 5.27)/6) \approx 12\%$ reduction in the number of decoding iterations. Thereafter the number of effective iterations more or less remains the same. Hence, BSD-TTCM yields a decoding complexity reduction of around 12% in the high-SNR region, when operating in uncorrelated Rayleigh fading channels, which is slightly less than the 17% reduction observed for the AWGN channel in Figure 4.13. Based on these results, it is reasonable to conclude that the decoding complexity of BSD-TTCM is only slightly higher in an uncorrelated Rayleigh fading channel than in an AWGN channel, but the attainable complexity savings are still quite significant. In Figure 4.17, we have also benchmarked the performance of our proposed BSD-TTCM decoder against the conventional hard-decision aided ET criterion of [194]. We may observe in Figure 4.17 that BSD-TTCM outperforms ET for all SNRs.

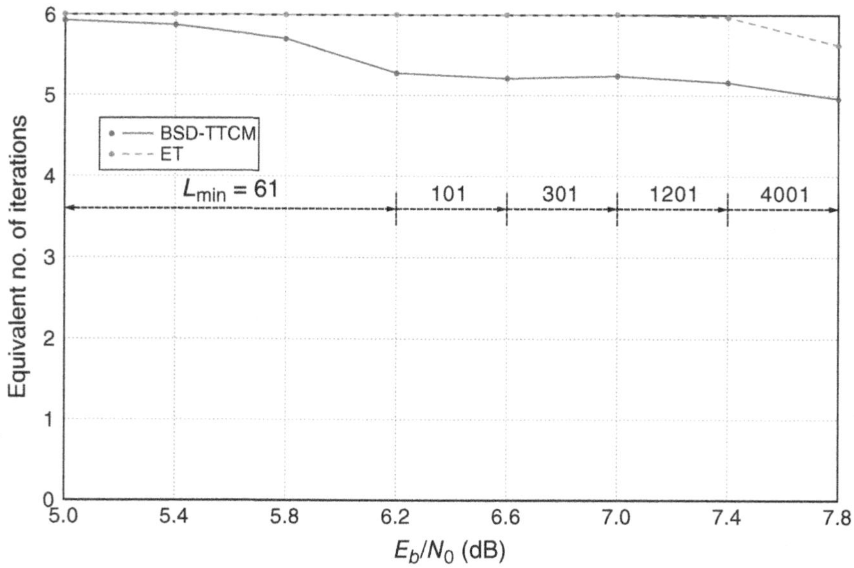


**Figure 4.17** Reduction in decoding complexity of the BSD-TTCM of Figure 4.15, quantified in terms of the "equivalent number of iterations."

**Table 4.4** Optimum $L_{min}$ for varying $E_b/N_0$ over uncorrelated Rayleigh fading channel using a frame of 500 symbols. Other TTCM parameters are same as that of Table 4.1.

| SNR range | $L_{min}$ |
|---|---|
| $E_b/N_0 \leq 6.6$ dB | 61 |
| $6.6 < E_b/N_0 \leq 7.0$ dB | 201 |
| $7.0 < E_b/N_0 \leq 7.4$ dB | 281 |
| $7.4 < E_b/N_0 \leq 7.8$ dB | 321 |

### 4.5.3 Effect of Frame Length on the Performance of BSD-TTCM

The high-SNR ET scheme, which we have used in Sections 4.5.1 and 4.5.2 as a benchmarker, offers higher reductions in the decoding complexity when shorter frames are used. Intuitively, shorter frames also improve the effective decoding complexity reduction of the BSD approach. Hence, BSD-TTCM is likely to outperform ET even for short frames. For the sake of substantiating this hypothesis, we have analyzed the performance of the 8-state TTCM relying on 8PSK transmissions over an uncorrelated Rayleigh fading channel using a frame length of 500 TTCM-8PSK symbols and six iterations. The corresponding SNR-based $L_{min}$ values are listed in Table 4.4.

The design parameter $L_{min}$ of Table 4.4 is heuristically optimized for a particular $E_b/N_0$ range, while ensuring that the BER performance curve of the resultant BSD-TTCM scheme is the same as that of the conventional TTCM, which is demonstrated in Figure 4.18. The corresponding decoding complexity is analyzed in Figures 4.19 and 4.20. Reducing the frame length from 12,000 to 500 symbols increases the percentage of non-decoded symbols at each iteration, as we can observe by comparing Figure 4.19 with Figure 4.13. Consequently, BSD-TTCM still out performs the ET technique, as shown in Figure 4.20.

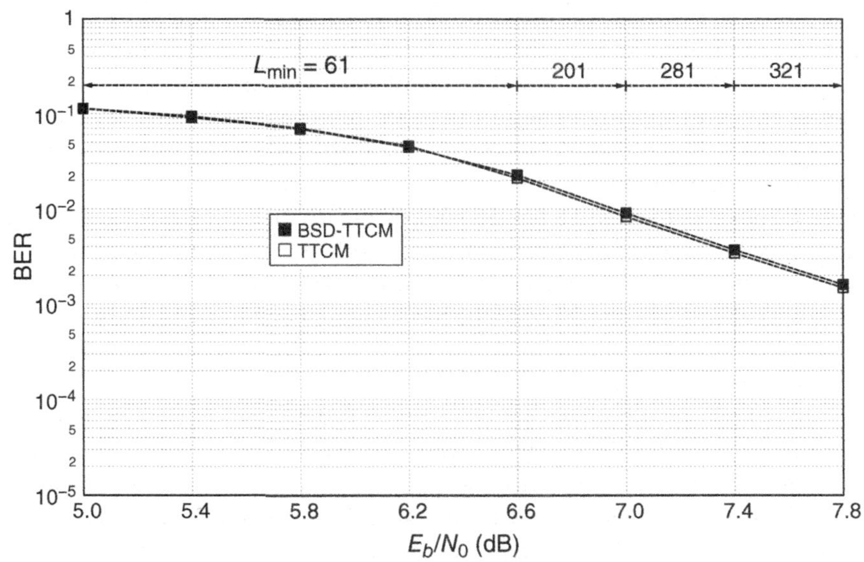


**Figure 4.18** Comparison of the BER performance curve of BSD-TTCM with the conventional TTCM decoding over an uncorrelated Rayleigh fading channel using the TTCM parameters of Table 4.1 but with a reduced frame length of 500. The corresponding optimized $L_{min}$ are listed in Table 4.3.

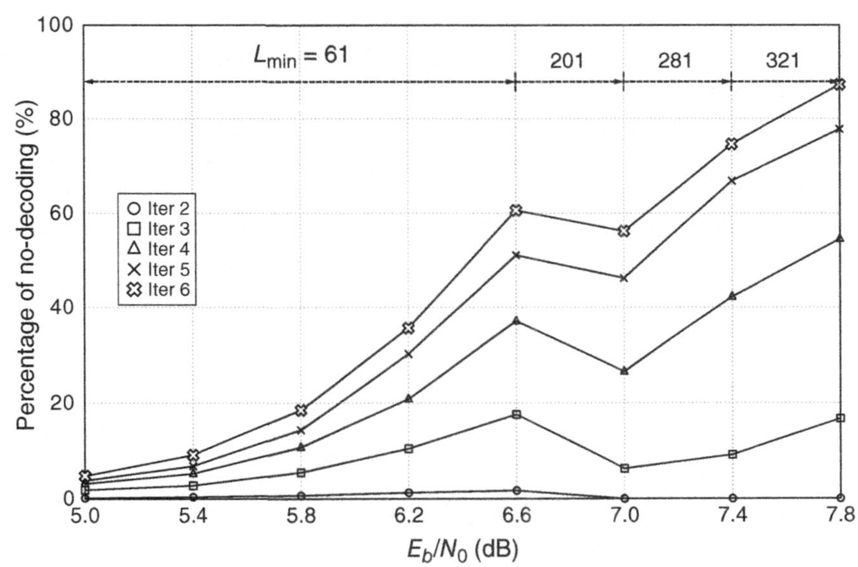


**Figure 4.19** Reduction in decoding complexity of the BSD-TTCM of Figure 4.18, quantified in terms of the "percentage of no-decoding."

## 4.6 Summary and Conclusions

Since quantum codes invoke the classical syndrome decoding based approach, as illustrated in Figure 4.1, in this chapter we discussed these decoding techniques operating in a classical channel. In contrast to the widely used codeword based decoding, which aims for identifying the most likely codeword, syndrome decoding characterizes the most likely channel error sequence. In this context, we commenced our discussions with the LUT-based syndrome decoding in Section 4.2, detailing the motivation behind the LUT-based syndrome decoding approach invoked for classical linear block codes. More specifically, it was demonstrated with the aid of a design example that the standard array-based codeword decoding imposes high storage requirements on long block codes. Fortunately, the same task may be achieved with the aid of an LUT-based decoder, which only requires a memory of size $2^{n-k} \times 2$, as depicted in Eq. (4.2), while the corresponding standard array of Eq. (4.1) has a size of $2^{n-k} \times 2^k$. We then proceeded with the construction of the error trellis of linear block codes and of convolutional codes in Sections 4.3.1 and 4.3.2, respectively. It was shown in Figures 4.6 and 4.7 that the conventional code trellis and the syndrome-based error trellis are equivalent. More explicitly, each path of a code trellis corresponds to a legitimate codeword, while each path of an error trellis is a legitimate error sequence for a given syndrome. When the syndrome is zero, the error trellis collapses to a code trellis. Finally, in Section 4.4, we detailed the reduced-complexity BSD approach. In particular, we conceived a syndrome-based block decoding approach for TTCM in Section 4.4.2. The proposed BSD-TTCM only decodes the blocks deemed to be erroneous, which are identified using the syndrome sequence, hence reducing the associated decoding complexity. Furthermore, a pre-correction sequence is estimated at each iteration for reducing the decoding complexity of the forthcoming iterations. Finally, we evaluated the performance of our proposed BSD-TTCM for transmission over both an AWGN channel as well as an uncorrelated Rayleigh fading channel in Section 4.5.

In Section 4.5.1, we compared the BER performance of the proposed BSD-TTCM to that of the classic full-complexity TTCM decoder for transmission over an AWGN channel. It was demonstrated in Figure 4.12 that the design parameter $L_{\min}$ may be heuristically optimized upon increasing the SNR values for the sake of achieving the same BER performance as that of a classic TTCM decoder. We further quantified the complexity reductions attained in terms of the percentage of non-decoded blocks at each iteration index as well as the number of effective decoding iterations in Figures 4.13 and 4.14, respectively. Quantitatively, we demonstrated in Figure 4.13 that a decoding complexity reduction of at least 17% is attained at high SNRs in terms of the effective number of iterations, with at least 20% and 45% reduction in the 5th and 6th iterations, respectively, for transmission over an AWGN channel. It was also shown in Figure 4.14 that reduced-complexity technique advocated outperforms the ET scheme at all SNRs. These results are summarized in Table 4.5.[8]

We further extended our analysis to the performance of BSD-TTCM over an uncorrelated Rayleigh fading channel in Section 4.5.2. Analogously to the AWGN channel, the design parameter $L_{\min}$ was optimized upon increasing SNR, so that the BSD-TTCM exhibits the same performance as that of a classic decoder, as evidenced in Figure 4.15. It was observed in Figures 4.16 and 4.17 and that the BSD approach offers a slightly less reduction in complexity for transmission over the uncorrelated Rayleigh fading channel than that offered over the AWGN channel. More specifically, the decoding complexity reduction for transmission over a Rayleigh fading channel in

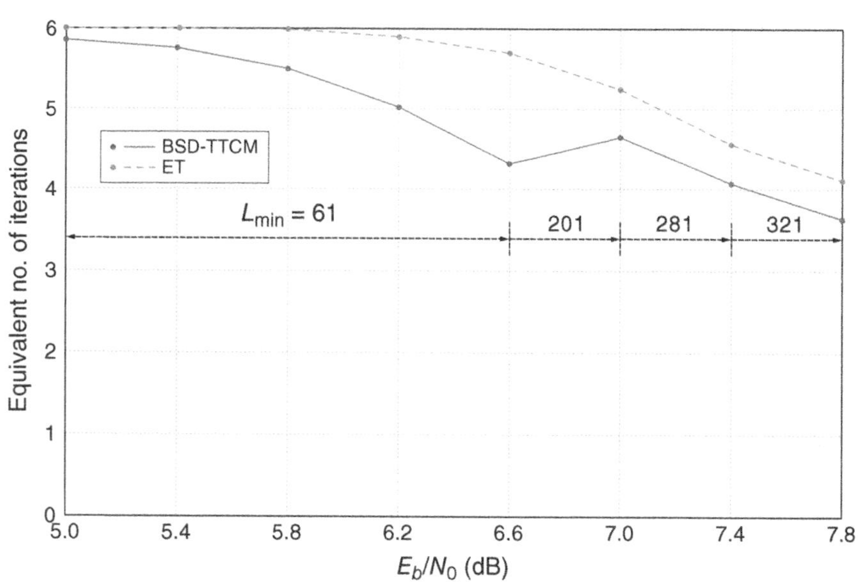


**Figure 4.20** Reduction in decoding complexity of the BSD-TTCM of Figure 4.18, quantified in terms of the "equivalent number of iterations."

8 "With respect to" is abbreviated as "w.r.t." in Table 4.5.

**Table 4.5** Summary of the achieved decoding complexity reduction, when BSD-TTCM is invoked using the simulation parameters of Table 4.1. Decoding complexity is quantified in terms of the percentage of no-decoding as well as the equivalent number of iterations $I_{avg}$. Complexity reduction is also compared with the high-SNR early termination technique.

| | | No-decoding | | | | |
|---|---|---|---|---|---|---|
| **Channel** | **SNR range** | $I = 5$ | $I = 6$ | $I_{avg}$ | **Reduction w.r.t. early termination** | **Reference figures** |
| AWGN | $\geq 3.5$ | $\geq 20\%$ | $\geq 45\%$ | $\leq 5$ | $\geq 0.5$ iteration | Figures 4.13 and 4.14 |
| Rayleigh | $\geq 6.2$ | $\geq 20\%$ | $\geq 30\%$ | $\leq 5.3$ | $\geq 0.5$ iteration | Figures 4.16 and 4.17 |

Figure 4.16 was found to be about 12% in the high-SNR region, with at least 20% and 30% reduction in the fifth and sixth iterations, respectively. In Section 4.5.3, we furthermore evaluated the performance of our BSD-TTCM scheme for a short frame length of 500 symbols. It was observed in Figure 4.20 that BSD-TTCM outperforms the popular ET technique, regardless of the frame length. These results are also tabulated in Table 4.5.

The classical-quantum communication system, which we conceived in Chapter 5, supports only the transmission of classical information. By contrast, quantum communication systems may transmit classical as well as quantum information. This in turn requires efficient quantum error correction codes (QECCs). QECCs are also vital for reliable quantum computation. In the next chapter, we will proceed with the design of QECCs, which is based on the classical to quantum isomorphism of Chapter 10 and on the classical syndrome decoding approach of Chapter 4.

# 5

# Near-capacity Codes for Entanglement-aided Classical Communication

## 5.1 Introduction

Throughout the previous three chapters we have laid the foundations for the more deep-routed discussions of this chapter inserted here for providing a more fast-paced portrayal of near-capacity code design principles in the classical domain first. In Section 5.5 we will highlight the classical capacity improvements that may be attained with the aid of entanglement and discuss the maximum code-rate capable of achieving an infinitesimally low BER at a given depolarizing probability. Then in Section 5.5 we will delve into sophisticated EXIT-chart-based near-capacity designs relying on so-called irregular convolutional codes and concatenated unity-rate codes iteratively exchanging *extrinsic* information. These powerful design tools will be heavily relied upon in the sophisticated frontier research of Part III of the book, but they are first introduced from a classical-domain perspective.

Quantum-domain communication constitutes an attractive solution for absolutely secure transmission [160]. More explicitly, any "measurement" or "observation" of the transmitted qubits by the eavesdropper perturbs the associated quantum superposition, thereby intimating the parties concerned [160]. In this context, entanglement-assisted transmission of classical information over quantum channels is of particular significance. This idea was conceived by Bennett [29] in his widely-cited 2-qubit SuperDense (2SD) coding protocol, which transmits two classical bits per channel use (cbits/use) over a noiseless quantum channel with the aid of a pre-shared maximally entangled qubit. The corresponding entanglement-assisted classical capacity (EACC) of the so-called quantum depolarizing channel was quantified in [207, 208].

Analogous to Shannon's well-known capacity theorem conceived for classical channels, the EACC quantifies the capacity limit of reliable transmission of classical information over a noisy quantum channel, when an unlimited amount of noiseless entanglement is shared between the transmitter and the receiver. The corresponding "classical-quantum-classical" conversion-based transmission model, whereby classical information is transmitted over a quantum channel with the aid of the SuperDense (SD) coding protocol, is depicted in Figure 5.1. Here, Alice intends to transmit her 2-bit classical message $x$ to Bob using a 2-qubit maximally entangled state $|\psi_x\rangle^{AB}$, where $A$ denotes the information qubit, while $B$ is a pre-shared entangled qubit transmitted over a noiseless channel. More specifically, the pre-shared qubit $B$ is transmitted to the receiver before the actual transmission commences, for example it can be shared during the off-peak hours, when the channel is underutilized. The classical message $x$ is encoded by the block $\mathcal{E}$ of Figure 5.1 into the corresponding quantum state using the 2SD coding protocol of [29]. The processed qubit $A'$ is passed through a quantum depolarizing channel, which is denoted as $\mathcal{N}^{A' \to B'}$. At the block $\mathcal{D}$ of Figure 5.1 Bob's receiver performs symbol-by-symbol Bell-basis measurement[1] [4, 160] on the received state $|\psi_y\rangle^{B'B}$, yielding the 2-bit classical message $y$. This transmission model was extended to a distributed network in [209], whereby the 2SD scheme of [29] was generalized to an $N$-particle system with the aid of an $N$-qubit entangled state. The resultant protocol facilitates the receiver to detect messages from $(N-1)$ users with the aid of a single $N$-qubit entangled quantum state as well as a single joint quantum measurement, albeit this is achieved at the cost of a reduced EACC.

1 Bell-basis measurement is a joint measurement on a 2-qubit composite system for the sake of detecting the orthonormal Bell states.

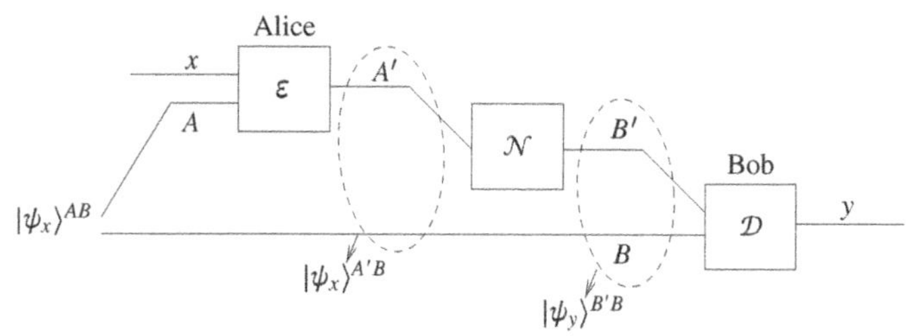


**Figure 5.1** Classical-quantum-classical transmission model employing 2-qubit SD. *Source:* Adapted from Babar et al. [210, 211].

Recently, Chiuri *et al.* [212] experimentally determined the achievable EACC of a quantum depolarizing channel, which paves the way for the practical implementation of future quantum-based communication systems. However, reliable transmission is impossible without efficient error correction codes.

Inspired by the near-capacity performance of concatenated classical code designs, in this chapter we design both bit-based and symbol-based concatenated classical-quantum code structures with the aid of *EXtrinsic* Information Transfer (EXIT) charts for the sake of achieving a performance close to the EACC of the quantum depolarizing channel. More explicitly, our novel contributions are as follows [210, 211]:

- We have conceived an SD-based near-capacity design for entanglement-assisted classical communication over a quantum depolarizing channel. Our design, referred to as an IRCC-URC-2SD arrangement, incorporates a classical irregular convolutional code (IRCC) and a unity rate code (URC). We have also introduced a soft-decision-aided SD decoder for facilitating iterative decoding.
- Our IRCC-URC-2SD design is bit-based, thereby incurring a capacity loss due to symbol-to-bit conversion. To circumvent this capacity loss, we have proposed an alternative iterative code design referred to as a symbol-based CC-URC-2SD. Our symbol-based design incorporates a single convolutional code (CC) as the outer component, while the URC and 2SD schemes constitute the amalgamated symbol-based inner code.

Again, the rest of the chapter is laid out as follows. We review the SD coding protocol in Section 5.2, while the EACC of $N$-qubit SD schemes is investigated in Section 5.3. The bit-based system model and our near-capacity design are detailed in Sections 5.4 and 5.5, respectively, while the corresponding simulation results are discussed in Section 5.6. Next we have detailed our symbol-based scheme in Section 5.7, and the associated results are discussed in Section 5.8. Finally, our conclusions are offered in Section 5.9.

## 5.2 Review of the SD Coding Protocol

### 5.2.1 2SD Coding

The 2SD protocol [29] invokes the peculiar law of quantum entanglement for transmitting two classical bits using a single qubit. Figure 5.2 shows the quantum circuit of 2SD [29]. Here, Alice intends to transmit two bits of classical information $x = (x_1\ x_2)$ to Bob. Alice initiates the process by generating a maximally entangled Bell state, also referred to as the Einstein–Podolsky–Rosen (EPR) pair [29], which is given by [29]:

$$|\psi_x\rangle^{AB} = \frac{|00\rangle + |11\rangle}{\sqrt{2}}. \tag{5.1}$$

This is achieved by applying the Hadamard gate (**H**) of Section 2.3.1.2 to two qubits initialized to the state $|0\rangle$, as depicted in the "EPR Generation" block of Figure 5.2. More explicitly, the Einstein–Podolsky–Rosen pair generation proceeds as follows:

***Step 1:***

Apply the Hadamard gate to the first qubit:

$$|00\rangle \to \frac{1}{\sqrt{2}}(|0\rangle + |1\rangle)\,|0\rangle. \tag{5.2}$$

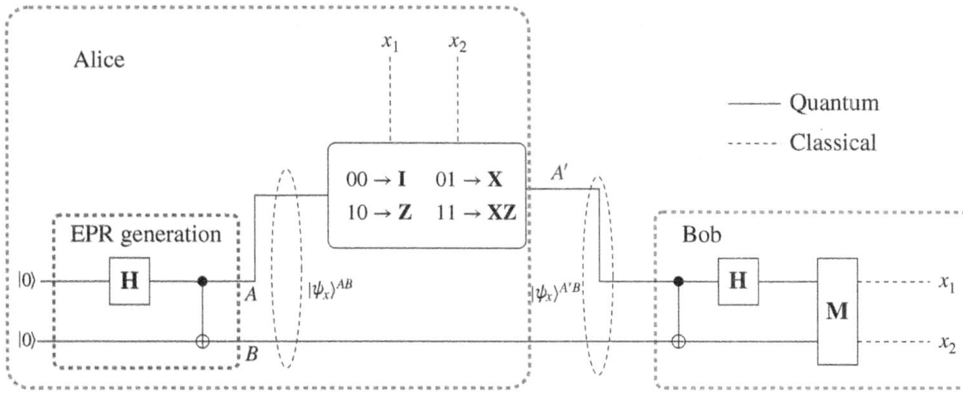


**Figure 5.2** The quantum circuit of 2-qubit SuperDense coding. Alice generates the Einstein–Podolsky–Rosen (EPR) pair $|\psi_x\rangle^{AB}$ using a **H** gate and CNOT gate, respectively. Qubit $A$ is used for encoding the 2-bit message, while the qubit $B$ is pre-shared with Bob. Bob performs Bell-basis measurement on the received state $|\psi_x\rangle^{A'B}$, yielding the original classical message.

**Table 5.1** Classical-to-quantum mapping for 2-qubit SuperDense coding. (The normalization factor $\frac{1}{\sqrt{2}}$ is ignored for simplicity.)

| $(x_1\ x_2)$ | $A$ | $\|\psi_x\rangle^{A'B}$ |
|---|---|---|
| 0 0 | **I** | $\|00\rangle + \|11\rangle$ |
| 0 1 | **X** | $\|10\rangle + \|01\rangle$ |
| 1 0 | **Z** | $\|00\rangle - \|11\rangle$ |
| 1 1 | **XZ** | $\|10\rangle - \|01\rangle$ |

***Step 2:***

Apply the CNOT gate to the second qubit, which is controlled by the first qubit:

$$\frac{1}{\sqrt{2}}(|00\rangle + |10\rangle) \rightarrow \frac{1}{\sqrt{2}}(|00\rangle + |11\rangle) \equiv |\psi_x\rangle^{AB}. \tag{5.3}$$

The resultant qubit $A$ is used for encoding the 2-bit classical message, while the qubit $B$ may be pre-shared with Bob before actual transmission takes place, for example during the instances, when the channel is not busy. During the encoding procedure, Alice performs either the **I**, **X**, **Z**, or **XZ** operation of Table 5.1 on her qubit $A$, depending on her 2-bit message. More specifically, the classical message is embedded in the qubit $A$ as follows:

- For $(x_1\ x_2) = (0\ 0)$, do not apply any operation,
- For $(x_1\ x_2) = (0\ 1)$, apply the **X** gate of Section 2.3.1.1 to $A$,

$$\frac{1}{\sqrt{2}}(|00\rangle + |11\rangle) \rightarrow \frac{1}{\sqrt{2}}(|10\rangle + |01\rangle). \tag{5.4}$$

- For $(x_1\ x_2) = (0\ 1)$, apply the **Z** gate of Section 2.3.1.1 to $A$,

$$\frac{1}{\sqrt{2}}(|00\rangle + |11\rangle) \rightarrow \frac{1}{\sqrt{2}}(|00\rangle - |11\rangle). \tag{5.5}$$

- For $(x_1\ x_2) = (0\ 1)$, apply the **Z** gate followed by the **X** gate to $A$,

$$\frac{1}{\sqrt{2}}(|00\rangle + |11\rangle) \rightarrow \frac{1}{\sqrt{2}}(|10\rangle - |01\rangle). \tag{5.6}$$

This classical-to-quantum mapping is summarized in Table 5.1.

Alice sends the appropriately processed qubit $A'$ over the quantum channel to Bob. Let us assume having a noiseless channel here. Since the four Bell states $\psi_x\rangle^{A'B}$ of Table 5.1 are orthonormal, they are distinguishable at the receiver. Recall that qubit $B$ is pre-shared with Bob. Upon receiving the processed qubit $A'$, Bob performs a collective Bell-basis measurement on the received state $|\psi_x\rangle^{A'B}$, which is carried out as follows:

***Step 1:***
Apply the CNOT gate to qubit $B$, which is controlled by the qubit $A'$:

$$\begin{aligned}
|\psi_{00}\rangle &= \frac{1}{\sqrt{2}}(|00\rangle + |11\rangle) \rightarrow \frac{1}{\sqrt{2}}(|00\rangle + |10\rangle),\\
|\psi_{01}\rangle &= \frac{1}{\sqrt{2}}(|10\rangle + |01\rangle) \rightarrow \frac{1}{\sqrt{2}}(|11\rangle + |01\rangle),\\
|\psi_{10}\rangle &= \frac{1}{\sqrt{2}}(|00\rangle - |11\rangle) \rightarrow \frac{1}{\sqrt{2}}(|00\rangle - |10\rangle),\\
|\psi_{11}\rangle &= \frac{1}{\sqrt{2}}(|10\rangle - |01\rangle) \rightarrow \frac{1}{\sqrt{2}}(|11\rangle - |01\rangle).
\end{aligned} \tag{5.7}$$

***Step 2:***
Apply the Hadamard gate to the first qubit:

$$\begin{aligned}
\frac{1}{\sqrt{2}}(|00\rangle + |10\rangle) &\rightarrow \frac{1}{\sqrt{2}}\frac{1}{\sqrt{2}}((|0\rangle + |1\rangle)|0\rangle + (|0\rangle - |1\rangle)|0\rangle) \equiv |00\rangle,\\
\frac{1}{\sqrt{2}}(|11\rangle + |01\rangle) &\rightarrow \frac{1}{\sqrt{2}}\frac{1}{\sqrt{2}}((|0\rangle - |1\rangle)|1\rangle) + (|0\rangle + |1\rangle)|1\rangle) \equiv |01\rangle,\\
\frac{1}{\sqrt{2}}(|00\rangle - |10\rangle) &\rightarrow \frac{1}{\sqrt{2}}\frac{1}{\sqrt{2}}((|0\rangle + |1\rangle)|0\rangle - (|0\rangle - |1\rangle)|0\rangle) \equiv |10\rangle,\\
\frac{1}{\sqrt{2}}(|11\rangle - |01\rangle) &\rightarrow \frac{1}{\sqrt{2}}\frac{1}{\sqrt{2}}((|0\rangle - |1\rangle)|1\rangle - (|0\rangle + |1\rangle)|1\rangle) \equiv -|11\rangle.
\end{aligned} \tag{5.8}$$

***Step 3:***
Measure the first qubit:

$$\begin{aligned}
|00\rangle &\rightarrow 00,\\
|01\rangle &\rightarrow 01,\\
|10\rangle &\rightarrow 10,\\
-|11\rangle &\rightarrow 11.
\end{aligned} \tag{5.9}$$

Hence, Alice transmits only a single qubit, namely $A'$, to Bob through the quantum channel for communicating a 2-bit classical message, resulting in a transmission rate of 2 cbits/use. Indeed, the transmission of the pre-shared entangled qubit $B$ also consumes transmission resources; hence, the overall transmission requirements remain the same as in a classical scenario. However, traditionally this is considered to be less of a problem, because the entangled qubit may be shared during off-peak hours, when the network is underutilized [29]. Alternatively, if both the transmitter and receiver are mobile, sharing may take place if and when they are close to each other [213].

### 5.2.2 *N*-Qubit SuperDense Coding

*N*-qubit SuperDense coding (NSD) [209] is a generalization of the 2SD scheme to a multi-qubit channel, which facilitates the receiver to read messages from multiple users with the aid of a single entangled quantum state as well as using a single joint quantum measurement. Let us consider a system supporting $N$ users sharing an $N$-qubit Greenberger–Horne–Zeilinger (GHZ) state [214], where each user possesses one qubit. Furthermore, one of the users intends to receive information from the $(N-1)$ other users (the source transmitters in this case). For $N$ qubits, there are $2^N$ unitary operations, which map the initial $N$-qubit state onto a unique quantum state. Therefore, the source transmitters mutually decide *a priori* to perform only certain operations on the qubit in their

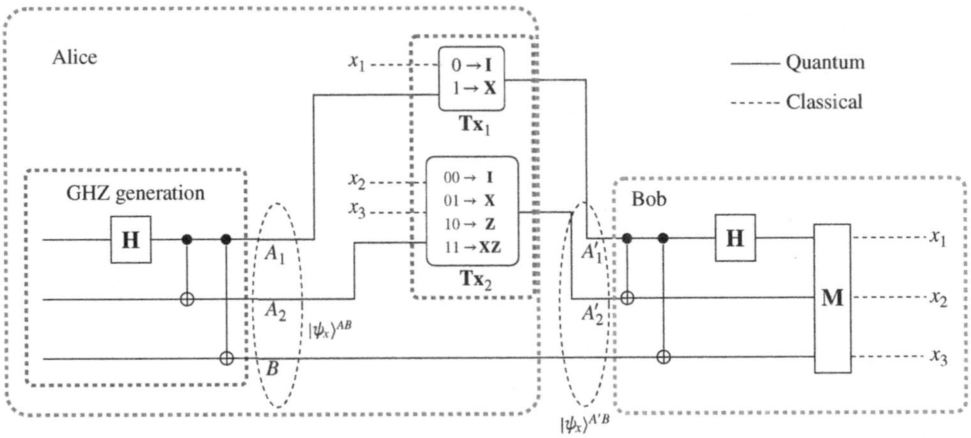


**Figure 5.3** The quantum circuit for 3-qubit SuperDense coding. Alice generates the Greenberger–Horne–Zeilinger state $|\psi_x\rangle^{AB}$ using an **H** gate and CNOT gates respectively. Qubits $A_1$ and $A_2$ are used for encoding the 3-bit message, while the qubit $B$ is pre-shared with Bob. Bob measures the received state $|\psi_x\rangle^{A'B}$ in the orthonormal basis, yielding the original classical message.

possession. Since there are $2^N$ operations and $(N-1)$ source transmitters, one transmitter can perform four operations on its qubit, while the remaining $(N-2)$ transmitters can perform two operations. Consequently, the former can transmit 2 cbits/use, while the latter can only transmit 1 cbit/use. The overall rate is therefore $\frac{N}{N-1}$ cbits/use. The receiver makes a collective measurement on the $N$-qubit state for determining the classical information transmitted by each transmitter.

Let us now consider the 3-qubit system of Figure 5.3, where two source transmitters intend to transmit three classical information bits to a receiver over a quantum channel. Since there are three users, the corresponding 3-qubit Greenberger–Horne–Zeilinger state, which is shared among the users, is given by:

$$|\psi_x\rangle^{AB} = \frac{|000\rangle + |111\rangle}{\sqrt{2}}. \tag{5.10}$$

Here $A$ constitutes a 2-qubit subsystem having qubits $A_1$ and $A_2$. The entangled triplet $|\psi_x\rangle^{AB}$ is prepared by the first transmitter ($Tx_1$) and shared with both the second source transmitter ($Tx_2$) and the receiver, i.e. with Bob, before actual communication takes place. For simplicity, we may combine the two source transmitters into a single device, namely into Alice's device, which wishes to transmit three classical bits to Bob. More explicitly, one bit is transmitted from $Tx_1$ of Figure 5.3, while two bits are transmitted from $Tx_2$ to Bob. The qubits $A_1$ and $A_2$ are used by $Tx_1$ and $Tx_2$, respectively, for mapping three classical bits onto two processed qubits, while the entangled qubit $B$ is pre-shared with Bob, as illustrated in Figure 5.3. Since Alice is in possession of the pair of qubits $A_1$ and $A_2$, she can perform the **I**, **X**, **Z**, or **XZ** Pauli operations on each of these qubits for generating distinct output qubit states $|\psi_x\rangle^{A'B}$, which are orthonormal and therefore distinguishable at the receiver. This may be achieved by adopting any set of classical-to-quantum mapping rules, which are capable of ensuring that the resultant states $|\psi_x\rangle^{A'B}$ are orthonormal. Table 5.2 lists one such mapping.

## 5.3 Entanglement-assisted Classical Capacity

Under the assumptions discussed in Section 5.2.1, 2SD doubles the capacity of a noiseless quantum channel. Conventionally it is assumed that the pre-sharing of the entangled qubit destined from Alice to Bob takes place over a noiseless channel, and only the processed qubit(s) is passed through a noisy quantum channel [207, 215]. The corresponding EACC of 2SD has already been derived in [207, 215] based on its equivalence to a 4-ary symmetric classical channel. In this section, we will generalize it to $N$-qubit SD by exploiting the well-known equivalent $M$-ary classical channel model ($M = 2^N$).

**Table 5.2** Classical-to-quantum mapping for 3-qubit SuperDense coding. *The normalization factor* $\frac{1}{\sqrt{2}}$ *is ignored for simplicity.*

| $(x_1\ x_2\ x_3)$ | $A_1$ | $A_2$ | $\lvert\psi_x\rangle^{A'B}$ |
|---|---|---|---|
| 0 0 0 | I | I | $\lvert 000\rangle + \lvert 111\rangle$ |
| 0 0 1 | I | X | $\lvert 010\rangle + \lvert 101\rangle$ |
| 0 1 0 | I | Z | $\lvert 000\rangle - \lvert 111\rangle$ |
| 0 1 1 | I | XZ | $\lvert 010\rangle - \lvert 101\rangle$ |
| 1 0 0 | X | I | $\lvert 100\rangle + \lvert 011\rangle$ |
| 1 0 1 | X | X | $\lvert 110\rangle + \lvert 001\rangle$ |
| 1 1 0 | X | Z | $\lvert 100\rangle - \lvert 011\rangle$ |
| 1 1 1 | X | XZ | $\lvert 110\rangle - \lvert 001\rangle)$ |

Let us recall that the capacity C of a classical channel is equivalent to the maximum value of the conveyed mutual information $I(x, y)$ between the transmitted symbol $x$ and the received symbol $y$, i.e. we have [53]:

$$\mathrm{C} = \max_{\mathrm{P}(x)} I(x, y) = \max_{\mathrm{P}(x)}[\mathrm{H}(y) - \mathrm{H}(y|x)], \tag{5.11}$$

where H is the classical entropy function. Since C is maximized for equiprobable source symbols, the capacity of an $M$-ary classical channel is given by:

$$\mathrm{C} = \log_2 M - \mathrm{H}(y|x), \tag{5.12}$$

which is further defined as follows [216, 217]:

$$\mathrm{C} = \log_2 M + \mathrm{E}\left[\sum_{m=0}^{M-1} \mathrm{P}(y|x = x^{(m)}) \log_2 \mathrm{P}(y|x = x^{(m)})\right], \tag{5.13}$$

using Eqs. (10) and (11) of [216]. Here E[.] is the expectation (or time average) of $y$ and $x^{(m)}$ is the $m$th hypothetically transmitted classical message for $m \in \{0, 1, \ldots, M-1\}$.

Based on Eq. (5.13), the capacity of NSD coding relying on a single noiseless pre-shared entangled qubit may be readily expressed as:

$$\mathrm{C}_{Nsd} = \frac{N + \sum_{m=0}^{M-1} \mathrm{P}(y|x = x^{(m)}) \log_2 \mathrm{P}(y|x = x^{(m)})}{N-1} \text{ cbits/use}, \tag{5.14}$$

where $\mathrm{P}(y|x)$ denotes the transition probabilities of the induced classical channel.[2]

Symbol-by-symbol measurements performed at the 2SD decoder reduce the transmission model of Figure 5.1 to a 4-ary classical channel. Consequently, the channel transition probabilities of the induced classical channel may be encapsulated as:

$$\mathrm{P}(y|x = x^{(m)}) = \begin{cases} 1-p, & \text{if } \mathtt{E} = 0 \\ p/3, & \text{if } \mathtt{E} \in \{1, 2, 3\}, \end{cases} \tag{5.15}$$

where $m \in \{0, 1, 2, 3\}$. Furthermore, $\mathtt{E}$ is the decimal equivalent of the $N$-bit classical error $e$, which is induced by the depolarizing channel. More specifically, the $N$-bit classical error $e = [e_1, \ldots, e_i, \ldots, e_N]$ relates the *ith* bit of $x = [x_1, \ldots, x_i, \ldots, x_N]$ to that of $y = [y_1, \ldots, y_i, \ldots, y_N]$ as follows:

$$y_i = x_i \oplus e_i \quad \text{or} \quad e_i = y_i \oplus x_i. \tag{5.16}$$

2 Due to the time-invariant nature of $\mathrm{P}(y|x)$, the average information is the same as the instantaneous value. The expectation operation of Eq. (5.13) can therefore be ignored.

Substituting Eq. (5.15) in Eq. (5.14) yields the entanglement-assisted classical capacity of 2SD over a quantum depolarizing channel, i.e we have:

$$C_{2sd} = 2 + (1-p)\log_2(1-p) + p\log_2(p/3), \tag{5.17}$$

which gives a maximum capacity of 2 cbits/use for the noiseless scenario.

Similarly, symbol-by-symbol measurements performed at the 3-qubit SuperDense (3SD) decoder reduce the overall transmission to an 8-ary classical channel. However, unlike the 2SD scheme, now 2 qubits are transmitted over the noisy quantum channel. All the possible quantum channel errors along with the corresponding probabilities of occurrence and the resultant classical error patterns $e$ are listed in Table 5.3. The resulting corrupted state $|\psi_y\rangle^{B'B}$ for the transmitted state $\frac{1}{\sqrt{2}}(|000\rangle + |111\rangle)$ is also tabulated in Table 5.3. It must be noted that different quantum errors may result in the same $e$, for example the third and sixth rows of Table 5.3 have the same classical error pattern. Consequently, we combined the probabilities corresponding to the same error patterns arriving at the following channel transition probabilities for the 3SD scheme:

$$P(y|x = x^{(m)}) = \begin{cases} (1-p)^2 + p^2/9, & \text{if } \mathbb{E} \in \{0\} \\ (1-p)(p/3) + p^2/9, & \text{if } \mathbb{E} \in \{2,3,6,7\} \\ 2(1-p)(p/3), & \text{if } \mathbb{E} \in \{4\} \\ 2p^2/9, & \text{if } \mathbb{E} \in \{1,5\}, \end{cases} \tag{5.18}$$

**Table 5.3** List of all the possible quantum errors when the first and second qubit, $A_1$ and $A_2$ respectively, of the 3-qubit Greenberger–Horne–Zeilinger state $\frac{1}{\sqrt{2}}(|000\rangle + |111\rangle)$ are transmitted over a quantum depolarizing channel. The normalization factor $\frac{1}{\sqrt{2}}$ is ignored for simplicity.

| Error on $A_1$ | Error on $A_2$ | $\|\psi_y\rangle^{B'B}$ | Error ($e/\mathbb{E}$) | Error probability |
|---|---|---|---|---|
| I | I | $\|000\rangle + \|111\rangle$ | 000/0 | $(1-p)(1-p)$ |
| X | I | $\|100\rangle + \|011\rangle$ | 011/3 | $(p/3)(1-p)$ |
| Z | I | $\|000\rangle - \|111\rangle$ | 100/4 | $(p/3)(1-p)$ |
| Y | I | $\|100\rangle - \|011\rangle$ | 111/7 | $(p/3)(1-p)$ |
| I | X | $\|010\rangle + \|101\rangle$ | 010/2 | $(1-p)(p/3)$ |
| I | Z | $\|000\rangle - \|111\rangle$ | 100/4 | $(1-p)(p/3)$ |
| I | Y | $\|010\rangle - \|101\rangle$ | 110/6 | $(1-p)(p/3)$ |
| X | X | $\|110\rangle + \|001\rangle$ | 001/1 | $(p/3)(p/3)$ |
| Z | X | $\|010\rangle - \|101\rangle$ | 110/6 | $(p/3)(p/3)$ |
| Y | X | $\|110\rangle - \|001\rangle$ | 101/5 | $(p/3)(p/3)$ |
| X | Z | $\|100\rangle - \|011\rangle$ | 111/7 | $(p/3)(p/3)$ |
| Z | Z | $\|000\rangle + \|111\rangle$ | 000/0 | $(p/3)(p/3)$ |
| Y | Z | $\|100\rangle + \|011\rangle$ | 011/3 | $(p/3)(p/3)$ |
| X | Y | $\|110\rangle - \|001\rangle$ | 101/5 | $(p/3)(p/3)$ |
| Z | Y | $\|010\rangle + \|101\rangle$ | 010/2 | $(p/3)(p/3)$ |
| Y | Y | $\|110\rangle + \|001\rangle$ | 001/1 | $(p/3)(p/3)$ |

where we have $m \in \{0, 1, \ldots, 7\}$. Eq. (5.18) may be substituted in Eq. (5.14) to compute the EACC of the 3SD scheme, when communicating over a quantum depolarizing channel. More explicitly, we have:

$$C_{3sd} = \frac{3}{2} + \frac{1}{2} \sum_{m=0}^{7} P(y|x=x^{(m)}) \log_2 P(y|x=x^{(m)}). \tag{5.19}$$

Hence, the 3SD scheme has a maximum capacity of 1.5 cbits/use when the channel is noiseless.

## 5.4 Bit-based Code Structure

In this section we will present the architecture of our proposed classical-quantum communication system, which is designed for approaching the EACC of the NSD code with the aid of EXIT charts [125, 218, 219]. Figure 5.4 shows the general schematic of the proposed system, which employs a classical IRCC [220, 221] for achieving the near-capacity performance. Furthermore, a classical symbol-based recursive URC having a generator polynomial of $G(D) = \frac{1}{1+D}$ [125] is used as a precoder for reaching the (1, 1) point of perfect decoding convergence in the EXIT chart [222]. We amalgamate our conceived soft-decision SD with the symbol-based URC, which hence constitutes an amalgamated inner component, while the bit-based IRCC is our outer component.

At the transmitter, the system is fed with classical bits $\{u_1\}$, which are encoded by an IRCC encoder. The IRCC-encoded bits $\{v_1\}$ of Figure 5.4 are then interleaved ($\pi$), yielding the permuted bit stream $\{u_2\}$, which is converted to symbols[3] and fed to the URC encoder of Figure 5.4. Classical to quantum domain conversion then takes place at the SD encoder, which maps the classical symbols $x$ onto the orthogonal quantum states $|\psi_x\rangle^{A'B}$ using the entangled state $|\psi_x\rangle^{AB}$, as discussed in Section 5.1. Hence, the SD encoder has a function similar to that of the classical phase-shift keying (PSK) or quadrature amplitude modulation (QAM) bit-to-symbol mapper, which maps several classical bits onto a complex-valued phasor for communication using the classical electromagnetic waves. The qubits of the resultant quantum state are then serially transmitted over the quantum depolarizing channel.[4]

At the receiver, iterative decoding is invoked for exchanging *extrinsic* information between the inner (URC-SD) and outer (IRCC) decoders. Here the notations $A(b)$ and $E(b)$ refer to the *a priori* and *extrinsic* probabilities of $b$, where we have $b \in \{v_1, u_2, x\}$, which are exploited for achieving decoding convergence to a vanishingly low bit error rate (BER). The SD decoder converts the received orthogonal states $|\psi_y\rangle^{B'B}$ to classical symbols $y$ by performing a joint measurement in the orthonormal basis. It must be highlighted here that a conventional SD decoder yields the

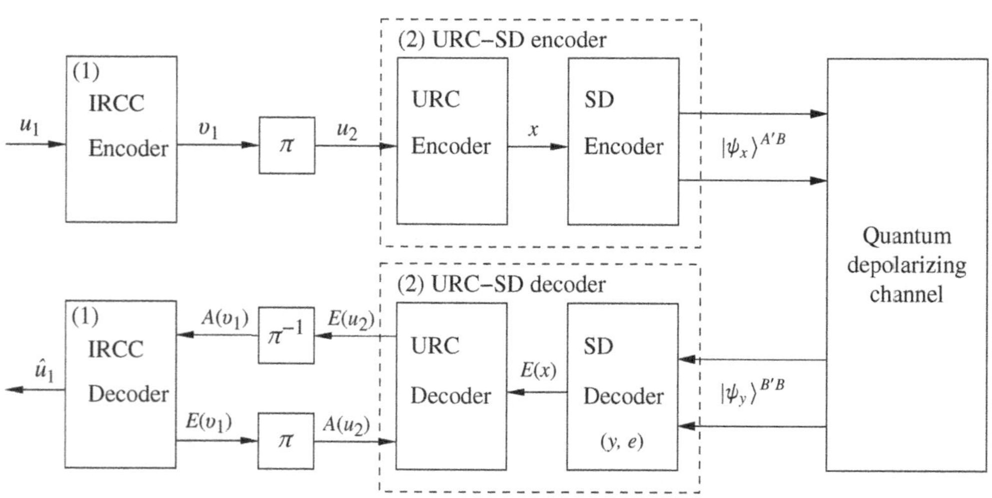


**Figure 5.4** Schematic of the proposed IRCC-URC-SD classical-quantum communication system. *Source:* [210]/IEEE.

3 Bit-to-symbol converter is assumed to be inside the URC Encoder block of Figure 5.4.

4 As illustrated earlier in Figure 5.1, the processed qubit(s) $A'$ is transmitted over the noisy quantum channel, while $B$ is shared between Alice and Bob over a noiseless channel.

hard-decision outputs. Instead, here we conceive a soft-decision SD decoder, which computes the corresponding *extrinsic* probability $E(x)$ for the transmitted classical symbol $x$, as follows:

$$E(x) \approx \mathrm{P}(y|x), \tag{5.20}$$

where $\mathrm{P}(y|x)$ is given by Eqs. (5.15) and (5.18) for the 2-qubit and 3-qubit schemes, respectively. The soft output $E(x)$ is then fed into the Maximum *A-Posteriori* (MAP) decoder of URC, which engages in iterative decoding with the IRCC decoder.

## 5.5 Near-capacity Design

### 5.5.1 EXIT Charts

EXIT charts [125, 218, 219] are capable of visualizing the convergence behavior of iterative decoding schemes by exploiting the input/output relations of the constituent decoders in terms of their average Mutual Information (MI) transfer characteristics. In the context of our proposed model of Figure 5.4, the EXIT chart visualizes the exchange of the following four MI terms:

**a.** average *a priori* MI between $u_2$ and $A(u_2)$: $I_{A(u_2)}$,
**b.** average *a priori* MI between $v_1$ and $A(v_1)$: $I_{A(v_1)}$,
**c.** average *extrinsic* MI between $u_2$ and $E(u_2)$: $I_{E(u_2)}$, and
**d.** average *extrinsic* MI between $v_1$ and $E(v_1)$: $I_{E(v_1)}$.

Here, $I_{A(u_2)}$ and $I_{E(u_2)}$ constitute the EXIT curve of the inner decoder, while $I_{A(v_1)}$ and $I_{E(v_1)}$ yield the EXIT curve of the outer decoder. For the sake of constructing the inner and outer EXIT curves, the Log Likelihood Ratios (LLRs)[5] related to the *a priori* probabilities of $A(u_2)$ and $A(v_1)$, respectively, are modeled using a Gaussian distribution, having a mean of $\sigma_A^2/2$ and a variance of $\sigma_A^2$, for a range of $I_{A(u_2)}, I_{A(v_1)} \in [0, 1]$. The corresponding average *extrinsic* MI can be formulated as [216, 217]:

$$I_{E(u_2)} = \log_2 M + \mathrm{E}\left[\sum_{m=0}^{M-1} E(u_2^{(m)}) \log_2(E(u_2^{(m)}))\right], \tag{5.21}$$

and

$$I_{E(v_1)} = \log_2 M + \mathrm{E}\left[\sum_{m=0}^{M-1} E(v_1^{(m)}) \log_2(E(v_1^{(m)}))\right]. \tag{5.22}$$

Furthermore, since we are employing symbol-to-bit conversion at the URC decoder, we incorporate binary EXIT charts in our design. This in turn implies that in Eqs. (5.21) and (5.22), we have $M = 2$ and $m \in \{0, 1\}$. The resultant inner EXIT function $T_{u_2}$ is given by:

$$I_{E(u_2)} = T_{u_2}[I_{A(u_2)}, p], \tag{5.23}$$

while the outer EXIT function $T_{v_1}$ is as follows:

$$I_{E(v_1)} = T_{v_1}[I_{A(v_1)}]. \tag{5.24}$$

More explicitly, unlike $T_{v_1}$, $T_{u_2}$ is a function of the depolarizing probability $p$, since the inner decoder is fed by the channel. Finally, the MI transfer characteristics of both the decoders encapsulated by Eqs. (5.23) and (5.24) are plotted in the same graph, with the $x$ and $y$ axes of the outer decoder swapped. The resultant EXIT chart is capable of visualizing the exchange of *extrinsic* MI as a staircase-shaped decoding trajectory, as the iterations proceed. Examples of EXIT charts will be given in Section 5.6.

---

5 The LLR $L(x)$ of a bit $x$ is the log of the ratio of the probabilities of the bit taking the two possible values of 0 and 1, which is given by [125]:

$$L(x) = \ln\left(\frac{\mathrm{P}(x=1)}{\mathrm{P}(x=0)}\right).$$

### 5.5.2 Near-capacity IRCC-URC-SD Design

We have exploited the area property of EXIT charts [223] for designing a near-capacity classical error correction code for our classical-quantum communication system of Figure 5.4. According to this property, the area under the normalized EXIT curve of the inner decoder is approximately equal to the attainable channel capacity [223], provided that the channel's input symbols are equiprobable. Since our system model of Figure 5.4 transmits classical information over a quantum depolarizing channel, the attainable channel capacity of the system is the entanglement-assisted classical capacity given in Eq. (5.14). However, as mentioned in Section 5.4, symbol-to-bit conversion takes place at the output of the URC decoder. This incurs a capacity loss [224]. More explicitly, the corresponding bit-based capacity of 2SD may be computed by marginalizing the symbol-based channel transition probabilities $P(y|x)$ of Eq. (5.15) to the bit-based probabilities $P(y_i|x_i)$ for $i \in \{1, 2\}$, assuming that the constituent bits are independent. More specifically, we get:

$$\begin{aligned} P(y_i = x_i|x_i) &= 1 - \frac{2}{3}p, \\ P(y_i \neq x_i|x_i) &= \frac{2}{3}p. \end{aligned} \tag{5.25}$$

Based on this marginalized perspective, the resultant 4-ary classical channel may be viewed as a pair of independent binary symmetric channels (BSCs) having a crossover probability of $2p/3$. The capacity of each BSC is given by:

$$C^i_{\text{BSC}} = 1 + (1 - \frac{2}{3}p)\ \log_2(1 - \frac{2}{3}p) + \frac{2}{3}p\ \log_2(\frac{2}{3}p), \tag{5.26}$$

for $i \in \{1, 2\}$. Since two classical bits are transmitted per channel use in the 2SD scheme, the symbol-based capacity of Eq. (5.17) is reduced to the sum of the capacity of these two BSCs, which is equivalent to:

$$\begin{aligned} C^{\text{bit}}_{2sd} &= \sum_{i=1}^{2} C^i_{\text{BSC}} \\ &= 2 \cdot \left[1 + (1 - \frac{2}{3}p)\ \log_2(1 - \frac{2}{3}p) + \frac{2}{3}p\ \log_2(\frac{2}{3}p)\right], \end{aligned} \tag{5.27}$$

where $C^i_{\text{BSC}}$ is the capacity of the $i$th BSC given in Eq. (5.26). More explicitly, the generalized formula of the bit-based capacity of an NSD scheme relying on a single noiseless pre-shared entangled qubit is given by:

$$C^{\text{bit}}_{Nsd} = \frac{1}{N-1} \cdot \sum_{i=1}^{N} C^i_{\text{BSC}}, \tag{5.28}$$

where $N = 2$ for the 2SD scheme.

Similarly, for computing the bit-based EACC of 3SD, the induced 8-ary channel may be viewed as three independent BSCs. For the sake of computing the channel transition probabilities associated with each of the three BSCs, we normalize the symbol-based conditional probability of Eq. (5.18) for each of the three constituent bits as follows:

$$\begin{aligned} P(y_1 = x_1|x_1) &= \sum_{e_1=0} P(y = x + e|x = x^{(m)}) = 1 - \frac{4}{3}p + \frac{8}{9}p^2, \\ P(y_1 \neq x_1|x_1) &= \sum_{e_1=1} P(y = x + e|x = x^{(m)}) = \frac{4}{3}p - \frac{8}{9}p^2, \\ P(y_2 = x_2|x_2) &= \sum_{e_2=0} P(y = x + e|x = x^{(m)}) = 1 - \frac{4}{3}p + \frac{8}{9}p^2, \\ P(y_2 \neq x_2|x_2) &= \sum_{e_2=1} P(y = x + e|x = x^{(m)}) = \frac{4}{3}p - \frac{8}{9}p^2, \\ P(y_3 = x_3|x_3) &= \sum_{e_3=0} P(y = x + e|x = x^{(m)}) = 1 - \frac{2}{3}p, \\ P(y_3 \neq x_3|x_3) &= \sum_{e_3=1} P(y = x + e|x = x^{(m)}) = \frac{2}{3}p. \end{aligned} \tag{5.29}$$

Using Eq. (5.13) as well as (5.29) and exploiting the fact that three classical bits are transmitted per two channel uses in 3SD, the symbol-based capacity of Eq. (5.19) is reduced to:

$$\begin{aligned} C_{3sd}^{\text{bit}} &= \frac{1}{2} \cdot \sum_{i=1}^{3} C_{\text{BSC}}^{i} \\ &= \frac{1}{2} \cdot [3 - 2 \times H_2(\frac{4}{3}p - \frac{8}{9}p^2) - H_2(\frac{2}{3}p)], \end{aligned} \tag{5.30}$$

where $C_{\text{BSC}}^{i}$ is the capacity of the $i$th BSC, while $H_2(z)$ is the binary entropy function, which is given by

$$H_2(z) = -z \log_2(z) - (1-z)\log_2(1-z). \tag{5.31}$$

The capacity loss for both the 2SD and 3SD schemes is quantified in Figure 5.5, which compares their bit-based and symbol-based capacities. Nevertheless, it must be pointed out that by virtue of being a unity rate code, the URC does not impose any capacity loss, as verified in Figure 5.5. The capacity of our inner decoder (URC-SD) is approximately equal to the attainable bit-based entanglement-assisted classical capacity for both 2SD and 3SD codes. The URC is only invoked for transforming the horizontal EXIT curve of the SD decoder to a slanted one for the sake of improving the scheme's decoding convergence, as detailed in the next section.

Furthermore, the area under the normalized EXIT curve of the outer decoder is equivalent to $(1 - R_o)$, where $R_o$ is its coding rate [223]. Therefore, our near-capacity design aims for creating a narrow but marginally open tunnel between the EXIT curves of the inner and outer decoders at the highest possible depolarizing probability, which corresponds to the lowest possible SNR for a classical channel. A feasible design option could be to create the EXIT curves of all the possible convolutional codes to find the optimal code $\mathcal{C}$, which gives the best match, i.e. whose EXIT curve yields a marginally open tunnel with the inner decoder's EXIT curve of URC-SD. To circumvent this tedious task, we have invoked the IRCC of [221], whereby a family of subcodes $\mathcal{C}_l$, $l \in \{1, 2, \ldots, L\}$, is used for constructing the target code $\mathcal{C}$. Due to its inherent flexibility, the resultant IRCC provides a better match than any single code. Furthermore, for the sake of reducing the encoding and decoding complexity, the family of subcodes $\mathcal{C}_l$ is constructed by selecting an $r_i$-rate convolutional code $\mathcal{C}_i$ as the mother code and obtaining the remaining $(L-1)$ subcodes $\mathcal{C}_l$ by puncturing the mother code for rate $r_l > r_1$ and by adding more generators and subsequently puncturing for $r_l < r_1$. The $l^{th}$ subcode has a coding rate of $r_l$ and it encodes a specifically designed fraction, $\varrho_l$, of

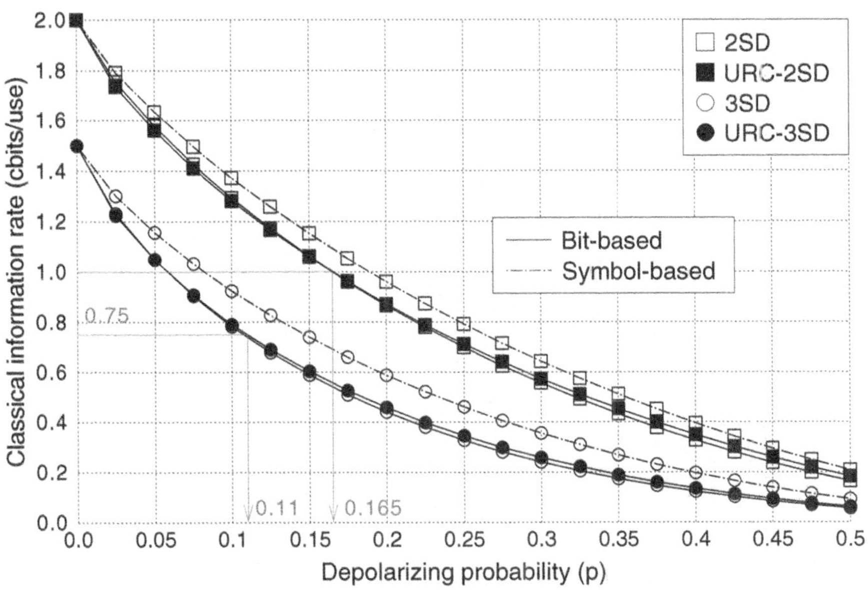


**Figure 5.5** Classical information rate (cbits/use) versus quantum depolarizing probability for 2-qubit and 3-qubit SuperDense codes with and without URC. Symbol-to-bit conversion incurs a capacity loss for 2SD as well as 3SD. *Source*: [210]/IEEE.

the original information bits to $\varrho_l N_c$ encoded bits. Here, $N_c$ is the total length of the coded frame. More specifically, for an $L$-subcode IRCC, $\varrho_l$ is the $l^{th}$ IRCC weighting coefficient satisfying the following constraints [220, 221]:

$$\sum_{l=1}^{L} \varrho_l = 1,\ R_o = \sum_{l=1}^{L} \varrho_l r_l,\ \varrho_l \in [0,1], \forall l, \tag{5.32}$$

which can be conveniently represented in the following matrix form:

$$\begin{bmatrix} 1 & 1\ldots & 1 \\ r_1 & r_2\ldots & r_L \end{bmatrix} \begin{bmatrix} \varrho_1 & \varrho_2\ldots & \varrho_L \end{bmatrix}^T = \begin{bmatrix} 1 \\ R_o \end{bmatrix} \tag{5.33}$$
$$\mathbf{C}\,\varrho = \mathbf{d}.$$

In our design, we have employed an IRCC relying on a set of 17 memory-4 convolutional subcodes having 17 different coding rates between 0 and 1, which were found in [221]. These 17 subcodes are derived such that they cover the complete range of coding rates from 0.1 to 0.9 with a rate-increment of 0.05, i.e. having rates of $r_l \in \{0.1, 0.15, 0.2, \ldots, 0.85, 0.9\}$. Figure 5.6 shows the inverted outer EXIT curves for each of the constituent subcodes of the IRCC scheme.

In physically tangible terms, the input bit stream is divided into 17 fractions corresponding to the 17 different-rate subcodes and the specific optimum fractions to be encoded by these codes are found by dynamic programming. More specifically, the EXIT curves of the 17 subcodes, given in Figure 5.6, are superimposed onto each other after weighting by the appropriate fraction-based weighting coefficients, which are determined by minimizing the area of the open EXIT-tunnel. To elaborate a little further, the transfer function of the IRCC is given by:

$$I_{E(v_1)} = T_{v_1}\left[I_{A(v_1)}\right] = \sum_{l=1}^{L} \varrho_l\, T_{v_1,l}\left[I_{A(v_1)}\right], \tag{5.34}$$

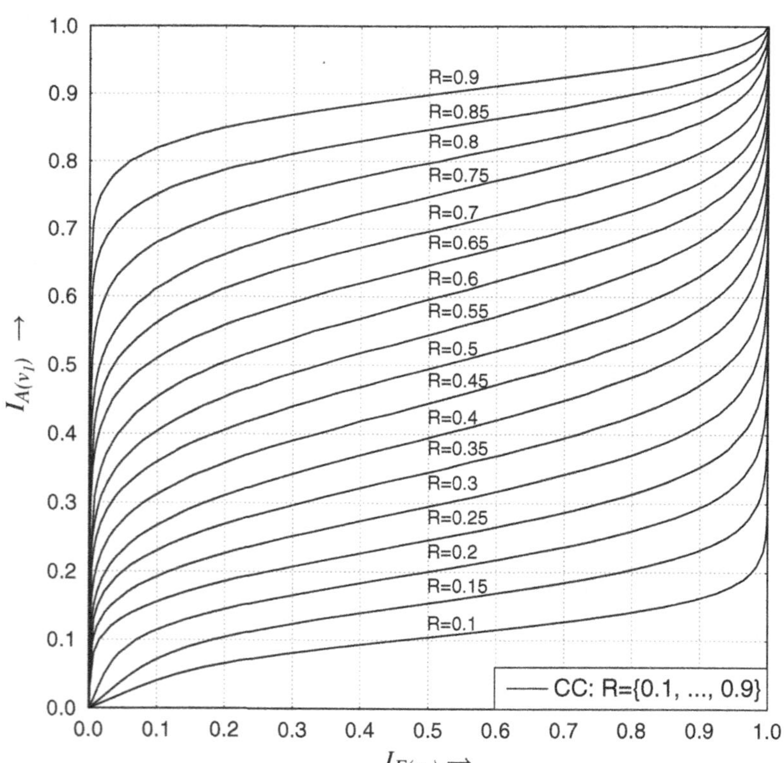


**Figure 5.6** Normalized outer EXIT curves (inverted) of the 17 IRCC subcodes. *Source*: [210]/IEEE.

where $T_{v_1,l}\left[I_{A(v_1)}\right] = I_{E(v_1),l}$ is the transfer function of the $l^{th}$ subcode. We employed the curve matching algorithm of [220, 221] for optimizing the weighting coefficients of the IRCC subcodes by ensuring that a narrow, yet open tunnel exists between the EXIT curves of the outer and inner decoder at the highest possible depolarizing probability; thus, guaranteeing that the system has a near-capacity performance.

## 5.6 Results and Discussion I

Based on the near-capacity design of Section 5.5, we have designed an SD-based near-capacity code for entanglement-assisted classical communication over the quantum depolarizing channel. We next evaluate the performance of our 2-qubit and 3-qubit designs in Sections 5.6.1 and 5.6.2, respectively.

### 5.6.1 Performance of IRCC-URC-2SD

Since we intend to design a system having a rate of 1 cbit/use, we have assumed a constant overall coding rate of 0.5 for the IRCC. Figure 5.7 shows the normalized EXIT curves for 2SD at a depolarizing probability of 0.15 and using an interleaver length of 30,000 bits. As expected, the EXIT curve of the 2SD decoder is a horizontal straight line. Hence, our URC is used as a precoder, to transform this horizontal EXIT curve into a slanted curve which terminates at the (1, 1) point of the EXIT chart; thus, facilitating a possible convergence to an infinitesimally low BER. More specifically, the area under the EXIT curve remains the same, yet reaches the (1, 1) point. Furthermore, using the curve matching algorithm of [220, 221], the IRCC weight vector of Eq. (5.33) was optimized to get a narrow open tunnel as evident in Figure 5.7. The corresponding simulation parameters are summarized in Table 5.4, where only seven subcodes are activated. The tunnel of Figure 5.7 is narrow, but wide enough for successful convergence, as visualized using the decoding trajectories. If the depolarizing probability is increased beyond $p = 0.15$, the EXIT curves of the inner and outer decoder would crossover, hence closing the tunnel. Thus, the system has a convergence threshold of $p = 0.15$. In other words, it can tolerate depolarizing probabilities up to $p = 0.15$, and yet achieve an infinitesimally low BER. However, this would require a high number of iterations between the IRCC and URC-2SD, hence imposing a high complexity.

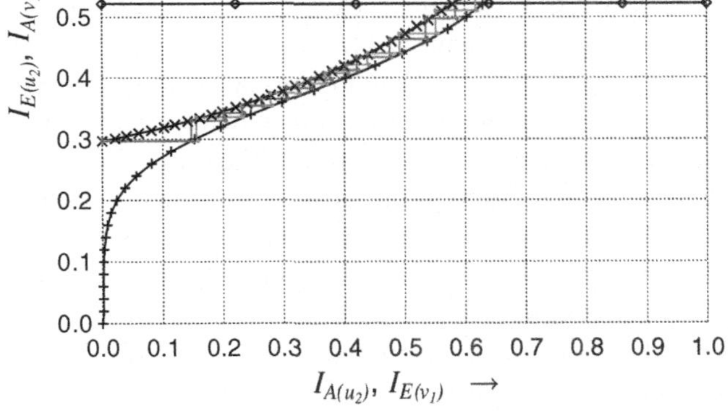


**Figure 5.7** Normalized EXIT curves of the IRCC-URC-2SD system of Figure 5.4 at a depolarizing probability of 0.15 using the simulation parameters of Table 5.4. *Source:* [210]/IEEE.

**Table 5.4** Simulation parameters of the IRCC-URC-SD scheme of Figure 5.4.

| SD scheme | 2-qubit |
|---|---|
| IRCC coding rate | 1/2 |
| IRCC active subcodes | $\varrho_4 = 0.0177, \varrho_5 = 0.0145, \varrho_7 = 0.6455, \varrho_{12} = 0.1797,$ $\varrho_{13} = 0.0580, \varrho_{16} = 0.0105, \varrho_{17} = 0.0742$ |
| Interleaver length | 30,000 bits |
| Overall system rate | 1 cbits/use |

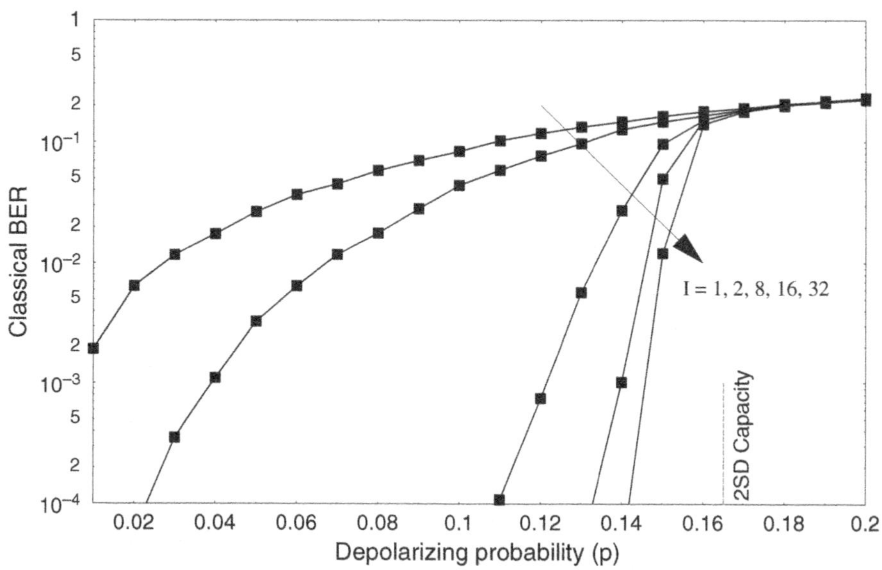


**Figure 5.8** Achievable BER performance of the IRCC-URC-2SD scheme of Figure 5.4 upon increasing the number of iterations, i.e. $\mathtt{I} = \{1, 2, 8, 16, 32\}$. The simulation parameters are summarized in Table 5.4. The dashed line at $p^* = 0.165$ marks the noise limit for a classical information rate of 1 cbit/use, which is obtained from the bit-based EACC curve of 2SD given in Figure 5.5.

The coding rate of the designed IRCC-URC-2SD system is 1 cbit/use, since a 1/2-rate IRCC is used. From the bit-based capacity curve of Figure 5.5, it can be found that the associated noise limit is $p^* = 0.165$. By contrast, the convergence threshold of our system is $p = 0.15$. Thus, it operates within $[10 \times \log_{10}(\frac{0.165}{0.15})] = 0.4$ dB of the noise limit.[6] Alternatively, this discrepancy may also be quantified in terms of the difference in the area under the inner and outer EXIT curves, which corresponds to the normalized capacity loss. The area under the normalized EXIT curve of our URC-2SD scheme is 0.531, whereas that under the IRCC is 0.5. Thus, the capacity of our IRCC-URC-2SD scheme is only $[0.031 \times 2] = 0.062$ cbits/use away from the capacity when $p = 0.15$.

We have further evaluated the BER performance of our IRCC-URC-2SD scheme in Figure 5.8 for the simulation parameters of Table 5.4. As it can be observed in Figure 5.8, the performance improves upon increasing the number of iterations. More specifically, the 2-qubit system starts to converge to a lower BER as the number of iterations increases at a depolarizing probability of $p = 0.15$, which matches the convergence threshold predicted using EXIT charts. More explicitly, since the EXIT chart tunnel closes beyond the depolarizing probability threshold of $p = 0.15$, the system fails to converge, if the depolarizing probability is increased further. Hence, the performance does not improve upon increasing the number of iterations if the depolarizing probability exceeds the threshold. By contrast, when the depolarizing probability is below the threshold, the BER improves at each successive iteration. Here, the trade-off between the complexity imposed and the performance attained comes into play. It should also be noted that the performance improves with diminishing returns at a higher number of iterations. For example, doubling the number of iterations from $\mathtt{I} = 8$ to $\mathtt{I} = 16$ for IRCC-URC-2SD increases the tolerable depolarizing

6 The difference in dB between two channel depolarizing probabilities $p_1$ and $p_2$ is calculated as follows [81, 82]: $\left(10 \times \log_{10} \frac{p_1}{p_2}\right)$.

probability by 0.0225, corresponding to a BER of $10^{-4}$. A further increase to $I = 32$ iterations only improves $p$ by around 0.01 at a BER of $10^{-4}$. We further demonstrate this in Figure 5.9, where we quantify the distance from the capacity, i.e. from the noise limit of $p^* = 0.165$, in terms of dB at a BER of $10^{-4}$ upon increasing the number of iterations. We may observe in Figure 5.9 that we approach the achievable noise limit with diminishing returns as the number of iterations is increased.

To elaborate further on the significance of using an IRCC rather than a conventional 1/2-rate CC, we have also conceived a corresponding setup, whereby the IRCC of Figure 5.4 is replaced by a memory-4 1/2-rate CC in the proposed IRCC-URC-2SD system. This is synonymous to employing an IRCC, which has only the ninth subcode active. Figure 5.10 shows the resultant EXIT curves for $p = 0.15$ and $p = 0.125$. It can be observed in Figure 5.10

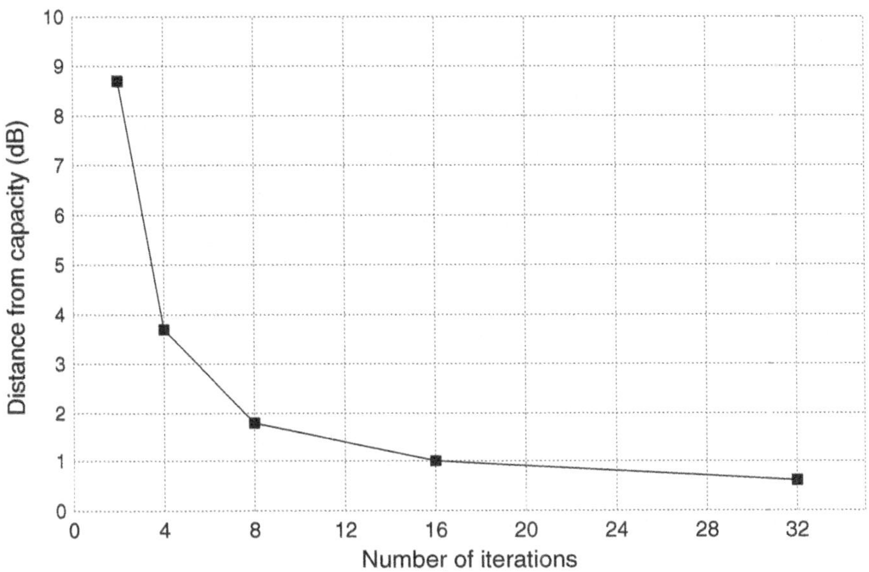


**Figure 5.9** Performance of the IRCC-URC-2SD scheme of Figure 5.8 at a BER of $10^{-4}$, which is quantified in terms of the distance from the bit-based EACC of 2SD, i.e. $p^* = 0.165$, as the number of iterations is increased.

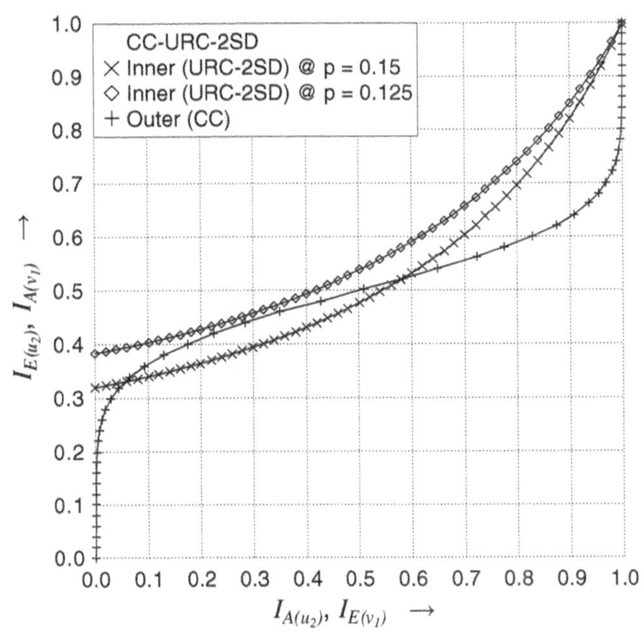


**Figure 5.10** Normalized EXIT curves of the CC-URC-2SD system using the simulation parameters of Table 5.4, but only the ninth subcode of IRCC is active. *Source*: [210]/IEEE.

that for $p=0.15$, which is the convergence threshold of our IRCC-URC-2SD design, the inner and outer EXIT curves of the CC-URC-2SD scheme exhibit a crossover. Thus, implying that the CC-URC-2SD configuration fails to converge at $p=0.15$. An open tunnel emerges only when $p$ is decreased to 0.125. Consequently, the convergence threshold of CC-URC-2SD is $p=0.125$, which is lower than that of our near-capacity design of Figure 5.7. It must also be pointed out here that the area between the inner and outer EXIT curves at the convergence threshold is wider than Figure 5.7. The wider the gap, the higher the capacity loss. Therefore, using a regular CC, rather than an IRCC, yields a poor match between the inner and outer decoders' EXIT curves.

### 5.6.2 Performance of IRCC-URC-3SD

As another example, we designed an IRCC-URC-3SD scheme having a classical transmission rate of 0.75 cbit-s/use. We have therefore assume a coding rate of 0.5 for the IRCC. Figure 5.11 shows the EXIT curves for our 3-qubit SD at a depolarizing probability of 0.1. The optimized IRCC weights are given in Table 5.5, where only five subcodes are activated. For $p \leq 0.1$, the system successfully converges and the decoding trajectory terminates at the $(1, 1)$ point of the EXIT chart. Since our 3SD transmits 1.5 cbits/use and we have used 1/2-rate IRCC, the effective throughput of the designed system is 0.75 cbits/use. The corresponding depolarizing probability according to the bit-based capacity curve of Figure 5.5 is $p^* = 0.11$. Thus, in terms of the depolarizing probability, our designed system operates within $\left[10 \times \log_{10}\left(\frac{0.11}{0.10}\right)\right] = 0.4$ dB of the capacity. Furthermore, the area under the normalized EXIT curve of the inner decoder is 0.5209. The deviation from the capacity curve is therefore $[0.0209 \times 1.5] \approx 0.031$ cbits/use.

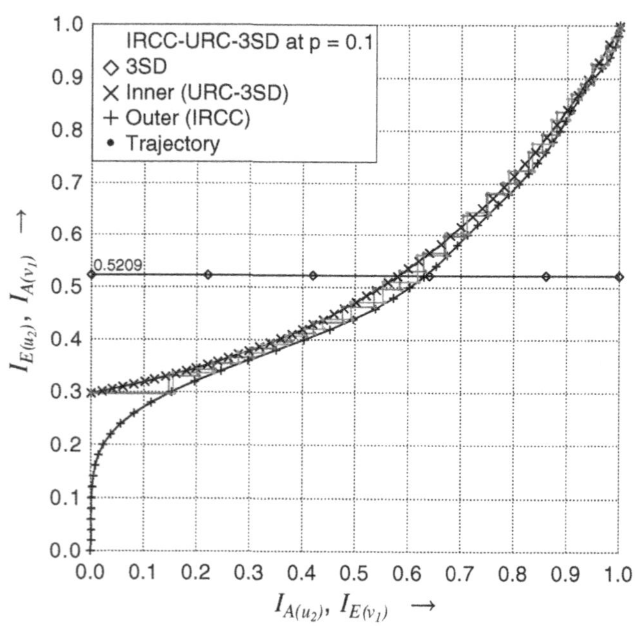


**Figure 5.11** Normalized EXIT curves of the IRCC-URC-3SD system at a depolarizing probability of 0.1 using the simulation parameters of Table 5.5. *Source*: [210]/IEEE.

**Table 5.5** Simulation parameters of the IRCC-URC-SD scheme of Figure 5.4.

| SD scheme | 3-qubit |
|---|---|
| IRCC coding rate | 1/2 |
| IRCC active subcodes | $\varrho_6 = 0.2641$, $\varrho_7 = 0.4062$, $\varrho_{12} = 0.1068$, $\varrho_{13} = 0.1247$, $\varrho_{17} = 0.0982$ |
| Interleaver length | 30,000 bits |
| Overall system rate | 0.75 cbits/use |

We have further evaluated the corresponding BER performance in Figure 5.12 for the simulation parameters of Table 5.5. Analogous to our IRCC-URC-2SD scheme in Figure 5.8, the performance in Figure 5.12 improves upon increasing the number of iterations. Particularly, the system converges for $p \leq 0.1$, which conforms to our EXIT chart predictions of Figure 5.11. Furthermore, for $p \leq 0.1$, the performance tends to approach the noise limit of $p^* = 0.11$. This is also demonstrated in Figure 5.13, which plots the distance from the capacity (dB) at a BER of $10^{-4}$ as a function of the number of iterations. As observed previously for our 2SD scheme, the performance converges towards the noise limit, as the number of iterations increases, but this happens with diminishing returns at higher number of iterations.

We have further benchmarked the performance of our IRCC-URC-SD system of Figure 5.4 against the classical turbo code (TC) in Figure 5.14 for both 2SD and 3SD designs. This was achieved by replacing the IRCC-URC unit

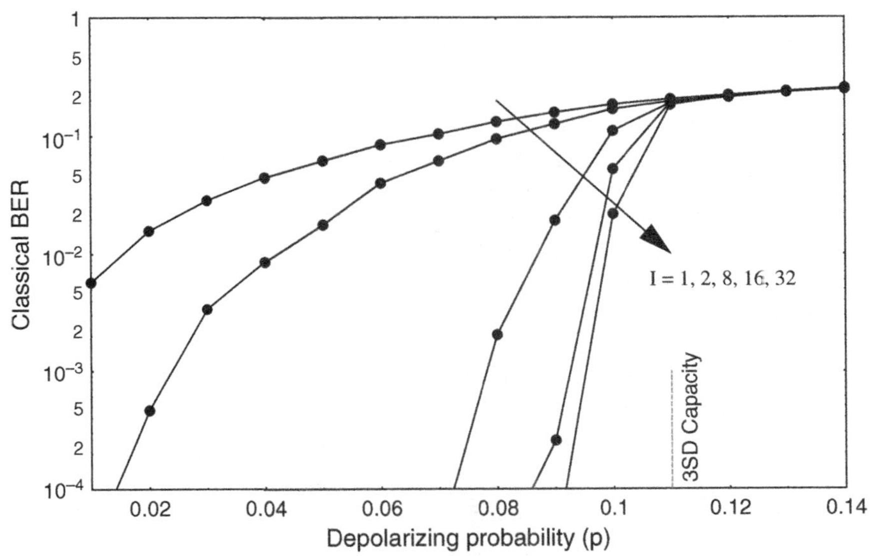


**Figure 5.12** Achievable BER performance of the IRCC-URC-3SD scheme of Figure 5.4 with increasing number of iterations, i.e. $\text{I} = \{1, 2, 8, 16, 32\}$. The simulation parameters are summarized in Table 5.5. The dashed line at $p^* = 0.11$ marks the noise limit for a classical information rate of 0.75 cbits/use, which is obtained from the bit-based EACC curve of 3SD given in Figure 5.5.

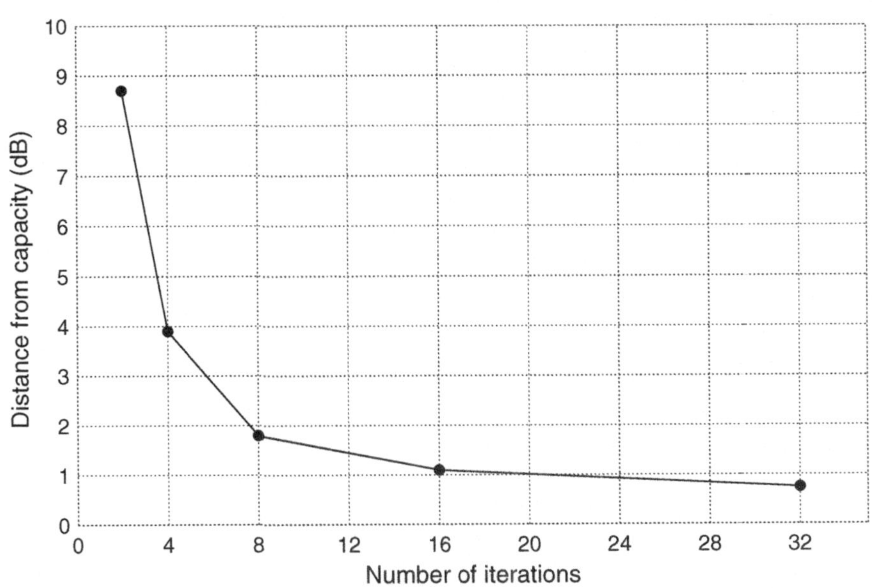


**Figure 5.13** Performance of the IRCC-URC-3SD scheme of Figure 5.12 at a BER of $10^{-4}$, which is quantified in terms of the distance from the bit-based EACC of 3SD, i.e. $p^* = 0.11$, as the number of iterations is increased.

of Figure 5.4 with TC.[7] We have used a memory-3 1/2-rate TC for our comparison, since it invokes 16 states in each iteration, which is the same as the number of states invoked per iteration in our design.[8] The uncoded BER curves of our 2SD and 3SD schemes are also plotted in Figure 5.14. Furthermore, we have used a sufficiently high number of iterations, i.e. $I = 32$, for our designed system to ensure that the system reaches the top right corner of the EXIT chart at a depolarizing probability that is close to the noise limit. More specifically, as observed in Figures 5.9 and 5.13 for the 2SD and 3SD schemes, respectively, doubling the number of iterations from 16 to 32 improves the performance only slightly. Therefore, we can safely assume that if the increasing the number of iterations may not improve the performance appreciably. By contrast, $I = 16$ iterations were used for TC since it did not yield any appreciable performance improvement, when the number of iterations was increased beyond $I = 8$, as evidenced in Figure 5.14. Our proposed IRCC-URC-SD system is capable of performing closer to the capacity, hence outperforming the turbo code for both 2SD and 3SD. The corresponding distances from the capacity expressed in terms of dB at a BER of $10^{-4}$ are tabulated in Table 5.6, where the noise limits for 2SD and 3SD are $p^* = 0.165$ and $p^*$ 0.11, respectively.

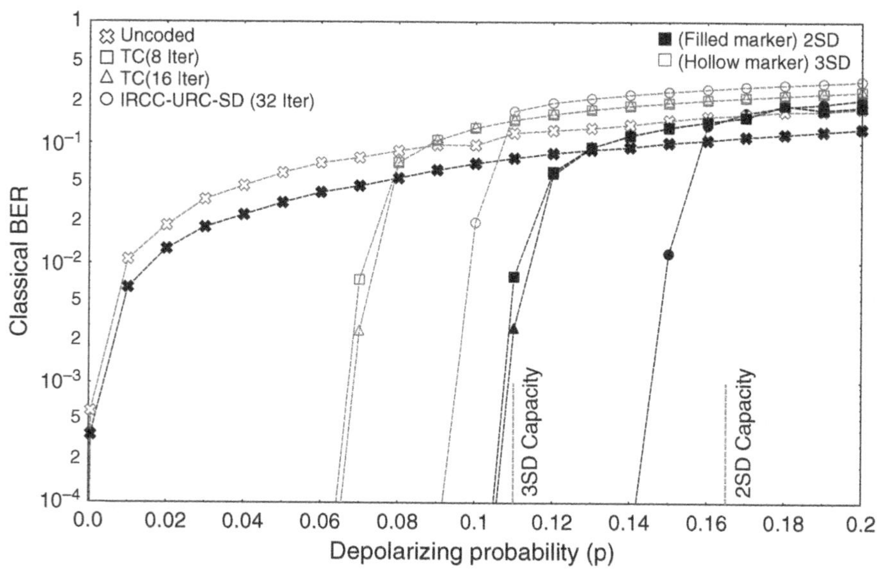


**Figure 5.14** Comparison of the achievable BER performance of our IRCC-URC-SD scheme with TC-SD having a memory-3 1/2-rate TC as the outer component. 2SD and 3SD schemes are plotted with filled and hollow markers, respectively, and their simulation parameters are summarized in Tables 5.4 and 5.5, respectively. Uncoded BER curves for both 2SD and 3SD are also plotted for comparison. Results are summarized in Table 5.6. *Source*: [210]/IEEE.

**Table 5.6** Distance of the TC-SD and IRCC-URC-SD schemes from the capacity at a BER of $10^{-4}$ using the performance curves of Figure 5.14.

| | TC-SD | IRCC-URC-SD |
|---|---|---|
| 2SD | 1.9 dB | 0.6 dB |
| 3SD | 2.2 dB | 0.75 dB |

7 Symbol-to-bit conversion takes place at the output of SD decoder. Consequently, the symbol-based probabilities of Eqs. (5.15) and (5.18) are converted to bit-based LLRs, assuming that the bits constituting the symbol are independent.
8 Since a memory-3 turbo code has two components with $2^3$ states, total number of states per iteration is $2 \times 2^3 = 16$. Similarly, a memory-4 IRCC invokes $2^4 = 16$ states per iteration.

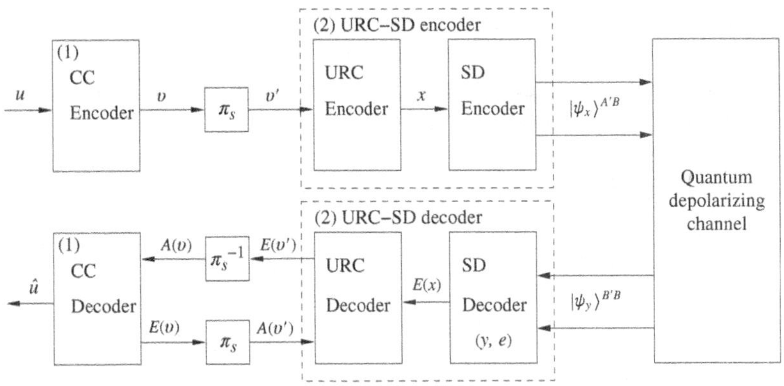


**Figure 5.15** Schematic of the proposed symbol-based CC-URC-SD classical-quantum communication system. *Source:* [211]/IEEE.

## 5.7 Symbol-based Code Structure

Since the design of Figure 5.4 uses a bit interleaver and hence bit-based iterative decoding, symbol-to-bit conversion is invoked before the related soft-information is fed from the inner decoder (URC-SD) to the outer decoder (IRCC). This in turn incurs a capacity loss. As gleaned from Figure 5.5, for a 2SD scheme having a classical information rate of 1 cbit/use, a bit-based system ensures reliable transmission for $p \leq 0.165$, while a symbol-based system would increase the noise limit to $p^* = 0.1875$. Therefore, a bit-based error correction scheme incurs a capacity loss of around 0.6 dB as compared to its symbol-based counterpart. This capacity loss was previously identified in [224] for classical discrete-memoryless channels, and a modified binary LDPC code was proposed to circumvent this issue. Similarly, to circumvent the quantum channel capacity loss, we have conceived an iterative code design for symbol-based CC-URC-2SD, which incorporates a single CC as the outer component, while the URC and 2SD schemes constitute the amalgamated inner code.

Figure 5.15 shows the proposed system model. At the transmitter, the system is fed with classical bits $\{u\}$, which are encoded by a 1/2-rate CC. The encoded 4-ary coded symbols $v = (v_1\ v_2)$ are then interleaved by a symbol interleaver ($\pi_s$), yielding the permuted symbol stream $v'$, which is fed to the symbol-based recursive URC having a generator polynomial of $G(D) = \frac{1}{1+D}$ [125]. Similar to the bit-based design of Figure 5.4, classical-to-quantum domain conversion then takes place at the SD encoder of Figure 5.15 and the encoded qubits $|\psi_x\rangle^{A'B}$ are serially transmitted over the quantum depolarizing channel. The receiver of Figure 5.15 is also same as that of Figure 5.4 with the bit interleaver replaced by a symbol interleaver.

Since our proposed model of Figure 5.15 relies on symbol-based iterative decoding, we invoke non-binary EXIT charts of [125, 216, 219] for the sake of achieving a near-capacity performance.

## 5.8 Results and Discussion II

Using the non-binary EXIT-charts, we have optimized our iterative code structure of Figure 5.15 to design a system with a coding rate of 1 cbit/use. According to the symbol-based capacity curve of Figure 5.5, the corresponding noise limit for our system is $p^* = 0.1875$.

**Design Objective I:** *For the sake of comparing the symbol-based scheme of Figure 5.15 with the bit-based scheme of Figure 5.4, which uses a 1/2-rate memory-4 IRCC, find the optimal 1/2-rate memory-4 convolutional code, which gives the best match with URC-2SD in the CC-URC-2SD configuration, when symbol-based iterative decoding is invoked.*

For the sake of achieving this objective, we created the EXIT curves of all the possible 1/2-rate memory-4 convolutional codes by evaluating all legitimate generator polynomials to find the optimal code $\mathcal{C}$, which yields a marginally open tunnel at the highest possible channel depolarizing probability. The EXIT characteristics of some of these (2, 1, 4) CCs are plotted in Figure 5.16 along with the inner decoder EXIT curve of the URC-2SD scheme at $p = 0.15$ and $p = 0.16$. As gleaned from the figure, all outer decoder EXIT curves plotted in "solid" lines exhibit a convergence threshold of $p_{\text{th}} = 0.15$, i.e. a marginally open tunnel exists for $p = 0.15$. If the depolarizing probability is increased beyond 0.15, the inner and outer decoder EXIT curves will cross over, thereby closing the tunnel.

By contrast, the pair of outer decoder EXIT curves plotted in "dashed" lines have $p_{\text{th}} < 0.15$. Hence, our desired optimal code $\mathcal{C}$ is one of those associated with $p_{\text{th}} = 0.15$. It may be further observed in Figure 5.16 that the EXIT curve labeled as "Optimal Outer", whose octally represented generator polynomials are $(g_1, g_2) = (31, 36)_8$, converges faster than the others.[9] Therefore, we have selected it as our optimal outer component.

The BER performance of the optimal CC of Figure 5.16 is recorded in Figure 5.17 using the simulation parameters of Figure 5.7. As it can be observed, the turbo-cliff formulation starts around $p = 0.15$, which matches the

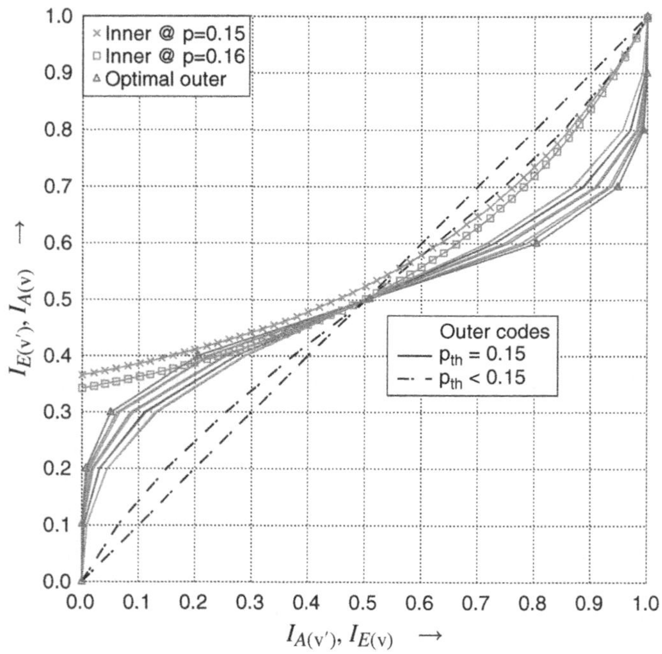


**Figure 5.16** Normalized EXIT curves of the CC-URC-2SD system. Various 1/2-rate memory-4 convolutional codes were used as outer components. The optimal outer code has generator polynomials $(g_1, g_2) = (31, 36)_8$. *Source*: [211]/IEEE.

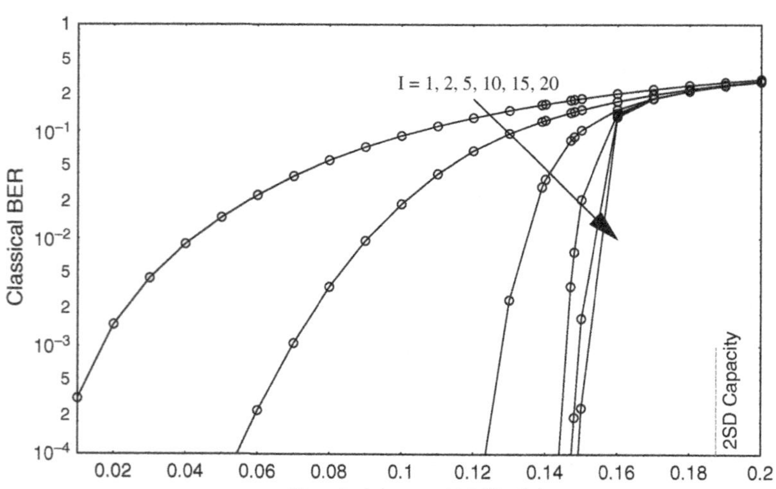


**Figure 5.17** Achievable BER performance of the CC-URC-2SD scheme of Figure 5.15 with increasing number of iterations, i.e. $\mathtt{I} = \{1, 2, 5, 10, 15, 20\}$. Simulation parameters are summarized in Table 5.7. The dashed line at $p^* = 0.1875$ marks the noise limit for a classical information rate of 1 cbit/use, which is obtained from the symbol-based EACC curve of 2SD given in Figure 5.5.

9 The optimal outer code yields the widest area between the inner and outer EXIT curves after the (0.5, 0.5)-point. This signifies that fewer decoding iterations are required.

**Table 5.7** Simulation parameters of the CC-URC-2SD scheme of Figure 5.15.

| | |
|---|---|
| SD scheme | 2-qubit |
| Interleaver length | 30,000 bits |
| Overall system rate | 1 cbits/use |
| **Convolutional code** | |
| Coding rate | 1/2 |
| Memory | 4 |
| $(g_1, g_2)$ | $(31, 36)_8$ |

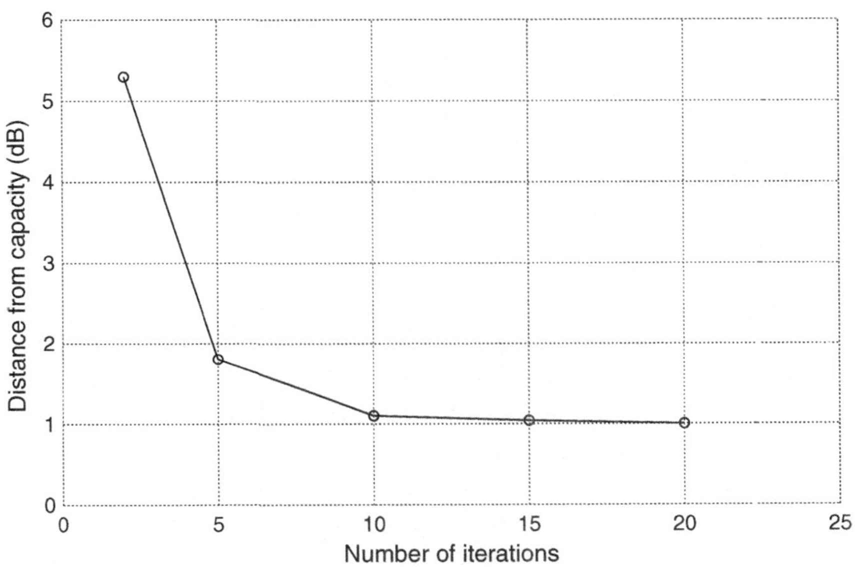


**Figure 5.18** Performance of the CC-URC-2SD scheme of Figure 5.17, at a BER of $10^{-4}$, which is quantified in terms of the distance from the symbol-based EACC of 2SD, i.e. $p^* = 0.1875$, as the number of iterations is increased.

convergence threshold predicted using EXIT charts. More specifically, at $p \leq 0.15$, the system converges to a low BER as the number of iterations increases, while for $p \geq 0.16$, the performance fails to improve upon increasing the number of iterations. This is because, as shown in Figure 5.16, the EXIT chart tunnel closes at $p = 0.16$. Thus, the system fails to converge to a low BER for $p \geq 0.16$. It may also be observed that the performance only moderately improves with diminishing returns at higher number of iterations. Furthermore, since doubling the number of iterations from $\mathtt{I} = 10$ to $\mathtt{I} = 20$ only improves the performance slightly at a BER of $10^{-4}$, we may conclude that $\mathtt{I} = 20$ iterations are sufficient to approach the $(1, 1)$-point of near-perfect convergence. This is also demonstrated in Figure 5.18, where the distance from the capacity in dBs is plotted at a BER of $10^{-4}$ for the increasing number of iterations. We may observe in Figure 5.18 that there is only a negligible improvement in performance when the number of iterations is increased from 15 to 20.

We further compare our symbol-based CC-URC-2SD to the bit-based IRCC-URC-2SD of Figure 5.4 in Figure 5.19, where the uncoded BER of 2SD is also plotted. It may be observed that both systems have the same convergence threshold of $p = 0.15$, which is within $[10 \times \log_{10}(\frac{0.15}{0.1875})] = 1$ dB of the achievable noise limit. Since an IRCC has a higher encoding and decoding structural complexity than a single-component CC, we can achieve the same convergence threshold at a lower encoding/decoding structural complexity using the symbol-based scheme. Furthermore, the CC-URC-2SD system exhibits an improved BER performance compared to the IRCC-URC-2SD scheme, as shown in Figure 5.19. After $\mathtt{I} = 2$ iterations, the IRCC-URC-2SD arrangement yields a BER of $10^{-4}$ at $p = 0.0225$, while the CC-URC-SD scheme has a BER of $10^{-4}$ at $p = 0.0525$. Therefore, CC-URC-2SD outperforms

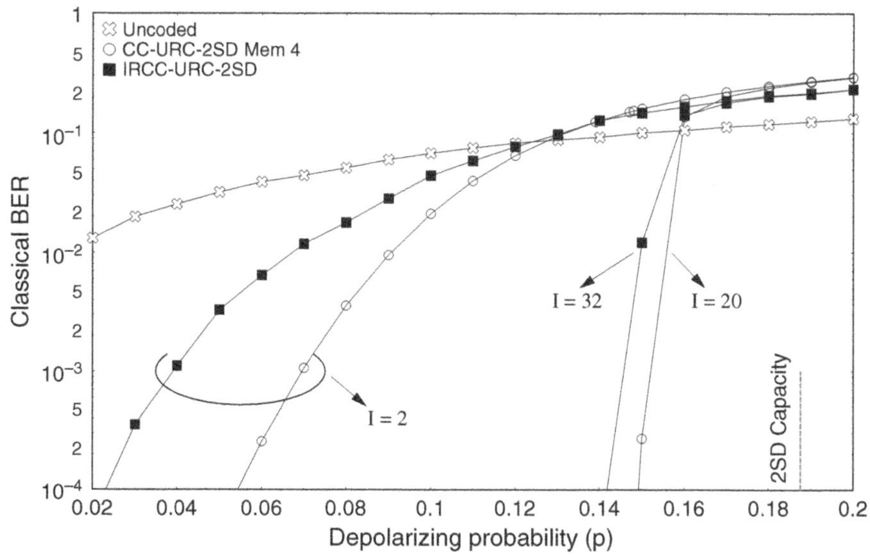


**Figure 5.19** Comparison of the achievable BER performance of the bit-based IRCC-URC-2SD of Figure 5.4 and the symbol-based CC-URC-2SD design of Figure 5.15 using the simulation parameters of Tables 5.4 and 5.7, respectively.

the IRCC-URC-2SD arrangement by $[10 \times \log_{10}(\frac{0.0225}{0.0525})] = 3.7$ dB. Moreover, as demonstrated in Figure 5.8, the IRCC-URC-2SD scheme achieves perfect convergence after about $\mathtt{I} = 32$ iterations, while only $\mathtt{I} = 20$ iterations are sufficient for the symbol-based CC-URC-2SD. We further benchmark the performance against the achievable symbol-based capacity of $p^* = 0.1875$. At a BER of $10^{-4}$ and after a sufficiently high number of iterations ($\mathtt{I} = 20$ for CC-URC-2SD and $\mathtt{I} = 32$ for IRCC-URC-2SD), the CC-URC-2SD scheme operates within $[10 \times \log_{10}(\frac{0.149}{0.1875})] =$ 1 dB of the capacity, while the IRCC-URC-2SD regime exhibits a deviation of $[10 \times \log_{10}(\frac{0.142}{0.1875})] = 1.2$ dB from the capacity. Thus, the performance of both systems becomes comparable, once perfect convergence is achieved. However, the IRCC-URC-2SD scheme requires 60% more iterations than the symbol-based CC-URC-2SD arrangement.

**Design Objective II:** *Find the optimal* 1/2*-rate memory-*2 *and memory-*3 *convolutional codes, which exhibit the best EXIT-curve shape match with URC-2SD in the CC-URC-2SD configuration, when symbol-based iterative decoding is invoked.*

Again, for the sake of finding the optimal memory-2 and memory-3 outer components, we created the EXIT curves for all the possible codes, as we previously did in Figure 5.16. It was found that the CC(2, 1, 2) having the generators $(g_1, g_2) = (7, 5)_8$ and the CC(2, 1, 3) with generators $(g_1, g_2) = (17, 15)_8$ yield the best match. The corresponding EXIT curves for the optimized memory-2 and memory-3 CCs are plotted in Figure 5.20 together with the optimal memory-4 CC of Figure 5.16. All codes have the same decoding convergence threshold. The corresponding BER performance is compared in Figure 5.21 after both 2 and 20 iterations. The CC associated with a higher constraint length exhibits a lower BER before perfect convergence is achieved, e.g. after 2 iterations as shown in Figure 5.21. Furthermore, after 20 iterations, all codes have a similar performance at a BER of $10^{-4}$. Codes having a lower constraint length have the additional benefit of a lower decoding complexity, since fewer states are invoked per iteration. We have further compared the optimized symbol-based CC-URC-2SD designs for varying constraint lengths to the bit-based IRCC-URC-2SD in Table 5.8 by quantifying their performance at a BER of $10^{-4}$ in terms of the distance (dB) from the noise limit of $p^* = 0.1875$. All the three symbol-based configurations outperform the bit-based IRCC-URC-2SD scheme.

## 5.9 Summary and Conclusion

In this chapter, we have conceived both bit-based as well as symbol-based concatenated classical-quantum code structures for entanglement-assisted classical communication over a quantum depolarizing channel. We commenced with a review of the SD protocol in Section 5.2, which facilitates the transmission of $N$ classical bits by sending only $(N-1)$ qubits over the noisy quantum channel, while one qubit is pre-shared with the receiver.

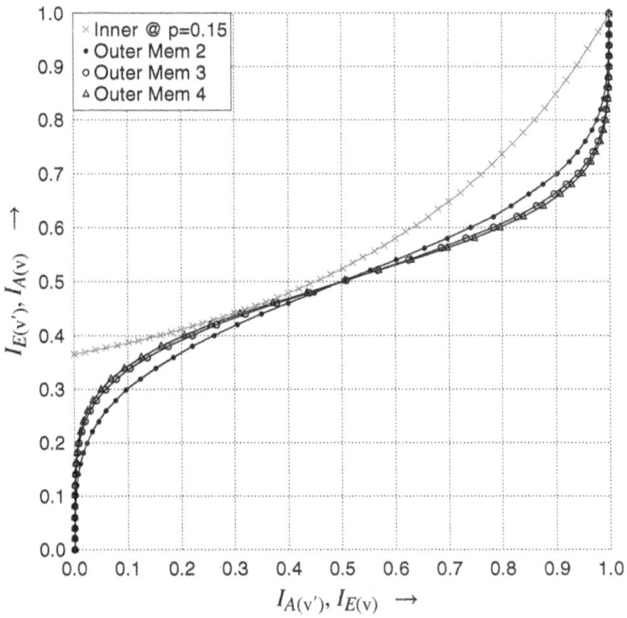


**Figure 5.20** Normalized EXIT curves of the CC-URC-2SD system optimized for varying constraint lengths. Optimal outer components are plotted here: CC(2, 1, 2) with $(g_1, g_2) = (7, 5)_8$, CC(2, 1, 3) with $(g_1, g_2) = (17, 15)_8$ and CC(2, 1, 4) with $(g_1, g_2) = (31, 36)_8$. *Source*: [211]/IEEE.

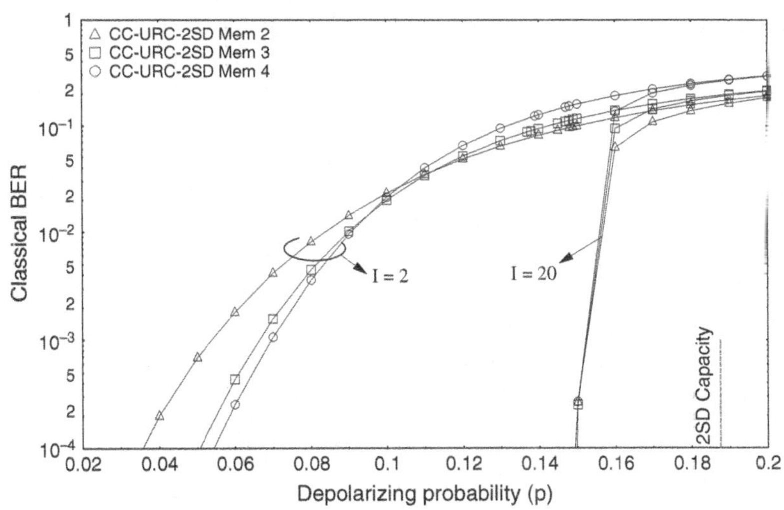


**Figure 5.21** Comparison of the achievable BER performance of the symbol-based CC-URC-2SD design of Figure 5.15 optimized for varying constraint lengths. Optimal CCs are: CC(2, 1, 2) with $(g_1, g_2) = (7, 5)_8$, CC(2, 1, 3) with $(g_1, g_2) = (17, 15)_8$ and CC(2, 1, 4) with $(g_1, g_2) = (31, 36)_8$. Other simulation parameters are same as Table 5.7.

This results in a transmission rate of 2 cbits/use for the 2SD protocol of Section 5.2.1 and a rate of $\frac{N}{N-1}$ cbits/use for the general NSD scheme of Section 5.2.2. We then derived the EACC for the general NSD transmission in Section 5.3, which was also customized for the 2SD and 3SD schemes. In Section 5.4, we presented our proposed bit-based IRCC-URC-SD system of Figure 5.4, which relies on channel coding operating in the classical domain by serially concatenating an IRCC and a URC-aided SD encoder. Furthermore, we have introduced a soft-decision-aided SD decoder facilitating iterative decoding. More specifically, the URC and SD constitute the amalgamated inner component, while the IRCC constitutes the outer component. Therefore, iterative decoding is invoked for

**Table 5.8** Comparison of the symbol-based CC-URC-2SD schemes having the optimized CC(2, 1, 2), CC(2, 1, 3), and CC(2, 1, 4) of Figure 5.21 to the bit-based IRCC-URC-2SD design of Figure 5.19 quantified in terms of the distance from the capacity (noise limit $p^* = 0.1875$) at a BER of $10^{-4}$. Here "$\infty$" denotes "sufficiently high" number of iterations for ensuring near-perfect convergence, which is assumed to be $\mathtt{I} = 20$ for CC-URC-2SD and $\mathtt{I} = 32$ for IRCC-URC-2SD.

| Outer code | $\mathtt{I} = 2$ | $\mathtt{I} \rightarrow \infty$ |
|---|---|---|
| CC(2, 1, 2) | 7.2 dB | 1 dB |
| CC(2, 1, 3) | 5.7 dB | 1 dB |
| CC(2, 1, 4) | 5.5 dB | 1 dB |
| IRCC | 9.2 dB | 1.2 dB |

exchanging *extrinsic* information between the inner (URC-SD) and outer (IRCC) decoders. Furthermore, we presented our EXIT-chart-aided near-capacity design criterion in Section 5.5 and demonstrated how the IRCC weighting coefficients have to be optimized for ensuring that a marginally open tunnel exists between the inner and outer decoders' EXIT curves at the highest possible depolarizing probability.

We then evaluated the performance of our bit-based IRCC-URC-SD design for 2SD and 3SD in Sections 5.6.1 and 5.6.2, respectively, which was benchmarked against the bit-based EACC given in Figure 5.5. It was demonstrated that our BER performance curves of Figures 5.8 and 5.12 conform to the EXIT chart predictions of Figures 5.7 and 5.11, respectively. Furthermore, the proposed system of Figure 5.4 operates within 0.4 dB of the achievable noise limit for both 2SD as well as 3SD schemes. More specifically, our design exhibits a deviation of only 0.062 and 0.031 cbits/use from the corresponding 2-qubit and 3-qubit capacity limits, respectively. We also benchmarked our system against the classical convolutional and turbo codes in Figures 5.10 and 5.14, respectively. It was shown in Figure 5.14 that the TC-2SD scheme operates within 1.9 dB of the capacity at a BER of $10^{-4}$, while the performance of our bit-based IRCC-URC-2SD is only 0.6 dB from the capacity. Similarly, the TC-3SD scheme is 2.5 dB from the capacity at a BER of $10^{-4}$ in contrast to the bit-based IRCC-URC-3SD, which operates within 0.75 dB.

Our bit-based code structure of Figure 5.4 incurs a capacity loss due to the symbol-to-bit conversion, as quantified in Figure 5.5. To overcome this capacity loss, we conceived a symbol-based code design in Section 5.7, which employs a single-component CC and a symbol interleaver in contrast to the IRCC and bit interleaver of Figure 5.4. We optimized our symbol-based CC-URC-2SD design with the aid of non-binary EXIT charts in Figure 5.16. Our simulation results of Section 5.8 demonstrated that the symbol-based CC-URC-2SD provides a significant BER performance improvement, despite its lower encoding/decoding complexity than that of the bit-based IRCC-URC-2SD. Quantitatively, after 2 iterations, our proposed symbol-based CC-URC-2SD design incorporating a memory-4 CC outperformed the bit-based IRCC-URC-2SD scheme by 3.7 dB at a BER of $10^{-4}$, as evidenced in Figure 5.19. Furthermore, the bit-based IRCC-URC-2SD arrangement required around 60% more iterations than the symbol-based CC-URC-2SD for achieving perfect decoding convergence. We also demonstrated in Figure 5.21 that the decoding complexity can be further reduced by using memory-2 and memory-3 CCs, which rely on only 4 and 8 states, respectively, per iteration. It was found in Figure 5.21 that even the memory-2 and memory-3 designs outperform the bit-based IRCC-URC-2SD. Finally, the performances of our bit-based IRCC-URC-SD ($\mathtt{I} = 32$) as well as the symbol-based CC-URC-SD ($\mathtt{I} = 20$) at a BER of $10^{-4}$ are summarized in Figure 5.22, along with the TC-SD ($\mathtt{I} = 16$) benchmark. To dispense with the exhaustive search, it may be helpful to conceive a symbol-based IRCC, whose weighting coefficients can be dynamically adapted to provide the best EXIT-curve match with that of a given inner code, as also discussed in Chapter 13.

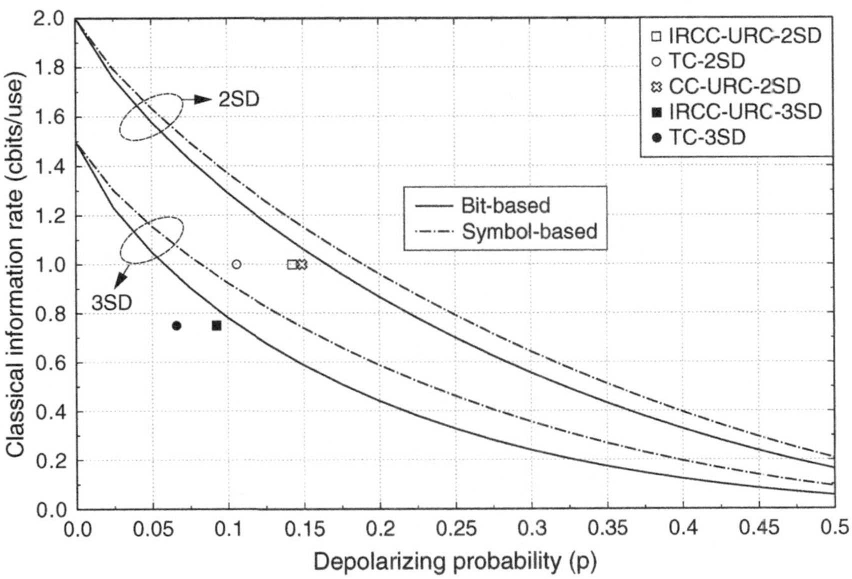


**Figure 5.22** Classical information rate (cbits/use) versus the quantum depolarizing probability for bit-based and symbol-based 2SD as well as 3SD schemes. The performance of our designed bit-based IRCC-URC-SD ($\mathtt{I} = 32$) and symbol-based CC-URC-SD ($\mathtt{I} = 20$), along with the TC-SD ($\mathtt{I} = 16$) benchmark, are compared at a BER of $10^{-4}$.

To conclude, in this chapter, we exploited classical redundancy for the reliable transmission of classical information over a quantum channel. Consequently, this design approach is only appropriate when the information to be transmitted is classical. For more general quantum communication systems, which may transmit classical as well as quantum information, and for quantum computation systems, it is vital to invoke quantum error correction codes, hence exploiting the redundancy in the quantum domain. In this spirit, we detail the design principles for constructing quantum codes from the known classical codes in the next chapter.

# Part II

# Near-term Quantum Codes

# 6

# Quantum Coding Bounds and a Closed-form Approximation of the Minimum Distance Versus Quantum Coding Rate

Having paved the way for the classical to quantum coding evolution throughout the chapters of Part I, in this chapter of Part II we commence by outlining some quantum coding bounds derived from the classical coding bounds as a function of code-rate and codeword length. In Chapter 7 we will then discuss the design and performance of diverse quantum topological error correction codes (QTECCs). These discussions will be followed in Chapter 8 by demonstrating how to apply them for the protection of quantum gates. The last chapter of Part II, namely Chapter 9, will finally highlight the so-called "universal decoding" principles, which are applicable for the decoding of any arbitrary linear codes. The associated performance results are based on Bose–Chaudhuri–Hocquenghem (BCH) and polar codes.

## 6.1 Introduction

To return to the subject of this chapter, the trade-off between the coding rate and the minimum distance as well as the codeword length is widely acknowledged in designing classical error correction codes. Since most of the QSCs are derived from their classical counterparts, the same problem persists. Even though extensive efforts have been invested in designing the QSCs, the question of how to determine the realistically achievable minimum distance $d$ of a QSC given the quantum coding rate $r_Q$ and codeword length $n$ remains unresolved. For example, for a given codeword length of $n = 128$ and quantum coding rate of $r_Q = 1/2$, the achievable minimum distance is loosely bounded by $11 < d < 22$, while for $n = 1024$ and $r_Q = 1/2$, the achievable minimum distance is bounded by $78 < d < 157$. Naturally, having such a wide range of estimated minimum distance is undesirable. For binary classical codes, this problem has been circumvented by the closed-form approximation proposed by Akhtman *et al.* [91]. Therefore, in this chapter, we present an appealingly simple and invertible closed-form approximation for determining the realistically achievable minimum distance of a QSC, given the codeword length $n$ and the quantum coding rate $r_Q$. Our formulation is suitable for both the idealized asymptotical case and for the practical finite-length codeword. Furthermore, our proposed closed-form approximation is also applicable to the family of EA-QSCs.

This chapter is organized as follows. In Section 6.2, we survey the existing quantum coding bounds and derive the bounds by exploiting the classical-to-quantum isomorphism. This is followed by our closed-form approximation proposed for the idealized asymptotical limit in Section 6.3. Since the asymptotical limit has limited relevance when it comes to practical implementations, we also proposed an approximation for practical finite-length codewords. To unify the quantum coding bound approximation for both entanglement-assisted and unassisted QSCs, we derive a closed-form approximation for arbitrarily entangled QSCs in Section 6.5. Finally, we conclude this chapter in Section 6.6.

## 6.2 On Classical to Quantum Coding Bounds

In this section, we present the quantum version of the most well-known classical coding bounds, namely the Singleton bound [225] and Hamming bound [226], which serve as the upper bounds, as well as the Gilbert–Varshamov (GV) bound [227], which acts as the lower bound. Although there are several ways of deriving the coding bounds in the quantum domain, we are interested in exploring the duality of coding bounds in the classical and quantum domains. Therefore, we present the derivation of quantum coding bounds using the classical-to-quantum isomorphism approach, and demonstrate that the final results agree with the coding bounds that are derived from a purely quantum-domain perspective.

### 6.2.1 Singleton Bound

The Singleton bound of classical binary code constructions $\mathcal{C}(n,k,d)$ is defined as

$$n-k \geq d-1, \tag{6.1}$$

where the notation $n$ denotes the codeword length, $k$ for the length of the uncoded information segment, and $d$ is the minimum distance among the legitimate codewords in the codebook $\mathcal{C}$. The Singleton bound acts as an upper bound in classical code constructions. The bound implies that the number of rows in a PCM associated with the length of the syndrome vector, which is equal to $(n-k)$, has to be greater than $(d-1)$. For the QSC $\mathcal{C}[n,k,d]$, the rows of the PCM correspond to the number of stabilizer operators. Since the stabilizer formalism has to correct both the bit-flip errors and the phase-flip errors, the classical Singleton bound of Eq. (6.1) can be readily transformed into the quantum Singleton bound as follows:

$$n-k \geq 2(d-1), \tag{6.2}$$

where $n$ now may also be referred to as the number of physical qubits and $k$ is the number of logical qubits. In order to show explicitly the trade-off between the minimum distance and the quantum coding rate, Eq. (6.2) can be modified to

$$\frac{k}{n} \leq 1-2\left(\frac{d-1}{n}\right). \tag{6.3}$$

In the quantum domain, the Singleton bound is also known as the Knill–Laflamme bound [85]. The QSCs achieving the quantum Singleton bound by satisfying the equality are classified as the quantum Maximum Distance Separable (MDS) codes. One of the well-known QSCs having a minimum distance of $d=3$ that reaches the quantum Singleton bound is the "perfect" 5-qubit code $\mathcal{C}[n,k,d]=\mathcal{C}[5,1,3]$.

### 6.2.2 Hamming Bound

In classical binary coding, a codebook $\mathcal{C}(n,k,d)$ maps the information words containing $k$ bits into a codeword of length $n$ bits. The maximal number of errors, which is denoted by $t$ that can be corrected by codebook $\mathcal{C}$ is given by

$$t=\lfloor\frac{d-1}{2}\rfloor. \tag{6.4}$$

Therefore the maximum size of a binary codebook $|\mathcal{C}|=2^k$ is bounded by the sphere-packing bound, which is defined as:

$$2^k \leq \frac{2^n}{\sum_{j=0}^{t=\left\lfloor\frac{d-1}{2}\right\rfloor}\binom{n}{j}}. \tag{6.5}$$

Since the QSCs have to correct three different types of errors – namely the bit-flip errors (**X**), phase-flip errors (**Z**), and both bit-flip and phase-flip errors (**Y**) – the size of the codebook for a QSC $\mathcal{C}[n,k,d]$ is now bounded by

$$2^k \leq \frac{2^n}{\sum_{j=0}^{t=\left\lfloor\frac{d-1}{2}\right\rfloor}\binom{n}{j}3^j}. \tag{6.6}$$

By modifying Eq. (6.6), we can express explicitly the bound of the quantum coding rate as a function of the minimum distance $d$ and codeword length $n$, as shown in the following:

$$\frac{k}{n} \leq 1 - \frac{1}{n}\log_2\left(\sum_{j=0}^{t=\left\lfloor \frac{d-1}{2} \right\rfloor} \binom{n}{j} 3^j\right). \tag{6.7}$$

If $n$ tends to $\infty$, we obtain

$$\frac{k}{n} \leq 1 - \left(\frac{d}{2n}\right)\log_2 3 - H\left(\frac{d}{2n}\right), \tag{6.8}$$

where $H(x)$ is the binary entropy of $x$ formulated as $H(x) = -x\log_2 x - (1-x)\log_2(1-x)$. Equations (6.7) and (6.8) are also known as the quantum Hamming bound [58], which constitutes the upper bound for QSC constructions.

### 6.2.3 Gilbert–Varshamov Bound

The analogy exploited to derive the quantum Hamming bound may also be used for transforming the classical Gilbert–Varshamov (GV) bound, namely the lower bound for classical code constructions, into its quantum counterpart. In the classical domain, the GV bound for classical codes $\mathcal{C}(n,k,d)$ is formulated as

$$2^k \geq \frac{2^n}{\sum_{j=0}^{d-1}\binom{n}{j}}. \tag{6.9}$$

Considering that the QSCs have to tackle three different types of errors, the size of the codebook $\mathcal{C}[n,k,d]$ is bounded by

$$2^k \geq \frac{2^n}{\sum_{j=0}^{d-1}\binom{n}{j}3^j}. \tag{6.10}$$

Hence, we can readily derive the quantum GV bound, the lower bound of the quantum coding rate as a function of the minimum distance $d$ and codeword length $n$ as follows:

$$\frac{k}{n} \geq 1 - \frac{1}{n}\log_2\left(\sum_{j=0}^{d-1}\binom{n}{j}3^j\right). \tag{6.11}$$

Again, if $n$ approaches $\infty$, we obtain

$$\frac{k}{n} \geq 1 - \left(\frac{d}{n}\right)\log_2 3 - H\left(\frac{d}{n}\right), \tag{6.12}$$

where $H(x)$ is the binary entropy of $x$. The quantum GV bounds in Eqs. (6.11) and (6.12) are valid for non-CSS QSCs. However, a special case should be considered for dual-containing quantum CSS codes. It will be shown in Section 6.4 that for some dual-containing CSS codes, the code constructions violate the quantum GV bound. Hence, a special bound has to be derived to accommodate the dual-containing CSS codes. In the classical domain, a binary code $\mathcal{C}(n,k,d)$ maps a $k$-bit information word into an $n$-bit encoded codeword. The number of syndrome measurement operators is determined by the number of rows in the PCM $\mathbf{H}$ of $\mathcal{C}(n,k,d)$, which is equal to $2^{(n-k)}$. With a simple modification of Eq. (6.9), the number of syndrome measurement operators in $\mathcal{C}(n,k,d)$ is bounded by

$$2^{(n-k)} \leq \left(\sum_{j=0}^{d-1}\binom{n}{j}\right). \tag{6.13}$$

**Table 6.1** Comparison of various classical and quantum coding bounds.

| Coding bound | Asymptotic | |
|---|---|---|
| | Classical | Quantum |
| Singleton | $\frac{k}{n} \leq 1-\left(\frac{d}{n}\right)$ | $\frac{k}{n} \leq 1-2\left(\frac{d}{n}\right)$ |
| Hamming | $\frac{k}{n} \leq 1-H\left(\frac{d}{2n}\right)$ | $\frac{k}{n} \leq 1-\left(\frac{d}{2n}\right)\log_2 3-H\left(\frac{d}{2n}\right)$ |
| GV | $\frac{k}{n} \geq 1-H\left(\frac{d}{n}\right)$ | $\frac{k}{n} \geq 1-\left(\frac{d}{n}\right)\log_2 3-H\left(\frac{d}{n}\right)$ |
| **Coding bound** | **Finite-length** | |
| | **Classical** | **Quantum** |
| Singleton | $\frac{k}{n} \leq 1-\left(\frac{d-1}{n}\right)$ | $\frac{k}{n} \leq 1-2\left(\frac{d-1}{n}\right)$ |
| Hamming | $\frac{k}{n} \leq 1-\frac{1}{n}\log_2\left(\sum_{j=0}^{t=\lfloor\frac{d-1}{2}\rfloor}\binom{n}{j}\right)$ | $\frac{k}{n} \leq 1-\frac{1}{n}\log_2\left(\sum_{j=0}^{t=\lfloor\frac{d-1}{2}\rfloor}\binom{n}{j}3^j\right)$ |
| GV | $\frac{k}{n} \geq 1-\frac{1}{n}\log_2\left(\sum_{j=0}^{d-1}\binom{n}{j}\right)$ | $\frac{k}{n} \geq 1-\frac{1}{n}\log_2\left(\sum_{j=0}^{d-1}\binom{n}{j}3^j\right)$ |

Recall that the dual-containing quantum CSS codes rely on dual-containing classical binary codes, which satisfy the symplectic criterion of Eq. (12.8) and also comply with the constraint of $\mathbf{H}_z = \mathbf{H}_x$. Explicitly, half of the stabilizer operators of $\mathcal{C}[n, k, d]$ are mapped onto $\mathbf{H}_z$, while the other half are mapped onto $\mathbf{H}_x$. Therefore, the number of stabilizer operators of a dual-containing quantum CSS code is bounded by

$$2^{\frac{(n-k)}{2}} \leq \left(\sum_{j=0}^{d-1}\binom{n}{j}\right). \tag{6.14}$$

Based on Eq. (6.14), we may formulate the lower bound on the quantum coding rate of a dual-containing quantum CSS code as follows:

$$\frac{k}{n} \geq 1-\frac{2}{n}\log_2\left(\sum_{j=0}^{d-1}\binom{n}{j}\right). \tag{6.15}$$

As $n$ approaches $\infty$, we obtain the quantum GV bound for CSS codes, as suggested in [86], which is formulated as

$$\frac{k}{n} \geq 1-2H\left(\frac{d}{n}\right), \tag{6.16}$$

where $H(x)$ is the binary entropy of $x$. Based on the discussions above, we compare the asymptotic classical and quantum coding bounds in Table 6.1 as well as in Figure 6.1. Since the QSCs are designed to mitigate both bit-flip errors and phase-flip errors, the bounds of QSCs are significantly lower than those of their classical counterparts. Nevertheless, the general concept still holds, the Singleton bound serves as a loose upper bound, whilst the Hamming bound is a tighter upper bound.

## 6.3 Quantum Coding Bounds in the Asymptotical Limit

Although the classical to binary isomorphism assists us in the development of QSCs from the well-known classical code designs, the issue of determining the actual achievable minimum distance, given the coding rate and the codeword length remains unresolved. In the classical domain as we described previously, finding the unique

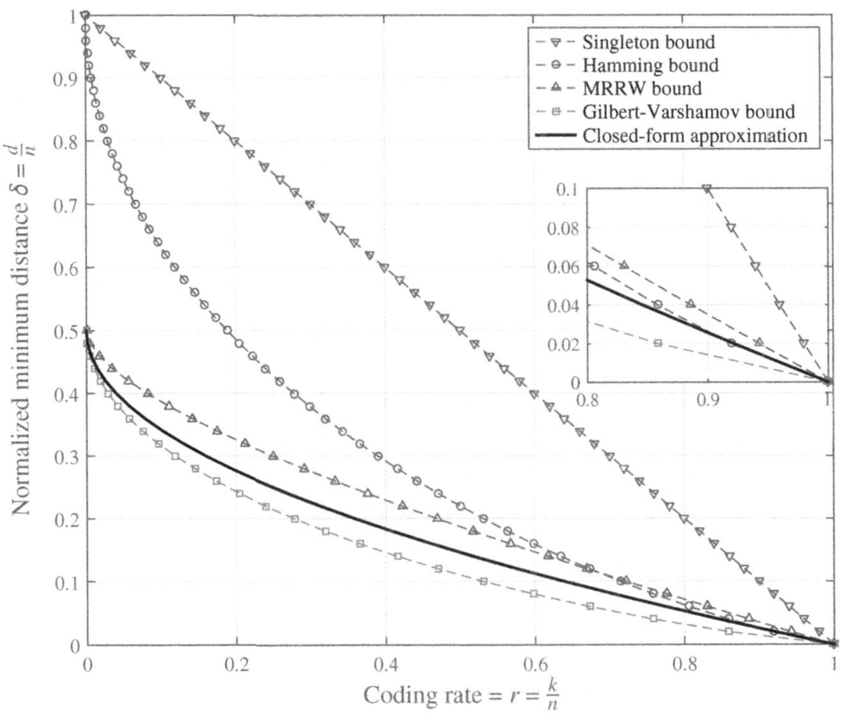


**Figure 6.1** The evolution from asymptotic classical binary coding bounds to the asymptotic quantum coding bounds. *Source*: [179]/IEE/CC BY 4.0.

**Table 6.2** The coding bounds for classical code constructions, with a minor modification.

| Classical bound | Finite | Asymptotic | Notes |
|---|---|---|---|
| Singleton [225] | $\frac{k}{n} \leq 1 - \left(\frac{d-1}{n}\right)$ | $\frac{k}{n} \leq 1 - \left(\frac{d}{n}\right)$ | a loose upper bound |
| Hamming [226] | $\frac{k}{n} \leq 1 - \frac{1}{n}\log_2\left(\sum_{j=0}^{t=\lfloor\frac{d-1}{2}\rfloor}\binom{n}{j}\right)$ | $\frac{k}{n} \leq 1 - H\left(\frac{d}{2n}\right)$ | tight upper bound for very high code rate |
| MRRW [228] | | $\frac{k}{n} \leq H\left(\frac{1}{2} - \sqrt{\frac{d}{n}\left(1-\frac{d}{n}\right)}\right)$ | tightest known asymptotic upper bound for medium and low rate codes |
| Plotkin [229] | $\frac{k}{n} \leq \frac{1}{n}\left(1 - \log_2\left(2 - \frac{n}{d}\right)\right)$ | | tight upper bound for finite-length at $\delta > \frac{1}{2}$ |
| GV [227] | $\frac{k}{n} \geq 1 - \frac{1}{n}\log_2\left(\sum_{j=0}^{d-1}\binom{n}{j}\right)$ | $\frac{k}{n} \geq 1 - H\left(\frac{d}{n}\right)$ | tightest known lower bound |

*Source*: Adapted from [91].

solution to the realistically achievable minimum distance of binary classical codes is still an open problem, even though the upper bound and lower bound of the quantum coding rate versus the achievable minimum distance can be found in the literature [225–229]. The bounds for the classical code constructions are listed in Table 6.2, while the corresponding asymptotic bounds are also plotted in Figure 6.2. Observe in the figure that we normalized $d$ by $n$ for the sake of being able to compare different-length codes under fair experimental conditions. To elaborate briefly, it is plausible that a longer code is capable of achieving a higher minimum distance and a higher error correction capability, but this normalized minimum distance allows us to gauge whether the code length extension does or does not yield an attractive increase in terms of $d$. This is particularly important because longer codes generally impose a higher decoding complexity. In the classical domain, the tightest known lower bound was derived by Gilbert [227]. The Hamming bound [226] serves as a tight upper bound for high coding rates, while the McEliece–Rodemich–Rumsey–Welch (MRRW) bound [228] serves as the tightest upper bound for moderate

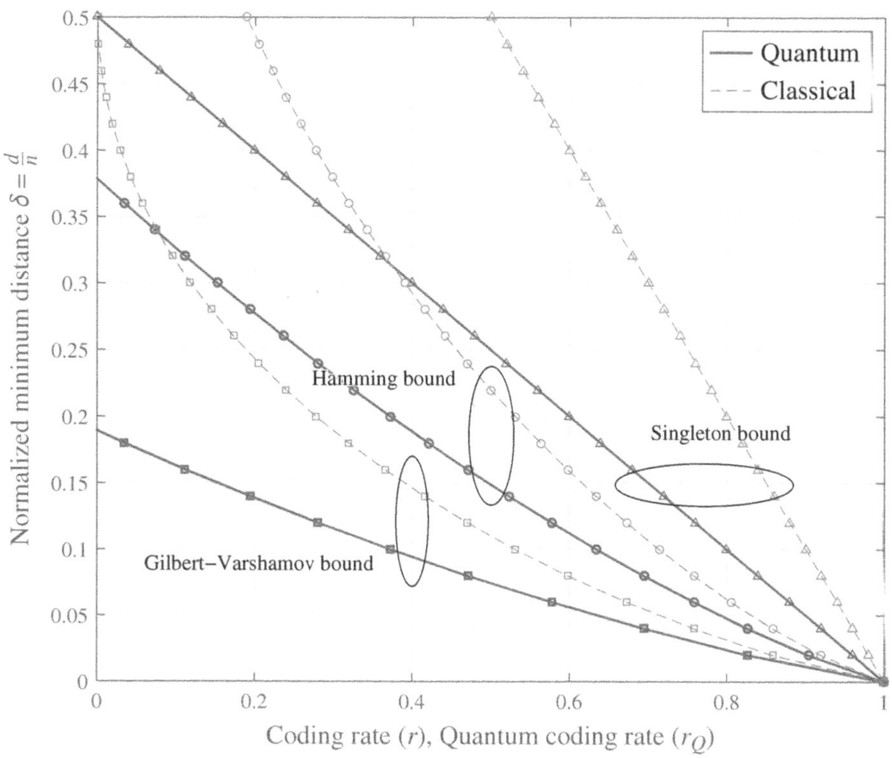


**Figure 6.2** The trade-off between classical coding rate $r$ and normalized minimum distance $\delta$ as described by classical binary coding bounds. A simple quadratic function $r(\delta) = (2\delta - 1)^2$, which satisfies all of the bounds, acts as a closed-form approximation for classical binary error correction codes as suggested in [91]. *Source*: [179]/IEE/CC BY 4.0.

**Table 6.3** The well-known quantum coding bounds found in the literature.

| Quantum bound | Finite-length | Asymptotic | Notes |
|---|---|---|---|
| Singleton [85] | $\frac{k}{n} \leq 1 - 2\left(\frac{d-1}{n}\right)$ | $\frac{k}{n} \leq 1 - 2\left(\frac{d}{n}\right)$ | very loose upper bound |
| Hamming [58] | $\frac{k}{n} \leq 1 - \frac{1}{n}\log_2\left(\sum_{j=0}^{t=\lfloor\frac{d-1}{2}\rfloor}\binom{n}{j}3^j\right)$ | $\frac{k}{n} \leq 1 - \left(\frac{d}{2n}\right)\log_2 3 - H\left(\frac{d}{2n}\right)$ | tight upper bound for moderate and high coding rate |
| Griesmer-Rain [169, 230] | $\frac{k}{n} \leq 1 - \left(\frac{3d-4}{n}\right)$ | $\frac{k}{n} \leq 1 - 3\left(\frac{d}{n}\right)$ | tighter upper bound for low coding rates CSS codes |
| Linear Programming [231] | | $\frac{k}{n} \leq H(\tau) + \tau\log_2 3 - 1$ | strengthen the upper |
| | | $\tau = \frac{3}{4} - \frac{1}{2}\delta - \frac{1}{2}\sqrt{3\delta(1-\delta)}$ | bound |
| GV [58] | $\frac{k}{n} \geq 1 - \frac{1}{n}\log_2\left(\sum_{j=0}^{d-1}\binom{n}{j}3^j\right)$ | $\frac{k}{n} \geq 1 - \left(\frac{d}{n}\right)\log_2 3 - H\left(\frac{d}{n}\right)$ | tight lower bound for general stabilizer codes |
| GV for CSS [86] | | $\frac{k}{n} \geq 1 - 2H\left(\frac{d}{n}\right)$ | tight lower bound for CSS codes |
| | $\frac{k}{n} \geq 1 - \frac{2}{n}\log_2\left(\sum_{j=0}^{d-1}\binom{n}{j}\right)$ | | lower bound for dual-containing CSS codes |

and low coding rates. As seen in Figure 6.1, the gap between the tight upper bounds and the lower bound is quite narrow. It was observed in [91] that a simple quadratic expression $r(\delta) = (2\delta - 1)^2$, where $\delta$ denotes the normalized minimum distance $d/n$, satisfies all the known asymptotic bounds.

The well-known bounds for QSC constructions are listed in Table 6.3 and they are also portrayed in Figure 6.3. The quantum Singleton bound serves as the loose upper bound, the quantum Hamming bound as a tighter upper

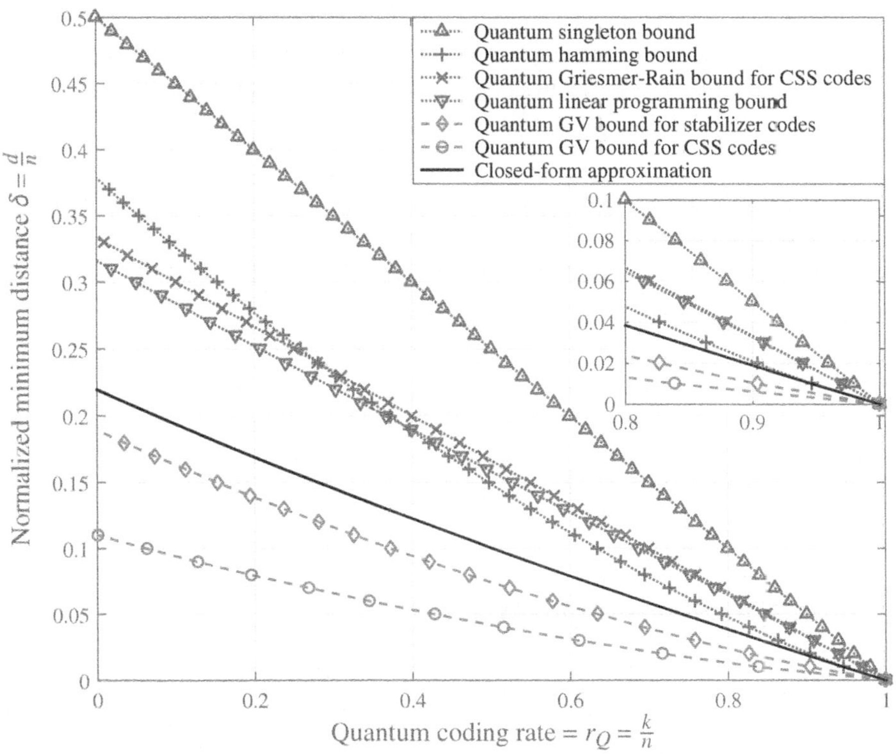


**Figure 6.3** The trade-off between quantum coding rate $r_Q$ and normalized minimum distance $\delta$ is characterized using quantum coding bounds. A simple quadratic closed-form $r_Q(\delta) = \frac{32}{9}\delta^2 - \frac{16}{3}\delta + 1$ satisfies all of the well-known quantum coding bounds, which is portrayed by black solid lines. The curves above the black solid line represent upper-bounds, while those below it are lower-bounds. *Source*: [179]/IEE/CC BY 4.0.

bound, and quantum GV bound as the tightest lower bound. However, a wide discrepancy can be observed between the upper bound and the lower bound. For the sake of narrowing this gap, the quantum Rain bound was derived using quantum weight enumerators [230]. To elaborate a little further, the quantum Rain bound states that any quantum code of length $n$ can correct at most $\left\lfloor \frac{n-1}{6} \right\rfloor$ errors. The resultant bound is only a function of codeword length $n$. Hence, under the asymptotic limit, the quantum Rain bound is a straight line at $\delta = 1/3$, which does not exhibit any further trade-off between the quantum coding rate and the minimum distance. In order to enhance the accuracy of the quantum Rain bound, Sarvepalli and Klappenecker derived a quantum version of the Griesmer bound [169]. By utilizing the quantum Griesmer bound and also the quantum Rain bound, a stronger bound was created for CSS type constructions. In this treatise, we will refer to this particular bound as the quantum Griesmer–Rain bound. For the sake of tightening the upper bound, Ashikhmin and Litsyn generalized the classical linear programming approach to the quantum domain using the MacWilliams identities [231]. The resultant quantum linear programming bound was proven to be tighter than the quantum Hamming bound in the low coding rate domain. As the quantum coding rate approaches zero, the achievable normalized minimum distance returned by the quantum Griesmer–Rain bound becomes $\delta = 0.33$, and that of the quantum linear programming bound becomes $\delta = 0.32$.

Recall from Section 3.3 that the QSCs may exhibit either a CSS or non-CSS structure. For CSS codes, the minimum distance is upper-bounded by the quantum Hamming bound for moderate to high quantum coding rates and by the quantum Griesmer–Rain bound for low coding rates, while it is also lower-bounded by the quantum GV bound for CSS codes. On the other hand, for non-CSS QSCs, the minimum distance is upper-bounded by the quantum Hamming bound for moderate to high coding rates and by the quantum linear programming bound for low coding rates. It is also lower-bounded by the quantum GV bound for general quantum stabilizer codes. Even though substantial efforts have been invested in tightening the gap between the upper and lower bounds, a significant amount of discrepancy persists. Hence, creating a simple approximation may be beneficial for giving us further insights into the realistic construction of QSCs.

Analogous to the classical closed-form approximation of [91], we also found that there exists a simple closed-form quadratic approximation, which satisfies all the well-known quantum coding bounds. Explicitly for quantum stabilizer codes, the following quadratic function was found to satisfy all the quantum coding bounds:

$$r_Q(\delta) = \frac{32}{9}\delta^2 - \frac{16}{3}\delta + 1 \text{ for } 0 \le \delta \le 0.2197. \tag{6.17}$$

We will further elaborate on the selection of this function in Section 6.5. It is important to note that the closed-form approximation is subject to the asymptotical bound for either CSS type or non-CSS type quantum code constructions. The closed-form approximation in Eq. (6.17) offers the benefit of simplicity, and it has the inverse function as given by

$$\delta(r_Q) = \frac{3\left(\sqrt{2} - \sqrt{r_Q + 1}\right)}{4\sqrt{2}} \text{ for } 0 \le r_Q \le 1. \tag{6.18}$$

This closed-form approximation suggests that it is possible to create a code construction whose minimum distance grows linearly with the codeword length at the asymptotical limit since for a given quantum coding rate $r_Q$, it will correspond to a unique constant value of $\delta$.

## 6.4 Quantum Coding Bounds on Finite-length Codes

The asymptotic limits are only relevant for $n \to \infty$. For practical applications, we require code constructions with shorter codeword length, which necessitates a different formulation for the quantum coding bounds. Finding a closed-form approximation will be beneficial for determining the realistically attainable minimum distance for the given code parameters. The well-known quantum coding bounds are listed in Table 6.3 and also portrayed in Figure 6.3. It is clearly seen that a simple quadratic approximation can satisfy all the well-known bounds. For the finite-length quantum codes, we propose the closed-form approximation of

$$r_Q(n, \delta) = a\delta^2 + b\delta + c. \tag{6.19}$$

To arrive at the closed-form approximation in Eq. (6.19), we have to determine three definitive points corresponding to realistic quantum code constructions. As an example in this treatise, we use three QSC constructions from the literature as listed in the following:

- For uncoded logical qubits and unity rate codewords, we have

$$r_Q(n, \delta) = r\left(n, \frac{1}{n}\right) = 1. \tag{6.20}$$

- For a high coding rate, we will use the construction given in [57]. For $n = 2^j$, there is a quantum stabilizer code construction $[n, k, d] = [n, n - j - 2, 3]$, which can be used to correct $t = 1$ error. This code construction reaches the quantum Hamming bound. For arbitrary $n$, it can be written as

$$r_Q(n, \delta) = r\left(n, \frac{3}{n}\right) = 1 - \frac{1}{n}\log_2(n) - \frac{2}{n}. \tag{6.21}$$

- For a very low coding rate, we are using the quantum stabilizer code constructions derived from quadratic residues [232, 233]. By using simple linear regression, we arrive at

$$r_Q(n, \delta) = r\left(n, \frac{2}{n} + \frac{1}{4}\right) = \frac{1}{n}. \tag{6.22}$$

Using the three definitive points from the constructions given in Eqs. (6.20), (6.21), and (6.22), we arrive at a system of three linear equations, which have a unique value of $a$, $b$ and $c$ for an arbitrary value of $n$. More explicitly, we have

$$r_1 = a\delta_1^2 + b\delta_1 + c, \tag{6.23}$$

$$r_2 = a\delta_2^2 + b\delta_2 + c, \tag{6.24}$$

$$r_3 = a\delta_3^2 + b\delta_3 + c. \tag{6.25}$$

The analytical solution of Eqs. (6.23), (6.24), and (6.25) is based on the following unique parameter values:

$$a=\frac{(r_3-r_2)\,\delta_1+(r_1-r_3)\,\delta_2+(r_2-r_1)\,\delta_3}{(\delta_2-\delta_1)(\delta_3-\delta_2)(\delta_1-\delta_3)},\tag{6.26}$$

$$b=\frac{(r_2-r_3)\,\delta_1^2+(r_3-r_1)\,\delta_2^2+(r_1-r_2)\,\delta_3^2}{(\delta_2-\delta_1)(\delta_3-\delta_2)(\delta_1-\delta_3)},\tag{6.27}$$

$$c=\frac{(r_3\delta_2-r_2\delta_3)\,\delta_1^2+(r_1\delta_3-r_3\delta_1)\,\delta_2^2+(r_2\delta_1-r_1\delta_2)\,\delta_3^2}{(\delta_2-\delta_1)(\delta_3-\delta_2)(\delta_1-\delta_3)}.\tag{6.28}$$

Despite the cluttered appearance of the analytical solution, it contains a simple closed-form approximation, because the value of $r_1$, $r_2$, $r_3$, $\delta_1$, $\delta_2$, and $\delta_3$ may be readily calculated using Eqs. (6.20), (6.21), and (6.22). Furthermore, the closed-form approximation derived for finite-length codewords has an inverse function of

$$\delta(n,r_Q)=\frac{-b-\sqrt{b^2-4a(c-r_Q)}}{2a}.\tag{6.29}$$

The accuracy of the proposed method is now tested for QSCs having codeword lengths of $n=\{31, 32, 63, 64, 127, 128\}$ as shown in Figure 6.4. The list of practical QSC constructions which are used in these plots can be seen in

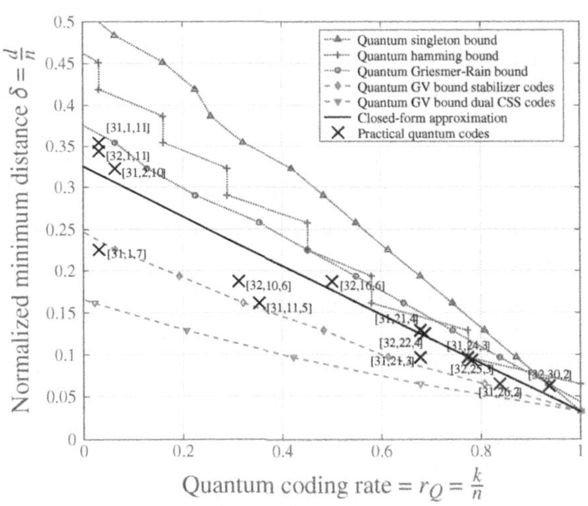

(a) $n = 31$ and $n = 32$.

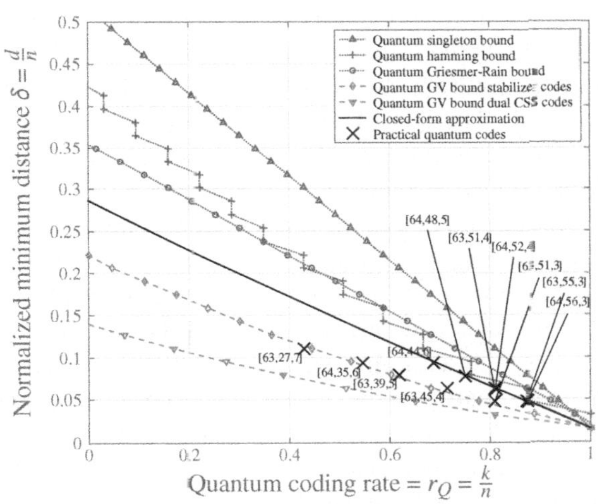

(b) $n = 63$ and $n = 64$.

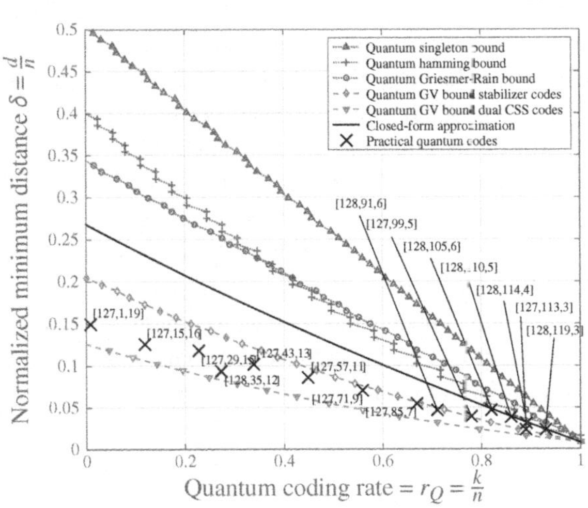

(c) $n = 127$ and $n = 128$.

**Figure 6.4** Quantum coding rate $r_Q$ versus normalized minimum distance $\delta$ for finite-length QSCs. The points for portraying the practical QSCs are taken from QBCH codes QRM codes, and quantum codes from *GF*(4) formulation. *Source*: Adapted from [60, 61, 64] Chandra et al. [179].

**Table 6.4** The list of QSC constructions that are used to plot practical code in Figure 6.4.

| | |
|---|---|
| | **C[*n*, *k*, *d*] for *n* = 31 and *n* = 32** |
| QBCH [61] | [31, 1, 7], [31, 11, 5], [31, 21, 3] |
| QRM [64] | [32, 10, 6], [32, 25, 3] |
| QGF(4) [60] | [31, 1, 11], [31, 2, 10], [31, 21, 4], [31, 26, 2], [32, 1, 11], [32, 16, 6], [32, 22, 4], [32, 25, 3], [32, 30, 2] |
| | **C[*n*, *k*, *d*] for *n* = 63 and *n* = 64** |
| QBCH [61] | [63, 27, 7], [63, 39, 5], [63, 45, 4], [63, 51, 3], [63, 57, 2] |
| QRM [64] | [64, 35, 6], [64, 56, 3] |
| QGF(4) [60] | [63, 51, 4], [63, 55, 3], [63, 60, 2], [64, 44, 6], [64, 48, 5], [64, 52, 4], [64, 56, 3], [64, 62, 2] |
| | **C[*n*, *k*, *d*] for *n* = 127 and *n* = 128** |
| QBCH [61] | [127, 1, 19], [127, 15, 16], [127, 29, 15], [127, 43, 13], [127, 57, 11], [127, 71, 9], [127, 85, 7], [127, 99, 5], [127, 113, 3] |
| QRM [64] | [128, 35, 12], [128, 91, 6], [128, 119, 3] |
| QGF(4) [60] | [127, 114, 4], [127, 118, 3], [127, 124, 2], [128, 105, 6], [128, 110, 5], [128, 114, 4], [128, 119, 3], [128, 126, 2] |

Table 6.4.[1] The closed-form approximation lies entirely between the upper and the lower quantum coding bounds. The practical QSCs are also plotted in the same figure to show the relative position with respect to the quantum coding bounds. The QSCs based on [60, 64] lay perfectly on the approximate curves, but it has been observed in [234] that as the codeword length increases and the quantum coding rate is reduced, the exact value of the minimum distance becomes unclear. As depicted in Figure 6.4b, c, we can hardly find definitive points associated with actual codes to plot in the low quantum coding-rate region constructed from quantum *GF*(4). However, the QBCH code constructions lie quite close to the GV lower bound for dual-containing CSS codes. As predicted, since the constructions of QBCH codes rely on dual-containing CSS type constructions, which employ two separate PCMs for their stabilizer operators, we expect a lower coding rate compared to their non-CSS relatives.

The proposed closed-form approximation offers substantial benefits for the development of QSCs. We can readily find an approximation of the realistically achievable minimum distance for given code parameters. For instance, for half-rate quantum stabilizer codes of length 128, the minimum distance is bounded by $11 < d < 22$. By using our formulation, we obtain $d(n = 128, r_Q = 1/2) = 17$ from our finite-length approximation. Likewise, for half-rate quantum stabilizer codes of length 1024, the minimum distance is bounded by $78 < d < 157$. Using our method, we can obtain $d(n = 1024, r_Q = 1/2) = 103$ from our asymptotic bound approximation. One of the logical questions that may arise is concerned with the existence of the corresponding codes. For example, does a half-rate QSCs relying on $n = 128$ physical qubits and a minimum distance of $d = 16$ exist? The answer to this question is not definitive. Let us refer to the code table given in [234], which is mainly based on the QSC constructions of [60]. Due to space limitations, we are unable to capture the entire table and the associated PCM formulation. However, it is shown in [234] that a half-rate QSC relying on $n = 128$ physical qubits indeed exists, although the minimum distance is only loosely specified by the bounds of $11 < d < 20$. The bound is similar to the quantum GV bound and to the quantum Hamming bound of the minimum distance given by $11 < d < 22$. By contrast, upon using our approximation, we have a minimum distance of $d = 17$, which is again only an approximation, and it does not imply the existence of a quantum code having a similar minimum distance. Nonetheless, we believe that our approximation is beneficial for approximating the attainable QBER performance of QSCs based on hard-decision syndrome decoding for short to moderate codeword length as follows (without considering degeneracy):

1 A comprehensive list of practical quantum stabilizer codes can be found online at [234]. In this treatise, we only consider quantum stabilizer codes with a definitive minimum distance in the list.

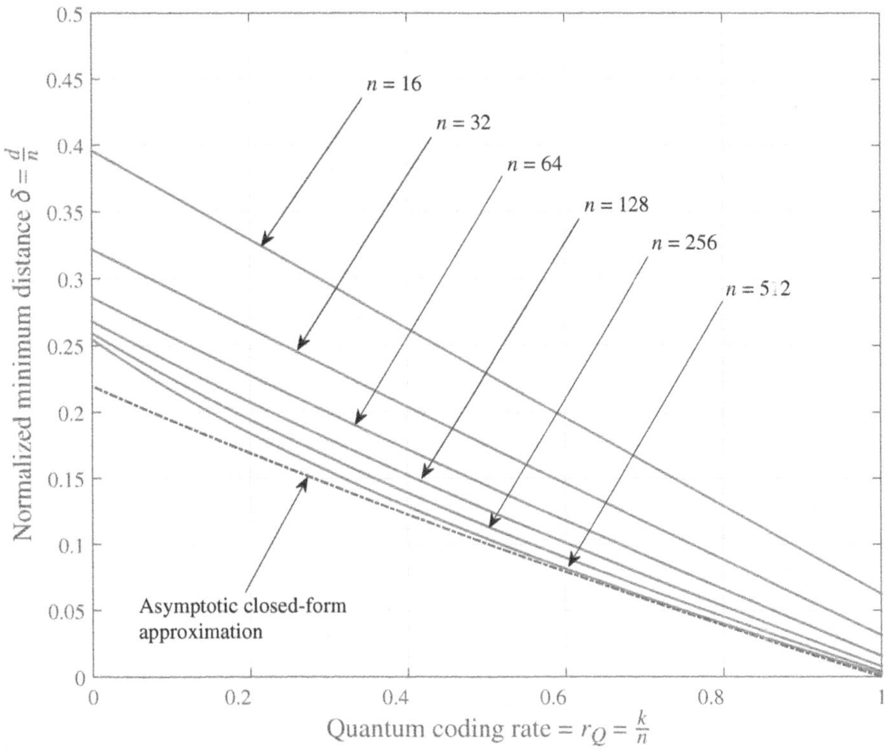


**Figure 6.5** The evolution of our closed-form approximation for finite-length codewords parameterized by the codeword length $n$. *Source*: [179]/IEE/CC BY 4.0.

$$\text{QBER}(n,d,p) = 1 - \sum_{i=0}^{t=\lfloor\frac{d-1}{2}\rfloor} \binom{n}{i} p^i(1-p)^{n-i}, \tag{6.30}$$

where the realistically achievable value of $d$ is obtained from our approximation. In our view, the combination of our closed-form approximation and the QBER of Eq. (6.30) constitutes a useful benchmark for the future development of QSCs, since it quantifies the realistically achievable QBER performance based on hard-decision syndrome-based decoding.

The evolution of our closed-form approximation as the codeword length increases for $n = \{31, 32, 63, 64, 127, 128\}$ can be seen in Figure 6.5. By using our example, it can be clearly observed that as the codeword length increases, the approximation derived for finite-length codes slowly approaches the closed-form approximation of the asymptotic bound. However, inaccuracies emerge as the codeword length increases. This phenomenon emerges because we do not have definitive QSC constructions to rely on in the low coding rate region. In our approximation example, we are using the QSCs from quadratic-residues-based construction for the low coding rate region and the number of QSC constructions is limited to a handful codeword lengths. By contrast, in the low coding rate region of classical codes, we have the simple repetition codes relying on the construction $\mathcal{C}(n, 1)$ having a normalized minimum distance of $\delta(n, r) = \delta\left(n, \frac{1}{n}\right) = 1$.

Albeit the finite and infinite-length-based approximation curves start to deviate for a very long codeword $n \gg 100$, the minimum distance still grows with the codeword length, as portrayed in Figure 6.6. Both the finite-length approximation and asymptotic approximation follow the same trend. For $n \gg 100$, we can simply utilize the asymptotic formulation given in Eq. (6.17) for calculating the quantum coding rate for a certain desired minimum distance, or the inverse of the asymptotic formulation in Eq. (6.18) to determine the realistically achievable minimum distance, given the quantum coding rate. We may conclude from this figure that it is indeed possible to have a QSC construction associated with a growing minimum distance, as the codeword length increases.

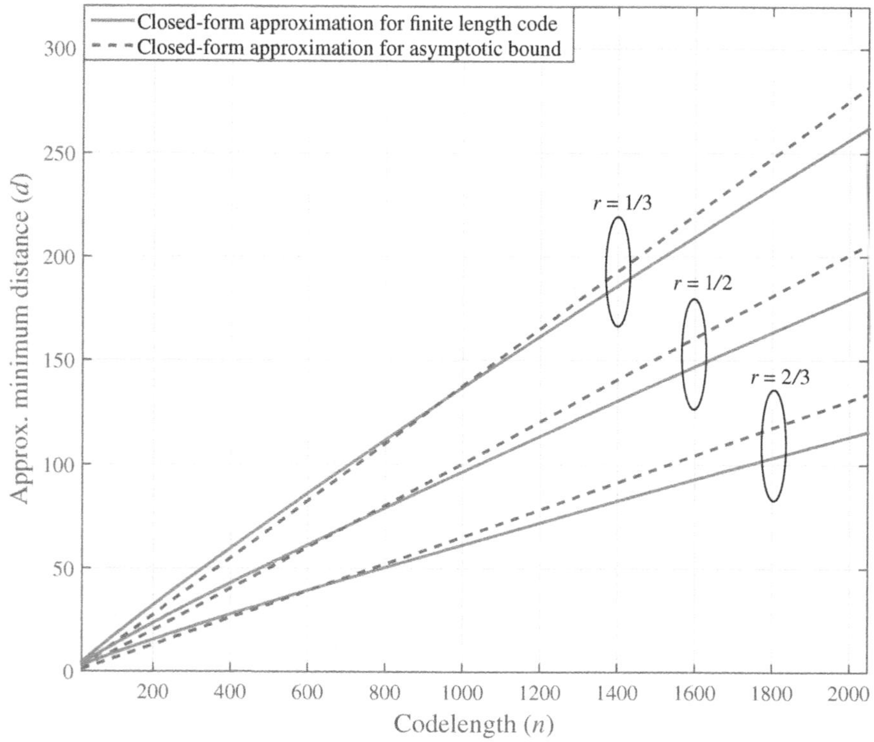


**Figure 6.6** The growth of achievable minimum distance for short block QSCs versus the codeword length. *Source*: [179]/IEE/CC BY 4.0.

## 6.5 The Bounds on Entanglement-assisted Quantum Stabilizer Codes

One of the distinctive characteristics of quantum systems, which does not bear any resemblance with the classical domain, is the ability of creating entanglement. This unique property can be exploited for increasing the achievable minimum distance of quantum codes, hence increasing the error correction capability of QSCs. The EA-QSC constructions are denoted by $\mathcal{C}(n, k, d; c)$, where $c$ denotes the number of preshared entangled qubits. It is important to note that even though the EA-QSCs expand the Pauli-group operators from $\mathcal{P}_n$ into $\mathcal{P}_{(n+c)}$, we only consider the error operators in $\mathcal{P}_n$. This is because the paradigm of EA-QSCs assumes that the preshared entangled qubits are not subjected to transmission error. Hence, for EA-QSCs, the quantum Hamming bound of Eq. (6.6) can be modified to

$$2^k \leq \frac{2^{n+c}}{\sum_{j=0}^{t=\left\lfloor \frac{d_{ea}-1}{2} \right\rfloor} \binom{n}{j} 3^j}, \tag{6.31}$$

where the notation $d_{ea}$ denotes the minimum distance of EA-QSCs. Equation (6.31) can be rewritten to show explicitly the trade-off between the quantum coding rate $r_Q$ and the minimum distance $d_{ea}$ of EA-QSCs as follows:

$$\frac{k}{n} \leq 1 - \frac{1}{n} \log_2 \left( \sum_{j=0}^{t=\left\lfloor \frac{d_{ea}-1}{2} \right\rfloor} \binom{n}{j} 3^j \right) + \left(\frac{c}{n}\right). \tag{6.32}$$

When $n$ tends to $\infty$, we have

$$\frac{k}{n} \leq 1 - \left(\frac{d_{ea}}{2n}\right) \log_2 3 - H\left(\frac{d_{ea}}{2n}\right) + \left(\frac{c}{n}\right). \tag{6.33}$$

As encapsulated in Eq. (6.33), an additional conflicting parameter is involved in determining the quantum coding bounds, namely the entanglement consumption rate. The entanglement consumption rate $E$ is the ratio of the number of preshared maximally entangled qubits $c$ to the number of physical qubits $n$ as encapsulated in the following:

$$E = \frac{c}{n}. \tag{6.34}$$

A maximally-entangled[2] QSCs requires $c = n - k$ preshared qubit pairs. Hence, for a maximally entangled QSCs, the quantum Hamming bound of Eq. (6.33) can be reformulated as follows by substituting $c = n - k$ into Eq. (6.33), yielding:

$$\frac{k}{n} \leq 1 - \frac{1}{2}\left(\left(\frac{d_{ea}}{2n}\right)\log_2 3 - H\left(\frac{d_{ea}}{2n}\right)\right). \tag{6.35}$$

Let us now consider the more general cases, where we may have a range of different entanglement ratios $0 \leq \theta \leq 1$. The entanglement ratio is defined as the ratio of the number of preshared qubits $c$ to that of the maximally-entangled preshared qubits $(n-k)$, yielding:

$$\theta = \frac{c}{n-k}. \tag{6.36}$$

The quantum Hamming bound for EA-QSCs with arbitrary entanglement ratios of $\theta$ is given by

$$\frac{k}{n} \leq 1 - \frac{1}{1+\theta}\left(\left(\frac{d_{ea}}{2n}\right)\log_2 3 - H\left(\frac{d_{ea}}{2n}\right)\right). \tag{6.37}$$

The rest of the quantum coding bounds can be readily derived using similar procedures. The entanglement-assisted quantum coding bounds found in the literature are summarized at a glance in Table 6.5. The resultant entanglement-assisted quantum coding bounds are portrayed in Figures 6.7 and 6.8. By substituting the entanglement ratio of $\theta = 0$, we arrive again at the quantum coding bounds derived for unassisted QSCs. By contrast, upon substituting the entanglement ratio of $\theta = 1$ into Eq. (6.37), we arrive at the quantum coding bounds of maximally-entangled QSCs. Figure 6.7 portrays the bounds on maximally-entangled QSCs. It is observed in Figure 6.7 that at the point ($\delta = 0.75$), the quantum GV bound (lower bound) intersects the quantum linear programming bound (upper bound). Indeed, it is confirmed by the quantum Plotkin bound of the maximally-entangled QSC constructions shown in Table 6.6 that for asymptotical maximally-entangled QSCs the highest normalized minimum distance that can be achieved is $\delta = 0.75$. Hence, based on this observation, we propose a

**Table 6.5** The entanglement-assisted quantum coding bounds found in the literature.

| Quantum bound | Finite-length | Asymptotic | Notes |
|---|---|---|---|
| Singleton [74] | $\frac{k}{n} \leq 1 - 2\left(\frac{d_{ea}-1}{n}\right) + \left(\frac{c}{n}\right)$ | $\frac{k}{n} \leq 1 - 2\left(\frac{d_{ea}}{n}\right) + \left(\frac{c}{n}\right)$ | very loose upper bound |
| Hamming [73] | $\frac{k}{n} \leq 1 - \frac{1}{n}\log_2\left(\sum_{j=0}^{t=\lfloor \frac{d_{ea}-1}{2} \rfloor} \binom{n}{j} 3^j\right) + \left(\frac{c}{n}\right)$ | $\frac{k}{n} \leq 1 - \left(\frac{d_{ea}}{2n}\right)\log_2 3 - H\left(\frac{d_{ea}}{2n}\right) + \left(\frac{c}{n}\right)$ | tight upper bound |
| Linear Progr. [235] | | $\frac{k}{n} \leq H(\tau) + \tau \log_2 3 - 1 + \left(\frac{c}{n}\right)$<br>$\tau = \frac{3}{4} - \frac{1}{2}\delta - \frac{1}{2}\sqrt{3\delta(1-\delta)}$ | strengthen the upper bound |
| Plotkin [236, 237] | $\frac{d_{ea}}{n} \leq \frac{3(4^k)}{8(4^k-1)}\left(1 + \left(\frac{k}{n}\right) + \left(\frac{c}{n}\right)\right)$ | $\frac{d_{ea}}{n} \leq \frac{3}{8}\left(1 + \left(\frac{k}{n}\right) + \left(\frac{c}{n}\right)\right)$ | upper bound for minimum distance |
| GV [237] | $\frac{k}{n} \geq 1 - \frac{1}{n}\log_2\left(\sum_{j=0}^{d_{ea}-1} \binom{n}{j} 3^j\right) + \left(\frac{c}{n}\right)$ | $\frac{k}{n} \geq 1 - \left(\frac{d_{ea}}{n}\right)\log_2 3 - H\left(\frac{d_{ea}}{n}\right) + \left(\frac{c}{n}\right)$ | tight lower bound |

2 For maximally-entangled QSCs, all of the auxiliary qubits required to generate the encoded state are already preshared using maximally entangled qubit pairs. Hence, the maximal number of entangled qubits that can be shared beforehand is equal to the total number of auxiliary qubits, which is equal to $(n-k)$.

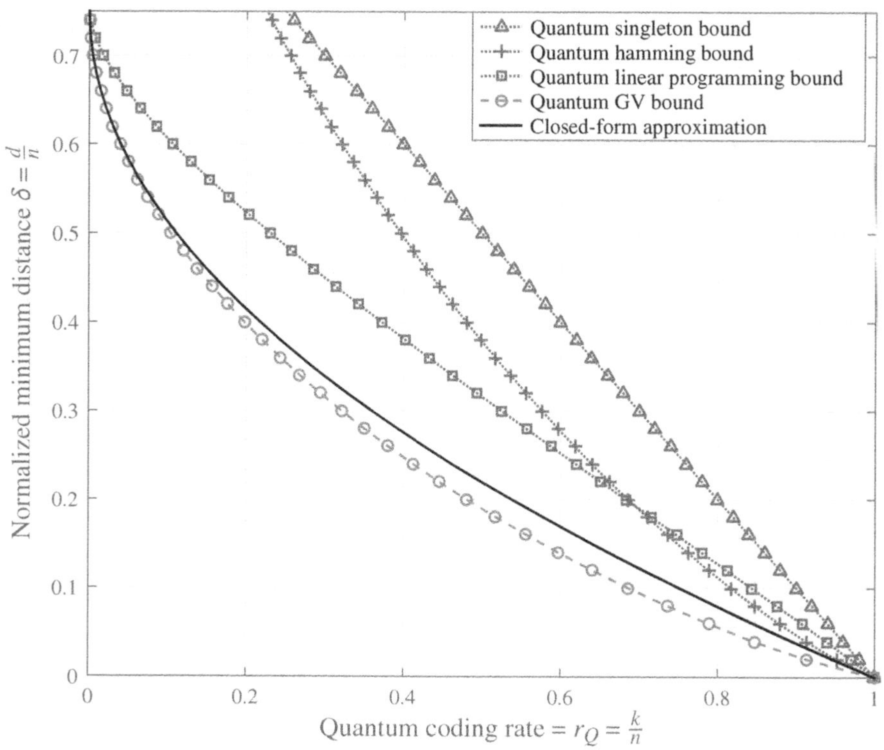


**Figure 6.7** The asymptotic quantum coding bounds on EA-QSCs for maximally-entangled constructions. A simple quadratic function $r(\delta) = \frac{16}{9}\delta^2 - \frac{8}{3}\delta + 1$ satisfies all of the quantum coding bounds. *Source*: [179]/IEE/CC BY 4.0.

**Table 6.6** The asymptotic quantum coding bounds for EA-QSCs given the arbitrary entanglement ratios of $\theta$.

| **Quantum Bound** | **Entanglement Ratio** $= \theta$ | **Maximally Entangled** $(\theta = 1)$ |
|---|---|---|
| Singleton [74] | $\frac{k}{n} \leq 1 - \left(\frac{2}{1+\theta}\right)\left(\frac{d_{ea}}{n}\right)$ | $\frac{k}{n} \leq 1 - \left(\frac{d_{ea}}{n}\right)$ |
| Hamming [73] | $\frac{k}{n} \leq 1 - \frac{1}{1+\theta}\left(\left(\frac{d_{ea}}{2n}\right)\log_2 3 - H\left(\frac{d_{ea}}{2n}\right)\right)$ | $\frac{k}{n} \leq 1 - \frac{1}{2}\left(\left(\frac{d_{ea}}{2n}\right)\log_2 3 - H\left(\frac{d_{ea}}{2n}\right)\right)$ |
| Linear Programming [235] | $\frac{k}{n} \leq \frac{1}{1+\theta}\left(H(\tau) + \tau \log_2 3 - 1 + \theta\right)$ | $\frac{k}{n} \leq \frac{1}{2}\left(H(\tau) + \tau \log_2 3\right)$ |
| Plotkin [236, 237] | $\frac{d_{ea}}{n} \leq \frac{3}{8}\left(1 + \theta + \frac{k}{n}(1-\theta)\right)$ | $\frac{d_{ea}}{n} \leq \frac{3}{4}$ |
| GV [237] | $\frac{k}{n} \geq 1 - \frac{1}{1+\theta}\left(\left(\frac{d_{ea}}{n}\right)\log_2 3 - H\left(\frac{d_{ea}}{n}\right)\right)$ | $\frac{k}{n} \geq 1 - \frac{1}{2}\left(\left(\frac{d_{ea}}{n}\right)\log_2 3 - H\left(\frac{d_{ea}}{n}\right)\right)$ |

*Source*: Adapted from [179].

simple quadratic function as the closed-form approximation of entanglement-assisted quantum stabilizer codes that will satisfy all of the well-known bounds. A quadratic function associated with a symmetry line at $(\delta = 0.75)$ and crossing the point of $(\delta, r) = (0, 1)$ is given by

$$r_Q(\delta) = \frac{16}{9}\delta^2 - \frac{8}{3}\delta + 1 \text{ for } 0 \leq \delta \leq 0.75. \tag{6.38}$$

The simple quadratic approximation given in Eq. (6.38) can also be inverted, yielding

$$\delta(r_Q) = \frac{3}{4}(1 - \sqrt{r_Q}) \text{ for } 0 \leq r_Q \leq 1. \tag{6.39}$$

From the simple quadratic function in Eq. (6.38), we can also derive a simple closed-form approximation for a given arbitrary entanglement ratio of $0 \leq \theta \leq 1$, as shown in the following:

$$r_Q(\delta) = \frac{1}{1+\theta}\left(\frac{32}{9}\delta^2 - \frac{16}{3}\delta + 1 + \theta\right), \tag{6.40}$$

for $0 \leq \delta \leq \frac{3}{4}\left(1 - \sqrt{\frac{1-\theta}{2}}\right)$ and $0 \leq \theta \leq 1$. The expression given in Eq. (6.40) may be inverted to arrive at the following equation:

$$\delta(r_Q) = \frac{3(\sqrt{2} - \sqrt{r_Q(1+\theta) + (1-\theta)})}{4\sqrt{2}}, \tag{6.41}$$

for $0 \leq r_Q \leq 1$ and $0 \leq \theta \leq 1$.

The simple closed-form approximation given in Eqs. (6.40) and (6.41) satisfies all entanglement-assisted quantum coding bounds for arbitrary entanglement ratios, as confirmed by Figure 6.8. We should point out at this stage

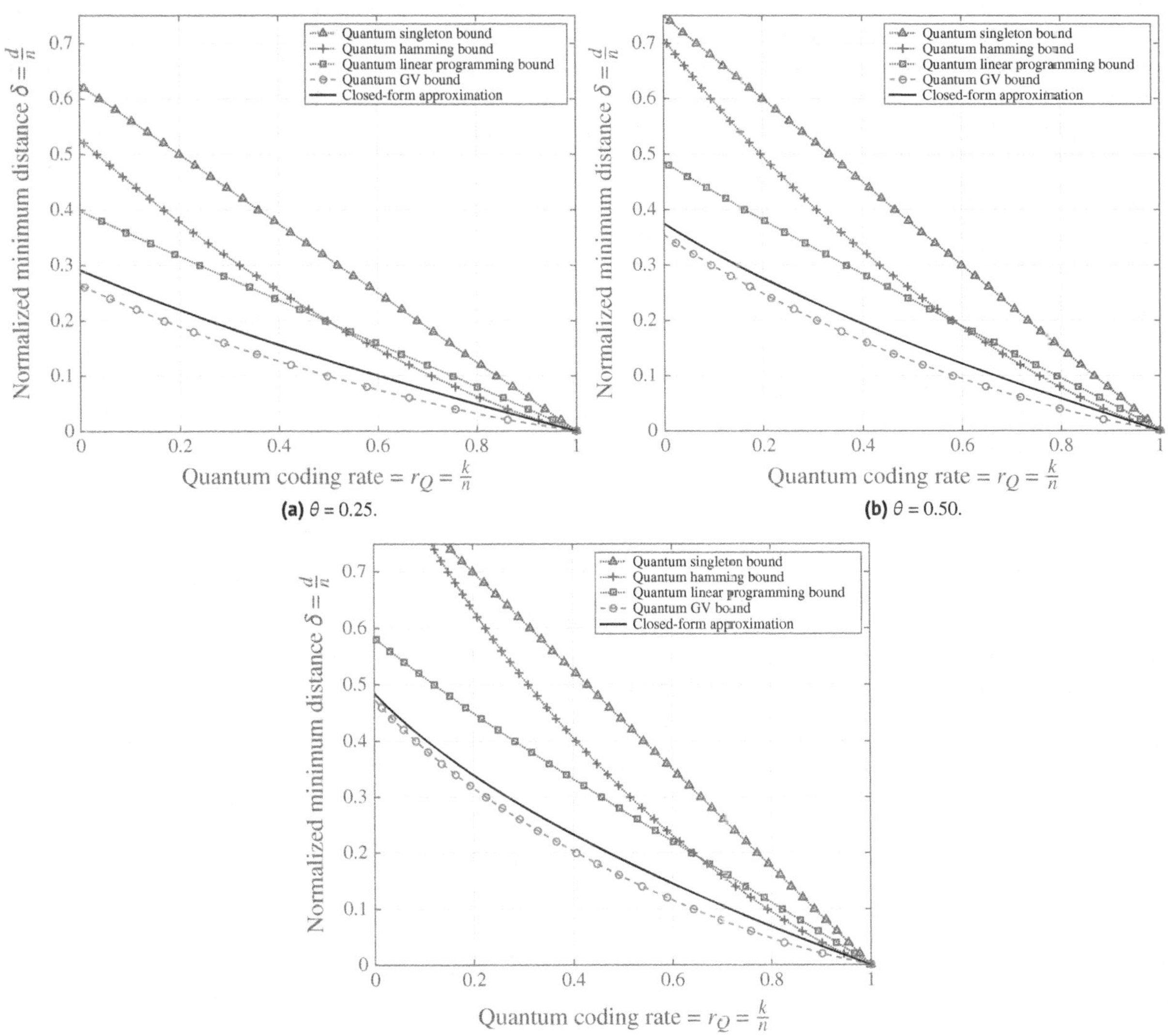


(a) $\theta = 0.25$.

(b) $\theta = 0.50$.

(c) $\theta = 0.75$.

**Figure 6.8** The asymptotic quantum coding bounds on EA-QSCs for entanglement ratios $\theta = \{0.25, 0.50, 0.75\}$.
*Source*: [179]/IEE/CC BY 4.0.

that as we substitute the value of $\theta = 0$ into Eqs. (6.40) and (6.41), we arrive at the closed-form approximation presented in the Eqs. (6.17) and (6.18) for unassisted asymptotic quantum coding bounds. Hence, we completed our closed-form approximations conceived for all of the different constructions of quantum stabilizer codes.

## 6.6 Summary and Conclusions

We have conducted a survey of quantum coding bounds, which describe the trade-off between the quantum coding rate and the error correction capability of a wide range of QSC constructions. Furthermore, we have provided insights into their relationships with their classical counterparts. For the family of unassisted QSCs, we have provided both lower and upper bounds for both CSS and non-CSS code constructions. For the EA-QSCs, we have presented the quantum coding bounds for maximally-entangled constructions and also for arbitrary entanglement ratios.

We have also proposed a closed-form approximation as a beneficial tool for analyzing the performance of QSCs. The resultant closed-form approximation may indeed be used as a simple benchmark for developing QSCs, because the resultant minimum distance $\delta$ and quantum coding rate $r_Q$ values from our approximations are unambiguous. For instance, for a half-rate quantum stabilizer code having a given codeword length of $n = 128$, the minimum distance is bounded by $11 < d < 22$. Upon using our approximation, we arrive at $d(n = 128, r_Q = 1/2) = 16$ from our finite-length approximation. Likewise, for a half-rate quantum stabilizer code having the codeword length of 1024, the minimum distance is bounded by $78 < d < 157$. By using our proposal, we have an approximate minimum distance of $d(n = 1024, r_Q = 1/2) = 103$ from our asymptotic bound approximation. Ultimately, the proposed method can be utilized as an efficient tool for the characterization of quantum stabilizer codes.

# 7

# Quantum Topological Error Correction Codes: The Classical-to-quantum Isomorphism Perspective

## 7.1 Introduction

In Chapters 3 and 6, we have demonstrated that classical error correction codes can be transformed into their quantum domain counterparts, and we can readily characterize their associated QBER performances by exploiting the classical-to-quantum isomorphism as a function of their code parameters. However, the real physical implementations of quantum computers impose additional challenges that prevent us from directly transplanting QSCs. Let us observe the layout of the physical qubits in some of IBM's quantum computers in Figure 7.1. In these figures, the circles represent the qubits, and the lines with the arrows represent the interactions among the qubits. Observe that any quantum computation task performed by the quantum computers is designed based on local qubit interactions. However, most of the QSCs derived from potent classical error correction codes may require interactions between distant qubits of a codeword, but arranging for this remains unrealistic at the current state of the art. This particular constraint motivated the invention of new families of short QSCs, which were specifically designed for circumventing the above mentioned limitation of local interactions. These codes belong to the family of QTECCs. The stabilizer operators of QTECCs can be explicitly defined by the underlying lattice structure accommodating the qubits. Following the same line of investigation as in Chapter 6, we will characterize the QBER performance of diverse QTECCs versus the code parameters given a certain lattice structure by exploiting the classical-to-quantum isomorphism.

The rest of this chapter is organized as follows. In Section 7.2, we commence with design examples of classical TECCs to pave the way for delving into the quantum domain. In Section 7.3, we detail our QSC design examples for QTECCs. We will continue by characterizing the QBER performance of QTECCs subjected to the quantum depolarizing channel, their distance from the hashing bound, and fidelity in Section 7.4. Finally, we conclude our discussions in Section 7.5.

## 7.2 Classical Topological Error Correction Codes: Design Examples

Classical error correction codes can be developed relying on diverse approaches [125]. We can find in the literature various families of codes based on algebraic formalisms, such as BCH codes and RS codes, codes based on conventional trellis structures, such as convolutional codes and turbo codes, codes based on bipartite graphs such as LDPC codes, and codes based on channel polarization, such as polar codes. Another approach that can be adopted to formulate a classical error correction code is by exploiting the topological or lattice structure. By mapping the bits of a codeword to a lattice structure we can create an error correction scheme [238]. For instance, let us assume that a codeword of classical bits is arranged on the square lattice given in Figure 7.2. The circles on the edges of the lattice define the encoded information bits, namely the codeword. The squares lying on the vertices of the lattice define the PCM of the code, which also directly defines the syndrome values of the received codeword. The number of circles is associated with the codeword length of $n$ bits and the number of squares is associated with the length of the syndrome vector or the number of rows in the PCM, which is equal to $(n-k)$ bits. For this particular square lattice seen in Figure 7.2, the codeword length $n$ is equal to 13 bits, and the length $(n-k)$ of the redundant part is 6. Hence, the number of information bits $k$ is equal to 7. Therefore, this code has $2^7 = 128$ legitimate codewords out of the theoretically possible $2^{13} = 8192$ received words. In conceptually simple terms one could

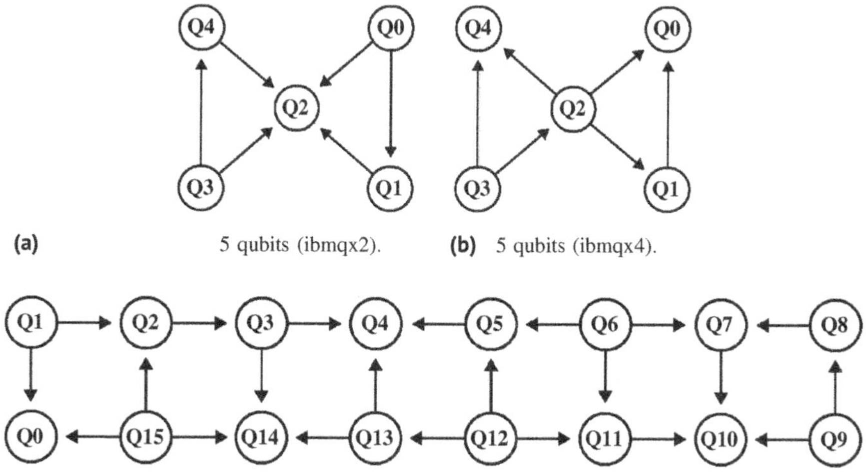


(a) 5 qubits (ibmqx2). (b) 5 qubits (ibmqx4).

(c) 16 qubits (ibmqx5).

**Figure 7.1** The qubit arrangement of IBM's superconducting quantum computers. The circles represent the qubits, while the arrows represent the possible qubit interactions within the computers. *Source*: Adapted from [99].

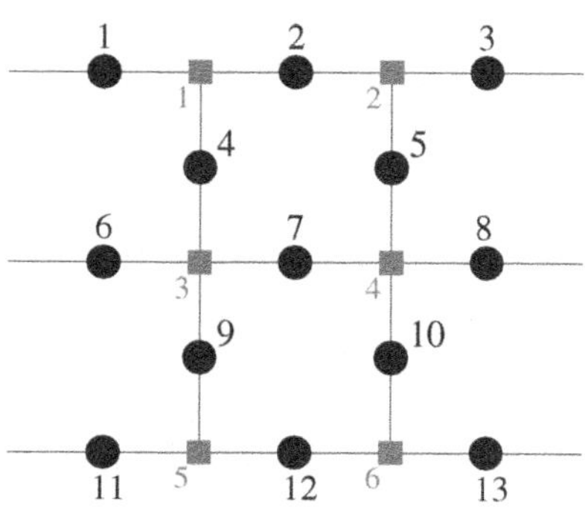

**Figure 7.2** Example of a classical bit arrangement on a square lattice structure. The circles lying on the edges of the lattice denote the bits of the codeword, while the vertices of the lattice denoted by the squares define the PCM and also the syndrome values. *Source*: [174]/IEEE/CC BY 4.0.

construct a look-up table for implementing the corresponding decoder, which has to find the specific legitimate codeword that has the lowest Hamming distance from the corrupted word.

For the sake of comparison, we could consider a classical BCH code having $n=15$, $k=7$ and $d=5$, which is capable of correcting two classical bit errors in a 15-bit codeword. In general, BCH codes do not have to satisfy the above mentioned topological constraint of only having localized interactions, and this design flexibility typically results in a higher error correction capability. This classical BCH code has $2^7=128$ legitimate codewords and $2^{15}=32\,768$ possible words. With the aid of its 8 parity bits we would be able to distinguish $2^{(15-7)} = 2^8 = 256$ distinct error patterns (including the error-free scenario) and correct two arbitrary bit errors.

The coding rate $r$ is defined by the ratio between the information bits $k$ and the codeword length $n$, yielding:

$$r = \frac{k}{n} \tag{7.1}$$

Hence, the coding rate of the square lattice code of Figure 7.2 is $r = 7/13$.

Now, let us delve deeper into how the error correction works. Let us revisit the square lattice of Figure 7.2. The $k$ information bits are encoded into $n$-bit codewords, where $n > k$. Noise or decoherence imposed by the channel corrupts the legitimate codeword. The syndrome computation is invoked to generate the $(n-k)$-bit syndrome vector, which tells us both the predicted number and the position of the errors. In Figure 7.2, each of the squares indicates a syndrome bit of $s_i$. Hence, the syndrome vector $\mathbf{s}$ is a 6-bit vector, which is given by

$$\mathbf{s} = [s_1\ s_2\ s_3\ s_4\ s_5\ s_6]. \tag{7.2}$$

In the case of an error-free received codeword, the resultant syndrome vector is $\mathbf{s} = [0\ 0\ 0\ 0\ 0\ 0]$. By contrast, if an error is imposed on the codeword, it triggers a syndrome bit value of 1 at the adjacent syndrome bit positions. For example, if an error occurs at the bit index 4 of Figure 7.2, it triggers the syndrome values of $s_1 = 1$ and $s_3 = 1$. The rest of the syndrome values remain equal to 0. Therefore, an error corrupting the bit index 4 generates a syndrome vector of $\mathbf{s} = [1\ 0\ 1\ 0\ 0\ 0]$. Hence, the decoder flips the value of bit index 4. Similarly, if an error occurs at bit number 3, it only triggers the syndrome value of $s_2 = 1$. Hence, it generates the syndrome vector of $\mathbf{s} = [0\ 1\ 0\ 0\ 0\ 0]$, and the error recovery procedure proceeds accordingly.

Now let us consider the occurrence of two bit errors in the codeword. For instance, let us assume that errors occur at bit indices of 6 and 7 of Figure 7.2. Note that both these errors affect $s_3$, therefore they cancel each other's effect on $s_3$, hence generating a syndrome bit value of $s_3 = 0$. However, we still do not receive an all-zero syndrome vector, because the bit index 7 results in the syndrome bit value of $s_4 = 1$ in Figure 7.2. Therefore, the resultant syndrome vector due to a bit error in both bits 6 and 7 is $\mathbf{s} = [0\ 0\ 0\ 1\ 0\ 0]$. Since the syndrome vector of $\mathbf{s} = [0\ 0\ 0\ 1\ 0\ 0]$ is also associated with the error incident upon bit index 8, the error recovery procedure decides to flip bit 8 instead, because for the error probability less than 1/2, a single error occurrence is more likely to happen than a double error. As a result, we end up having three errors. This example is an illustration that the occurrence of two bit errors in the codeword is beyond the error correction capability of the code given in Figure 7.2. We conclude that the code based on the square lattice illustrated in Figure 7.2 is capable of correcting only a single bit error. The error correction capability of $t$ bits for a given code construction is defined by the minimum distance $d$ of the code as formulated by

$$t = \left\lfloor \frac{d-1}{2} \right\rfloor. \tag{7.3}$$

Hence, a code that is only capable of correcting a single error has a minimum distance of $d = 3$, as exemplified by the square lattice code given in Figure 7.2. Moreover, the minimum distance of a square lattice code is defined by dimension of the lattice. Therefore, to increase the error correction capability of the code, we can simply increase the dimension of the lattice, which directly translates into increasing the minimum distance. The square lattice considered in our example can be generalized to a rectangular lattice structure having a dimension of $(l \times h)$, where $l$ is the length of the lattice and $h$ is the height of the lattice. In the case of a rectangular structure, the minimum distance is defined by

$$d = \min(l, h). \tag{7.4}$$

The codeword length is also uniquely defined by the dimension of the lattice. More explicitly, for a rectangular lattice of dimension $(l \times h)$, the codeword length is equal to the number of the lattice edges, which is given by

$$n\text{-edges} = n_{\text{square}} = 2lh - l - h + 1. \tag{7.5}$$

The number of rows in the PCM of a square lattice is defined by the number of faces or plaquettes of the rectangular lattice, which is formulated as follows:

$$n\text{-vertices} = n_{\text{square}} - k_{\text{square}} = h(l-1). \tag{7.6}$$

Hence, from Eqs. (7.5) and (7.6), the number of information bits $k$ encoded by the rectangular lattice codes is

$$\begin{aligned} k_{\text{square}} &= n_{\text{square}} - (n_{\text{square}} - k_{\text{square}}) \\ &= lh - l + 1. \end{aligned} \tag{7.7}$$

The most efficient code can be constructed by a square lattice, where $d = l = h$. Therefore, the expression given in Eqs. (7.5) and (7.7) can be simplified to

$$n_{\text{square}} = 2d^2 - 2d + 1 \tag{7.8}$$

$$k_{\text{square}} = d^2 - d + 1. \tag{7.9}$$

Hence, the coding rate of square lattice-based codes can be formulated as follows:

$$r_{\text{square}} = \frac{k_{\text{square}}}{n_{\text{square}}} = \frac{d^2 - d + 1}{2d^2 - 2d + 1}. \tag{7.10}$$

**Table 7.1** Constructing the PCM of the square lattice code of Figure 7.2 with minimum distance of $d = 3$. Each row is associated with the syndrome operators denoted by squares in Figure 7.2.

| | **1** | **2** | **3** | **4** | **5** | **6** | **7** | **8** | **9** | **10** | **11** | **12** | **13** |
|---|---|---|---|---|---|---|---|---|---|---|---|---|---|
| $\mathbf{h}_1$ | 1 | 1 | 0 | 1 | 0 | 0 | 0 | 0 | 0 | 0 | 0 | 0 | 0 |
| $\mathbf{h}_2$ | 0 | 1 | 1 | 0 | 1 | 0 | 0 | 0 | 0 | 0 | 0 | 0 | 0 |
| $\mathbf{h}_3$ | 0 | 0 | 0 | 1 | 0 | 1 | 1 | 0 | 1 | 0 | 0 | 0 | 0 |
| $\mathbf{h}_4$ | 0 | 0 | 0 | 0 | 1 | 0 | 1 | 1 | 0 | 1 | 1 | 0 | 0 |
| $\mathbf{h}_5$ | 0 | 0 | 0 | 0 | 0 | 0 | 0 | 0 | 1 | 0 | 1 | 1 | 0 |
| $\mathbf{h}_6$ | 0 | 0 | 0 | 0 | 0 | 0 | 0 | 1 | 0 | 1 | 0 | 0 | 1 |

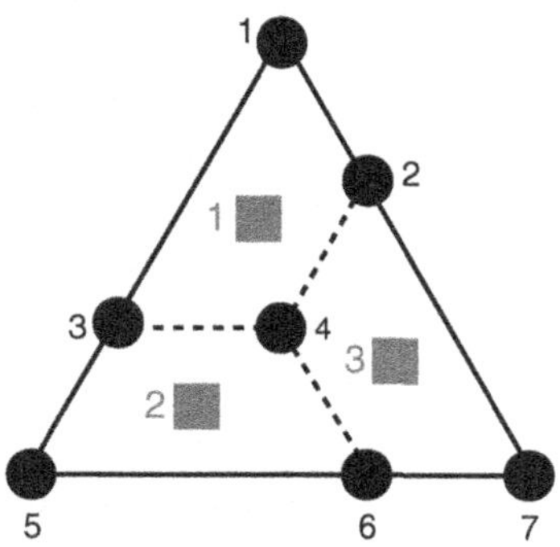


**Figure 7.3** Example of a classical bit arrangement constructed over a triangular lattice structure. The circles lying on the vertices of the lattice represent the codeword bits, while the faces or the plaquettes of the lattice denoted by squares define the parity-check matrix and the syndrome bits of the error correction code. This configuration bears a resemblance to the $C(7, 4)$ classical Hamming code. *Source*: [174]/IEEE/CC BY 4.0.

The PCM can be readily constructed in a similar fashion. Each square of Figure 7.2 represents the row of the PCM, where the adjacent circles denote the index of the column containing a value of 1. For example, the first square is adjacent to the circles numbered 1, 2, and 4. Therefore, in the first row of the PCM, there are only three elements containing a value of 1 and those are marked by the index 1, 2, and 4. The remaining rows of the PCM are generated using the same principle. Explicitly, each row of the PCM of the square lattice code of Figure 7.2 is portrayed in Table 7.1. Finally, the PCM $\mathbf{H}$ of the square lattice code of Figure 7.2 is given by

$$\mathbf{H} = \left[\mathbf{h}_1\ \mathbf{h}_2\ \mathbf{h}_3\ \mathbf{h}_4\ \mathbf{h}_5\ \mathbf{h}_6\right]^T. \tag{7.11}$$

The code construction based on the general lattice structure is not limited to a rectangular lattice. Let us consider, for instance, the triangular lattice of Figure 7.3. The circles lying on the vertex of the lattice define the codeword and the squares on the faces of the lattice define the syndrome vector. The error correction principle of the triangular lattice code is similar to that of its square counterpart. Hence, the PCM of the triangular lattice code is readily derived using the following equation:

$$\mathbf{H} = \left[\mathbf{h}_1\ \mathbf{h}_2\ \mathbf{h}_3\right]^T, \tag{7.12}$$

where $\mathbf{h}_1$, $\mathbf{h}_2$, and $\mathbf{h}_3$ correspond to the syndrome bits given in Table 7.2. It is important to point out that the resultant triangular lattice code bears a strong resemblance to the classical $C(7, 4, 3)$ Hamming code. Specifically, both codes have a codeword length of $n = 7$ and the number of information bits is $k = 4$. Hence, the length of the syndrome vector is 3 bits. Consequently, the codes have $2^4$ legitimate codewords out of the $2^7$ possible received words. Based on the sphere packing bound, the codes are capable of distinguishing $2^3 = 8$ distinct error patterns including the error-free scenario. Therefore, both constructions are capable of correcting exactly a single error with an identical coding rate of $r = 4/7$.

Similar to its rectangular counterpart, increasing the error correction capability of a triangular lattice code is achieved by expanding the underlying lattice configuration. However, increasing the number of vertices of the

**Table 7.2** Constructing the PCM of the triangular lattice code with minimum distance of $d = 3$. Each row is associated with the syndrome operators denoted by circles in Figure 7.3.

| | 1 | 2 | 3 | 4 | 5 | 6 | 7 |
|---|---|---|---|---|---|---|---|
| $\mathbf{h}_1$ | 1 | 1 | 1 | 1 | 0 | 0 | 0 |
| $\mathbf{h}_2$ | 0 | 0 | 1 | 1 | 1 | 1 | 0 |
| $\mathbf{h}_3$ | 0 | 1 | 0 | 1 | 0 | 1 | 1 |

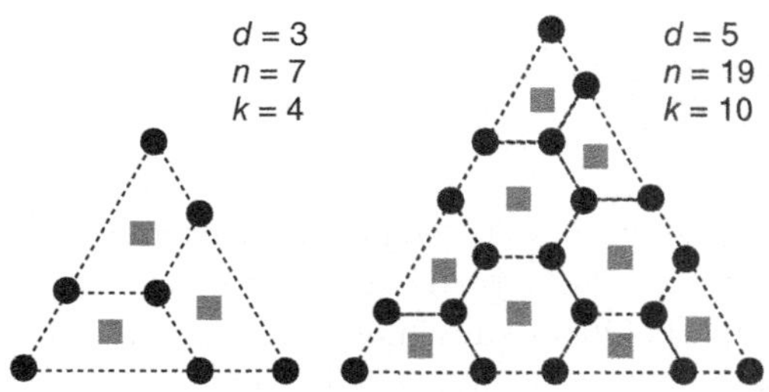


**Figure 7.4** Extending the length of the triangular lattice code, which directly increases the numbers of error corrected. *Source*: [174]/IEEE/CC BY 4.0.

triangular lattice structure is not as straightforward as that of its rectangular counterpart because it can be carried out in several different ways. In this example, we use the construction proposed in [100], and Figure 7.4 illustrates how to increase the number of encoded bits of the triangular lattice code of Figure 7.3 by using hexagonal tiles.

Following the pattern of Figure 7.4, the codeword length, which is also given by the number of vertices of the given lattices, is explicitly formulated as follows:

$$n\text{-vertices} = n_{\text{triangular}} = \frac{1}{4}(3d^2 + 1). \tag{7.13}$$

Hence for $d$=3 we have 7 and for $d$=5 we have 19 vertices. The number of faces in the triangular lattice, which corresponds to the number of rows of the PCM and also to the syndrome vector length, can be expressed as

$$n\text{-faces} = n_{\text{triangular}} - k_{\text{triangular}} = \frac{1}{8}(3d^2 - 3). \tag{7.14}$$

Hence, the number of information bits can be expressed as

$$\begin{aligned} k_{\text{triangular}} &= n_{\text{triangular}} - (n-k)_{\text{triangular}} \\ &= \frac{1}{8}(3d^2 + 5). \end{aligned} \tag{7.15}$$

Finally, the coding rate of the triangular lattice codes of Figure 7.4 is formulated as follows:

$$r_{\text{triangular}} = \frac{k_{\text{triangular}}}{n_{\text{triangular}}} = \frac{3d^2 + 5}{2(3d^2 + 1)}. \tag{7.16}$$

Then, the normalized minimum distance, which directly corresponds to the error correction capability per-bit of a code may be defined as:

$$\delta = \frac{d}{n} \tag{7.17}$$

For square lattice and triangular lattice codes, the normalized minimum distances are given by

$$\begin{aligned} \delta_{\text{square}} &= \frac{d}{2d^2 - 2d + 1} \\ \delta_{\text{triangular}} &= \frac{4d}{3d^2 + 1}. \end{aligned} \tag{7.18}$$

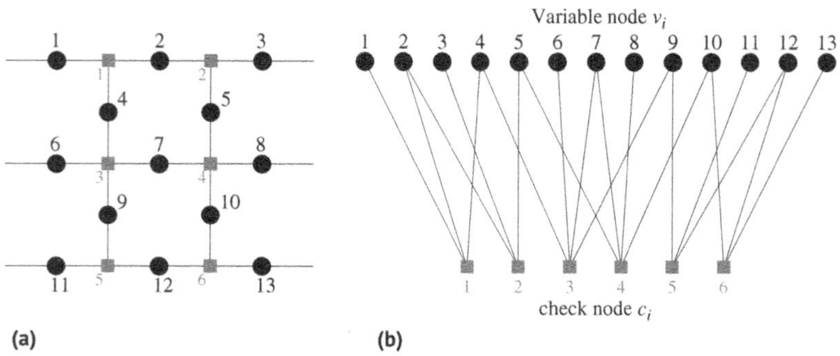


**Figure 7.5** Example of how to represent the square lattice code. (a) The representation in lattice structure. (b) The representation in Tanner or bipartite graph. *Source*: [174]/IEEE/CC BY 4.0.

In the rest of this treatise, we will consider the family of error correction codes based on lattice structures as a prominent representative of classical topological error correction codes (TECC). The lattice structures given in Figures 7.2 and 7.3 can be transformed into Tanner graphs [239]. The dual representation of TECCs in the rectangular lattice domain and in the Tanner graph domain is given in Figure 7.5 as exemplified by the square lattice code. We can observe that TECCs based on square lattices have a maximum row weight of $\rho_{\max} = 4$ and a maximum column weight of $\gamma_{\max} = 2$. By contrast, the codes based on triangular lattices have $\rho_{\max} = 6$ and $\gamma_{\max} = 3$. For a very long codeword, these properties lead to sparse PCMs. Hence, classical TECCs can be viewed as a specific family of LDPC codes. The asymptotical limit of the coding rate for LDPC codes based on TECCs can be directly derived from Eqs. (7.10) and (7.16). As the codeword length tends to infinity ($n \to \infty$), the minimum distance $d$ is also expected to tend to infinity. Hence, for the asymptotical limit we have

$$r^{\infty}_{\text{square}} = \lim_{d\to\infty} \frac{d^2 - d + 1}{2d^2 - 2d + 1} = \frac{1}{2}, \tag{7.19}$$

$$r^{\infty}_{\text{triangular}} = \lim_{d\to\infty} \frac{3d^2 + 5}{2(3d^2 + 1)} = \frac{1}{2}. \tag{7.20}$$

Let us observe Figure 7.6, where we plot the minimum distance ($d$) versus coding rate ($r$) of TECCs based on Eqs. (7.10) and (7.16). We also include the classical codes based on the sphere packing concept, namely the Hamming codes and the BCH codes, whose parameters are portrayed in Tables 7.3 and 7.4, respectively. Additionally, we include some labels for several codes in the figure, in order to show how to convert the code parameters into constellation points in the figure. More explicitly, let us consider the specific triangular codes T1 and T2, where T1 represents the triangular code having a minimum distance of 3, which we have already used in the example in Figure 7.3. As it has been elaborated on earlier, the resultant code T1 is $C(7, 4, 3)$. Hence, the coding rate is $r = 4/7 \approx 0.57$. Again, the triangular code T1 has identical code parameters to the Hamming code $C(7, 4, 3)$, which is labeled H1. Hence, the same point in Figure 7.6 represents both T1 and H1. Next, the code parameters of the triangular code T2 having a minimum distance of $d = 5$ are obtained using Eqs. (7.13) and (7.15) for determining the codeword length $n$ and the information length $k$, respectively. Explicitly, by substituting $d = 5$ into Eqs. (7.13) and (7.15), we have $n = 19$ and $k = 10$. Finally, we arrive at the coding rate of $r = k/n = 10/19 \approx 0.53$ for the triangular code T2. The rest of the code parameters for square codes, triangular codes, Hamming codes, and BCH codes are portrayed in the same way in Figure 7.6.

In general, increasing the minimum distance of the codes while maintaining the codeword length can be achieved at the expense of reducing the coding rate. This phenomenon is perfectly reflected by the behavior of classical BCH codes in Figure 7.6. Explicitly, in Figure 7.6 we portray BCH codes having a constant codeword length of $n = 255$, which are described in Table 7.4. As seen, upon increasing the minimum distance of BCH codes, the coding rate is gradually reduced. Next, increasing the coding rate while maintaining the minimum distance of the code can indeed be achieved by increasing the codeword length. In this case, the Hamming codes, whose code parameters are described in Table 7.3, perfectly reflect this phenomenon. Observe in Figure 7.6, that for the Hamming codes exhibiting a constant minimum distance of $d = 3$, we can see the gradual increase of coding rate upon increasing the codeword length. However, the behavior of the BCH and Hamming codes is not reflected by the TECCs. Let us elaborate on the TECCs behavior in Figure 7.6. The increase of the minimum distance of TECCs upon increasing the codeword length looks very impressive since they do not seem to require much sacrifice in

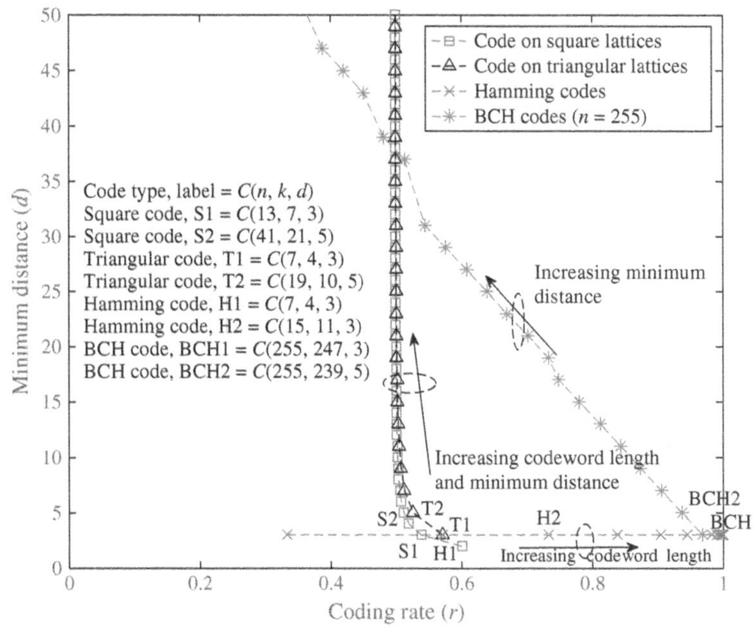


**Figure 7.6** The coding rate versus minimum distance of TECCs. For asymptotical limit, the TECCs may be categorized into LDPC codes and the coding rates converge to $r = \frac{1}{2}$. We also include the BCH codes and Hamming codes for the sake of comparison. The coding rate for the square-lattice-based codes and the triangular-lattice-based codes are defined in Eqs. (7.10) and (7.16), respectively. The code parameters for classical Hamming and BCH codes are described in Tables 7.3 and 7.4, respectively. We put labels only for several codes as examples on how to convert the given code parameters into the figure. *Source*: [174]/IEEE/CC BY 4.0.

**Table 7.3** Code parameters of classical Hamming code having a single error correction capability, which is used in Figures 7.6 and 7.7. The coding rate $r$ and normalized minimum distance $\delta$ are calculated using Eqs. (7.1) and (7.17), respectively.

| *n* | *k* | *d* | *n* | *k* | *d* |
|---|---|---|---|---|---|
| 3 | 1 | 3 | 127 | 120 | 3 |
| 7 | 4 | 3 | 255 | 247 | 3 |
| 15 | 11 | 3 | 511 | 502 | 3 |
| 31 | 26 | 3 | 1023 | 1013 | 3 |
| 63 | 57 | 3 | ... | ... | ... |

terms of coding rate reduction. In fact, the coding rate is saturated at approximately $r = 1/2$ for long codewords. This is indeed a rather different behavior compared to that of the classical BCH codes. However, it is of pivotal importance to mention again that the increasing error correction capability per codeword does not necessarily imply the improvement of error correction capability per bit. Therefore, we have to normalize the performance to the codeword length for a fair comparison.

Let us now observe Figure 7.7, where we plot the normalized minimum distance ($\delta$) versus the coding rate ($r$) of TECCs based on Eq. (7.18). We include both the BCH codes and the Hamming codes for the sake of comparison. We also plot the classical Hamming bound [226] and GV bound [227] in this figure to portray the upper bound and lower bound of the normalized minimum distance, which correspond directly to the normalized error correction capability, given the coding rate. The classical Hamming bound is formulated as follows [226]:

$$\frac{k}{n} \leq 1 - H\left(\frac{d}{2n}\right), \tag{7.21}$$

**Table 7.4** Code parameters of classical BCH codes having codeword length of $n = 255$, which is used in Figures 7.6 and 7.7. The coding rate $r$ and normalized minimum distance $\delta$ are calculated using Eqs. (7.1) and (7.17), respectively.

| *n* | *k* | *d* | *n* | *k* | *d* | *n* | *k* | *d* |
|---|---|---|---|---|---|---|---|---|
| 255 | 1 | 255 | 255 | 87 | 53 | 255 | 171 | 23 |
| 255 | 9 | 127 | 255 | 91 | 51 | 255 | 179 | 21 |
| 255 | 13 | 119 | 255 | 99 | 47 | 255 | 187 | 19 |
| 255 | 21 | 111 | 255 | 107 | 45 | 255 | 191 | 17 |
| 255 | 29 | 95 | 255 | 115 | 43 | 255 | 199 | 15 |
| 255 | 37 | 91 | 255 | 123 | 39 | 255 | 207 | 13 |
| 255 | 45 | 87 | 255 | 131 | 37 | 255 | 215 | 11 |
| 255 | 47 | 85 | 255 | 139 | 31 | 255 | 223 | 9 |
| 255 | 55 | 63 | 255 | 147 | 29 | 255 | 231 | 7 |
| 255 | 63 | 61 | 255 | 155 | 27 | 255 | 239 | 5 |
| 255 | 71 | 59 | 255 | 163 | 25 | 255 | 247 | 3 |
| 255 | 79 | 55 | | | | | | |

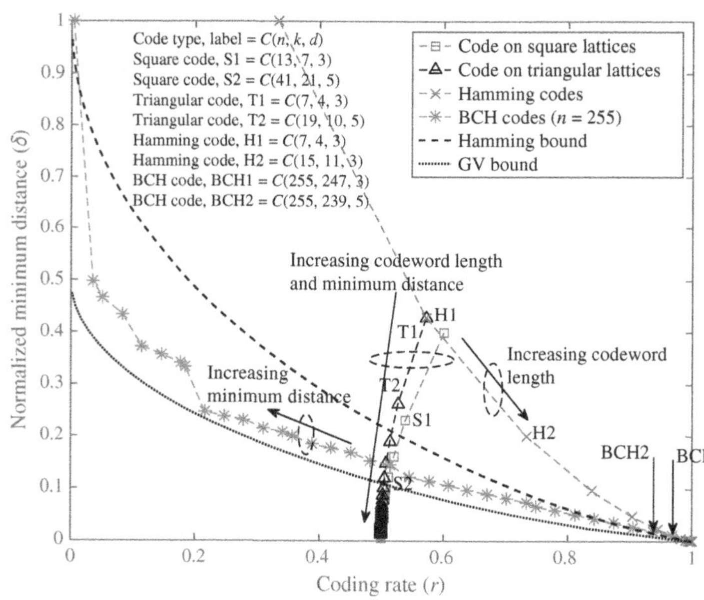


**Figure 7.7** The coding rate versus normalized minimum distance of TECCs. For asymptotical limit, the TECCs may be categorized into LDPC codes and the coding rates converge to $r = \frac{1}{2}$, while the normalized minimum distances ($\delta$) vanish to zero. In addition, we also include the classical Hamming and BCH codes, which constructed based on sphere packing bound, for the sake of comparison. The code parameters for classical Hamming and BCH codes are portrayed in Tables 7.3 and 7.4, respectively. We put labels only for several codes as examples on how to convert the given code parameters into the figure. *Source*: [174]/IEEE/CC BY 4.0.

where $H(x)$ is the binary entropy of $x$ defined by $H(x) = -x \log_2 x - (1-x) \log_2(1-x)$, while the classical GV bound is expressed as [227]

$$\frac{k}{n} \geq 1 - H\left(\frac{d}{n}\right). \tag{7.22}$$

The classical Hamming bound and GV bound defined in Eqs. (7.21) and (7.22) are valid for asymptotical limit where $n \to \infty$.

**Table 7.5** The code parameters of TECC-based LDPC codes.

| Parameter | Square lattice | Triangular lattice |
|---|---|---|
| $r$ | $\approx \frac{1}{2}$ | $\approx \frac{1}{2}$ |
| $d$ | $\mathcal{O}(\sqrt{n})$ | $\mathcal{O}(\sqrt{n})$ |
| $\delta$ | $\frac{d}{2d^2-2d+1}$ | $\frac{4d}{3d^2+1}$ |
| $\rho_{\max}$ | 4 | 6 |
| $\gamma_{\max}$ | 2 | 3 |
| Girth | 6 | 4 |

The classical Hamming codes constitute the so-called *perfect codes* for a finite-length, since they always achieve the Hamming bound for finite-length codes.[1] Therefore, the Hamming codes also mark the upper bound of normalized minimum distance, given the coding rate of finite-length codewords. Secondly, the classical BCH codes having a codeword length of $n = 255$ lay perfectly—as expected—between the Hamming and GV bound in the asymptotical limit, as shown in Figure 7.7. However, we observe an unusual behavior for the family of TECCs, since the normalized minimum distance drops to zero upon increasing the codeword length, while the coding rate saturates at $r = 1/2$. We hypothesize that since these codes were not designed using the sphere packing concept—which the Hamming and BCH codes are based on—the Hamming distance radius of the associated decoding sphere in the TECCs code space is most likely to be nonidentical for the different codewords. Also, the minimum distance of TECCs is only on the order of $\mathcal{O}(\sqrt{n})$, which implies that the codeword length of TECCs is proportional to the factor of $\mathcal{O}(d^2)$. By contrast, for classical BCH and Hamming codes the growth of the minimum distance is approximately linear, i.e. of order $\mathcal{O}(n)$. It can be seen that even though the growth of minimum distance per codeword of the TECCs appears to be impressive in Figure 7.6, it is not fast enough to compensate for the undesired effect of the increasing codeword length. Hence, the TECC error correction capability per bit tends to zero in the asymptotical limit. Nevertheless, we leave the definitive answer for this peculiar phenomenon open for future research, since our focus in this treatise is on finding the classical-to-quantum isomorphism of TECCs.

Since the TECCs associated with the asymptotical limit of $n \to \infty$ belong to the family of LDPC codes, an efficient LDPC decoder such as the belief propagation (BP) technique [240] can be invoked for these code constructions. However, the normalized minimum distance of the LDPC codes based on topological order tends to zero, as the codeword length increases. Nevertheless, TECC-based LDPC codes exhibit several desirable code properties, such as an attractive coding rate ($r \approx 1/2$), structured construction, and unbounded minimum distance. However, another aspect worth considering for TECC-based LDPC codes is the fact that we can find numerous cycles of length 4 in triangular constructions and cycles of length 6 in square constructions, which potentially degrades the performance of the codes. A summary of the specific code parameters of TECC-based LDPC codes is given in Table 7.5.

## 7.3 Quantum Topological Error Correction Codes: Design Examples

Let us now delve deeper into the TECC concept in the quantum domain. The quantum version of TECCs, namely the QTECCs, constitute a member of the QSC family, whose stabilizer operators are defined by the underlying lattice structure. This formalism offers several benefits for the implementation of quantum computers. Firstly, it explicitly accommodates the physical implementation of quantum memory by mapping the qubits to the lattice arrangement exemplified by Figures 7.2 and 7.3. Secondly, the localized nature of the stabilizer measurements confines the interaction among qubits and also eliminates the interaction of qubits associated with specific quantum gates that are physically far from each other within the topology. Thirdly, the number of errors corrected can

1 The Hamming bound for finite length codes has a different formulation from that of asymptotical limit. Therefore, we refer to [179] for further explanations.

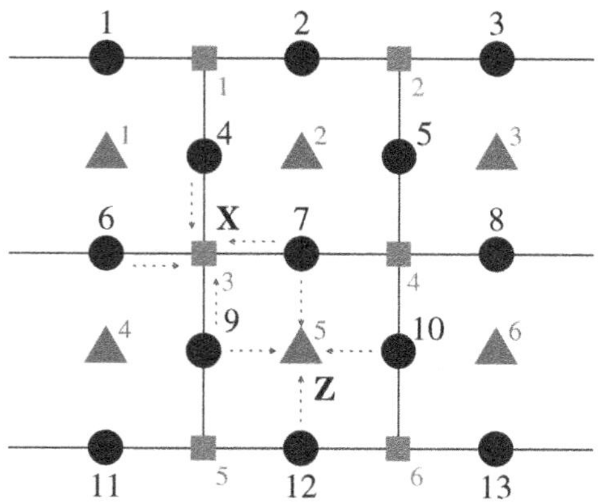


**Figure 7.8** Example of qubit arrangement on a rectangular lattice structure. The circle-based qubits on the edges of the lattice represent the physical qubits or the encoded state, the square-based qubits lying on the vertices of the lattice act as the **X** stabilizer operators, while the triangle-based qubits lying on the plaquettes (faces) of the lattice constitute the **Z** stabilizer operators. *Source*: [174]/IEEE/CC BY 4.0.

be increased simply by extending the size of the lattice. For now, let us assume having a square-shaped lattice structure similar to Figure 7.2 for defining the stabilizer operators of a surface code illustrated in Figure 7.8 [98]. Explicitly, surface codes represent the quantum equivalent of classical TECCs defined on rectangular lattice structures. The physical qubits are portrayed by the circles lying on the edge of the lattice, the **X** stabilizer operators are defined by the squares on the lattice vertices, while the **Z** stabilizers are defined by the triangles on the lattice plaquettes (faces). The stabilizer operators of QTECCs are defined as follows:

$$A_v = \prod_{i \in \text{vertex}(v)} \mathbf{X}_i \,, B_p = \prod_{i \in \text{plaquette}(p)} \mathbf{Z}_i, \tag{7.23}$$

where $i$ indicates the index of stabilizer operators containing the Pauli matrix **X** as well as **Z** and the rest of the stabilizer operators are given by the Pauli identity matrix **I**. Hence, the encoded state of the physical qubits of QTECCs is constrained within a code space $C$ satisfying

$$C = \{|\overline{\psi}\rangle \in \mathcal{H} | A_v|\overline{\psi}\rangle = |\overline{\psi}\rangle,\ B_p|\overline{\psi}\rangle = |\overline{\psi}\rangle;\ \forall v, p\}. \tag{7.24}$$

More specifically, let us revisit Figure 7.8 for exemplifying the construction of the stabilizer operators of a QTECC, namely of a surface code, which is one of the QTECC constructions whose stabilizer operators are defined by a rectangular lattice structure [98]. For instance, the square on the vertex number 3 of Figure 7.8 represents the **X** stabilizer operator of $A_3 = \mathbf{X}_4\mathbf{X}_6\mathbf{X}_7\mathbf{X}_9$, as seen in the row $S_3$ of Table 7.6. Similarly, the triangle on the plaquette number 5 of Figure 7.8 defines the **Z** stabilizer operator of $B_5 = \mathbf{Z}_7\mathbf{Z}_9\mathbf{Z}_{10}\mathbf{Z}_{12}$, as seen in the line $B_5$ of Table 7.6. By performing the same evaluation for all of the squares and triangles, we arrive at the stabilizer operators for the quantum surface codes, as listed in Table 7.6.

Let us now consider an example of how the error correction procedure works by revisiting Figure 7.8 using QTECCs, which are similar to classical TECCs. For instance, let us assume that the quantum decoherence imposes a bit-flip (**X**) error on the physical qubit index 7. Since, the **X**-type error commutes with the **Z** stabilizer operators, which are represented by the triangles, the adjacent **Z** stabilizer operators return the eigenstate values of $-1$ upon measurement. Consequently, the **Z** stabilizer measurements yield a syndrome vector of $\mathbf{s}_z = [0\ 1\ 0\ 0\ 1\ 0]$, where only the vector elements of $i = 2, 5$ have the value of 1. For a short block code considered in Figure 7.8, the error recovery operators $\mathcal{R}$ to be detailed later in Figure 8.3 are determined based on hard-decision maximum-likelihood (ML) decoding, which is translated into a simple look-up table (LUT) decoder. Therefore, based on the syndrome vector of $\mathbf{s}_z$, the error recovery operator $\mathcal{R}$ of Figure 8.3 is given by $\mathcal{R} = \mathbf{X}_7$. Likewise, let us now assume that the qubit on index 7 also suffers from a **Z**-type error imposed by the quantum channel. The associated syndrome vector gleaned from the **X** stabilizer operators is $\mathbf{s}_x = [0\ 0\ 1\ 1\ 0\ 0]$, where only the vector elements of $i = 3, 4$ have the value of 1. Thus, based on the syndrome vector of $\mathbf{s}_x$, the decoder applies the error recovery operator of $\mathcal{R} = \mathbf{Z}_7$.

**Table 7.6** The stabilizer operators ($S_i$) of the quantum surface code having the lattice construction of Figure 7.8. The code has a minimum distance of 3 ($d = 3$), which means that it is only capable of correcting a single qubit error.

| $S_i$ | $A_v$ | $S_i$ | $B_p$ |
|---|---|---|---|
| $S_1$ | $\mathbf{X}_1\mathbf{X}_2\mathbf{X}_4$ | $S_7$ | $\mathbf{Z}_1\mathbf{Z}_4\mathbf{Z}_6$ |
| $S_2$ | $\mathbf{X}_2\mathbf{X}_3\mathbf{X}_5$ | $S_8$ | $\mathbf{Z}_2\mathbf{Z}_4\mathbf{Z}_5\mathbf{Z}_7$ |
| $S_3$ | $\mathbf{X}_4\mathbf{X}_6\mathbf{X}_7\mathbf{X}_9$ | $S_9$ | $\mathbf{Z}_3\mathbf{Z}_5\mathbf{Z}_8$ |
| $S_4$ | $\mathbf{X}_5\mathbf{X}_7\mathbf{X}_8\mathbf{X}_{10}$ | $S_{10}$ | $\mathbf{Z}_6\mathbf{Z}_9\mathbf{Z}_{11}$ |
| $S_5$ | $\mathbf{X}_9\mathbf{X}_{11}\mathbf{X}_{12}$ | $S_{11}$ | $\mathbf{Z}_7\mathbf{Z}_9\mathbf{Z}_{10}\mathbf{Z}_{12}$ |
| $S_6$ | $\mathbf{X}_{10}\mathbf{X}_{12}\mathbf{X}_{13}$ | $S_{12}$ | $\mathbf{Z}_8\mathbf{Z}_{10}\mathbf{Z}_{13}$ |

The error correction capability $t$ of a QSC $\mathcal{C}[n, k, d]$ can be determined by its minimum distance $d$ as follows:

$$t = \left\lfloor \frac{d-1}{2} \right\rfloor. \tag{7.25}$$

Therefore, in order to verify the error correction capability of a QSC $\mathcal{C}$, first, we have to evaluate the minimum distance $d$ based on the stabilizer operators $S_i \in \mathcal{S}$. Let the normalizer $\mathcal{N}(\mathcal{S}) \in \mathcal{P}_n$ be the set of operators $P_i \in \mathcal{P}_n$ so that $PS_iP^\dagger = S_j \in \mathcal{S}$ for all $S_i \in \mathcal{S}$ and $i$ is not necessarily equal to $j$. It is clear that all the stabilizer operators $S_i \in \mathcal{S}$ are automatically in $\mathcal{N}(\mathcal{S})$. Now, we are interested in the set of operators in the normalizer $\mathcal{N}(\mathcal{S})$ that does not belong to the stabilizer operators $\mathcal{S}$, which is denoted by $\mathcal{N}(\mathcal{S}) - \mathcal{S}$. The minimum distance of a QSC $\mathcal{C}$ is equal to $d$ if and only if $\mathcal{N}(\mathcal{S}) - \mathcal{S}$ contains no elements with weight less than $d$, where the weight of a Pauli operator $P_i \in \mathcal{P}_n$ is the number of nonidentity Pauli operators. In other words, the minimum distance of a QSC $\mathcal{C}$ can be defined by the minimum weight of the operators $P_i$, which commute with all stabilizer operators $S_i \in \mathcal{S}$, but are not element of $\mathcal{S}$.

In the case of the rectangular lattice structure of Figure 7.8, a good example of such an operator $P_i$ is represented by the specific chain connecting the two boundaries of the lattice. To elaborate a little further, let us take a Pauli operator $P$ represented by the shortened version $P = \mathbf{X}_2\mathbf{X}_7\mathbf{X}_{12}$ connecting the boundaries of the lattice given in Figure 7.8. It can be readily checked that this specific Pauli operator $P$ commutes with all the stabilizer generators $G_i \in \mathcal{S}$, but it cannot be represented as the product of any stabilizer generators $G_i \in \mathcal{S}$. Since $P_i$ represents the lowest weight Pauli operator $P_i$ commuting with all the stabilizer operators $S_i \in \mathcal{S}$, but not an element of $\mathcal{S}$, the weight of $P_i$ determines the minimum distance of the QSC defined by the rectangular lattice of Figure 7.8. Therefore, we conclude that based on the stabilizer generators given in Table 7.6, the minimum distance of the QSC defined by the rectangular lattice of Figure 7.8 is $d = 3$. Furthermore, the dimension of the lattices defining the stabilizer operators $G_i \in \mathcal{S}$ can be used to calculate the minimum distance $d$, the number of logical qubits and physical qubits, as well as the quantum coding rate $r_Q$.

Again, similar to the classical TECCs, the construction of QTECCs is not limited to the square lattice structure. In this spirit, let us now elaborate on another construction inspired by [100] using a triangular lattice based on the classic example of Figure 7.3. In the proposal of [100], this specific code construction is often referred to as the (triangular) color code, since the underlying triangular lattice may be composed by three distinct colored tiles, each representing a nonoverlapping topological region of interaction and protection. However, constructing the stabilizer operators of color codes slightly differs from that of the surface codes. Explicitly, the color codes use the lattice plaquettes to define both the $\mathbf{Z}$ and $\mathbf{X}$ stabilizer operators, rather than having separate stabilizers. Consequently, the resultant color codes belong to the family of dual-containing CSS codes, which is in contrast to the rectangular-shaped surface codes constellation that belong to the class of non-dual-containing CSS codes. For color codes, defining both the $\mathbf{Z}$ and $\mathbf{X}$ stabilizer operators using the same plaquette always guarantees to satisfy the symplectic criterion of Eq. (12.8). However, for the rectangular-shaped surface code constellations, we cannot always satisfy the symplectic criterion by using the same procedure. Therefore, the dual pair of the lattice is used for defining half of the stabilizer operators of the surface codes to satisfy the symplectic criterion.[2]

2 The dual pair of a lattice or a graph $G$ is the graph that has a vertex for each plaquette of the graph.

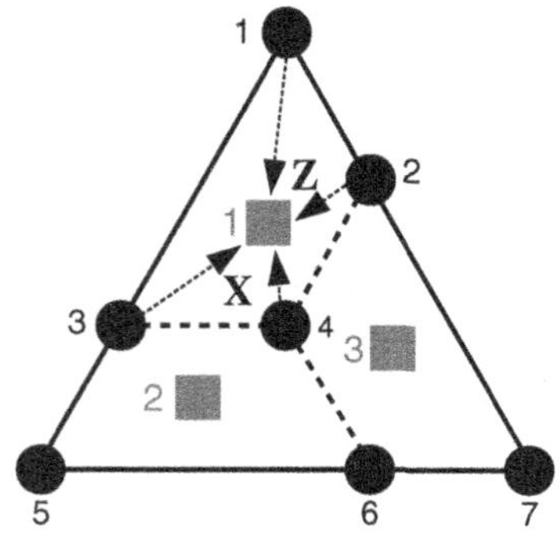


**Figure 7.9** Example of a qubit arrangement for a color code, which is a type of QTECCs whose stabilizer operators are defined by a triangular lattice structure. The circle-based qubits on the vertices of the lattice represent the physical qubits, while the faces or the plaquettes of the lattice denoted by squares define stabilizer operators of the color code. The resultant code has a minimum distance of $d = 3$ and hence becomes capable of correcting a single qubit error. This specific configuration bears resemblance to Steane's 7-qubit code $\mathcal{C}[7, 1, 3]$. *Source*: [174]/IEEE/CC BY 4.0.

Let us consider Figure 7.9 for constructing the stabilizer operators of distance-3 color codes, which are only capable of correcting a single qubit error. The plaquette denoted by square at index 3 is used to define both the **Z** and **X** stabilizer operators. Thus, the resultant **X** stabilizer operator is $A_3 = \mathbf{X}_2\mathbf{X}_4\mathbf{X}_6\mathbf{X}_7$ and the resultant of **Z** stabilizer operator is $B_3 = \mathbf{Z}_2\mathbf{Z}_4\mathbf{Z}_6\mathbf{Z}_7$. The stabilizer operators for the color code having the minimum distance 3 in Figure 7.9 are listed in Table 7.7. We can observe that the color code of Figure 7.3 exhibits a strong resemblance to Steane's 7-qubit code.

To draw on the parallelism between classical TECCs and QTECCs, let us consider the stabilizer operators of the color code having a minimum distance of $d = 3$, as seen in Table 7.7. Since the distance-3 color code belongs to the family of quantum CSS codes, the PCM **H** obtained by using Eqs. (3.18) and (3.21) as well as Table 7.7 may be formulated as follows:

$$\mathbf{H} = \left(\begin{array}{ccccccc|ccccccc} 1 & 1 & 1 & 1 & 0 & 0 & 0 & 0 & 0 & 0 & 0 & 0 & 0 & 0 \\ 0 & 0 & 1 & 1 & 1 & 1 & 0 & 0 & 0 & 0 & 0 & 0 & 0 & 0 \\ 0 & 1 & 0 & 1 & 0 & 1 & 1 & 0 & 0 & 0 & 0 & 0 & 0 & 0 \\ 0 & 0 & 0 & 0 & 0 & 0 & 0 & 1 & 1 & 1 & 1 & 0 & 0 & 0 \\ 0 & 0 & 0 & 0 & 0 & 0 & 0 & 0 & 0 & 1 & 1 & 1 & 1 & 0 \\ 0 & 0 & 0 & 0 & 0 & 0 & 0 & 0 & 1 & 0 & 1 & 0 & 1 & 1 \end{array}\right). \tag{7.26}$$

A CSS stabilizer code $\mathcal{C}[n, k, d]$ having $(n - k)$ stabilizer operators can be portrayed as a classical code having a PCM **H** containing $(n - k) \times 2n$ elements. Therefore, the coding rate of the classical dual of a quantum CSS code can be expressed as follows [83]:

$$\begin{aligned} r_C &= \frac{2n - (n - k)}{2n}, \\ &= \frac{n + k}{2n}, \\ &= \frac{1}{2}\left(1 + \frac{k}{n}\right), \\ &= \frac{1}{2}(1 + r_Q), \end{aligned} \tag{7.27}$$

where $r_C$ is the coding rate of the classical dual of the stabilizer code $C[n, k, d]$ exhibiting a quantum coding rate of $r_Q$. The relationship between the classical and quantum coding rate in Eq. (7.27) can be rewritten as

$$r_Q = 2r_C - 1. \tag{7.28}$$

**Table 7.7** The stabilizer operators ($S_i$) of the color code seen in Figure 7.9. The code has a minimum distance of 3 ($d = 3$), which means that it is only capable of correcting a single qubit error.

| $S_i$ | $A_p$ | $S_i$ | $B_p$ |
|---|---|---|---|
| $S_1$ | $\mathbf{X}_1\mathbf{X}_2\mathbf{X}_3\mathbf{X}_4$ | $S_4$ | $\mathbf{Z}_1\mathbf{Z}_2\mathbf{Z}_3\mathbf{Z}_4$ |
| $S_2$ | $\mathbf{X}_3\mathbf{X}_4\mathbf{X}_5\mathbf{X}_6$ | $S_5$ | $\mathbf{Z}_3\mathbf{Z}_4\mathbf{Z}_5\mathbf{Z}_6$ |
| $S_3$ | $\mathbf{X}_2\mathbf{X}_4\mathbf{X}_6\mathbf{X}_7$ | $S_6$ | $\mathbf{Z}_2\mathbf{Z}_4\mathbf{Z}_6\mathbf{Z}_7$ |

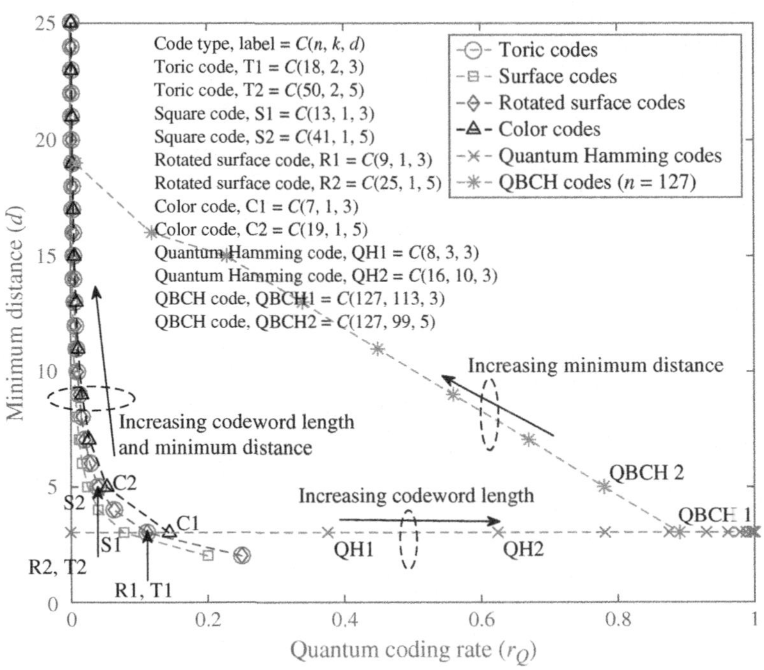


**Figure 7.10** The minimum distance ($d$) versus the quantum coding rate ($r_Q$) of QTECCs based on the parameter given in Table 7.8. For QTECCs, the quantum coding rate tends to zero as we increase the minimum distance. We also include the QBCH codes having the physical qubits of $n = 127$ and quantum Hamming codes for the sake of comparing the QTECCs with the non-topological QSCs. *Source*: [174]/IEEE/CC BY 4.0.

For instance, let us consider the distance-3 color codes $C[n, k, d] = \mathcal{C}[7, 1, 3]$, as exemplified in Figure 7.9, and its classical dual $C(n, k, d) = C(7, 4, 3)$, as seen in Figure 7.3. Explicitly, we have the classical coding rate of $r_C = 4/7$ for the $C(7, 4, 3)$ code. By substituting $r_C = 4/7$ into Eq. (7.28), we obtain the quantum coding rate for its quantum counterpart as $r_Q = 1/7$, which is the quantum coding rate of the distance-3 color code $C[7, 1, 3]$. The same goes for the classical square codes and their quantum counterpart, namely for the surface codes. Let us consider the distance-5 classical square code, which is labeled by S2 in Figure 7.6 and its quantum pair, which is labeled by S2 in Figure 7.10. We can readily determine the quantum coding rate of the surface code S2 $C[41, 1, 5]$, which is $r_Q = 1/41$. Therefore, by substituting $r_Q = 1/41$ into Eq. (7.27), we arrive at the coding rate of its classical dual given by $r_C = 21/41$, which is indeed the coding rate of the classical square code S2 $C(41, 21, 5)$.

Similar to their classical counterparts, the code parameters of QTECCs, such as the number of logical qubits $k$, the number of physical qubits $n$, the minimum distance of the code $d$, as well as the quantum coding rate $r_Q$, depend on the size of the lattices. Following the same line of investigation as for the classical TECCs, in Table 7.8 we characterize the family of QTECCs.

Explicitly, we plot the minimum distance ($d$) versus quantum coding rate ($r_Q$) of QTECCs in Figure 7.10 for color codes [100] for the family of rotated surface codes [99], for surface codes [98] and for toric codes [95]. We also include the family of non-topological QBCH codes [61] having $n = 127$ physical qubits and the quantum

**Table 7.8** The code parameters for various QTECCs based on the minimum distance $d$ of the code.

| Codes type | Dimension | Number of physical qubits | Number of stabilizers | Number of logical qubits |
|---|---|---|---|---|
| Color | $d$ | $\frac{1}{4}(3d^2+1)$ | $\frac{1}{4}(3d^2-3)$ | 1 |
| Rotated-surface | $d \times d$ | $d^2$ | $d^2-1$ | 1 |
| Surface | $d \times d$ | $2d^2-2d+1$ | $2d^2-2d$ | 1 |
| Toric | $d \times d$ | $2d^2$ | $2d^2-2$ | 2 |

a. For triangular color codes the dimension is defined by the side length of the equilateral triangle.

**Table 7.9** Code parameters of quantum Hamming codes having a single error correction capability, which is used in Figures 7.10 and 7.11. The quantum coding rate $r_Q$ and normalized minimum distance $\delta$ are calculated using Eqs. (7.1) and (7.17), respectively.

| $n$ | $k$ | $d$ | $n$ | $k$ | $d$ |
|---|---|---|---|---|---|
| 8 | 3 | 3 | 256 | 246 | 3 |
| 16 | 10 | 3 | 512 | 501 | 3 |
| 32 | 25 | 3 | 1024 | 1012 | 3 |
| 64 | 56 | 3 | 2048 | 2035 | 3 |
| 128 | 119 | 3 | … | … | … |

**Table 7.10** Code parameters of QBCH codes having codeword length of $n = 127$, which is used in Figures 7.10 and 7.11. The quantum coding rate $r_Q$ and normalized minimum distance $\delta$ are calculated using Eqs. (7.1) and (7.17), respectively.

| $n$ | $k$ | $d$ | $n$ | $k$ | $d$ |
|---|---|---|---|---|---|
| 127 | 1 | 19 | 127 | 71 | 9 |
| 127 | 15 | 16 | 127 | 85 | 7 |
| 127 | 29 | 15 | 127 | 99 | 5 |
| 127 | 43 | 13 | 127 | 113 | 3 |
| 127 | 57 | 11 | | | |

Hamming codes, which constitute the quantum-domain pair of the Hamming code constructions [57]. Similarly to the classical domain, the behavior of both the QBCH codes and the quantum Hamming codes listed in Table 7.9 and 7.10 is as expected, namely reminiscent of the behavior inherited from their classical-domain counterparts. However, it is interesting to observe that the quantum coding rate of QTECCs tends to zero for long codewords, which is not unexpected, if we consider the classical to quantum isomorphism in the context of the coding rate given in Eqs. (7.27) and (7.28). For the classical TECCs, the coding rate $r_C$ approaches the value of $r_C = 1/2$ for long codewords. Hence, by substituting $r_C = 1/2$ into Eq. (7.28), we arrive at $r_Q = 0$, which is the phenomenon we observe in Figure 7.10.

Next, we plot the normalized minimum distance ($\delta$) versus the quantum coding rate ($r_Q$) in Figure 7.11. Once again, for the sake of comparison, we also include the quantum Hamming bound [58] and the quantum GV bound derived for CSS codes [86] in addition to the QBCH codes and the quantum Hamming codes. The quantum Hamming bound is defined by [58]

$$\frac{k}{n} \leq 1 - \left(\frac{d}{2n}\right)\log_2 3 - H\left(\frac{d}{2n}\right), \tag{7.29}$$

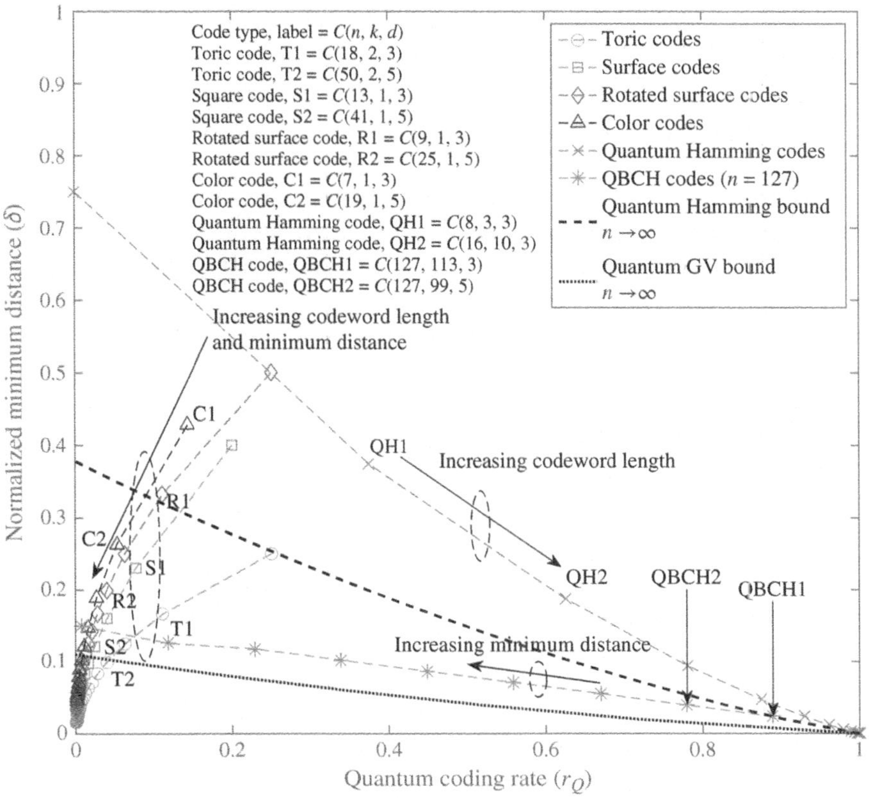


**Figure 7.11** The normalized minimum distance ($\delta$) versus the quantum coding rate ($r_Q$) of QTECCs based on the parameter given in Table 7.8. For QTECCs, the normalized minimum distance and quantum coding rate tend to zero as we increase the minimum distance. We also include the QBCH codes having the physical qubits of $n = 127$, quantum Hamming codes, quantum Hamming bound and also quantum GV bound for CSS codes for the sake of comparing the QTECCs with the non-topological QSCs. *Source*: [174]/IEEE/CC BY 4.0.

while the quantum GV bound for CSS codes is given by [86]

$$\frac{k}{n} \geq 1 - 2H\left(\frac{d}{n}\right). \tag{7.30}$$

Both the quantum Hamming bound and the quantum GV bound of Figure 7.11 serve the same purpose as the classical Hamming bound and the GV bound seen in Figure 7.7. Explicitly, they portray the upper bound and the lower bound of normalized minimum distance versus quantum coding rate trade-off. Once again, the puzzling behavior of classical TECCs resurfaces for the QTECCs, as observed in Figure 7.11. Since all the QBCH codes, quantum Hamming codes and QTECCs inherit the properties of their classical counterparts, their behavior is reminiscent of that of their classical counterparts. As for the QTECCs, the definitive interpretation of this unusual behavior is left for future exploration in our research. Nonetheless, for a relatively long codeword, the QTECCs are reminiscent of QLDPC codes. Observe from Figure 7.11 that both the normalized minimum distance and the quantum coding rate of QTECCs tend to zero upon increasing the minimum distance by increasing the codeword length. Therefore, the QTECCs are deemed to be more favorable for short to medium codeword lengths.

## 7.4 Performance of Quantum Topological Error Correction Codes

In this section we consider the performance of QTECCs in the face of quantum depolarizing channels. Explicitly, the quantum depolarizing channel is characterized by the quantum depolarizing probability $p$ inflicting an error pattern constituted by the Pauli operators $P \in \mathcal{P}_n$ upon the state of physical qubits. Each qubit may independently experience a bit-flip error ($\mathbf{X}$), a phase-flip error ($\mathbf{Z}$), or both bit-flip and phase-flip errors ($\mathbf{Y}$) with an equal probability of $p/3$. In order to get a more precise insight into the performance trends of QTECCs, we have to distinguish how the different error patterns affect the state representing the physical qubits. Explicitly, the $n$-tuple Pauli error patterns exemplified in Figures 7.12 and 7.13 may be classified as follows:

a. **Harmful detected error pattern**. This specific type of error pattern has a similarity to the conventional bit errors experienced in the classical domain. The error pattern of $\mathcal{P}$ anti-commutes with the stabilizer operators $S_i \in \mathcal{S}$, hence it triggers nontrivial syndrome values.
b. **Harmful undetected error pattern**. The error pattern commutes with all of the stabilizer operators, but it does not belong to the stabilizer group $\mathcal{S}$. In the classical domain, this is similar to an error pattern that returns an all-zero syndrome. The error pattern is harmful, since it does not result in a nontrivial syndrome value, yet it corrupts the legitimate state of the physical qubits.
c. **Harmless undetected error pattern**. This particular error pattern does not have any classical counterpart. The error pattern is harmless because it belongs to the stabilizer group $\mathcal{S}$. This is also referred to as a degenerate error pattern. Consequently, the error pattern does not alter the legitimate state of the physical qubits. By considering the phenomenon referred to as degeneracy, the actual performance of QTECCs are potentially improved.

To illustrate both the harmless and harmful undetected error patterns, we refer to Figures 7.12 and 7.13. We commence by considering the *harmless undetected error patterns*, which are illustrated in Figure 7.12. In this example, we consider a surface code having a minimum distance of 5, which implies that it is only capable of correcting 2-qubit errors. Following the stabilizer formulation of QTECCs discussed in Section 7.3, the physical qubits are arranged along the edges of the square lattice, while the **X** stabilizer operators are located at the vertices. Therefore, the **X** stabilizer operators on the vertices are used for indicating the **Z** errors, which will trigger eigenvalues of $-1$ if they anticommute with the **X** stabilizer operators. Let us assume that the quantum depolarizing channel inflicts three **Z** errors on the physical qubits, which are denoted by the filled circles in Figure 7.12, while the hollow circles represent the error-free physical qubits. All of the error patterns given in Figure 7.12 a–c trigger

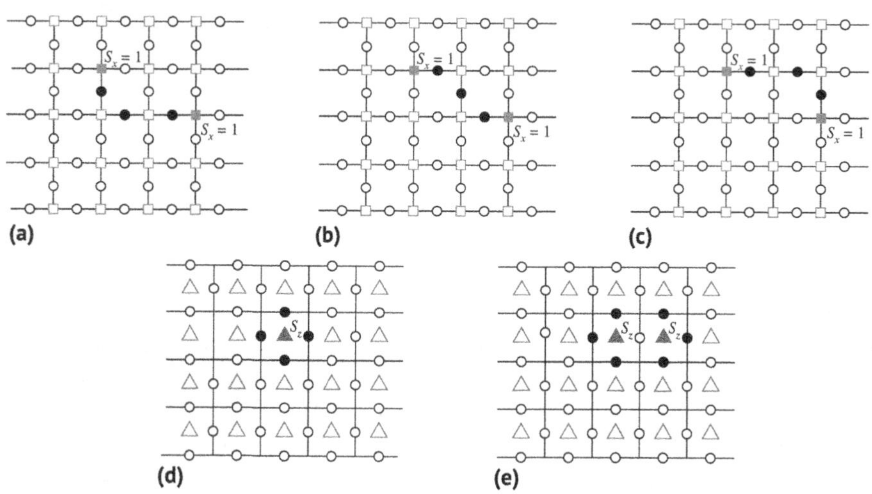


**Figure 7.12** Illustration of how the error recovery operator $\mathcal{R}$ creates the degenerate error patterns and how the degeneracy nature of QECCs may improve the performance of QTECCs. All of the error patterns given in (a), (b) and (c) represent error patterns generating an identical syndrome value. Without loss of generality, let us assume that based on the generated syndrome value, the decoder always decides to perform error recovery operator $\mathcal{R}$ of (a) on the corrupted state of physical qubits. If the actual error pattern is (a), the corrupted state of physical qubits will be fully recovered. By contrast, figure (d) shows the resultant error pattern if the actual error pattern is (b), but it is corrected using the error pattern given in (a). Moreover, figure (e) represents the resultant error pattern if the actual error pattern is (c) and it is corrected using the error recovery pattern of (a). As a result, the error pattern (d) represents a stabilizer operator of a plaquette, while the error pattern (e) resembles the product of two adjacent stabilizer operators. Both error patterns of (d) and (e) constitute the *harmless undetectable error patterns*, since they belong to the stabilizer group $\mathcal{S}$. Therefore, the state of physical qubits is not altered after the recovery operator $\mathcal{R}$ of (a) is applied to all error patterns of (a), (b) and (c). In classical setup, both error patterns (d) and (e) are considered as error events. However, in the quantum domain, both error patterns (d) and (e) are considered as error-free cases. This specific error-type has no similarity in the classical domain and hence potentially improves the performance of QTECCs. *Source*: [174]/IEEE/CC BY 4.0.

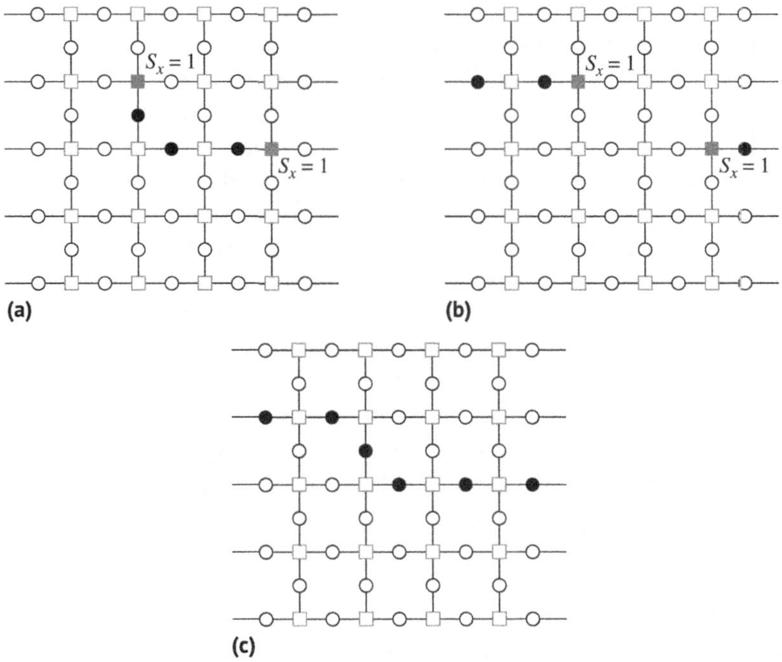


**Figure 7.13** Illustration of the harmful undetectable error pattern in the quantum domain. The actual error pattern inflicts the state of physical qubits is given in (b), while the decoder always decides to perform a recovery operator given in (a). Instead of recovering the legitimate state of the physical qubits, the specified error recovery procedure generates a chain of error that commutes with all of the stabilizer operators, as shown in (c). In the quantum domain, it constitutes the *harmful undetectable error patterns*. In the classical domain, it resembles the error pattern that generates all-zero syndrome values. *Source*: [174]/IEEE/CC BY 4.0.

the eigenvalues of $-1$ for the stabilizer operators denoted by filled squares, while the rest of the stabilizer operators are represented by hollow squares, which return eigenvalues of $+1$. Since the decoder relies on hard-decision ML decoding, all of the error patterns given in Figures 7.12 a–c have the same probability of occurrence. Let us assume that the decoder always decides to apply the error recovery pattern of Figure 7.12 a for the specified values of stabilizer measurement. When the actual error pattern is the one given in Figure 7.12 a, the states of the physical qubits are fully recovered. By contrast, if the actual error pattern is the one seen in Figure 7.12 b, but it is corrected using the error recovery operator of Figure 7.12 a, we arrive at the accumulated error pattern shown in Figure 7.12 d. Lastly, when the actual error pattern is the one given by Figure 7.12 c, but we attempt to correct it using the error recovery of Figure 7.12 a, we obtain the error pattern seen in Figure 7.12 e. However, if we observe closely the error pattern illustrated in Figure 7.12 d, it is reminiscent of a plaquette **Z** stabilizer operator denoted by the filled triangle. Therefore, based on the definition of stabilizer operators, the error pattern given in Figure 7.12 d does not alter the legitimate state of physical qubits. Similarly, the error pattern of Figure 7.12 e resembles the product of two adjacent plaquette stabilizer operators. Since the product between a pair of stabilizer operators returns another valid stabilizer operator, the error pattern given in Figure 7.12 e belongs to the stabilizer group $\mathcal{S}$. Once again, by definition, the error pattern given in Figure 7.12 e does not corrupt the legitimate state of physical qubits. This is an example of *harmless undetectable error patterns*.

To elaborate a little further, a harmless undetected error can be directly generated by the quantum decoherence, where the Pauli operator $P \in \mathcal{P}_n$ imposed by the quantum depolarizing channel is identical to the stabilizer operator $S_i$. Another possibility is that it is generated by the associated error recovery procedure when trying to recover an ambiguous error pattern, where there are more than one possible error pattern associated with a specific syndrome value, as illustrated in Figure 7.12. The degeneracy property, which is associated with the harmless undetectable error patterns, does not have a classical analogue, because the resultant error patterns illustrated in Figures 7.12 d, e will always be considered as an error in the classical setup. Ultimately, considering the degeneracy potentially improves the performance of QECCs.

Let us consider a range of different scenarios for illustrating the presence of harmful undetected error patterns, which is portrayed in Figure 7.13. Similar to the previous example of Figure 7.12, three **Z** errors are imposed on the state of logical qubits by the quantum depolarizing channel. The error patterns given in Figures 7.13 a, b trigger the eigenvalues of −1 for the stabilizer operators denoted by filled squares in Figure 7.13, while the rest of the stabilizer operators represented by hollow squares return eigenvalues of +1. Given the associated syndrome value, the decoder always decides to apply the error recovery operator of Figure 7.13 a. In the specific scenario, where the actual error pattern is the one given by Figure 7.13 b, the resultant error pattern is given in Figure 7.13 c. We can observe that the resultant error pattern of Figure 7.13 c commutes with all of the stabilizer operators in Figure 7.13. However, this specific error pattern does not belong to the stabilizer operator $\mathcal{S}$, since we cannot represent a chain of errors by the product of stabilizer operators. Consequently, this undetectable error pattern inevitably corrupts the legitimate state representing the physical qubits. This is an example of the *harmful undetectable error patterns*. This error pattern is similar to that of its counterpart in the classical domain, where the error pattern returns the all-zero syndrome.

Therefore, based on these conditions, by appropriately modifying the probability of correct decoding in the classical domain [241], we can readily formulate the worst-case upper bound QBER performance of QTECCs as

$$\text{QBER}_{\text{upper}}(n,d,p) = 1 - \sum_{i=0}^{t=\lfloor\frac{d-1}{2}\rfloor} \binom{n}{i} p^i (1-p)^{n-i} - \sum_{i=1,\forall S_i\in\mathcal{S}}^{|\mathcal{S}|} p^{w(S_i)}(1-p)^{n-w(S_i)}, \tag{7.31}$$

where $w(S_i)$ is the weight of the stabilizer operator $S_i$, which is defined by the number of non-identity Pauli operators within the stabilizer operators. The second term of Eq. (7.31) represents all the correctable error patterns of QTECCs, while the last term of Eq. (7.31) represents the degenerate error patterns that belong to the stabilizer operators. For example, let us revisit the construction of the surface codes of Figure 7.8. There are 12 stabilizer generators for a distance-3 surface code, as seen in Table 7.6. Hence, we can potentially generate $2^{12}$ unique stabilizer operators, since the product of the stabilizer operators returns another valid stabilizer operator. However, in order to further simplify the expression given in Eq. (7.31), we only consider the specific error patterns resembling the specified stabilizer operators given in Table 7.6, since they exhibit a lower weight of nonidentity Pauli matrices and hence have a higher probability of occurrence. Therefore, for surface codes, the last term of Eq. (7.31) can be approximated as $(2d^2-2d)p^4(1-p)^{n-4}$. The term $(2d^2-2d)$ represents the number of stabilizer operators, which is given in Table 7.8, and we assume that all the weights of the stabilizer operators $w(S_i)$ are equal to 4.

### 7.4.1 QBER Versus Depolarizing Probability

In order to characterize the performance of QTECCs by simulations, we exploit the fact that the QTECCs belong to the family of CSS codes, which handle the bit-flips (**X**) and phase-flips (**Z**) separately. Hence, we invoke two independent binary symmetric channels (BSC), one for the **X** channel and one for the **Z** channel, where each channel is characterized by the flip probability of $2p/3$, where $p$ is the associated depolarizing probability of the quantum depolarizing channel [67, 80]. The decoder utilizes hard-decision ML decoding relying on a simple LUT decoder, as exemplified in Section 3.3. However, this classical-domain simulation only represents the performance of QTECCs without considering the degenerate error patterns. To elaborate a little further, we transmitted all-zero information bits. Therefore, we always consider the non-all-zero bits at the decoder output as an error. In order to additionally consider several cases of degenerate error patterns, which is exemplified in Figure 7.12, we performed another evaluation step. We evaluate the non-all-zero corrected received words and check for the degenerate error patterns. If it satisfies the degenerate error pattern criterion that we have above, we conclude that this is an error-free case. However, we are not capable of providing a complete list of all possible degenerate error patterns. Here we only consider the error patterns resembling the stabilizer generators of $S_i$, as exemplified in Tables 7.6 and 7.7 for surface codes and triangular codes, respectively. The QBER performance of distance-3 QTECCs versus the quantum depolarizing probability is portrayed in Figure 7.14, where the code parameters are given in Table 7.11. We also include the upper bound of the QTECC performance of Eq. (7.31) in Figure 7.14. It can be observed that the upper bounds match the QTECCs performance recorded without considering the degenerate error patterns.

As we mentioned earlier, there are two sources of degenerate error patterns at the output of the decoder. Firstly, the degenerate error pattern that was imposed directly by the quantum channel, where the error exhibits an

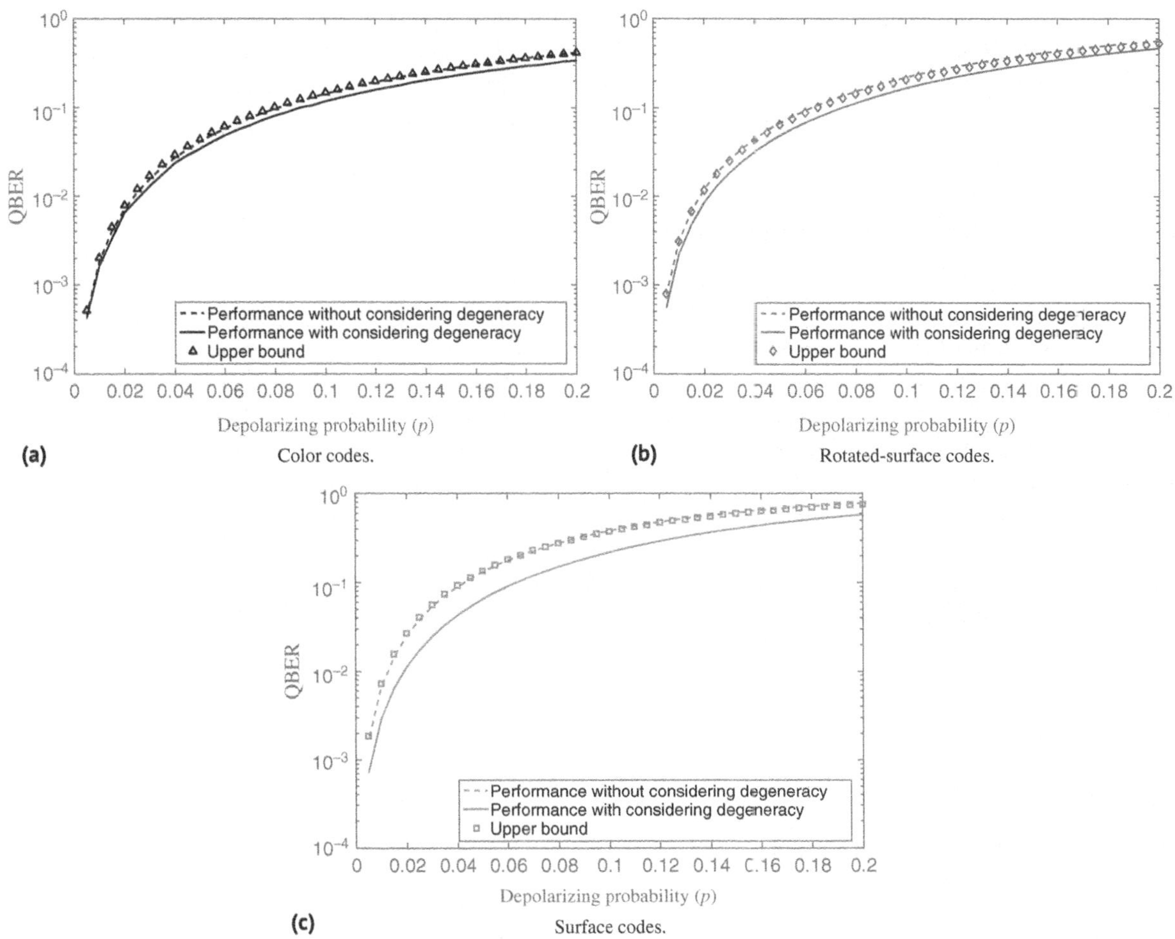


**Figure 7.14** QBER performance of the distance-3 QTECCs over the quantum depolarizing channel, which is capable of correcting a single qubit error. The code parameters are given in Table 7.11. For this scenario, the decoder using hard-input ML decoding approach for predicting the error pattern. *Source*: [174]/IEEE/CC BY 4.0.

**Table 7.11** Code parameters for distance-3 color code, rotated-surface code, and surface code.

| **Code type** | $n$ | $k$ | $d$ | $r_Q$ |
|---|---|---|---|---|
| Color code | 7 | 1 | 3 | 1/7 |
| Rotated-surface code | 9 | 1 | 3 | 1/9 |
| Surface code | 13 | 1 | 3 | 1/13 |

identical pattern to the stabilizer operator $S_i$. Secondly, the degenerate error pattern generated by the recovery operator $\mathcal{R}$, when it tries to recover the legitimate physical qubits, as illustrated in Figure 7.12. The second case is more dominant than the first one. The reason can be explained as follows. Let us consider the **Z** stabilizer operators of the distance-3 surface code given in Table 7.6. There are six **Z** stabilizer operators corresponding to the $2^6 = 64$ possible syndrome vector, including the error-free scenario. Remember that the distance-3 surface code can only correct a single qubit error within a block of 13 physical qubits, where each of the single-qubit error patterns is associated with a single syndrome vector. In other words, among all of the 64 possible syndrome vectors, there are only 13 syndrome vectors used for uniquely distinguishing the correctable error patterns, while the rest of the syndrome vectors are associated with an error pattern ambiguity, as exemplified in Figures 7.12 and 7.13.

For this reason, QTECCs are highly degenerate QSCs. Hence, the upper bound of the QBER performance matches the simulation-based performance recorded without considering the degeneracy, since it considers the first case of degeneracy, where we only consider a portion of all valid stabilizer operators $S_i \in \mathcal{S}$ in Eq. (7.31). As expected, by accommodating both of the degeneracy cases, the QBER performance of QTECCs is improved, as portrayed in Figure 7.14.

### 7.4.2 QBER Versus Distance from Hashing Bound

Increasing the minimum distance of a given QSC construction, which directly improves its per-codeword error correction capability ($t$), is achieved by increasing the number of physical qubits ($n$) or by decreasing the quantum coding rate. Specifically for QTECCs, increasing the minimum distance means increasing the number of physical qubits ($n$) and decreasing the quantum coding rate ($r_Q$) simultaneously. Naturally, the goal of increasing the minimum distance of the QSC is to achieve a better QBER performance. However, a QBER improvement can only be observed below a certain depolarizing probability ($p$), which may be referred to as the threshold probability ($p_{th}$). Using the QBER upper bound performance of Eq. (7.31), we plot the QBER curves for color, rotated-surface, surface and toric codes in Figure 7.15. For each of the QTECC constructions, we portray the upper bound QBER performance for the minimum distance values of $d = \{3, 5, 7, 9, 11\}$. The threshold probability of each code is represented by the crossover points, which are marked by dashed lines. Quantitatively the threshold probability of color codes, rotated-surface, surface, and toric codes are $1.83 \times 10^{-2}$, $1.34 \times 10^{-2}$, $6.28 \times 10^{-3}$, and $6.77 \times 10^{-3}$, respectively.

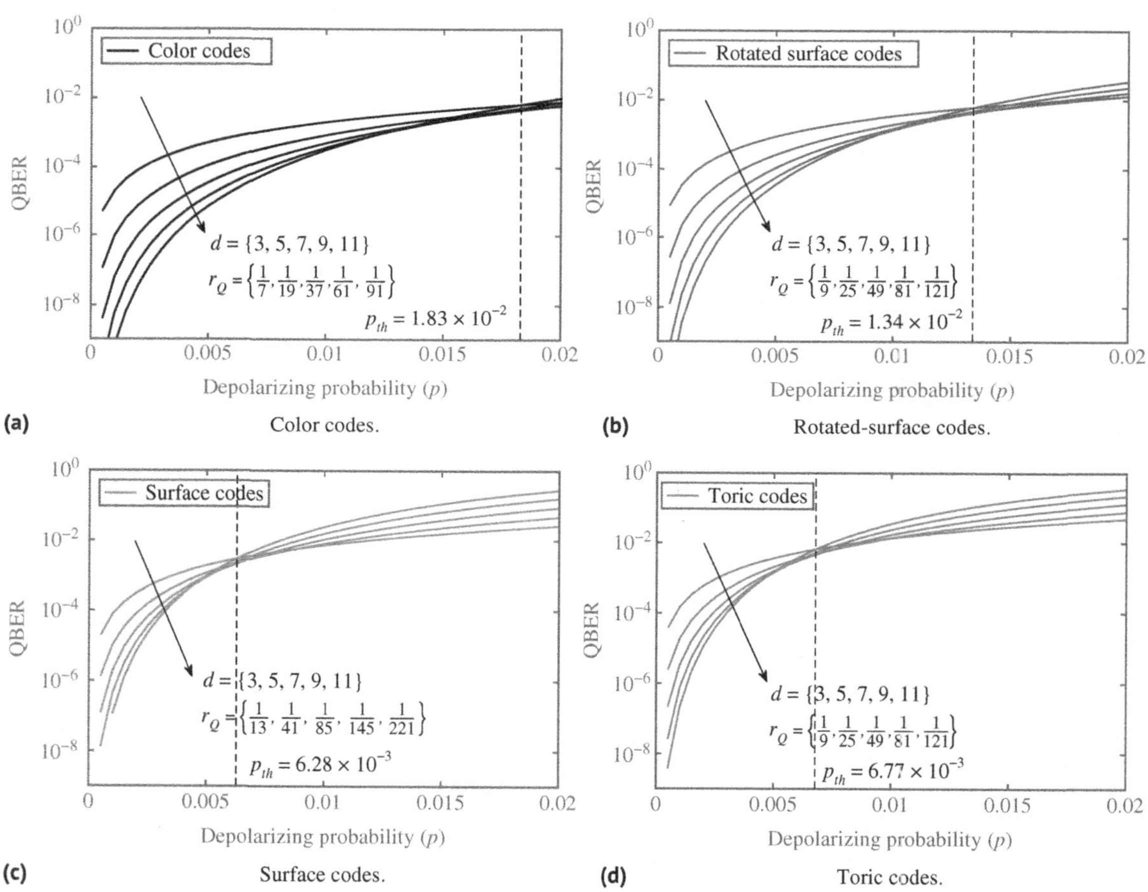


**Figure 7.15** Upper bound QBER performance of QTECCs for the minimum distance of $d = \{3, 5, 7, 9, 11\}$ based on Eq. (7.31) and code parameters given in Table 7.8. The crossover amongst the QBER curves represents the threshold probability ($p_{th}$), which is portrayed in dashed line. *Source*: [174]/IEEE/CC BY 4.0.

However, presenting the performance of QTECCs over quantum depolarizing channels by portraying the QBER curves versus the depolarizing probability ($p$) does not take the quantum coding rate ($r_Q$) into consideration. As we mentioned earlier, we can simply decrease the quantum coding rate further and further to increase the error correction capability of the QTECCs. Nonetheless, for the sake of depicting a fair comparison upon reducing the quantum coding rate, we have to scrutinize how much performance improvement we obtain upon decreasing the quantum coding rate. Therefore, to demonstrate how much performance improvement we attain compared to how much we decrease the quantum coding rate, we normalize the QBER performance by incorporating the quantum hashing bound. More explicitly, the quantum hashing bound can be expressed as follows [242]:

$$C_Q(p) = 1 - H(p) - p \cdot \log_2(3), \tag{7.32}$$

where $H(p)$ is the binary entropy of $p$. More specifically, the quantum hashing bound of Eq. (7.32) dictates that a random quantum code $\mathcal{C}$ having a sufficiently long codeword and a quantum coding rate $r_Q \leq C_Q(p)$ may yield an infinitesimally low QBER for a given depolarizing probability $p$. Alternatively, we can refer to $C_Q(p)$ as the hashing limit for the quantum coding rate $r_Q$ associated with a given depolarizing probability $p$. In terms of its classical dual pair, the value of $C_Q$ is similar to the capacity limit. Similarly, for a given coding rate $r_Q$, we can find a value of $p^*$ satisfying $r_Q = C_Q(p^*)$, where $p^*$ denotes the maximum value of depolarizing probability $p$ so that a quantum code $\mathcal{C}$ having quantum coding rate of $r_Q$ can operate at an infinitesimally low QBER. The value of $p^*$ may be referred to as the hashing limit for the depolarizing probability of $p$ associated with a given quantum coding rate of $r_Q$. In the classical domain, the value of $p^*$ is similar to the noise limit. Therefore, in general, the aim is that of finding a QSC that is capable of performing as close as possible to the quantum hashing bound. For example, let us consider the distance-3 and distance-5 rotated-surface codes having quantum coding rates of $r_Q = 1/9$ and $r_Q = 1/25$, respectively. By substituting $C_Q = 1/9$ and $C_Q = 1/25$ into the Eq. (7.32), we obtain the noise limits of $p^* = 0.160$ and $p^* = 0.179$, respectively. It can be concluded that the noise limit is higher for the quantum code exhibiting a lower quantum coding rate. To incorporate the quantum hashing bound into the QBER performances of QTECCs, we define the distance from the hashing bound as follows:

$$D \triangleq p(r_Q) - p. \tag{7.33}$$

In other words, by changing the horizontal axis from the depolarizing probability $p$ to the distance $D$ from the hashing bound, we shift all the QBER curves according to their hashing bounds, so that all the hashing bounds are at the reference point of $D = 0$.

Several pertinent questions arise from the quantum hashing bound formulation. Firstly, is there a noise limit where no QSC constructions are capable of achieving a satisfactorily low QBER? Indeed, the answer is yes. By substituting $C_Q = 0$ into Eq. (7.32), which is the lowest possible value of achievable quantum coding rate, we arrive at the ultimate hashing bound of $p(0) \approx 0.1893$. Secondly, what is the farthest possible distance from the quantum hashing bound for any QSC construction? To answer this question, we have to consider the worst-case scenario where a QSC exhibiting a near-zero quantum coding rate ($r_Q \approx 0$) achieves an infinitesimally low QBER at near-zero quantum depolarizing probability ($p \approx 0$). By substituting the value of $r_Q = 0$ and $p = 0$ into Eq. (7.33), we define the ultimate distance $D_0$ from the hashing bound as

$$\begin{aligned} D_0 &= p(0) - p \\ &= 0.1893 - 0 \\ &= 0.1893. \end{aligned} \tag{7.34}$$

Therefore, the desirable performance of any QSCs quantified in terms of the QBER versus distance from the quantum hashing bound is represented by the curves exhibiting a reasonably low QBER as close as possible to the reference point of $D = 0$. Naturally, this implies having a low QBER as far as possible from the ultimate distance of $D_0 = 0.1893$ wrt the hashing bound. In simpler terms, any QSCs can only operate at a reasonably low QBER within the hashing bound range of $0 \leq D \leq D_0$. Furthermore, we should only consider the quantum coding rate reduction of $r_Q$ to be beneficial if the associated QBER performance curve moves closer to the reference point of $D = 0$. Otherwise, it is more advisable to find a better code construction exhibiting an identical quantum coding rate. Alternatively, we may invoke a more powerful decoding scheme, for example by utilizing a soft-decision-aided decoder. The QBER performance of QTECCs versus their distances from the quantum hashing bound is

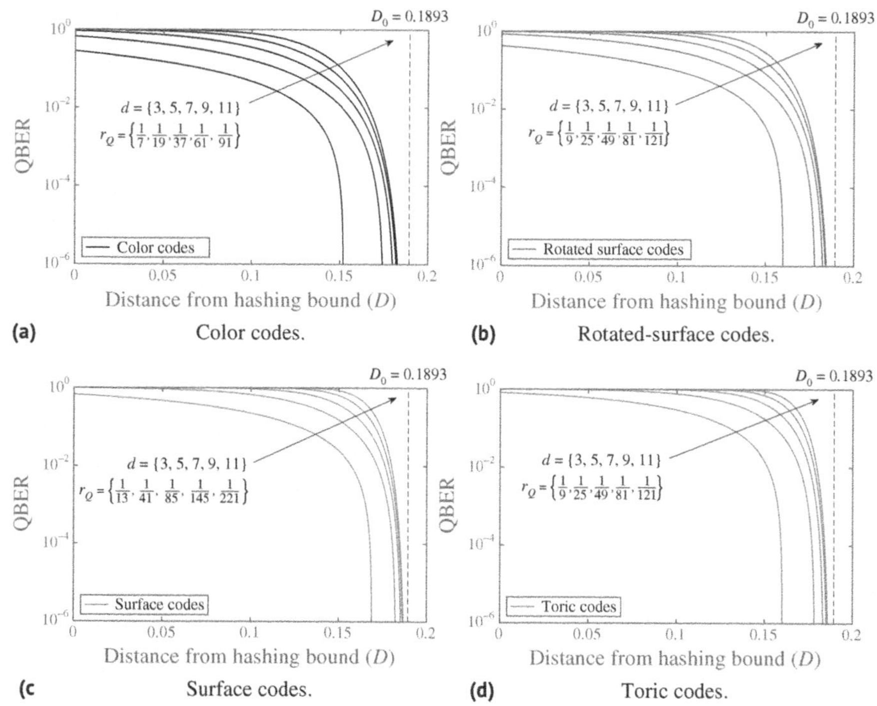


(a) Color codes.
(b) Rotated-surface codes.
(c Surface codes.
(d) Toric codes.

**Figure 7.16** Upper bound performance of QTECCs in term of the QBER versus the distance $D$ from the hashing bound. The dashed lines portray the ultimate distance to the quantum hashing bound of $D_0 = 0.1893$. *Source*: [174]/IEEE/CC BY 4.0.

portrayed in Figure 7.16. It can be observed in Figure 7.16 that increasing the minimum distance of the QTECCs yields a performance improvement in terms of their QBER versus depolarizing probability $p$ and also in terms of their distance from the hashing bound $D$. However, at low QBERs the curves become crowded in the vicinity of the ultimate hashing bound distance of $D_0$. Moreover, the results show an agreement with the quantum coding rate versus minimum distance evolution of QTECCs seen in Figure 7.11. The improvement of the minimum distance – which is directly linked to the error correction capability – is not fast enough upon reducing the quantum coding rate to compensate for the rapidly increasing number of physical qubits. Therefore, the QTECCs may be recommended for short to moderate codeword lengths.

### 7.4.3 Fidelity

From an implementational perspective, a quantum gate or quantum channel is often characterized by the so-called fidelity, which represents the closeness of a pure quantum state of $|\overline{\psi}\rangle$ compared to the mixed states having the quantum density operator of $\rho$. More explicitly, since the quantum channel imposes decoherence on our legitimate quantum states representing the physical qubits $|\overline{\psi}\rangle$, the decoder may not successfully recover the legitimate state. Therefore, the ensemble of all the possible predicted legitimate states of physical qubits $|\widehat{\overline{\psi}}\rangle$ can be represented using the state of $|\psi_i\rangle$ having a probability of $p_i$. The fidelity can be formulated as follows [85, 243, 244]:

$$F = \langle\overline{\psi}|\rho|\overline{\psi}\rangle, \tag{7.35}$$

while $\rho$, which portrays the statistical characteristics of a the mixed states, is defined by

$$\rho = \sum_{i=1}^{N} p_i |\psi_i\rangle\langle\psi_i|, \tag{7.36}$$

where $|\psi_i\rangle$ represents all the possible states in the ensemble and $p_i$ is the probability of having state $|\psi_i\rangle$ in the ensemble, which is subject to the unity constraint of $\sum_{i=1}^{N} p_i = 1$.

In order to demonstrate the benefit of QTECCs in the context of quantum depolarizing channels, we compare the so-called initial fidelity $F_{\text{in}}$ and final fidelity $F_{\text{out}}$. The initial fidelity is the fidelity of the pure quantum state of $|\psi\rangle$ over the quantum depolarizing channel $\mathcal{P}$ unprotected by any QSCs scheme. Therefore, the initial fidelity $F_{\text{in}}$ can be expressed as follows:

$$F_{\text{in}} = 1 - p. \tag{7.37}$$

The final fidelity is that of the pure state of the desired output $|\psi'\rangle$ protected by a QSC scheme after the recovery procedure $\mathcal{R}$ and inverse encoder $\mathcal{V}^{\dagger}$ of Figure 8.3. Therefore, the final fidelity $F_{\text{out}}$ of the quantum system can be readily described as

$$F_{\text{out}} = 1 - \text{QBER}. \tag{7.38}$$

The fidelity performance of the distance-3 QTECCs are depicted in Figure 7.17. The solid line represents the condition of $F_{\text{in}} = F_{\text{out}}$. The crossover point between the line of $F_{\text{in}} = F_{\text{out}}$ and fidelity performance curve of QTECCs is the break-even point, which we may refer to as the *threshold fidelity* $F_{\text{th}}$. The break-even point denotes the minimal initial fidelity required for ensuring that we do acquire a fidelity improvement upon the application of the QSC scheme, which is invoked for protecting the state of the physical qubits. The upper bound of threshold fidelity $F_{\text{th}}$ for the different types of QTECCs is depicted in Figure 7.18. It can be observed that different code families having various minimum distances $d$ result in different threshold fidelity $F_{\text{th}}$. For the QSCs utilizing

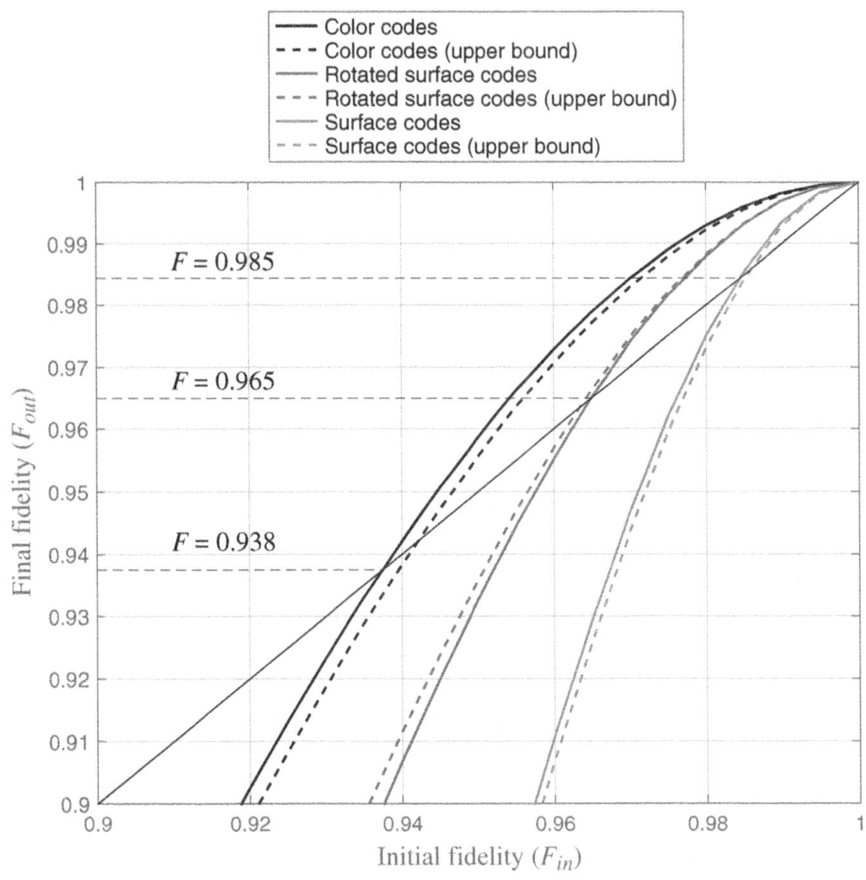


**Figure 7.17** The fidelity performance of QTECCs having a minimum distance of 3 in term of fidelity of Eq. (7.35). The color code reaches the fidelity threshold earlier than the rotated-surface and surface code, since the color code has the lowest number of physical qubits compared to the rotated-surface code and the surface code. The code parameters are given in Table 7.11. *Source*: [174]/IEEE/CC BY 4.0.

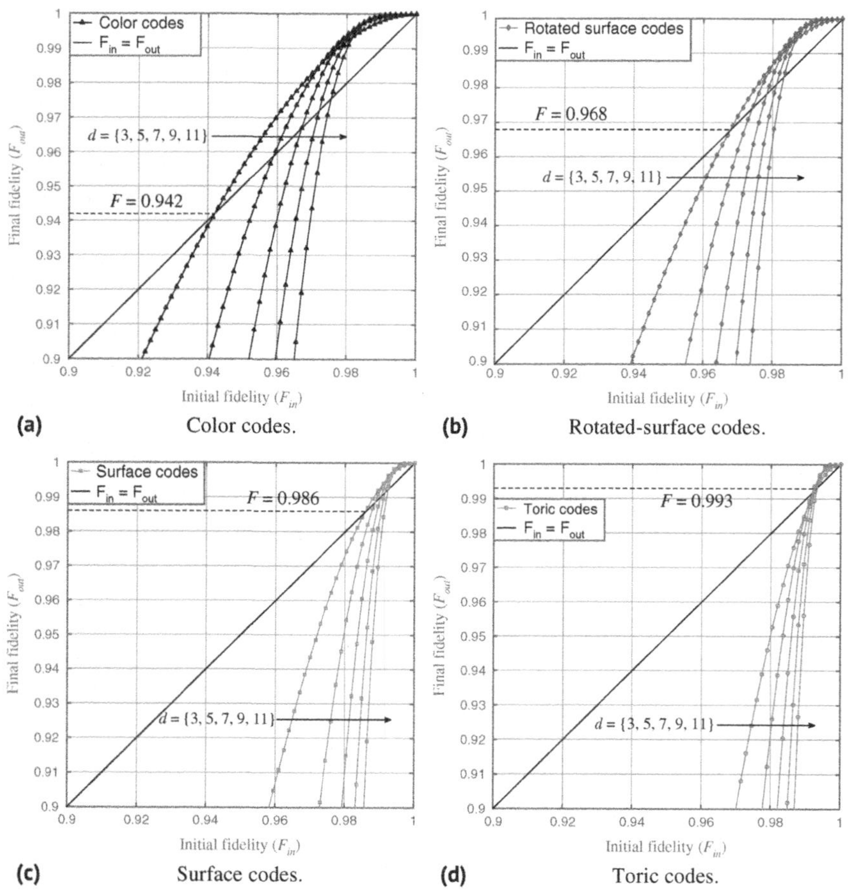


**Figure 7.18** Upper bound fidelity performance of QTECCs. *Source*: [174]/IEEE/CC BY 4.0.

hard-decision syndrome decoding, we derive the upper bound approximation formula for $F_{\text{th}}$. First, from Eqs. (7.31) and (7.38), we arrive at

$$
\begin{aligned}
F_{\text{out}} &= 1 - \text{QBER}_{\text{upper}} \\
&= 1 - \left( 1 - \sum_{i=0}^{t=\left\lfloor \frac{d-1}{2} \right\rfloor} \binom{n}{i} p^i (1-p)^{n-i} \right) \\
&= 1 - \sum_{\left\lfloor \frac{d-1}{2} \right\rfloor + 1}^{n} \binom{n}{i} p^i (1-p)^{n-i}.
\end{aligned}
\tag{7.39}
$$

For a low depolarizing probability $p$, the expression given in Eq. (7.39) can be approximated in order to determine the upper bound of the output fidelity as follows:

$$
F_{\text{out}} \approx 1 - \binom{n}{\lfloor \frac{d-1}{2} \rfloor + 1} p^{\lfloor \frac{d-1}{2} \rfloor + 1}. \tag{7.40}
$$

Since the threshold fidelity satisfies the relationship of $F_{\text{th}} = F_{\text{in}} = F_{\text{out}}$, we can substitute $F_{\text{out}} = F_{\text{th}}$ and $p = 1 - F_{\text{th}}$ into Eq. (7.40). Finally, the upper bound of the threshold probability can be formulated as

$$
F_{\text{th}}(n, d) = 1 - \binom{n}{\lfloor \frac{d-1}{2} \rfloor + 1}^{-1/\lfloor \frac{d-1}{2} \rfloor}. \tag{7.41}
$$

For example, the threshold for a distance-3 color code having a quantum coding rate of $r_Q = 1/7$ based on Figure 7.18a is $F_{th} = 0.942$, while using the upper bound approximation of the fidelity threshold in Eq. (7.41) we have $F_{th} = 0.952$. For the distance-3 rotated-surface code, surface code, and toric code, the threshold fidelity values based on Figures 7.18 b–d are $F_{th} = 0.968$, $F_{th} = 0.986$ and $F_{th} = 0.993$, respectively. By using the approximation of Eq. (7.41), the fidelity threshold upper bounds are given by $F_{th} = 0.972$, $F_{th} = 0.987$, and $F_{th} = 0.994$, respectively for the distance-3 rotated-surface code, surface code, and toric code. Here, we used the family of QTECCs as our representative examples, while the threshold fidelity of Eq. (7.41) is generically applicable for any QSCs using hard-decision syndrome decoding. Ultimately, the QTECCs are capable of reducing the quantum decoherence, which is demonstrated both by the QBER reduction and the fidelity improvement attained.

## 7.5 Summary and Conclusions

We portrayed the evolution of the topological error correction codes designed in the classical domain to that of their quantum-domain dual pairs. We showed that by arranging the bits of the codeword on a lattice structure in the classical domain provides a beneficial inherent error correction capability. Furthermore, for a long codeword, the classical topological error correction codes correspond to the family of LDPC codes exhibiting attractive properties, such as unbounded minimum distance as a function of the codeword length, structured construction, and a coding rate of $r = 1/2$. By contrast, the quantum topological error correction codes are more suitable for applications requiring short to moderate codeword lengths, since the quantum coding rate of QTECCs tends to zero for a long codeword. We characterized the performance of QTECCs in the face of the quantum depolarizing channel in terms of the QBER attained. First, we showed that QTECCs are highly degenerate quantum codes; therefore, the classical simulation is only capable of portraying the performance of QTECCs without considering the degeneracy property. Secondly, we demonstrated that increasing the minimum distance of the QTECCs improves the QBER performance. Additionally, we normalized the performance by considering the coding rate, which was achieved by defining the *distance from the hashing bound*. Explicitly, we have shown that the growth of minimum distance of QTECCs upon increasing the codeword length is not fast enough to compensate for the increased codeword length. Consequently, the QBER performance of QTECCs gradually tends to the *ultimate distance from the hashing bound*. Finally, we determined the fidelity threshold for QSCs based on hard-decision syndrome decoding, which represents the minimum fidelity value required for a quantum system to glean benefits from QSCs. Ultimately, the employment of QSCs will improve the reliability of quantum computers.

# 8

# Protecting Quantum Gates Using Quantum Topological Error Correction Codes

## 8.1 Introduction

So far, we have described the classical-to-quantum isomorphism for deriving and characterizing QSCs. In the classical domain, the error correction codes are invoked for dealing with the imperfections of the communication channel, either in a form of imperfections imposed by the transmission medium or by information storage. However, in the quantum domain, the quantum decoherence is imposed by the entanglement between the quantum information and environment, or by the coherence time of qubits, or by the imperfection of quantum gates. In the classical domain, we often assume that the information is contaminated by the transmission medium or by the storage medium. The imperfections of the encoding and decoding operations tend to have a negligible effect, hence they are usually ignored. However, in the quantum domain, the impact of imperfect quantum gates cannot be neglected. Fortunately, the QSC can also be designed specifically for handling the imperfections caused by the quantum gates. Although the general principle is similar to that of protecting quantum information during its passage through realistic noisy quantum channels, substantial modifications are needed and additional constraints have to be considered.

In this chapter, we present the general framework of protecting quantum gates using QSCs. The ultimate goal of invoking QSCs is to answer the cardinal question: "is it possible to build reliable quantum computers using unreliable quantum circuits?" The concept of reliable computation using unreliable components can be traced back to Von Neumann's work in 1956 [245]. However, the work of Von Neumann is not directly applicable in the context of quantum computers, since he dealt with classical computation heavily relying on irreversible logic gates, while quantum computers are composed of reversible quantum gates. Realizing that in order to invoke QSCs we have to introduce additional unreliable quantum gates into the system, the field of fault-tolerant quantum computers was introduced [52, 87, 89, 93, 246]. The quest for finding the answer was partly settled, when the threshold theorem was proposed [148]. The main result suggested that it is indeed possible to create a reliable quantum computer from unreliable quantum gates, given that the error probability of the quantum gates is below a certain probability threshold value and a reasonable redundant overhead is tolerable.

Now, it is pertinent to mention that throughout this part of the book, we consider gate-based quantum computation [160, 247], noting that there are many other models for quantum computation, such as measurement-based quantum computation [248], quantum cellular automata [249], topological quantum computation [250], and adiabatic quantum computation [251]. Therefore, in this chapter, we refer the readers to the method presented in [180, 181, 252] for creating an efficient quantum encoder $\mathcal{V}$ for QSCs. To elaborate a little further, given the so-called stabilizer operators $S_i \in \mathcal{S}$, we can transform the stabilizer operators $S_i \in \mathcal{S}$ into their classical binary PCM using the so-called Pauli-to-binary isomorphism [170, 179]. The resultant binary PCM $\mathbf{H}$ derived from the stabilizer formalism $S_i \in \mathcal{S}$ is utilized for constructing the quantum encoder $\mathcal{V}$ of the associated QECC $\mathcal{C}$. Since we deal with the family of gate-based quantum computers, naturally, the quantum encoder $\mathcal{V}$ is also composed of quantum gates.

The method specified in [180, 181, 252] is applicable to both CSS [55, 86, 92] and non-CSS codes [60, 94]. However, color codes [100], which belong to the QTECCs family, can also be classified further as the member of a more specific category of quantum CSS codes, namely, the family of dual-containing CSS codes. For dual-containing CSS codes, a specific technique can be invoked for creating the associated quantum encoder $\mathcal{V}$. This method of generating the quantum encoder $\mathcal{V}$ of dual-containing CSS codes has been detailed in [67, 163]. It is important to note that upon using the method detailed in [67, 163, 180, 181, 252], the number of quantum gates required for constructing a quantum encoder $\mathcal{V}$ for a QSC $\mathcal{C}$ is linearly proportional to the number of physical qubits [180, 252].

However, the need for invoking a quantum encoder $\mathcal{V}$ can be eliminated by simply preparing all the auxiliary qubits in the state of $|+\rangle$ and then performing stabilizer measurements, as suggested in [253, 254]. By initializing all the $(n-k)$ auxiliary qubits in the $|+\rangle$ states, we create the superposition of all possible combinations of all $(n-k)$-bit sequences. Therefore, to generate a legitimate encoded state of the physical qubits, we only require stabilizer measurements for projecting the space created by the above mentioned initialization into a specific code space based on the classical bits obtained from the stabilizer measurements.

The rest of this chapter is organized as follows. We provide the formulation of our framework in Section 8.2. This is followed by the design examples of QSC-protected Hadamard gates and CNOT gates in Section 8.3, where we invoke a simple quantum repetition code as our QSC. To evaluate the performance of our proposed framework, in Section 8.4, we present the decoherence model utilized in our simulations. Then in Section 8.5, we quantify the performance of QTECC-protected transversal Hadamard gates and CNOT gates both in terms of their QBER and fidelity along with the derivation of the QBER upper bound. The lower bound of the depolarization fidelity threshold is also determined. Finally, we conclude in Section 8.6.

## 8.2 Protecting Transversal Gates

In this section, we present the design of QSC-protected quantum gates along with the pivotal theory in quantum information processing required for formulating the proposed framework.

### 8.2.1 Quantum Clifford Gates

The quantum gates manipulating the state of the qubits are represented using the unitary transformation $U$, which satisfies

$$U^{\dagger}U = \mathbf{I}. \tag{8.1}$$

Since the quantum gates themselves also potentially impose the deleterious effect of quantum decoherence, which is represented by the Pauli group $\mathcal{P}_n$, the evolution of quantum decoherence through the quantum gates can be described using the conjugation of the unitary transformation.

Let us assume that a unitary transformation of $M$ is applied to a quantum state of $N|\psi\rangle$, where $N$ is also a unitary transformation that has been applied previously. Therefore, the final quantum state is given by $MN|\psi\rangle$. Since $M$ is a unitary transformation, we have $M^{\dagger}M = \mathbf{I}$. The quantum state of $MN|\psi\rangle$ can be transformed as follows:

$$\begin{aligned} MN|\psi\rangle &= MNM^{\dagger}M|\psi\rangle \\ &= VM|\psi\rangle, \end{aligned} \tag{8.2}$$

where we have $V = MNM^{\dagger}$, which is the conjugate of $N$ under the unitary transformation $M$. Consequently, Eq. (8.2) implies that the unitary transformation $MNM^{\dagger}$ after the operator $M$ acts similarly to the unitary transformation $N$ before the operator $M$. For instance, a Hadamard gate is defined by a unitary matrix as follows:

$$\mathbf{H} = \frac{1}{\sqrt{2}}\begin{pmatrix} 1 & 1 \\ 1 & -1 \end{pmatrix}. \tag{8.3}$$

The transformation carried out by the Hadamard gate maps a quantum state represented in the specific computational basis used into the Hadamard basis, as described below:

$$\begin{aligned} \mathbf{H}|0\rangle &= \frac{|0\rangle + |1\rangle}{\sqrt{2}} \equiv |+\rangle, \\ \mathbf{H}|1\rangle &= \frac{|0\rangle - |1\rangle}{\sqrt{2}} \equiv |-\rangle \end{aligned} \tag{8.4}$$

and vice versa. Based on the conjugation of Eq. (8.2), we arrive at the following transformations:

$$\begin{aligned} \mathbf{HXH}^{\dagger} &= \mathbf{Z}, \\ \mathbf{HZH}^{\dagger} &= \mathbf{X}, \\ \mathbf{HYH}^{\dagger} &= -\mathbf{Y}. \end{aligned} \tag{8.5}$$

One way to interpret the transformation given in Eq. (8.5) is that a bit-flip (**X**) error before the Hadamard gate is equivalent to a phase-flip (**Z**) error after the Hadamard gate. Similarly, a phase-flip (**Z**) error before the Hadamard gate can be treated as an **X** error after the Hadamard gate. Another example is the phase gate (**S**), which is defined by the unitary transformation of

$$\mathbf{S} = \begin{pmatrix} 1 & 0 \\ 0 & i \end{pmatrix}. \tag{8.6}$$

Based on Eq. (8.2) and on the unitary matrix of **S** in Eq. (8.6), we arrive at the following transformations:

$$\begin{aligned} \mathbf{SXS}^{\dagger} &= \mathbf{Y} \\ \mathbf{SZS}^{\dagger} &= \mathbf{Z} \\ \mathbf{SYS}^{\dagger} &= -\mathbf{X}. \end{aligned} \tag{8.7}$$

Moreover, the relationship given in Eq. (8.2) can also be applied to the model of the conjugation over 2-qubit quantum gates. An example of a 2-qubit quantum gate is the CNOT gate, whose unitary transformation is defined by the following unitary matrix:

$$\mathbf{CNOT} = \begin{pmatrix} 1 & 0 & 0 & 0 \\ 0 & 1 & 0 & 0 \\ 0 & 0 & 0 & 1 \\ 0 & 0 & 1 & 0 \end{pmatrix}. \tag{8.8}$$

Again, the CNOT gate is a 2-qubit quantum gate, where the first qubit is the control qubit and the second qubit is referred to as the target qubit. The value of the target qubit is flipped if and only if the value of the control qubit is equal to one. Based on Eq. (8.2), the 2-qubit conjugation over the CNOT gate can be readily formulated as follows:

$$\begin{aligned} (\mathbf{CNOT})(\mathbf{X} \otimes \mathbf{I})(\mathbf{CNOT})^{\dagger} &= \mathbf{X} \otimes \mathbf{X}, \\ (\mathbf{CNOT})(\mathbf{I} \otimes \mathbf{X})(\mathbf{CNOT})^{\dagger} &= \mathbf{I} \otimes \mathbf{X}, \\ (\mathbf{CNOT})(\mathbf{Z} \otimes \mathbf{I})(\mathbf{CNOT})^{\dagger} &= \mathbf{Z} \otimes \mathbf{I}, \\ (\mathbf{CNOT})(\mathbf{I} \otimes \mathbf{Z})(\mathbf{CNOT})^{\dagger} &= \mathbf{Z} \otimes \mathbf{Z}. \end{aligned} \tag{8.9}$$

We can also interpret the result as an error transformation or an error propagation process, illustrated in Figure 8.1. It can be observed that a bit-flip or **X**-type error imposed on the control qubit before the CNOT gate will propagate to the target qubit after the CNOT gate. Meanwhile, a **Z**-type error inflicted upon the target qubit before the CNOT gate will impose another **Z**-type error on the control qubit after the CNOT gate.

In this chapter, we limit our discussions to quantum gates belonging to the Clifford group, since the stabilizer formalism of QTECCs will be preserved under conjugation [51, 161]. The theory of protecting quantum circuits using QSCs has been widely investigated [52, 87–89, 93, 246, 256] and in this chapter, we provide a comparative study of the quantum circuits protected by QSCs, specifically by the family of QTECCs. The most reasonable way of embedding QSCs into quantum gates is by the transversal implementation of quantum gates. The physical interpretation of the transversal implementation of QTECCs, specifically that of CNOT gates, is illustrated in

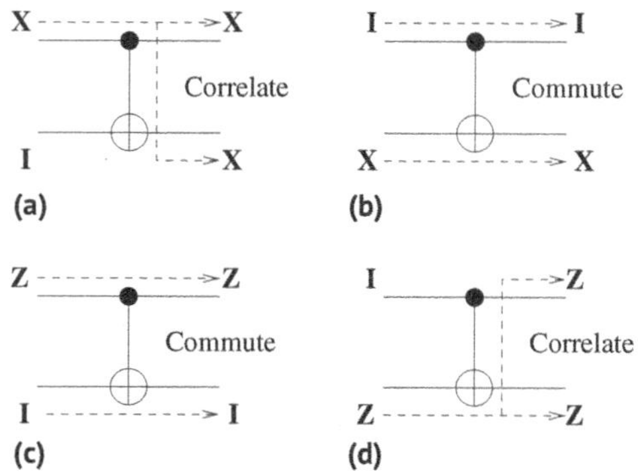


**Figure 8.1** The evolution of 2-qubit unitary transformation over the CNOT quantum gate, which is the circuit-level interpretation of Eq. (8.9). For example, an **X**-type error imposed on the control qubit will propagate to the target qubit after the CNOT gate, as we can observe in (a). By contrast, a **Z**-type error inflicting the target qubit will propagate to the control qubit after the CNOT gate, as shown in (d). *Source*: [255]/IEEE/CC BY 4.0.

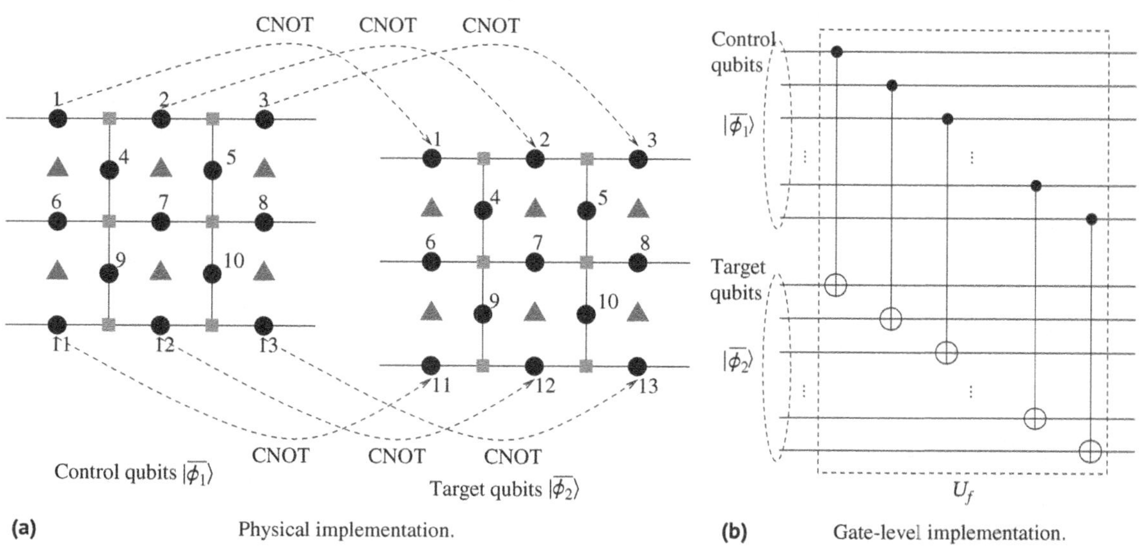


**Figure 8.2** The physical and gate-level implementation of the transversal CNOT gates. In the physical implementation, we can imagine two layers of physical qubits, where on each layer the physical qubits are arranged over a lattice structure portrayed in Figure 7.8. The CNOT interactions are performed accordingly on each of the pairs of physical qubits. The CNOT interactions between the physical qubits number #4 to #10 are removed from the figure for the sake of avoiding obfuscation. In the gate-level implementation, the physical layout portrayed in (a) can be translated into a chain of CNOT gates illustrated in (b). *Source*: [255]/IEEE/CC BY 4.0.

Figure 8.2. In the physical implementation, we can imagine having a pair of lattice structures arranged on a wafer, where each of the physical qubit layers is encoded using a QTECC scheme. The first qubit from the upper layer acts as the control qubit, while the first qubit from the lower layer serves as the target qubit. It is followed by the second, the third, and all the remaining physical qubits from the upper as well as the lower layer.

### 8.2.2 Design Formulation

The employment of QSCs for protecting the quantum circuits indeed increases the reliability of quantum computing, as shown in [163]. However, in order to avoid a perpetual encoding and decoding process throughout the quantum circuit before the number of errors exceeds the error correction capability of the QSC, we present a more efficient framework where we encode the logical qubits at the input of the quantum circuit and decode them afterwards at the output of the computational step. However, the unitary transformation $U_f$ applied to the state of physical qubits alters the legitimate state of physical qubits. Therefore, the initial stabilizer operators $S_i \in \mathcal{S}$

designed for stabilizing the legitimate state of physical qubits are no longer valid after the application of the unitary transformation $U_f$. Fortunately, we are able to conceive an *effective stabilizer formalism* and *effective inverse encoder* for successfully circumvent the problem.[1]

To elaborate a little further, let us observe the basic QSC model portrayed in Figure 8.3 and the basic scheme of protecting quantum gates using QSC, as depicted in Figure 8.4. Let us now highlight the main differences between the conventional QSC scheme of Figure 8.3 and the QSC scheme conceived for protecting the quantum gates shown in Figure 8.4. Firstly, in Figure 8.3, the stabilizer operators $S_i \in \mathcal{S}$ are designed for stabilizing the state of the physical qubits $|\overline{\psi}\rangle$, while the effective stabilizer operators $\hat{S}_i \in \hat{\mathcal{S}}$ in Figure 8.4 are constructed for stabilizing the state of physical qubits after the unitary transformation $U_f|\overline{\psi}\rangle = |\overline{\psi_2}\rangle$. Consequently, the recovery procedures of $R_i \in \mathcal{R}$ based on stabilizer operators $\mathcal{S}$ are also modified according to the effective stabilizer operators $\hat{\mathcal{S}}$ into the effective recovery operators $\widehat{R}_i \in \widehat{\mathcal{R}}$. Secondly, the inverse encoder $\mathcal{V}^\dagger$ of Figure 8.3 is designed to recover the original state of the logical qubit $|\psi\rangle$, while in Figure 8.4, the block $\widehat{\mathcal{V}}^\dagger$ is invoked for restoring the state of the logical qubits $|\overline{\psi_0}\rangle$, which has been transformed by the unitary transformation $U_f$ into $U_f|\overline{\psi_0}\rangle$.

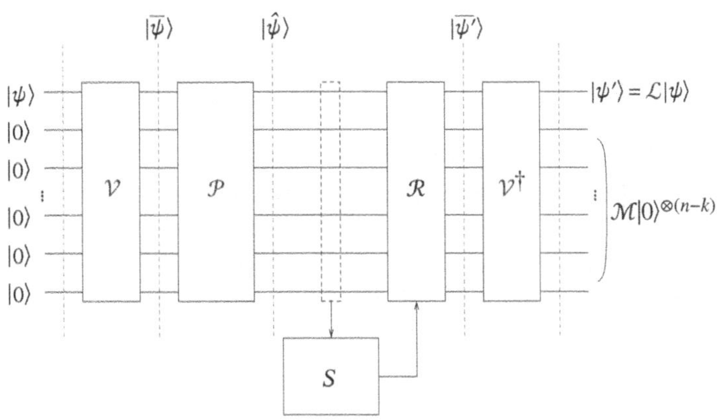


**Figure 8.3** The basic model of a QSC's implementation over the quantum depolarizing channel. The standard scheme for protecting the encoded state of physical qubits $|\overline{\psi}\rangle$. In this scheme, the purpose of applying a QSC is to recover the state of logical qubit $|\psi\rangle$ by stabilizing the state $|\overline{\psi}\rangle$ using the stabilizer operators $S_i \in \mathcal{S}$ in the presence of the depolarizing channel $\mathcal{P}$. *Source*: [255]/IEEE/CC BY 4.0.

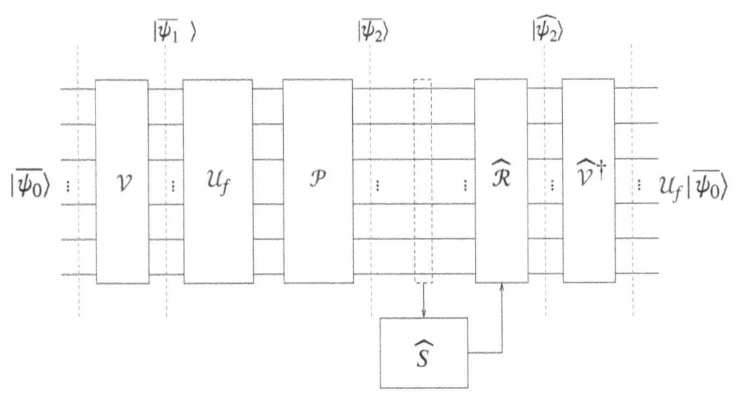


**Figure 8.4** The basic model of QSC-protected quantum gates, where the unitary transformation $\mathcal{U}_f$ precedes the quantum depolarizing channel $\mathcal{P}$. It portrays the modified scheme conceived for protecting the encoded state of physical qubits $|\overline{\psi_2}\rangle$, which is the encoded state after the unitary transformation $\mathcal{U}_f$. In this scheme, instead of stabilizing the state of $|\overline{\psi_1}\rangle$, the stabilizer operators have to stabilize the state of $|\overline{\psi_2}\rangle$. Since the stabilizer operator $S_i \in \mathcal{S}$ is only valid for the encoded state of $|\overline{\psi_1}\rangle$, we have to reformulate the stabilizer operators $S_i$ for stabilizing the encoded state $|\overline{\psi_2}\rangle$, which we refer to as the *effective stabilizer operators* $\hat{S}_1 \in \hat{\mathcal{S}}$. *Source*: [255]/IEEE/CC BY 4.0.

1 The term *effective* means that the stabilizer formalism and the inverse encoder at the output of computational step take into account both the initial stabilizer formalism and quantum encoder when we encode the logical qubits at the input and the unitary transformation applied to the input physical qubits.

Now, we proceed to specifically elaborate further on the scheme proposed for protecting quantum gates using QSCs, as shown in Figure 8.3. Let us commence with the logical qubits in the state of $|\psi\rangle$ representing the input of the quantum circuit. In order to encode the logical qubits, we require $(n-k)$ auxiliary qubits (ancillas) all in the state of $|0\rangle$. We assume that fresh ancillas are always available provided by a quantum memory. Hence, the state of the logical qubits and of the ancillas can be expressed as

$$|\overline{\psi_0}\rangle = |\psi\rangle \otimes |0\rangle^{\otimes(n-k)}. \tag{8.10}$$

The quantum encoder $\mathcal{V}$ of Figure 8.4 maps the input state of $|\overline{\psi_0}\rangle$ into the state of encoded logical qubits or physical qubits $|\overline{\psi_1}\rangle$ as follows:

$$|\overline{\psi_1}\rangle = \mathcal{V}|\overline{\psi_0}\rangle. \tag{8.11}$$

The unitary operation $U_f$ of Figure 8.4, which is the unitary transformation that we wish to protect, maps the physical qubits in the state of $|\overline{\psi_1}\rangle$ onto $|\overline{\psi_2}\rangle$ as follows:

$$|\overline{\psi_2}\rangle = U_f|\overline{\psi_1}\rangle = U_f\mathcal{V}|\overline{\psi_0}\rangle. \tag{8.12}$$

It is important to note that the unitary transformation of $U_f$ may impose quantum errors $\mathcal{P}$ on the encoded state $|\overline{\psi_2}\rangle$, as it will be shown later in Section 8.4.

Due to the unitary transformation $U_f$ after the quantum encoder $\mathcal{V}$, the stabilizer operators of $S_i \in \mathcal{S}$ are not applicable for the encoded state of $|\overline{\psi_2}\rangle$, because the stabilizer formalism $\mathcal{S}$ was designed for stabilizing the encoded state of $|\overline{\psi_1}\rangle$. Since the aim of this scheme is to protect the state of $|\overline{\psi_2}\rangle$ instead of $|\overline{\psi_1}\rangle$, a different stabilizer formalism, which we refer to as the effective stabilizer operators $\hat{S}_i \in \hat{\mathcal{S}}$, should be designed for stabilizing the state of $|\overline{\psi_2}\rangle$ by taking into account the unitary transformation $U_f$. Given the formulation in Eq. (8.2), we formulate the effective stabilizer operator $\hat{S}$ as follows:

$$\begin{aligned} |\overline{\psi_2}\rangle &= U_f|\overline{\psi_1}\rangle \\ &= U_fS|\overline{\psi_1}\rangle \\ &= U_fSU_f^{\dagger}U_f|\overline{\psi_1}\rangle \\ &= \hat{S}U_f|\overline{\psi_1}\rangle \\ &= \hat{S}|\overline{\psi_2}\rangle, \end{aligned} \tag{8.13}$$

where $\hat{S}$ is the effective stabilizer for $|\overline{\psi_2}\rangle$, which is defined by

$$\hat{S} = U_fSU_f^{\dagger}, \tag{8.14}$$

for stabilizing the state of $|\overline{\psi_2}\rangle$ in Figure 8.4.

Given a unitary function $U_f$ and a set of stabilizer operators $S_i \in \mathcal{S}$, there are three possible outcomes due to the effective stabilizer formalism of Eq. (8.14). Firstly, the set of stabilizer operators does not change ($\hat{\mathcal{S}} = \mathcal{S}$). In other words, the overall stabilizer operators are preserved. This specific result can be obtained, given that the unitary transformation $U_f$ is constituted by some types of transversal quantum Clifford gates, for instance, transversal Hadamard gates or CNOT gates, and $S_i \in \mathcal{S}$ belongs to dual-containing CSS-type QSCs.

Secondly, the stabilizer operators change ($\hat{\mathcal{S}} \neq \mathcal{S}$). One of the possible reasons that we can obtain the second result is that we apply the stabilizer codes to non-transversal quantum Clifford gates. Since the set of stabilizer operators is changed, there is a possibility that the resultant stabilizer operators $\hat{S}_i \in \hat{\mathcal{S}}$ are associated with a QSC exhibiting a higher error correction capability. This idea is reminiscent of the idea of code deformation presented in [257–260]. Defining $U_f$ for the non-transversal configurations of the quantum Clifford gates to obtain a higher error correction capability is a deep research question in its own right. We will set aside this question as one of our future research directions.

Thirdly, the resultant $\hat{S}_i$ is no longer a set of $n$-tuple Pauli operators. This means that the unitary transformation $U_f$ is containing non-Clifford quantum gates. More specifically, if the unitary transformation $U_f$ is not a quantum

Clifford gate, for example, it is a Toffoli gate [160], the QSCs cannot be used directly for protecting the quantum gates as presented in this chapter. To tackle this problem, a method of protecting the non-Clifford quantum gates—namely magic state distillation—was proposed [147]. In this chapter, we focus our attention on the first possible outcome, since we are dealing with the transversal quantum Clifford gates. Nevertheless, the two remaining implications of effective stabilizer formalism are also interesting research directions.

Next, after performing the stabilizer measurements of $\hat{S}_i \in \hat{\mathcal{S}}$, the error recovery procedure $\hat{\mathcal{R}}$ of Figure 8.4 acts according to the effective stabilizer measurements and we obtain the predicted legitimate physical qubit state of $|\widehat{\psi_2}\rangle$. The final task of our system given in Figure 8.4 is to perform a unitary transformation in order to transform the final state of $|\widehat{\psi_2}\rangle$ into the state of $U_f|\overline{\psi_0}\rangle$. Similar to the stabilizer formalism $\mathcal{S}$ in Figure 8.3, the inverse encoder $\mathcal{V}$ was also designed for recovering the state of $|\overline{\psi}_1\rangle$, which is based on the stabilizer formalism $\mathcal{S}$. Therefore, we require the *effective inverse encoder* $\hat{\mathcal{V}}^\dagger$ – which is designed based on the effective stabilizer operators $\hat{\mathcal{S}}$ seen in Figure 8.4 – to recover the state of $U_f|\overline{\psi_0}\rangle$. The formulation used for describing the effective inverse encoder $\hat{\mathcal{V}}^\dagger$ is given by

$$\begin{aligned} U_f|\overline{\psi_0}\rangle &= U_f(U_f\mathcal{V})^\dagger (U_f\mathcal{V})\,|\overline{\psi_0}\rangle \\ &= U_f(U_f\mathcal{V})^\dagger|\overline{\psi_2}\rangle \\ &= U_f\mathcal{V}^\dagger U_f^\dagger|\overline{\psi_2}\rangle \\ &= \hat{\mathcal{V}}^\dagger|\overline{\psi_2}\rangle, \end{aligned} \tag{8.15}$$

where $\hat{\mathcal{V}}^\dagger$ is the effective inverse encoder for $|\overline{\psi_2}\rangle$, defined as follows:

$$\hat{\mathcal{V}}^\dagger = U_f\mathcal{V}^\dagger U_f^\dagger. \tag{8.16}$$

Finally, as seen in Eq. (8.15), the effective inverse encoder $\hat{\mathcal{V}}^\dagger$ successfully transforms the state $|\overline{\psi_2}\rangle$ into the state of $U_f|\overline{\psi_0}\rangle$.

## 8.3 Design Examples

One of the strategies we may rely on for creating high-reliability quantum gates is that of invoking the unitary transformation $U_f$, representing a sequence of quantum gates arranged in a transversal fashion. For example, let us consider a quantum gate protected by a 1/3-rate quantum repetition code, as shown in Figure 8.5. Naturally, this code can only correct bit-flips, and for phase-flips we would need a second 1/3-rate code. More explicitly, based on the model depicted in Figure 8.4, we describe the transversal implementation of both the Hadamard gates and of the CNOT gates protected by the 1/3-rate quantum repetition code against bit-flip errors.

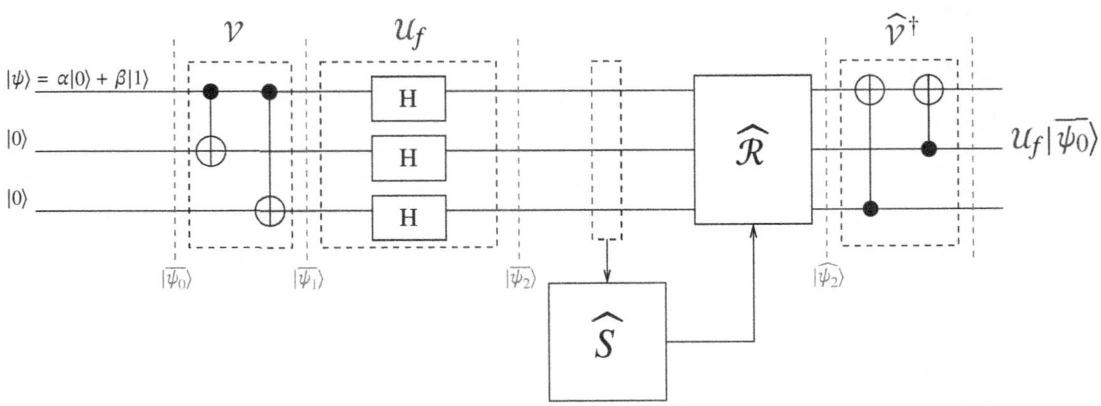


**Figure 8.5** Example of the transversal implementation of Hadamard gates protected by a 1/3-rate quantum repetition code relying on a quantum encoder $\mathcal{V}$. *Source*: [255]/IEEE/CC BY 4.0.

### 8.3.1 Transversal Hadamard Gates

**Design 1:** First, we would like to elaborate on the transversal implementation of Hadamard gates protected by a 1/3-rate quantum repetition code. Let us refer to Figure 8.5. The procedure begins with encoding the state of a single logical qubit $|\psi\rangle = \alpha|0\rangle + \beta|1\rangle$ and two auxiliary qubits in the state of $|0\rangle$ into the state of physical qubits of $|\overline{\psi_1}\rangle$ with the aid of quantum encoder $\mathcal{V}$ as follows:

$$\begin{aligned}|\overline{\psi_1}\rangle &= \mathcal{V}(|\psi\rangle \otimes |0\rangle^{\otimes 2}) \\ &= \mathcal{V}((\alpha|0\rangle + \beta|1\rangle) \otimes |0\rangle^{\otimes 2}) \\ &= \alpha|000\rangle + \beta|111\rangle \\ &\equiv \alpha|0\rangle_L + \beta|1\rangle_L,\end{aligned} \tag{8.17}$$

where $|0\rangle_L = |000\rangle$, $|1\rangle_L = |111\rangle$, and the quantum encoder $\mathcal{V}$ for this mapping is portrayed by the part marked by $\mathcal{V}$ in Figure 8.5. The encoded state of the physical qubits given in Eq. (8.17) is stabilized by the stabilizer operators generated by $S_i$:

$$\begin{aligned}S_1 &= \mathbf{Z}_1 \otimes \mathbf{I}_2 \otimes \mathbf{Z}_3, \\ S_2 &= \mathbf{Z}_1 \otimes \mathbf{Z}_2 \otimes \mathbf{I}_3,\end{aligned} \tag{8.18}$$

which can be invoked for correcting a single bit-flip (**X**) error. Recall that for the corresponding classical code the parity checks are 110 and 101. The Hadamard gates, which carry out the unitary transformation we wish to protect, are arranged transversally, where the Hadamard gate is applied to each of the encoded logical qubits as seen in Figure 8.5. Hence, the unitary transformation $U_f$ can be expressed as

$$U_f = \mathbf{H}^{\otimes n}, \tag{8.19}$$

where the superscript $\otimes n$ of $\mathbf{H}$ represents the $n$-fold tensor product. The unitary transform $U_f$ transforms the quantum state $|\overline{\psi_1}\rangle$ into quantum state $|\overline{\psi_2}\rangle$ as follows:

$$|\overline{\psi_2}\rangle = \alpha|+++\rangle + \beta|---\rangle. \tag{8.20}$$

Based on Eq. (8.14), the stabilizer operators of Eq. (8.18) and the unitary transformation $U_f$ of Eq. (8.19), we obtain the effective stabilizer generators $\hat{S}_i$ for stabilizing the quantum state $|\overline{\psi_2}\rangle$ in Figure 8.5 as follows:

$$\begin{aligned}\hat{S}_1 &= (\mathbf{H}^{\otimes 3})(\mathbf{Z}_1 \otimes \mathbf{I}_2 \otimes \mathbf{Z}_3)(\mathbf{H}^{\otimes 3})^\dagger \\ &= (\mathbf{HZH}^\dagger)_1 \otimes (\mathbf{HIH}^\dagger)_2 \otimes (\mathbf{HZH}^\dagger)_3 \\ &= \mathbf{X}_1 \otimes \mathbf{I}_2 \otimes \mathbf{X}_3,\end{aligned} \tag{8.21}$$

$$\begin{aligned}\hat{S}_2 &= (\mathbf{H}^{\otimes 3})(\mathbf{Z}_1 \otimes \mathbf{Z}_2 \otimes \mathbf{I}_3)(\mathbf{H}^{\otimes 3})^\dagger \\ &= (\mathbf{HZH}^\dagger)_1 \otimes (\mathbf{HZH}^\dagger)_2 \otimes (\mathbf{HIH}^\dagger)_3 \\ &= \mathbf{X}_1 \otimes \mathbf{X}_2 \otimes \mathbf{I}_3,\end{aligned} \tag{8.22}$$

which are capable of correcting a single phase-flip (**Z**) error. Finally, to transform the physical qubits in the state of $|\overline{\psi_2}\rangle$ to the state of $U_f|\overline{\psi_0}\rangle$, we design the effective inverse encoder of $\hat{\mathcal{V}}^\dagger$ based on Eq. (8.16) and we obtain the quantum circuit portrayed in Figure 8.5. Therefore, the final state of $U_f|\overline{\psi_0}\rangle$ can be described as follows:

$$\begin{aligned}U_f|\overline{\psi_0}\rangle &= \mathbf{H}^{\otimes n}(|\psi\rangle \otimes |0\rangle^{\otimes(n-k)}) \\ &= \mathbf{H}^{\otimes k}|\psi\rangle \otimes (\mathbf{H}^{\otimes(n-k)} \otimes |0\rangle^{\otimes(n-k)}) \\ &= \mathbf{H}^{\otimes k}|\psi\rangle \otimes |+\rangle^{\otimes(n-k)}.\end{aligned} \tag{8.23}$$

The last term of $|+\rangle^{\otimes(n-k)}$ can be discarded during measurement, since it is no longer entangled. In this example, we arrive at $|++\rangle$. Finally, from the design example specified in Figure 8.5, we acquire the desired output in the state of $\mathbf{H}^{\otimes k}|\psi\rangle = \mathbf{H}|\psi\rangle = \alpha|+\rangle + \beta|-\rangle$, given that we have $k = 1$ and $|\psi\rangle = \alpha|0\rangle + \beta|1\rangle$.

**Design 2:** Let us now consider another technique of utilizing QSCs for protecting transversal quantum Clifford gates, while dispensing with the quantum encoder $\mathcal{V}$. In order to relax the assumption of having a perfect quantum encoder $\mathcal{V}$, all of the $(n-k)$ auxiliary qubits required for creating the encoded state of the physical qubits are initialized in the $|+\rangle$ state and are followed by stabilizer measurements. The implementation of the quantum circuit of transversal Hadamard gates protected by a 1/3-rate quantum repetition code is portrayed in Figure 8.6. Let us denote the encoded state of physical qubits $\alpha|000\rangle + \beta|111\rangle$ of Eq. (8.17) as $|\overline{\psi_1}\rangle$ and the encoded state of physical qubits $\alpha|+++\rangle + \beta|---\rangle$ of Eq. (8.20) as $|\overline{\psi_2}\rangle$. The quantum state $|\overline{\psi_0}\rangle$ of Figure 8.6 can be expressed as

$$|\overline{\psi_0}\rangle = (\alpha|0\rangle + \beta|1\rangle) \otimes |+\rangle \otimes |+\rangle. \tag{8.24}$$

Given that $|+\rangle = \frac{|0\rangle+|1\rangle}{\sqrt{2}}$, we can expand and rewrite the quantum state $|\overline{\psi_0}\rangle$ of Eq. (8.24) in terms of $|\overline{\psi_1}\rangle = \alpha|000\rangle + \beta|111\rangle$ as follows:

$$|\overline{\psi_0}\rangle = |\overline{\psi_1}\rangle + \mathbf{X}_2|\overline{\psi_1}\rangle + \mathbf{X}_3|\overline{\psi_1}\rangle + \mathbf{X}_2\mathbf{X}_3|\overline{\psi_1}\rangle, \tag{8.25}$$

where the notation of $\mathbf{X}_i$ indicates that the Pauli matrix $\mathbf{X}$ is applied to the $i$-th qubit. The current quantum state of $|\overline{\psi_0}\rangle$ is based on a superposition, where the action of the stabilizer measurements $(S_i \in \mathcal{S})$ will result in collapsing the quantum state $|\overline{\psi_0}\rangle$ into one of the following possibilities: $|\overline{\psi_1}\rangle$, $\mathbf{X}_2|\overline{\psi_1}\rangle$, $\mathbf{X}_3|\overline{\psi_1}\rangle$, and $\mathbf{X}_2\mathbf{X}_3|\overline{\psi_2}\rangle$ with equal probabilities. Following this measurement, the resultant quantum state $|\overline{\psi_1}\rangle$ will be in one of the $\pm 1$ values acquired from the stabilizer measurements. Hence, the error recovery operator $\mathcal{R}$ can restore the resultant collapsed quantum state back into the legitimate quantum state $|\overline{\psi_1}\rangle$, which is similar to Design 1 associated with the quantum encoder $\mathcal{V}$. Next, the action of the unitary operator $U_f$ –which is represented by the transversal Hadamard gates of Eq. (8.19) – transforms the quantum state $|\overline{\psi_1}\rangle$ into the quantum state $|\overline{\psi_2}\rangle$ as follows:

$$\begin{aligned} |\overline{\psi_2}\rangle &= U_f|\overline{\psi_1}\rangle \\ &= \alpha|+++\rangle + \beta|---\rangle. \end{aligned} \tag{8.26}$$

From this point onwards, the recovery operators $\hat{\mathcal{R}}$ as well as the effective quantum inverse encoder $\hat{\mathcal{V}}^\dagger$ of both Design 1 and 2 operating with and without quantum encoder $\mathcal{V}$ are identical. Therefore, the error correction performances of Design 1 and 2 are also expected to be identical.

### 8.3.2 Transversal CNOT Gates – Advanced Design

In our next example, namely **Design 3** we aim for conceiving the transversal implementation of CNOT gates protected by the 1/3-rate quantum repetition code against bit-flip errors. The model is depicted in Figures 8.7 and 8.8.

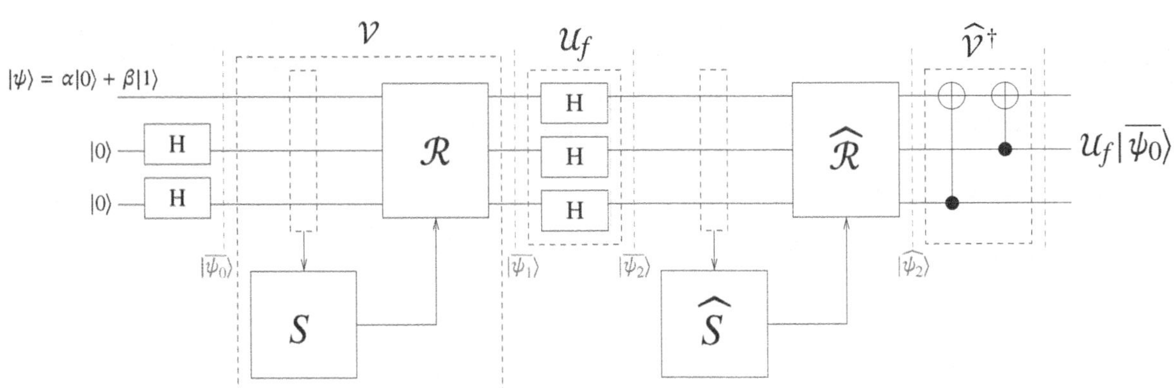


**Figure 8.6** Example of the transversal implementation of Hadamard gates protected by a 1/3-rate quantum repetition code relying on repeated stabilizer measurements. *Source:* [255]/IEEE/CC BY 4.0.

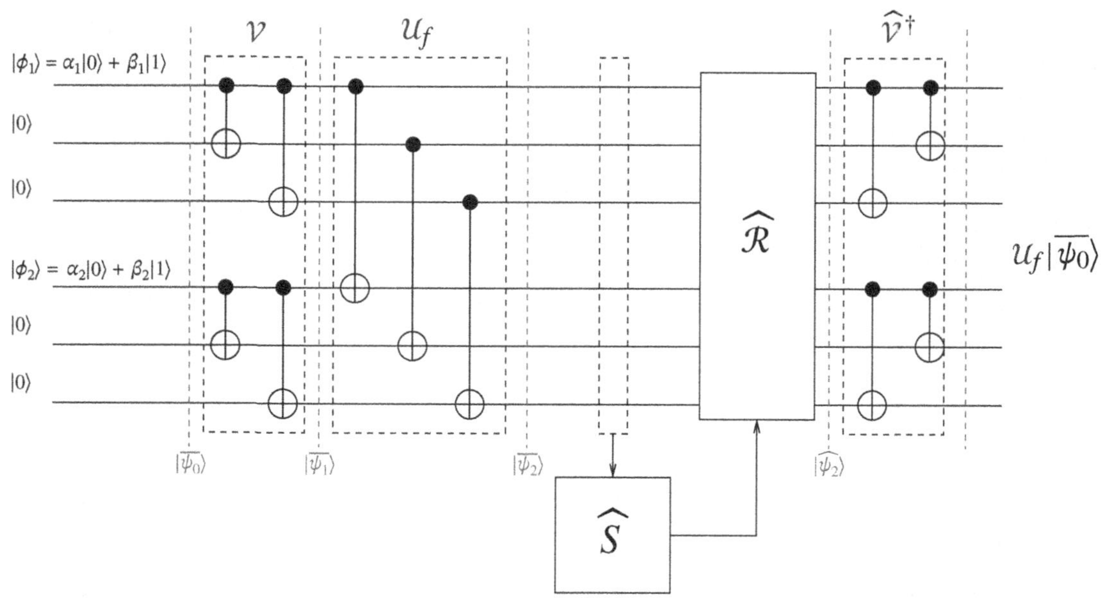


**Figure 8.7** Example of the transversal implementation of CNOT gates protected by a 1/3-rate quantum repetition code relying on the quantum encoder $\mathcal{V}$. *Source*: [255]/IEEE/CC BY 4.0.

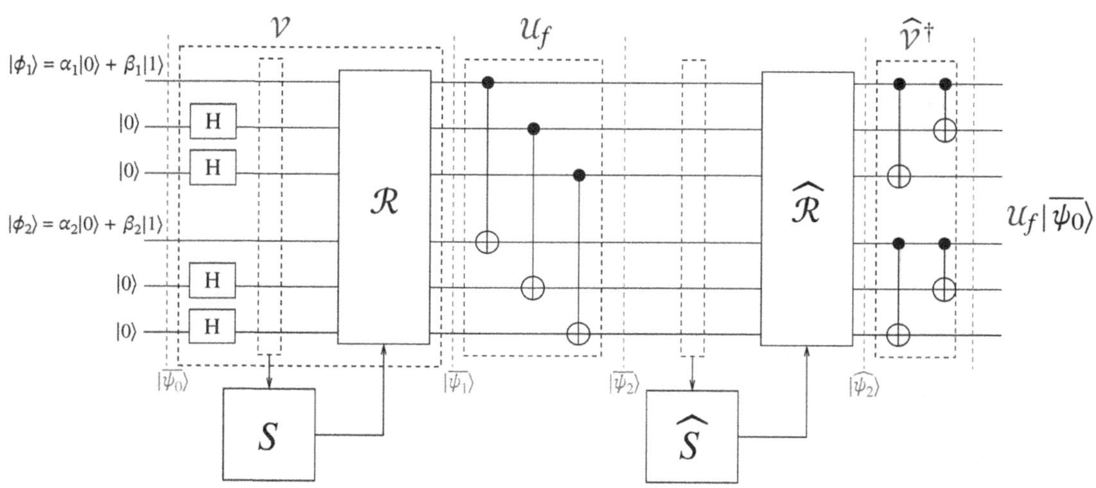


**Figure 8.8** Example of the transversal implementation of CNOT gates protected by a 1/3-rate quantum repetition code relying on repeated stabilizer measurements. *Source*: [255]/IEEE/CC BY 4.0.

For the scheme portrayed in Figure 8.7, the initial state is defined by $|\psi\rangle = |\phi_1\rangle \otimes |\phi_2\rangle$ and our desired output is $\mathbf{CNOT}(|\phi_1\rangle \otimes |\phi_2\rangle)$, where $|\phi_1\rangle$ acts as the control qubit and $|\phi_2\rangle$ serves as the target qubit. The quantum encoder $\mathcal{V}$ of Figure 8.8 encodes each of the logical qubits in the state of $|\phi_1\rangle$ and $|\phi_2\rangle$ independently, yielding the physical qubits in the state of $|\overline{\psi_1}\rangle = |\overline{\phi_1}\rangle \otimes |\overline{\phi_2}\rangle$, where $|\overline{\phi_1}\rangle$ and $|\overline{\phi_2}\rangle$ are the encoded logical qubits of $|\phi_1\rangle$ and $|\phi_2\rangle$, respectively. Therefore, the stabilizer operators $S_i$ provided for the physical qubits in the state of $|\overline{\psi_1}\rangle$ in Figure 8.7 are generated by the following stabilizer generators:

$$\begin{aligned} S_1 &= \mathbf{Z}_1 \otimes \mathbf{I}_2 \otimes \mathbf{Z}_3 \otimes \mathbf{I}_4 \otimes \mathbf{I}_5 \otimes \mathbf{I}_6, \\ S_2 &= \mathbf{Z}_1 \otimes \mathbf{Z}_2 \otimes \mathbf{I}_3 \otimes \mathbf{I}_4 \otimes \mathbf{I}_5 \otimes \mathbf{I}_6, \\ S_3 &= \mathbf{I}_1 \otimes \mathbf{I}_2 \otimes \mathbf{I}_3 \otimes \mathbf{Z}_4 \otimes \mathbf{I}_5 \otimes \mathbf{Z}_6, \\ S_4 &= \mathbf{I}_1 \otimes \mathbf{I}_2 \otimes \mathbf{I}_3 \otimes \mathbf{Z}_4 \otimes \mathbf{Z}_5 \otimes \mathbf{I}_6. \end{aligned} \tag{8.27}$$

In this example, the quantum gate that we want to protect is the CNOT gate. Therefore, the unitary transformation $U_f$ of Figures 8.7 and 8.8 represents the unitary matrix of the transversal CNOT gates. Let us now denote the unitary matrix of the $n$ transversal CNOT gates as $\overline{\textbf{CNOT}}^{n}$. Therefore, the unitary transformation $U_f$ of Figures 8.7 and 8.8 can be expressed as a $64 \times 64$-element matrix by expanding the following transformation:

$$\begin{aligned} U_f &= \overline{\textbf{CNOT}}^{3} \\ &= |000\rangle\langle 000| \otimes \mathbf{I} \otimes \mathbf{I} \otimes \mathbf{I} + |001\rangle\langle 001| \otimes \mathbf{I} \otimes \mathbf{I} \otimes \mathbf{X} \\ &\quad + |010\rangle\langle 010| \otimes \mathbf{I} \otimes \mathbf{X} \otimes \mathbf{I} + |011\rangle\langle 011| \otimes \mathbf{I} \otimes \mathbf{X} \otimes \mathbf{X} \\ &\quad + |100\rangle\langle 100| \otimes \mathbf{X} \otimes \mathbf{I} \otimes \mathbf{I} + |101\rangle\langle 101| \otimes \mathbf{X} \otimes \mathbf{I} \otimes \mathbf{X} \\ &\quad + |110\rangle\langle 110| \otimes \mathbf{X} \otimes \mathbf{X} \otimes \mathbf{I} + |111\rangle\langle 111| \otimes \mathbf{X} \otimes \mathbf{X} \otimes \mathbf{X}. \end{aligned} \tag{8.28}$$

Based on the stabilizer generators $S_i$ in Eq. (8.27) and the unitary transformation $U_f$ of Eq. (8.28), we can obtain the effective stabilizer operators $\hat{S}_i$ by applying Eq. (8.14), which was formulated for protecting the state of $|\overline{\psi_2}\rangle$ in Figure 8.7. Explicitly, the effective stabilizer operators $\hat{S}_i$ are generated by the following stabilizer generators:

$$\begin{aligned} \hat{S}_1 &= \mathbf{Z}_1 \otimes \mathbf{I}_2 \otimes \mathbf{Z}_3 \otimes \mathbf{I}_4 \otimes \mathbf{I}_5 \otimes \mathbf{I}_6, \\ \hat{S}_2 &= \mathbf{Z}_1 \otimes \mathbf{Z}_2 \otimes \mathbf{I}_3 \otimes \mathbf{I}_4 \otimes \mathbf{I}_5 \otimes \mathbf{I}_6, \\ \hat{S}_3 &= \mathbf{Z}_1 \otimes \mathbf{I}_2 \otimes \mathbf{Z}_3 \otimes \mathbf{Z}_4 \otimes \mathbf{I}_5 \otimes \mathbf{Z}_6, \\ \hat{S}_4 &= \mathbf{Z}_1 \otimes \mathbf{Z}_2 \otimes \mathbf{I}_3 \otimes \mathbf{Z}_4 \otimes \mathbf{Z}_5 \otimes \mathbf{I}_6. \end{aligned} \tag{8.29}$$

Based on the commutative nature of stabilizer operators, where the multiplication among stabilizer operators will produce another valid stabilizer operator, we may rewrite the list of stabilizer generators given in Eq. (8.29). Hence, upon multiplying $\hat{S}_1$ by $\hat{S}_3$ and also multiplying $\hat{S}_2$ by $\hat{S}_4$, we obtain the following effective stabilizer operators $\hat{S}_i$ generated by the stabilizer generators of:

$$\begin{aligned} \hat{S}_1 &= \mathbf{Z}_1 \otimes \mathbf{I}_2 \otimes \mathbf{Z}_3 \otimes \mathbf{I}_4 \otimes \mathbf{I}_5 \otimes \mathbf{I}_6, \\ \hat{S}_2 &= \mathbf{Z}_1 \otimes \mathbf{Z}_2 \otimes \mathbf{I}_3 \otimes \mathbf{I}_4 \otimes \mathbf{I}_5 \otimes \mathbf{I}_6, \\ \hat{S}_3 &= \mathbf{I}_1 \otimes \mathbf{I}_2 \otimes \mathbf{I}_3 \otimes \mathbf{Z}_4 \otimes \mathbf{I}_5 \otimes \mathbf{Z}_6, \\ \hat{S}_4 &= \mathbf{I}_1 \otimes \mathbf{I}_2 \otimes \mathbf{I}_3 \otimes \mathbf{Z}_4 \otimes \mathbf{Z}_5 \otimes \mathbf{I}_6. \end{aligned} \tag{8.30}$$

As we can observe, the resultant effective stabilizer operators $\hat{S}_i \in \hat{\mathcal{S}}$ of Eq. (8.30) are identical to the stabilizer operators $S_i \in \mathcal{S}$ of Eq. (8.27). Consequently, this demonstrates the convenience of exploiting the transversal implementation of CNOT gates. Since the effective stabilizer operators $\hat{S}_i$ of Eq. (8.30) are identical to the stabilizer operators $S_i$ of Eq. (8.27), the quantum circuit of the effective inverse encoder $\hat{\mathcal{V}}^{\dagger}$ of Figure 8.7 is also identical to the inverse encoder $\mathcal{V}^{\dagger}$ designed for transforming the state $|\overline{\psi_1}\rangle$ to the state $|\overline{\psi_0}\rangle$. Finally, the desired state for the physical output qubits based on the transversal configuration given in Figure 8.7 can be formulated as

$$\begin{aligned} U_f|\overline{\psi_0}\rangle &= \overline{\textbf{CNOT}}^{n}(|\phi_1\rangle \otimes |0\rangle^{\otimes(n-k)}, (|\phi_2\rangle \otimes |0\rangle^{\otimes(n-k)})) \\ &= \overline{\textbf{CNOT}}^{k}(|\phi_1\rangle, |\phi_2\rangle) \otimes |00\rangle^{\otimes(n-k)}, \end{aligned} \tag{8.31}$$

where the last term represents the auxiliary qubits in the state of $|00\rangle^{\otimes(n-k)}$ that can be discarded after measurement, since they are no longer entangled with the logical qubits in the state of $\overline{\textbf{CNOT}}^{k}(|\phi_1\rangle, |\phi_2\rangle)$. Given that we have $k = 1$ and $n = 3$ for our example in Figure 8.7, we successfully protect the unitary transformation of $\textbf{CNOT}(|\phi_1\rangle, |\phi_2\rangle)$ at the output of our scheme. Therefore, we have outlined the general framework of QSC-protected transversal quantum gates.

**Design 4:** Additionally, in Figure 8.8 we also present an alternative scheme designed for protecting transversal CNOT gates without the quantum encoder $\mathcal{V}$. Briefly, instead of using the quantum encoder $\mathcal{V}$ portrayed in Figure 8.7, we can also utilize the scheme of Figure 8.8, where the quantum encoder $\mathcal{V}$ is replaced by a stabilizer measurement to create the code space. More specifically, the quantum state of the physical qubits $|\overline{\psi_1}\rangle$ of Figure 8.7 is given by

$$\begin{aligned}|\overline{\psi_1}\rangle &= (\alpha_1|000\rangle + \beta_1\rangle|111\rangle) \otimes (\alpha_2|000\rangle + \beta_2\rangle|111\rangle) \\ &= \alpha_1\alpha_2|000\rangle|000\rangle + \alpha_1\beta_2|000\rangle|111\rangle + \alpha_2\beta_1|111\rangle|000\rangle + \beta_1\beta_2|111\rangle|111\rangle.\end{aligned} \tag{8.32}$$

In Figure 8.8, the physical qubits are prepared in the quantum state of $|\overline{\psi_0}\rangle$ as follows:

$$|\overline{\psi_0}\rangle = (\alpha_1|0\rangle + \beta_1|1\rangle) \otimes |+\rangle \otimes |+\rangle \otimes (\alpha_2|0\rangle + \beta_2|1\rangle) \otimes |+\rangle \otimes |+\rangle. \tag{8.33}$$

Given that $|+\rangle = \frac{|0\rangle+|1\rangle}{\sqrt{2}}$, we can expand and rewrite the quantum state $|\overline{\psi_0}\rangle$ of Eq. (8.33) in terms of $|\overline{\psi_1}\rangle$ of Eq. (8.32) as follows:

$$\begin{aligned}|\overline{\psi_0}\rangle = {} & |\overline{\psi_1}\rangle + \mathbf{X}_2|\overline{\psi_1}\rangle + \mathbf{X}_3|\overline{\psi_1}\rangle + \mathbf{X}_2\mathbf{X}_3|\overline{\psi_1}\rangle \\ & + \mathbf{X}_5|\overline{\psi_1}\rangle + \mathbf{X}_2\mathbf{X}_5|\overline{\psi_1}\rangle + \mathbf{X}_3\mathbf{X}_5|\overline{\psi_1}\rangle + \mathbf{X}_2\mathbf{X}_3\mathbf{X}_5|\overline{\psi_1}\rangle \\ & + \mathbf{X}_6|\overline{\psi_1}\rangle + \mathbf{X}_2\mathbf{X}_6|\overline{\psi_1}\rangle + \mathbf{X}_3\mathbf{X}_6|\overline{\psi_1}\rangle + \mathbf{X}_2\mathbf{X}_3\mathbf{X}_6|\overline{\psi_1}\rangle \\ & + \mathbf{X}_5\mathbf{X}_6|\overline{\psi_1}\rangle + \mathbf{X}_2\mathbf{X}_5\mathbf{X}_6|\overline{\psi_1}\rangle + \mathbf{X}_3\mathbf{X}_5\mathbf{X}_6|\overline{\psi_1}\rangle + \mathbf{X}_2\mathbf{X}_3\mathbf{X}_5\mathbf{X}_6|\overline{\psi_1}\rangle,\end{aligned} \tag{8.34}$$

where the notation of $\mathbf{X}_i$ indicates that a Pauli matrix $\mathbf{X}$ is applied to the $i$-th qubit. Observe that the stabilizer operators of Eq. (8.27) are associated with 16 possible classical syndrome vectors, where each of the syndrome vectors is associated with one of the superimposed states given in Eq. (8.34). When the stabilizer measurements are performed, the superposition state of Eq. (8.34) will collapse to one of the following 16 possibilities: $|\overline{\psi_1}\rangle$, $\mathbf{X}_2|\overline{\psi_1}\rangle$, $\mathbf{X}_3|\overline{\psi_1}\rangle$, $\mathbf{X}_2\mathbf{X}_3|\overline{\psi_1}\rangle$, $\mathbf{X}_5|\overline{\psi_1}\rangle$, $\mathbf{X}_2\mathbf{X}_5|\overline{\psi_1}\rangle$, $\mathbf{X}_3\mathbf{X}_5|\overline{\psi_1}\rangle$, $\mathbf{X}_2\mathbf{X}_3\mathbf{X}_5|\overline{\psi_1}\rangle$, $\mathbf{X}_6|\overline{\psi_1}\rangle$, $\mathbf{X}_2\mathbf{X}_6|\overline{\psi_1}\rangle$, $\mathbf{X}_3\mathbf{X}_6|\overline{\psi_1}\rangle$, $\mathbf{X}_2\mathbf{X}_3\mathbf{X}_6|\overline{\psi_1}\rangle$, $\mathbf{X}_5\mathbf{X}_6|\overline{\psi_1}\rangle$, $\mathbf{X}_2\mathbf{X}_5\mathbf{X}_6|\overline{\psi_1}\rangle$, $\mathbf{X}_3\mathbf{X}_5\mathbf{X}_6|\overline{\psi_1}\rangle$, $\mathbf{X}_2\mathbf{X}_3\mathbf{X}_5\mathbf{X}_6|\overline{\psi_1}\rangle$, where the collapsed quantum state can be inferred from the classical syndrome vector obtained from stabilizer measurements. Therefore, we can apply the recovery operator $\mathcal{R}$ to obtain the encoded state of physical qubits of $|\overline{\psi_1}\rangle$ from Eq. (8.32). Once the recovery operator has been applied, the unitary transformation $U_f$ is carried out, which transforms the quantum state of $|\overline{\psi}_1\rangle$ into the quantum state $|\overline{\psi}_1\rangle$ as follows:

$$|\overline{\psi_2}\rangle = U_f|\overline{\psi}_1\rangle. \tag{8.35}$$

Similar to the case of transversal Hadamard gates, from this point onwards, all the effective stabilizer measurements, error recovery operators, and inverse encoder of Figure 8.8 are identical to those of Figure 8.7. Hence, we expect the performance of the scheme illustrated in Figure 8.7 to be identical to the one in Figure 8.8.

## 8.4 Error Model

In order to show the benefit of utilizing the framework exemplified in Section 8.3, we have to opt for a realistic quantum decoherence model of the system to produce the most realistic performance results. However, several assumptions have to be made to justify the proposed error model. Based on [261–264], we stipulate the idealized simplifying assumption that quantum decoherence may be imposed by single-qubit quantum gates, 2-qubit quantum gates, as well as by the deleterious effects of the stabilizer measurements. In order to consider the decoherence inflicted by multiple components within our framework, we offer the following two propositions:

**Proposition 1.** An error-infested quantum encoder $\mathcal{V}$ and a unitary transformation $U_f$ can be modeled as a perfect quantum encoder $\mathcal{V}$ and a perfect unitary transformation $U_f$ followed by the quantum channel $P \in \mathcal{P}_n$. To elaborate a little further, the encoder of QSCs can be fully constructed from the quantum gates belonging to the Clifford group. Consequently, we can use the formulation of Eq. (8.2), which is illustrated in Figure 8.1, to model the error propagation through it. More explicitly, let us provide an example using the quantum encoder of Steane's 7-qubit code, which is equivalent to the quantum encoder of the distance-3 color code, as portrayed in Figure 8.9. We can observe from Figure 8.9a that a single bit-flip (**X**) error at the input of the quantum encoder is transformed into three separated bit-flip (**X**) errors, which are accumulated at the output of the encoder $\mathcal{V}$. Similarly in Figure 8.9b, a phase-flip (**Z**) at the input of the quantum encoder propagating through it is transformed into three different phase-flip errors at three different locations at the output of the quantum encoder $\mathcal{V}$. Hence, in general, the severity of error propagation within the quantum encoder $\mathcal{V}$ is determined by the number of constituent 2-qubit quantum Clifford gates.

**Proposition 2.** An error-infested stabilizer measurement of the QSC protecting the transversal quantum gates of Figure 8.4 can be substituted by a perfect stabilizer measurement and the quantum channel $P \in \mathcal{P}$ after the transversal configuration of quantum gates, which is illustrated in Figure 8.10. This is also one of the natural consequences of the conjugation given in Eq. (8.2). Since the **X** stabilizer operators anti-commute with the **Z** Pauli operator, only **Z**-type errors are considered for **X** stabilizer measurements. Equivalently, since the **Z** stabilizer operators anti-commute with the **X** Pauli operator, only **X**-type errors affect the result of **Z** stabilizer measurements.

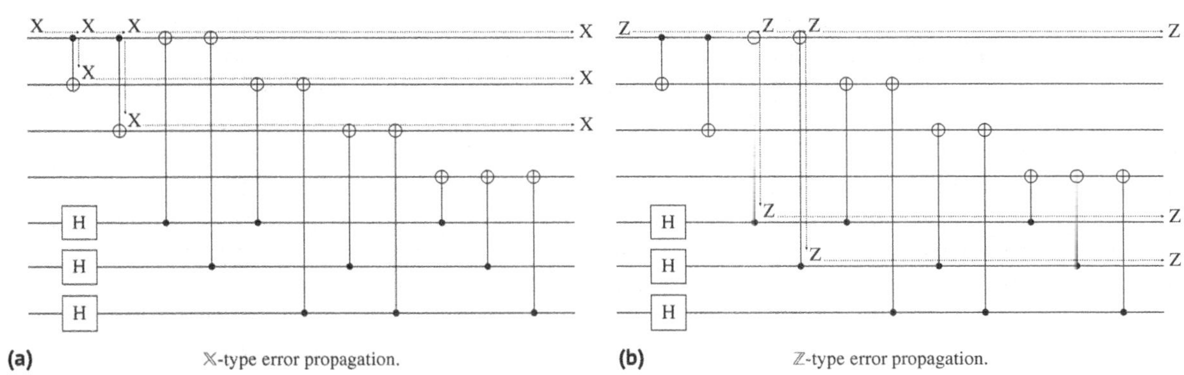


**Figure 8.9** The quantum encoder of Steane's 7-qubit code can be implemented purely consisting of quantum gates from the Clifford group. Therefore, a faulty quantum encoder of any QSC can be assumed to be modeled as a perfect quantum encoder followed by the quantum depolarizing channel. A single bit-flip (**X**) error at the input may in fact be transformed into three bit-flip errors at the output of the quantum encoder $\mathcal{V}$. Similarly, a phase-flip (**Z**) inflicted at the input of the quantum encoder **V** may propagate, hence resulting in three phase-flip errors at the output. *Source*: [255]/IEEE/CC BY 4.0.

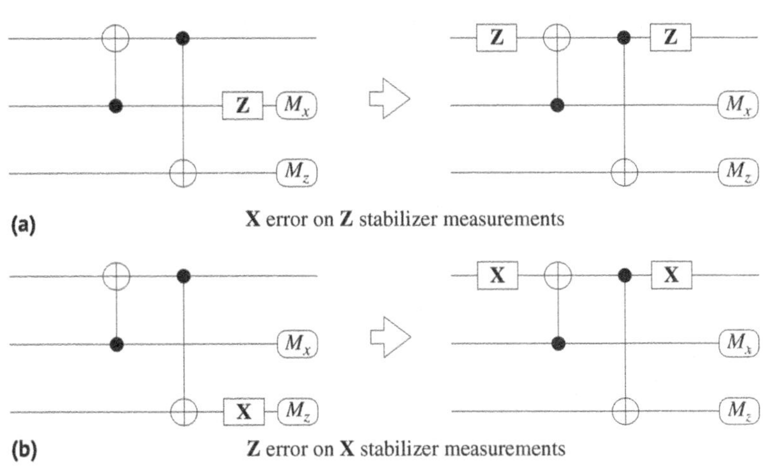


**Figure 8.10** Error on stabilizer measurements. *Source*: [255]/IEEE/CC BY 4.0.

### 8.4.1 Source of Decoherence

By considering the potential sources of quantum decoherence based on our proposed framework and also the nature of error propagation, we conclude that diverse sources of decoherence can be efficiently modeled as the accumulated quantum decoherence before and after the transversal quantum gates $U_f$, as explicitly shown in Figure 8.11. To elaborate a little further, the quantum decoherence before the transversal quantum gates is constituted by $P_1 \in \mathcal{P}_n$ that corrupts the physical qubits in the state of $|\overline{\psi_1}\rangle$ by **X**, **Z** and **Y**-type errors independently with depolarizing probability of $p_X = p_Y = p_Z = p_1/3$. Similarly, the quantum decoherence after the transversal gates is denoted by $P_2 \in \mathcal{P}_n$), which is described by the depolarizing probability of $p_2$, corrupting the physical qubits in the state of $|\overline{\psi_2}\rangle$.

It is important to note that each of the error operators $P_1$ and $P_2$ may encapsulate several sources of quantum decoherence. For example, observe from Figures 8.11a, b that the error operator $P_1$ represents the decoherence from the quantum encoder $\mathcal{V}$ of Figure 8.4, which is denoted by $P_v$. The error operator of $P_v \in \mathcal{P}_n$ is characterized by the depolarizing probability of $p_v$. The error operator of $P_2 \in \mathcal{P}_n$ encapsulates both the quantum decoherence imposed by the quantum gates $P_u$ as well as that imposed by the stabilizer measurement $P_m$. If the error operator $P_u$ is specified by the depolarizing probability of $p_u$ and the error operator $P_m$ is specified by the depolarizing probability of $p_m$, the error operator $P_2$ can be determined by $P_m \cdot P_u = P_2 \in \mathcal{P}_n$.

Let us now consider various error models available in the literature. Most of the error models used for evaluating the performance of QSCs harnessed for protecting quantum gates consist of three parameters namely, the error probability imposed by a single-qubit gate denoted by $p_a$, the error probability imposed by 2-qubit quantum gates denoted by $p_b$, and that inflicted by the stabilizer measurements denoted by $p_m$. The *standard error model* [262] assumes that $p_a = p_b = p_m = p$. By contrast, the *balanced error model* [262] assumes that the error rate imposed by the single-qubit quantum gate is $p_a = 4p/5$, that by the 2-qubit quantum gate is $p_b = p$, and that by the stabilizer measurements is given by $p_m = 8p/15$. From an experimental perspective, let us consider the *ion trap error model* [262], where the parameters are defined by $p_1 = p/1000$, $p_2 = p$, and $p_m = p/100$. In this chapter, one of our main goals is to investigate the overall scheme using the quantum-to-classical isomorphism. Therefore, we simulate the quantum decoherence contaminating each of the physical qubits as an individual and independent binary symmetric channel (BSC) as suggested in [67, 83]. Consequently, for the classical simulation based on independent BSCs, we have the parameters of $p_a = p_m = p$ and $p_b \approx 2p$. A more detailed description of the error model used for this investigation is provided in the following subsection.

Different error models are valid for the different technology platforms available for developing quantum computers. In this chapter, however, we focus our attention on how we can investigate the performance of transversal quantum Clifford gates protected by two-dimensional QTECCs using classical simulations. Intuitively, we want to have a depolarizing probability, which is as low as possible. However, state-of-the-art quantum gates typically have relatively high error probability, ranging between 90.00% and 99.90% across various technology platforms, such as spin electronics, photonics, superconducting, trapped-ion, and silicon implementations [37–40, 42, 44–46, 145]. Fortunately, based on the threshold theorem [148], it is possible to construct relatively reliable quantum computers from modest-fidelity quantum gates, provided that the error probability of the quantum gates is

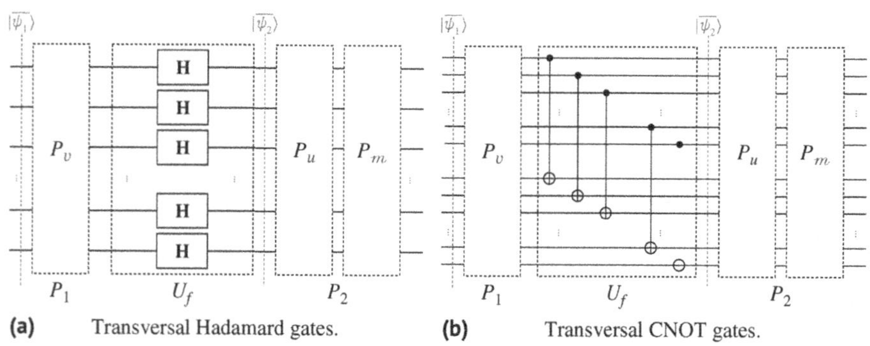


**Figure 8.11** The potential quantum decoherence model imposed in QSC-protected transversal Hadamard and CNOT gates. There are several potential sources of quantum decoherence including the quantum encoder, quantum gates, and stabilizer measurement, denoted by $P_v$, $P_u$, and $P_m$, respectively. *Source*: [255]/IEEE/CC BY 4.0.

below a certain probability threshold value and a reasonable coding overhead is affordable. Therefore, most of the studies dedicated to QECCs are focused on finding the specific value of gate error probabilities $p_a$, $p_b$, and $p_m$ so that QECCs can be harnessed for significantly improving the reliability of the resultant quantum computers.

### 8.4.2 Faulty Quantum Gates

In this chapter, we rely on the model illustrated in Figure 8.12, where each qubit experiences an independent quantum depolarizing channel characterized by its depolarizing probability. The metric used for evaluating the performance of our system is the qubit error rate (QBER) and the fidelity ($F$). Naturally, the QBER is defined as the ratio between the number of erroneous qubits and the total number of qubits. For a single-qubit quantum gate, which is exemplified by the Hadamard gate **H**, the QBER can be represented as

$$\text{QBER}_{\text{Had}} = p, \tag{8.36}$$

where $p$ is the depolarizing probability of the single-qubit quantum decoherence caused by the imperfection of the quantum gate.

Secondly, the reliability of a quantum gate can also be quantified using its *fidelity*. Explicitly, the fidelity may be used to reflect the closeness of an ensemble of quantum states in the mixed-state to the desired pure state, which is formulated as follows [85, 243, 244]:

$$F = \langle \overline{\psi} | \rho | \overline{\psi} \rangle, \tag{8.37}$$

where $|\overline{\psi}\rangle$ is the desired pure state and $\rho$ is the density matrix encapsulating the statistical characteristics of the mixed-states. The density matrix $\rho$ is defined by

$$\rho = \sum_{i=1}^{N} p_i |\psi_i\rangle\langle\psi_i|, \tag{8.38}$$

where $|\psi_i\rangle$ represents all the possible quantum states in the ensemble and $p_i$ is the probability of obtaining the quantum state $|\psi_i\rangle$, which is consequently constrained by the unity requirement of $\sum_{i=1}^{N} p_i = 1$. For a quantum Clifford gate, the relationship between the fidelity and the QBER is as simple as

$$F = 1 - \text{QBER}, \tag{8.39}$$

where QBER is the qubit error ratio of the unprotected gate. Consequently, we obtain the analytical expression of the initial fidelity ($F_{\text{in}}$) for a Hadamard gate as a function of the depolarizing probability $p$ as follows:

$$F_{\text{in}} = 1 - p. \tag{8.40}$$

Similar to the Hadamard gate, the fidelity of the CNOT gate can be defined using Eq. (8.39). Since a CNOT gate is a 2-qubit quantum gate, the fidelity can be explicitly formulated as the probability of having the Pauli operator **I** on both the control qubit and the target qubit, which can be formulated as

$$\begin{aligned} F_{\text{in}} &= (1-p)(1-p) \\ &= 1 - 2p + p^2. \end{aligned} \tag{8.41}$$

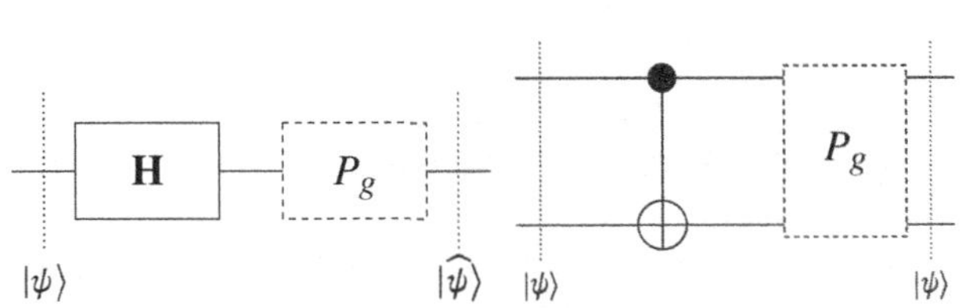

**(a)** Faulty Hadamard gate. **(b)** Faulty CNOT gate.

**Figure 8.12** The model of faulty quantum gates. The Pauli channel $Pg \in \mathcal{P}$ is inflicted after the quantum gates.
*Source:* [255]/IEEE/CC BY 4.0.

Therefore, the QBER of a CNOT gate can be rewritten as follows:

$$\text{QBER}_{\text{CNOT}} = 2p - p^2 \approx 2p, \tag{8.42}$$

for $p \ll 1$. Therefore, given that $p_a$ is the error rate or the QBER of a single-qubit quantum gate and $p_b$ is the error rate or the QBER of a 2-qubit quantum gate, we obtain the relationship between $p_a$ and $p_b$ for classical simulations relying on a BSC as follows:

$$p_b \approx 2p_a. \tag{8.43}$$

Additionally, the relationship between the error rate $p_a$ of a single-qubit quantum gate and that of a stabilizer measurement – namely $p_m$ – can be simply formulated as

$$p_m = p_a. \tag{8.44}$$

### 8.4.3 Effective Depolarizing Channel

As we have described in Subsection 8.4.1, in the QSC-protected quantum transversal gates, there are multiple sources of decoherence. For example, in Figure 8.11, the decoherence effects imposed by the transversal quantum gates and stabilizer measurements can be modeled by multiple subsequent quantum depolarizing channels. To simplify the analytical calculations and their approximation, we introduce the notion of *effective depolarizing channel*.

For example, let us assume that the first depolarizing channel is constituted by the error operator $P_1 \in \mathcal{P}_n$, which is characterized by the depolarizing probability $p_1 = p$, while the second depolarizing channel is constituted by the error operator $P_2 \in \mathcal{P}_n$, which is characterized by the depolarizing probability $p_2 = p$. Then, the probability of obtaining the Pauli matrix **I** at the output of two consecutive Pauli channels can be expressed as follows:

$$\begin{aligned} p_{\mathbf{I},f} &= p_{\mathbf{I},1}p_{\mathbf{I},2} + p_{\mathbf{X},1}p_{\mathbf{X},2} + p_{\mathbf{Y},1}p_{\mathbf{Y},2} + p_{\mathbf{Z},1}p_{\mathbf{Z},2} \\ &= (1-p)(1-p) + \left(\frac{p}{3}\right)\left(\frac{p}{3}\right) + \left(\frac{p}{3}\right)\left(\frac{p}{3}\right) + \left(\frac{p}{3}\right)\left(\frac{p}{3}\right) \\ &= 1 - 2p + \frac{4}{3}p^2. \end{aligned} \tag{8.45}$$

Consequently, we obtain the following probability of experiencing the Pauli error **X**, **Y**, and **Z**:

$$p_{\mathbf{X},f} = p_{\mathbf{Y},f} = p_{\mathbf{Z},f} = \frac{2}{3}p - \frac{4}{9}p^2. \tag{8.46}$$

In other words, the effective depolarizing probability can be expressed as

$$p_f = 2p - \frac{4}{3}p^2 \approx 2p. \tag{8.47}$$

In can be concluded that a pair of depolarizing channels – each characterized by the depolarizing probability $p$ – can be effectively viewed as a single quantum depolarizing channel associated with the aggregated depolarizing probability of $p_f = 2p$. Furthermore, the effective depolarizing probability $p_f$ for $c$ number of consecutive depolarizing channels – where each of the channels is characterized by an identical depolarizing probability $p$ – can be approximated as

$$p_f \approx cp, \tag{8.48}$$

for $p \ll 1$.The expression given in Eq. (8.48) is our basis for deriving the analytical upper-bound expressions in Section 8.5.

We have to emphasize once again that this is one of the desirable properties of QTECCs compared to the rest of the QSC family, namely that the number of stabilizer measurements applied to each physical qubit remains constant upon increasing the number of physical qubits $n$ due to the convenient construction of the underlying lattice structure. We can observe that the effective depolarizing probability $p_f$ is governed by the value of $c$ and it is dependent on the number of stabilizer measurements experienced by each of the physical qubits. In the case of the

QTECCs, the value of $c$ remains constant as we increase the minimum distance $d$ of the code and the number $n$ of the physical qubits. For instance, for color codes, the number of stabilizer measurements is defined by the number of adjacent plaquettes for a given vertex. More specifically, each of the physical qubits of color codes experiences at most six stabilizer measurements, which is independent of the minimum distance $d$ of the code and of the number $n$ of physical qubits. Similar observations are valid for surface codes. The number of stabilizer measurements experienced by each of the physical qubits is defined by the number of vertices and plaquettes, given an edge of a lattice. Each of the physical qubits of surface codes experiences at most four stabilizer measurements, which is also independent of the minimum distance $d$ of the code and of the number $n$ of physical qubits.

## 8.5 Simulation Results and Performance Analysis

To evaluate the performance of the system considered, we exploited the classical-to-quantum Pauli isomorphism [83, 179]. To elaborate further, we generated two independent binary symmetric channels, where one of the channels modeled the bit-flips, while the other emulated the phase-flips. Since it is impossible to perfectly mimic the actual quantum depolarizing channel using two independent binary symmetric channels (BSCs), for approximating the quantum depolarizing channel having an equal probability of **X**, **Z**, and **Y**-type of errors ($p_{\mathbf{X}} = p_{\mathbf{Z}} = p_{\mathbf{Y}} = p/3$), it is widely accepted that the flip probability of each BSCs in the classical simulation is adjusted to $p_{\mathbf{X}} = p_{\mathbf{Z}} = 2p/3$ [67], [80]. The maximum-likelihood hard-decision decoding technique was invoked, which was translated into a look-up table (LUT)-based decoder. For the full explanation of how we conceived the LUT decoder, we refer the reader to [179]. We take the value of frame error rate (FER) from the classical simulation to portray the QBER, since we are concerned with unitary transformation of the arbitrary unknown quantum state.

### 8.5.1 Simple Examples

In this section, we present the simplest scenario of transversal Hadamard gates and CNOT gates protected by quantum repetition codes. Let us revisit Figures 8.5 and 8.6 and observe the associated QBER performance. Based on the error model described in Section 8.4, the quantum depolarizing channel $P_g \in \mathcal{P}_n$ associated with the depolarizing probability $p$ corrupted the quantum state of the physical qubits $|\overline{\psi_2}\rangle$. For the simplest scenario, here we assumed that the quantum encoder $\mathcal{V}$ and the syndrome measurement were also error-free.

For the transversal Hadamard gates protected by a 1/3-rate quantum repetition code, which is illustrated in Figures 8.5 and 8.6, the simulation results are portrayed in Figure 8.13a. We have also included the performance results for transversal Hadamard gates protected by 1/5-rate and 1/7-rate quantum repetition codes. Naturally,

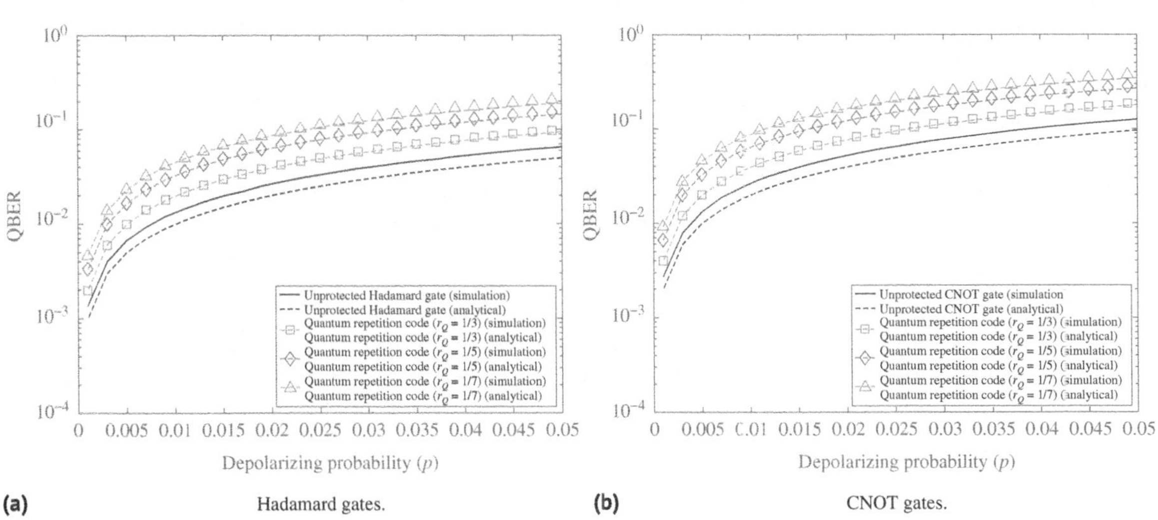


**Figure 8.13** QBER performance of the transversal Hadamard and CNOT gates protected by 1/3-, 1/5-, and 1/7-rate quantum repetition codes. We applied the depolarizing channel after the transversal configuration of the quantum gates, where the depolarizing channel is characterized by depolarizing probability $p$. *Source*: [255]/IEEE/CC BY 4.0.

the quantum repetition codes can only protect the transversal Hadamard gates from one type of error, either the phase-flip or the bit-flip errors. In other words, they are not capable of protecting the quantum gates from a more realistic quantum depolarizing channel. Furthermore, reducing the quantum coding rate—for quantum repetition codes this only allows increasing the error correction capability for either bit-flip or phase-flip errors—imposes increased quantum decoherence on our system, which is shown explicitly by the increase of QBER in Figure 8.13a. To elaborate further, upon increasing the number of qubits, we only increase the error correction capability for either phase-flip or bit-flip errors. Consequently, the deleterious effect of other types of errors imposed by the quantum depolarizing channel is accumulated and left uncorrected.

We have also invoked our QSC-protected scheme for transversal 2-qubit Clifford quantum gates, as exemplified by the CNOT gate. We portray the performance of an unprotected CNOT gate along with that of its QSC-protected counterpart utilizing a 1/3-rate quantum repetition code, as illustrated in Figures 8.7 and 8.8, in Figure 8.13b. Furthermore, we have also included the QBER performance curves of 1/5-rate and 1/7-rate quantum repetition codes. As expected, similar to transversal Hadamard gates, the QBER performance of transversal CNOT gates is degraded upon reducing the quantum coding rate. Again, invoking QSCs for protecting quantum gates remains futile if we only consider protecting one type of errors, i.e. mitigate either bit-flips or phase-flips in isolation. In conclusion, we have to employ QSCs, which are capable of correcting the bit-flip, phase-flip, as well as the simultaneous bit-flip and phase-flip errors.

### 8.5.2 QTECC-protected Transversal Hadamard Gates

In this section, we utilized the QTECCs as opposed to the above mentioned quantum repetition codes, since the QTECCs are capable of mitigating both bit-flip and phase-flip errors. More specifically, we considered color codes [100], rotated-surface codes [99], and surface codes [98], exhibiting a minimum distance of $d = 3$ in our model of Figure 8.4. For this scenario, we stipulated the assumption that the encoded physical qubits can be created fault-tolerantly, hence the quantum encoder $\mathcal{V}$ was assumed to be error-free. Alternatively, we can utilize the scheme without the quantum encoder $\mathcal{V}$, as we have described earlier in Section 8.3. The quantum depolarizing channel was modeled by the quantum unitary operation $U_f$ and also by the stabilizer measurements. The error operator $P_u \in \mathcal{P}_n$ imposed by the unitary operation $U_f$ was characterized by the depolarizing probability $p_u = p$. However, for the stabilizer measurements, as we have mentioned in Chapter 7, each of the physical qubits will have a constant number of interactions with the adjacent qubits for each **X** and **Z** stabilizer operators. More explicitly, for surface codes and rotated-surface codes, each of the physical qubits will have at most two interactions for each **X** and **Z** stabilizer measurement, while for color codes each of the physical qubits will have at most three interactions for each **X** and **Z** stabilizer measurements.

To elaborate a little further, due to the stabilizer measurements, we encountered four additional consecutive depolarizing channels after the error operator $P_u$ imposed by the unitary operation $U_f$ for surface and rotated-surface codes. Therefore, we had five consecutive depolarizing channels, where each of the error operators $P_i \in \mathcal{P}_n$ for $i = \{1, 2, 3, 4, 5\}$ was characterized by the depolarizing probability $p_i = p$. Similarly, for color codes we incorporated six additional consecutive depolarizing channels after the error operator $P_u$ imposed by the unitary operation $U_f$. Hence we imposed a total of seven consecutive depolarizing channels after unitary operation $U_f$, where each of the error operators $P_i \in \mathcal{P}_n$ for $i = \{1, 2, 3, 4, 5, 6, 7\}$ was also characterized by the depolarizing probability of $p_i = p$.

Formally, the effective error operator $P_f$ after $c$ consecutive error operators $P_i$ can be expressed as

$$P_f = \prod_{i=1}^{c} P_i \text{ for } P_i \in \mathcal{P}_n. \tag{8.49}$$

For $c$ consecutive depolarizing channels, the $j$th qubit from the set of $n$ physical qubits will independently experience the effective error operators $P_f$, which is formulated as

$$P_{f,j} = \prod_{i=1}^{c} P_i, \text{ for } \forall P_i \in \mathcal{P}_1^*. \tag{8.50}$$

Since there are $c$ consecutive depolarizing channels, the probability of obtaining the identity matrix **I** is equal to the sum of all probabilities from all the possible combinations of $P_{f,j}$ resulting in the Pauli matrix **I**, where we assume that $p_{\mathrm{I}} = (1-p)$ and $p_{\mathrm{X}} = p_{\mathrm{Y}} = p_{\mathrm{Z}} = p/3$. Therefore, the effective probability of obtaining the Pauli matrix **I** for five consecutive depolarizing channels can be expressed as shown in Eq. (8.74) as follows:

$$\begin{aligned} p_{\mathrm{I},f} &= (1-p)^5 + 30(1-p)^3\left(\frac{p}{3}\right)^2 + 60(1-p)^2\left(\frac{p}{3}\right)^3 + 105(1-p)\left(\frac{p}{3}\right)^4 + 60\left(\frac{p}{3}\right)^5 \\ &= 1 - 5p + \frac{40}{3}p^2 - \frac{160}{9}p^3 + \frac{320}{27}p^4 - \frac{256}{81}p^5. \end{aligned} \quad (8.74)$$

$$\begin{aligned} p_f &= 1 - p_f^{\mathrm{I}} \\ &= 5p - \frac{40}{3}p^2 + \frac{160}{9}p^3 - \frac{320}{27}p^4 + \frac{256}{81}p^5. \end{aligned} \quad (8.75)$$

To elaborate a little further, we can infer from Eq. (8.74) that there are 30 possible combinations from $\prod_{i=1}^{5} P_i$ which give us $P_{f,j} = \mathbf{I}$ consisting of two nonidentity Pauli operators $P_i \in \mathcal{P}_1^*$, 60 combinations consisting of three nonidentity Pauli operators, 105 combinations consisting of four nonidentity Pauli operators, and finally, 60 combinations consisting of five nonidentity Pauli operators. Therefore, the effective depolarizing probability $p_f$ for $c = 5$ can be formulated as shown in Eq. (8.75). However, in case of $p \ll 1$, the effective depolarizing probability can be approximated as

$$p_f \approx 5p, \quad (8.76)$$

as we have suggested earlier in Eq. (8.48).

Similarly, for $c = 7$, the sum of the probabilities from all of the possible combinations $P_{f,j}$ resulting in the Pauli matrix **I** can be expressed as shown in Eq. (8.77). Therefore, the effective depolarizing probability $p_f$ for $c = 7$ can be expressed as portrayed in Eq. (8.78).

$$\begin{aligned} p_{\mathrm{I},f} &= (1-p)^7 + 63(1-p)^5\left(\frac{p}{3}\right)^2 + 210(1-p)^4\left(\frac{p}{3}\right)^3 + 735(1-p)^3\left(\frac{p}{3}\right)^4 + 1260(1-p)^2\left(\frac{p}{3}\right)^5 \\ &\quad + 966(1-p)\left(\frac{p}{3}\right)^6 + 756\left(\frac{p}{3}\right)^7 \\ &= 1 - 7p + 28p^2 - \frac{560}{9}p^3 + \frac{2270}{27}p^4 - \frac{1792}{27}p^5 + \frac{5488}{243}p^6 - \frac{3711}{729}p^7. \end{aligned} \quad (8.77)$$

$$\begin{aligned} p_f &= 1 - p_f^{\mathrm{I}} \\ &= 7p - 28p^2 + \frac{560}{9}p^3 - \frac{2270}{27}p^4 + \frac{1792}{27}p^5 - \frac{5488}{243}p^6 + \frac{3711}{729}p^7. \end{aligned} \quad (8.78)$$

Again, for $p \ll 1$, the value of $p_f$ in Eq. (8.78) can be approximated as

$$p_f \approx 7p, \quad (8.79)$$

as we have suggested in Eq. (8.48).

We have simulated the system using the quantum-to-classical Pauli isomorphism for simulating the QSCs. The simulation results are portrayed in Figure 8.14. The performance of the proposed scheme is quantified using the QBER values of the vertical axis versus the depolarizing probability values $p$ represented by the horizontal axis. For a minimum distance of $d = 3$, the quantum coding rate $r_Q$ of color codes, of rotated-surface codes, and of surface codes are given by 1/7, 1/9, and 1/13, respectively, based on the code parameters given in Table 8.1. We can observe the QBER performance improvement upon applying the scheme given in Figure 8.4 compared to the unprotected quantum gates, especially for depolarizing probability values of $p < 2 \times 10^{-3}$.

In general, the analytical QBER performance of QSC-protected single-qubit quantum gates can be calculated as follows:

$$\mathrm{QBER}_{\mathrm{approx}}^{(1)}(n, d, p) = 1 - \sum_{i=0}^{n} A_i \binom{n}{i} p^i (1-p)^{n-i}, \quad (8.80)$$

where $A_i$ is a real number representing the success probability of correcting the error patterns having a weight of $i$. For a large number of $n$, finding the value of $A_i$ for each of $i$ becomes an intractable problem. A particular example of finding these $A_i$ values specifically for color codes can be seen in [265], where the authors successfully

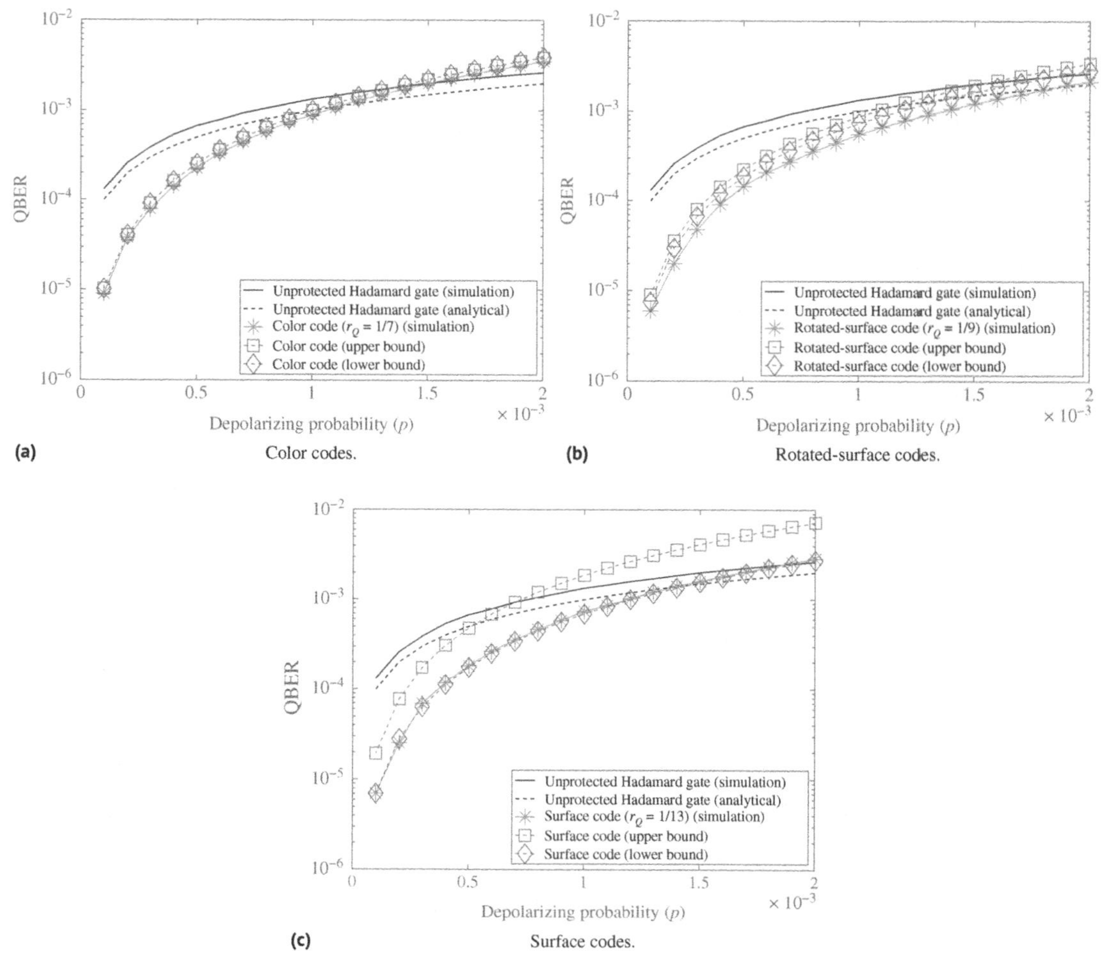


**Figure 8.14** QBER performance for transversal Hadamard gates protected by distance-3 QTECCs over quantum depolarizing channel. The quantum decoherence is inflicted after the transversal configuration of Hadamard gates, where the error operators of $\prod_{i=1}^{c} P_i \in \mathcal{P}_n$ are defined by $p_i = p$. The number of consecutive error operators is $c = 7$ for color codes and $c = 5$ for rotated-surface and surface codes. *Source*: [255]/IEEE/CC BY 4.0.

**Table 8.1** The code parameters for various QTECCs based on the minimum distance $d$ of the code.

| Code type | Dimension | Physical qubits ($n$) | Stabilizers ($\lvert\mathcal{S}\rvert$) | Logical qubits ($k$) |
|---|---|---|---|---|
| Color [100] | $d$ [a] | $\frac{1}{4}(3d^2+1)$ | $\frac{1}{4}(3d^2-3)$ | 1 |
| Rotated-surface [99] | $d \times d$ | $d^2$ | $d^2-1$ | 1 |
| Surface [98] | $d \times d$ | $2d^2-2d+1$ | $2d^2-2d$ | 1 |
| Toric [95] | $d \times d$ | $2d^2$ | $2d^2-2$ | 2 |

*Source*: [153]/IEEE/CC BY 4.0.
a. For triangular color codes the dimension is defined by the side length of the equilateral triangle

characterized the $A_i$ values for color codes having a minimum distance up to $d = 7$. However, for nondegenerate-QSCs, the analytical QBER performance can be approximated using the following upper bound as described in [153, 179]:

$$\text{QBER}_{\text{upper}}^{(1)}(n,d,p) = 1 - \sum_{i=0}^{t=\lfloor\frac{d-1}{2}\rfloor} \binom{n}{i} p^i (1-p)^{n-i} = \sum_{i=t+1}^{n} \binom{n}{i} p^i (1-p)^{n-i}, \tag{8.81}$$

where for QSC-protected transversal single-qubit gates we have $p = p_f$. In our case this is the effective depolarizing probability defined by Eq. (8.75) for both rotated-surface as well as for surface codes and by Eq. (8.78) for color codes.

To elaborate a little further, the upper bound of Eq. (8.81) provides the worst-case scenario performance assuming that any syndrome associated with the error pattern beyond the error correction capability of the quantum code is ignored, because attempting to correct the error will potentially introduce additional errors. However, this decoding method is not utilizing the full benefit of the remaining syndromes. For instance, for a distance-3 surface code, we have $n = 13$ and $k = 1$, and hence we have $|\mathcal{G}| = n - k = 12$. Since the surface codes belong to the CSS-type quantum codes, the syndrome operator $G_i \in \mathcal{G}$ is invoked to correct the bit-flip and phase-flip error separately. Consequently, for a distance-3 surface code, we have six stabilizer operators dedicated for correcting bit-flip errors ($|\mathcal{G}_z| = 6$) and six stabilizer operators dedicated for correcting phase-flip errors ($|\mathcal{G}_x| = 6$). Since each of the syndrome measurement values is associated with an element of the syndrome vector **s**, we have a total of 64 possible syndrome vectors **s**. We know that a distance-3 surface code is capable of correcting a single-qubit error from both bit-flip and phase-flip errors.

Consequently, from the total of 64 possible syndrome vectors **s**, only 14 syndrome vectors are actually associated with recoverable error patterns. More explicitly, one syndrome vector is the all-zero syndrome vector associated with the error-free quantum state of the physical quits, and 13 syndrome vectors associated with either a single bit-flip or phase-flip error pattern. The remaining 50 syndromes are capable of detecting error patterns exhibiting error weights beyond the error correction capability of the distance-3 surface code, although the decoder cannot make a definitive error recovery decision from these remaining syndromes, since each of them may be associated with multiple error patterns having identical error weight. In the upper bound formulation of Eq. (8.81), these remaining 50 syndrome vectors are ignored, considering that making a wrong decision, for instance by making a random decision for the error recovery operator, will further degrade the received quantum state of the physical qubits.

In order to provide a confidence interval for the QBER performance of QSC-protected single-qubit quantum gates, we introduce the lower bound performances of CSS-type quantum codes based on the classical sphere-packing bound [266, 267], also known as the quantum GV bound [86, 179]. Formally, the lower bound of the analytical QBER performance can be defined as follows [266, 267]:

$$\text{QBER}^{(1)}_{\text{lower}}(n, d, p) = 1 - \sum_{i=0}^{t'+1} A(i) p^i (1-p)^{n-i}, \tag{8.82}$$

where for QSC-protected transversal single-qubit gates we have $p = pf$ and $A(i)$ is an integer number obeying:

$$\sum_{i=0}^{t'+1} A_i \leq 2^{(n-k)/2}, \text{ where } A_i = \binom{n}{i}. \tag{8.83}$$

Consequently, the final coefficient of $A_{t'+1}$ can be formulated as:

$$A_{t'+1} = 2^{(n-k)/2} - \sum_{i=0}^{t'} A_i. \tag{8.84}$$

If the final coefficient obeys $A_{t'+1} = 0$, the code construction is referred to as a perfect CSS-type QSC. Otherwise, the code is referred to as a quasi-perfect CSS-type QSC.

For instance, based on Eq. (8.81), the upper bound QBER performance of a distance-3 surface code can be approximated as

$$\text{QBER}^{(1)}_{\text{upper}}(13, 3, p_f) = 1 - (1 - p_f)^{13} - 13 p_f (1 - p_f)^{12}. \tag{8.85}$$

As a comparison, based on Eq. (8.82), the lower bound QBER performance of a distance-3 surface code can be approximated as

$$\text{QBER}^{(1)}_{\text{lower}}(13, 3, p_f) = 1 - (1 - p_f)^{13} - 13p(1 - p_f)^{12} - 50 p_f^2 (1 - p_f)^{11} \tag{8.86}$$

Let us revisit the analytical QBER upper bound performance of Eq. (8.81) and the lower bound of Eq. (8.82), as well as the simulation results for the transversal Hadamard gates protected by selected distance-3 QTECCs, as depicted in Figure 8.14. We observe that the analytical QBER upper bound of Eq. (8.81) is a good approximation for the QBER performance of a distance-3 color code based on the simulation results of Figure 8.14a. This is because the construction of the distance-3 color code is identical to that of the 7-qubit Steane code, which is a nondegenerate QSC. In general, Eq. (8.81) is a good approximation for nondegenerate QSCs. By contrast, a slightly different phenomenon can be observed in Figure 8.14b, c, where the simulation results are closer to the analytical lower bound QBER performance owing to their highly degenerate nature.

Next, in Figure 8.15, we portray the analytical QBER upper bound and the lower bound performance of transversal Hadamard gates protected by QTECCs for various minimum distance values. More specifically, we calculate the QBER upper bound performance of color codes, rotated-surface codes, surface codes, and toric codes having the minimum distances of $d=\{3,5,7,9,11\}$ using Eq. (8.81) and their lower bound QBER performances using Eq. (8.82). The code parameters of the QTECCs used for calculating the QBER upper bound and lower bound performance are summarized in Table 8.1. One of the unique properties of QTECCs is that upon increasing the minimum distance of the code $d$, we simultaneously increase the number of physical qubits $n$ and decrease the quantum coding rate $r_Q$ [153]. The quantum coding rate $r_Q$ portrayed in Figure 8.15 is calculated using $r_Q=k/n$, where the number of logical qubits $k$ and the number of physical qubits $n$ are also given in Table 8.1.

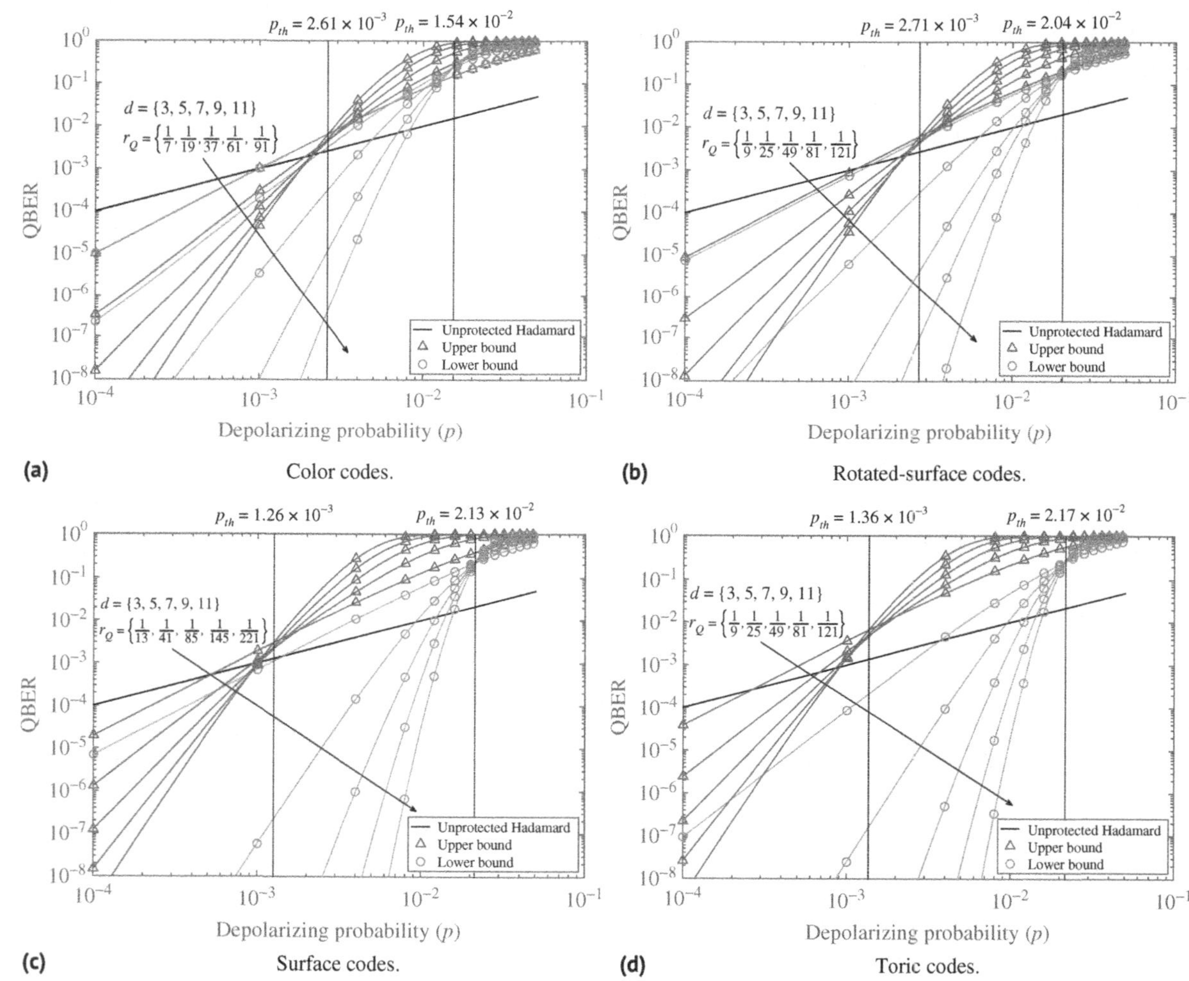


**Figure 8.15** The upper and lower bound QBER analytical performance curves of the transversal implementation of Hadamard gates protected by various QTECCs. *Source:* [255]/IEEE/CC BY 4.0.

Increasing the error correction capability of QTECCs means that we simultaneously increase the number of auxiliary qubits and reduce the quantum coding rate $r_Q$. On the other hand, at high qubit error rates, low-rate QECCs often carry out flawed corrections, hence actually degrading the QBER. To elaborate a little further, given the higher minimum distance of low-rate codes than that of their high-rate counterparts, a flawed corrective action of a low-rate code tends to inflict more errors than that of a low-distance higher-rate code. The superior error correction capability of the low-rate quantum codes starts to become more pronounced below a specific depolarizing probability $p$, where the probability of flawed corrections is reduced. This *depolarizing probability threshold* ($p_{th}$) is marked in Figure 8.15 by vertical lines. More specifically, $p_{th}$ represents the point below which increasing the error correction capability of a quantum code is considered to be beneficial. Additionally, the value of $p_{th}$ can also be used to infer the asymptotic performance of the QTECCs exhibiting a large number of physical qubits, where the quantum coding rate $r_Q$ tends zero.

Again, in Figure 8.15, $p_{th}$ is denoted by a vertical line at the cross-over point of the QBER performance curves. Briefly, observe that the upper bound of $p_{th}$ for color codes, rotated-surface codes, surface codes, and toric codes is seen to be as follows: $2.61\times10^{-3}$, $2.71\times10^{-3}$, $1.26\times10^{-3}$, and $1.36\times10^{-3}$, respectively. These specific $p_{th}$ values are obtained by taking into account the erroneous stabilizer measurements. Specifically, each of the physical qubits of rotated-surface and surface codes experiences at most two **X** and two **Z** stabilizer measurements, while for color codes, each of the physical qubits experiences at most three **X** and three **Z** stabilizer measurements. These numbers of the stabilizer measurements experienced by each of the physical qubits are independent of the total number of the physical qubits. In the idealized scenario of having perfect stabilizer measurements, indeed we can achieve a higher $p_{th}$ value. We can simply use Eqs. (8.75) and (8.78) to obtain the $p_{th}$ values associated with error-free stabilizer measurements. More specifically, we obtain the $p_{th}$ values as follows: $1.83\times10^{-2}$, $1.36\times10^{-2}$, $6.30\times10^{-3}$, and $6.80\times10^{-3}$, respectively, for color, rotated-surface, surface, and toric codes.

Secondly, in Figure 8.15, we can also observe the lower bound of the $p_{th}$ values as follows: $1.54\times10^{-2}$, $2.04\times10^{-2}$, $2.13\times10^{-2}$, and $2.17\times10^{-2}$, respectively, for color, rotated-surface, surface, and toric codes, which are associated with erroneous stabilizer measurements. Similarly, in a case where we assume that we have the error-free stabilizer measurements, the $p_{th}$ values observed are: 10.78%, 10.20%, 10.65%, and 10.85%, respectively, for color, rotated-surface, surface, and toric codes. We observe that all of the $p_{th}$ lower bound values are in the proximity of $p_{th}\approx 11\%$, which is close to the quantum hashing limit of dual-containing CSS-type QSCs. This is formulated as:

$$C_Q = 1 - 2H(p), \tag{8.87}$$

where $H(p)$ is the binary entropy of $p$ defined by $H(p) = -p\log_2 p - (1-p)\log_2(1-p)$. Since the quantum coding rate of two-dimensional of QTECCs tends to zero ($r_Q \to 0$) for a very large $n$ ($n \to \infty$), we can show that for the asymptotical limit, the QBER performance of QTECCs approaches the ultimate hashing limit of dual-containing CSS-type QSCs. This is given by $p^* = 11\%$ for $r_Q = 0$. It is important to note that the quantum GV bound is a strong lower bound for nondegenerate QSCs. We also have to mention that the value $p^* = 11\%$ is confirmed in a different way in [265].

Finally, we present the performance of the transversal single-qubit quantum gates protected by QSCs in terms of the fidelity ($F_{\text{th}}$) of each of the single-qubit quantum gate. Based on Eq. (8.37), we define the output fidelity as follows:

$$F_{\text{out}} = 1 - \text{QBER}_{\text{protected}}. \tag{8.88}$$

Since for asymptotical limit of $n \to \infty$ the QBER performance approaches the $p_{th}$ value, we can also determine the fidelity threshold ($F_{\text{th}}$), which is defined as the minimum fidelity required for each of the quantum gates in order to benefit from employing the transversal quantum gates protected by the QSCs. Explicitly, the value of $F_{\text{th}}$ for a single-qubit quantum gate can be simply determined as follows:

$$F_{\text{th}} = 1 - p_{th}. \tag{8.89}$$

Based on all the results presented in Figure 8.15, we can obtain the upper bound of the fidelity $F_{\text{th}}$ for single-qubit quantum Clifford gates as follows: 99.74%, 99.73%, 99.87%, and 99.86%, respectively, for color codes, rotated-surface codes, surface codes, and toric codes. Similarly, we also obtain the lower bound of the fidelity $F_{\text{th}}$ for single-qubit quantum Clifford gates as follows: 98.48%, 97.96%, 97.87%, and 97.83%, respectively, for color codes, rotated-surface codes, surface codes, and toric codes. These $F_{th}$ values mark the minimum requirement for the physical implementation of the single-qubit quantum gates if the implementation of QECCs within the quantum computers is considered. We have demonstrated that having quantum gates exhibiting lower $F_{th}$ values will not provide any reliability improvement by the QECCs. Finally, all the results presented in this subsection are summarized in Table 8.2.

### 8.5.3 QTECC-protected Transversal CNOT Gates

Following similar investigations to those in Subsection 8.5.2, we also employed the family of QTECCs for protecting the transversal CNOT gates. For the transversal configuration of CNOT gates, we have two sets of QSCs. One of the QSCs is invoked for protecting the physical control qubits, while the other one is for the physical target qubits. We assumed that the QSCs used for both target and control qubits are identical. Due to the stabilizer preservation of QSCs after the transversal CNOT gates, as demonstrated in Section 8.3, each of the QSCs handles the errors inherent in the target qubits and in the control qubits independently. Decoding success is declared if the QSCs of both the control and target qubits carry out flawless error correction. Therefore, the QBER upper bound performance of the QSC-protected 2-qubit quantum gates can be expressed by modifying Eq. (8.81) as follows:

$$\begin{aligned} \text{QBER}^{(2)}_{\text{upper}}(n,d,p) &= 1-\left(1-\text{QBER}^{(1)}_{\text{upper}}(n,d,p)\right)^2 \\ &= 1-\left(\sum_{i=0}^{t=\left\lfloor\frac{d-1}{2}\right\rfloor}\binom{n}{i}p^i(1-p)^{n-i}\right)^2. \end{aligned} \tag{8.90}$$

In this case, we assume that $p=p_f$ considering the erroneous stabilizer measurements, which is given by Eq. (8.75) for $c$=5 for rotated-surface codes, surface codes, as well as toric codes. By contrast, for $c$=7 Eq. (8.78) is valid.

Similar to the transversal Hadamard gates discussed in the previous subsection, we also harness Eq. (8.82) for determining the lower bound of the QBER performance of the transversal CNOT gates protected by QSCs, formulated as follows:

$$\begin{aligned} \text{QBER}^{(2)}_{\text{upper}}(n,d,p) &= 1-\left(1-\text{QBER}^{(1)}_{\text{lower}}(n,d,p)\right)^2 \\ &= 1-\left(1-\sum_{i=0}^{t'+1}A(i)p^i(1-p)^{n-i}\right)^2 \end{aligned} \tag{8.91}$$

**Table 8.2** Performance summary of QTECC-protected transversal quantum Clifford gates.

| Results | Color codes | Rotated-surface codes | Surface codes | Toric codes |
|---|---|---|---|---|
| Upper bound $p_{th}$ (error-free measurement) | 1.83% | 1.36% | 0.63% | 0.68% |
| Lower bound $p_{th}$ (error-free measurement) | 10.78% | 10.20% | 10.65% | 10.85% |
| Upper bound $p_{th}$ (with erroneous measurement) | 0.26% | 0.27% | 0.13% | 0.14% |
| Lower bound $p_{th}$ (with erroneous measurement) | 1.54% | 2.04% | 2.13% | 2.17% |
| Upper bound $F_{th}$ for Hadamard gates | 99.74% | 99.73% | 99.87% | 99.86% |
| Lower bound $F_{th}$ for Hadamard gates | 98.46% | 97.96% | 97.87% | 97.83% |
| Upper bound $F_{th}$ for CNOT gates | 99.48% | 99.46% | 99.74% | 99.72% |
| Lower bound $F_{th}$ for CNOT gates | 96.92% | 95.92% | 95.74% | 95.66% |

given that $A(i)$ is an integer obeying:

$$\sum_{i=0}^{t'+1} A_i \leq 2^{(n-k)/2}, \text{ where } A_i = \binom{n}{i}. \tag{8.92}$$

Consequently, the final coefficient $A_{t'+1}$ can be expressed as:

$$A_{t'+1} = 2^{(n-k)/2} - \sum_{i=0}^{t'} A_i. \tag{8.93}$$

To verify the accuracy of the analytical expression in Eq. (8.90), we have evaluated the performance of QTECC-protected transversal CNOT gates by simulations. More explicitly, they were protected by a distance-3 color code, rotated-surface code, and surface code, exploiting the classical-to-quantum Pauli isomorphism. The results are depicted in Figure 8.16. As expected, similar trends to those of the QBER performance of the transversal Hadamard gates protected by QTECCs were found. An improvement in terms of QBER can be observed for depolarizing probabilities obeying $p < 2 \times 10^{-3}$. Therefore, we conclude that our design seen in Figure 8.4 does indeed improve the reliability of both Hadamard gates as well as of CNOT gates.

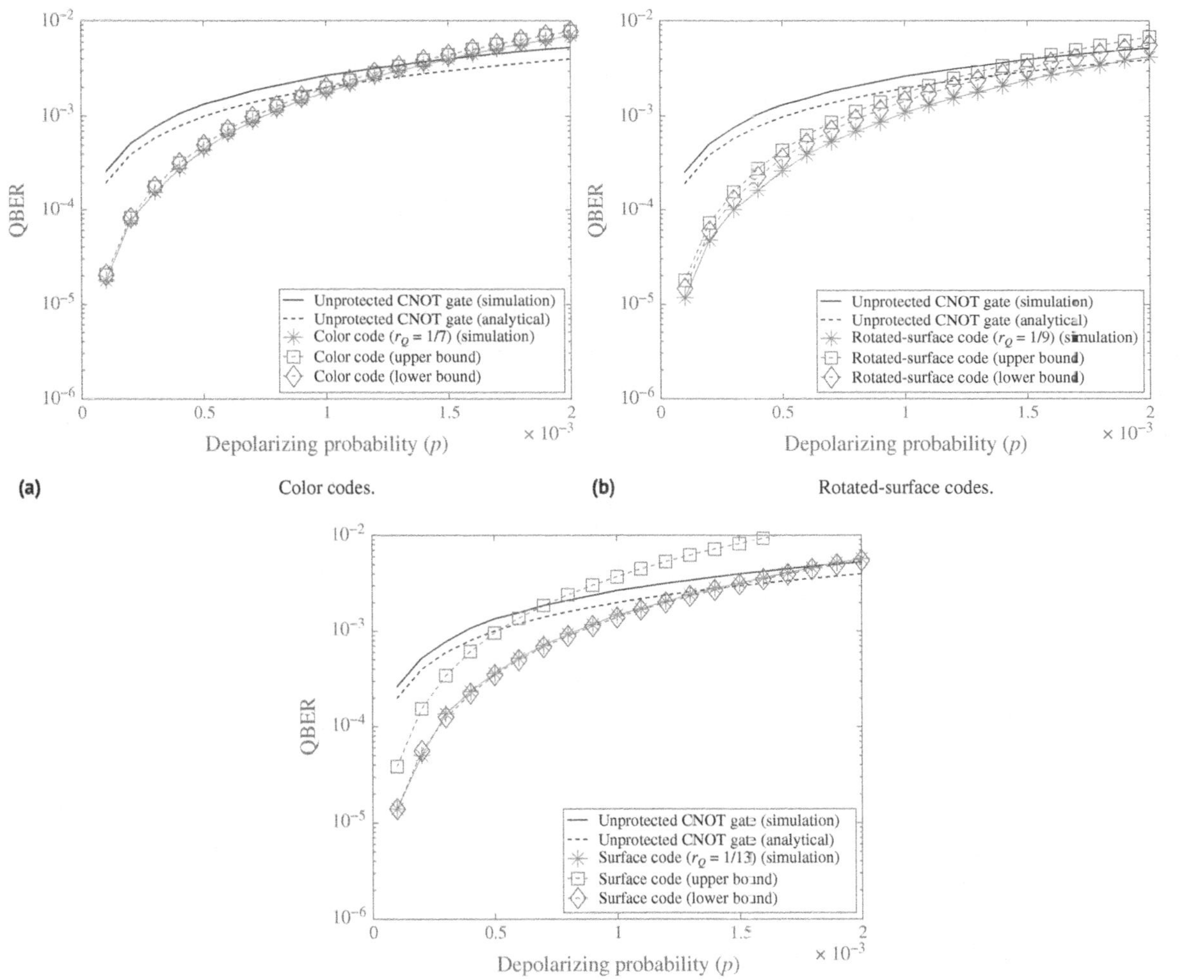


(a) Color codes. (b) Rotated-surface codes. (c) Surface codes.

**Figure 8.16** QBER performance for transversal CNOT gates protected by distance-3 QTECCs over quantum depolarizing channel. The quantum decoherence is inflicted after the transversal configuration of CNOT gates, where the error operators of $\prod_{i=1}^{c} P_i \in \mathcal{P}_n$ are defined by $p_i = p$. The number of consecutive error operators is $c = 7$ for color codes and $c = 5$ for rotated-surface and surface codes. *Source*: [255]/IEEE/CC BY 4.0.

Furthermore, we have plotted the upper and lower bounds of the analytical QBER performance given in Eq. (8.90) for the transversal implementation of CNOT gates employing various types of QTECCs for different minimum distances $d$ based on the code parameters of Table 8.1. The corresponding QBER performance curves are portrayed in Figure 8.17. We can also infer the specific $p_{\text{th}}$ values, which define the depolarizing probability value where we can start observing QBER improvements upon decreasing the quantum coding rate. Again, they also mark the QBER performance of the QSCs at the asymptotical limit. The $p_{\text{th}}$ value is represented by vertical lines, where we have $2.61 \times 10^{-3}$, $2.71 \times 10^{-3}$, $1.26 \times 10^{-3}$, and $1.36 \times 10^{-3}$, respectively, for color codes, rotated-surface codes, surface codes, and toric codes. Similarly, we have also plotted the lower bound of the analytical QBER performance of the transversal CNOT gates protected by various QTECCs in Figure 8.17 based on Eq. (8.91). In this case, we have the $p_{\text{th}}$ values of $1.54 \times 10^{-2}$, $2.04 \times 10^{-2}$, $2.13 \times 10^{-2}$, and $2.17 \times 10^{-2}$, respectively, for color, rotated-surface, surface, and toric codes.

Since the QBER improvement can indeed be clearly observed, it is logical that a corresponding fidelity improvement can also be achieved. The salient question is then – what level of the fidelity the quantum gates have to attain for ensuring that the QSC-protected quantum gates succeed in improving the overall fidelity of the system. Firstly, we have defined the output fidelity of the CNOT gates in Eq. (8.41), which is repeated here for convenience as follows:

$$F_{\text{out}} = 1 - \text{QBER}_{\text{protected}}. \tag{8.94}$$

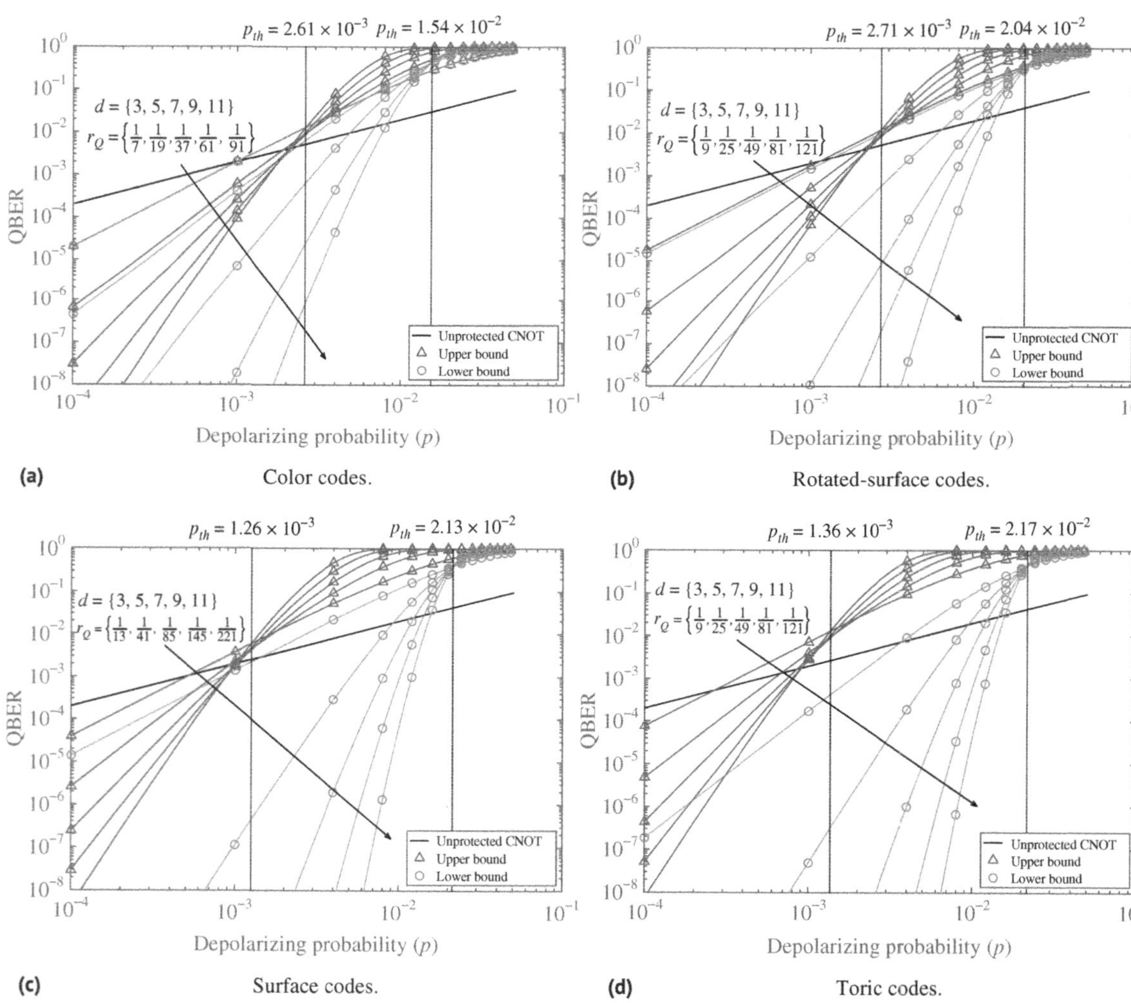


**Figure 8.17** The upper and lower bound QBER analytical performance curves of the transversal implementation of CNOT gates protected by various QTECCs. *Source*: [255]/IEEE/CC BY 4.0.

For the asymptotical limit based on Eq. (8.41) we can determine the threshold fidelity ($F_{th}$) as follows:

$$F_{th} = 1 - 2p_{th} + p_{th}^2 \approx 1 - 2p_{th}, \quad (8.95)$$

for $p_{th} \ll 1$. First, based on the upper bound of the analytical QBER performance curves portrayed in Figure 8.17, we can obtain the fidelity upper bound $F_{th}$ required by each of the CNOT gates in order to glean the benefit of employing QSCs for protecting the transversal CNOT gates. By using Eq. (8.95), we have the upper bound of the $F_{th}$ values of 99.48%, 99.46%, 99.74%, and 99.72%, respectively, for color codes, rotated-surface codes, surface codes, and toric codes. Additionally, the lower bound of the fidelity $F_{th}$ can also be obtained using Eq. (8.95), where we have: 99.48%, 99.46%, 99.74%, and 99.72%, respectively, for color codes, rotated-surface codes, surface codes, and toric codes. All of the results presented in this subsection are summarized in Table 8.2. Finally, we have shown that our framework proposed for protecting transversal quantum Clifford gates will provide a reliability improvement for both single-qubit and 2-qubit gates, provided that the fidelity threshold required for each of the quantum gates is satisfied.

## 8.6 Conclusions and Future Research

### 8.6.1 Conclusions

We have presented a general framework conceived for protecting quantum Clifford gates using QSCs along with the notion of effective stabilizer formalism. In this chapter, we have also provided examples of how to utilize the framework proposed for protecting quantum Clifford gates. More specifically, in order to protect quantum Clifford gates, we arrange the gates in a transversal configuration to exploit the benefit of stabilizer operator preservation. Furthermore, since we considered imperfect quantum gates and also imperfect stabilizer measurements in our scheme, we harnessed the QTECCs for applying error correction to the erroneous physical qubits. The additional benefit of employing QTECCs is that the number of stabilizer measurements experienced by each of the physical qubits remains constant as we increase the number of physical qubits. Hence, the propagation or even proliferation of decoherence due to the interaction between qubits during stabilizer measurements can be effectively circumvented. We have shown that by combining the transversal implementation of quantum Clifford gates and the QTECCs, we can indeed improve the reliability of quantum Clifford gates – provided that they satisfy a minimum depolarization fidelity threshold $F_{th}$. In order to determine the approximate value of $F_{th}$, first, we provide the upper bound and the lower bound of the analytical QBER performance for a single-qubit and for 2-qubit transversal gates protected by QSCs. Based on the upper bound of the QBER performance, we obtain the $F_{th}$ values for single-qubit quantum gates as follows: 99.74%, 99.73%, 99.87%, and 99.86%, respectively, protected using color, rotated-surface, surface, and toric codes. These $F_{th}$ values were obtained at the asymptotical limit, meaning that the number of physical qubits are extremely large – obeying $n \rightarrow \infty$ – and the quantum coding rates are approaching zero ($r_Q \rightarrow 0$). We have to highlight that the upper bound of the analytical QBER performance portrays the worst-case scenario, where the error correction performance is purely defined by the minimum distance of the QSCs, while disregarding the advantage of exploiting the degeneracy inherited by QSCs. As a comparison, based on the upper bound of the QBER performance, we obtained the following $F_{th}$ values for single-qubit quantum gates: 98.46%, 97.96%, 97.87%, and 97.83%, respectively, protected by color, rotated-surface, surface, and toric codes. By contrast, the lower bound analytical QBER performance portrays the optimistic scenario, where we assume that the degeneracy inherited by QTECCs can be exploited to approach the sphere-packing bound for nondegenerate QSCs.

By following the same line of investigation, we have also obtained the minimum depolarization fidelity threshold $F_{th}$ values for 2-qubit quantum gates, which are exemplified by CNOT gates in this chapter. The upper bounds of the $F_{th}$ values are given by, 99.48%, 99.46%, 99.74%, and 99.72%, respectively, protected by color, rotated-surface, surface, and toric codes. Similarly, the lower bounds of the $F_{th}$ values are 96.92%, 95.92%, 95.74%, and 95.66%, respectively, protected using color, rotated-surface, surface, and toric codes. Ultimately, all the $F_{th}$ values presented in this chapter mark the minimum requirements to be satisfied by the physical implementation of quantum gates, if we want to exploit the benefit of reliability improvements offered by QECCs for quantum computation.

### 8.6.2 Future Research

Our main goal in this chapter was to propose a general framework for protecting quantum gates utilizing QSCs. In these preliminary results, we assume that each of the physical qubits experiences an individual uncorrelated quantum depolarizing channel. Each of the quantum depolarizing channels is influenced by the number of quantum gates interacting with the associated physical qubit. However, it is important to note that the existence of 2-qubit quantum gates, such as the CNOT gate, potentially introduces error propagation between the physical qubits and hence creates some level of correlation among the quantum depolarizing channels of each of the physical qubits. Therefore, our next step is to include this correlation into our error model to glean more realistic insights concerning the error correction performance of the proposed scheme.

We have exemplified the application of the framework for protecting transversal Hadamard and CNOT gates, which is equivalent to a single-step operation of Hadamard gates and CNOT gates. The natural extension of this work is to try to implement the framework for much more complex circuits. Additionally, we have mentioned in this chapter that we only exploited the effective stabilizer formalism for transversal quantum Clifford gates. Therefore, combining the scheme with the family of both Clifford and non-Clifford gates will indeed create the universal set of quantum gates for quantum computation. Ultimately, the final goal is to conceive a universal framework of protecting large-scale quantum computers using QECCs.

# 9

# Universal Decoding of Quantum Stabilizer Codes via Classical Guesswork

## 9.1 Introduction

As discussed in the previous chapters, quantum error correction codes (QECCs) [54, 55, 94] constitute a potent solution for mitigating the quantum decoherence prevalent in quantum systems. The primary concept of QECCs is reminiscent of that of classical forward error-correction (FEC) codes. Specifically, the quantum state of logical qubits is mapped into the encoded state of physical qubits by incorporating auxiliary qubits during the encoding step. These auxiliary qubits are then exploited by the decoder for determining the appropriate recovery operator. However, due to the short coherence time of the quantum bits (qubits), the QECCs' encoding and decoding procedures should be completed before the qubits decohere further. Unfortunately, most of the QECCs available in the open literature require a high number of physical qubits and exhibit a very low quantum coding rate because, in contrast to classical FEC codes, QECCs have to correct not only bit-flip errors, but also phase-flip errors as well as the combination of both. Thus, it is a challenge to conceive QECCs for a moderate number of physical qubits, while maintaining a very low quantum bit error ratio (QBER).

Although at first sight seemingly unrelated, the development of ultra-reliable low-latency communications (URLLCs) faces similar challenges to those encountered in quantum error correction coding (QECC) research. For example, one of the challenges is that the decoding of the QECC must be completed before the qubits start to lose coherence, since the coherence time of the qubits is very limited. In other words, similar to URLLC, QECCs also require prompt and reliable decoding. Another challenge is finding an error correction code with a short- to moderate-length codeword that has a high error correction capability and hence attains a low bit error ratio (BER).

In the classical regime, the powerful maximum-likelihood (ML) decoder has been proposed for meeting the stringent requirements imposed by URLLC. However, ML decoding exhibits potentially excessive complexity, which hinders its hardware implementation. As a remedy, an innovative decoder based on classical guesswork was proposed as an attractive solution for short- to moderate-length classical FEC codes, but without imposing the excessive complexity of the standard ML decoder, which is referred to as Guessing Random Additive Noise Decoding (GRAND) [268–271]. The complexity reduction achievable by GRAND exploits the classical guesswork concept, where the decoder generates the channel-induced error patterns from the most likely to the least likely and in turn verifies whether the sequence that remains after the error removal is part of the legitimate codebook. As an additional benefit, GRAND is eminently suitable for a large family of classical FEC codes, since it operates in an error-pattern-centric manner. Thus, GRAND might be utilized for a wide range of classical FEC codes having no efficient decoder.

Inspired by this solution advocated in the classical domain, we aim for conceiving a universal decoder for QECCs. As a benefit of the classical-to-quantum isomorphism, a wide range of classical FEC codes can be transplanted into the quantum domain. More specifically, we focus our attention on the family of quantum stabilizer codes (QSCs), which belong to the class of syndrome-based QECCs [59, 167, 170, 179].

Against this background, our contributions offered in this chapter can be summarized as follows:

**(a)** We devise a universal decoding scheme for QSCs by further evolving the GRAND decoding philosophy. We demonstrate that the decoding scheme conceived may be adopted for two different QSC decoding paradigms, namely for both stabilizer-measurement-based and the inverse-encoder-based decoding.

**(b)** We then apply the resultant decoder for both quantum BCH codes as well as quantum polar codes and quantify their quantum block error ratio (QBLER), QBLER per logical qubits, and their decoding complexity.

**(c)** We conclude with a parametric study of the associated design trade-offs and provide the design guideline for the implementation of quantum-GRAND-aided QSC decoding.[1]

The rest of this chapter is organized as follows. Section 9.2 introduces the decoding classical FEC codes via guesswork, while Section 9.3 introduces the quantum stabilizer codes. Then, a pair of quantum-GRAND-aided QSC decoding paradigms is discussed in Section 9.4, namely the stabilizer-measurement-based decoder and the inverse-encoder-based decoder. Section 9.5 provides simulation results for characterizing the family of quantum BCH and polar codes. Explicitly, we portray the performance versus complexity of quantum-GRAND-aided QSC decoders, relying on both stabilizer-measurement-based and on inverse-encoder-based schemes. Finally, Section 9.6 offers our conclusions and some future research directions.

## 9.2 Decoding Classical FEC Codes via Guesswork

Let $\mathcal{C}(n,k,d)$ denote a classical FEC code mapping the information word of length $k$ bits into the codeword of length $n$ bits. Let $\boldsymbol{c}^n$ denote the legitimate codeword $\boldsymbol{c} \in \mathbb{F}_2^n$ as an input of the channel and $\boldsymbol{y}^n$ denote the received word after an error pattern $\boldsymbol{e}^n$ is inflicted by the channel. The transformation can be explicitly written as

$$\boldsymbol{y}^n = \boldsymbol{x}^n \oplus \boldsymbol{e}^n, \tag{9.1}$$

where $\oplus$ denotes modulo-2 addition. If the error pattern $\boldsymbol{e}^n$ is known, the legitimate codeword $\boldsymbol{c}^n$ is recoverable by applying the following transformation:

$$\boldsymbol{x}^n = \boldsymbol{y}^n \oplus \boldsymbol{e}^n. \tag{9.2}$$

In this scenario, the standard ML decoding is defined as

$$\boldsymbol{c}^{n,*} = \arg\max_{\boldsymbol{c}_i^n} p(\boldsymbol{y}^n|\boldsymbol{c}_i^n),\ \forall \boldsymbol{c}_i^n \in \mathcal{C}, \tag{9.3}$$

where $\boldsymbol{c}^{n,*}$ is the codeword solution $\boldsymbol{c}^n$ that maximizes the conditional probability $p(\boldsymbol{y}^n|\boldsymbol{c}_i^n)$ over all possible values of $\boldsymbol{c}_i^n$, so that $\boldsymbol{c}_i^n$ is an element of the codebook $\mathcal{C}$.

Based on Eq. (9.3), the number of evaluations of $p(\boldsymbol{y}^n|\boldsymbol{c}_i^n)$ required for finding the solution $\boldsymbol{c}^{n,*}$ is equal to the cardinality of the codebook $\mathcal{C}(n,k,d)$, which is given by $C = |\mathcal{C}| = 2^k$. It is clear that exhaustive sequential evaluation of all entries in the codebook $\mathcal{C}$ using ML decoder is excessively complex.

Recently, a new classical paradigm of ML decoding was introduced by exploiting the concept of classical guesswork [270, 271], which is formulated as follows:

- Given the received word $\boldsymbol{y}^n$, initialize $i = 1$ and set $\boldsymbol{g}^n$ to be the first guess based on the most likely error pattern.
- While $\boldsymbol{x}^n = \boldsymbol{y}^n \oplus \boldsymbol{g}^n \notin \mathcal{C}$, increase $i$ by 1 and set $\boldsymbol{g}^n$ to be the next guess based on next most likely error pattern.
- The process ends when we find $\boldsymbol{x}^n = \boldsymbol{y}^n \oplus \boldsymbol{g}^n \in \mathcal{C}$ in this while loop, and the final value of $i$ determines the computational complexity of this decoder.

A compelling benefit of hard-decision GRAND is its ability to verify whether the sequence left behind after the error removal $\boldsymbol{x}^n$ is part of the legitimate codebook. We can observe that since GRAND operates in an error-pattern-centric manner, the decoder does not require the entire codebook to be stored in memory. The decoder simply needs the parity check matrices $\boldsymbol{H}$ or the generator matrices $\boldsymbol{G}$ or even only the kernel of the codes in the case of

1 Please note that the similar term of QGRAND was used by the authors of [272] to represent "quantized" GRAND in a different context.

polar codes. It has been proven in the seminal paper of GRAND [270] that the average complexity of GRAND for the binary symmetric channel (BSC) is given by

$$C = 2^{n \cdot \min\{1-k/n, H_{1/2}(p)\}}, \tag{9.4}$$

where $p$ is the flip probability of the BSC, and $H_{\alpha} = H_{1/2}$ is the Rényi entropy for $\alpha = 1/2$ [273]. The complexity expression of Eq. (9.4) demonstrates the significant complexity reduction against the standard ML decoder. Furthermore, the hardware complexity of the hard-decision GRAND has been demonstrated to be appealingly low, as presented in [274].

To explicitly portray the complexity reduction achieved by GRAND, Figure 9.1 depicts the complexity of standard ML decoding compared to the average complexity of GRAND for classical FEC codes having codeword lengths of $n = \{128, 64, 32\}$ in the face of the BSC. The complexity is portrayed as the function of coding rate $r = k/n$. Observe in Figure 9.1 that since GRAND is an error-pattern-centric decoder, its complexity is driven by the channel's error probability. For the BSC, it is given by the flip probability $p$. For instance, let us observe in Figure 9.1 the average complexity of GRAND for $n = 128$, which is significantly lower for $p = 10^{-3}$ than that of $p = 10^{-2}$. Similar trends can also be observed for $n = 64$ and $n = 32$. For the BSC, the likelihood of the error patterns is rank-ordered based on their Hamming weight. Thus, for a lower value of $p$, the probability that the channel inflicts an error sequence $\boldsymbol{e}^n$ having a high Hamming weight is extremely low. Consequently, the number of error patterns that have to be evaluated before finding the legitimate codeword is also lower, since it is far more likely that the channel inflicts a lower Hamming weight error pattern than a higher one.

As the coding rate decreases, we can see that the complexity of the standard ML decoding also decreases. Thus, we can find the cross-over point below which the standard ML decoder has a lower complexity than GRAND. For instance, for $n = 128$, the ML decoder exhibits a lower complexity when $k < 34$ for $p = 10^{-2}$ and $k < 12$ for $p = 10^{-3}$. Similarly, for $n = 64$, we find that the complexity of the ML decoder is lower than GRAND when $k < 18$ for $p = 10^{-2}$ and $k < 6$ for $p = 10^{-3}$. Finally, the cross-over point for $n = 32$ is given by $k < 9$ and $k < 3$, for $p = 10^{-2}$ and $p = 10^{-3}$, respectively. In the region where the ML decoder exhibits a lower complexity, the size of the legitimate codebook $\mathcal{C}$ is significantly smaller than the average number of evaluations required by GRAND for finding the correct solution.

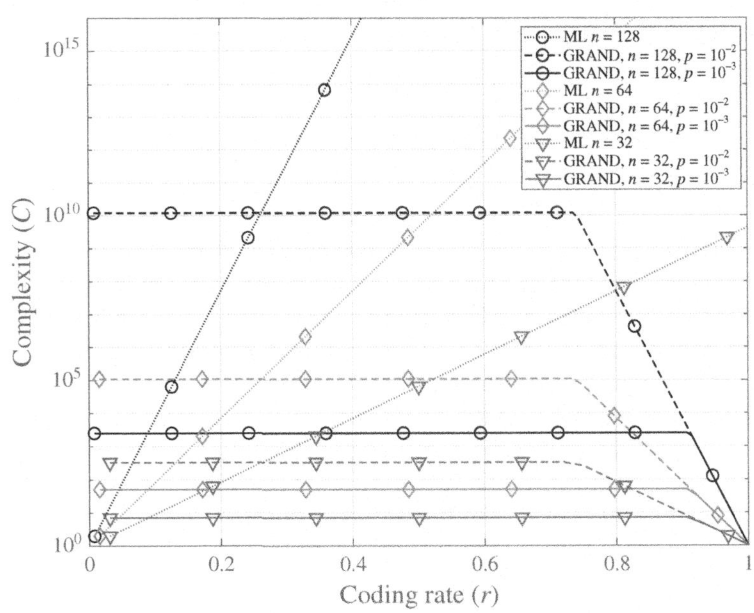


**Figure 9.1** The complexity $C$ of standard ML decoding compared to the average complexity of ML GRAND for classical error-correction codes having codeword length of $n = \{128, 64, 32\}$ over BSC. *Source:* [275]/IEEE/CC BY 4.0.

## 9.3 Quantum Stabilizer Codes

Since the concept of protecting quantum information is similar to that of classical FEC codes, it is natural to aim for transplanting the classical FEC codes philosophy into the quantum domain. In this chapter, we focus our attention on the QSCs, which constitute a class of syndrome-based QECCs. Specifically, QSCs can be constructed by exploiting the so-called classical-to-quantum isomorphism [59, 167, 170, 179]. A QSC denoted by $\mathcal{C}[[N,K,D]]$ maps $K$ logical qubits having the original quantum state $|\psi\rangle$ into $N$ physical qubits having the encoded quantum state $|\overline{\psi}\rangle$ with the aid of $(N-K)$ auxiliary qubits. The minimum distance of the QSC is denoted by $D$ and its error correction capability is given by $T=\lfloor(D-1)/2\rfloor$.

In this chapter we consider the class of quantum Pauli channels for modeling the quantum decoherence imposed on the encoded physical qubits. Explicitly, the qubit errors imposed by the quantum Pauli channels may be described by the linear combinations of Pauli matrices $\{\boldsymbol{I},\boldsymbol{X},\boldsymbol{Y},\boldsymbol{Z}\}\in\mathcal{G}$, where $\mathcal{G}$ denotes the Pauli group.[2] Physically, the Pauli $\boldsymbol{X}$ error constitutes a bit-flip error, the Pauli $\boldsymbol{Z}$ error represents the phase-flip error, while the Pauli $\boldsymbol{Y}$ describes the simultaneous bit-flip and phase-flip errors.

The encoded state of physical qubits is designed by ensuring that it is projected onto the $(+1)$ eigenspace of the group of Pauli operators $\mathcal{S}\subset\mathcal{G}_N$ known as the stabilizer group so that we have $\boldsymbol{S}_i|\overline{\psi}\rangle=(+1)|\overline{\psi}\rangle$ for every stabilizer operator $\boldsymbol{S}_i\in\mathcal{S}$. If the encoded state of physical qubits is subject to a Pauli error $\boldsymbol{E}$ that anti-commutes with a stabilizer operator $\boldsymbol{S}_j\in\mathcal{S}$, the measurement of this stabilizer operator will collapse the encoded state of the logical qubits onto its $(-1)$ eigenspace given by

$$\boldsymbol{S}_j\boldsymbol{E}|\overline{\psi}\rangle=(-1)|\overline{\psi}\rangle. \tag{9.5}$$

The results of the stabilizer measurements form a "syndrome" that can be used for determining the appropriate recovery operator $\mathcal{R}$.

A QSC $\mathcal{C}$ that encodes $K$ logical qubits has a set of logical operators $\mathcal{L}$ that are defined as operators that commute with all of the stabilizer operators $\boldsymbol{S}_i\in\mathcal{S}$, but they themselves do not constitute stabilizer operators. The initial state of the logical qubits $|\psi\rangle$ will experience a so-called logical error if a Pauli error constituted by a logical operator $\mathcal{L}$ is imposed on the encoded state of the physical qubits $|\overline{\psi}\rangle$. The minimum Pauli weight of the logical operator $\mathcal{L}$ therefore defines the minimum distance $D$ of the QSC $\mathcal{C}$.

By exploiting the classical-to-quantum isomorphism [59, 167, 170, 179], we may perform the mapping of Pauli operators $\boldsymbol{P}\in\mathcal{G}_N$ to a classical binary vector in $\mathbb{F}_2^{2n}$, which allows us to transform various classes of classical FEC codes into QSCs. More specifically, the Pauli-to-binary mapping may be explicitly defined as follows:

$$\boldsymbol{I}\mapsto(0|0),\ \boldsymbol{X}\mapsto(1|0),\ \boldsymbol{Y}\mapsto(1|1),\ \boldsymbol{Z}\mapsto(0|1). \tag{9.6}$$

Therefore, an $N$-qubit Pauli operator $\boldsymbol{P}\in\mathcal{G}_N$ can be mapped to a $2n$-bit binary vector as follows:

$$\boldsymbol{P}\in\mathcal{G}_N\mapsto\boldsymbol{g}=(\boldsymbol{g}_x|\boldsymbol{g}_z)\in\mathbb{F}_2^{2n}, \tag{9.7}$$

where $\boldsymbol{g}_x$ is an $n$-bit binary vector having an element equal to 1 in the particular location, where the Pauli operator $\boldsymbol{P}$ has a Pauli matrix $\boldsymbol{X}$. Similarly, $\boldsymbol{g}_z$ is an $n$-bit binary vector having an element equal to 1 in the specific location, where Pauli the operator $\boldsymbol{P}$ having a Pauli matrix $\boldsymbol{Z}$. Consequently, a Pauli operator associated with a Pauli matrix $\boldsymbol{Y}$ results in an element equal to 1 in the corresponding position of both vectors $\boldsymbol{g}_x$ and $\boldsymbol{g}_z$. As an example, the 2-qubit Pauli operator $\boldsymbol{P}=\boldsymbol{X}\otimes\boldsymbol{Y}$ maps to the binary representation of $\boldsymbol{g}=(11|01)$.

Again, by exploiting the classical-to-quantum isomorphism, a QSC can be derived from classical FEC codes. Explicitly, given a pair of parity-check matrices (PCMs) $\boldsymbol{H}_x$ and $\boldsymbol{H}_z$, we may construct a QSC, whose binary PCM $\boldsymbol{H}$ is formulated by

$$\boldsymbol{H}=\left[\boldsymbol{H}_z\,\middle|\,\boldsymbol{H}_x\right]. \tag{9.8}$$

2 A single-qubit Pauli group $\mathcal{G}_1=\{\boldsymbol{I},\boldsymbol{X},\boldsymbol{Y},\boldsymbol{Z}\}$ is constituted by the following matrices: $\boldsymbol{I}=\begin{bmatrix}1&0\\0&1\end{bmatrix}$, $\boldsymbol{X}=\begin{bmatrix}0&1\\1&0\end{bmatrix}$, $\boldsymbol{Y}=\begin{bmatrix}0&-i\\i&0\end{bmatrix}$ and $\boldsymbol{Z}=\begin{bmatrix}1&0\\0&-1\end{bmatrix}$. The $N$-qubit Pauli group is given by $\mathcal{G}_N=\otimes_{i=0}^{N}\mathcal{G}_i$.

To conceive a valid QSC, the pair of classical PCMs $\boldsymbol{H}_x$ and $\boldsymbol{H}_z$ has to satisfy the symplectic criterion given by [60, 94]

$$\boldsymbol{H}_z \cdot \boldsymbol{H}_x^T + \boldsymbol{H}_x \cdot \boldsymbol{H}_z^T = 0. \tag{9.9}$$

Thus, the stabilizer operators of a QSC can be written as a binary PCM having $M \times 2N$ elements, where each row corresponds to one of the $M$ stabilizer operators. Now, let us assume that a Pauli error operator $\boldsymbol{E}$ associated with the corresponding binary vector $\boldsymbol{e}_Q = (\boldsymbol{e}_x|\boldsymbol{e}_z)$ is inflicted by the quantum channel $\mathcal{P}$. Thus, the stabilizer measurements will generate the syndrome vector given by

$$\boldsymbol{s}_Q = (\boldsymbol{e}_x|\boldsymbol{e}_z) \cdot [\boldsymbol{H}_z|\boldsymbol{H}_x]^T = (\boldsymbol{s}_x|\boldsymbol{s}_z). \tag{9.10}$$

The subscript $x$ of $\boldsymbol{s}_x$ implies that the syndrome vector is used for determining the number and the location of Pauli $\boldsymbol{X}$ errors and similarly, the subscript $z$ of $\boldsymbol{s}_z$ is for Pauli $\boldsymbol{Z}$ errors.

The Calderbank–Shor–Steane (CSS)-type QSCs [55, 86] constitute a specific subset of QSCs that have disjoint $\boldsymbol{X}$ and $\boldsymbol{Z}$ stabilizer operators such that the nonidentity part of each stabilizer operator is made up either exclusively of $\boldsymbol{X}$ Pauli matrices or exclusively of $\boldsymbol{Z}$ Pauli operators. In the binary representation, the PCM of a CSS-type QSC can be expressed as

$$\boldsymbol{H}_{\text{CSS}} = \left[\begin{array}{c|c} \boldsymbol{H}_z & 0 \\ 0 & \boldsymbol{H}_x \end{array}\right]. \tag{9.11}$$

For CSS-type QSC codes, the symplectic criterion can be further simplified into

$$\boldsymbol{H}_z \cdot \boldsymbol{H}_x{}^T = 0. \tag{9.12}$$

Furthermore, if the construction satisfies $\boldsymbol{H}_z = \boldsymbol{H}_x$, the resultant QSC is referred to as dual-containing CSS-type QSC.

By accounting for Eqs. (9.10) and (9.11), the syndrome vector of CSS-type QSCs can be obtained as follows:

$$\boldsymbol{s}_Q = \boldsymbol{e}_x \cdot \boldsymbol{H}_z{}^T + \boldsymbol{e}_z \cdot \boldsymbol{H}_x{}^T = (\boldsymbol{s}_x|\boldsymbol{s}_z). \tag{9.13}$$

Consequently, the syndrome vector $\boldsymbol{s}_Q$ of CSS-type QSCs allows the bit-flip and phase-flip errors to be corrected using separate classical FEC codes. Therefore, for the rest of this chapter, we employ the classical GRAND for CSS-type QSCs.

## 9.4 Decoding Quantum Stabilizer Codes

In the previous section, we have explicitly demonstrated how to transform classical FEC codes into their quantum domain counterparts. Let us now discuss how to decode QSCs in the presence of quantum impairments by exploiting GRAND. Generally speaking, there is a pair of paradigms that can be utilized for decoding QSCs. The first one is constituted by stabilizer-measurement-based decoding [59], while the second one is by inverse-encoder-based decoding [68]. The stabilizer-measurement-based decoding is widely utilized in the literature for QSCs, where the classical FEC codes forming the basis of the QSCs exploit the symplectic condition of the PCM formulation, as exemplified by quantum linear block codes [276], quantum Bose–Chaudhuri–Hocquenghem (BCH) codes [277], and quantum low-density parity-check codes [67]. By contrast, the inverse-encoder-based decoding is invoked for QSCs, whose classical FEC codes forming the QSCs are defined by their corresponding encoders, such as quantum convolutional codes [65], quantum turbo codes [68], as well as quantum polar codes [278]. In this chapter, we aim for demonstrating that by further evolving the classical-domain GRAND philosophy of [270], we can further develop this decoder for both decoding paradigms.

We will use the Steane's 7-qubit code as an example for both decoding paradigms, where a total of six stabilizer operators are required for correcting a single-qubit error. These stabilizer operators $\mathbf{S}_i \in \mathcal{S}$ are given as follows:

$$\begin{aligned} \mathbf{S}_1 &= \mathbf{ZZIZZII}, \\ \mathbf{S}_2 &= \mathbf{ZIZZIZI}, \\ \mathbf{S}_3 &= \mathbf{IZZZIIZ}, \\ \mathbf{S}_4 &= \mathbf{XXIXXII}, \\ \mathbf{S}_5 &= \mathbf{XIXXIXI}, \\ \mathbf{S}_6 &= \mathbf{IXXXIIX}. \end{aligned} \tag{9.14}$$

Thus, based on the Pauli-to-binary mapping of Eq. (9.6) and based on the binary PCM of the CSS-type QSCs of Eq. (9.11), we have

$$\mathbf{H}_z = \mathbf{H}_x = \begin{bmatrix} 1 & 1 & 0 & 1 & 1 & 0 & 0 \\ 1 & 0 & 1 & 1 & 0 & 1 & 0 \\ 0 & 1 & 1 & 1 & 0 & 0 & 1 \end{bmatrix}. \tag{9.15}$$

Steane's 7-qubit code has a quantum coding rate of $r_Q = K/N = 1/7$ and a minimum distance of $D = 3$, which means that it is capable of correcting a single-qubit error ($T = 1$).

### 9.4.1 Stabilizer-measurement-based Decoding

The general schematic of QSC encoding and decoding based on stabilizer measurements is depicted in Figure 9.2. The initial state of $K$ logical qubits is mapped into the encoded state of $N$ physical qubits with the aid of $(N-K)$ auxiliary qubits using the quantum encoder $\mathcal{V}$, which can be formulated as follows:

$$|\overline{\psi}\rangle = \mathcal{V}\left(|\psi\rangle \otimes |0\rangle^{\otimes(N-K)}\right). \tag{9.16}$$

The quantum channel $\mathcal{P}$ imposes errors represented by the $N$-tuple Pauli operator $\mathbf{E} \in \mathcal{G}_N$, which can be formally expressed as

$$|\hat{\overline{\psi}}\rangle = \mathbf{E}|\overline{\psi}\rangle. \tag{9.17}$$

The measurements of the stabilizer operators $\mathbf{S}_i \in \mathcal{S}$ generate the eigenvalues of $\pm 1$, which are analogous to the classical syndrome values as described in Section 9.3. We have also demonstrated how Pauli-to-binary mapping

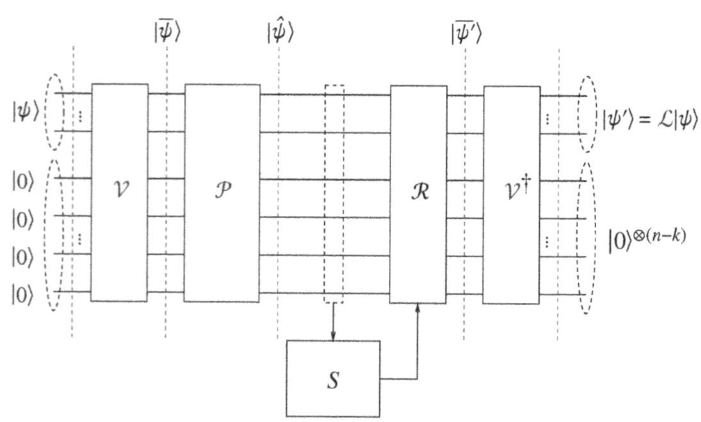


**Figure 9.2** The general schematic of the encoding and decoding of QSCs based on the stabilizer measurements. *Source*: [275]/IEEE/CC BY 4.0.

is utilized for transforming the stabilizer operators $\boldsymbol{S}_i \in \mathcal{S}$ into the binary PCM $\mathbf{H}$. Finally, the error recovery $\mathcal{R}$ is applied according to the specific syndrome values and decoding algorithm utilized. Finally, the inverse encoder $\mathcal{V}^\dagger$ transforms the corrected state of physical qubits $|\overline{\psi'}\rangle$ back to the corrected state of logical qubits $|\psi'\rangle$.

Based on the description of the classical-domain GRAND philosophy in Section 9.2, the observation of the received word $\boldsymbol{y}^n$ is pivotal in the evaluation process for determining the legitimate codeword. However, in the quantum domain, such measurements cannot be performed on the physical qubits, since this would collapse the superposition of the encoded quantum states to the classical values. Consequently, the ML decoding of QSCs based on the measurement of stabilizer operators may be reformulated as finding the most likely error pattern $\boldsymbol{e}^{2n}$ based on the syndrome value $s_Q$ from the received quantum state as follows:

$$\boldsymbol{e}^{2n,*} = \arg\max_{\boldsymbol{e}_i^{2n}} p(\boldsymbol{e}_i^{2n}|\boldsymbol{s}_Q),\ \forall \boldsymbol{e}_i^{2n} \in \mathbb{F}_2^{2n}, \tag{9.18}$$

where $\boldsymbol{e}^{2n,*}$ is the most likely error pattern $\boldsymbol{e}^{2n}$ imposed on the physical qubits that maximizes the conditional probability $p(\boldsymbol{e}_i^{2n}|\boldsymbol{s}_Q)$ over all possible values of $\boldsymbol{e}_i^{2n}$, such that $\boldsymbol{e}_i^{2n}$ is an element of $\mathbb{F}_2^{2n}$.

For CSS-type QSCs, $\boldsymbol{s}_Q = (\boldsymbol{s}_x|\boldsymbol{s}_z)$ may be obtained using Eq. (9.13). Thus, instead of relying on the measurement of the received quantum states, we may perform GRAND by relying on the syndrome vector $\boldsymbol{s}_Q$ obtained from the stabilizer measurements. More specifically, the quantum-GRAND-aided QSC decoder relying on the stabilizer measurements can be described as follows:

- Given the Pauli error operator $\boldsymbol{E} \in \mathcal{G}_N$ having the binary vector representation of $\boldsymbol{e}^{2n} = (\boldsymbol{e}_x^n|\boldsymbol{e}_z^n)$, calculate $\hat{\boldsymbol{s}}_x = \boldsymbol{e}_x^n \cdot \boldsymbol{H}_z^T$ and $\hat{\boldsymbol{s}}_z = \boldsymbol{e}_z^n \cdot \boldsymbol{H}_x^T$.
- Initialize $i = 1$ and set $\boldsymbol{g}_x^n$ to be the initial guess based on the most likely error vector for the Pauli $\boldsymbol{X}$ error pattern and calculate $\boldsymbol{s}_x = \boldsymbol{g}_x^n \cdot \boldsymbol{H}_z^T$.
- While $\hat{\boldsymbol{s}}_x \neq \boldsymbol{s}_x$, increase $i$ by 1 and set $\boldsymbol{g}_x^n$ to be the next guess based on the next most likely error vector for the Pauli $\boldsymbol{X}$ error pattern and calculate $\boldsymbol{s}_x = \boldsymbol{g}_x^n \cdot \boldsymbol{H}_z^T$.
- The process ends when we find $\hat{\boldsymbol{s}}_x = \boldsymbol{s}_x$ in this while loop and the final value of $i$ determines the computational complexity of Pauli $\boldsymbol{X}$ error decoding.
- Initialize $j = 1$ and set $\boldsymbol{g}_z^n$ to be the initial guess based on the most likely error vector for the Pauli $\boldsymbol{Z}$ error pattern and calculate $\boldsymbol{s}_z = \boldsymbol{g}_z^n \cdot \boldsymbol{H}_x^T$.
- While $\hat{\boldsymbol{s}}_z \neq \boldsymbol{s}_z$, increase $j$ by 1 and set $\boldsymbol{g}_z^n$ to be the next guess based on the next most likely error vector for the Pauli $\boldsymbol{Z}$ error pattern and calculate $\boldsymbol{s}_z = \boldsymbol{g}_z^n \cdot \boldsymbol{H}_x^T$.
- The process ends when we find $\hat{\boldsymbol{s}}_z = \boldsymbol{s}_z$ in this while loop and the final value of $j$ determines the computational complexity of Pauli $\boldsymbol{Z}$ error decoding.
- The recovery operator $\mathcal{R} \in \mathcal{G}_N$ is constituted by the Pauli operator represented by the binary vector $(\boldsymbol{g}_x^n|\boldsymbol{g}_z^n)$ and the total complexity is given by $C = i + j$.

Table 9.1 portrays the syndrome vector associated with the most likely Pauli $\boldsymbol{X}$ and Pauli $\boldsymbol{Z}$ error patterns of Steane's 7-qubit code. We have a total of 16 syndromes for correcting both the Pauli $\boldsymbol{X}$ and Pauli $\boldsymbol{Z}$ errors. Explicitly, seven of them represent seven single-qubit bit-flip error patterns and seven correspond to single-qubit phase-flip error patterns. Additionally, we have a pair of (0 0 0) syndrome vectors indicating the absence of bit-flip and phase-flip errors. Thus, each of the syndrome vector is capable of identifying a unique single-qubit error pattern. The error pattern $\boldsymbol{E}$ in Table 9.1 is rank-ordered based on its likelihood in the face of quantum Pauli channels, which means the first error pattern is constituted by the error-free pattern, followed by the single-qubit error patterns. Since all the single-qubit error patterns exhibit an equal probability of occurrence, they can be rank-ordered arbitrarily.

Let us provide a small-scale example of quantum-GRAND-aided stabilizer-measurement-based QSC decoding by utilizing Steane's 7-qubit code, assuming that the quantum Pauli channel $\mathcal{P}$ induces the error pattern of $\boldsymbol{E} = \boldsymbol{IIXIIZI}$. Thus, by using the Pauli-to-binary mapping of Eq. (9.6), the syndrome calculation of Eq. (9.13), and the binary PCM of Steane's 7-qubit code of Eq. (9.15), we obtain $\hat{\boldsymbol{s}}_x = (0\ 1\ 1)$ and $\hat{\boldsymbol{s}}_z = (0\ 1\ 0)$. Upon relying on these syndrome vectors, GRAND will generate the error patterns commencing the most likely to the least likely one and evaluates the syndrome vector. This evaluation process will stop when the decoder finally finds the error pattern that produces the same syndrome vector as $\hat{\boldsymbol{s}}_x$ and $\hat{\boldsymbol{s}}_z$. In this example, GRAND will find the specific Pauli $\boldsymbol{X}$ error pattern from Table 9.1 after four evaluations ($i = 4$) and identify the Pauli $\boldsymbol{Z}$ error pattern after seven evaluations ($j = 7$). Thus, the total complexity of GRAND in this scenario is given by $C = i + j = 4 + 7 = 11$. In a more complex

**Table 9.1** Syndrome values and the associated error-recovery operator $\mathcal{R}$.

| Error operator | Syndrome | Error recovery | Error operator | Syndrome | Error recovery |
|---|---|---|---|---|---|
| $E$ | $s_x$ | $\mathcal{R}$ | $E$ | $s_z$ | $\mathcal{R}$ |
| $IIIIII$ | $(0\,0\,0)$ | $IIIIII$ | $IIIIII$ | $(0\,0\,0)$ | $IIIIII$ |
| $XIIIII$ | $(1\,1\,0)$ | $XIIIII$ | $ZIIIII$ | $(1\,1\,0)$ | $ZIIIII$ |
| $IXIIII$ | $(1\,0\,1)$ | $IXIIII$ | $IZIIII$ | $(1\,0\,1)$ | $IZIIII$ |
| $IIXIII$ | $(0\,1\,1)$ | $IIXIII$ | $IIZIII$ | $(0\,1\,1)$ | $IIZIII$ |
| $IIIXII$ | $(1\,1\,1)$ | $IIIXII$ | $IIIZII$ | $(1\,1\,1)$ | $IIIZII$ |
| $IIIIXI$ | $(1\,0\,0)$ | $IIIIXI$ | $IIIIZI$ | $(1\,0\,0)$ | $IIIIZI$ |
| $IIIIIX$ | $(0\,1\,0)$ | $IIIIIX$ | $IIIIIZ$ | $(0\,1\,0)$ | $IIIIIZ$ |
| $IIIIIIX$ | $(0\,0\,1)$ | $IIIIIIX$ | $IIIIIIZ$ | $(0\,0\,1)$ | $IIIIIIZ$ |

scenario, where a QSC is capable of correcting multiple-qubits error, the evaluation process will continue to the 2-qubit error patterns, 3-qubit error patterns, and so on until GRAND finds the specific error pattern that generates the same syndrome vector as the channel-induced syndrome vector.

In our quantum-GRAND-aided simulation of stabilizer-measurement-based QSC decoding, the observation of errors is carried out for the quantum state $|\overline{\psi'}\rangle$ after the error recovery operator $\mathcal{R}$ is applied as shown in Figure 9.2. For the stabilizer-measurement-based QSC decoder, we declare a quantum block error for every instance when we find $(\boldsymbol{e}_x^n|\boldsymbol{e}_z^n) \neq (\boldsymbol{g}_x^n|\boldsymbol{g}_z^n)$. Thus, the quantum block error rate (QBLER) $Q$ is the ratio between the number of quantum block errors observed and the total number of quantum blocks simulated. Therefore, to compare the performance of various QSCs having different quantum coding rates $r_Q$ as well as different number of logical qubits $K$, we may utilize the notion of normalized QBLER per logical qubits. The QBLER per logical qubits $P$ inferred from the QBLER $Q$ observed may be calculated as

$$P = 1 - (1 - Q)^{1/K}. \tag{9.19}$$

### 9.4.2 Inverse-encoder-based Decoding

In contrast to Figure 9.2, the general schematic of the QSC encoding and decoding based on inverse encoding is depicted in Figure 9.3. The quantum encoder $\mathcal{V}$ and the quantum Pauli channel $\mathcal{P}$ act in the same way as those in Figure 9.2. The main difference is that instead of applying stabilizer measurements to the corrupted quantum state $|\widehat{\psi}\rangle$, we apply the inverse encoder $\mathcal{V}^\dagger$. The effect of $\mathcal{V}^\dagger$ can be explicitly expressed as

$$\mathcal{V}^\dagger \left(\boldsymbol{E}|\overline{\psi}\rangle\right) = \boldsymbol{L}\,|\psi\rangle \otimes \boldsymbol{S}|0\rangle^{\otimes(N-K)}. \tag{9.20}$$

To elaborate briefly on the effect of the inverse encoder $\mathcal{V}^\dagger$ in Figure 9.3, it effectively decomposes the error operator $\boldsymbol{E}$ into two components, namely the logical error component $\boldsymbol{L}$ imposed on the $K$ logical qubits and the auxiliary error component $\boldsymbol{S}$ inflicted upon the $(N-K)$ auxiliary qubits. In this case, the measurement of the error operator contaminating the auxiliary qubits $\boldsymbol{S}|0\rangle^{(N-K)}$ may be carried out either by using the computational ($\boldsymbol{Z}$) basis $\{|0\rangle, |1\rangle\}$ or the Hadamard ($\boldsymbol{X}$) basis $\{|+\rangle, |-\rangle\}$. The measurement results represent the syndrome vector to be used by the inverse-encoding-based decoder. More specifically, the measurement results are constituted by a syndrome vector $\boldsymbol{s}_Q = (\boldsymbol{s}_x|\boldsymbol{s}_z)$, where $\boldsymbol{s}_x$ is obtained from the measurement of error operators using the $\boldsymbol{Z}$ basis and $\boldsymbol{s}_z$ is from the measurement using the $\boldsymbol{X}$ basis.[3]

By exploiting the Pauli-to-classical mapping, the quantum encoder $\mathcal{V}$ harnessed for creating $N$ physical qubits from $K$ logical qubits can be unambiguously represented by a binary matrix $\boldsymbol{V}$ having $(2n \times 2n)$ elements. Similarly, the inverse encoder $\mathcal{V}^\dagger$ can be expressed as a binary matrix $\boldsymbol{V}^{-1}$ and the measurement operators $\mathcal{M}$ can be

3 The syndrome vector $\boldsymbol{s}_x$ obtained from the measurement using the $\boldsymbol{Z}$ basis is used for decoding the Pauli $\boldsymbol{X}$ errors because the Pauli $\boldsymbol{Z}$ operator is anti-commute with Pauli $\boldsymbol{X}$ operator and vice versa.

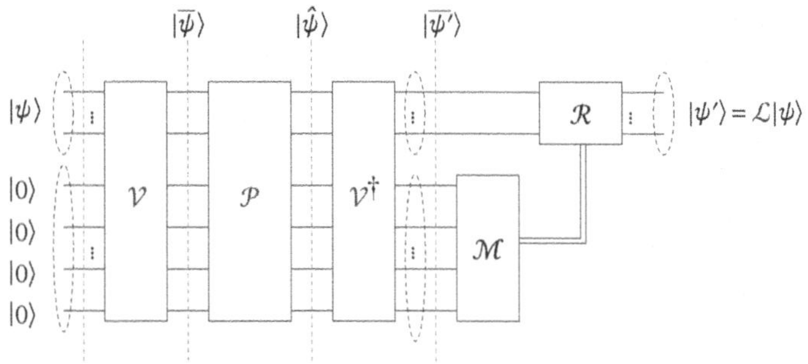


**Figure 9.3** The general schematic of the encoding and decoding of QSCs based on the inverse encoding philosophy. *Source*: [275]/IEEE/CC BY 4.0.

represented by a binary matrix $\boldsymbol{M}$. Therefore, the effect of the Pauli error operator $\boldsymbol{E}$ after the application of the inverse encoder $\mathcal{V}^\dagger$ and of the measurement operators $\mathcal{M}$ can be represented in binary form as

$$(\boldsymbol{e}_x|\boldsymbol{e}_z)\cdot \boldsymbol{V}^{-1}\cdot \boldsymbol{M} = (\boldsymbol{l}_x : \boldsymbol{s}_x : \boldsymbol{0} \mid \boldsymbol{l}_z : \boldsymbol{0} : \boldsymbol{s}_z). \tag{9.21}$$

Observe in Eq. (9.21) that there are zero components $\boldsymbol{0}$ within the vector $(\boldsymbol{l}_x : \boldsymbol{s}_x : \boldsymbol{0})$ and $(\boldsymbol{l}_z : \boldsymbol{0} : \boldsymbol{s}_z)$. This is because the measurements performed on the auxiliary qubits in the $\boldsymbol{Z}$ basis make the auxiliary qubits inaccessible in the $\boldsymbol{X}$ basis and vice versa.

Therefore, based on the results in Eq. (9.21), the ML decoding process for inverse-encoder-based QSCs may be formulated as finding the most likely logical error operator $\boldsymbol{l} = (\boldsymbol{l}_x|\boldsymbol{l}_z)$, given the syndrome vector extracted from the measurements of the auxiliary qubits $\boldsymbol{s}_Q = (\boldsymbol{s}_x|\boldsymbol{s}_z)$ as follows:

$$\boldsymbol{l}^{2k,*} = \arg\max_{\boldsymbol{l}_i^{2k}} p(\boldsymbol{l}_i^{2k}|\boldsymbol{s}_Q),\ \forall \boldsymbol{l}_i^{2k} \in \mathbb{F}_2^{2k}, \tag{9.22}$$

where $\boldsymbol{l}^{2k,*}$ is the most likely logical error operator $\boldsymbol{l}^{2k}$ that maximizes the conditional probability $p(\boldsymbol{l}_i^{2k}|\boldsymbol{s}_Q)$ over all possible values of $\boldsymbol{l}_i^{2k}$, so that $\boldsymbol{l}_i^{2k}$ is an element of $\mathbb{F}_2^{2k}$.

Thus, the quantum-GRAND-aided inverse-encoder-based QSC decoder is defined as follows:

- Given the Pauli error operator $\boldsymbol{E} \in \mathcal{G}_N$ having the binary representation of $\boldsymbol{e}^{2n} = (\boldsymbol{e}_x^n|\boldsymbol{e}_z^n)$, calculate $(\hat{\boldsymbol{l}}_x|\hat{\boldsymbol{s}}_x|\boldsymbol{0}_z) = \boldsymbol{e}_x^n \cdot \boldsymbol{V}_x^{-1} \cdot \boldsymbol{M}_z$ and $(\hat{\boldsymbol{l}}_z|\boldsymbol{0}_x|\hat{\boldsymbol{s}}_z) = \boldsymbol{e}_z^n \cdot \boldsymbol{V}_z^{-1} \cdot \boldsymbol{M}_x$.
- Initialize $i = 1$ and set $\boldsymbol{g}_x^n$ to be the initial guess based on the most likely error vector for the Pauli $\boldsymbol{X}$ error pattern and calculate $(\boldsymbol{l}_x|\boldsymbol{s}_x|\boldsymbol{0}_z) = \boldsymbol{g}_x^n \cdot \boldsymbol{V}_x^{-1} \cdot \boldsymbol{M}_z$.
- While $\hat{\boldsymbol{s}}_x \neq \boldsymbol{s}_x$, increase $i$ by 1 and set $\boldsymbol{g}_x^n$ to be the next guess based on the next most likely error vector for the Pauli $\boldsymbol{X}$ error pattern and calculate $(\boldsymbol{l}_x|\boldsymbol{s}_x|\boldsymbol{0}_z) = \boldsymbol{g}_x^n \cdot \boldsymbol{V}_x^{-1} \cdot \boldsymbol{M}_z$.
- The process ends when we find $\hat{\boldsymbol{s}}_x = \boldsymbol{s}_x$ in this while loop and the final value of $i$ determines the computational complexity of Pauli $\boldsymbol{X}$ error decoding.
- Initialize $j = 1$ and set $\boldsymbol{g}_z^n$ to be the initial guess based on the most likely error vector for the Pauli $\boldsymbol{Z}$ error pattern and calculate $(\boldsymbol{l}_z|\boldsymbol{0}_x|\boldsymbol{s}_z) = \boldsymbol{g}_z^n \cdot \boldsymbol{V}_z^{-1} \cdot \boldsymbol{M}_x$.
- While $\hat{\boldsymbol{s}}_z \neq \boldsymbol{s}_z$, increase $j$ by 1 and set $\boldsymbol{g}_z^n$ to be the next guess based on the next most likely error vector for the Pauli $\boldsymbol{Z}$ error pattern and calculate $(\boldsymbol{l}_z|\boldsymbol{0}_x|\boldsymbol{s}_z) = \boldsymbol{g}_z^n \cdot \boldsymbol{V}_z^{-1} \cdot \boldsymbol{M}_x$.
- The process ends when we find $\hat{\boldsymbol{s}}_z = \boldsymbol{s}_z$ in this while loop and the final value of $j$ determines the computational complexity of Pauli $\boldsymbol{Z}$ error decoding.
- The recovery operator $\mathcal{R} \in \mathcal{G}_K$ is constituted by the Pauli operator represented by the binary vector $(\boldsymbol{l}_x|\boldsymbol{l}_z)$ and the total complexity is given by $C = i + j$.

To provide a clearer picture of the Quantum GRAND-aided inverse-encoder-based QSC decoder, Figure 9.4 portrays the circuit diagram of the quantum encoder $\mathcal{V}$ and of the inverse encoder $\mathcal{V}^\dagger$ for Steane's 7-qubit code based on the PCM given in Eq. (9.15). For the inverse encoder $\mathcal{V}^\dagger$ illustrated in Figure 9.4, the binary matrix representation $\boldsymbol{V}^{-1}$ is given by

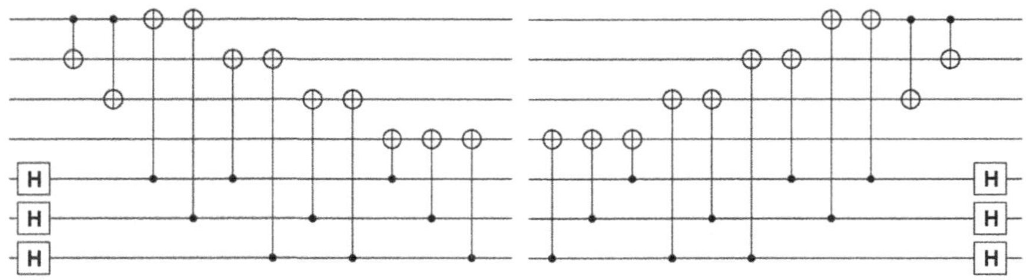


(a) The quantum encoder $\mathcal{V}$ (b) The inverse-encoder $\mathcal{V}^\dagger$

**Figure 9.4** The quantum encoder and inverse-encoder of Steane's 7-qubit code. *Source*: [275]/IEEE/CC BY 4.0.

$$\boldsymbol{V}^{-1} = \left[\begin{array}{c|c} \boldsymbol{V}_x^{-1} & 0 \\ 0 & \boldsymbol{V}_z^{-1} \end{array}\right], \tag{9.23}$$

where $\boldsymbol{V}_x^{-1}$ and $\boldsymbol{V}_z^{-1}$ are formulated as

$$\boldsymbol{V}_x^{-1} = \begin{bmatrix} 1 & 1 & 1 & 0 & 0 & 0 & 0 \\ 0 & 1 & 0 & 0 & 0 & 0 & 0 \\ 0 & 0 & 1 & 0 & 0 & 0 & 0 \\ 0 & 0 & 0 & 1 & 0 & 0 & 0 \\ 1 & 0 & 1 & 1 & 1 & 0 & 0 \\ 1 & 1 & 0 & 1 & 0 & 1 & 0 \\ 0 & 1 & 1 & 1 & 0 & 0 & 1 \end{bmatrix}, \tag{9.24}$$

$$\boldsymbol{V}_z^{-1} = \begin{bmatrix} 1 & 0 & 0 & 0 & 1 & 1 & 0 \\ 1 & 1 & 0 & 0 & 1 & 0 & 1 \\ 1 & 0 & 1 & 0 & 0 & 1 & 1 \\ 0 & 0 & 0 & 1 & 1 & 1 & 1 \\ 0 & 0 & 0 & 0 & 1 & 0 & 0 \\ 0 & 0 & 0 & 0 & 0 & 1 & 0 \\ 0 & 0 & 0 & 0 & 0 & 0 & 1 \end{bmatrix}. \tag{9.25}$$

For deeper insights on how to transform the PCM $\boldsymbol{H}$ of CSS-type QSCs into the quantum encoder $\mathcal{V}$ and the inverse encoder $\mathcal{V}^\dagger$ as well as their associated binary matrices $\boldsymbol{V}$ and $\boldsymbol{V}^{-1}$, we refer enthusiastic readers to [67, 279].

For Steane's 7-qubit code, the first qubit is allocated to the logical qubit, the next three qubits are dedicated to the auxiliary qubits, which are subject to the measurement in the $\boldsymbol{Z}$ basis and finally, the next three qubits are the auxiliary qubits measured in the $\boldsymbol{X}$ basis. Therefore, the measurement operator $\mathcal{M}$ can be represented using the binary matrices $\boldsymbol{M}_x$ and $\boldsymbol{M}_z$ formulated as follows:

$$M_x = \begin{bmatrix} 1 & 0 & 0 & 0 & 0 & 0 & 0 \\ 0 & 0 & 0 & 0 & 0 & 0 & 0 \\ 0 & 0 & 0 & 0 & 0 & 0 & 0 \\ 0 & 0 & 0 & 0 & 0 & 0 & 0 \\ 0 & 0 & 0 & 0 & 1 & 0 & 0 \\ 0 & 0 & 0 & 0 & 0 & 1 & 0 \\ 0 & 0 & 0 & 0 & 0 & 0 & 1 \end{bmatrix}, \tag{9.26}$$

$$M_z = \begin{bmatrix} 1 & 0 & 0 & 0 & 0 & 0 & 0 \\ 0 & 1 & 0 & 0 & 0 & 0 & 0 \\ 0 & 0 & 1 & 0 & 0 & 0 & 0 \\ 0 & 0 & 0 & 1 & 0 & 0 & 0 \\ 0 & 0 & 0 & 0 & 0 & 0 & 0 \\ 0 & 0 & 0 & 0 & 0 & 0 & 0 \\ 0 & 0 & 0 & 0 & 0 & 0 & 0 \end{bmatrix}. \tag{9.27}$$

Observe that the binary representation of the measurement operator $\boldsymbol{M}_x$ of Eq. (9.26) is constituted by a specific identity matrix having zero elements for those specific diagonal element $\boldsymbol{M}_{x,ii}$, where the $i$th qubit is auxiliary qubit measured in the $\boldsymbol{Z}$ basis. Similarly, the binary representation of the measurement operator $\boldsymbol{M}_z$ of Eq. (9.27) is represented by a specific identity matrix having the element of $\boldsymbol{M}_{z,jj}$ set to zero, where $j$th qubit is auxiliary qubit measured in the $\boldsymbol{X}$ basis.

Let us assume that the quantum Pauli channel $\mathcal{P}$ induces an error pattern of $\boldsymbol{E} = \boldsymbol{IZIIXII}$. Thus, by using the Pauli-to-binary mapping of Eq. (9.6) and the syndrome calculation of Eq. (9.21), we obtain $\boldsymbol{s}_x = (0\ 1\ 1)$ and $\boldsymbol{s}_z = (1\ 0\ 1)$. Relying on these syndrome vectors, GRAND will generate the error pattern commencing from the most likely to the least likely and evaluate the syndrome vector. This evaluation process will be terminated when the decoder finally finds the specific error pattern that produces the same syndrome vector as $\hat{\boldsymbol{s}}_x$ and $\hat{\boldsymbol{s}}_z$. In this example, GRAND will find from Table 9.2 the Pauli $\boldsymbol{X}$ error pattern after six evaluations ($i = 6$) and the Pauli $\boldsymbol{Z}$ error pattern after three evaluations ($j = 3$). Thus, the total complexity of GRAND in this example is given by $C = i + j = 6 + 3 = 9$.

In contrast to the GRAND simulation used for stabilizer-measurement-based QSC decoding, the observation of errors is carried out for the quantum state $|\psi'\rangle$ after the inverse encoder $\mathcal{V}^\dagger$ and error recovery operator $\mathcal{R}$ are applied, as shown Figure 9.3. For the inverse-encoder-based QSC decoder, we declare a quantum block error for every instance, when we find $(\hat{\boldsymbol{l}}_x|\hat{\boldsymbol{l}}_z) \neq (\boldsymbol{l}_x|\boldsymbol{l}_z)$. Furthermore, instead of performing normalization of the QBLER performance using Eq. (9.19), we are able to measure the actual QBLER per logical qubits. More specifically, the number of errors in the logical qubits can be defined as

$$\text{wt}\{(\hat{\boldsymbol{l}}_x \oplus \boldsymbol{l}_x) \vee (\hat{\boldsymbol{l}}_z \oplus \boldsymbol{l}_z)\}, \tag{9.28}$$

where wt$\{\cdot\}$ denotes the Hamming weight of a vector, $\oplus$ represents the modulo-2 addition, and $\vee$ denotes the bit-wise logical OR operation. Therefore, the QBLER per logical qubits can be calculated as the ratio of the total number of errors divided by the total number of logical qubits simulated.

**Table 9.2** Syndrome values and the associated error-recovery operator $\mathcal{R}$.

| Error operator | Syndrome | Error recovery | Error operator | Syndrome | Error recovery |
|---|---|---|---|---|---|
| $P$ | $s_x$ | $\mathcal{R}$ | $P$ | $s_z$ | $\mathcal{R}$ |
| $IIIIII$ | (0 0 0) | $I$ | $IIIIII$ | (0 0 0) | $I$ |
| $XIIIII$ | (1 1 0) | $X$ | $ZIIIII$ | (1 1 0) | $Z$ |
| $IXIIII$ | (1 0 0) | $I$ | $IZIIII$ | (1 0 1) | $Z$ |
| $IIXIII$ | (0 1 0) | $I$ | $IIZIII$ | (0 1 1) | $Z$ |
| $IIIXII$ | (0 0 1) | $I$ | $IIIZII$ | (1 1 1) | $I$ |
| $IIIIXI$ | (0 1 1) | $X$ | $IIIIZI$ | (1 0 0) | $I$ |
| $IIIIIX$ | (1 0 1) | $X$ | $IIIIIZ$ | (0 1 0) | $I$ |
| $IIIIIIX$ | (1 1 1) | $I$ | $IIIIIIZ$ | (0 0 1) | $I$ |

## 9.5 Results and Discussion

In this section, we present our Monte–Carlo simulation results for quantum-GRAND-aided QSC decoding relying on both decoding philosophies represented in Section 9.4. To evaluate the decoding performance, we utilize the quantum depolarizing channel represented by the $N$-tuple Pauli operator $\boldsymbol{E} \in \mathcal{G}_N$, which is characterized by the depolarizing probability $p$. To elaborate a little further, each qubit within the $N$ physical qubits may independently experience a Pauli $\boldsymbol{X}$ error, a Pauli $\boldsymbol{Z}$ error, or a Pauli $\boldsymbol{Y}$ error, where the probability of each qubit experiencing one of these errors is given by $p_x$, $p_z$, and $p_y$, respectively. Thus, we have $p_x + p_z + p_y = p$ and $p_x = p_z = p_y = p/3$. To demonstrate the generic nature of our solution, we utilize quantum BCH codes for characterizing the quantum-GRAND-aided stabilizer-measurement-based decoder and quantum polar codes for the quantum-GRAND-aided inverse-encoder-based decoder.

### 9.5.1 Quantum BCH Codes

In this chapter, we consider the family of dual-containing CSS-type quantum BCH codes, whose PCM $\boldsymbol{H}$ is taken from the primitive narrow-sense classical BCH codes. More specifically, the PCM of classical binary BCH codes $\boldsymbol{H}$ can be expressed in the form of

$$\boldsymbol{H}_{\mathrm{BCH}} = \begin{bmatrix} \alpha^0 & \alpha^1 & \alpha^2 & \cdots & \alpha^{n-1} \\ \alpha^0 & (\alpha^3) & (\alpha^3)^2 & \cdots & (\alpha^3)^{n-1} \\ \alpha^0 & (\alpha^5) & (\alpha^5)^2 & \cdots & (\alpha^5)^{n-1} \\ \vdots & \vdots & \vdots & \ddots & \vdots \\ \alpha^0 & (\alpha^{2t-1}) & (\alpha^{2t-1})^2 & \cdots & (\alpha^{2t-1})^{n-1} \end{bmatrix}, \tag{9.29}$$

where the entries $\alpha^i$ of the PCM $\boldsymbol{H}$ are the elements of $GF(2^m)$ written in binary column vector, $n = 2^m - 1$ is the length of classical codewords and $t = \lfloor (d-1)/2) \rfloor$ is the error correction capability of the classical BCH codes. Finally, the PCM of quantum BCH codes takes the form of Eq. (9.11) with $\boldsymbol{H}_x = \boldsymbol{H}_z = \boldsymbol{H}_{\mathrm{BCH}}$. We summarize the quantum BCH codes used in our Monte-Carlo simulation in Table 9.3.

### 9.5.2 Quantum Polar Codes

Furthermore, we utilize the quantum polar code constructions presented in [278]. The kernel of the quantum polar encoder can be separated into two types, namely the kernel for the Pauli $\boldsymbol{X}$ matrix – namely the quantum bit-flip

**Table 9.3** The list of quantum BCH codes considered in this chapter for evaluating the performance of quantum-GRAND-aided stabilizer-measurement-based decoding using Monte–Carlo simulations.

| Power | Primitive polynomial | Error correction | Code parameters | Classical codes | Code rate |
|---|---|---|---|---|---|
| $m$ | $p(X)$ | $t$ | $[[N,K,D]]$ | $(n,k,d)$ | $r_Q$ |
| 3 | $1+X+X^3$ | 1 | $[[7,1,3]]$ | $(7,4,3)$ | 0.14 |
| 4 | $1+X+X^4$ | 1 | $[[15,7,3]]$ | $(15,11,3)$ | 0.47 |
| 5 | $1+X^2+X^5$ | 1 | $[[31,21,3]]$ | $(31,26,3)$ | 0.68 |
| | | 2 | $[[31,11,5]]$ | $(31,21,5)$ | 0.35 |
| | | 3 | $[[31,1,7]]$ | $(31,16,7)$ | 0.03 |
| 6 | $1+X+X^6$ | 1 | $[[63,51,3]]$ | $(63,57,3)$ | 0.81 |
| | | 2 | $[[63,39,5]]$ | $(63,51,5)$ | 0.62 |
| | | 3 | $[[63,27,7]]$ | $(63,45,7)$ | 0.43 |
| 7 | $1+X+X^7$ | 1 | $[[127,113,3]]$ | $(127,120,3)$ | 0.89 |
| | | 2 | $[[127,99,5]]$ | $(127,113,5)$ | 0.78 |
| | | 3 | $[[127,85,7]]$ | $(127,106,7)$ | 0.67 |

channel and the kernel for the Pauli $\boldsymbol{Z}$ matrix – namely the quantum phase-flip channel. The Pauli $\boldsymbol{Y}$ matrix can be readily modeled as the combination of the Pauli $\boldsymbol{X}$ and $\boldsymbol{Z}$ channel. The kernel of the quantum polar encoder for the Pauli $\boldsymbol{X}$ matrix is given by

$$\boldsymbol{G}_{0,x} = \begin{bmatrix} 0 & 1 \\ 1 & 1 \end{bmatrix}. \tag{9.30}$$

Therefore, the binary representation of the quantum polar encoder $\boldsymbol{V}_x$ having $N=2^m$ physical qubits is given by

$$\boldsymbol{V}_x = \boldsymbol{G}_{0,x}^{\otimes m}. \tag{9.31}$$

By contrast, the kernel of the quantum polar encoder for the Pauli $\boldsymbol{Z}$ matrix channel is given by

$$\boldsymbol{G}_{0,z} = \begin{bmatrix} 1 & 1 \\ 0 & 1 \end{bmatrix}. \tag{9.32}$$

Therefore, the binary representation of the quantum polar encoder $\boldsymbol{V}_z$ having $N=2^m$ physical qubits is represented by

$$\boldsymbol{V}_z = \boldsymbol{G}_{0,z}^{\otimes m}. \tag{9.33}$$

Furthermore, the kernels of Eqs. (9.30) and (9.32) are used for determining the frozen qubits of the quantum polar encoder. As detailed further in [278], the channel polarization of quantum bit-flip ($\boldsymbol{X}$) channels takes place in the reverse order of the channel polarization of quantum phase-flip ($\boldsymbol{Z}$) channels. Therefore, the channel capacity of the qubit's index for the quantum phase-flip error can be inferred from the reverse ordered rank of the quantum bit-flip channel.

We utilize the binary erasure channel (BEC) based approximation for determining the location of the frozen (auxiliary) qubits. Explicitly, we used the erasure probability of $\epsilon = 0.5$. It is important to note that, in the idealistic implementation of quantum polar codes, the location of the auxiliary qubits may be different for a different depolarizing probability value. This also means that the encoder-decoder pair of the quantum polar codes has the perfect knowledge of the quantum channel's depolarizing probability. In this chapter, we are focusing only on the capability of our quantum-GRAND-aided inverse-encoder-based decoder to decode quantum polar codes. Thus,

**Table 9.4** The rank-ordered qubit index spanning from the most reliable to the least reliable qubit in the presence of quantum bit-flip ($\boldsymbol{X}$) channels used for determining the location of auxiliary qubits in quantum polar codes. For quantum phase-flip ($\boldsymbol{Z}$) channel, the rank-ordered index of the qubit is reversed.

| Number of physical qubits | Rank-ordered qubit's index |
|---|---|
| $N$ | $i$ |
| 8 | 1, 5, 3, 2, 7, 6, 4, 8 |
| 16 | 1, 9, 5, 3, 2, 13, 11, 7, 10, 6, 4, 15, 14, 12, 8, 16 |
| 32 | 1, 17, 9, 5, 3, 2, 25, 21, 13, 19, 11, 18, 7, 10, 29, 6 |
| | 27, 4, 23, 26, 15, 22, 14, 20, 12, 8, 31, 30, 28, 24, 16, 32 |
| 64 | 1, 33, 17, 9, 5, 3, 49, 2, 41, 25, 37, 21, 13, 35, 19, 11 |
| | 34, 57, 18, 7, 53, 10, 45, 51, 29, 6, 43, 27, 50, 4, 39, 42 |
| | 23, 26, 61, 15, 38, 22, 59, 36, 14, 20, 55, 12, 58, 47, 8, 31 |
| | 54, 46, 30, 52, 44, 28, 40, 24, 63, 16, 62, 60, 56, 48, 32, 64 |

optimizing the location of the auxiliary qubits will be left for our future work. The rank-ordered qubit's index spanning from the most reliable qubit to the least reliable is in the presence of a quantum bit-flip ($\boldsymbol{X}$) channel is portrayed in Table 9.4. Thus, the rank-ordered qubit's index for quantum phase-flip ($\boldsymbol{Z}$) channels can be determined by reverse-ordering the index presented in Table 9.4.

### 9.5.3 QBLER and QBLER per Logical Qubits

In this section, we present the QBLER and QBLER per logical qubits performance results of both decoding philosophies represented in Section 9.4, namely the quantum BCH codes for characterizing the quantum-GRAND-aided stabilizer-measurement-based decoder and the quantum polar codes for the quantum-GRAND-aided inverse-encoder-based decoder.

As mentioned in Section 9.4, the QBLER is determined by the ratio of quantum block errors observed to the total number of quantum blocks simulated. Figure 9.5a shows the performance of various QSCs codes represented by $\mathcal{C}[[N, K, D]]$, as well as having the quantum coding rates $r_Q$ of Table 9.3, for quantum BCH codes relying on the quantum-GRAND-aided stabilizer-measurement-based decoder. As shown in Figure 9.5a, when a fixed number of $N$ physical qubits is considered such as $N = 63$, as in $[[63, 51, 3]]$, $[[63, 39, 5]]$ and $[[63, 27, 7]]$, the higher the minimum distance $D$, the better the performance becomes. Hence, as expected $[[63, 27, 7]]$ outperforms the $[[63, 51, 3]]$ and $[[63, 39, 5]]$ schemes.

Additionally, Figure 9.5b provides performance of the normalized QBLER per logical qubits for the quantum BCH codes, which is calculated using Eq. (9.19). This normalized metric provides a fairer comparison than the QBLER of Figure 9.5a. Interestingly, quantum BCH $[[63, 27, 7]]$ and quantum BCH $[[31, 1, 7]]$ have very similar error correction performances, which have however vastly different quantum coding rates of $r_Q = 0.43$ and $r_Q = 0.03$, respectively. Hence, the former is much preferred for practical systems.

Furthermore, Figure 9.6a characterizes the performance of quantum polar codes for the quantum-GRAND-aided inverse-encoder-based decoder. It is important to highlight that the minimum distance $D$ is unknown for the quantum polar codes. Observe in Figure 9.6a when the same number of $N$ physical qubits is considered such as $N = 64$, as in $[[64, 32, D]]$, $[[64, 16, D]]$ and $[[64, 8, D]]$, the quantum polar code having a lower quantum coding rates $r_Q$ attains a better error correction performance. The best overall QBLER performance is achieved by the $[[16, 2, D]]$ having a quantum coding rate of $r_Q = 0.125$. Furthermore, we also quantified the QBLER per logical qubit for the quantum polar codes using the quantum-GRAND-aided inverse-encoder-based decoder relying on Eq. (9.28) (Figure 9.6b). In this context, the best performance is attained by the $[[64, 8, D]]$ scheme associated with $r_Q = 0.125$.

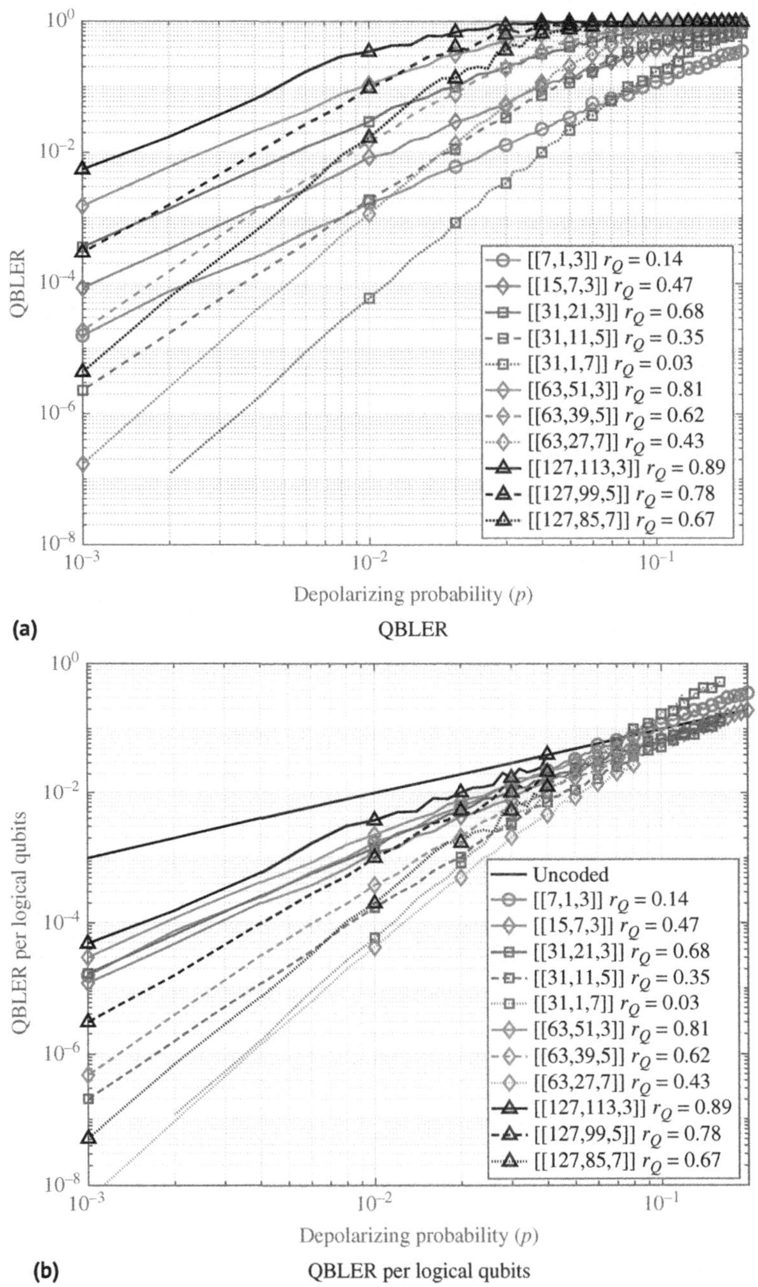


**Figure 9.5** The QBLER and QBLER per logical qubits of quantum BCH codes. *Source:* [275]/IEEE/CC BY 4.0.

### 9.5.4 Complexity

In this section, we present the complexity and complexity per logical qubits of both the quantum BCH codes and of the quantum polar codes. As mentioned in Section 9.4, in both the quantum-GRAND-aided stabilizer-measurement-based decoder and the quantum-GRAND-aided inverse-encoder-based decoder, the complexity estimated in terms of the number of guessing $i$ and $j$, where the total complexity is given by $C = i + j$.

Figure 9.7a shows the quantum-GRAND-aided decoder complexity of the quantum BCH codes, which predominantly depends on the $N$ value. More specifically, as shown in Figure 9.7a, a lower $N$ requires fewer number of guesses to find the correct decoded codeword and vice versa. Observe in Figure 9.7a, that $[[127, 85, 7]]$ invokes the

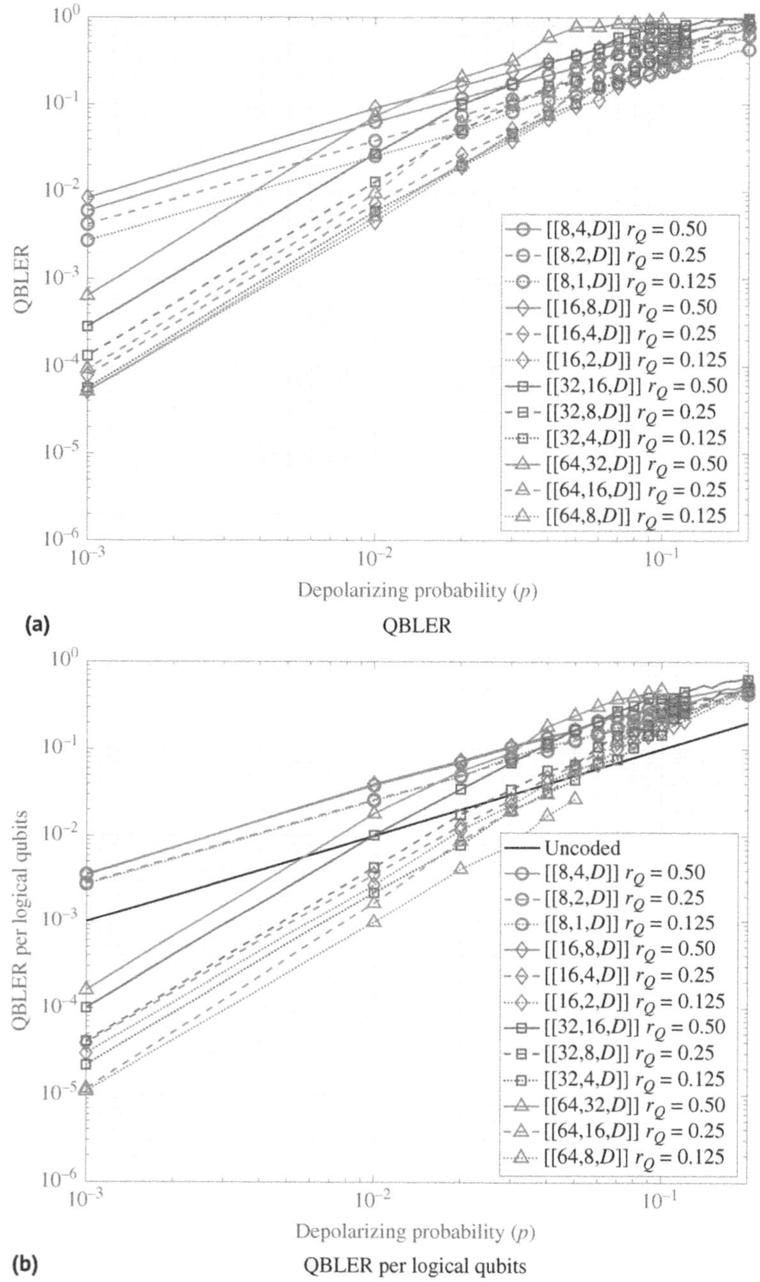


**Figure 9.6** The QBLER and QBLER per logical qubits of quantum polar codes. *Source*: [275]/IEEE/CC BY 4.0.

highest complexity, while $[[7,1,3]]$ imposes the lowest complexity. On the other hand, in terms of the complexity per logical qubits, Figure 9.7b shows that $[[127,85,7]]$ requires the highest complexity per logical qubits and $[[31,21,3]]$ induces the lowest normalized complexity when $p = 10^{-2}$.

Furthermore, Figure 9.8a shows the quantum-GRAND-aided decoder complexity of the quantum polar codes, which again predominantly depends on the $N$ value. More specifically, as shown in Figure 9.8a, a lower $N$ requires fewer number guesses to find the correct decoded codeword and vice versa. Observe in Figure 9.8a, that $[[64,8,D]]$ requires the highest, while $[[8,4,D]]$ the lowest complexity. On the other hand, in terms of the complexity per logical qubits, Figure 9.8b shows that $[[64,8,D]]$ requires the highest and $[[8,4,D]]$ the lowest normalized complexity.

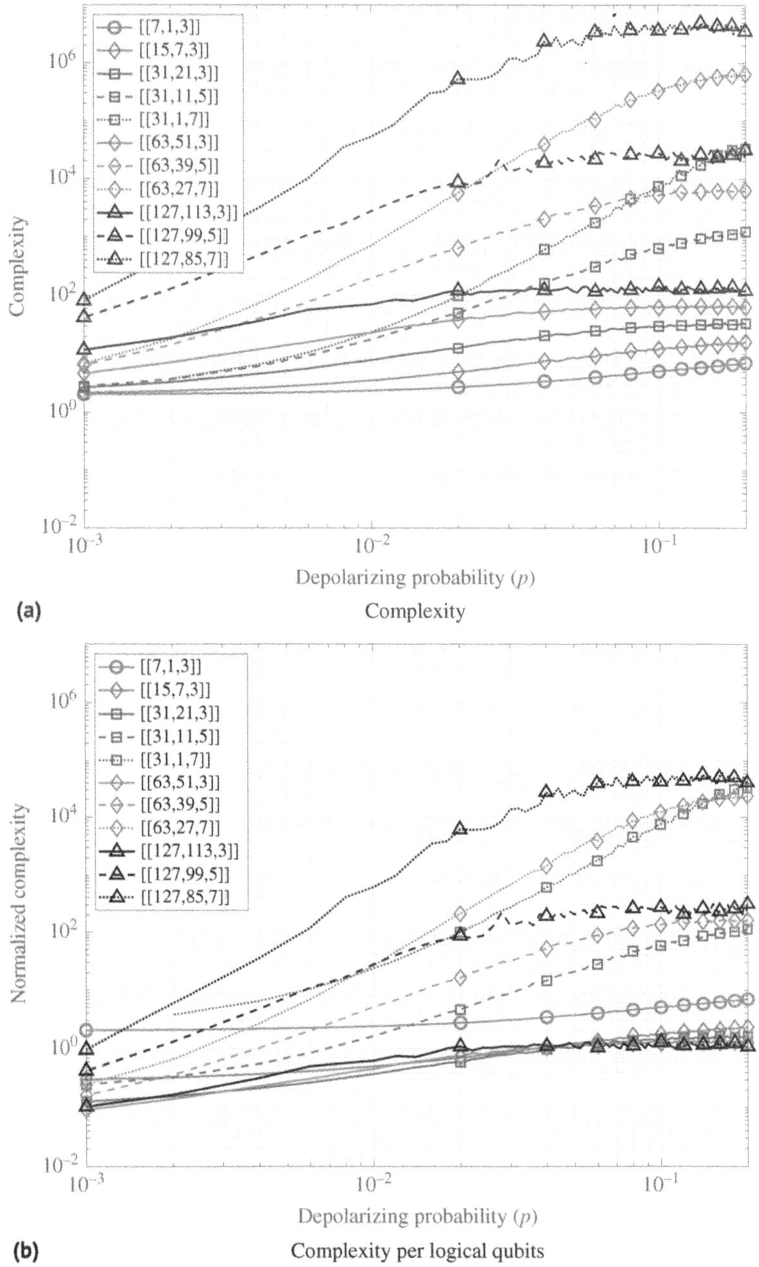


**Figure 9.7** The complexity and the normalized complexity of quantum-GRAND-aided stabilizer-measurement-based decoder for quantum BCH codes. *Source:* [275]/IEEE/CC BY 4.0.

## 9.6 Conclusions and Future Work

In conclusion, we devised a universal decoding scheme for QSCs by further evolving the GRAND decoding philosophy for employment in the quantum domain. We demonstrated that the decoding scheme conceived may be adopted for two different QSC decoding paradigms, namely for both stabilizer-measurement-based as well as the inverse-encoder-based decoding. We then applied the resultant decoder for both quantum BCH codes and quantum polar codes and quantified their QBLER, QBLER per logical qubits as well as their decoding complexity. We concluded with a parametric study of the associated design trade-offs and provided design guidelines for the implementation of quantum-GRAND-aided QSC decoders. Based on our QBLER simulations, we demonstrated

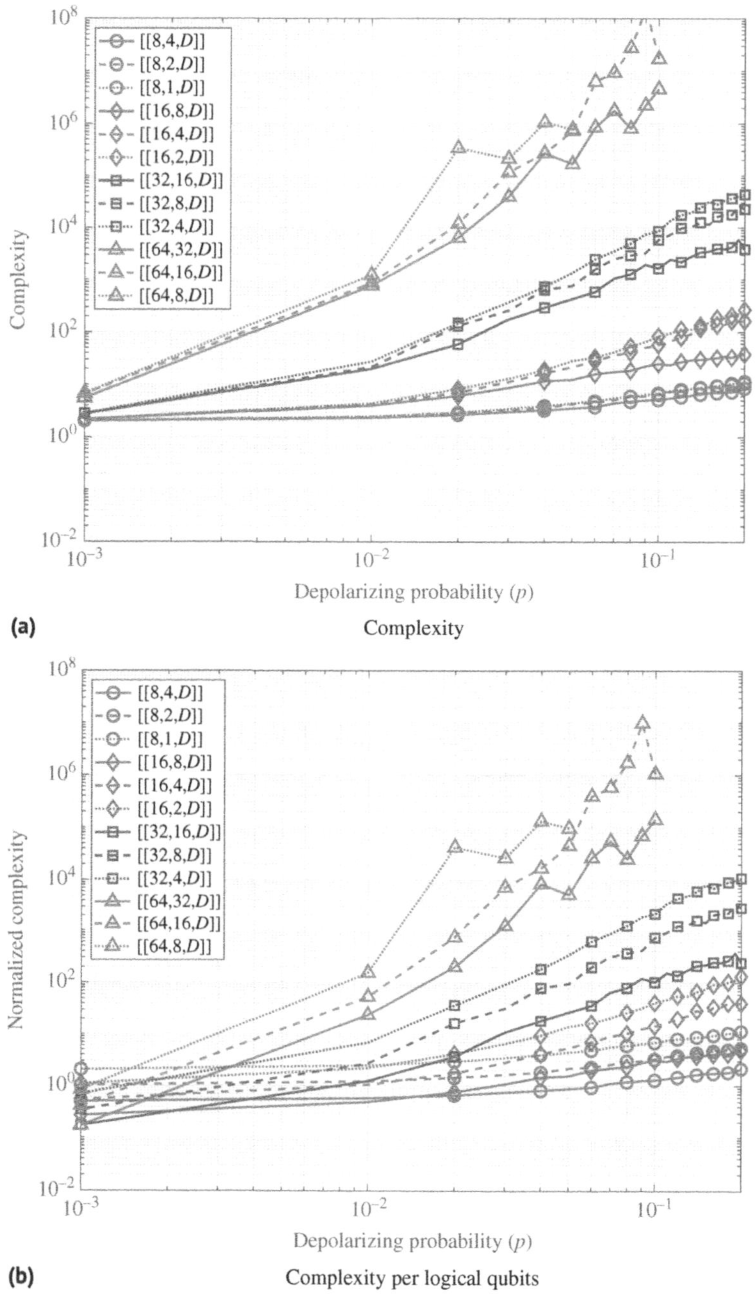


**Figure 9.8** The complexity and the normalized complexity of quantum-GRAND-aided inverse-encoder-based decoder for quantum polar codes. *Source*: [275]/IEEE/CC BY 4.0.

that when a fixed number of $N$ physical qubits is considered, the higher the minimum distance $D$, the better the performance becomes. According to the list of quantum BCH codes considered in Table 9.3, our simulations showed that the quantum BCH [[63, 27, 7]] is much preferred for practical systems upon applying the quantum-GRAND-aided stabilizer-measurement-based decoder. On the other hand, for quantum polar codes relying on the quantum-GRAND-aided inverse-encoder-based decoder, the best overall QBLER performance is achieved by the [[16, 2, $D$]] having quantum coding rate of $r_Q = 0.125$. Furthermore, based on our simulations, the quantum-GRAND-aided decoder complexity of quantum BCH codes and quantum polar codes is dominated by $N$, because a lower $N$ requires a lower number of guesses to find the correct decoded codeword. Our future research might also explore the employment of soft-information-aided GRAND [271, 280, 281], which can also be done efficiently from the complexity point of view.

In this chapter, we have concentrated on using quantum-GRAND-aided QSC decoding for the family of CSS-type QSCs. Our next goal is to expand the proposed decoding method to the family of non-CSS codes, such as the QSCs presented in [60, 282].

Our simulation results confirm the findings presented in [283], namely that quantum polar codes do not offer the best error correction capability in the face of quantum depolarizing channels. This motivates us to explore the use of quantum-GRAND-aided QSC decoding for more realistic scenarios. Firstly, quantum channels are inherently asymmetric [146]. As a result, the number of frozen qubits in quantum polar codes harnessed for the quantum bit-flip ($\boldsymbol{X}$) and quantum phase-flip ($\boldsymbol{Z}$) channels can be made different. Secondly, the encoding and decoding process of QSC is not error-free [255]. Modeling the error proliferation within the quantum error correction circuit is a complex task. Therefore, performing quantum error correction decoding with the knowledge that the quantum encoder and decoder of QSCs are not error-free has been a long-standing challenge in fault-tolerant quantum computation. So far, progress has been made mostly for quantum topological error correction codes (QTECCs) [153], because the locality of stabilizer measurements ensures that errors only propagate to a fixed number of qubits, thus minimizing the error proliferation phenomenon. However, quantum polar codes may provide an alternative solution to this problem as a benefit of the systematic structure of the quantum encoder and decoder, making it simpler to model and to predict the error proliferation within the quantum error correction circuit. Therefore, in our future research we will also consider the utilization of quantum-GRAND-aided QSC decoding for quantum polar codes under realistic fault-tolerance assumptions.

# Part III

# Advanced Quantum Codes

# 10

# Revisiting the Classical to Quantum Coding Evolution

The subject of Part I was the classical to quantum coding evolution. Then, in Chapter 6 of Part II we set out by providing some quantum coding bounds derived from the classical coding bounds as a function of the code-rate and codeword length. Furthermore, in Chapter 7 we considered a suite of near-term quantum topological error correction code (QTECC) solutions relying on a limited number of qubits, while in Chapter 8 we demonstrated, how to apply them for the protection of quantum gates. Part II of the book was concluded by outlining the so-called "universal decoding" principles in Chapter 9, which are applicable for the decoding of any arbitrary linear codes, such as Bose–Chaudhuri–Hocquenghem (BCH) and polar codes.

The remaining chapters of the book are dedicated to recent radical advances in the field, aiming for designing sophisticated iteratively detected quantum codes. Experts of classical coding might like to turn directly to this part of the book, since Chapter 10 revisits the classical to quantum evolution to ease their entry into quantum coding. Chapter 11 delves into the extrinsic information transfer (EXIT) chart based design of serially concatenated turbo codes. Hence readers who are unfamiliar with EXIT-chart based designs might like to consult Chapter 5 first concerning the EXIT-chart based near-capacity design principles in the context of classical codes. Our discourse continues in Chapter 12 with the design of short quantum block codes relying on EXIT-chart assisted iterative near-hashing-bound principles. Following a similar approach, in Chapter 13 we conceive so-called irregular short quantum block codes for near-hashing-bound operation, which are designed for having an adaptive rate. Hence they can be reconfigured for accommodating time-variant depolarizing probabilities. Finally, Chapter 14 concludes the monograph with a detailed characterization of quantum low-density parity-check (LDPC) codes, followed by a summary chapter.

## 10.1 Introduction

In Chapter 5, we invoked near-capacity classical code designs for classical transmission over a quantum communication channel. Our classical-quantum code design, which amalgamates the classical codes with a quantum superdense code, is only suitable when the transmitted information is classical. For reliable quantum information transmission as well as for quantum computing systems, we have to resort to the family of quantum error correction codes (QECCs), which exploit redundancy in the quantum domain in contrast to the classical-domain redundancy of Chapter 5. Again, meritorious families of QECCs can be derived by exploring the duality between classical and quantum codes, while from the known classical codes by exploiting the underlying quantum-to-classical isomorphism, while also taking into account the peculiar laws of quantum mechanics. This transition from the classical to the quantum domain has to address the following challenges [160]:

- **No-cloning Theorem:** Most classical codes are based on the transmission of multiple replicas of the same bit, e.g. in a simple rate-1/3 repetition code each information bit is transmitted thrice. This is not possible in the quantum domain according to the no-cloning theorem [284], which states that quantum states must not be copied/cloned.
- **Continuous Nature of Quantum Errors:** In contrast to the classical errors, which are discrete with bit-flip being the only type of error, recall from Section 2.7 that a qubit may experience both a bit-flip as well as

a phase-flip or in fact both. These impairments have a continuous nature and the erroneous qubit may lie anywhere on the surface of the Bloch sphere.

- **Qubits Collapse Upon Measurement:** "Measurement" of the received bits is a vital step representing a hard-decision operation in the field of classical error correction. However, this is not feasible in the quantum domain, since qubits collapse to classical bits upon measurement.

In a nutshell, a classical $(n, k)$ binary code is designed to protect discrete-valued message sequences of length $k$ by encoding them into one of the $2^k$ discrete codewords of length $n$. By contrast, since a quantum state of $k$ qubits is specified by $2^k$ continuous-valued complex coefficients, quantum error correction aims for encoding a $k$-qubit state into an $n$-qubit state, so that all the $2^k$ complex coefficients can be perfectly restored [67]. For example, let $k = 2$, then the 2-qubit information word $|\psi\rangle$ is given by:

$$|\psi\rangle = \alpha_0|00\rangle + \alpha_1|01\rangle + \alpha_2|10\rangle + \alpha_3|11\rangle. \tag{10.1}$$

Consequently, the error correction algorithm would aim for correctly preserving all the four coefficients, i.e. $\alpha_0$, $\alpha_1$, $\alpha_2$, and $\alpha_3$. It is interesting to note here that although the coefficients $\alpha_0$, $\alpha_1$, $\alpha_2$, and $\alpha_3$ are continuous in nature, yet the entire continuum of errors can be corrected, if we can correct a discrete set of errors, i.e. bit (Pauli-**X**), phase (Pauli-**Z**) as well as both (Pauli-**Y**) errors inflicted on either or both qubits [160]. This is because the act of measurement collapses the entire continuum of errors to a discrete set. More explicitly, for $|\psi\rangle$ of Eq. (10.1), the discrete error set is as follows:

$$\begin{aligned}&\{\mathbf{IX}, \mathbf{IZ}, \mathbf{IY}, \mathbf{XI}, \mathbf{XX}, \mathbf{XZ}, \mathbf{XY}, \mathbf{ZI}, \mathbf{ZX}, \mathbf{ZZ},\\ &\mathbf{ZY}, \mathbf{YI}, \mathbf{YX}, \mathbf{YZ}, \mathbf{YY}\}.\end{aligned} \tag{10.2}$$

However, the errors **X**, **Y**, and **Z** may occur with varying frequencies. In this discourse, we will focus on the specific design of codes conceived for mitigating the deleterious effects of the quantum depolarizing channel, which has been extensively investigated in the context of QECCs [67, 69, 141].

Most of the quantum codes developed to date owe their existence to the theory of stabilizer codes, which allows us to import any arbitrary classical binary as well as quaternary code to the quantum domain. In this chapter, we will delve deeper into the stabilizer formalism, providing insights into the construction of quantum codes based on the family of known classical codes. This allows us to pave the way for a smooth transition from the classical to the quantum domain.

Since the stabilizer codes owe their existence to the classical linear block codes, we commence with a review of the classical linear block codes in Section 10.2. Then the family of stabilizer codes is revisited in Section 10.3 with a particular emphasis on the general stabilizer formalism, on the underlying quantum-to-classical isomorphism, and on the classification of quantum errors, which are discussed in Sections 10.3.1–10.3.3, respectively. We next detail the construction of quantum convolutional codes in Section 10.4, while the class of entanglement-assisted quantum codes is discussed in Section 10.5. Finally, the highlights of the chapter are provided in Section 10.6.

## 10.2 Review of Classical Linear Block Codes

The stabilizer formalism derives its existence from the theory of classical linear block codes. A classical linear block code $C(n, k)$ maps $k$-bit information blocks onto $n$-bit codewords. For small values of $k$ and $n$, this can be readily achieved using a look-up table, which maps the input information blocks onto the encoded message blocks. However, for large values of $k$ and $n$, the process may be simplified using a $k \times n$ generator matrix $G$ as follows:

$$\overline{x} = xG, \tag{10.3}$$

where $x$ and $\overline{x}$ are row vectors of the original information and encoded messages, respectively. Furthermore, $G$ may be decomposed as:

$$G = (I_k|P), \tag{10.4}$$

where $I_k$ is a $(k \times k)$-element identity matrix and $P$ is a $k \times (n-k)$-element matrix. This in turn implies that the first $k$ bits of the encoded message are information bits, followed by $(n-k)$ parity bits. Hence this is a systematic code.

At the decoder, syndrome decoding is invoked, which determines the position of the channel-induced error using the syndromes observed rather than directly acting on the received codewords. More precisely, each generator matrix is associated with an $(n-k)\times n$-element parity check matrix (PCM) $H$ which is given by:

$$H=(P^T|I_{n-k}), \tag{10.5}$$

and is defined such that $\bar{x}$ is a valid codeword only if,

$$\bar{x}H^T=0. \tag{10.6}$$

For a received vector $y=\bar{x}+e$, where $e$ is the error incurred during transmission, the error syndrome of length $(n-k)$ is computed as:

$$s=yH^T=(\bar{x}+e)H^T=\bar{x}H^T+eH^T=eH^T, \tag{10.7}$$

which is then used for identifying the erroneous bit. Recall that since a $C(n,k)$ is a linear block code having $n-k$ parity bits, we have $2^{n-k}$ possible $(n-k)$-bit unique syndromes. Consequently, we can identify $2^{n-k}$ possible unique $n$-bit error patterns.

Let us consider a simple 3-bit repetition code, which makes three copies of the intended information bit. More precisely, $k=1$ and $n=3$. It is specified by the following generator matrix:

$$G=\begin{pmatrix}1 & 1 & 1\end{pmatrix}, \tag{10.8}$$

which yields the pair of legitimate codewords [111] and [000] having a minimum distance of 3. At the receiver, a decision may be made on the basis of simple majority logic decision by reading the received bits. For example, if $y=[011]$ is received, then we may conclude that the transmitted bit was 1. Alternatively, we may invoke the PCM-based syndrome decoding. According to Eq. (10.5), the corresponding PCM is given by:

$$H=\begin{pmatrix}1 & 1 & 0\\ 1 & 0 & 1\end{pmatrix}. \tag{10.9}$$

It may be readily seen that we have $yH^T=0$ only for the pair of valid codewords [111] and [000]. For all other received codewords, at least one of the two syndrome elements is 1. For example, when the first bit is corrupted, i.e. if we have $y=[011]$ or [100], then we arrive at $s=[11]$. The look-up table (LUT) for the PCM of Eq. (10.9) is given in Table 10.1, which enlists all the 1-bit errors that may be identified using this syndrome based decoding procedure.

This process of error correction using the generator and parity check matrices is usually preferred due to its compact nature. Generally, a $C(n,k)$ code, which encodes a $k$-bit information message into an $n$-bit codeword, would require $2^k$ legitimate $n$-bit codewords. Thus, it would require a total of $n2^k$ bits to completely specify the code space. By contrast, the aforementioned approach only requires $kn$ bits of the generator matrix. Hence, memory resources are saved exponentially, while encoding and decoding operations are efficiently implemented. These attractive features of classical block linear codes and the associated PCM-based syndrome decoding have led to the development of quantum stabilizer codes.

**Table 10.1** Look-up table for the PCM of Eq. (10.9), which enlists the single-bit errors along with the corresponding syndromes.

| Syndrome ($s$) | Index of error |
|---|---|
| [11] | 1 |
| [10] | 2 |
| [01] | 3 |

## 10.3 Quantum Stabilizer Codes

### 10.3.1 Stabilizer Formalism

Since qubits collapse to classical bits upon measurement [160], this prevents us from directly applying the family of classical error correction techniques for reliable quantum transmission. Inspired by the PCM-based syndrome decoding of classical codes, Gottesman [57, 59] introduced the notion of stabilizer formalism, which facilitates the design of quantum codes from the classical ones. Analogous to Shor's pioneering 9-qubit code [54], the stabilizer formalism circumvents the measurements by observing the error syndromes without reading the actual quantum information. More specifically, quantum stabilizer codes (QSCs) rely on the PCM-based syndrome decoding approach of classical linear block codes for estimating the errors incurred during transmission.

Figure 10.1 shows the general schematic of a quantum communication system relying on a QSC for reliable transmission. An $[n, k]$ QSC[1] encodes the information qubits $|\psi\rangle$ into the coded sequence $|\overline{\psi}\rangle$ with the aid of $(n-k)$ auxiliary (also called ancilla) qubits, which are initialized to the state $|0\rangle$. The noisy sequence $|\hat{\psi}\rangle = \mathcal{P}|\overline{\psi}\rangle$, where $\mathcal{P}$ is the $n$-qubit channel error vector, is received by the receiver (RX), which engages in a three-step process for the sake of recovering the intended transmitted information. More explicitly, RX computes the syndrome of the received sequence $|\hat{\psi}\rangle$ and uses it to estimate the channel error $\tilde{\mathcal{P}}$ with the aid of the classical syndrome decoding. The recovery operator $\mathcal{R}$ then uses the estimated error $\tilde{\mathcal{P}}$ to restore the transmitted coded stream. Finally, the decoder, or more specifically the inverse encoder, processes the recovered coded sequence $|\tilde{\overline{\psi}}\rangle$, yielding the estimated transmitted information qubits $|\tilde{\psi}\rangle$.

*An $[n, k]$ QSC, constructed over a code space $\mathcal{C}$, which maps the information word (logical qubits) $|\psi\rangle \in \mathbb{C}^{2^k}$ onto the codeword (physical qubits) $|\overline{\psi}\rangle \in \mathbb{C}^{2^n}$, where $\mathbb{C}^d$ denotes the d-dimensional Hilbert space, is defined by a set of $(n-k)$ independent commuting n-tuple Pauli operators $g_i$, for $1 \leq i \leq (n-k)$. The corresponding stabilizer group $\mathcal{H}$ contains both $g_i$ and all the products of $g_i$ for $1 \leq i \leq (n-k)$ and forms an Abelian subgroup of $\mathcal{G}_n$. A unique feature of these operators is that they do not change the state of valid codewords, while yielding an eigenvalue of $-1$ for corrupted states.*

Let us now elaborate on this definition of the stabilizer code by considering a simple 3-qubit **bit-flip correcting repetition code**, which is capable of correcting single-qubit bit-flip errors, but no phase flips. Since the laws of quantum mechanics do not permit cloning of the information qubit, we cannot encode $|\psi\rangle$ to $(\psi \otimes \psi \otimes \psi)$. Instead, the 3-qubit bit-flip repetition code entangles two auxiliary qubits with the information qubit such that the basis states $|0\rangle$ and $|1\rangle$ are copied thrice in the superposition of basis states of the resulting 3-qubit codeword, i.e. $|0\rangle$ and $|1\rangle$ are mapped as follows:

$$\begin{aligned} |0\rangle &\rightarrow |\overline{0}\rangle \equiv |000\rangle, \\ |1\rangle &\rightarrow |\overline{1}\rangle \equiv |111\rangle. \end{aligned} \tag{10.10}$$

Consequently, the information word $|\psi\rangle = \alpha|0\rangle + \beta|1\rangle$ is encoded as:

$$\alpha|0\rangle + \beta|1\rangle \rightarrow \alpha|\overline{0}\rangle + \beta|\overline{1}\rangle \equiv \alpha|000\rangle + \beta|111\rangle, \tag{10.11}$$

using the quantum circuit of Figure 10.2. The resultant codeword $|\overline{\psi}\rangle$ is stabilized by the operators $g_1 = \mathbf{ZZI}$ and $g_2 = \mathbf{ZIZ}$. Here the term "stabilize" implies that the valid codewords are not affected by the generators $g_1$ and $g_2$ and yield an eigenvalue of $+1$, as shown here:

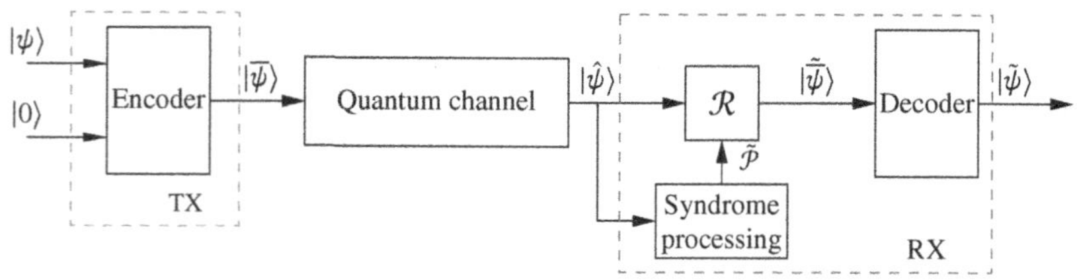


**Figure 10.1** System Model: Quantum communication system relying on a quantum stabilizer code. *Source:* [80]/IEEE.

1 We use round brackets (.) for classical codes, while the square brackets [.] are used for quantum codes.

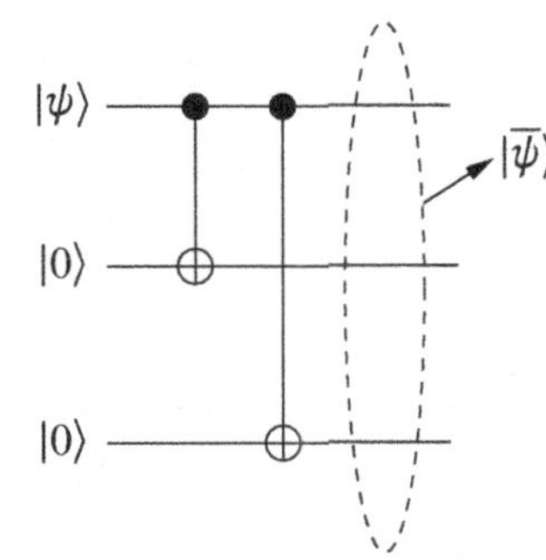


**Figure 10.2** Circuit for 3-qubit bit-flip repetition code. The information qubit $|\psi\rangle$ is encoded into $|\overline{\psi}\rangle$ using two auxiliary qubits, which are entangled with $|\psi\rangle$ using CNOT gates.

$$\begin{aligned} g_1\left[|\overline{\psi}\rangle\right] &= \alpha|000\rangle + \beta|111\rangle \equiv |\overline{\psi}\rangle, \\ g_2\left[|\overline{\psi}\rangle\right] &= \alpha|000\rangle + \beta|111\rangle \equiv |\overline{\psi}\rangle. \end{aligned} \tag{10.12}$$

On the other hand, if a corrupted state $|\hat{\psi}\rangle$ is received, then the stabilizer generators yield an eigenvalue of $-1$, e.g. let $|\hat{\psi}\rangle = |100\rangle + \beta\,|011\rangle$ where $\mathcal{P} = \mathbf{XII}$, then we have:

$$\begin{aligned} g_1\left[|\hat{\psi}\rangle\right] &= -\alpha|100\rangle - \beta|011\rangle \equiv -|\hat{\psi}\rangle, \\ g_2\left[|\hat{\psi}\rangle\right] &= -\alpha|100\rangle - \beta|011\rangle \equiv -|\hat{\psi}\rangle. \end{aligned} \tag{10.13}$$

More specifically, the stabilizer generators have a role similar to the PCM of a classical linear block code. The eigenvalue is $-1$ if the $n$-tuple Pauli error $\mathcal{P}$ acting on the transmitted codeword $|\overline{\psi}\rangle$ anti-commutes with the stabilizer $g_i$ (analogous to $yH^T \neq 0$ in Eq. [10.7]) and it is $+1$ if $\mathcal{P}$ commutes with $g_i$ (analogous to $yH^T = 0$ in Eq. [10.7]). Therefore, we have:

$$g_i\,|\hat{\psi}\rangle = \begin{cases} |\overline{\psi}\rangle, & g_i\mathcal{P} = \mathcal{P}g_i \\ -|\overline{\psi}\rangle, & g_i\mathcal{P} = -\mathcal{P}g_i, \end{cases} \tag{10.14}$$

where $|\hat{\psi}\rangle = \mathcal{P}\,|\overline{\psi}\rangle$. The resultant $\pm 1$ eigenvalue gives the corresponding error syndrome $s$, which is 0 for an eigenvalue of $+1$ and 1 for an eigenvalue of $-1$. This computation of the syndrome using the $\mathbf{Z}$ operators is realized by employing the quantum circuit of Figure 10.3, where the circuit on the left is popular, while the one on the right is the equivalent circuit suitable for implementation [160]. In both circuits of Figure 10.3, the top qubit is the auxiliary qubit used for computing the syndrome, while the bottom qubit is the coded qubit subjected to the $\mathbf{Z}$ operator. The resultant syndromes are listed in Table 10.2 along with the corresponding single-qubit bit-flip errors, eigenvalues, and the location of the single-bit errors, which may be identified using the syndrome decoding approach. Here $X_i$ and $Z_i$ represent the application of $\mathbf{X}$ and $\mathbf{Z}$ gates to the $i$th qubit. An interesting point to note is that $|\overline{\psi}\rangle$, given in Eq. (10.14), is a unique quantum state which can be stabilized by the operators $g_1 = \mathbf{XX}$ and $g_2 = \mathbf{ZZ}$. Hence the quantum states can be completely and unambiguously represented by the stabilizers. Consequently, quantum codes can be easily described in terms of the stabilizers rather than the state vector descriptions [160, p. 454].

A 3-qubit **phase-flip based repetition code** may be constructed using a similar approach. This is because phase errors in the Hadamard basis $\{|+\rangle, |-\rangle\}$ are similar to the bit errors in the computational basis $\{|0\rangle, |1\rangle\}$. More explicitly, the states $|+\rangle$ and $|-\rangle$ are defined as:

$$\begin{aligned} |+\rangle &\equiv \mathbf{H}|0\rangle = \frac{|0\rangle + |1\rangle}{\sqrt{2}}, \\ |-\rangle &\equiv \mathbf{H}|1\rangle = \frac{|0\rangle - |1\rangle}{\sqrt{2}}, \end{aligned} \tag{10.15}$$

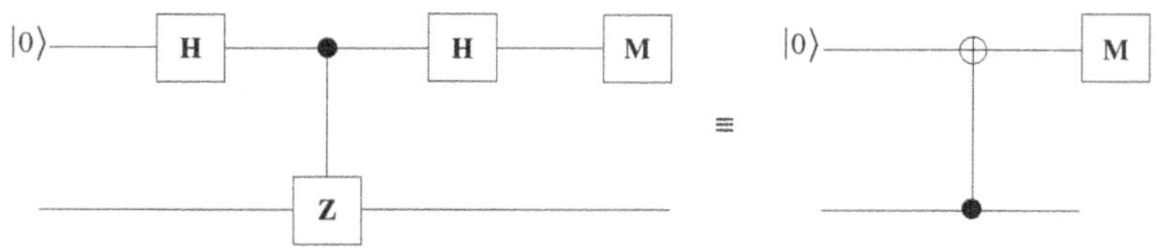


**Figure 10.3** Quantum circuit for measuring the **Z** operator acting on the bottom qubit. *Source*: [160]/Cambridge University Press. The top qubit is the auxiliary qubit used for computing syndrome. The circuit on the left is popular, while the one on the right is suitable for implementation.

**Table 10.2** Single-qubit bit-flip errors along with the corresponding eigenvalues for 3-qubit bit-flip repetition code having $g_1 = \mathbf{ZZI}$ and $g_2 = \mathbf{ZIZ}$.

| $\lvert\hat{\psi}\rangle = \mathscr{P}\lvert\overline{\psi}\rangle$ | $g_1\lvert\hat{\psi}\rangle$ | $g_2\lvert\hat{\psi}\rangle$ | Syndrome (*s*) | Index of error |
|---|---|---|---|---|
| $\alpha\lvert 100\rangle + \beta\lvert 011\rangle$ | −1 | −1 | [11] | 1 |
| $\alpha\lvert 010\rangle + \beta\lvert 101\rangle$ | −1 | +1 | [10] | 2 |
| $\alpha\lvert 001\rangle + \beta\lvert 110\rangle$ | +1 | −1 | [01] | 3 |

where **H** is a single-qubit Hadamard gate, which is given by [160]:

$$\mathbf{H} = \frac{1}{\sqrt{2}}\begin{pmatrix} 1 & 1 \\ 1 & -1 \end{pmatrix}. \tag{10.16}$$

Therefore, Pauli-**Z** gate acting on the states $|+\rangle$ and $|-\rangle$ yields:

$$\begin{aligned} \mathbf{Z}|+\rangle &= |-\rangle, \\ \mathbf{Z}|-\rangle &= |+\rangle, \end{aligned} \tag{10.17}$$

which is similar to the effect of the Pauli-**X** gate on the states $|0\rangle$ and $|1\rangle$, i.e. we have:

$$\begin{aligned} \mathbf{X}|0\rangle &= |1\rangle, \\ \mathbf{X}|1\rangle &= |0\rangle. \end{aligned} \tag{10.18}$$

Consequently, analogous to Eq. (10.10), a 3-qubit phase-flip repetition code encodes $|0\rangle$ and $|1\rangle$ in the Hadamard basis as follows:

$$\begin{aligned} |0\rangle &\rightarrow |\bar{0}\rangle \equiv |+++\rangle, \\ |1\rangle &\rightarrow |\bar{1}\rangle \equiv |---\rangle, \end{aligned} \tag{10.19}$$

for protection against the single-qubit phase errors. Based on Eq. (10.19), $|\psi\rangle$ is encoded as:

$$\alpha|0\rangle + \beta|1\rangle \rightarrow \alpha|\bar{0}\rangle + \beta|\bar{1}\rangle \equiv \alpha|+++\rangle + \beta|---\rangle, \tag{10.20}$$

using the quantum circuit of Figure 10.4, where Hadamard gates are used at the end of the circuit of Figure 10.2 to transform the computational basis into the Hadamard basis. The resultant encoded state of Eq. (10.20) is stabilized by the generators $g_1 = \mathbf{XXI}$ and $g_2 = \mathbf{XIX}$, where the computation of the syndrome using the **X** operators is realized in Figure 10.5. We may also observe in these design examples that the Pauli-**X** operators are used in the stabilizer generators for phase-error (**Z**) correction, while the Pauli-**Z** operators are used for bit-error (**X**) correction.

The overall transition from the classical 3-bit repetition code of Section 10.2 to the quantum repetition code is depicted in Figure 10.6, which can be summarized as follows:

- **Encoder**: In classical codes, the information bit may be cloned (or copied) during the encoding process, e.g. in a 3-bit repetition code. By contrast, this is not permissible in the quantum domain owing to the

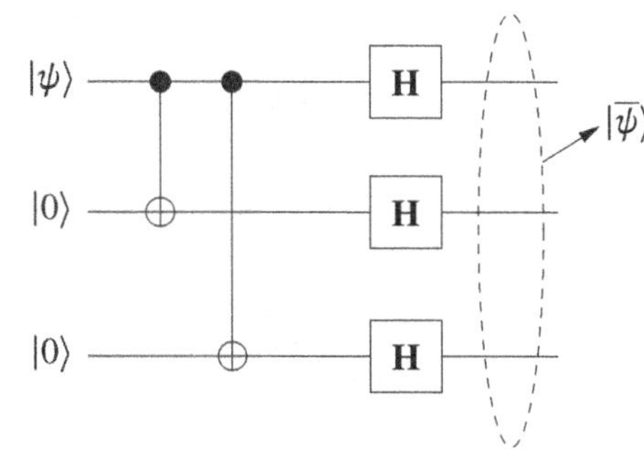


**Figure 10.4** Circuit for 3-qubit phase-flip repetition code. The information qubit $|\psi\rangle$ is encoded into $|\overline{\psi}\rangle$ using two auxiliary qubits, which are entangled with $|\psi\rangle$ using CNOT gates. Finally, the **H**-gate transforms the computational basis into the Hadamard basis for phase-error correction.

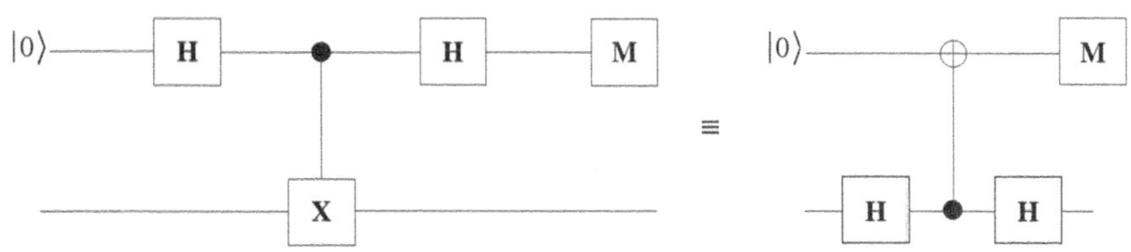


**Figure 10.5** Quantum circuit for measuring the **X** operator acting on the bottom qubit. *Source*: [160]/Cambridge University Press. The top qubit is the auxiliary qubit used for computing syndrome. The circuit on the left is the usual construction, while the one on the right is suitable for implementation.

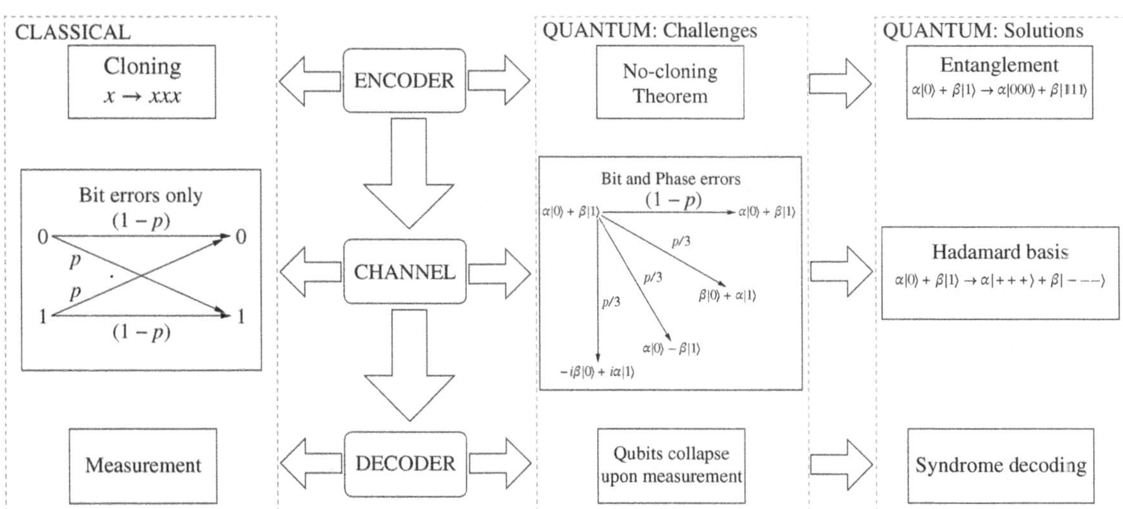


**Figure 10.6** Transition from the classical to quantum codes. *Source*: [83]/IEEE.

no-cloning theorem. Instead, in quantum codes, the information qubit is entangled with the auxiliary qubits as in Eq. (10.10) for the 3-qubit bit-flip repetition code and in Eq. (10.19) for the 3-qubit phase-flip repetition code.

- **Channel:** Only bit errors occur during the transmission over a classical channel, e.g. a binary symmetric channel having a channel crossover probability of $p$. By contrast, a qubit may experience a bit-flip or a phase-flip as well as both, when subjected to the depolarizing channel having a depolarizing probability of $p$. Since phase errors in the Hadamard basis $\{|+\rangle, |-\rangle\}$ are similar to the bit errors in the computational basis $\{|0\rangle, |1\rangle\}$, phase errors may be corrected in the same way as the bit errors by exploiting the Hadamard basis.
- **Decoder:** In classical codes, the received bits are measured during the decoding process, e.g. in a 3-bit repetition code a decision may be made on the basis of majority voting. Unfortunately, the qubits collapse upon measurement. Consequently, quantum codes invoke the classical syndrome decoding approach, which circumvents any observation.

Stabilizer generators $g_i$ constituting the stabilizer group $\mathcal{H}$ must exhibit the following two characteristics:

a. **Any two operators in the stabilizer set must commute** so that the stabilizer operators can be applied simultaneously, i.e. we have:

$$g_1 g_2 |\overline{\psi}\rangle = g_2 g_1 |\overline{\psi}\rangle. \tag{10.21}$$

This is because the stabilizer leaves the codeword unchanged as encapsulated here:

$$g_i |\overline{\psi}\rangle = |\overline{\psi}\rangle. \tag{10.22}$$

Hence, evaluating the left-hand and right-hand sides of Eq. (10.21) gives:

$$g_1 g_2 |\overline{\psi}\rangle = g_1 |\overline{\psi}\rangle = |\overline{\psi}\rangle, \tag{10.23}$$

and

$$g_2 g_1 |\overline{\psi}\rangle = g_2 |\overline{\psi}\rangle = |\overline{\psi}\rangle, \tag{10.24}$$

respectively. This further imposes the constraint that the stabilizers should have an even number of places with different non-identity (i.e. **X**, **Y**, or **Z**) operations. This is derived from the fact that the **X**, **Y**, and **Z** operations anti-commute with one another. More explicitly, it may be readily shown that:

$$\mathbf{XY} = \begin{pmatrix} 0 & 1 \\ 1 & 0 \end{pmatrix} \begin{pmatrix} 0 & -i \\ i & 0 \end{pmatrix} = \begin{pmatrix} i & 0 \\ 0 & -i \end{pmatrix} = i\mathbf{Z}, \tag{10.25}$$

while we have:

$$\mathbf{YX} = \begin{pmatrix} 0 & -i \\ i & 0 \end{pmatrix} \begin{pmatrix} 0 & 1 \\ 1 & 0 \end{pmatrix} = \begin{pmatrix} -i & 0 \\ 0 & i \end{pmatrix} = -i\mathbf{Z}. \tag{10.26}$$

This implies that:

$$\mathbf{XY} = -\mathbf{YX}. \tag{10.27}$$

Similarly, we can readily show that:

$$\begin{aligned} \mathbf{YZ} &= i\mathbf{X}, \quad & \mathbf{ZY} &= -i\mathbf{X} \quad \rightarrow \quad \mathbf{YZ} = -\mathbf{ZY} \\ \mathbf{ZX} &= i\mathbf{Y}, \quad & \mathbf{XZ} &= -i\mathbf{Y} \quad \rightarrow \quad \mathbf{ZX} = -\mathbf{XZ}. \end{aligned} \tag{10.28}$$

Thus, for example the operators **ZZI** and **XYZ** commute, whereas **ZZI** and **YZI** anti-commute.

b. **Generators constituting the stabilizer group $\mathcal{H}$ are closed under multiplication**, i.e. multiplication of the constituent generators $g_i$ yields another generator, which is also part of the stabilizer group $\mathcal{H}$. For example, the full stabilizer group $\mathcal{H}$ of the 3-qubit bit-flip repetition code will also include the operator **IZZ**, which is the product of $g_1$ and $g_2$.

### 10.3.2 Quantum-to-classical Isomorphism

#### 10.3.2.1 Pauli-to-binary Isomorphism

QSCs may be characterized in terms of an equivalent classical PCM notation satisfying the commutativity constraint of stabilizers [67, 285] given in Eq. (10.21). This is achieved by mapping the **I**, **X**, **Y**, and **Z** Pauli operators onto $(\mathbb{F}_2)^2$ as follows:

$$\mathbf{I} \rightarrow (00), \qquad \mathbf{X} \rightarrow (01), \qquad \mathbf{Y} \rightarrow (11), \qquad \mathbf{Z} \rightarrow (10), \tag{10.29}$$

where a binary 1 at the first index represents a **Z** operator, while a binary 1 at the second index represents an **X** operator. More explicitly, the $(n-k)$ stabilizers of an $[n, k]$ stabilizer code constitute the rows of the binary

PCM $H$, which can be represented as a concatenation of a pair of $(n-k)\times n$ binary matrices $H_z$ and $H_x$ based on Eq. (10.29), as illustrated here:

$$H=(H_z|H_x). \tag{10.30}$$

Each row of $H$ corresponds to a stabilizer of $\mathcal{H}$, so that the $i$th column of $H_z$ and $H_x$ corresponds to the $i$th qubit and a binary 1 at these locations represents a **Z** and **X** Pauli operator, respectively, in the corresponding stabilizer. For the 3-qubit bit-flip repetition code, which can only correct bit-flip errors, the PCM $H$ is given by:

$$H=\left(\begin{array}{ccc|ccc}1&1&0&0&0&0\\1&0&1&0&0&0\end{array}\right). \tag{10.31}$$

It must be pointed out here that $H_z$ of Eq. (10.31) is the same as the $H$ of the classical repetition code of Eq. (10.9), yielding the same syndrome patterns in Tables 10.1 and 10.2.

Let us now elaborate further on the process by considering Shor's [9, 1] code, which consists of the Pauli-**Z** as well as the Pauli-**X** operators. The corresponding stabilizer generators are given in Table 10.3. They can be mapped onto the binary matrix $H$ as follows:

$$H=\left(\begin{array}{ccccccccc|ccccccccc}1&1&0&0&0&0&0&0&0&0&0&0&0&0&0&0&0&0\\0&1&1&0&0&0&0&0&0&0&0&0&0&0&0&0&0&0\\0&0&0&1&1&0&0&0&0&0&0&0&0&0&0&0&0&0\\0&0&0&0&1&1&0&0&0&0&0&0&0&0&0&0&0&0\\0&0&0&0&0&0&1&1&0&0&0&0&0&0&0&0&0&0\\0&0&0&0&0&0&0&1&1&0&0&0&0&0&0&0&0&0\\0&0&0&0&0&0&0&0&0&1&1&1&1&1&1&0&0&0\\0&0&0&0&0&0&0&0&0&0&0&0&1&1&1&1&1&1\end{array}\right). \tag{10.32}$$

Given the matrix notation of Eq. (10.30), the multiplication of Pauli operators is transformed into the bit-wise addition of the equivalent binary representation. For example, multiplying the set of Pauli operators $\{\mathbf{I},\mathbf{X},\mathbf{Z},\mathbf{Y}\}$ with Pauli-**X** is equivalent to the second column of Table 10.4, when the Pauli operators are mapped onto $(\mathbb{F}_2)^2$ according to Eq. (10.29). Furthermore, the commutative property of stabilizers given in Eq. (10.21) is transformed into the orthogonality of rows with respect to the symplectic product (also referred to as a twisted product). If row $i$ is $H_i=(H_{z_i},H_{x_i})$, where $H_{z_i}$ and $H_{x_i}$ are the binary strings for **Z** and **X** respectively, then the symplectic product of rows $i$ and $i'$ is given by,

**Table 10.3** Stabilizers of the 9-qubit Shor code.

| | Stabilizer |
|---|---|
| $g_1$ | ZZIIIIIII |
| $g_2$ | IZZIIIIII |
| $g_3$ | IIIZZIIII |
| $g_4$ | IIIIZZIII |
| $g_5$ | IIIIIIZZI |
| $g_6$ | IIIIIIIZZ |
| $g_7$ | XXXXXXIII |
| $g_8$ | IIIXXXXXX |

**Table 10.4** $(\mathbb{F}_2)^2$ addition.

| + | 00 | 01 | 10 | 11 |
|---|---|---|---|---|
| 00 | 00 | 01 | 10 | 11 |
| 01 | 01 | 00 | 11 | 10 |
| 10 | 10 | 11 | 00 | 01 |
| 11 | 11 | 10 | 01 | 00 |

$$H_i \star H_{i'} = (H_{z_i} \cdot H_{x_{i'}} + H_{z_{i'}} \cdot H_{x_i}) \bmod 2. \tag{10.33}$$

This symplectic product is zero if there are even number of places where the non-identity operators (**X**, **Y**, or **Z**) in the row $i$ and $i'$ are different; thus meeting the commutativity requirement. In other words, if $H$ is written as $H = (H_z|H_x)$, then the symplectic product is satisfied for all the rows only if we have:

$$H_z H_x^T + H_x H_z^T = 0 \bmod 2, \tag{10.34}$$

which may be readily verified for the $H$ of Eq. (10.32). Consequently, any classical binary codes satisfying Eq. (10.34) may be used for constructing QSCs. A special class of these stabilizer codes is constituted by the family of Calderbank–Shor–Steane (CSS) codes, which are defined as follows:

*An $[n, k_1 - k_2]$ CSS code, which is capable of correcting $(d-1)/2$ bit-flips as well as phase-flips, can be constructed from classical linear block codes $C_1(n, k_1)$ and $C_2(n, k_2)$, if $C_2 \subset C_1$ and both $C_1$ as well as the dual of $C_2$, i.e. $C_2^{\perp}$, have a minimum Hamming distance d.*

In CSS construction, the PCM $H_z'$ of $C_1$ is used for correcting bit-flips, while the PCM $H_x'$ of $C_2^{\perp}$ is used for phase-flip correction. Consequently, the PCM of the resultant CSS code assumes the following form:

$$H = \left(\begin{array}{c|c} H_z' & \mathbf{0} \\ \mathbf{0} & H_x' \end{array}\right), \tag{10.35}$$

where we have $H_z = \begin{pmatrix} H_z' \\ \mathbf{0} \end{pmatrix}$, $H_x = \begin{pmatrix} \mathbf{0} \\ H_x' \end{pmatrix}$, with $H_z'$ and $H_x'$ being $(n-k_1) \times n$ and $k_2 \times n$ binary matrices, respectively. Furthermore, since $C_2 \subset C_1$, the symplectic condition of Eq. (10.34) is reduced to $H_z' H_x'^T = 0$. In this scenario, $(n - k_1 + k_2)$ stabilizers are applied to $n$ qubits. Therefore, the resultant quantum code encodes $(k_1 - k_2)$ information qubits into $n$ qubits. Furthermore, if $H_z' = H_x'$, the resultant structure is termed as a dual-containing (or self-orthogonal) code because $H_z' H_z'^T = 0$, which is equivalent to $C_1^{\perp} \subset C_1$. Hence, the stabilizer codes may be subdivided into various code structures based on the binary matrix $H$ of Eq. (10.30), as summarized in Figure 10.7.

Let us consider the classical (7, 4) Hamming code, whose PCM is given by:

$$H = \begin{pmatrix} 1 & 1 & 0 & 1 & 1 & 0 & 0 \\ 1 & 0 & 1 & 1 & 0 & 1 & 0 \\ 0 & 1 & 1 & 1 & 0 & 0 & 1 \end{pmatrix}. \tag{10.36}$$

Since $H$ of Eq. (10.36) yields $HH^T = 0$, it is used for constructing the dual-containing rate-1/7 Steane code [55]. The corresponding stabilizer generators are listed in Table 10.5.

Based on the Pauli-to-binary isomorphism encapsulated in Eq. (10.29), a Pauli error $\mathcal{P} \in \mathcal{G}_n$ experienced by an $n$-qubit block subjected to a depolarizing channel can be modeled by an effective error-vector $P$, which is a binary vector of length $2n$. The effective error vector $P$ may be represented as $P = (P_z, P_x)$, where both $P_z$ and $P_x$ are $n$-bit long and represent **Z** and **X** errors, respectively, as seen in Figure 10.8. This implies that an **X** error imposed on the $t$th qubit will yield a 0 and a 1 at the $t$th and $(n+t)$th index of $P$, respectively. Similarly, a **Z** error imposed on

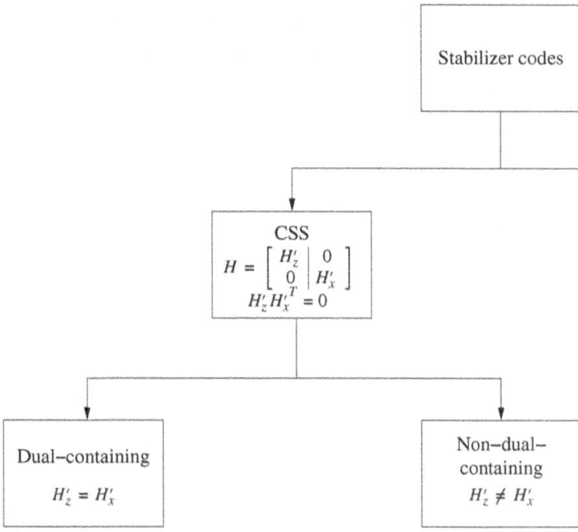


**Figure 10.7** Family of stabilizer codes. *Source*: [83]/IEEE.

**Table 10.5** Stabilizers for the Steane code.

| | Stabilizer |
|---|---|
| $g_1$ | ZZIZZII |
| $g_2$ | ZIZZIZI |
| $g_3$ | IZZZIIZ |
| $g_4$ | XXIXXII |
| $g_5$ | XIXXIXI |
| $g_6$ | IXXXIIX |

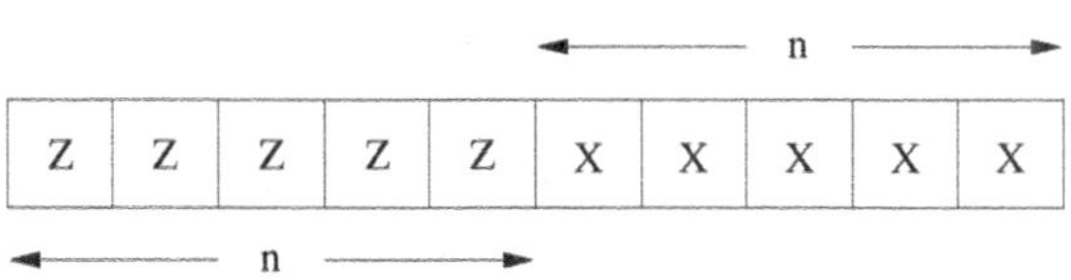


**Figure 10.8** Effective classical error $P$ corresponding to the error $\mathcal{P}$ imposed on an $n$-qubit frame. *Source*: [83]/IEEE.

the $t$th qubit will give a 1 and a 0 at the $t$th and $(n + t)$th index of $P$, respectively, while a **Y** error on the $t$th qubit will result in a 1 at both the $t$th as well as $(n + t)$th index of $P$. The resultant quantum-domain syndrome is given by the symplectic product of $H$ and $P$, which is formulated as follows:

$$s = H \star P^T = \left(H_z P_x^T + H_x P_z^T\right) \bmod 2, \tag{10.37}$$

where the Pauli-**X** operator is used for correcting **Z** errors, while the Pauli-**Z** operator is used for correcting **X** errors, as previously discussed in the context of 3-qubit bit-flip and phase-flip repetition codes. The resultant syndrome has either a value of 0 or 1. Thus, the quantum-domain syndrome is equivalent to the classical-domain binary syndrome and a basic quantum-domain decoding procedure is similar to the syndrome-based decoding of the equivalent classical code [67]. However, due to the degenerate nature of quantum codes (discussed in Section 10.3.3), quantum decoding aims for finding the most likely error coset, while the classical syndrome decoding finds the most likely error.

Hence, an $[n,k]$ QSC associated with $(n-k)$ stabilizers can be effectively modeled using an $(n-k)\times 2n$-element classical PCM satisfying Eq. (10.34). The coding rate of the equivalent classical code $R_c$ can be determined as follows:

$$\begin{aligned} R_c &= \frac{2n-(n-k)}{2n} \\ &= \frac{n+k}{2n} \\ &= \frac{1}{2}\left(1+\frac{k}{n}\right) \\ &= \frac{1}{2}(1+R_Q), \end{aligned} \tag{10.38}$$

where $R_Q$ is its quantum coding rate. Using Eq. (10.38), the coding rate of the classical equivalent of Shor's rate-1/9 quantum code is 5/9, while that of the Steane code is 4/7.

#### 10.3.2.2 Pauli-to-quaternary Isomorphism Revisited

Since the **I**, **X**, **Y**, and **Z** Pauli operators have the equivalent 2-bit representation of Eq. (10.29), they may also be expressed in the Galois Field GF(4) by the equivalent 4-ary symbols. More specifically, the Pauli-to-quaternary isomorphism may be formulated as:

$$\mathbf{I}\rightarrow 0,\quad \mathbf{X}\rightarrow 1,\quad \mathbf{Y}\rightarrow \overline{\omega},\quad \mathbf{Z}\rightarrow \omega, \tag{10.39}$$

where 0, 1, $\omega$, and $\overline{\omega}$ are the elements of GF(4), which conform to the additive and multiplicative rules of Tables 10.6 and 10.7[2], respectively. According to this isomorphism, the multiplication of Pauli operators is transformed to the addition of the corresponding elements in GF(4), while the commutativity (symplectic product) criterion is mapped onto the trace[3] inner product [59]. For example, multiplying the set of Pauli operators $\{\mathbf{I},\mathbf{X},\mathbf{Z},\mathbf{Y}\}$ with Pauli-**X** is equivalent to the second column of Table 10.6. On the other hand, the commutative relationship between $\hat{A}$ and $\hat{B}$ in GF(4) is computed using the trace inner product as follows[4]:

$$\mathrm{Tr}\langle\hat{A},\hat{B}\rangle = \mathrm{Tr}(\hat{A}\times\overline{\hat{B}}) = 0, \tag{10.40}$$

**Table 10.6** GF(4) addition.

| + | **0** | **1** | $\omega$ | $\overline{\omega}$ |
|---|---|---|---|---|
| 0 | 0 | 1 | $\omega$ | $\overline{\omega}$ |
| 1 | 1 | 0 | $\overline{\omega}$ | $\omega$ |
| $\omega$ | $\omega$ | $\overline{\omega}$ | 0 | 1 |
| $\overline{\omega}$ | $\overline{\omega}$ | $\omega$ | 1 | 0 |

**Table 10.7** GF(4) multiplication.

| × | **0** | **1** | $\omega$ | $\overline{\omega}$ |
|---|---|---|---|---|
| 0 | 0 | 0 | 0 | 0 |
| 1 | 0 | 1 | $\omega$ | $\overline{\omega}$ |
| $\omega$ | 0 | $\omega$ | $\overline{\omega}$ | 1 |
| $\overline{\omega}$ | 0 | $\overline{\omega}$ | 1 | $\omega$ |

2 The addition and multiplication rules for GF($p$), having a prime $p$, are the same as the modulo $p$ addition and multiplication, while the rules for GF($p^m$), having $m>1$, do not follow the conventional rules for modulo $p^m$ addition and multiplication. For example, the addition of the elements of GF(4) is equivalent to the bitwise modulo 2 addition of the equivalent 2-bit patterns.

3 In GF(4), the trace operator maps $x$ to $(x+\overline{x})$. where $\overline{x}$ is the conjugate of $x$ [60].

4 We denote GF(4) variables with a ˆ on top, e.g. $\hat{x}$.

**Table 10.8** GF(4) Hermitian inner product.

| $\langle , \rangle$ | **0** | **1** | $\omega$ | $\overline{\omega}$ |
|---|---|---|---|---|
| 0 | 0 | 0 | 0 | 0 |
| 1 | 0 | 1 | $\omega$ | $\overline{\omega}$ |
| $\omega$ | 0 | $\overline{\omega}$ | 1 | $\omega$ |
| $\overline{\omega}$ | 0 | $\omega$ | $\overline{\omega}$ | 1 |

**Table 10.9** GF(4) trace inner product.

| tr$\langle , \rangle$ | **0** | **1** | $\omega$ | $\overline{\omega}$ |
|---|---|---|---|---|
| 0 | 0 | 0 | 0 | 0 |
| 1 | 0 | 0 | 1 | 1 |
| $\omega$ | 0 | 1 | 0 | 1 |
| $\overline{\omega}$ | 0 | 1 | 1 | 0 |

where $\langle , \rangle$ represents the Hermitian inner product and $\overline{\hat{B}}$ denotes the conjugate[5] of $\hat{B}$. Moreover, $\mathrm{Tr}(0) = \mathrm{Tr}(1) = 0$, while $\mathrm{Tr}(\omega) = \mathrm{Tr}(\overline{\omega}) = 1$. Explicitly, both the Hermitian inner product and the trace inner product between the elements of GF(4) are tabulated in Tables 10.8 and 10.9, respectively.

Based on Eq. (10.40), the symplectic product of Eq. (10.33) is transformed into the trace inner product in GF(4). For example, the symplectic product of the $i$th and $i'$th row of $\hat{H}$, which is defined in GF(4), is formulated as:

$$\hat{H}_i \star \hat{H}_{i'} = \mathrm{Tr}\langle \hat{H}_i, \hat{H}_{i'} \rangle = \mathrm{Tr}\left( \sum_{t=1}^{n} \hat{H}_{it} \times \overline{\hat{H}}_{i't} \right), \tag{10.41}$$

where $\hat{H}_{it}$ denotes the element in the $i$th row and $t$th column of $\hat{H}$.

Let us now prove the equivalence of Eqs. (10.33) and (10.41). Given $H_i = (H_{z_i}, H_{x_i})$ and the mapping of Eq. (10.39), $\hat{H}_i$ may be expressed as:

$$\hat{H}_i = \omega H_{z_i} + H_{x_i}. \tag{10.42}$$

Substituting Eq. (10.42) into Eq. (10.41) yields:

$$\begin{aligned} \hat{H}_i \star \hat{H}_{i'} &= \mathrm{Tr}\left\langle (\omega H_{z_i} + H_{x_i}), (\omega H_{z_{i'}} + H_{x_{i'}}) \right\rangle \\ &= \mathrm{Tr}\left( (\omega H_{z_i} + H_{x_i})(\overline{\omega} H_{z_{i'}} + H_{x_{i'}}) \right) \\ &= \mathrm{Tr}\left( H_{z_i} H_{z_{i'}} + \omega H_{z_i} H_{x_{i'}} + \overline{\omega} H_{x_i} H_{z_{i'}} + H_{x_i} H_{x_{i'}} \right). \end{aligned} \tag{10.43}$$

Since $\mathrm{Tr}(1) = 0$ and $\mathrm{Tr}(\omega) = \mathrm{Tr}(\overline{\omega}) = 1$, Eq. (10.43) reduces to:

$$\hat{H}_i \star \hat{H}_{i'} = H_{z_i} H_{x_{i'}} + H_{x_i} H_{z_{i'}}, \tag{10.44}$$

which is the same as Eq. (10.33). Consequently, analogous to Eq. (10.37), the syndrome in the quaternary domain is computed as:

$$s_i = \mathrm{Tr}(\hat{s}_i) = \mathrm{Tr}\left( \sum_{t=1}^{n} \hat{H}_{it} \times \overline{\hat{P}}_t \right), \tag{10.45}$$

where $s_i$ is the syndrome corresponding to the $i$th row of $\hat{H}$ and $\hat{P}_t$ is the $t$th element of $\hat{P}$, which represents the error inflicted on the $t$th qubit.

---

5 In GF(4), the conjugate operation is defined as $\overline{x} = x^2$ [60]. Consequently, conjugation swaps the elements $\omega$ and $\overline{\omega}$, while leaving 0 and 1 intact.

Any arbitrary classical quaternary linear code, which is self-orthogonal with respect to the trace inner product of Eq. (10.41), can be used for constructing a QSC. Since a quaternary linear code is closed under multiplication by the elements of GF(4), this condition reduces to satisfying the Hermitian inner product, rather than the trace inner product [60]. This can be proved as follows.

Let $C$ be a classical linear code in GF(4) having codewords $u$ and $v$. Furthermore, let us assume that:

$$\langle u, v\rangle = \alpha + \beta\omega. \tag{10.46}$$

For the sake of satisfying the symplectic product, we must have:

$$\mathrm{Tr}\langle u, v\rangle = 0. \tag{10.47}$$

Since $\mathrm{Tr}(\omega) = 1$, Eq. (10.47) is only valid, when $\beta$ is zero in Eq. (10.46). Furthermore, since the code $C$ is GF(4)-linear, Eq. (10.47) leads to:

$$\mathrm{Tr}\langle u, \overline{\omega}v\rangle = 0, \tag{10.48}$$

which in turn implies that $\alpha$ should also be zero in Eq. (10.46). Hence, for a classical GF(4)-linear code, the Hermitian inner product of Eq. (10.46) must be zero when the trace inner product of Eq. (10.47) is zero. Based on this notion, Calderbank, Rains, Shor, and Sloane proposed [60]:

*An [n,k] QSC, which is capable of correcting $(d-1)/2$ bit-flips as well as phase-flips, can be constructed in the quaternary domain from a classical self-orthogonal (under the Hermitian inner product) GF(4)-linear block code $C(n,(n-k)/2)$, if the orthogonal code $C^{\perp}(n,(n+k)/2)$ has a minimum Hamming distance d.*

The PCM of the resultant QSC is characterized as:

$$\hat{H} = \begin{pmatrix} \hat{H}_c \\ \omega\hat{H}_c \end{pmatrix}, \tag{10.49}$$

where $\hat{H}_c$ is the PCM of the orthogonal code $C^{\perp}(n,(n+k)/2)$. For example, there exists a classical self-orthogonal GF(4)-linear code $C(5,2)$, whose orthogonal code $C^{\perp}(5,3)$ is a Hamming code having the PCM $\hat{H}_c$ given by [119]:

$$\hat{H}_c = \begin{pmatrix} 0 & \overline{\omega} & \omega & \omega & \overline{\omega} \\ \overline{\omega} & 0 & \overline{\omega} & \omega & \omega \end{pmatrix}. \tag{10.50}$$

Consequently, the (5, 1) quantum Hamming code can be constructed as:

$$\hat{H} = \begin{pmatrix} 0 & \overline{\omega} & \omega & \omega & \overline{\omega} \\ \overline{\omega} & 0 & \overline{\omega} & \omega & \omega \\ 0 & 1 & \overline{\omega} & \overline{\omega} & 1 \\ 1 & 0 & 1 & \overline{\omega} & \overline{\omega} \end{pmatrix}. \tag{10.51}$$

Based on the Pauli-to-GF(4) mapping of Eq. (10.39), $\hat{H}$ is mapped onto the stabilizer generators listed in Table 10.10.

Hence, a Pauli operator may be expressed in terms of the equivalent binary or quaternary representation, which is summarized in Table 10.11. This in turn facilitates the design of quantum codes from the known classical codes.

### 10.3.3 Classification of Quantum Errors

The error set of a classical linear block code $C$ having a PCM $H$ can be categorized as:

(a) **Detected Error Patterns:** These error patterns yield a nontrivial syndrome, i.e. $eH^T \neq 0$, which may be corrected by the code.

**Table 10.10** Stabilizers for 5-qubit Hamming code.

| | Stabilizer |
|---|---|
| $g_1$ | IYZZY |
| $g_2$ | YIYZZ |
| $g_3$ | IXYYX |
| $g_4$ | XIXYY |

**Table 10.11** Quantum-to-classical isomorphism.

| Pauli | $(\mathbb{F}_2)^2$ | GF(4) |
|---|---|---|
| **I** | 00 | 0 |
| **X** | 01 | 1 |
| **Y** | 11 | $\bar{\omega}$ |
| **Z** | 10 | $\omega$ |
| Multiplication | Bit-wise addition | Addition |
| Commutativity | Symplectic product | Trace inner product |

**(b) Undetected Error Patterns:** This set of error patterns results in a trivial syndrome, i.e. $eH^T = 0$, which cannot be detected by the code. More specifically, an undetected error maps the transmitted codeword onto another valid codeword. Since the resultant codeword still lies in the code space $C$, it does not trigger a nonzero syndrome. These error patterns are attributed to the small minimum distance of the code.

Analogous to the classical detected error patterns, detected quantum-domain error patterns anti-commute with at least one of the stabilizer generators, which results in a nontrivial syndrome. Similarly, the undetected quantum-domain error patterns commute with all the stabilizer generators, yielding an all-zero syndrome. This commuting set of error patterns is also known as the centralizer (or normalizer) of the stabilizer code having the stabilizer group $\mathcal{H}$, which is denoted as $C(\mathcal{H})$ (or $N(\mathcal{H})$). In particular, the centralizer of an $[n, k]$ QSC is a dual subspace consisting of $n$-tuple Pauli errors $\mathcal{P} \in \mathcal{G}_n$, which are orthogonal to all the stabilizers of the stabilizer group $\mathcal{H}$. Furthermore, since the $\mathcal{H}$ is itself an Abelian group consisting of mutually orthogonal generators, it is contained in the centralizer, i.e. we have $\mathcal{H} \subset N(\mathcal{H})$. Recall from Section 10.3.1 that the stabilizer generators do not affect the state of valid codewords. This in turn implies that errors which belong to the stabilizer group – i.e. for which we have $\mathcal{P} \in \mathcal{H}$ – do not corrupt the transmitted codewords and therefore may be classified as harmless undetected error patterns. This class of errors does not have any classical counterpart. By contrast, those error patterns, which lie in the subspace $N(\mathcal{H}) \setminus \mathcal{H}$, are the harmful undetected errors, which map one valid codeword onto another. Hence, as depicted in Figure 10.9, quantum error patterns can be classified as follows:

**(a) Detected Errors Patterns:** These error patterns fall outside the normalizer subspace, i.e. they satisfy $\mathcal{P} \in \mathcal{G}_n \setminus N(\mathcal{H})$.
**(b) Harmful Undetected Error Patterns:** This set of error patterns is defined as $N(\mathcal{S}) \setminus \mathcal{H}$.
**(c) Harmless Undetected Errors Patterns:** These error patterns fall in the stabilizer group $\mathcal{H}$.

The set of harmless undetected error patterns gives quantum codes the intrinsic property of "degeneracy" [124]. More explicitly, Pauli errors which differ only by the elements of the stabilizer group have the same impact on all the codewords and therefore can be corrected by the same recovery operations. For example, the errors $\mathcal{P}$ and $\mathcal{P}' = g_i\mathcal{P}$ have the same impact on the transmitted codeword, because we have:

$$\mathcal{P}'[|\overline{\psi}\rangle] = g_i\mathcal{P}[|\overline{\psi}\rangle] = \mathcal{P}g_i[|\overline{\psi}\rangle]. \tag{10.52}$$

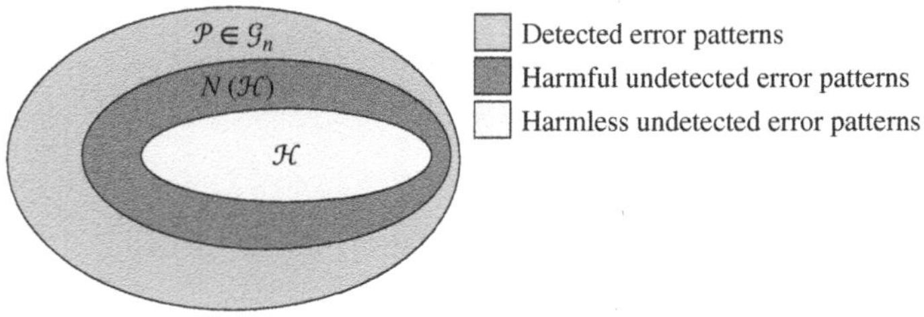


**Figure 10.9** Error pattern classification for stabilizer codes. *Source:* [80]/IEEE.

Since $g_i[|\overline{\psi}\rangle] = |\overline{\psi}\rangle$, we get:

$$\mathcal{P}'[|\overline{\psi}\rangle] = \mathcal{P}[|\overline{\psi}\rangle]. \tag{10.53}$$

Therefore, degenerate errors can be corrected by the same recovery operation. Getting back to our example of the 3-qubit bit-flip repetition code of Section 10.3.1, let $\mathcal{P} = \mathbf{IIX}$ and $\mathcal{P}' = g_1\mathcal{P} = \mathbf{ZZX}$. Both $\mathcal{P}$ and $\mathcal{P}'$ corrupt the transmitted codeword of Eq. (10.11) to $\alpha\,|001\rangle + \beta\,|110\rangle$. Consequently, $\mathcal{P}$ and $\mathcal{P}'$ do not have to be differentiated and are therefore classified as degenerate errors. Thus, degeneracy allows a quantum code to convey more information than the underlying classical design.

## 10.4 Quantum Convolutional Codes

Quantum convolutional codes (QCCs) are derived from the corresponding classical convolutional codes using stabilizer formalism. This is based on the equivalence between the classical convolutional codes (CCC) and the classical linear block codes having semi-infinite length, which is subsequently derived [182].

Consider a $(2, 1, m)$ classical convolutional code having the generators of

$$\begin{aligned} g^{(0)} &= (g_0^{(0)}, g_1^{(0)}, \ldots, g_m^{(0)}), \\ g^{(1)} &= (g_0^{(1)}, g_1^{(1)}, \ldots, g_m^{(1)}). \end{aligned} \tag{10.54}$$

For an input sequence $[u = (u_0, u_1, u_2, \ldots)]$, the output sequences $[v^{(0)} = (v_0^{(0)}, v_1^{(0)}, v_2^{(0)}, \ldots)]$ and $[v^{(1)} = (v_0^{(1)}, v_1^{(1)}, v_2^{(1)}, \ldots)]$ are given as follows:

$$\begin{aligned} v^{(0)} &= u \circledast g^{(0)}, \\ v^{(1)} &= u \circledast g^{(1)}, \end{aligned} \tag{10.55}$$

where $\circledast$ denotes discrete convolution (modulo 2), which implies that for all $l \geq 0$ we have:

$$v_l^{(j)} = \sum_{i=0}^{m} u_{l-i} g_i^{(j)} = u_l g_0^{(j)} + u_{l-1} g_1^{(j)} + \cdots + u_{l-m} g_m^{(j)}, \tag{10.56}$$

where $j = 0, 1$, and $u_{l-i} \triangleq 0$ for all $l < i$. The pair of encoded sequences are multiplexed into a single codeword sequence $v$ given by:

$$v = (v_0^{(0)}, v_0^{(1)}, v_1^{(0)}, v_1^{(1)}, v_2^{(0)}, v_2^{(1)}, \ldots) \tag{10.57}$$

This encoding process can also be represented in matrix notation by interlacing the generators $g^{(0)}$ and $g^{(1)}$ and arranging them in matrix form as follows,[6]

6 Blank spaces in the matrix indicate zeros.

$$G=\begin{pmatrix} g_0^{(0)(1)} & g_1^{(0)(1)} & \cdots & g_m^{(0)(1)} & & & \\ & g_0^{(0)(1)} & g_1^{(0)(1)} & \cdots & g_m^{(0)(1)} & & \\ & & g_0^{(0)(1)} & g_1^{(0)(1)} & \cdots & g_m^{(0)(1)} & \\ & & \ddots & & \cdots & & \ddots \end{pmatrix}, \tag{10.58}$$

where $g_i^{(0)(1)} \triangleq \left(g_i^{(0)} g_i^{(1)}\right)$. The encoding operation of Eq. (10.56) is therefore equivalent to,

$$v = uG. \tag{10.59}$$

Since the information sequence $u$ is of arbitrary length, $G$ is semi-infinite. Furthermore, each row of $G$ is identical to the previous row, but is shifted to the right by two places (since $n=2$). In practice, $u$ has a finite length $N$. Therefore, $G$ has $N$ rows and $2(m+N)$ columns for CCC(2, 1, $m$). For CCC($n$, $k$, $m$), $G$ can be generalized as follows:

$$G=\begin{pmatrix} G_0 & G_1 & \cdots & G_m & & & \\ & G_0 & G_1 & \cdots & G_m & & \\ & & G_0 & G_1 & \cdots & G_m & \\ & & \ddots & & \cdots & & \ddots \end{pmatrix}, \tag{10.60}$$

where $G_l$ is a ($k$ x $n$) submatrix with entries,

$$G_l=\begin{pmatrix} g_{1,l}^{(0)} & g_{1,l}^{(1)} & \cdots & g_{1,l}^{(n-1)} \\ g_{2,l}^{(0)} & g_{2,l}^{(1)} & \cdots & g_{2,l}^{(n-1)} \\ \vdots & \vdots & & \vdots \\ g_{k,l}^{(0)} & g_{k,l}^{(1)} & \cdots & g_{k,l}^{(n-1)} \end{pmatrix}. \tag{10.61}$$

The corresponding PCM $H$ can be represented as a semi-infinite matrix consisting of submatrices $H_l$ with dimensions of $(n-k)\times n$. For a convolutional code having $m$ memory elements, $H$ is given by:

$$H=\begin{pmatrix} H_0 & & & & & \\ H_1 & H_0 & & & & \\ H_2 & H_1 & H_0 & & & \\ \vdots & \vdots & \vdots & & & \\ H_m & H_{m-1} & H_{m-2} & \cdots & H_0 & \\ & H_m & H_{m-1} & H_{m-2} & \cdots & H_0 \\ & & \vdots & \vdots & & \vdots \end{pmatrix}. \tag{10.62}$$

Therefore, a CCC can be represented as a linear block code with semi-infinite block length. Furthermore, if each row of the submatrices $H_l$ is considered as a single block and $h_{j,i}$ is the $i$th row of the $j$th block, then $H$ has a block-band structure after the first $m$ blocks, whereby the successive blocks are time-shifted versions of the first block ($j=0$) and the adjacent blocks have an overlap of $m$ submatrices. This has been depicted in Figure 10.10 and can be mathematically represented as follows:

$$h_{j,i} = [\mathbf{0}^{j\times n}, h_{0,i}],\ 1 \le i \le (n-k),\ 0 \le j, \tag{10.63}$$

where $\mathbf{0}^{j\times n}$ is a row-vector with $(j\times n)$ zeros.

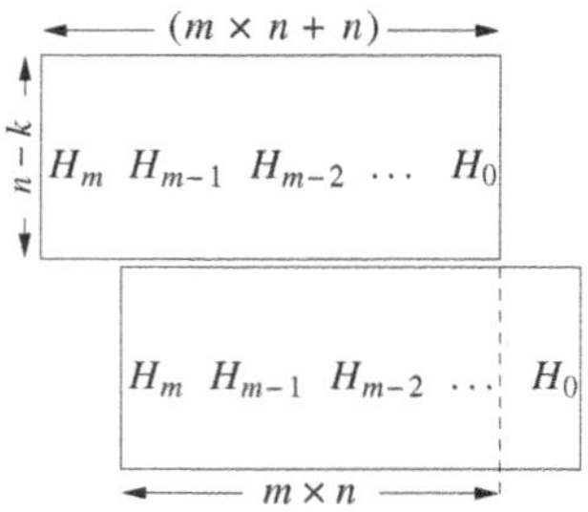


**Figure 10.10** Block-band structure of the semi-infinite classical PCM *H*. *Source*: [83]/IEEE.

As discussed in Section 10.3.2, the rows of a classical PCM correspond to the stabilizers of a quantum code. Hence, the quantum stabilizer group $\mathcal{H}$ of an $[n, k, m]$ stabilizer convolutional code is given by [116]:

$$\mathcal{H} = sp\{g_{j,i} = I^{\otimes jn} \otimes g_{0,i}\},\ 1 \leq i \leq (n-k),\ 0 \leq j, \tag{10.64}$$

where $g_{j,i}$ is the $i$th stabilizer of the $j$th block of the stabilizer group $\mathcal{H}$. Furthermore, $sp$ represents a symplectic group, thus implying that all the stabilizers $g_{j,i}$ must be independent and must commute with each other.

As proposed by Forney in [118, 119], CSS-type QCCs can be derived from the classical self-orthogonal binary convolution codes. Let us consider the rate 1/3 QCC of [118, 119], which is constructed from a binary rate-1/3 CCC with generators:

$$G = \left(\begin{array}{ccc|ccc|ccc|ccc|c} 1 & 1 & 1 & 1 & 0 & 0 & 1 & 1 & 0 & 0 & 0 & 0 & \cdots \\ 0 & 0 & 0 & 1 & 1 & 1 & 1 & 0 & 0 & 1 & 1 & 0 & \cdots \\ & & & & \cdots & & & & & & & & \end{array}\right). \tag{10.65}$$

In $D$-transform notation, these generators are represented as $(1 + D + D^2, 1 + D^2, 1)$. Each generator is orthogonal to all other generators under the binary inner product, making it a self-orthogonal code. Moreover, the dual $C^{\perp}$ has the capability of correcting 1 bit. Therefore, based on the CSS construction, the basic stabilizers of the corresponding single-error correcting [3, 1] QCC are as follows:

$$g_{0,1} = (\mathbf{XXX}, \mathbf{XII}, \mathbf{XXI}), \tag{10.66}$$

$$g_{0,2} = (\mathbf{ZZZ}, \mathbf{ZII}, \mathbf{ZZI}). \tag{10.67}$$

Other stabilizers of $\mathcal{H}$ are the time-shifted versions of these basic stabilizers as depicted in Eq. (10.64).

Let us further consider a non-CSS QCC construction given by Forney in [118, 119]. It is derived from the classical self-orthogonal rate-1/3 quaternary ($\mathbb{F}_4$) convolutional code $C$ having generators $(1 + D, 1 + wD, 1 + \bar{w}D)$, where $\mathbb{F}_4 = \{0, 1, w, \overline{w}\}$. These generators can also be represented as follows:

$$G = \left(\begin{array}{ccc|ccc|ccc|c} 1 & 1 & 1 & 1 & w & \bar{w} & 0 & 0 & 0 & \cdots \\ 0 & 0 & 0 & 1 & 1 & 1 & 1 & w & \bar{w} & \cdots \\ & & & & \cdots & & & & & \end{array}\right). \tag{10.68}$$

Since all these generators are orthogonal under the Hermitian inner product, $C$ is self-orthogonal. Therefore, a [3, 1] QCC can be derived from this classical code. The basic generators $g_{0,i}$, for $1 \leq i \leq 2$, of the corresponding stabilizer group, $\mathcal{H}$, are created by multiplying the generators of Eq. (10.68) with $w$ and $\bar{w}$, and mapping $0, w, 1, \bar{w}$ onto **I**, **X**, **Y**, and **Z** respectively. The resultant basic stabilizers are as follows:

$$g_{0,1} = (\mathbf{XXX}, \mathbf{XZY}), \tag{10.69}$$

$$g_{0,2} = (\mathbf{ZZZ}, \mathbf{ZYX}), \tag{10.70}$$

and all other constituent stabilizers of $\mathcal{H}$ can be derived using Eq. (10.64).

## 10.5 Entanglement-assisted Quantum Codes

Let us recall that the classical binary and quaternary codes may only be used for constructing stabilizer codes if they satisfy the symplectic criterion of Eq. (10.34). Consequently, some of the well-known classical codes cannot be directly transformed to the quantum domain. This limitation can be readily overcome by using the entanglement-assisted stabilizer formalism, which exploits pre-shared entanglement between the transmitter and receiver to embed a set of non-commuting stabilizer generators into a larger set of commuting generators.

Figure 10.11 shows the general schematic of a quantum communication system, which incorporates an entanglement-assisted quantum stabilizer code (EA-QSC). An $[n, k, c]$ EA-QSC, having a coding rate $R_Q = k/n$ and an entanglement consumption rate of $\mathrm{E} = c/n$, encodes the information qubits $|\psi\rangle$ into the coded sequence $|\overline{\psi}\rangle$ with the aid of $(n-k-c)$ auxiliary qubits, which are initialized to the state $|0\rangle$. Furthermore, the transmitter and receiver share $c$ entangled qubits (ebits) before their actual transmission takes place. This may be carried out during the off-peak hours, when the channel is under-utilized, thus efficiently distributing the transmission requirements in time. More specifically, the state $|\phi^+\rangle$ of an ebit is given by the following Bell state:

$$|\phi^+\rangle = \frac{|00\rangle^{T_XR_X} + |11\rangle^{T_XR_X}}{\sqrt{2}}, \tag{10.71}$$

where $T_X$ and $R_X$ denote the transmitter's and receiver's half of the ebit, respectively. Similar to the superdense coding protocol of [29], it is assumed that the receiver's half of the $c$ ebits are transmitted over a noiseless quantum channel, while the transmitter's half of the $c$ ebits together with the $(n-k-c)$ auxiliary qubits are used for encoding the intended $k$ information qubits into $n$ coded qubits. The resultant $n$-qubit codewords $|\overline{\psi}\rangle$ are transmitted over a noisy quantum channel. The receiver then combines his half of the $c$ noiseless ebits with the received $n$-qubit noisy codewords $|\hat{\psi}\rangle$ to compute the syndrome, which is used for estimating the error pattern $\tilde{\mathcal{P}}$ incurred on the $n$-qubit codewords. The rest of the processing at the receiver is the same as that in Figure 10.1.

The entangled state of Eq. (10.71) has unique commutativity properties, which assist us in transforming a set of non-Abelian generators into an Abelian set. The state $|\phi^+\rangle$ is stabilized by the operators $\mathbf{X}^{T_X}\mathbf{X}^{R_X}$ and $\mathbf{Z}^{T_X}\mathbf{Z}^{R_X}$, which commute with each other. Therefore, we have[7]:

$$[\mathbf{X}^{T_X}\mathbf{X}^{R_X}, \mathbf{Z}^{T_X}\mathbf{Z}^{R_X}] = 0. \tag{10.72}$$

However, local operators acting on either of the qubits anti-commute, i.e. we have:

$$\{\mathbf{X}^{T_X}, \mathbf{Z}^{T_X}\} = \{\mathbf{X}^{R_X}, \mathbf{Z}^{R_X}\} = 0. \tag{10.73}$$

Therefore, if we have two single qubit operators $\mathbf{X}^{T_X}$ and $\mathbf{Z}^{T_X}$, which anti-commute with each other, then we can resolve the anti-commutativity by entangling another qubit and choosing the local operators on this additional qubit for ensuring that the resultant 2-qubit generators ($\mathbf{X}^{T_X}\mathbf{X}^{R_X}$ and $\mathbf{Z}^{T_X}\mathbf{Z}^{R_X}$ in this case) commute. This additional qubit constitutes the receiver's half of the ebit. In other words, we entangle an additional qubit for the sake of ensuring that the resultant 2-qubit operators have an even number of places with different non-identity operators, which in turn ensures commutativity.

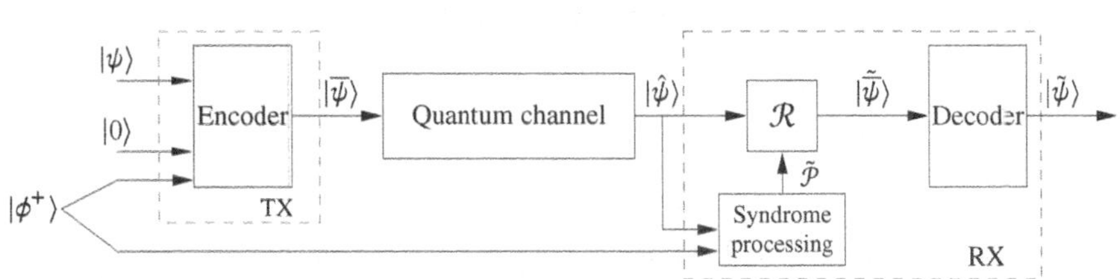


**Figure 10.11** System Model: Quantum communication system relying on an entanglement-assisted quantum stabilizer code. *Source:* [83]/IEEE.

7 $[a, b]$ represents the commutative relation between $a$ and $b$, while $\{a, b\}$ denotes the anti-commutative relation.

Let us now consider a pair of classical binary codes associated with the following PCMs:

$$H_z = \begin{pmatrix} 0 & 1 & 0 & 0 \\ 0 & 0 & 0 & 0 \\ 1 & 1 & 1 & 0 \\ 0 & 1 & 1 & 1 \end{pmatrix}, \tag{10.74}$$

and

$$H_x = \begin{pmatrix} 1 & 0 & 1 & 0 \\ 1 & 1 & 0 & 1 \\ 1 & 0 & 0 & 1 \\ 1 & 1 & 1 & 0 \end{pmatrix}, \tag{10.75}$$

which are used to construct a non-CSS quantum code having $H = (H_z|H_x)$. The PCM $H$ does not satisfy the symplectic criterion. The resultant non-Abelian set of Pauli generators are as follows:

$$H_Q = \begin{pmatrix} \mathrm{X} & \mathrm{Z} & \mathrm{X} & \mathrm{I} \\ \mathrm{X} & \mathrm{X} & \mathrm{I} & \mathrm{X} \\ \mathrm{Y} & \mathrm{Z} & \mathrm{Z} & \mathrm{X} \\ \mathrm{X} & \mathrm{Y} & \mathrm{Y} & \mathrm{Z} \end{pmatrix}. \tag{10.76}$$

In Eq. (10.76), the first two generators (i.e. the first and second row) anti-commute, while all other generators commute with each other. This is because the local operators acting on the second qubit in the first two generators anti-commute, while the local operators acting on all other qubits in these two generators commute. In other words, there is a single index (i.e. 2) with different non-identity operators. To transform this non-Abelian set into an Abelian set, we may extend the generators of Eq. (10.76) with a single additional qubit, whose local operators also anti-commute for the sake of ensuring that the resultant extended generators commute. Therefore, we get:

$$H_Q = \left(\begin{array}{cccc|c} \mathrm{X} & \mathrm{Z} & \mathrm{X} & \mathrm{I} & \mathrm{Z} \\ \mathrm{X} & \mathrm{X} & \mathrm{I} & \mathrm{X} & \mathrm{X} \\ \mathrm{Y} & \mathrm{Z} & \mathrm{Z} & \mathrm{X} & \mathrm{I} \\ \mathrm{X} & \mathrm{Y} & \mathrm{Y} & \mathrm{Z} & \mathrm{I} \end{array}\right), \tag{10.77}$$

where the operators to the left of the vertical bar (|) act on the transmitted $n$-qubit codewords, while those on the right of the vertical bar act on the receiver's half of the ebits.

## 10.6 Summary and Conclusions

Qubits cannot be cloned or copied and they collapse to classical bits upon measurement. Moreover, in contrast to a classical channel, which imposes only bit errors, the quantum channel inflicts both bit as well as phase errors. Hence, classical coding techniques cannot be directly applied to the quantum domain. Against this background, in this chapter we have provided insights into the quantum stabilizer formalism, which aids in the development of quantum codes from the known classical codes.

In Section 10.2, we reviewed the classical linear block codes, which is the basis of the stabilizer formalism. We then discussed the stabilizer codes in Section 10.3. More specifically, we laid out the general stabilizer formalism in Section 10.3.1 and detailed the transition from the classical codes to the quantum codes, which was summarized in Figure 10.6. More particularly, it was demonstrated with the aid of design examples – namely the 3-qubit bit-flip repetition code and the 3-qubit phase-flip repetition code – that entanglement can be invoked for circumventing the cloning issue, the Hadamard basis can be exploited for phase-error correction, while the classical syndrome decoding approach can be used for observing the channel errors without reading the actual received qubits. In a nutshell:

**a.** Entanglement of the auxiliary qubits with the intended information qubit can be invoked for circumventing the issues of cloning.
**b.** In contrast to the computational basis used for bit-error correction, the Hadamard basis can be used for phase-error correction.
**c.** The classical syndrome decoding approach can be harnessed for observing the channel errors without reading the actual received qubits.

We then derived the equivalence between the quantum codes and the classical binary and quaternary codes in Sections 10.3.2.1 and 10.3.2.2, respectively, which was summarized in Table 10.11. Based on this quantum-to-classical isomorphism, arbitrary classical binary and quaternary codes can be used for constructing QSCs, provided they meet the stringent commutativity criterion, which is characterized by the symplectic product in the binary domain and by the Hermitian inner product in the quaternary domain. Following this design rule, we constructed the $[7,1]$ and $[5,1]$ QSCs from the classical dual-containing $(7,4)$ Hamming code and the classical self-orthogonal GF(4)-linear $(5,2)$ code, respectively. Furthermore, various code structures, namely dual-containing CSS, non-dual-containing CSS and non-CSS codes associated with the binary PCM of a stabilizer code were summarized in Figure 10.7. In Section 10.3.3, we presented the classification of quantum errors. It was pointed out that quantum codes are inherently degenerate. Consequently, errors, which differ by an element of the stabilizer group, can be corrected with the same recovery operation. Furthermore, errors, which belong to the stabilizer group, constitute the class of harmless undetected errors, which has no classical analogue. In Section 10.4, we laid out the design of QCCs from the CCCs. Since convolutional codes are equivalent to semi-infinite block codes, it was shown that the designs of Section 10.3 can be readily extended to the QCCs. Finally, in Section 10.5, EA-QSCs were presented, which facilitate the design of quantum codes from arbitrary classical codes when they do not meet the commutativity requirement. Hence a rich selection of classical codes can be transformed to the quantum domain. However, this is achieved at the cost of pre-shared transmission of entangled qubits, which is a valuable resource and therefore should be minimized.

As discussed in this chapter, QSCs invoke the classical PCM-based syndrome decoding approach. More explicitly, the stabilizer generators of a QSC are used for computing the syndrome, which collapses to a binary 0 or 1 upon measurement. Since the resultant syndrome is binary and the generators of a QSC can be mapped onto an equivalent classical PCM, the observed syndromes are fed to a classical PCM-based syndrome decoder for estimating the channel error. Therefore, in Chapter 5 we will focus our attention on the family of classical syndrome decoding techniques.

# 11

# EXIT-chart Aided Near-hashing-bound Concatenated Quantum Codes

## 11.1 Introduction

In Chapter 5, we conceived a classical-quantum communication system, relying on near-capacity classical code designs. The designs of Chapter 5 are restricted to the transmission of classical information. By contrast, a more general quantum communication system may transmit both classical as well as quantum information, which in turn requires efficient quantum error correction codes (QECCs). QECCs are also indispensable for reliable quantum computation. In this spirit, in Chapter 10, we presented the methodology of constructing QECCs from known classical codes, while the associated classical syndrome decoding techniques were discussed in Chapter 4. Pursuing further the design of QECCs, in this chapter we aim for designing hashing bound approaching QECCs, based on the foundation laid down in Chapters 4 and 10.

Similar to the family of classical error correction codes [125, 182], which aim for operating close to Shannon's capacity limit, QECCs are designed to approach the quantum capacity [286–288], or more specifically the hashing bound, which is a lower bound of the achievable quantum capacity. A significant amount of work has been carried out over the last few decades to achieve this ambitious objective. However, the field of QECCs is still not as mature as that of their classical counterparts. Recently, inspired by the family of classical near-capacity concatenated codes, which rely on iterative decoding schemes, e.g. [218, 289], substantial efforts have been invested into constructing concatenated quantum codes [68, 82], which we refer to as serially concatenated quantum turbo codes (QTCs).

The concatenated coding philosophy relying on iterative turbo detection principles has already been introduced in Chapter 12 in the context of short block codes, while relying on EXIT charts. However, the search for the optimal components of a QTC has been predominantly confined to the analysis of the distance spectra of the constituent quantum convolutional codes (QCCs), followed by intensive Monte-Carlo simulations for determining the iterative decoding convergence threshold of the resultant QTC, as detailed in [68, 82]. While the distance spectrum dominates a turbo code's performance in the bit error rate (BER) floor region, it has a relatively insignificant impact on the convergence properties in the low signal-to-noise ratio (SNR) turbo-cliff region [218]. Therefore, having a good distance spectrum does not guarantee having a near-capacity performance – in fact, often there is a trade-off between them. To circumvent this problem and to dispense with time-consuming Monte-Carlo simulations, we extend the application of EXtrinsic information transfer (EXIT) charts to the design of QTCs. More specifically, in the light of the increasing interest in conceiving near-hashing-bound concatenated quantum code design principles, the novel contributions of this chapter are [83, 290]:

- We have appropriately adapted the conventional non-binary EXIT chart based design approach to the family of QTCs based on the underlying quantum-to-classical isomorphism of Chapter 10. We have analyzed the behavior of both an unassisted (non-recursive) and of an entanglement-assisted (recursive) inner convolutional code using EXIT charts for demonstrating that, similar to their classical counterparts, recursive inner

quantum codes constitute families of QTCs having an unbounded minimum distance.[1] We have further optimized the constituent inner and outer components of the concatenated structure using EXIT charts for the sake of approaching the hashing bound.
- We have conceived a generically applicable structure for quantum irregular convolutional codes (QIRCCs), which can be dynamically adapted to a specific application scenario for the sake of facilitating a near-hashing-bound performance. We also provide a detailed design example by constructing a 10-subcode based QIRCC and use it as an outer code in a concatenated structure for evaluating its performance.

This chapter is organized as follows. We commence by outlining our design objectives in Section 11.2. We then present the circuit-based representation of QCCs in Section 11.3, which is essential for understanding the iterative decoding procedure employed by concatenated quantum codes. Then, the system model of a quantum communication system relying on concatenated quantum codes is laid out in Section 11.4.1, followed by the associated degenerate decoding algorithm in Section 11.4.2. We present our proposed EXIT chart aided near-capacity quantum code design in Section 11.5, followed by our simulation results in Section 11.6. We then proceed with our proposed QIRCC in Section 11.7, whose performance is recorded in Section 11.8. Finally, our conclusions are offered in Section 11.9.

## 11.2 Design Objectives

An ideal code $\mathcal{C}$ designed for a quantum depolarizing channel may be characterized in terms of the channel's depolarizing probability $p$ and its coding rate $R_Q$. Here the coding rate $R_Q$ is measured in terms of the number of information qubits transmitted per channel use, i.e. we have $R_Q = k/n$, where $k$ and $n$ are the lengths of the information word to be protected and the resultant codeword, respectively. Analogously to Shannon's classical capacity, the relationship between $p$ and $R_Q$ for the depolarizing channel is defined by the hashing bound, which sets a lower limit on the achievable quantum capacity.[2] The hashing bound is given by [82, 242]:

$$C_Q(p) = 1 - H_2(p) - p\,\log_2(3), \tag{11.1}$$

where $H_2(p)$ is the binary entropy function.

More explicitly, for a given $p$, if a random code $\mathcal{C}$ of a sufficiently long codeword-length is chosen for ensuring that its coding rate obeys $R_Q \le C_Q(p)$, then $\mathcal{C}$ may yield an infinitesimally low qubit error rate (QBER) for a depolarizing probability of $p$. It must be noted here that intuitively a low QBER corresponds to a high fidelity between the transmitted and the decoded quantum state. More explicitly, for a given value of $p$, $C_Q(p)$ gives the hashing limit on the coding rate. Alternatively, for a given coding rate $R_Q$, where we have $R_Q = C_Q(p^*)$, $p^*$ gives the hashing limit on the channel's depolarizing probability. In parallel to the classical domain, this may also be referred to as the noise limit. An ideal quantum code should be capable of ensuring reliable transmission close to the noise limit $p^*$. Furthermore, for any arbitrary depolarizing probability $p$, its discrepancy with respect to the noise limit $p^*$ may be computed in decibels (dB) as follows [82]:

$$\text{Distance from hashing bound} \triangleq 10 \times \log_{10}\left(\frac{p^*}{p}\right). \tag{11.2}$$

Consequently, our quantum code design objective is to minimize the discrepancy with respect to the hashing bound, thereby yielding a near-hashing bound code design.

It is pertinent to recall here the entanglement-assisted (EA) regime discussed in Section 10.5, where the EA code $\mathcal{C}$ is characterized by an additional parameter $c$. Here $c$ is the number of entangled qubits pre-shared between the transmitter and the receiver, thus leading to the terminology of being entanglement-assisted.[3] It is assumed

1 The unbounded minimum distance of a code implies that its minimum distance increases almost linearly with the interleaver length.

2 Recall from Section 10.3.3 that quantum codes are inherently degenerate in nature, because different errors may have the same impact on the quantum state. Due to this degenerate nature, the real capacity of a quantum channel can be higher than that defined by the hashing bound [291, 292]. However, none of the codes known at the time of writing outperform the hashing bound at practically feasible frame lengths.

3 A quantum code without pre-shared entanglement, i.e. $c = 0$, may be termed as an unassisted quantum code.

furthermore that these pre-shared entangled qubits are transmitted over a noiseless quantum channel. The resultant EA hashing bound is given by [82, 237]:

$$C_Q(p) = 1 - H_2(p) - p\ \log_2(3) + \mathrm{E}, \tag{11.3}$$

where the so-called entanglement consumption rate is $\mathrm{E} = \frac{c}{n}$. Furthermore, the value of $c$ may be varied from 0 to a maximum of $(n-k)$. For the family of maximally entangled codes associated with $c = (n-k)$, the EA hashing bound of Eq. (11.3) is reduced to [82, 237]:

$$C_Q(p) = 1 - \frac{H_2(p) - p\ \log_2(3)}{2}. \tag{11.4}$$

Therefore, the resultant hashing region of the EA communication is bounded by Eqs. (11.1) and (11.4), which is also illustrated in Figure 11.1. To elaborate a little further, let us assume that the desired coding rate is $R_Q = 0.4$. Then, as seen from Figure 11.1, the noise limit for the "unassisted" quantum code is around $p^* = 0.095$, which increases to around $p^* = 0.25$ with the aid of maximum entanglement, i.e. we have $\mathrm{E} = 1 - R_Q = 0.6$. Furthermore, $0 < \mathrm{E} < 0.6$ will result in having noise limits in the range of $0.095 < p^* < 0.25$. Let us assume furthermore that we design a maximally entangled code $\mathcal{C}$ for $R_Q = 0.4$, so that it ensures reliable transmission for $p \leq 0.15$. Based on Eq. (11.2), the performance of this code (marked with a circle in Figure 11.1) is around $\left[10 \times \log 10\left(\frac{0.25}{0.15}\right)\right] = 2$ dB away from the noise limit. We may approach the noise limit more closely by striking a trade-off amongst a range of conflicting design challenges, which are illustrated in the stylized representation of Figure 11.2. For example, we may achieve a lower QBER by increasing the code length. However, this in turn incurs longer delays and higher complexity. Alternatively, we may resort to more complex code designs for reducing the QBER. However, a lower QBER may also be attained by employing codes having lower coding rates or higher entanglement consumption rates, thus requiring more entangled qubits. Hence striking an appropriate compromise, which meets these conflicting design challenges is required.

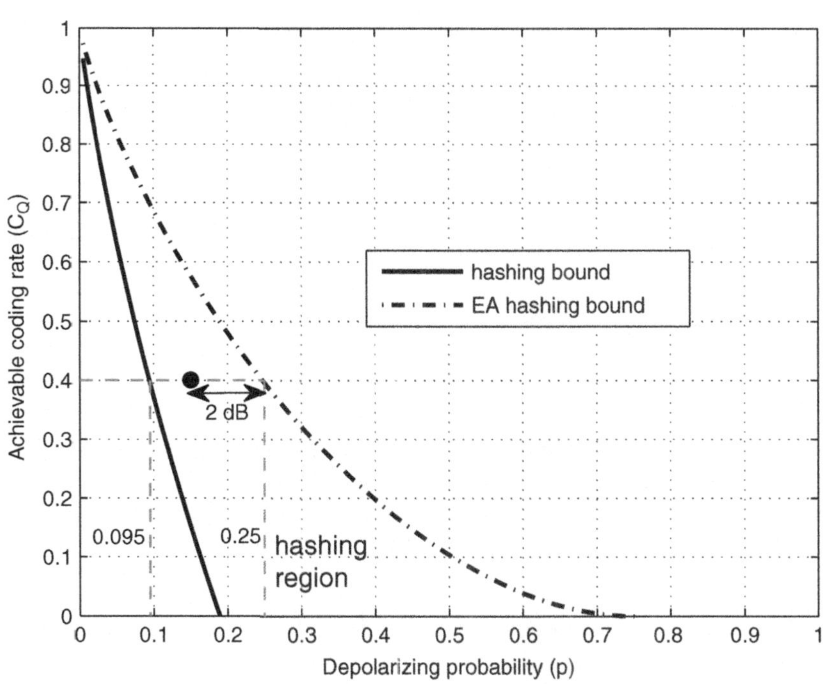


**Figure 11.1** Unassisted and EA hashing bounds characterized by Eqs. (11.1) and (11.4), respectively, for the quantum depolarizing channel. The region enclosed by these two bounds, which is labeled the hashing region, defines the capacity for varying number of pre-shared entangled qubits ($c$). At $R_Q = 0.4$, the unassisted hashing bound gives a noise limit of $p^* = 0.095$, while the maximally entangled hashing bound increases the limit to $p^* = 0.25$. The circle represents a maximally entangled code with $R_Q = 0.4$, which ensures reliable transmission for $p \leq 0.15$, thus operating at a distance of 2 dB from the noise limit. *Source*: [83]/IEEE.

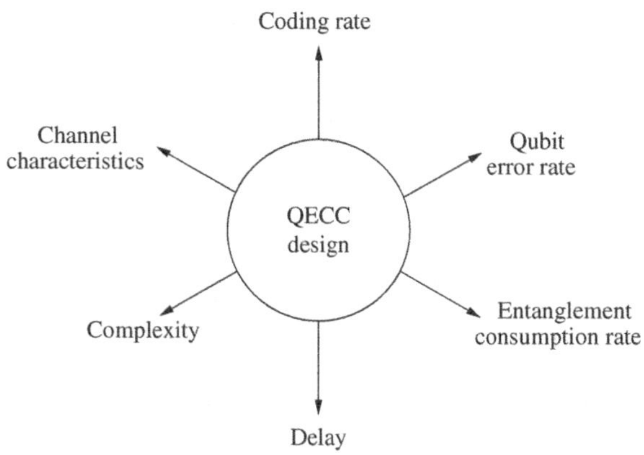


**Figure 11.2** Stylized illustration of the conflicting design challenges, which are involved in the design of quantum codes. *Source*: [83]/IEEE.

## 11.3 Circuit-based Representation of Stabilizer Codes

Circuit-based representation of quantum codes facilitates the design of concatenated code structures. More specifically, for decoding concatenated quantum codes it is more convenient to exploit the circuit-based representation of the constituent codes, rather than the conventional trellis-based syndrome decoding. Therefore, in this section, we will review the circuit-based representation of quantum codes. This discussion is based on [68].

Let us recall from Section 4.3.1 that an $(n, k)$ classical linear block code constructed over the code space $C$ maps the information word $x \in \mathbb{F}_2^k$ onto the corresponding codeword $\bar{x} \in \mathbb{F}_2^n$. In the circuit-based representation, this encoding procedure can be encapsulated as follows:

$$C = \{\bar{x} = (x : 0_{n-k})\, V\}, \tag{11.5}$$

where $V$ is an $(n \times n)$-element invertible encoding matrix over $\mathbb{F}_2$ and $0_{n-k}$ is an $(n-k)$-bit vector initialized to 0. Furthermore, given the generator matrix $G$ and the parity check matrix (PCM) $H$, the encoding matrix $V$ may be specified as:

$$V = \begin{pmatrix} G \\ \left(H^{-1}\right)^T \end{pmatrix}, \tag{11.6}$$

and its inverse is given by:

$$V^{-1} = \begin{pmatrix} G^{-1} & H^T \end{pmatrix}. \tag{11.7}$$

The encoding matrix $V$ specifies both the code space as well as the encoding operation, while its inverse $V^{-1}$ specifies the error syndrome. More specifically, let $y = \bar{x} + e$ be the received codeword, where $e$ is the $n$-bit error incurred during transmission. Then, passing the received codeword $y$ through the inverse encoder $V^{-1}$ yields:

$$yV^{-1} = (\tilde{x} : s), \tag{11.8}$$

where $\tilde{x} = x + l$ for the logical error $l \in \mathbb{F}_2^k$ inflicted on the information word $x$ and $s \in \mathbb{F}_2^{n-k}$ is the syndrome, which is equivalent to $yH^T$. Equation (11.8) may be further decomposed as:

$$\begin{aligned} (\bar{x} + e)\, V^{-1} &= (x + l : s), \\ \bar{x}V^{-1} + eV^{-1} &= (x : 0_{n-k}) + (l : s), \end{aligned} \tag{11.9}$$

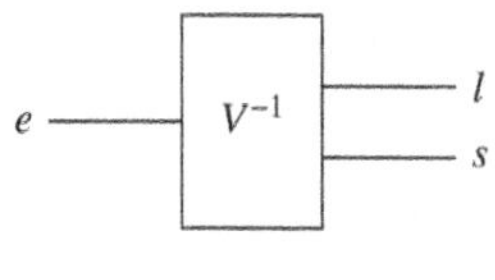


**Figure 11.3** Circuit representation of the inverse encoder $eV^{-1} = (l : s)$. *Source:* [83]/IEEE.

which is a linear superposition of the inverse of Eq. (11.5) and $eV^{-1} = (l : s)$. Hence, the inverse encoder $V^{-1}$ decomposes the channel error $e$ into the logical error $l$ and the error syndrome $s$, which is also depicted in Figure 11.3.

Analogously to Eq. (11.5), the unitary encoding operation $\mathcal{V}$ of an $[n, k]$ QSC, constructed over a code space $\mathcal{C}$, which maps the information word (logical qubits) $|\psi\rangle \in \mathbb{C}^{2^k}$ onto the codeword (physical qubits) $|\overline{\psi}\rangle \in \mathbb{C}^{2^n}$, may be mathematically formulated as follows:

$$\mathcal{C} = \{|\overline{\psi}\rangle = \mathcal{V}(|\psi\rangle \otimes |0_{n-k}\rangle)\}, \tag{11.10}$$

where $|0_{n-k}\rangle$ are $(n-k)$ auxiliary qubits initialized to the state $|0\rangle$. The unitary encoder $\mathcal{V}$ of Eq. (11.10) carries out an $n$-qubit Clifford transformation, which maps an $n$-qubit Pauli group $\mathcal{G}_n$ onto itself under conjugation [293], i.e. we have:

$$\mathcal{V}\mathcal{G}_n\mathcal{V}^{\dagger} = \mathcal{G}_n. \tag{11.11}$$

In other words, a Clifford operation preserves the elements of the Pauli group under conjugation such that for $\mathcal{P} \in \mathcal{G}_n$, $\mathcal{V}\mathcal{P}\mathcal{V}^{\dagger} \in \mathcal{G}_n$. Furthermore, any Clifford unitary matrix is completely specified by a combination of Hadamard (**H**) gates, phase (**S**) gates and controlled-NOT (C-NOT) gates, which are defined as follows[4] [160]:

$$\mathbf{H} = \frac{1}{\sqrt{2}}\begin{pmatrix} 1 & 1 \\ 1 & -1 \end{pmatrix}, \quad \mathbf{S} = \begin{pmatrix} 1 & 0 \\ 0 & i \end{pmatrix},$$
$$\text{C-NOT} = \begin{pmatrix} 1 & 0 & 0 & 0 \\ 0 & 1 & 0 & 0 \\ 0 & 0 & 0 & 1 \\ 0 & 0 & 1 & 0 \end{pmatrix}. \tag{11.12}$$

A Hadamard gate preserves the elements of a single-qubit Pauli group $\mathcal{G}_1$ under conjugation as follows:

$$\begin{aligned} \mathbf{X} &\rightarrow \mathbf{H}\mathbf{X}\mathbf{H}^{\dagger} = \mathbf{Z}, \\ \mathbf{Z} &\rightarrow \mathbf{H}\mathbf{Z}\mathbf{H}^{\dagger} = \mathbf{X}, \\ \mathbf{Y} &\rightarrow \mathbf{H}\mathbf{Y}\mathbf{H}^{\dagger} = -\mathbf{Y}, \end{aligned} \tag{11.13}$$

while a phase gate preserves them under conjugation as:

$$\begin{aligned} \mathbf{X} &\rightarrow \mathbf{S}\mathbf{X}\mathbf{S}^{\dagger} = \mathbf{Y}, \\ \mathbf{Z} &\rightarrow \mathbf{S}\mathbf{Z}\mathbf{S}^{\dagger} = \mathbf{Z}, \\ \mathbf{Y} &\rightarrow \mathbf{S}\mathbf{Y}\mathbf{S}^{\dagger} = -\mathbf{X}, \end{aligned} \tag{11.14}$$

4 The standard gates invoked here may not be optimum. There is no evidence in literature pertaining to the optimality of these gates.

The C-NOT gate of Eq. (11.12) is a 2-qubit gate, where the first qubit is the control qubit, while the second is the target. Since C-NOT is a 2-qubit gate, it acts on the elements of $\mathcal{G}_2$, transforming the standard basis of $\mathcal{G}_2$ under conjugation as illustrated here:

$$\begin{aligned} &\mathbf{X} \otimes \mathbf{I} \rightarrow \mathbf{X} \otimes \mathbf{X}, \\ &\mathbf{I} \otimes \mathbf{X} \rightarrow \mathbf{I} \otimes \mathbf{X}, \\ &\mathbf{Z} \otimes \mathbf{I} \rightarrow \mathbf{Z} \otimes \mathbf{I}, \\ &\mathbf{I} \otimes \mathbf{Z} \rightarrow \mathbf{Z} \otimes \mathbf{Z}. \end{aligned} \tag{11.15}$$

Let us further emphasize the significance of the Clifford encoding operation. *Since $\mathcal{V}$ belongs to the Clifford group, it preserves the elements of the stabilizer group $\mathcal{H}$ under conjugation.* If $g_i'$ is the $i$th stabilizer of the unencoded state $|\psi\rangle$, then this may be proved as follows:

$$|\psi\rangle \otimes |0_{n-k}\rangle = g_i' (|\psi\rangle \otimes |0_{n-k}\rangle). \tag{11.16}$$

Encoding $|\psi\rangle$ with $\mathcal{V}$ yields:

$$\mathcal{V}(|\psi\rangle \otimes |0_{n-k}\rangle) = \mathcal{V}(g_i' (|\psi\rangle \otimes |0_{n-k}\rangle)), \tag{11.17}$$

which is equivalent to:

$$\mathcal{V}(|\psi\rangle \otimes |0_{n-k}\rangle) = \mathcal{V}(g_i' \mathcal{V}^\dagger \mathcal{V}(|\psi\rangle \otimes |0_{n-k}\rangle)), \tag{11.18}$$

since $\mathcal{V}^\dagger \mathcal{V} = \mathbb{I}_n$. Substituting Eq. (11.10) into Eq. (11.18) gives:

$$|\overline{\psi}\rangle = (\mathcal{V} g_i' \mathcal{V}^\dagger) |\overline{\psi}\rangle. \tag{11.19}$$

Hence, the encoded state $|\overline{\psi}\rangle$ is stabilized by $g_i = \mathcal{V} g_i' \mathcal{V}^\dagger$. From this it appears as if any arbitrary $\mathcal{V}$ (not necessarily Clifford) can be used to preserve the stabilizer subspace, which is not true. Since we assume that the stabilizer group $\mathcal{H}$ is a subgroup of the Pauli group, we impose the additional constraint that $\mathcal{V}$ must yield the elements of Pauli group under conjugation as in Eq. (11.11), which is only true for Clifford operations.

Furthermore, *the Clifford encoding operation also preserves the commutativity of stabilizers.* Let $g_i'$ and $g_j'$ be a pair of unencoded stabilizers. Then the above statement can be proved as follows:

$$g_i g_j = (\mathcal{V} g_i' \mathcal{V}^\dagger)(\mathcal{V} g_j' \mathcal{V}^\dagger) = \mathcal{V} g_i' g_j' \mathcal{V}^\dagger. \tag{11.20}$$

Since $g_i'$ and $g_j'$ commute, we have:

$$\mathcal{V} g_i' g_j' \mathcal{V}^\dagger = \mathcal{V} g_j' g_i' \mathcal{V}^\dagger. \tag{11.21}$$

Using $\mathcal{V}^\dagger \mathcal{V} = \mathbb{I}_n$, gives:

$$\mathcal{V} g_j' \mathcal{V}^\dagger \mathcal{V} g_i' \mathcal{V}^\dagger. = g_j g_i. \tag{11.22}$$

Since the $n$-qubit Pauli group forms a basis for the $(2^n \times 2^n)$-element matrices of Eq. (11.12), the Clifford encoder $\mathcal{V}$, which acts on the $2^n$-dimensional Hilbert space, can be completely defined by specifying its action under conjugation on the Pauli-**X** and **Z** operators acting on each of the $n$ qubits, as seen in Eqs. (11.13)–(11.15). However, $\mathcal{V}$ and $\mathcal{V}'$, which differ only through a global phase such that $\mathcal{V}' = e^{j\theta}\mathcal{V}$, have the same impact under conjugation. Therefore, the global phase has no physical significance in the context of Eq. (11.11) and the $n$-qubit encoder $\mathcal{V}$ can be completely specified by its action on the binary equivalent of the Pauli operators. More specifically, the $n$-qubit encoder $\mathcal{V}$ maps $\mathcal{P} \in \mathcal{G}_n$ to $\mathcal{P}' \in \mathcal{G}_n$ as follows:

$$\mathcal{P}' = \mathcal{V} \mathcal{P} \mathcal{V}^\dagger, \tag{11.23}$$

which is equivalent to mapping the equivalent $2n$-bit vector $P = [\mathcal{P}]$ onto $P' = [\mathcal{P}']$, where [.] denotes the effective Pauli group $G_n$ such that $P = [\mathcal{P}]$ differs from $\mathcal{P}$ by a multiplicative constant. More explicitly, we have

$P = \mathcal{P}/\{\pm 1, \pm i\}$, and the elements of $G_n$ are represented by $2n$-tuple binary vectors based on the mapping given in Eq. (10.29). Consequently, Eq. (11.23) can be rewritten as:

$$P' = [\mathcal{P}'] = [\mathcal{V}\mathcal{P}\mathcal{V}^\dagger]. \tag{11.24}$$

Since the effective mapping of Eq. (11.24) is binary, i.e. $P \rightarrow P'$, we may characterize it in terms of an equivalent $(2n \times 2n)$-element binary matrix $V$, which is defined as follows:

$$P' = [\mathcal{V}\mathcal{P}\mathcal{V}^\dagger] = [\mathcal{P}]V = PV. \tag{11.25}$$

Furthermore, since the Clifford transformation $\mathcal{V}$ preserves the commutativity relationship, the associated binary matrix $V$ is always a symplectic matrix [68]. As a consequence of this equivalence, any Clifford unitary can be efficiently simulated on a classical system as stated by the Gottesman–Knill theorem [161].

We next define $\mathcal{V}$ by specifying its action on the elements of the Pauli group $\mathcal{G}_n$. More precisely, we consider $2n$ $n$-qubit unencoded operators $Z_i, X_i, \ldots, Z_n, X_n$, where $Z_i$ and $X_i$ represents the Pauli **Z** and **X** operator, respectively, acting on the $i$th qubit and the identity **I** on all other qubits. The unencoded operators $Z_{k+1}, \ldots, Z_n$ stabilizes the unencoded state of Eq. (11.10), i.e. $(|\psi\rangle \otimes |0_{n-k}\rangle)$, and are therefore called the unencoded stabilizer generators. On the other hand, $X_{k+1}, \ldots, X_n$ are the unencoded pure errors since $X_i$ anti-commutes with the corresponding unencoded stabilizer generator $Z_i$, yielding an error syndrome of 1. Furthermore, the unencoded logical operators acting on the information qubits are $Z_i, X_i, \ldots, Z_k, X_k$, which commute with the unencoded stabilizers $Z_{k+1}, \ldots, Z_n$. The encoder $\mathcal{V}$ maps the unencoded operators $Z_i, X_i, \ldots, Z_n, X_n$ onto the encoded operators $\overline{Z}_i, \overline{X}_i, \ldots, \overline{Z}_n, \overline{X}_n$, which may be represented as follows:

$$\overline{X}_i = [\mathcal{V}X_i\mathcal{V}^\dagger] = [X_i]\,V, \qquad \overline{Z}_i = [\mathcal{V}Z_i\mathcal{V}^\dagger] = [Z_i]\,V. \tag{11.26}$$

Since Clifford transformations do not perturb the commutativity of the operators, the resultant encoded stabilizers $\overline{Z}_{k+1}, \ldots, \overline{Z}_n$ are equivalent to the stabilizers $g_i$ of Eq. (10.14), while $\overline{X}_{k+1}, \ldots, \overline{X}_n$ are the pure errors $t_i$ of the resultant stabilizer code, which trigger a nontrivial syndrome. Moreover, $\overline{Z}_i, \overline{X}_i, \ldots, \overline{Z}_k, \overline{X}_k$ are the encoded logical operators, which commute with the stabilizers $g_i$. Logical operators merely map one codeword onto the other, without affecting the code space $\mathcal{C}$ of the stabilizer code. It also has to be mentioned here that the stabilizer generators $g_i$ together with the encoded logical operations constitute the normalizer of the stabilizer code. The $(2n \times 2n)$-element binary symplectic encoding matrix $V$ is therefore given by:

$$V = \begin{pmatrix} \overline{Z}_1 \\ \vdots \\ \overline{Z}_k \\ \overline{Z}_{k+1} \\ \vdots \\ \overline{Z}_n \\ \overline{X}_1 \\ \vdots \\ \overline{X}_k \\ \overline{X}_{k+1} \\ \vdots \\ \overline{X}_n \end{pmatrix} = \begin{pmatrix} \overline{Z}_1 \\ \vdots \\ \overline{Z}_k \\ g_1 \\ \vdots \\ g_{n-k} \\ \overline{X}_1 \\ \vdots \\ \overline{X}_k \\ t_1 \\ \vdots \\ t_{n-k} \end{pmatrix}, \tag{11.27}$$

where the Pauli **Z** and **X** operators are mapped onto the classical bits using the Pauli-to-binary isomorphism of Section 10.3.2.1.

Analogously to the classical inverse encoder of Eq. (11.8), the inverse encoder of a quantum code is the Hermitian conjugate $\mathcal{V}^\dagger$. Let $|\hat{\psi}\rangle = \mathcal{P}|\overline{\psi}\rangle$ be the received codeword such that $\mathcal{P}$ is the $n$-qubit channel error. Then, passing the received codeword $|\hat{\psi}\rangle$ through the inverse encoder $\mathcal{V}^\dagger$ yields:

$$\begin{aligned}\mathcal{V}^\dagger\mathcal{P}|\overline{\psi}\rangle &= \mathcal{V}^\dagger\mathcal{P}\mathcal{V}(|\psi\rangle \otimes |0_{(n-k)}\rangle) \\ &= (\mathcal{L}|\psi\rangle) \otimes (\mathcal{S}|0_{(n-k)}\rangle),\end{aligned} \tag{11.28}$$

where $\mathcal{V}^\dagger\mathcal{P}\mathcal{V} \equiv (\mathcal{L} \otimes \mathcal{S})$ and $\mathcal{L} \in \mathcal{G}_k$ denotes the error imposed on the information word, while $\mathcal{S} \in \mathcal{G}_{n-k}$ represents the error inflicted on the remaining $(n-k)$ auxiliary qubits. In the equivalent binary representation, Eq. (11.28) may be modeled as follows:

$$PV^{-1} = (L : S), \tag{11.29}$$

where we have $P = [\mathcal{P}]$, $L = [\mathcal{L}]$ and $S = [\mathcal{S}]$.

Let us now derive the encoding matrix $V$ for the 3-qubit bit-flip repetition code $C(3,1)$. Recall from Section 10.3.2.1 that the corresponding binary PCM $H$ is given by:

$$H = \left(\begin{array}{ccc|ccc} 1 & 1 & 0 & 0 & 0 & 0 \\ 1 & 0 & 1 & 0 & 0 & 0 \end{array}\right), \tag{11.30}$$

and the circuit of Figure 11.4 constitutes the encoder. Its unencoded operators are as follows:

$$\begin{pmatrix} Z_1 \\ Z_2 \\ Z_3 \\ X_1 \\ X_2 \\ X_3 \end{pmatrix} = \begin{pmatrix} \mathbf{ZII} \\ \mathbf{IZI} \\ \mathbf{IIZ} \\ \mathbf{XII} \\ \mathbf{IXI} \\ \mathbf{IIX} \end{pmatrix} \equiv \left(\begin{array}{ccc|ccc} 1 & 0 & 0 & 0 & 0 & 0 \\ 0 & 1 & 0 & 0 & 0 & 0 \\ 0 & 0 & 1 & 0 & 0 & 0 \\ \hline 0 & 0 & 0 & 1 & 0 & 0 \\ 0 & 0 & 0 & 0 & 1 & 0 \\ 0 & 0 & 0 & 0 & 0 & 1 \end{array}\right). \tag{11.31}$$

A C-NOT gate is then applied to the second qubit, which is controlled by the first. As seen in Eq. (11.15), the C-NOT gate copies the Pauli **X** operator forward from the control qubit to the target qubit, while **Z** is copied in the opposite direction. Therefore, we get:

$$\begin{pmatrix} \mathbf{ZII} \\ \mathbf{IZI} \\ \mathbf{IIZ} \\ \mathbf{XII} \\ \mathbf{IXI} \\ \mathbf{IIX} \end{pmatrix} \xrightarrow{\text{C-NOT}(1,2)} \begin{pmatrix} \mathbf{ZII} \\ \mathbf{ZZI} \\ \mathbf{IIZ} \\ \mathbf{XXI} \\ \mathbf{IXI} \\ \mathbf{IIX} \end{pmatrix} \equiv \left(\begin{array}{ccc|ccc} 1 & 0 & 0 & 0 & 0 & 0 \\ 1 & 1 & 0 & 0 & 0 & 0 \\ 0 & 0 & 1 & 0 & 0 & 0 \\ \hline 0 & 0 & 0 & 1 & 1 & 0 \\ 0 & 0 & 0 & 0 & 1 & 0 \\ 0 & 0 & 0 & 0 & 0 & 1 \end{array}\right). \tag{11.32}$$

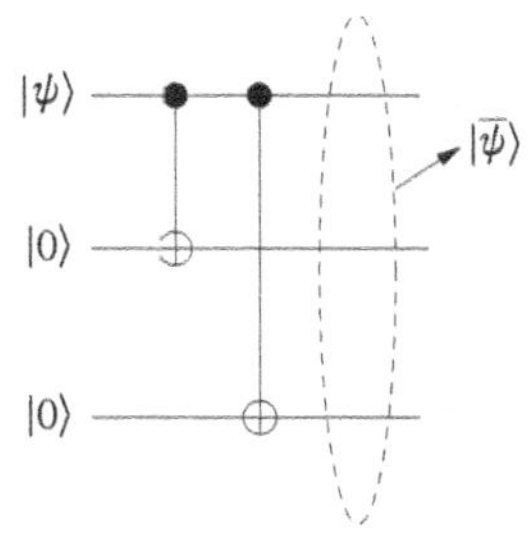


**Figure 11.4** Encoding Circuit for 3-qubit bit-flip repetition code. *Source*: [83]/IEEE.

Another C-NOT gate is then applied to the third qubit, which is also controlled by the first, yielding:

$$\begin{pmatrix} \mathbf{ZII} \\ \mathbf{ZZI} \\ \mathbf{IIZ} \\ \mathbf{XXI} \\ \mathbf{IXI} \\ \mathbf{IIX} \end{pmatrix} \xrightarrow{\text{C-NOT(1,3)}} \begin{pmatrix} \mathbf{ZII} \\ \mathbf{ZZI} \\ \mathbf{ZIZ} \\ \mathbf{XXX} \\ \mathbf{IXI} \\ \mathbf{IIX} \end{pmatrix} \equiv \left(\begin{array}{ccc|ccc} 1 & 0 & 0 & 0 & 0 & 0 \\ 1 & 1 & 0 & 0 & 0 & 0 \\ 1 & 0 & 1 & 0 & 0 & 0 \\ \hline 0 & 0 & 0 & 1 & 1 & 1 \\ 0 & 0 & 0 & 0 & 1 & 0 \\ 0 & 0 & 0 & 0 & 0 & 1 \end{array}\right) = V. \tag{11.33}$$

We can also express the binary matrix $V$ of Eq. (11.33) in decimal notation as:

$$V \equiv \{32, 48, 40, 7, 2, 1\}_{10}, \tag{11.34}$$

where each index corresponds to a row of $V$, e.g. the first row (1 0 0 0 0 0) is equivalent to the decimal number 32.

As observed from Eq. (11.33), the stabilizer generators of the 3-qubit bit-flip repetition code are $g_1 = \mathbf{ZZI}$ and $g_2 = \mathbf{ZIZ}$ according to Eq. (11.27), where $k = 1$ and $n = 3$. More explicitly, rows 2 and 3 of $V$ constitute the PCM $H$ of Eq. (11.30). The encoded logical operators are $\overline{Z}_1 = \mathbf{ZII}$ and $\overline{X}_1 = \mathbf{XXX}$, which commute with the stabilizers $g_1$ and $g_2$. Finally, the pure errors are $t_1 = \mathbf{IXI}$ and $t_2 = \mathbf{IIX}$, which anti-commute with $g_1$ and $g_2$, respectively, yielding a nontrivial syndrome.

Based on the above discussions, we now proceed to lay out the circuit-based model for a convolutional code, which is given in [68]. As discussed in Section 10.4, convolutional codes are equivalent to linear block codes associated with semi-infinite block lengths. More specifically, as illustrated in Figure 10.10, the PCM $H$ of a $C(n, k, m)$ convolutional code has a block-band structure, where the adjacent blocks have an overlap of $m$ submatrices. Similarly, the encoder $V$ of a classical convolutional code can be constructed from the repeated applications of a linear invertible seed transformation $U$, which is an $(n + m) \times (n + m)$-element encoding matrix, as shown in Figure 11.5. The inverse encoder $V^{-1}$ can be readily obtained by moving backward in time, i.e. by reading Figure 11.5 from right to left. Let us elaborate further by stating that at time instant $j$, the seed transformation matrix $U$ takes as its input the memory bits $m_{j-1} \in \mathbb{F}_2^m$, the logical bits $l_j \in \mathbb{F}_2^k$ and the syndrome bits $s_j \in \mathbb{F}_2^{n-k}$ to generate the output bits $e_j \in \mathbb{F}_2^n$ and the memory state $m_j$. More explicitly, we have:

$$(m_j : e_j) = (m_{j-1} : l_j : s_j)\, U, \tag{11.35}$$

and the overall encoder is formulated as [68]:

$$\begin{aligned} V &= U_{[1,\ldots,n+m]} U_{[n+1,\ldots,2n+m]} \cdots U_{[(N-1)n+1,\ldots,Nn+m]}, \\ &= \prod_{j=1}^{N} U_{[(j-1)n+1,\ldots,jn+m]}, \end{aligned} \tag{11.36}$$

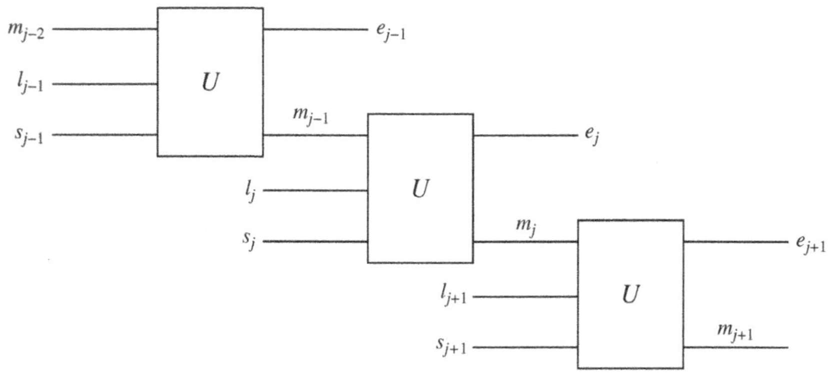


**Figure 11.5** Circuit representation of the encoder $V$ of a convolutional code. *Source*: Adapted from [68].

where $N$ denotes the length of the convolutional code and $U_{[(j-1)n+1,\ldots,jn+m]}$ acts on $(n+m)$ bits, i.e. $(m_{j-2} : l_{j-1} : s_{j-1})$. For an $C[n,k,m]$ quantum convolutional code, the seed transformation $U$ is a $2(n+m)\times 2(n+m)$-element symplectic matrix and Eq. (11.35) may be re-written as:

$$(M_j : P_j) = (M_{j-1} : L_j : S_j)\, U, \tag{11.37}$$

where $M$ represents the memory state with an $m$-qubit Pauli operator.

The aforementioned methodology conceived for constructing the circuit-based model of unassisted quantum codes may be readily extended to the class of EA codes [82]. The unitary encoding operation $\mathcal{V}$ of an $C[n,k,c]$ EA-QSC, which acts on the $n$ transmitter qubits, i.e $k$ information qubits, $a$ auxiliary qubits and $c$ pre-shared entangled qubits, may be mathematically modeled as follows:

$$\mathcal{C} = \{|\overline{\psi}\rangle = \mathcal{V}(|\psi\rangle^{T_X} \otimes |0_a\rangle^{T_X} \otimes |\phi_c^+\rangle^{T_X R_X})\}, \tag{11.38}$$

where the superscripts $T_X$ and $R_X$ denote the transmitter's and receiver's qubits, respectively. Furthermore, $|0_a\rangle^{T_X}$ are $a$ auxiliary qubits initialized to the state $|0\rangle$, where $a = (n-k-c)$, and $|\phi_c^+\rangle^{T_X R_X}$ are the $c$ entangled qubits. Analogously to Eq. (11.28), the inverse encoder of an EA quantum code $\mathcal{V}^\dagger$ gives:

$$\begin{aligned}\mathcal{V}^\dagger \mathcal{P}|\overline{\psi}\rangle &= \mathcal{V}^\dagger \mathcal{P}\mathcal{V}(|\psi|^{T_X} \otimes |0_a|^{T_X} \otimes |\phi_c^+|^{T_X R_X}) \\ &= (\mathcal{L}^{T_X}|\psi|^{T_X}) \otimes (\mathcal{S}^{T_X}|0_a|^{T_X} \otimes (\mathcal{E}^{T_X}|\phi_c^+|^{T_X R_X}),\end{aligned} \tag{11.39}$$

where $\mathcal{L}^{T_X} \in \mathcal{G}_k$ denotes the error imposed on the information word, while $\mathcal{S}^{T_X} \in \mathcal{G}_a$ represents the error inflicted on the transmitter's $a$ auxiliary qubits and $\mathcal{E}^{T_X} \in \mathcal{G}_c$ is the error corrupting the transmitter's half of $c$ ebits. The equivalent binary representation of Eq. (11.39) is given by:

$$PV^{-1} = (L : S : E), \tag{11.40}$$

where we have $P = [\mathcal{P}^{T_X}]$, $L = [\mathcal{L}^{T_X}]$, $S = [\mathcal{S}^{T_X}]$ and $E = [\mathcal{E}^{T_X}]$. Similarly, Eq. (11.37) can be re-modeled as follows:

$$(M_j : P_j) = (M_{j-1} : L_j : S_j : E_j)\, U. \tag{11.41}$$

## 11.4 Revisiting Concatenated Quantum Codes

### 11.4.1 System Model

Recall that the family of short concatenated quantum codes was introduced in Section 12.1. Hence basic familiarity with the schematic of Figure 12.1 is assumed, including the terminologies of *intrinsic, extrinsic, a-posteriori,* and *a-priori* information.

Based on this principle, in this chapter we elaborate further on this potent quantum coding family. Figure 11.6 shows the general schematic of a quantum communication system relying on a pair of concatenated quantum

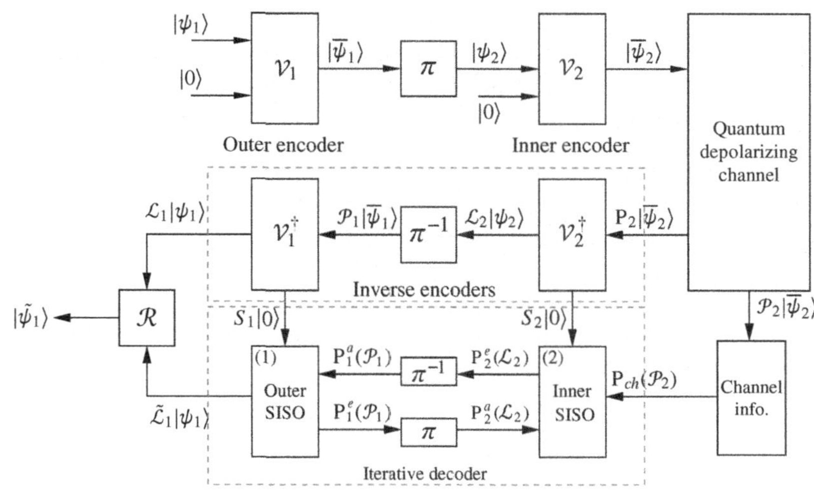


**Figure 11.6** System Model: Quantum communication system relying on concatenated quantum stabilizer codes. $P_i^a(.)$, $P_i^e(.)$, and $P_i^o(.)$ *denote the a-priori, extrinsic, and a-posteriori probabilities related to the ith decoder. Source*: [83]/IEEE.

stabilizer codes. In our work, both the inner as well as the outer codes are assumed to be convolutional codes. Furthermore, analogously to the classical concatenated codes, the inner code must have a so-called recursive architecture, exemplified by a recursive systematic convolutional code, as detailed in [125] in the context of classical turbo convolutional codes. Furthermore, both the inner as well the outer code must be of non-catastrophic nature. To elaborate briefly, using a recursive inner code is essential for the sake of ensuring that the resultant families of codes have an unbounded minimum distance, when the code length or the turbo interleaver length is increased. On the other hand, the non-catastrophic nature of both the inner and the outer codes guarantees that a decoding convergence to an infinitesimally low error rate may be achieved. However, it was found in [141, 142] that QCCs cannot be simultaneously recursive and non-catastrophic. In order to overcome this problem, Wilde *et al.* [81, 82] proposed to employ EA inner codes, which are both recursive as well as non-catastrophic. Therefore, the inner code should be an entanglement-assisted recursive and non-catastrophic code, while the outer code can be either an unassisted or an entanglement-assisted non-catastrophic code.

At the transmitter, the intended quantum information $|\psi_1\rangle$ is encoded by an $C[n_1, k_1]$ outer encoder $\mathcal{V}_1$ using $(n_1 - k_1)$ auxiliary qubits, which are initialized to the state $|0\rangle$, as depicted in Eq. (11.10). The encoded qubits $|\overline{\psi}_1\rangle$ are passed through a quantum interleaver ($\pi$), which acts as a randomizer or scrambler. This is required for ensuring that during iterative decoding the *extrinsic* information to be provided by the surrounding bits concerning the current bit to be decoded remains as uncorrelated as possible. Recall that the minimum distance is expected grow linearly upon increasing the codeword length, i.e. the turbo interleaver length.

The resultant permuted qubits $|\psi_2\rangle$ are fed to an $C[n_2, k_2]$ inner encoder $\mathcal{V}_2$, which encodes them into the codewords $|\overline{\psi}_2\rangle$ using $(n_2 - k_2)$ auxiliary qubits initialized to the state $|0.\rangle$.[5] The $n$-qubit codewords $|\overline{\psi}_2\rangle$, where we have $n = n_1 n_2$, are then serially transmitted over a quantum depolarizing channel, which imposes an $n$-tuple error $\mathcal{P}_2 \in \mathcal{G}_n$ on the transmitted codewords.

The received codeword $|\hat{\psi}_2\rangle = \mathcal{P}_2 |\overline{\psi}_2\rangle$ is then passed through the inverse encoder $\mathcal{V}_2^\dagger$, which yields the corrupted information word of the inner encoder $\mathcal{L}_2 |\psi_2\rangle$ and the associated $(n_2 - k_2)$-qubit syndrome $\mathcal{S}_2 |0_{(n_2-k_2)}\rangle$. Recall that this was encapsulated in Eq. (11.28), where $\mathcal{L}_2$ denotes the error imposed on the logical qubits of the inner encoder, while $\mathcal{S}_2$ represents the error inflicted on the remaining $(n_2 - k_2)$ qubits. The corrupted logical qubits of the inner encoder are de-interleaved, resulting in $\mathcal{P}_1 |\overline{\psi}_1\rangle$, which is then passed through the inverse outer encoder $\mathcal{V}_1^\dagger$. This gives the corrupted information word of the outer encoder $\mathcal{L}_1 |\psi_1\rangle$ and the associated $(n_1 - k_1)$-qubit syndrome $\mathcal{S}_1 |0_{(n_1-k_1)}\rangle$.

The next step is to estimate the error $\mathcal{L}_1$ for the sake of ensuring that the original logical qubit $|\psi_1\rangle$ can be restored by applying the recovery operation $\mathcal{R}$. For estimating $\mathcal{L}_1$, both the syndromes $\mathcal{S}_2 |0_{(n_2-k_2)}\rangle$ and $\mathcal{S}_1 |0_{(n_1-k_1)}\rangle$ are

5 Please note that this is a general schematic. The inner code can be either an unassisted or an EA code. However, it is advisable to use an EA inner code for the sake of ensuring an unbounded minimum distance of the resultant concatenated code.

fed to the syndrome-based[6] inner and outer soft-in soft-out (SISO) decoders [125], respectively, which engage in iterative decoding [68, 82] in order to yield the estimated error $\tilde{\mathcal{L}}_1$. The corresponding block is marked as "iterative decoder" in Figure 11.6. Here, $\mathrm{P}_i^a(.)$, $\mathrm{P}_i^e(.)$, and $\mathrm{P}_i^o(.)$ denote the *a-priori*, *extrinsic*, and *a-posteriori* probabilities [125] related to the *i*th decoder. Based on this notation, the turbo decoding process can be summarized as follows:

- The inner SISO decoder of Figure 11.6 uses the channel information $\mathrm{P}_{\mathrm{ch}}(\mathcal{P}_2)$, the *a-priori* information gleaned from the outer decoder $\mathrm{P}_2^a(\mathcal{L}_2)$ (initialized to be equiprobable for the first iteration, because at this stage no *extrinsic* information is available from the other decoder) and the syndrome $\mathcal{S}_2$ to compute the *extrinsic* information $\mathrm{P}_2^e(\mathcal{L}_2)$. For a coded sequence of length $N$, we have $\mathcal{P}_2 = [\mathcal{P}_{2,1}, \mathcal{P}_{2,2}, \ldots, \mathcal{P}_{2,t}, \ldots, \mathcal{P}_{2,N}]$, where $\mathcal{P}_{2,t} = [\mathcal{P}_{2,t}^1, \mathcal{P}_{2,t}^2, \ldots, \mathcal{P}_{2,t}^n]$. The channel information $\mathbf{P}_{\mathrm{ch}}\left(P_{2,t}\right)$ is computed assuming that each qubit is independently transmitted over a quantum depolarizing channel having a depolarizing probability of $p$, whose channel transition probabilities are given by [68]:

$$\mathbf{P}_{\mathrm{ch}}\left(P_{2,t}^i\right) = \begin{cases} 1-p, & \text{if } \mathcal{P}_{2,t}^i = \mathbf{I} \\ p/3, & \text{if } \mathcal{P}_{2,t}^i \in \{\mathbf{X}, \mathbf{Z}, \mathbf{Y}\}. \end{cases} \tag{11.42}$$

- $\mathrm{P}_2^e(\mathcal{L}_2)$ is passed through the quantum deinterleaver $(\pi^{-1})$ of Figure 11.6 to generate the *a-priori* information for the outer decoder $\mathrm{P}_1^a(\mathcal{P}_1)$.
- Based on both the *a-priori* information $\mathrm{P}_1^a(\mathcal{P}_1)$ and on the syndrome $\mathcal{S}_1$, the outer SISO decoder of Figure 11.6 computes both the *a-posteriori* information $\mathrm{P}_1^o(\mathcal{L}_1)$ and the *extrinsic* information $\mathrm{P}_1^e(\mathcal{P}_1)$.
- $\mathrm{P}_1^e(\mathcal{P}_1)$ is then interleaved to obtain $\mathrm{P}_2^a(\mathcal{L}_2)$, which is fed back to the inner SISO decoder of Figure 11.6. This iterative procedure continues, until either convergence is achieved or the maximum affordable number of iterations is reached.
- Finally, a qubit-based MAP decision is made for determining the most likely error coset $\mathcal{L}_1$. It must be mentioned here that both the inner and outer SISO decoders employ the degenerate decoding approach of [68], which aims for finding the "most likely error coset" rather than the "most likely error" acting on the logical qubits $\mathcal{L}_i$, as we will further detail in the next section.

### 11.4.2 Degenerate Iterative Decoding

As discussed in Section 10.3.3, quantum codes exhibit degeneracy, which becomes plausible from Eq. (11.28). More explicitly, we have:

$$\mathcal{S}\,|0_{n-k}\rangle = \mathcal{S}_1|0\rangle \otimes \cdots \otimes \mathcal{S}_{n-k}|0\rangle. \tag{11.43}$$

Since, we have $\mathcal{S}_j \in \{\mathbf{I}, \mathbf{X}, \mathbf{Y}, \mathbf{Z}\}$, we can rewrite Eq. (11.43) as follows [68]:

$$\mathcal{S}\,|0_{n-k}\rangle \equiv \epsilon|s_1\rangle \otimes \cdots \otimes |s_{n-k}\rangle, \tag{11.44}$$

where $\epsilon \in \{\pm 1, \pm i\}$, and:

$$\begin{aligned} s_j &= 0 \quad \text{if } \mathcal{S}_j = \mathbf{I} \text{ or } \mathcal{S}_j = \mathbf{Z}, \\ s_j &= 1 \quad \text{otherwise.} \end{aligned} \tag{11.45}$$

For example, if $\mathcal{S}_1 = \mathbf{Y}$ and $\mathcal{S}_j = \mathbf{I}$ for $j \neq 1$, since $\mathbf{Y} = i\mathbf{XZ}$, we get $\mathcal{S}\,|0_{n-k}\rangle = i\,|1\rangle \otimes |0\rangle \otimes \cdots \otimes |0\rangle$.

Upon observing the $(n-k)$ syndrome qubits of Eq. (11.44) they collapse to the classical syndrome $s = \{s_1, \ldots, s_{n-k}\}$, which is equivalent to the symplectic product of $P$ and $H$, i.e. $s = \left(P \star H_j\right)_{1 \le j \le n-k}$. More precisely, the syndrome sequence $|0_{n-k}\rangle$ is invariant to the $\mathbf{Z}$-component of $\mathcal{S}$ since $\mathbf{Z}\,|0\rangle = |0\rangle$. Let $S$ be the effective $2(n-k)$-bit error on the syndrome, which may be decomposed as $S = S^x + S^z$, where $S^x$ and $S^z$ are the $\mathbf{X}$ and $\mathbf{Z}$ components of $S$, respectively. Then $s$ only reveals $S^x$. Hence, two distinct error sequences $P = (L : S^x + S^z)V$ and $P' = (L : S^x + S'^z)V$, which only differ in the $\mathbf{Z}$-component of $\mathcal{S}$, yield the same syndrome $s$. Furthermore, it must

6 See Section 4.4.2.2 for details of syndrome-based SISO or maximum *a-posteriori* (MAP) decoder.

be noted that both $P$ and $P'$ have the same logical error $L$. Therefore, $P$ and $P'$ differ only by the stabilizer group and are known as degenerate errors, which do not have to be distinguished, since they can be corrected by the same recovery operation $L^{-1}$.

The classic syndrome-based MAP decoder aims for finding the most likely error for a given syndrome, which may be modeled as:

$$L(S) = \text{argmax}_L \, \text{P}(L|S), \tag{11.46}$$

where $\text{P}(L|S)$ denotes the probability of experiencing the logical error $L$ imposed on the transmitted qubits, given that the syndrome of the received qubits is $S$. By contrast, quantum codes employ degenerate decoding, which aims for finding the most likely error coset $C(L, S^x)$ associated with the observed syndrome $S^x$. The coset $C(L, S^x)$ is defined as [68]:

$$C(L, S^x) = \{P = (L : S^x + S^z)V\} \quad \forall S^z \in \{\mathbf{I}, \mathbf{Z}\}^{n-k}. \tag{11.47}$$

Therefore, a degenerate MAP decoder yields:

$$L(S^x) = \text{argmax}_L \, \text{P}(L|S^x), \tag{11.48}$$

where we have:

$$\text{P}(L|S^x) \equiv \sum_{S^z \in \{\mathbf{I},\mathbf{Z}\}^{n-k}} \text{P}(L|(S^x + S^z)). \tag{11.49}$$

The iterative decoder of Figure 11.6 consists of two serially concatenated SISO decoders, which employ the aforementioned degenerate decoding approach. Figure 11.7 shows the general schematic of a SISO decoder, where the Pauli operators $\mathcal{P}$, $\mathcal{L}$ and $\mathcal{S}$ are replaced by the effective operators $P$, $L$, and $S^x$, respectively. The SISO decoder of Figure 11.7 yields the *a-posteriori* information pertaining to the logical error $L$ and channel error $P$ based on the classic forward–backward recursive coefficients $\alpha$ and $\beta$, which are computed over the quantum circuit of Figure 11.8 (analogous to a classic trellis) as follows [68]:

- For a coded sequence of duration $N$, let us denote the channel error sequence by $P = [P_1, P_2, \dots, P_t, \dots, P_N]$ and the logical error sequence by $L = [L_1, L_2, \dots, L_t, \dots, L_N]$, where we have $P_t \in G_n$ and $L_t \in G_k$. More explicitly, $P_t = [P_t^1, P_t^2, \dots, P_t^n]$ and $L_t = [L_t^1, L_t^2, \dots, L_t^k]$.
- Let us decompose the $2(n+m) \times 2(n+m)$-element binary symplectic matrix $U$ of Figure 11.8 as $U = (U_M : U_P)$, where $U_M$ is the binary matrix formed by the first $2m$ columns of $U$, while $U_P$ is the binary matrix formed by the last $2n$ columns of $U$. Therefore, Eq. (11.37) can be decomposed as:

$$M_t = (M_{t-1} : L_t : S_t)\, U_M, \tag{11.50}$$

$$P_t = (M_{t-1} : L_t : S_t)\, U_P. \tag{11.51}$$

- The forward recursive coefficient $\alpha_t(M_t)$ is the probability that the memory state of the $t$th seed transformation $U$ in the circuit of Figure 11.8 is $M_t$ at time instant $t$, given the syndrome sequence up to this point, i.e.

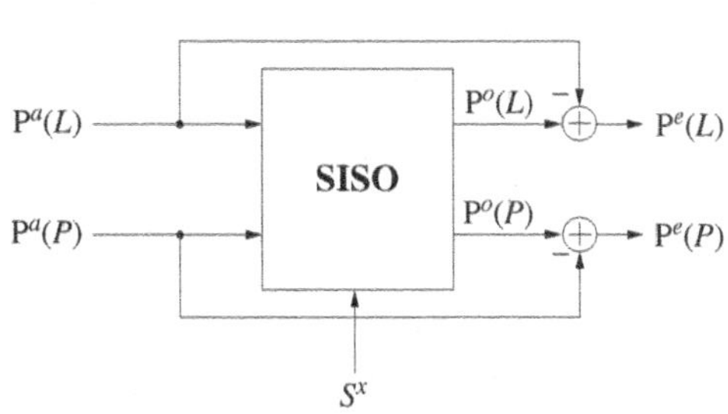


**Figure 11.7** General schematic of a SISO decoder. $P^a(.)$, $P^e(.)$, *and* $P^o(.)$ *denote the a-priori, extrinsic and a posteriori probabilities. Source*: [83]/IEEE.

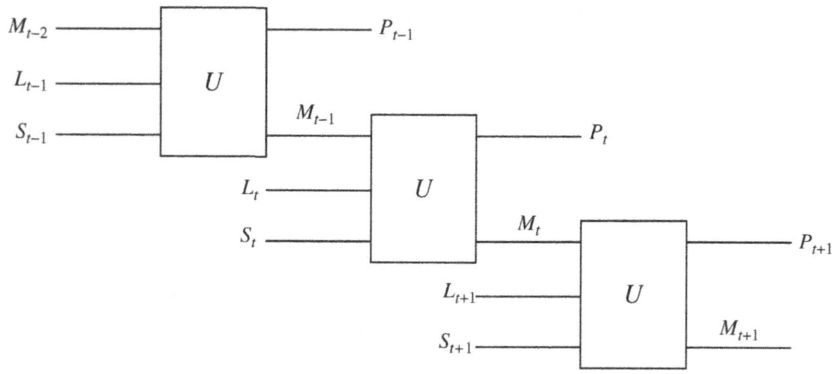


**Figure 11.8** Circuit representation of the encoder $V$ of a quantum convolutional code. *Source*: Adapted from [68]. The operation of the $t$th seed transformation can be characterized as $(M_t : P_t) = (M_{t-1} : L_t : S_t)U$, where $M_t \in G_m$, $P_t \in G_n$, $L_t \in G_k$ and $S_t \in G_{n-k}$, while $U$ is a $2(n+m) \times 2(n+m)$-element binary symplectic matrix.

$S^x_{\leq t} \triangleq \left(S^x_j\right)_{0 \leq j \leq t}$, which can be mathematically modeled as:

$$\alpha_t(M_t) \triangleq \mathrm{P}\left(M_t | S^x_{\leq t}\right),$$
$$\propto \sum_{\substack{(\mu,\lambda,\sigma)\Rightarrow \\ M_t=(\mu:\lambda:\sigma)U_M}} \mathrm{P}^a(L_t=\lambda)\,\mathrm{P}^a(P_t=(\mu:\lambda:\sigma)U_P)\,\alpha_{t-1}(M_{t-1}=\mu), \tag{11.52}$$

where the summation implies adding all the probabilities associated with those specific values of the memory state $M_{t-1} = \mu \in G_m$, of the logical error $L_t = \lambda \in G_k$ and of the error inflicted on the auxiliary qubits $S_t = \sigma \in G_{n-k}$, which yield a particular value of $M_t$ according to Eq. (11.50). Furthermore, $\sigma$ can be decomposed into the **X** and **Z** components such that $\sigma = \sigma_x + \sigma_z$, having $\sigma_x = S^x_t$, while $\sigma_z$ can assume all possible values, as seen in Eq. (11.49).

- The backward recursive coefficient $\beta_t(M_t)$ is the probability that the memory state of the $t$th seed transformation $U$ in the circuit of Figure 11.8 is $M_t$, given the future syndrome sequence, i.e. $S^x_{>t} \triangleq \left(S^x_j\right)_{t<j\leq N}$. This can be formulated as:

$$\beta_t(M_t) \triangleq \mathrm{P}\left(M_t | S^x_{>t}\right),$$
$$\propto \sum_{\lambda,\sigma} \mathrm{P}^a(L_{t+1}=\lambda)\,\mathrm{P}^a(P_{t+1}=(M_t:\lambda:\sigma)U_P)\,\beta_{t+1}(M_{t+1}=(M_t:\lambda:\sigma)\,U_M), \tag{11.53}$$

where the summation implies adding the probabilities for all possible values of logical errors $L_{t+1} = \lambda \in G_k$ plus the errors inflicted on the auxiliary qubits $S_{t+1} = \sigma \in G_{n-k}$, given furthermore that $\sigma = \sigma_x + \sigma_z$, having $\sigma_x = S^x_{t+1}$.

- Finally, we have the *a-posteriori* probabilities $\mathrm{P}^o(L_t)$ and $\mathrm{P}^o(P_t)$, which are given by:

$$\mathrm{P}^o(L_t) \triangleq \mathrm{P}(L_t|S^x),$$
$$\propto \sum_{\mu,\sigma} \mathrm{P}^a(L_t)\mathrm{P}^a(P_t=(\mu:L_t:\sigma)U_P)\alpha_{t-1}(M_{t-1}=\mu)\,\beta_t(M_t=(\mu:L_t:\sigma)\,U_M), \tag{11.54}$$

$$\mathrm{P}^o(P_t) \triangleq \mathrm{P}(P_t|S^x),$$
$$\propto \sum_{\substack{\mu,\lambda,\sigma\Rightarrow \\ P_t=(\mu:\lambda:\sigma)U_P}} \mathrm{P}^a(P_t)\mathrm{P}^a(L_t=\lambda)\alpha_{t-1}(M_{t-1}=\mu)\,\beta_t(M_t=(\mu:\lambda:\sigma)\,U_M), \tag{11.55}$$

where $S^x \triangleq \left(S^x_t\right)_{0\leq t\leq N}$, while the memory state $M_{t-1} = \mu \in G_m$, logical error $L_t = \lambda \in G_k$ and the error inflicted on the auxiliary qubits $S_t = \sigma \in G_{n-k}$, given further that $\sigma = \sigma_x + \sigma_z$, having $\sigma_x = S^x_t$.

- The marginalized probabilities $\mathrm{P}^o(L_t^j)$, for $j \in \{0, k-1\}$, and $\mathrm{P}^o(P_t^j)$, for $j \in \{0, n-1\}$, are then computed from $\mathrm{P}^o(L_t^j)$ and $\mathrm{P}^o(P_t^j)$, respectively. The *a-priori* information is then removed in order to yield the *extrinsic* probabilities [82]. Therefore, in the logarithmic domain, we have:

$$\ln[\mathrm{P}^e(L_t^j)] = \ln[\mathrm{P}^o(L_t^j)] - \ln[\mathrm{P}^a(L_t^j)], \tag{11.56}$$

$$\ln[\mathrm{P}^e(P_t^j)] = \ln[\mathrm{P}^o(P_t^j)] - \ln[\mathrm{P}^a(P_t^j)]. \tag{11.57}$$

It has to be mentioned here that the property of degeneracy is only an attribute of auxiliary qubits and the ebits of an EA code do not contribute to it. This is because both **X** as well as **Z** errors acting on the transmitter's half of ebits give distinct results, when measured in the Bell basis, i.e. $\mathcal{E}^{T_X}|\phi_c^+\rangle^{T_X R_X}$ gives four distinct Bell states for $\mathcal{E}_j^{T_X} \in \{\mathbf{I}, \mathbf{X}, \mathbf{Z}, \mathbf{Y}\}$. Consequently, degeneracy is a function of the number of auxiliary qubits $a$ and reduces to zero for $a = 0$.

## 11.5 EXIT Chart Aided Quantum Code Design

The popular EXIT chart analysis allows us to dispense with time-consuming Monte-Carlo simulations, while facilitating the design of near-capacity codes without resorting to the tedious analysis of their distance spectra.[7] For further details please refer to [125, 219]. Therefore, they have been extensively employed for designing near-capacity classical codes [294–296], as we previously demonstrated in Chapter 5. Let us recall furthermore from Section 5.5.1 that the EXIT chart of a serially concatenated scheme visualizes the exchange of four mutual information (MI) terms, i.e. the average *a-priori* MI of the outer decoder $I_A^1$, the average *a-priori* MI of the inner decoder $I_A^2$, the average *extrinsic* MI of the outer decoder $I_E^1$, and the average *extrinsic* MI of the inner decoder $I_E^2$. More specifically, $I_A^1$ and $I_E^1$ constitute the EXIT curve of the outer decoder, while $I_A^2$ and $I_E^2$ yield the EXIT curve of the inner decoder. The MI transfer characteristics of both the decoders are plotted in the same graph, with the $x$ and $y$ axes of the outer decoder swapped. The resultant EXIT chart quantifies the improvement in the mutual information as the iterations proceed, which can be viewed as a stair-case-shaped decoding trajectory. An open tunnel between the two EXIT curves ensures that the decoding trajectory reaches the $(1, y)$ point of perfect convergence to a vanishingly low error ratio.

In this section, we extended the application of EXIT charts to the quantum domain by appropriately adapting the conventional non-binary EXIT chart generation technique [216, 297] for the quantum syndrome decoding approach. Before proceeding with the application of EXIT charts for quantum codes, let us elaborate on the quantum-to-classical isomorphism of Section 10.3.2, which forms the basis of our EXIT chart aided approach. As discussed in Section 10.3.2.1, a Pauli error operator $\mathcal{P}$ experienced by an $N$-qubit frame transmitted over a depolarizing channel can be modeled by an effective error-vector $P$, which is a binary vector of length $2N$. The first $N$ bits of $P$ denote $Z$ errors, while the remaining $N$ bits represent **X** errors. More explicitly, an **X** error imposed on the 1st qubit will yield a 0 and a 1 at the 1st and $(N+1)$th index of $P$, respectively. Similarly, a **Z** error imposed on the 1st qubit will give a 1 and a 0 at the 1st and $(N+1)$st index of $P$, respectively, while a **Y** error on the 1st qubit will result in a 1 at both the 1st as well as $(N+1)$st index of $P$. Since a depolarizing channel characterized by the probability $p$ incurs **X**, **Y** and **Z** errors with an equal probability of $p/3$, the effective error-vector $P$ reduces to two binary symmetric channels (BSCs) having a crossover probability of $2p/3$, where we have one channel for the **Z** errors and the other for the **X** errors. Hence, a quantum depolarizing channel has been considered analogous to a BSC [67, 298], whose capacity is given by:

$$\mathrm{C}_C^{\mathrm{BSC}}(p) = 1 - \mathrm{H}_2(2p/3), \tag{11.58}$$

where $\mathrm{H}_2$ is the binary entropy function. Let us recall from Eq. (10.38) that the code rate $R_Q$ of an $[n, k]$ QSC is related to the equivalent classical code rate $R_C$ as follows [67, 137]:

$$R_C = \frac{1}{2}(1 + R_Q). \tag{11.59}$$

7 In this chapter familiarity with EXIT charts is assumed, but a rudimentary conceptual introduction was provided in Section 12.1, while a detailed discourse may be found in Chapter 19 of [125].

**Table 11.1** Correlation between **X** and **Z** errors on the *i*th qubit in terms of the corresponding probability of occurrence.

| | **Z** = 0 | **Z** = 1 |
|---|---|---|
| **X** = 0 | $1-p$ | $p/3$ |
| **X** = 1 | $p/3$ | $p/3$ |

The corresponding quantum capacity can be computed by substituting Eq. (11.58) into Eq. (11.59) such that $R_C = \mathrm{C}_C^{\mathrm{BSC}}(p)$, which yields [67, 137]:

$$\mathrm{C}_Q^{\mathrm{BSC}}(p) = 1 - 2\mathrm{H}_2(2p/3). \tag{11.60}$$

However, the two BSCs constituting a quantum depolarizing channel are not entirely independent. There is an inherent correlation between the **X** and **Z** errors [67], which is characterized in Table 11.1. This correlation is taken into account by the iterative decoder of Section 11.4.2.

Alternatively, a quantum depolarization channel can also be considered equivalent to a 4-ary symmetric channel based on the Pauli-to-quaternary isomorphism of Section 10.3.2.2. More explicitly, the $i$th and $(N+i)$th index of $P$ constitute the 4-ary symbol according to the Pauli-to-quaternary isomorphism of Section 10.3.2.2. Hence, the corresponding classical capacity is equivalent to the maximum rate achievable over each half of the 4-ary symmetric channel, or more explicitly the normalized capacity of a 4-ary symmetric channel [67, 137]. Since the **X**, **Y**, and **Z** errors occur with an equal probability of $p/3$ over a depolarizing channel, the normalized capacity of the equivalent 4-ary classical channel is given by:

$$\begin{aligned}\mathrm{C}_C^{\text{4-ary}}(p) &= \frac{1}{2}\left(2+(1-p)\log_2(1-p)+\frac{p}{3}\log_2\left(\frac{p}{3}\right)+\frac{p}{3}\log_2\left(\frac{p}{3}\right)+\frac{p}{3}\log_2\left(\frac{p}{3}\right)\right)\\ &= \frac{1}{2}\left(2+(1-p)\log_2(1-p)+p\log_2(p)-p\log_2(3)\right)\\ &= \frac{1}{2}\left(2-\mathrm{H}_2(p)-p\log_2(3)\right).\end{aligned} \tag{11.61}$$

Substituting Eq. (11.61) into Eq. (11.59) yields the hashing bound of Eq. (11.1), i.e. we have:

$$\mathrm{C}_Q(p) = 1 - \mathrm{H}_2(p) - p\log_2(3). \tag{11.62}$$

Recall that a quantum code is equivalent to a classical code through Eq. (10.30). Additionally, the decoding of a quantum code is essentially carried out with the aid of the equivalent classical code by exploiting the additional property of degeneracy. More particularly, quantum codes employ the syndrome decoding approach of Chapter 4, which yields information about the **error-sequence** rather than the information-sequence or coded qubits, hence avoiding the observation of the latter sequences, which would collapse them back to the classical domain.

Since a quantum code has an equivalent classical representation and the depolarizing channel is analogous to a BSC, we employ the power EXIT chart based technique of [125, 219] for designing concatenated quantum codes that can approach the hashing bound. The major difference between the EXIT charts conceived for the classical and quantum domains is that while the former models the *a-priori* information concerning the input bits of the inner encoder (and similarly the output bits of the outer encoder), the latter models the *a-priori* information concerning the corresponding error-sequence, i.e. the error-sequence related to the input qubits of the inner encoder $L_2$ (and similarly the error-sequence related to the output qubits of the outer encoder $P_1$).

Similar to the classical EXIT charts, it is assumed that the interleaver length is sufficiently high to ensure that [125, 218]:

- the *a-priori* values are fairly uncorrelated;
- the *a-priori* information has a Gaussian distribution.

Figure 11.9 shows the system model used for generating the EXIT chart of the inner decoder. Here, a quantum depolarizing channel having a depolarizing probability of $p$ generates the error sequence $P_2$, which is passed

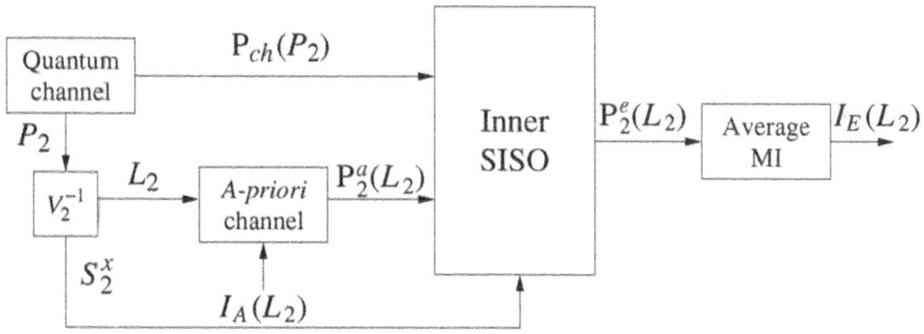


**Figure 11.9** System model for generating the EXIT chart of the inner decoder. *Source:* [290]/IEEE.

through the inverse inner encoder $V_2^{-1}$. This yields both the error imposed on the logical qubits $L_2$ and the syndrome $S_2^x$. The *a-priori* channel block then models the *a-priori* probability $P_2^a(L_2)$ such that the average MI between the actual error $L_2$ and the *a-priori* probabilities $P_2^a(L_2)$ is given by $I_A(L_2)$ [125, 218, 219]. More explicitly, we have $I_A(L_2) = I[L_2, P_2^a(L_2)]$, where $I$ denotes the average MI function. Moreover, the $i$th and $(N+i)$th bits of the effective error vector $L_2$ can be visualized as 4-ary symbols. Consequently, similar to classical non-binary EXIT charts [216, 297], the logarithmic *a-priori* probability is modeled using an independent Gaussian distribution with a mean of $\sigma_A^2/2$ and variance of $\sigma_A^2$, assuming that the **X** and **Z** errors constituting the 4-ary symbols are independent.[8] Based on the channel probability $P_{ch}(P_2)$, on the syndrome $S_2^x$ and on the *a-priori* probability $P_2^a(L_2)$, the inner SISO decoder generates the *extrinsic* probability $P_2^e(L_2)$ by using the degenerate decoding approach of Section 11.4.2. Finally, the *extrinsic* average MI $I_E(L_2) = I[L_2, P_2^e(L_2)]$ between $L_2$ and $P_2^e(L_2)$ is computed. Since the equivalent classical capacity of a quantum channel is given by the capacity achievable over each half of the 4-ary symmetric channel, $I_E(L_2)$ is the normalized MI of the 4-ary symbols, which can be computed based on [216, 217] as:

$$I_E(L_2) = \frac{1}{2}\left(2 + \mathrm{E}\left[\sum_{\mathrm{m}=0}^{3} P_2^e(L_2^{j(\mathrm{m})}) \log_2 P_2^e(L_2^{j(\mathrm{m})})\right]\right), \tag{11.63}$$

where E is the expectation (or time average) operator and $L_2^{j(\mathrm{m})}$ is the $m$th hypothetical error imposed on the logical qubits. More explicitly, since the error on each qubit is represented by an equivalent pair of classical bits, $L_2^{j(\mathrm{m})}$ is a 4-ary classical symbol associated with $\mathrm{m} \in \{0, 3\}$. The process is repeated for a range of $I_A(L_2) \in [0, 1]$ values for the sake of obtaining the *extrinsic* information transfer characteristics at the depolarizing probability $p$. The resultant inner EXIT function $T_2$ of the specific inner decoder may be defined as follows:

$$I_E(L_2) = T_2[I_A(L_2), p], \tag{11.64}$$

which is a function of the channel's depolarizing probability $p$.

The system model used for generating the EXIT chart of the outer decoder is depicted in Figure 11.10. As inferred from Figure 11.10, the EXIT curve of the outer decoder is independent of the channel's output information. The *a-priori* information is generated by the *a-priori* channel based on $P_1$ (error on the physical qubits of the second decoder) and $I_A(P_1)$, which is the average MI between $P_1$ and $P_1^a(P_1)$. Furthermore, as for the inner decoder, $P_1$ is passed through the inverse outer encoder $V_1^{-1}$ to compute $S_1^x$, which is fed to the outer SISO decoder to yield the *extrinsic* probability $P_1^e(P_1)$. The average MI between $P_1$ and $P_1^e(P_1)$ is then calculated similar to Eq. (11.63) as follows:

$$I_E(P_1) = \frac{1}{2}\left(2 + \mathrm{E}\left[\sum_{\mathrm{m}=0}^{3} P_1^e(P_1^{j(\mathrm{m})}) \log_2 P_1^e(P_1^{j(\mathrm{m})})\right]\right). \tag{11.65}$$

The resultant EXIT chart is characterized by the following MI transfer function:

$$I_E(P_1) = T_1[I_A(P_1)], \tag{11.66}$$

where $T_1$ is the outer EXIT function, which is dependent on the specific outer decoder, but it is independent of the depolarizing probability $p$.

8 Under the idealized asymptotic conditions of having an infinite-length interleaver, $I_A(L_2)$ may be accurately modeled by the Gaussian distribution. As and when shorter interleavers are used, the Gaussian assumption becomes less accurate, hence in practice a histogram-based approximation may be relied upon.

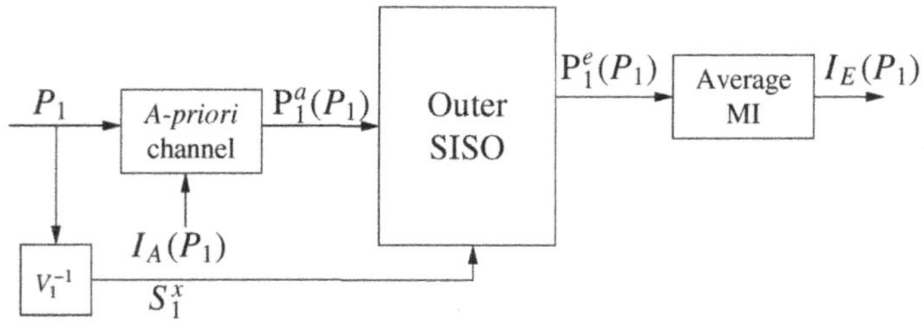


**Figure 11.10** System model for generating the EXIT chart of the outer decoder. *Source*: [290]/IEEE.

Finally, the MI transfer characteristics of both decoders characterized by Eqs. (11.64) and (11.66) are plotted in the same graph, with the $x$ and $y$ axes of the outer decoder swapped. The area under the EXIT curve of the inner decoder is approximately equal to the attainable channel capacity [223], provided that the channel's input symbols are equiprobable, while the area under the EXIT curve of the outer decoder is approximately equivalent to $(1 - R)$ [223], where $R$ is the coding rate of the equivalent classical code given by Eq. (10.38).

In this spirit, for the sake of approaching the achievable capacity of Figure 11.1, *our EXIT chart aided design aims for creating a narrow, but marginally open tunnel between the EXIT curves of the inner and outer decoders at the highest possible depolarizing probability (analogous to the lowest possible SNR for a classical channel).* For a given noise limit $p^*$ and the desired code parameters, this may be achieved in two steps:

- We first find that specific inner code, which yields the largest area under its EXIT curve at the noise limit $p^*$.
- Once the optimal inner code is selected, we find the optimal outer code, whose EXIT curve gives the best shape-match with the inner code chose. The narrower the tunnel-area between the inner and outer decoder's EXIT curve, the lower is the deviation from the achievable capacity or the hashing bound, which may be quantified using Eq. (11.2).

## 11.6 Results and Discussion I

### 11.6.1 Accuracy of EXIT Chart Predictions

In order to verify the accuracy of our EXIT chart-based approach, we have analyzed the convergence behavior of a rate-1/9 QTC, consisting of two identical rate-1/3 QCCs, whose parameters are listed in Table 11.2. More specifically, for both the inner and outer decoders, we have used the configuration termed as "PTO1R" in [81, 82], which is a non-catastrophic but quasi-recursive code.

Our first aim was to predict the convergence threshold using EXIT charts, which would otherwise require time-consuming word error rate (WER) or QBER simulations. The convergence threshold can be determined by finding the maximum depolarizing probability $p$, which results in a marginally open EXIT tunnel between the EXIT curves of the inner and outer decoder, hence facilitating an infinitesimally low error rate. Figure 11.11 shows the EXIT curves for the inner and outer decoders, where the area under the EXIT curve of the inner decoder decreases upon increasing $p$. Eventually, the inner and outer decoder curves cross each other, when $p$ is increased to $p = 0.13$. More explicitly, increasing $p$ beyond 0.125, closes the EXIT tunnel. Hence, the convergence threshold is around $p = 0.125$. Figure 11.12 further shows two decoding trajectories superimposed on the EXIT chart of Figure 11.11 at $p = 0.125$. We have used a 30,000-qubit long interleaver. As seen from Figure 11.12, the trajectory successfully reaches the $(x, y) = (1, y)$ point of the EXIT chart. This in turn guarantees an infinitesimally low WER/QBER at $p = 0.125$ for an interleaver of infinite length.

We have further verified the validity of our EXIT chart predictions using WER simulations. Figure 11.13 shows the WER performance curve for the simulation parameters of Table 11.2. The achievable performance of Figure 11.13 improves upon increasing the number of iterations from 1 to 8. More specifically, the turbo-cliff region starts to emerge around $p = 0.125$ (marked with a dashed-line in Figure 11.13), whereby the WER drops as the iterations proceed. Therefore, our EXIT chart predictions of Figure 11.11 follow the Monte-Carlo simulation results of Figure 11.13 to a reasonable degree.

**Table 11.2** Simulation parameters of the concatenated scheme of Figure 11.6. The inner/outer QCC is the "PTO1R" configuration which is an unassisted rate-1/3 QCC (quasi-recursive and non-catastrophic).

| | |
|---|---|
| Coding rate | $R = 1/9$ |
| Entanglement consumption rate | $\mathrm{E} = 0$ |
| Interleaver length | $N = 3000$ qubits |
| Iterations | $\mathrm{I} = 8$ |
| **Inner QCC** | |
| Coding rate | $R_i = 1/3$ |
| Entanglement consumption rate | $\mathrm{E}_i = 0$ |
| Memory | 3 |
| Seed transformation | $U_i = \{1355, 2847, 558, 2107, 3330, 739, 2009, 286, 473, 1669, 1979, 189\}_{10}$ |
| **Outer QCC** | |
| Coding rate | $R_o = 1/3$ |
| Entanglement consumption rate | $\mathrm{E}_o = 0$ |
| Memory | 3 |
| Seed transformation | $U_o = \{1355, 2847, 558, 2107, 3330, 739, 2009, 286, 473, 1669, 1979, 189\}_{10}$ |

*Source*: Adapted from [81, 82].

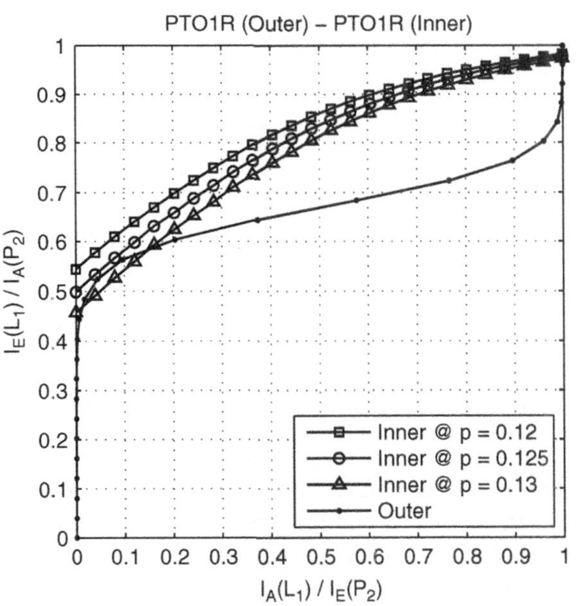


**Figure 11.11** The EXIT curves of a QTC parametrized by the increasing depolarizing probability $p$. The parameters of the inner and outer QCC are listed in Table 11.2. *Source*: [290]/IEEE.

### 11.6.2 Entanglement-assisted and Unassisted Inner Codes

All non-catastrophic QCCs are non-recursive [68]. Therefore, the resultant families of QTCs have a bounded minimum distance and they do not have a true iterative threshold. To circumvent this limitation of QTCs, Wilde *et al.*

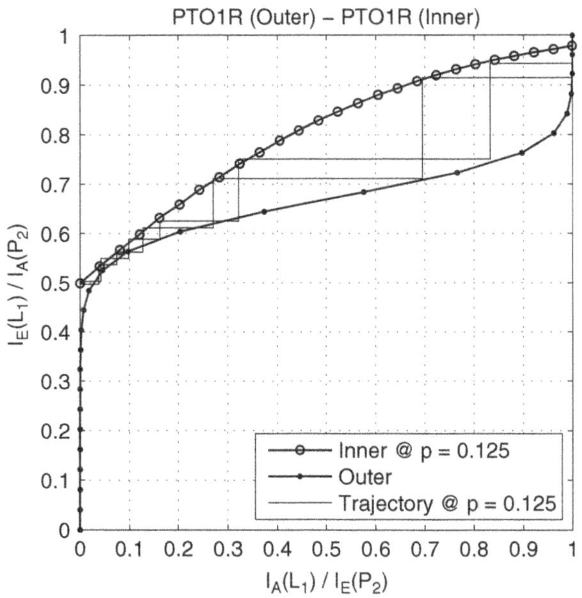


**Figure 11.12** The EXIT chart of a QTC with decoding trajectories at $p = 0.125$. We have used the QTC of Table 11.2 with an increased interleaver length of 30,000 qubits. *Source*: [290]/IEEE.

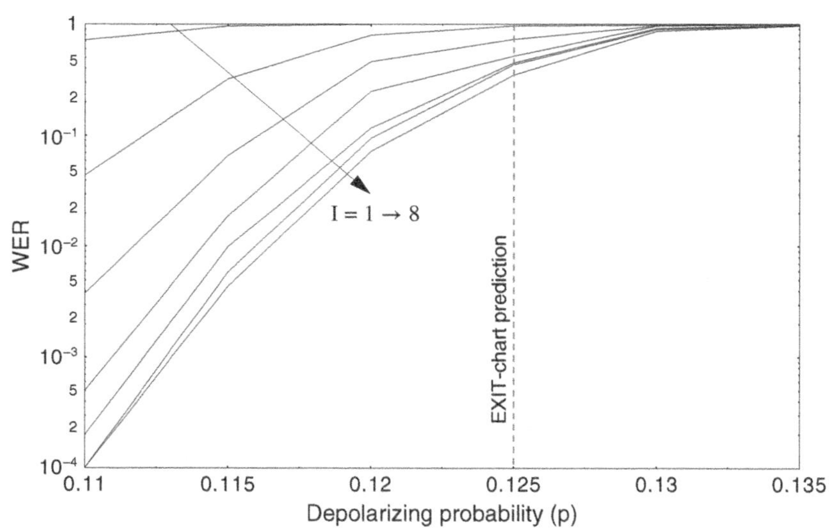


**Figure 11.13** Achievable WER performance of the QTC of Figure 11.6 as the number of iterations (I) is increased from 1 to 8. Simulation parameters are summarized in Table 11.2. The dashed-line at $p = 0.125$ marks the convergence threshold predicted using the EXIT chart of Figure 11.12.

[81, 82] proposed to employ EA inner codes, which are recursive as well as non-catastrophic. The resultant families of EA-QTCs have an unbounded minimum distance [81, 82], i.e. their minimum distance increases almost linearly with the interleaver length. Here, we verify this by analyzing the inner decoder's EXIT curves for both the unassisted (non-recursive) and the EA (recursive) inner convolutional codes.

For classical recursive inner codes, the inner decoder's EXIT curve reaches the $(x, y) = (1, 1)$ point,[9] which guarantees perfect decoding convergence to a vanishingly low WER/QBER as well as having an unbounded minimum distance for the family of QTCs [68] based on these inner codes. Consequently, the resultant families of QTCs

9 Note that we only need $(x, y) = (1, y)$ for achieving decoding convergence to an infinitesimally low error rate. However, this requires an outer code having a sufficiently large minimum distance for the sake of ensuring that the outer code's EXIT curve does not intersect with that of the inner code before reaching the $(1, y)$ point. Unfortunately, an outer code having a large minimum distance would result in an EXIT curve having a large open-tunnel area. Thus, it will operate far from the capacity.

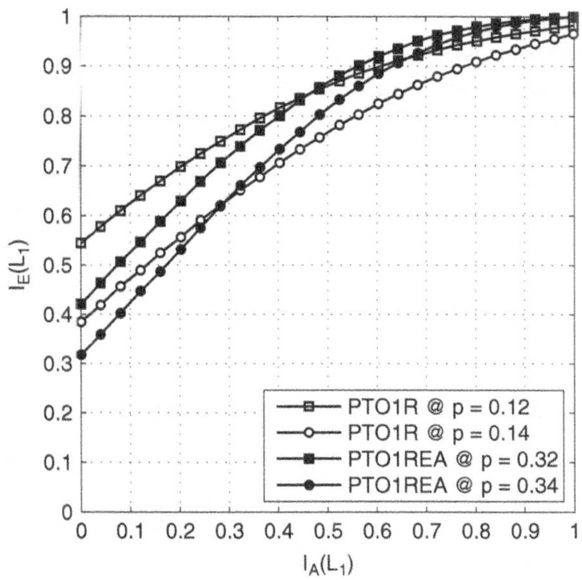


**Figure 11.14** Comparison of the inner EXIT curves of both unassisted and entanglement-assisted QCCs, labeled as PTO1R and PTO1REA respectively. PTO1R is the inner code of Table 11.2, while PTO1REA is the same as PTO1R but requires 2 e-bits. *Source*: [290]/IEEE.

have unbounded minimum distance and hence an arbitrarily low WER/QBER can be achieved for an infinitely long interleaver. This also holds true for the recursive QCCs, as shown in Figure 11.14. In this figure, we compare the inner decoder's EXIT curves of both the unassisted QCC (non-recursive) and the EA-QCC (recursive) of [81], which are labeled "PTO1R" and "PTO1REA," respectively. More explicitly, PTO1REA is the maximally entangled[10] version of PTO1R, which has the same configuration as that of the PTO1R given in Table 11.2, but with an increased entanglement consumption rate of 2/3. We may observed in Figure 11.14 that, for the PTO1R configuration, decreasing the depolarizing probability from $p = 0.14$ to $p = 0.12$ shifts the inner decoder's EXIT curve upward and toward the $(1, 1)$ point. Hence, the EXIT curve will only succeed in reaching the $(1, 1)$ point at very low values of depolarizing probability. By contrast, the EXIT curve of PTO1REA always terminates at $(1, 1)$, regardless of the value of $p$. Therefore, provided an open EXIT tunnel exists and the interleaver length is sufficiently long, the decoding trajectories of an EA-QTC will always reach the $(1, 1)$ point; thus, guaranteeing an arbitrarily low WER/QBER for the family of QTCs based on these inner codes. Hence the performance improves upon increasing the interleaver length. This implies that the minimum distance increases upon increasing the interleaver length. Therefore, the resultant QTCs have an unbounded minimum distance.

### 11.6.3 Optimized Quantum Turbo Code Design

The QTC design of [81, 82] characterized in Figure 11.12 exhibits a large area between the inner and outer decoder's EXIT curves. The larger the "open-tunnel" area, the farther the WER/QBER performance from the achievable noise limit $p^*$ [125]. For an unassisted rate-1/9 code, the noise limit is $p^* = 0.16028$ according to the hashing bound of Figure 11.1. Consequently, the design of Figure 11.12 operates within $\left[10 \times \log_{10}\left(\frac{0.125}{0.16028}\right)\right] = 1.1$ dB of the noise limit. Various other distance spectra based QTCs investigated in [82], which exhibit a wide EXIT chart tunnel analogous to Figure 11.12, operate within 0.9 dB of the hashing bound. For the sake of achieving a hashing bound approaching performance, we minimize the area between the inner and outer EXIT curves, so that a narrow, but still marginally open tunnel exists at the highest possible depolarizing probability.

**Design Objective:** *Congenially with the rate-1/9 QTC of [82], find the optimal inner and outer components of a rate-1/9 QTC relying on a maximally entangled inner code (recursive and non-catastrophic) and an unassisted*

10 For a maximally entangled code, we have $c = (n - k)$, resulting in an entanglement consumption rate of $(1 - R_Q)$, where $R_Q$ is its coding rate.

*outer code (non-catastrophic), both having a memory of 3 and a rate of 1/3. The resultant QTC has an entanglement consumption rate of 6/9 (or equivalently 2/3), for which the corresponding noise limit is $p^* = 0.3779$ according to Eq. (11.3). Consequently, the optimized QTC should operate at a channel depolarizing probability close to the noise limit* $p^* = 0.3779$. For the sake of finding the optimized inner and outer components, which minimize the area between the corresponding EXIT curves at a depolarizing probability close to the noise limit, we randomly selected both the inner and outer encoders from the Clifford group according to the algorithm of [299]. Based on this design criterion, we found the optimal inner and outer code pair, whose seed transformations (decimal representation) are given by:

$$U_i = \{4091, 3736, 2097, 1336, 1601, 279, 3093, 502, 1792, 3020, 226, 1100\}_{10}; \tag{11.67}$$

$$U_o = \{1048, 3872, 3485, 2054, 983, 3164, 3145, 1824, 987, 3282, 2505, 1984\}_{10}. \tag{11.68}$$

Code parameters of our optimized design are also summarized in Table 11.3.

Figure 11.15 shows the EXIT curves of our optimized QTC at the convergence threshold of $p = 0.35$. As observed in Figure 11.15, a marginally open EXIT tunnel exists between the two curves, which would facilitate for the decoding trajectories to reach the $(1, 1)$ point of perfect convergence. Hence, our optimized QTC has a convergence threshold of $p = 0.35$, which is only $\left[10 \times \log_{10}\left(\frac{0.35}{0.3779}\right)\right] = 0.3$ dB from the noise limit of $p^* = 0.3779$. We have quantified the corresponding achievable performance in Figure 11.16, where the interleaver length was increased from 1500 to 12,000. All other simulation parameters are kept the same as that of Table 11.3. We have recorded both the WER as well as the QBER performance. Analogous to the classical turbo codes, increasing the interleaver length improves the attainable performance for $p < 0.35$, hence providing a better performance at the cost of an increased delay, which was also pointed out in Figure 11.2 in the context of our conflicting design challenges.

In Figure 11.17, we further compare our optimized design, using the parameters of Table 11.3, to the "PTO1REA-PTO1R" configuration of [82], whose parameters are summarized in Table 11.4. Both configurations employ a rate-1/3 EA-QCC (recursive and non-catastrophic) as the inner code, while an unassisted rate-1/3 QCC (non-catastrophic) is used as the outer code. For the "PTO1REA-PTO1R" design, the turbo cliff region emerges around

**Table 11.3** Simulation parameters of the optimized QTC, having a rate-1/3 EA-QCC (recursive and non-catastrophic) as the inner code, while an unassisted rate-1/3 QCC (non-catastrophic) is used as the outer code.

| | |
|---|---|
| Coding rate | $R = 1/9$ |
| Entanglement consumption rate | $\mathrm{E} = 6/9$ |
| Interleaver length | $N = 3000$ qubits |
| Iterations | $\mathrm{I} = 15$ |
| **Inner QCC** | |
| Coding rate | $R_i = 1/3$ |
| Entanglement consumption rate | $\mathrm{E}_i = 2/3$ |
| Memory | 3 |
| Seed transformation | $U_i = \{4091, 3736, 2097, 1336, 1601, 279, 3093, 502, 1792, 3020, 226, 1100\}_{10}$ |
| **Outer QCC** | |
| Coding rate | $R_o = 1/3$ |
| Entanglement consumption rate | $\mathrm{E}_o = 0$ |
| Memory | 3 |
| Seed transformation | $U_o = \{1048, 3872, 3485, 2054, 983, 3164, 3145, 1824, 987, 3282, 2505, 1984\}_{10}$ |

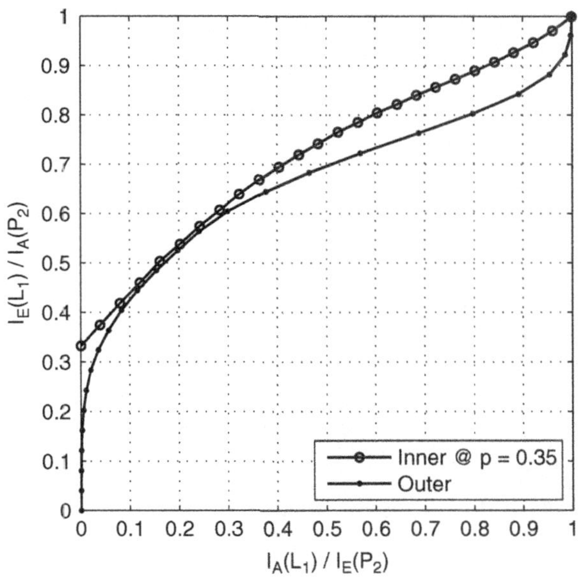


**Figure 11.15** The EXIT curves of the optimized rate-1/9 QTC. The parameters of the inner and outer QCC are listed in Table 11.3. *Source*: [290]/IEEE.

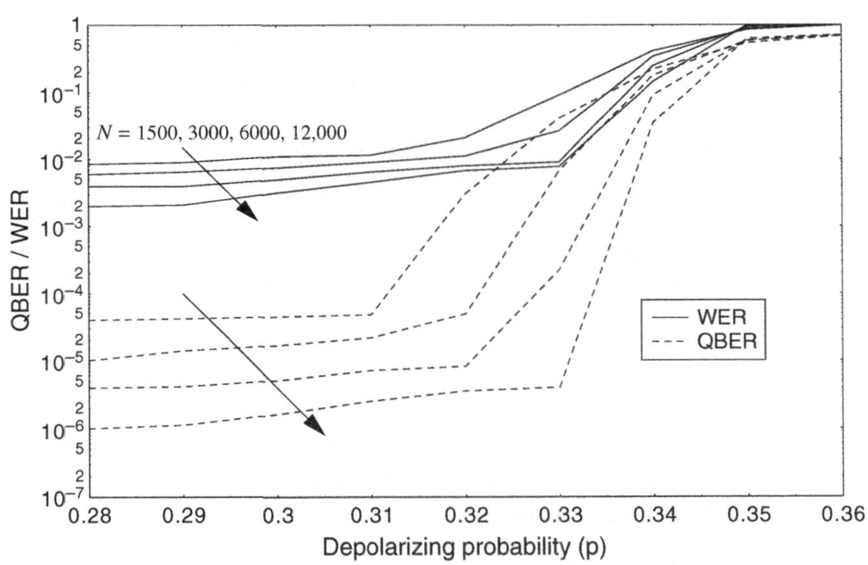


**Figure 11.16** Achievable QBER and WER performance of the optimized QTC of Figure 11.6 as the interleaver length ($N$) is increased from 1500 to 12,000. All other simulation parameters are summarized in Table 11.3.

$p = 0.31$, which is within 0.9 dB of the noise limit. It may also be observed in Figure 11.17 that our optimized design outperforms the "PTO1REA-PTO1R" in terms of having a better convergence threshold, albeit at the cost of a higher error-floor. This is because our optimized outer code has a low minimum distance of only 3. Its truncated distance spectrum is as follows:

$$D(x) = 2x^3 + 19x^4 + 108x^5 + 530x^6 + 2882x^7 + 14179x^8 + 62288x^9 + 243234x^{10}$$
$$+845863x^{11} + 1165784x^{12} + 2501507x^{13} + 744394x^{14}.$$

By contrast, the truncated distance spectrum of "PTO1R," which has a minimum distance of 5, is given by [82]:

$$D(x) = 11x^5 + 47x^6 + 253x^7 + 1187x^8 + 6024x^9 + 30529x^{10} + 153051x^{11} + 771650x^{12}.$$

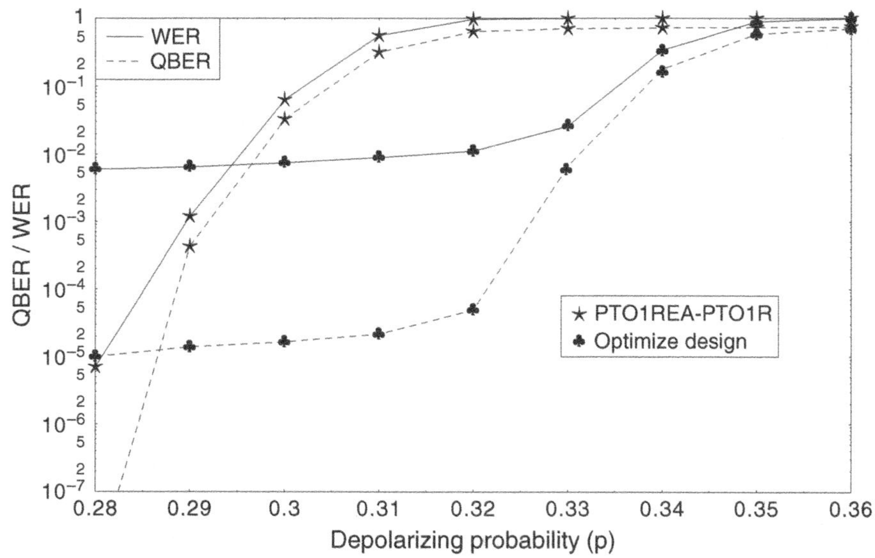


**Figure 11.17** Comparison of the achievable QBER/WER performance of our optimized QTC having the parameters of Table 11.3 and the "PRO1REA-PTO1R" configuration. *Source*: Adapted from [81, 82] whose parameters are summarized in Table 11.4.

Consequently, as seen from Figure 11.17, the "PTO1REA-PTO1R" configuration has a much lower error floor ($< 10^{-6}$), since the outer code "PTO1R" has a higher minimum distance. However, this enlarges the area between the inner and outer decoder's EXIT curves. hence pushing the performance curve farther away from the achievable capacity. Hence, there is a trade-off between the minimization of the error floor and achieving a hashing bound approaching performance. More specifically, while the distance-spectrum based design primarily aims for achieving a lower error floor, the EXIT chart-based design strives for achieving a near-capacity performance. Note that the error floor can also be reduced by employing a longer interleaver.

Furthermore, we invoked a maximum of eight decoding iterations for the "PTO1REA-PTO1R" design, while a maximum of 15 iterations were used for our optimized design. Again, this can be attributed to the large EXIT tunnel area between the inner and outer decoders' EXIT curves of the "PTO1REA-PTO1R" construction. Generally, the wider the gap between the inner and outer decoders' EXIT curves, the faster the decoding convergence, since a lower number of decoding iterations are required for reaching the $(1, 1)$ point of perfect convergence. In this section, we did not intend to carry out an exhaustive code search for finding the best code. Instead, our intention was to optimize our design in terms of its convergence threshold for the sake of demonstrating the explicit benefit of our EXIT chart technique conceived for approaching the hashing bound. Nevertheless, in the next section, we have conceived a QIRCC, which reduces the error floor.

## 11.7 Quantum Irregular Convolutional Codes

In this section we further pursue our design objective, namely *that of finding the optimal outer code $\mathcal{C}$ having a coding rate $R_o$, which gives the best match with the given inner code, i.e. whose EXIT curve yields a marginally open tunnel with the given inner decoder's EXIT curve at a depolarizing probability close to the hashing bound.* For the sake of achieving this objective, a feasible design option could be to create the outer EXIT curves of all the possible convolutional codes to find the optimal code $\mathcal{C}$, which gives the best match, as we did in Section 11.6.3. To circumvent this exhaustive code search, in this section we advocate the QIRCC design philosophy detailed in Chapter 19 of [125] for achieving accurate EXIT curve matching.

Similar to the classical irregular convolutional code (IRCC) of [221], our proposed QIRCC employs a family of $\Omega$ subcodes $\mathcal{C}_q$, $q \in \{1, 2, \ldots, \Omega\}$, for constructing the target code $\mathcal{C}$. As a benefit of its inherent flexibility, the resultant QIRCC provides a better EXIT curve match than any single code, when used as the outer component in the concatenated structure of Figure 11.6. The $q$th subcode has a coding rate of $r_q$ and it encodes a specifically

**Table 11.4** Simulation parameters of the "PRO1REA-PTO1R" configuration which is used as a benchmark. Similar to the QTC of Table 11.3, inner code is a rate-1/3 EA-QCC (recursive and non-catastrophic), while the outer code is an unassisted rate-1/3 QCC (non-catastrophic).

| | |
|---|---|
| Coding rate | $R = 1/9$ |
| Entanglement consumption rate | $\mathrm{E} = 6/9$ |
| Interleaver length | $N = 3000$ qubits |
| Iterations | $\mathrm{I} = 8$ |
| **Inner QCC** | |
| Coding rate | $R_i = 1/3$ |
| Entanglement consumption rate | $\mathrm{E}_i = 2/3$ |
| Memory | 3 |
| Seed transformation | $U_i = \{1355, 2847, 558, 2107, 3330, 739,$ $2009, 286, 473, 1669, 1979, 189\}_{10}$ |
| **Outer QCC** | |
| Coding rate | $R_o = 1/3$ |
| Entanglement consumption rate | $\mathrm{E}_o = 0$ |
| Memory | 3 |
| Seed transformation | $U_o = \{1355, 2847, 558, 2107, 3330, 739,$ $2009, 286, 473, 1669, 1979, 189\}_{10}$ |

*Source*: Adapted from [81, 82].

designed fraction of the original information qubits to $\varrho_q N$ encoded qubits. Here, $N$ is the total length of the coded frame. More specifically, for a $\Omega$-subcode IRCC, $\varrho_q$ is the $q$th IRCC weighting coefficient satisfying the following constraints [220, 221]:

$$\sum_{q=1}^{\Omega} \varrho_q = 1,\ R_o = \sum_{q=1}^{\Omega} \varrho_q r_q,\ \varrho_q \in [0,1], \forall q, \tag{11.69}$$

which can be conveniently represented in the following matrix form:

$$\begin{pmatrix} 1 & 1 & \dots & 1 \\ r_1 & r_2 & \dots & r_\Omega \end{pmatrix} \begin{pmatrix} \varrho_1 & \varrho_2 \dots & \varrho_\Omega \end{pmatrix}^T = \begin{pmatrix} 1 \\ R_o \end{pmatrix} \tag{11.70}$$
$$\mathbf{r}\,\varrho = \mathbf{R}.$$

Hence, as shown in Figure 11.18, the input stream is partitioned into $\Omega$ sub-frames,[11] which are assembled back into a single $N$-qubit stream after encoding.

In the context of classical IRCCs, the subcodes $\mathcal{C}_q$ are constructed from a mother code [220, 221]. More specifically, high-rate subcodes are obtained by puncturing the mother code, while the lower rates are obtained by adding more generators. However, in contrast to classical codes, puncturing is not easy to implement for quantum codes, since the resultant punctured code must satisfy the symplectic criterion, as in [300].[12] In this context, in order to design the constituent subcodes of our proposed QIRCC, we selected five strong randomly constructed memory-3 quantum convolutional codes having the quantum code rates of $\{1/4, 1/3, 1/2, 2/3, 3/4\}$,

11 This is only true if all subcodes are active. If $\varrho_q = 0$ for the $q^{th}$ subcode, then $\mathcal{C}_q$ is not activated. Therefore, the input stream is only divided among the active subcodes.

12 Puncturing represents the removal of some of the specifically selected encoded bits for the sake of adjusting the coding rate.

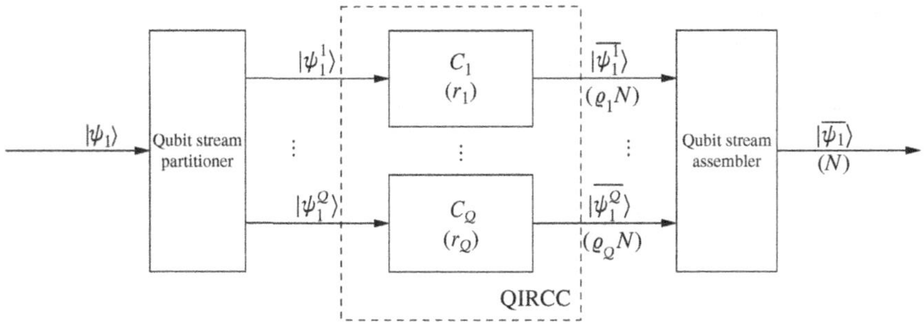


**Figure 11.18** Structure of a $Q$-subcode QIRCC encoder. *Source*: [83]/IEEE.

which met the non-catastrophic requirement of [68]. More explicitly, for the sake of creating a random construction for the Clifford encoder specifying the quantum convolutional code, we used the classical random walk algorithm over the $(n+m)$-qubit Clifford group as in [299]. The seed transformations of the resultant subcodes having rates $\{1/4, 1/3, 1/2, 2/3, 3/4\}$ are provided as follows:

$$
\begin{aligned}
U_1 &= \{9600, 691, 11713, 4863, 1013, 6907, 1125, 828, 10372, 6337, 5590, 11024, 12339, 3439\}_{10},\\
U_2 &= \{3968, 1463, 2596, 3451, 1134, 3474, 657, 686, 3113, 1866, 2608, 2570\}_{10},\\
U_3 &= \{848, 1000, 930, 278, 611, 263, 744, 260, 356, 880\}_{10},\\
U_4 &= \{529, 807, 253, 1950, 3979, 2794, 956, 1892, 3359, 2127, 3812, 1580\}_{10},\\
U_5 &= \{62, 6173, 4409, 12688, 7654, 10804, 1763, 15590, 6304, 3120, 2349, 1470, 9063, 4020\}_{10}.
\end{aligned} \tag{11.71}
$$

The EXIT curves of these QIRCC subcodes are shown in Figure 11.19, whereby the memory-3 subcodes of Eq. (11.71) are indicated by solid lines. Furthermore, in order to facilitate accurate EXIT curve matching with the aid of a sufficiently versatile and diverse set of inner EXIT functions, we also selected 5 weak randomly constructed memory-1 subcodes for the same range of coding rates, i.e. $\{1/4, 1/3, 1/2, 2/3, 3/4\}$. The corresponding seed transformations are as follows:

$$
\begin{aligned}
U_6 &= \{475, 194, 526, 422, 417, 988, 426, 611, 831, 84\}_{10},\\
U_7 &= \{26, 147, 149, 99, 112, 184, 64, 139\}_{10},\\
U_8 &= \{37, 55, 58, 35, 57, 54\}_{10},\\
U_9 &= \{57, 248, 99, 226, 37, 93, 244, 54\}_{10},\\
U_{10} &= \{469, 634, 146, 70, 186, 969, 387, 398, 807, 452\}_{10},
\end{aligned} \tag{11.72}
$$

and their EXIT curves are plotted in Figure 11.19, which are marked by the dotted lines. It must be mentioned here that the range of coding rates chosen for the QIRCC subcodes can be expanded for ensuring that the EXIT curves cover a larger portion of the EXIT plot, which would further improve the curve matching accuracy. However, this increases the encoding and decoding complexity.

Based on our proposed QIRCC, relying on the 10 subcodes specified by Eqs. (11.71) and (11.72), the input bit stream is divided into 10 fractions corresponding to the 10 different-rate subcodes. The specific optimum fractions to be encoded by these codes are found by dynamic programming. More specifically, since the QCCs belong to the class of linear codes, the EXIT curves of the 10 subcodes, given in Figure 11.19, are superimposed onto each other after weighting by the appropriate fraction-based weighting coefficients, which are determined by minimizing the area of the open EXIT tunnel. To elaborate a little further, the transfer function of the QIRCC is given by the weighted sum of each subcode's transfer function as illustrated:

$$
I_E(P_1) = T_1[I_A(P_1)] = \sum_{q=1}^{Q} \varrho_q\, T_1^q\,[I_A(P_1)]\,, \tag{11.73}
$$

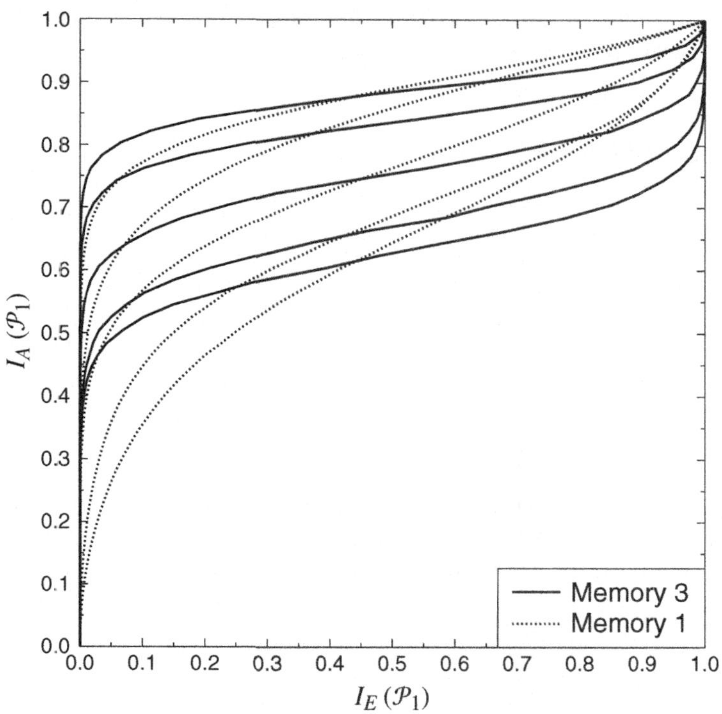


**Figure 11.19** Outer EXIT curves (inverted) of our QIRCC subcodes having code rates {1/4, 1/3, 1/2, 2/3, 3/4} for both memory-3 as well as memory-1. *Source*: [83]/IEEE.

where $T_1^q\,[I_A(P_1)]$ is the transfer function of the $q$th subcode. For a given inner EXIT curve and outer code rate $R_Q$, we employ the curve matching algorithm of [220, 221] for optimizing the weighting coefficients $\boldsymbol{\varrho}$ of our proposed QIRCC such that the square of the error between the inner and inverted outer EXIT curves is minimized subject to Eq. (11.69). More explicitly, the error function may be modeled as:

$$e(i) = T_2[i, p] - T_1^{-1}[i], \tag{11.74}$$

where $p = (p^* - \epsilon)$ given that $p^*$ is the noise limit defined by the hashing bound and $\epsilon$ is an arbitrarily small number. The corresponding matrix-based notation may be formulated as [220, 221]:

$$\mathbf{e} = \mathbf{b} - \mathbf{A}\boldsymbol{\varrho}, \tag{11.75}$$

where we have:

$$\mathbf{b} = \begin{pmatrix} T_2[i_1, p] \\ T_2[i_2, p] \\ \vdots \\ T_2[i_N, p] \end{pmatrix}, \text{and}$$
$$\mathbf{A} = \begin{pmatrix} T_1^{1^{-1}}[i_1] & T_1^{2^{-1}}[i_1] & \dots & T_1^{Q^{-1}}[i_1] \\ T_1^{1^{-1}}[i_2] & T_1^{2^{-1}}[i_2] & \dots & T_1^{Q^{-1}}[i_2] \\ \vdots & \vdots & \vdots & \vdots \\ T_1^{1^{-1}}[i_N] & T_1^{2^{-1}}[i_N] & \dots & T_1^{Q^{-1}}[i_N] \end{pmatrix}. \tag{11.76}$$

Here, $N$ denotes the number of sample points such that $i \in \{i_1, i_2, \ldots, i_N\}$ and it is assumed that $N > \mathcal{Q}$. Furthermore, the error should be higher than zero for the sake of ensuring an open tunnel, i.e. we have:

$$e(i) > 0, \ \forall i \in [0, 1]. \tag{11.77}$$

The resultant cost function, i.e. sum of the square of the errors, is given by [220]:

$$\mathcal{J}(\varrho_1, \ldots, \varrho_{\mathcal{Q}}) = \int_0^1 e(i)^2 di, \tag{11.78}$$

which may also be written as:

$$\mathcal{J}(\varrho) = \mathbf{e}^T\mathbf{e}. \tag{11.79}$$

The overall process may be encapsulated as follows:

$$\varrho_{opt} = \arg\min_{\varrho} \mathcal{J}(\varrho), \tag{11.80}$$

subject to Eqs. (11.69) and (11.77), which is a convex optimization problem. The unconstrained optimal solution for Eq. (11.80) is found iteratively using the steepest descent approach with a gradient of $\partial\mathcal{J}(\varrho)/\partial\varrho = 2\mathbf{e}$, which is then projected onto the constraints defined in Eqs. (11.69) and (11.77). Further details of this optimization algorithm can be found in [125, 220, 221].

## 11.8 Results and Discussion II

For the sake of demonstrating the EXIT curve matching capability of our proposed QIRCC, we designed a rate-1/9 concatenated code relying on the rate-1/3 EA inner code of Table 11.4, namely "PTO1REA" [81, 82], in conjunction with our proposed QIRCC, which constitutes the outer code. Since the entanglement consumption rate of "PTO1REA" is 2/3, the resultant code has an entanglement consumption rate of 6/9, for which the corresponding noise limit is $p^* = 0.3779$ according to Eq. (11.3) [82]. Furthermore, since we intend to design a rate-1/9 scheme with the aid of a rate-1/3 inner code, we have $R_o = 1/3$. Hence, for a target coding rate of 1/3, we used the optimization algorithm discussed in Section 11.7 for the sake of finding the optimum weighting coefficients of Eq. (11.80) at the highest possible depolarizing probability $p = p^* - \epsilon$.

It was found that we only need to invoke two subcodes out of the 10 possible subcodes, based on $\varrho = [0\,0\,0\,0\,0.168\ 0.832\,0\,0\,0\,0]^T$, for attaining a marginally open tunnel, which occurs at $p = 0.345$, as shown in Figure 11.20 using the simulation parameters of Table 11.5. Hence, the resultant code has a convergence threshold of $p = 0.345$, which is only $\left[10 \times \log_{10}\left(\frac{0.345}{0.3779}\right)\right] = 0.4$ dB away from the noise limit of $p^* = 0.3779$. Figure 11.20 also shows two decoding trajectories at $p = 0.34$ for a 30,000 qubit long interleaver, which approaches the ultimate bound of an infinitely long interleaver. As seen from the figure, the decoding trajectories closely follow the EXIT curves reaching the $(1, 1)$ point of perfect convergence.

The corresponding WER performance curves recorded for our QIRCC-based optimized design, having the simulation parameters of Table 11.5, are seen in Figure 11.21, where the WER is reduced upon increasing the number of iterations from 1 to 15. More explicitly, our code converges to a low WER for $p \leq 0.345$. Hence this convergence threshold matches the one predicted using EXIT charts in Figure 11.20. More explicitly, since the EXIT chart tunnel closes for $p > 0.345$, the system fails to converge, if the depolarizing probability is increased beyond 0.345. Hence, the performance does not improve upon increasing the number of iterations if the depolarizing probability exceeds the threshold. By contrast, when the depolarizing probability is below the threshold, the WER improves at each successive iteration. It should also be noted that the performance only improves marginally, with diminishing returns at a higher number of iterations.

Figure 11.22 compares our QIRCC-based optimized design associated with the rate-1/9 "PTO1REA-PTO1R" configuration of [82]. An interleaver length of 000 qubits was used. For the "PTO1REA-PTO1R" configuration, the turbo cliff region emerges around 0.31, which is within 0.9 dB of the noise limit. Therefore, our QIRCC-based design outperforms the "PTO1REA-PTO1R" configuration of [82]. More specifically, the "PTO1REA-PTO1R" configuration yields a WER of $10^{-3}$ at $p = 0.29$, while our design gives a WER of $10^{-3}$ at $p = 0.322$. Hence, our optimized design outperforms the "PTO1REA-PTO1R" configuration by about $\left[10 \times \log_{10}\left(\frac{0.29}{0.322}\right)\right] = 0.5$ dB at a WER

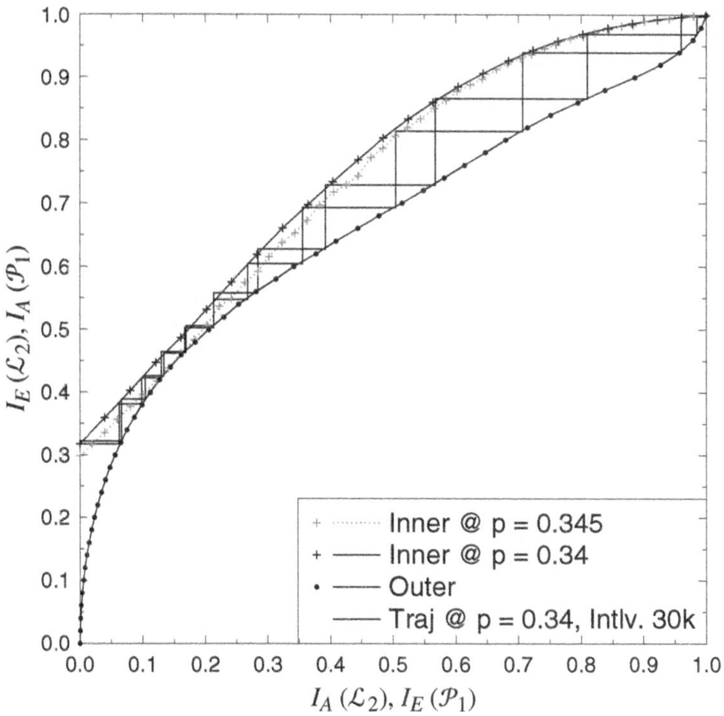


**Figure 11.20** EXIT curves of the concatenated rate-1/9 system, with PTO1REA as the inner code and QIRCC as the outer, at $p = 0.345$ and $p = 0.34$. The parameters of the inner and outer code are summarized in Table 11.5, while the trajectories are plotted for a 30,000-qubit long interleaver. *Source*: [83]/IEEE.

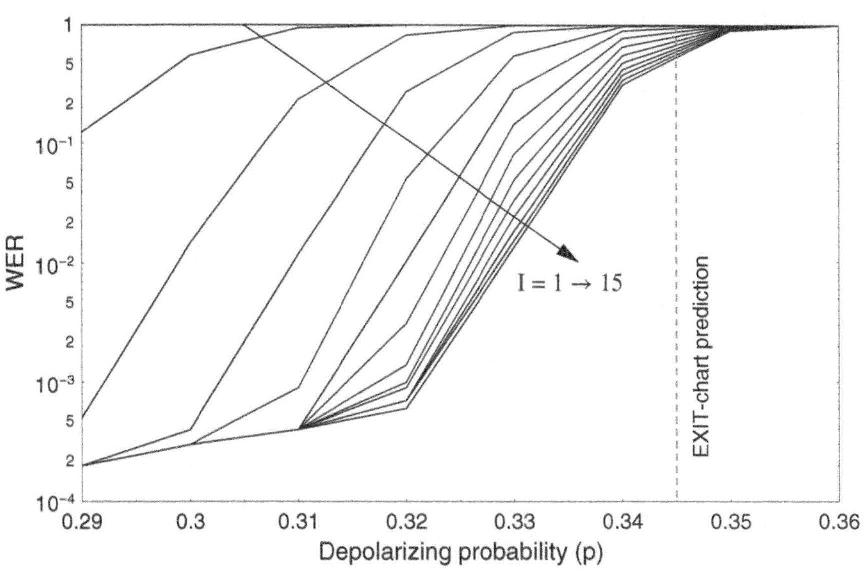


**Figure 11.21** Achievable WER performance of our QIRCC-based optimized design, having the parameters of Table 11.5, as the number of iterations (I) is increased from 1 to 15.

of $10^{-3}$. It must be mentioned here that the "PTO1REA-PTO1R" configuration may have a lower error floor than our design for low value of $p$, yet our design exhibits a better performance in the turbo cliff region. We further compare our QIRCC-based optimized design with the exhaustive-search based optimized turbo code of Section 11.6.3 in Figure 11.22. Our QIRCC-based design does not provide any improvement in terms of its convergence threshold as compared to the optimized QTC of Section 11.6.3. However, our QIRCC-based design has a much

**Table 11.5** Simulation parameters of the QIRCC-aided configuration. Inner code is the same as that in Table 11.4, while the QIRCC is used as the outer code, whose weighting coefficients are optimized with the aid of EXIT charts for the sake of approaching the hashing bound.

| | |
|---|---|
| Coding rate | $R = 1/9$ |
| Entanglement consumption rate | $\mathrm{E} = 6/9$ |
| Interleaver length | $N = 3000$ qubits |
| Iterations | $\mathrm{I} = 15$ |
| **Inner QCC** | |
| Coding rate | $R_i = 1/3$ |
| Entanglement consumption rate | $\mathrm{E}_i = 2/3$ |
| Memory | 3 |
| Seed transformation | $U_i = \{1355, 2847, 558, 2107, 3330, 739, 2009, 286, 473, 1669, 1979, 189\}_{10}$ |
| **Outer QIRCC** | |
| Coding rate | $R_o = 1/3$ |
| Entanglement consumption rate | $\mathrm{E}_o = 0$ |
| Weighting coefficients | $\varrho = [0\ 0\ 0\ 0\ 0.168\ 0.832\ 0\ 0\ 0\ 0]^T$ |

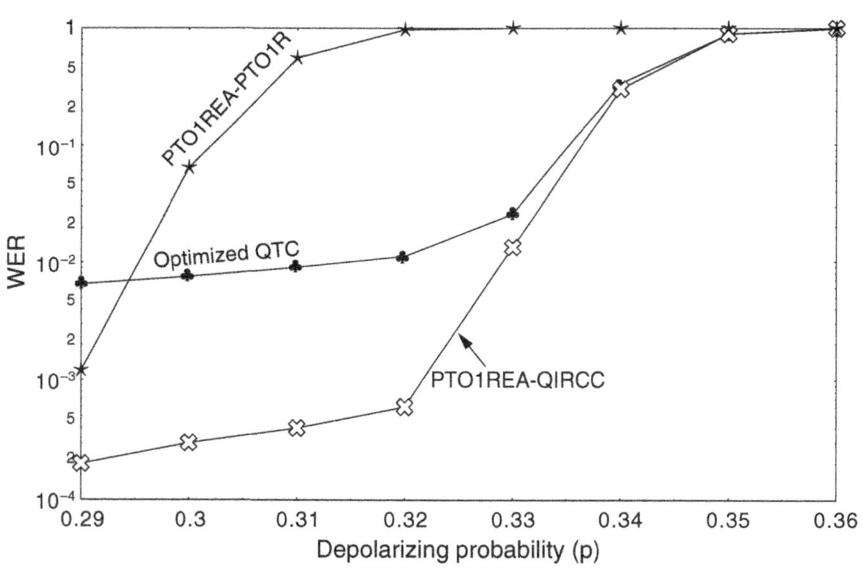


**Figure 11.22** Comparison of the achievable WER performance of our QIRCC-based optimized QTC having the parameters of Table 11.5 with the "PRO1REA-PTO1R" configuration. *Source*: Adapted from [81, 82]. Table 11.4 and our exhaustive-search based optimized QTC of Section 11.6.3 (Table 11.3).

lower error rate associated with a lower error floor, as observed from Figure 11.22. Furthermore, the QIRCC-based design allows us to dispense with the exhaustive-search based optimization of Section 11.6.3. It must be pointed out here that we may accrue an improvement in the convergence threshold by increasing the number of QIRCC subcodes, which would facilitate better curve matching.

## 11.9 Summary and Conclusions

Powerful QECCs are required for stabilizing and protecting the fragile constituent qubits of both quantum computation as well as of communication systems against the deleterious effects of decoherence. In line with the developments in the field of classical channel coding theory, this may be achieved by exploiting concatenated codes designs, which invoke iterative decoding. Therefore, in this chapter we have provided a slow-paced tutorial for designing hashing bound approaching concatenated quantum codes using EXIT charts, which is based on the insights developed in Chapters 4 and 10.

We commenced our discourse by highlighting our design objectives in Section 11.2. In particular, we characterized the performance of an ideal code in terms of its performance, its coding rate and its entanglement consumption rate. They all are related to each other through the hashing bound, or more specifically the hashing region of Figure 11.1. We next presented the circuit based representation of QCCs in Section 11.3, which facilitates the degenerate iterative decoding of concatenated quantum codes. We also discussed the construction of a Clifford unitary encoder, which is completely specified by the Hadamard, phase and controlled-NOT gates of Eq. (11.12). We next presented our system model in Section 11.4.1, which relies on the circuit-based representation of a pair of concatenated QSCs.

The degenerate iterative decoding approach, which is invoked in the system model of Section 11.4.1, is then detailed in Section 11.4.2. In contrast to the classic syndrome-based MAP algorithm, which aims for finding the most likely error for a given syndrome, a degenerate MAP algorithm aims for finding the most likely error coset. More explicitly, the probabilities corresponding to degenerate errors are accumulated, as depicted in Eq. (11.49), in order to cater for the specific errors, which can be corrected by the same recovery operation. Finally, in Section 11.5, we extended the application of classical non-binary EXIT charts to the circuit-based syndrome decoder of QTCs, to facilitate the EXIT chart aided hashing bound approaching design of QTCs. While the classical EXIT charts aim for modeling the *a-priori* information concerning the input bits of the inner encoder (and similarly the output bits of the outer encoder), the EXIT charts conceived for quantum codes have the objective of modeling the *a-priori* information concerning the corresponding error-sequence, i.e. the error-sequence related to the input qubits of the inner encoder (and similarly the error-sequence related to the output qubits of the outer encoder).

We evaluated the performance of our EXIT chart based code design in Section 11.6. More specifically, we first quantified the accuracy of our EXIT chart approach in Section 11.6.1, where it was demonstrated that our EXIT chart predictions of Figure 11.12 match the Monte-Carlo simulation results to a reasonable degree, as seen in Figure 11.13. We next in Section 11.6.2 we analyzed the behavior of both an unassisted (non-recursive) and an EA (recursive) inner QCC using EXIT charts. We demonstrated in Figure 11.14 that similar to their classical counterparts, the recursive inner quantum codes constitute families of QTCs having an unbounded minimum distance. In Section 11.6.3, we optimized the constituent inner and outer components of the QTC of Figure 11.6 using EXIT charts. In this context, our design guidelines formulated for achieving a hashing bound approaching performance may be summarized as follows:

- As discussed in the context of our design objectives in Section 11.2, we commence our design by determining the noise limit $p^*$ for the desired code parameters, i.e the coding rate and the entanglement consumption rate of the resultant concatenated quantum code, using the capacity curves of Figure 11.1.
- We then proceed with the selection of the inner stabilizer code of Figure 11.6, which has to be both recursive as well as non-catastrophic, as argued in Section 11.4.1. Since the unassisted quantum codes cannot be simultaneously both recursive as well as non-catastrophic, we employ an EA code. Furthermore, the EA inner code of Figure 11.6 may be either derived from the family of known classical codes, as discussed in Chapter 10, or it may be constructed using the random Clifford operations, which were discussed in Section 11.3. At this point, the EXIT curves of Section 11.5 may be invoked for the sake of finding that specific inner code, which yields the largest area under its EXIT curve at the noise limit $p^*$.
- Finally, we find the optimal non-catastrophic outer code of Figure 11.6, which gives the best EXIT curve match to that of a carefully chosen inner code having the largest area under its EXIT curve. Our EXIT chart aided design of Section 11.5 aimed for creating a narrow, but marginally open tunnel between the EXIT curves of the inner and outer decoders at the highest possible depolarizing probability, as demonstrated in the EXIT

**Table 11.6** Comparison of the performance of the QTC of [82], i.e. PRO1REA-PTO1R, with our exhaustive-search optimized QTC of Section 11.6.3 and the PRO1REA-QIRCC of Section 11.8. All the three configurations rely on a rate-1/3 EA-QCC (recursive and non-catastrophic) as the inner code, while the outer code is an unassisted rate-1/3 QCC (non-catastrophic).

| | Distance from capacity | | |
|---|---|---|---|
| **Code structure** | **Convergence threshold** | **Performance at WER = $10^{-2}$** | **Performance at WER = $10^{-3}$** |
| QTC of [82] | 0.9 dB | 1.1 dB | 1.15 dB |
| Exhaustive-search based optimized QTC | 0.3 dB | 0.8 dB | Error floor < $10^{-3}$ |
| QIRCC-based QTC | 0.4 dB | 0.6 dB | 0.7 dB |

curves of Figure 11.15. The narrower the tunnel-area, the lower is the deviation from the hashing bound, which may be quantified using Eq. (11.2).

Recall that the desired code structure may also be optimized on the basis of a range of conflicting design challenges, which were illustrated in Figure 11.2.

We demonstrated in Section 11.6.3 that in contrast to the distance spectra based QTCs of [82], whose convergence threshold is within 0.9 dB of the hashing bound, the convergence threshold of our optimized QTC is within 0.3 dB of the noise limit, as evidenced in Figure 11.15. However, the resultant optimized QTC has a higher error floor and worse WER performance, which was recorded in Figure 11.16 and compared to the performance of [82] in Figure 11.17. Nevertheless, the error floor may be reduced upon increasing the interleaver length, which would in turn incur a longer delay. For example, upon increasing the interleaver length from $N = 1500$ to $N = 12{,}000$ in Figure 11.16, the WER floor was reduced from WER $= 10^{-2}$ to WER $= 2 \times 10^{-3}$, which is about an order of magnitude. It is important to mention here that we did not intend to carry out an exhaustive code search for finding the best code, but our aim was rather to find a design optimized in terms of improving the convergence threshold for the sake of demonstrating the explicit benefit of our EXIT chart based design in terms of approaching the hashing bound.

For the sake of further characterizing the near-hashing-bound code design philosophy, we proposed the QIRCC structure in Section 11.7, which constitutes the outer component of a concatenated quantum code. The proposed QIRCC allows us to dispense with exhaustive code-search based methods, since it can be dynamically adapted to match any given inner code using EXIT charts. We constructed a 10-subcode QIRCC and used it as an outer code in concatenation with the non-catastrophic and recursive EA-QCC of [81, 82]. We optimized our design using EXIT charts, as demonstrated in Figure 11.20, while the achievable performance was recorded in Figure 11.21. Finally, we compared the designs of Tables 11.3–11.5 in Figure 11.22. The corresponding results are summarized in Table 11.6.

In the spirit of designing iterative code structures, in this chapter we conceived hashing bound approaching designs for concatenated quantum codes. Pursuing further the iterative code design, in the next chapter we will focus our efforts on the family of quantum low density parity check (QLDPC) codes from the perspective of code design as well as on the associated iterative decoding algorithms.

# 12

# Near-hashing-bound Quantum Turbo Short-block Codes

## 12.1 Introduction to Iterative Decoding

We have established that QSCs [54, 55, 59, 60, 86, 92, 94] are capable of estimating both the number and the position of quantum bit (qubit) errors without collapsing the quantum state of physical qubits into their classical state. Hence, they can be viewed as syndrome-based QECCs. In Chapters 7 and 8, we have shown that the family of QTECCs suffer from a lower quantum coding rate ($r_Q$) than their classical counterparts, since they have to tackle not only the bit-flip (**X**) errors but also the phase-flip (**Z**) errors [179]. In this chapter, in order to circumvent the issue of having low quantum coding rates, we present a QTC scheme having high quantum coding rates by concatenating quantum error detection codes (QEDCs) inspired by QTECCs with quantum-domain unity rate codes (QURCs).

The above mentioned concatenated design philosophy of this chapter is motivated by [301], where it has been demonstrated that concatenating a quantum linear block code with a unity-rate quantum convolutional code (QCC) facilitates soft-decision-aided iterative decoding. The above mentioned QCC is also referred to as a QURC. Again, we will demonstrate that a dramatic performance improvement may be attained without reducing the quantum coding rate.

The iterative decoding philosophy of the classical domain dates back all the way to Gallagher's seminal paper as early as 1962 [126], in which he proposed to iteratively exchange information between the so-called variable nodes and parity check nodes of the decoder in the interest of improving the decoding performance at the cost of increasing the decoding complexity. In simple plausible terms the iterative information exchange between these nodes of the decoder is beneficial, because statistically speaking the different nodes tend to be contaminated by impairments, which are typically independent of each other. This is particularly plausible in the presence of uncorrelated noise-induced contamination or in quantum systems case of uncorrelated decoherence. Therefore the chances are that if for example an information bit is gravely contaminated by a noise sample, the corresponding redundant parity bits are less likely to be affected, unless a prolonged burst of errors is experienced.

In case of prolonged error bursts it is especially beneficial to have a longer separation between the position of the information and the redundant parity bits for ensuring their uncorrelated contamination. Therefore it maybe surmised that because the redundant bits are related to the original information bits, their uncorrelated corruption allows us these bits to assist in each other's recovery by harnessing iterative information exchange or "negotiation" between them. Since longer channel codes are capable of maintaining a potentially higher separation between the information and redundant bits, they tend to perform better, albeit they also impose higher decoding complexity. Hence the higher-complexity decoding also contributes toward improving their performance. These trends directly follow from Shannon's channel-coding theorem, loosely speaking stating that if the codeword-length tends to infinity, near-capacity performance may be attained. The historic evolution of concatenated coding and a rich set of iterative decoding techniques was detailed in [125, 219], including both parallel and serial concatenated schemes.

To elaborate a little further, the specific concept of *serial code component concatenation* of classical coding was conceived by Benedetto *et al.*, which is portrayed in Figure 12.1. Again, it is advantageous to have a longer separation between the position of the information and the redundant parity bits for ensuring their uncorrelated contamination. This is why the interleaver or scrambler Π is inserted between the pair of serially concatenated encoders, namely the outer and inner encoders.

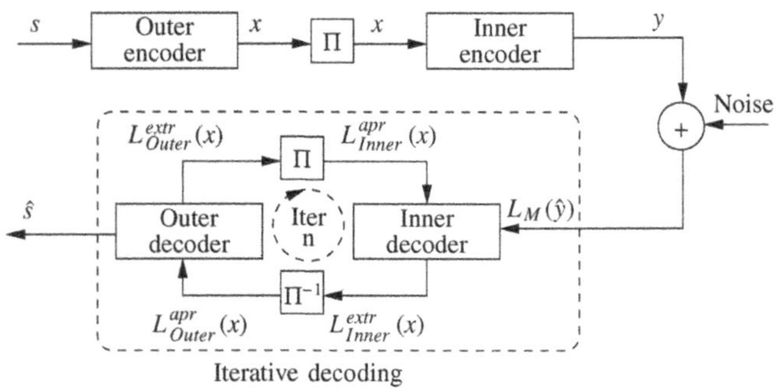


**Figure 12.1** Serially concatenated encoder and decoder relying on the outer and inner encoders/decoders and an interleaver.

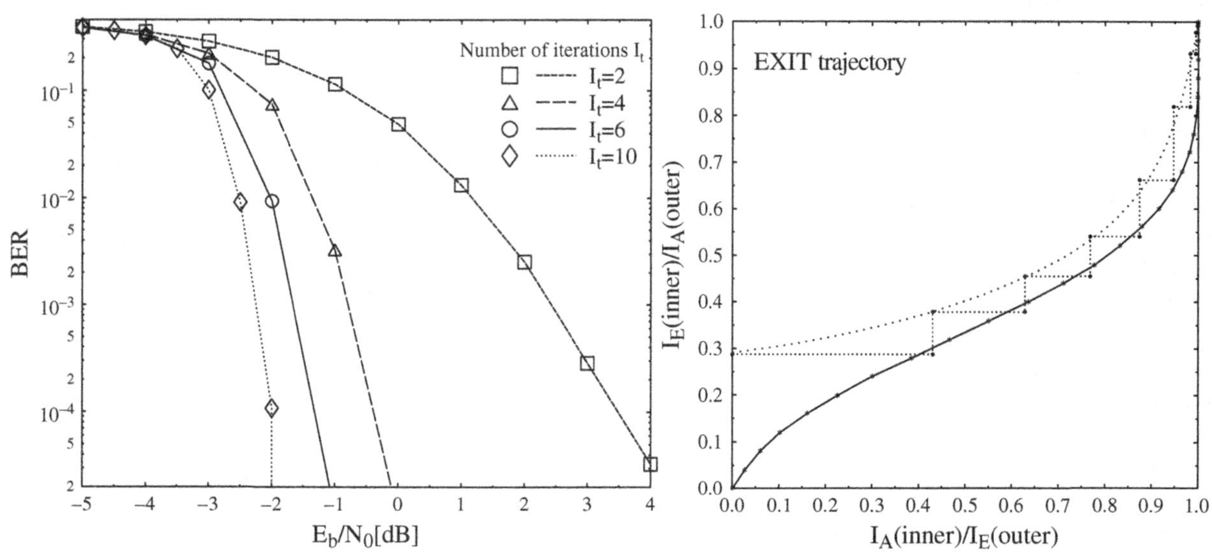


**Figure 12.2** Stylized classical BER and EXIT chart relationship.

At the decoder we have four variables, which play a salient role in the ensuing iterative detection. These are $L^{\text{apr}}_{\text{Inner}}, L^{\text{apr}}_{\text{Outer}}, L^{\text{extr}}_{\text{Inner}}, L^{\text{extr}}_{\text{Outer}}$, representing soft-decision based probability values, rather than hard-decision based binary values. At the beginning of iterations the inner decoder has to process its noise-contaminated input information, but it has no other source of information. It then makes a tentative decision in order to share its decision with the outer decoder in form of the so-called *a-priori* information $L^{\text{apr}}_{\text{Outer}}$ after appropriately positioning the bits at the output of the deinterleaver $\Pi^{-1}$. Explicitly, the *extrinsic* information ${}^{\text{extr}}_{\text{Inner}}$ produced by the inner decoder becomes the *a-priori* information $L^{\text{apr}}_{\text{Outer}}$ at the deinterleaver's output. Based on this *a-priori* information the outer decoder produces $L^{\text{extr}}_{\text{Outer}}$, which becomes $L^{\text{apr}}_{\text{Inner}}$ for the inner decoder. The inner decoder now has both the channel's output and $L^{\text{apr}}_{\text{Inner}}$ and hence it becomes capable of iteratively improving its tentative decisions. Once the affordable number of iterations has been exhausted, the outer decoder makes a final hard-decision.

Observe in the stylized illustration at the top of Figure 12.2 that upon increasing the number of iterations $I$ the BER of such a serially concatenated scheme gradually improves, but beyond $I=4$ the gain becomes more limited. This iterative decoding process may also be tangibly visualized with the aid of the so-called extrinsic information transfer (EXIT) chart seen in the lower stylized illustration of Figure 12.2. For a detailed tutorial on EXIT charts the enthusiastic reader might like to consult [125, 219], but here we assume familiarity with the basic concept.

Suffice to say that when the *a-priori* mutual information (MI) $I_A(inner)$ is zero before the beginning of iterations, this EXIT chart indicates having an *extrinsic* MI of about $I_e(inner) = 0.3$ on the vertical axis, which becomes the $I_a(outer)$ at input of the outer decoder after deinterleaving. This outer decoder generates $I_e(outer)$, which becomes $I_a(inner) \approx 0.4$ after deinterleaving, as seen on the horizontal axis at the end of the first horizontal step of the staircase-shaped iterative decoding characteristic. Given the *a-priori* MI gleaned from the outer decoder, the inner encoder now provides the improved *extrinsic* MI $I_e(inner0$, generating $I_a(outer0$ after deinterleaving. The iterations continue in the same way, gradually improving MI upon each extra iteration and the BER improvements seen in the upper illustration of Figure 12.2 correspond to each step in the MI trajectory. Explicitly, a total of 10 steps may be observed during the 10 iterations. Perfect convergence to an infinitesimally low BER may be observed, when the decoder produces near-unity *extrinsic* MI upon having near-unity *a-priori* MI.

Let us now return to the inspirational solution in [301]. This impressive early solution constituted a mile-stone, but unfortunately it suffered from a relatively high error floor. This was somewhat unexpected, because it relied on a low overall quantum coding rate of $r_Q = 1/8$, when using a block code having a minimum distance of $d = 3$ as the outer code. Additionally, to eliminate the error floor, this specific code construction required the insertion of auxiliary bits relying on a so-called doping mechanism for supporting the convergence of iterative decoding.

As a further advance, it was shown in [302] that by carefully selecting the inner and the outer codes using an EXIT chart [125, 219] aided code search, a half-rate QTC can be conceived, which is capable of performing relatively close to the quantum hashing bound. Explicitly, this excellent error correction performance was achieved by a half-rate quantum irregular convolutional codes (QIrCCs) used as the outer codes combined with a QURC as the inner code. This specific code was referred to as the QIrCC-QURC scheme.

Again, that the above mentioned concatenated coding philosophy of Figure 12.1 is well established in the literature of classical codes, as detailed for example in [125]. One of the components of Figure 12.1 may also have a unity rate for ensuring that the code-rate is not unduly reduced. Hence in simple plausible terms, the unity-rate outer encoder may be serially concatenated with an interleaver, which rearranges the unity-rate encoder's output sequence before entering it into an appropriately selected inner encoder. The inner and outer encoders connected by the interleaver jointly constitute a serially concatenated encoder. Given that the outer encoder has a coding-rate of unity, it does not result in the undesired reduction of the coding rate, i.e. of the throughput, but we will demonstrate that it is capable of improving the quBit error ratio (QBER) without substantially increasing the decoding complexity, i.e. the number of quantum gates. This QBER improvement is an explicit benefit of iteratively exchanging *extrinsic* information between the inner and outer decoders a number of times before making a final hard decision concerning the original transmitted sequence. in this context the role of the above mentioned interleaver – also often termed as a scrambler – is to beneficially rearrange the relative position of the original information and redundant symbols for ensuring that each information symbol is adequately protected by the surrounding redundant symbols. This way the inner and outer decoders become capable of providing independent *extrinsic* information for each other, which is the source of the iterative turbo detection gain.

As an important result in the classical domain, it was shown that an outer code exhibiting a minimum distance of $d = 2$ is capable of guaranteeing the convergence of iterative decoding to a vanishingly low bit error ratio (BER) [303, 304], as exemplified by the family of single parity-check codes (SPCs) or short-block codes (SBCs) [305, 306]. This may be deemed somewhat surprising, because simple logic would dictate that it is necessary to have a minimum distance of three for correcting a single error. A low-complexity technique of constructing codes having a minimum distance of two is to concatenate a single parity-checking bit to $k$ information bits. Then the code-rate becomes $k/(k + 1)$.

Returning to our main discussions cast in the quantum domain, by exploiting the classical-to-quantum isomorphism [153, 179], we can indeed conceive the quantum-domain counterpart of the classical SBCs, which we may refer to as quantum short-block codes (QSBCs). As an additional benefit, the QSBCs can also be viewed as QTECCs. More specifically, the QTECC construction exhibits an inherent error detection and error correction capability, when the physical qubits are appropriately arranged on a lattice structure. However, most of the conventional techniques of constructing the QTECCs suffer from a low quantum coding rate as well as from the lack of flexibility, when choosing both the number of logical qubits and the quantum coding rate [153]. By contrast, when a similar approach relying on utilizing a lattice structure is invoked for constructing quantum error detection codes (QEDCs) instead of QECCs, we found that the resultant topological QEDCs are flexible and exhibit high quantum coding rates.

The rest of this chapter is organized as follows. In Section 12.2, we present the general formulation of QSBCs in terms of their code construction, encoder, and stabilizer measurement. This is followed by Section 12.3, where we propose serially concatenated QTCs by utilizing QSBCs as the outer codes and a QURC as the inner code, which we refer to as the QSBC-QURC scheme. We analyze the convergence behavior of our iterative-decoding-aided QSBC-QURC scheme using EXIT charts and evaluate both its QBER and its goodput in Section 12.4. Finally, we conclude the chapter and present some promising directions for future research in Section 12.5.

## 12.2 Quantum Short-block Codes

In this section, we introduce the quantum version of classical SBCs by describing their general construction, the structure of the quantum encoder, as well as the quantum circuit required for the stabilizer measurements. This section will also characterize both the flexibility and scalability of the QSBC encoders and the associated stabilizer measurements, as the natural evolution from their PCM structure. Furthermore, we present a short tutorial on conducting the classical simulation of QSBCs. In order to avoid ambiguity, throughout the rest of this chapter the notation $\mathcal{C}(n, k, d)$ is used to denote the classical error correction code having a codeword length of $n$ bits, information word length of $k$ bits, and a minimum distance of $d$. By contrast, the notation of $\mathcal{C}[n, k, d]$ is used for the quantum stabilizer code. More explicitly, the round brackets in $(n, k, d)$ represent the classical codes, while the square brackets in $[n, k, d]$ indicate quantum codes.

### 12.2.1 Code Construction

The classical SBCs are systematic linear binary block codes $\mathcal{C}\,(n, k, d)$, whose generator matrix $\mathbf{G}$ is defined by:

$$\mathbf{G} = [\mathbf{I}_k | \mathbf{P}_{k,(n-k)}] = [\mathbf{I}_k | \mathbf{J}_{k,1}], \tag{12.1}$$

where $\mathbf{I}_k$ is a $k$-dimensional identity matrix, $\mathbf{P}_{(n-k),k}$ is a $[k \times (n-k)]$-element binary matrix and $\mathbf{J}_{m,n}$ is a $(m \times n)$-element matrix having all-one elements. Hence, the PCM $\mathbf{H}$ of a systematic linear block code is encapsulated in

$$\mathbf{H} = [\mathbf{I}_{n-k} | \mathbf{P}^T]. \tag{12.2}$$

Therefore, the PCM $\mathbf{H}$ of the classical SBCs is given by

$$\mathbf{H} = \mathbf{J}_{1,n}, \tag{12.3}$$

which is an all-one $(1 \times n)$—element matrix. Finally, the resultant coding rate is given by

$$r = \frac{k}{n} = \frac{k}{k+1} = \frac{n-1}{n}. \tag{12.4}$$

The minimum distance of the SBCs conceived is $d = 2$, hence this guarantees the convergence of iterative decoding to a vanishingly low BER, when they constitute the outer code [303, 304].

By exploiting the classical-to-quantum isomorphism [179], this specific type of classical SBCs can be readily transformed into their quantum counterparts. To elaborate a little further, given a pair of classical codes $\mathcal{C}_1(n, k_1, d_1)$ and $\mathcal{C}_2(n, k_2, d_2)$ having PCMs $\mathbf{H}_1$ and $\mathbf{H}_2$, respectively, a QSC $\mathcal{C}[\tilde{n}, \tilde{k}, \tilde{d}]$ having a binary PCM $\mathbf{H}$ can be constructed from $\mathbf{H}_x = \mathbf{H}_1$ and $\mathbf{H}_z = \mathbf{H}_2$. Then $\mathbf{H}_x$ will be used for mitigating the bit-flip errors and $\mathbf{H}_z$ will be used for mitigating the phase-flip errors, where we have $\tilde{n} = n$, $\tilde{k} = k_1 + k_2 - n$, and $\tilde{d} = \min(d_1, d_2)$. In general, there are two ways of constructing the binary PCM $\mathbf{H}$ of a QSC $\mathcal{C}$ given a pair of PCMs $\mathbf{H}_x$ and $\mathbf{H}_z$. Firstly, we may construct a CSS type quantum code, whose binary PCM $\mathbf{H}$ is as follows [86]:

$$\mathbf{H} = \left[\begin{array}{c|c} \mathbf{H}_z & \mathbf{0} \\ \mathbf{0} & \mathbf{H}_x \end{array}\right]. \tag{12.5}$$

Second, we may also construct a non-CSS type quantum code, whose binary PCM $\mathbf{H}$ is given by [94]

$$\mathbf{H} = \left[\mathbf{H}_z \,\middle|\, \mathbf{H}_x\right]. \tag{12.6}$$

Recall that in order to conceive a valid PCM $\mathbf{H}$ for a QSC $\mathcal{C}$, a pair of PCMs $\mathbf{H}_x$ and $\mathbf{H}_z$ has to satisfy the symplectic criterion, which is defined as [94]

$$\mathbf{H}_z \cdot \mathbf{H}_x^T + \mathbf{H}_x^T \cdot \mathbf{H}_z = 0. \tag{12.7}$$

Therefore, the symplectic criterion formulated for a CSS type quantum code can be reduced to

$$\mathbf{H}_z \cdot \mathbf{H}_x^T = 0. \tag{12.8}$$

A specific case of CSS type quantum codes, where we have $\mathbf{H}_x = \mathbf{H}_z$, is referred to as a dual-containing CSS quantum code. Therefore, the dual-containing CSS quantum codes can be instantly derived from the classical SBCs having the following PCMs:

$$\mathbf{H}_z^T = \mathbf{H}_x^T = \mathbf{J}_{1,n}, \tag{12.9}$$

where $n$ is an even number. This automatically satisfies the symplectic criterion of Eq. (12.8). Ultimately, the resultant PCM of QSBCs is given by:

$$\mathbf{H} = \left[\begin{array}{c|c} \mathbf{J}_{1,n} & \mathbf{0} \\ \mathbf{0} & \mathbf{J}_{1,n} \end{array}\right]. \tag{12.10}$$

Hence, for dual-containing CSS quantum codes, the relationship between the classical coding rate $r_C$ and the quantum coding rate $r_Q$ can be described as follows [83, 153, 170]

$$r_Q = 2r_C - 1. \tag{12.11}$$

Since the quantum coding rate $r_Q$ has to be positive ($r_Q > 0$), the original classical code must exhibit a classical coding rate of $r_C > 1/2$.

For QSCs, the PCM $\mathbf{H}$ is associated with stabilizer operators $S_i \in \mathcal{S}$. For example, let us consider a classical SBC $\mathcal{C}(4, 3, 2)$ having a PCM of

$$\mathbf{H}_x = \mathbf{H}_z = [1\,1\,1\,1], \tag{12.12}$$

exhibiting a classical coding rate of $r_C = 3/4$, which is associated with a QSBC of $\mathcal{C}[n, k, d] = \mathcal{C}[4, 2, 2]$ having a quantum coding rate of $r_Q = 1/2$. The stabilizer operators of $\mathcal{C}[4, 2, 2]$ are given by

$$\begin{aligned} S_1 &= \mathbf{Z}_1\mathbf{Z}_2\mathbf{Z}_3\mathbf{Z}_4, \\ S_2 &= \mathbf{X}_1\mathbf{X}_2\mathbf{X}_3\mathbf{X}_4, \end{aligned} \tag{12.13}$$

where $\mathbf{X}$ and $\mathbf{Z}$ are the Pauli matrices. By exploiting the classical-to-quantum isomorphism, we arrive at the PCM $\mathbf{H}$ of the $\mathcal{C}[4, 2, 2]$ dual-containing CSS quantum code formulated as

$$\mathbf{H}_{[4,2,2]} = \left[\begin{array}{cccc|cccc} 1 & 1 & 1 & 1 & 0 & 0 & 0 & 0 \\ 0 & 0 & 0 & 0 & 1 & 1 & 1 & 1 \end{array}\right]. \tag{12.14}$$

Similarly, we can readily extend the construction to a higher quantum coding rate, as exemplified by $\mathcal{C}[n, k, d] = \mathcal{C}[6, 4, 2]$, which is derived from a classical SBC of $\mathcal{C}(6, 5, 2)$. Hence, the stabilizer operators for $\mathcal{C}[6, 4, 2]$ are defined by

$$\begin{aligned} S_1 &= \mathbf{Z}_1\mathbf{Z}_2\mathbf{Z}_3\mathbf{Z}_4\mathbf{Z}_5\mathbf{Z}_6, \\ S_2 &= \mathbf{X}_1\mathbf{X}_2\mathbf{X}_3\mathbf{X}_4\mathbf{X}_5\mathbf{X}_6. \end{aligned} \tag{12.15}$$

For this construction, the resultant quantum coding rate is $r_Q = 2/3$. The same analogy can be used for constructing $\mathcal{C}[n, k, d] = \mathcal{C}[8, 6, 2]$ derived from a classical SBC $\mathcal{C}(8, 7, 2)$. Therefore, the stabilizer operators are as follows:

$$\begin{aligned} S_1 &= \mathbf{Z}_1\mathbf{Z}_2\mathbf{Z}_3\mathbf{Z}_4\mathbf{Z}_5\mathbf{Z}_6\mathbf{Z}_7\mathbf{Z}_8, \\ S_2 &= \mathbf{X}_1\mathbf{X}_2\mathbf{X}_3\mathbf{X}_4\mathbf{X}_5\mathbf{X}_6\mathbf{X}_7\mathbf{X}_8. \end{aligned} \tag{12.16}$$

The resultant QSBC exhibits a quantum coding rate of $r_Q = 3/4$. The discussion on how the stabilizer operators $S_i$ can be invoked for detecting quantum errors will be provided in subsection 12.2.3.

Furthermore, the QSBCs can also be classified as a family of QTECCs, as shown in Figure 12.3. Assuming that we can arrange the physical qubits on the vertices of a lattice structure, we can satisfy the localized stabilizer

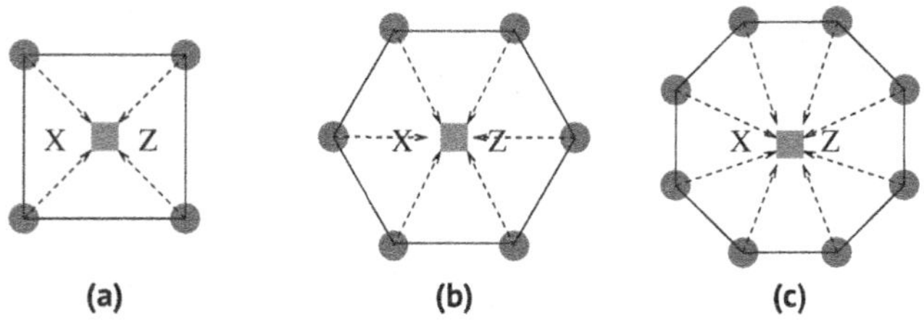


**Figure 12.3** QSBCs can be arranged to match the qubit layout on a lattice structure. The circles represent the physical qubits, while the squares denote the stabilizer operators. Each square is utilized for measuring both the **X** and **Z** operator. Hence, the resultant quantum codes belong to the family of dual-containing CSS codes. The quantum coding rate $r_Q$ for construction (a) is 1/2, for (b) is 2/3, and for (c) is 3/4. All of the QSBCs exhibit a minimum distance of $d = 2$. *Source*: [279]/IEEE/CC BY 4.0.

measurement property. Since the resultant QSC constructions are only capable of error detection, which is a consequence of having a minimum distance of $d = 2$, the stabilizer measurements can only indicate the presence or absence of quantum errors, but not the specific number or the position of the errors. However, we will show later that this error detection capability can be transformed into error correction capability by concatenating QSBCs with a carefully selected inner code.

### 12.2.2 Quantum Encoder

In the quantum domain, an information word having $k$ logical qubits in the state of $|\psi\rangle$ can be transformed into a codeword having $n$ physical qubits in the state of $|\overline{\psi}\rangle$, where we have $n > k$. This can be arranged with the aid of $(n - k)$ auxiliary qubits initialized in the state of $|0\rangle$. This specific transformation, which is carried out by a unitary transformation $\mathcal{V}$ referred to as a quantum encoder, can be formally described as follows[1]:

$$\mathcal{V}\left(|\psi\rangle^k \otimes |0\rangle^{\otimes(n-k)}\right) = |\overline{\psi}\rangle^n. \tag{12.17}$$

This is reminiscent of the encoding process of classical error correction codes. To elaborate, in the classical domain, we can transform a $k$-bit information word into an $n$-bit codeword with the aid of the generator matrix $\mathbf{G}$, where the additional $(n - k)$ bits are referred to as the redundant bits.

Based on the description of QSBCs in subsection 12.2.1, they can be classified as a member of the dual-containing CSS code family. For this specific class of quantum codes, the design of the quantum encoder $\mathcal{V}$ can be readily derived from its classical PCMs [67, 163]. More specifically, the PCM of the classical code $\mathcal{C}(n, k, d)$ may be utilized to obtain the quantum encoder $\mathcal{V}$ of a QSC $\mathcal{C}[\tilde{n}, \tilde{k}, \tilde{d}]$, where $\tilde{n} = n$, $\tilde{k} = 2k - n$, and $\tilde{d} = d$.

Let us now embark on creating the quantum encoder $\mathcal{V}$ of dual-containing CSS codes derived from the classical codes $\mathcal{C}(n, k, d)$. The PCM of the classical code $\mathcal{C}(n, k, d)$ can be represented by a full-rank matrix $\mathbf{H}$ having $n \times (n - k)$ elements. Naturally, every PCM $\mathbf{H}$ of linear block codes can be transformed into the corresponding systematic form of

$$\widetilde{\mathbf{H}} = \left[\mathbf{I}_{n-k} | \mathbf{A}_{n-k,k}\right] \tag{12.18}$$

by using row operations and column permutations, where $\mathbf{I}_{n-k}$ is a $(n - k)$-dimension identity matrix, and the matrix $\mathbf{A}$ has $(n - k) \times k$ elements. For the next step, we may further transform the matrix $\mathbf{A}$ into the systematic form of

$$\widetilde{\mathbf{A}} = \left[\mathbf{I}_{n-k} | \mathbf{B}_{n-k,2k-n}\right], \tag{12.19}$$

where $\mathbf{I}_{n-k}$ is another $(n - k)$-dimensional identity matrix and the matrix $\mathbf{B}$ has $(n - k) \times (2k - n)$ elements.

Ultimately, the quantum encoder $\mathcal{V}$ of a dual-containing CSS code can be described as a two-stage encoder. The first stage of the quantum encoder is used for initializing a set of codewords $\mathcal{C}$, which must not have a difference exactly corresponding to a specific legitimate codeword of $\mathcal{C}^\perp$, where $\mathcal{C}^\perp$ is the dual code of $\mathcal{C}$. Therefore, it can be utilized for generating the unique cosets of $\mathcal{C}$ relative to $\mathcal{C}^\perp$. Then, the second stage of the quantum encoder $\mathcal{V}$

1 The superscript of $n$ in the notation $|\psi\rangle^n$ represents the number of physical qubits, which is $n$, given a quantum state $|\psi\rangle$. This notation will be used throughout this chapter.

is invoked for generating the code space of $\mathcal{C}^{\perp}$ according to the PCM $\widetilde{\mathbf{H}}$. Hence, the resultant states after the first and the second stage are constituted by the superposition of all the codewords of $\mathcal{C}^{\perp}$ generated by the second stage added to the codewords of $\mathcal{C}$ generated in the first stage. The more general method of constructing the quantum encoder $\mathcal{V}$ for all types of QSCs, including both non-dual-containing CSS codes and non-CSS codes, can be found in [180, 181].

For developing a clearer idea about the two-stage quantum encoder $\mathcal{V}$, let us consider the QSBC $\mathcal{C}\,[6, 4, 2]$ and construct its quantum encoder $\mathcal{V}$ based on the classical PCM $\mathbf{H}$ derived from the classical code $\mathcal{C}(6, 5, 2)$ as follows:

$$\mathbf{H} = [1\ 1\ 1\ 1\ 1\ 1]. \tag{12.20}$$

Fortunately, the PCM $\mathbf{H}$ has already a systematic structure, hence we have $\mathbf{H} = \widetilde{\mathbf{H}}$ without any extra transformation. From the PCM $\mathbf{H}$ in Eq. (12.20), matrix $\mathbf{A}$ is readily given by

$$\mathbf{A} = [1\ 1\ 1\ 1\ 1]. \tag{12.21}$$

Consequently, given that $\mathbf{A} = \widetilde{\mathbf{A}}$, we obtain the matrix $\mathbf{B}$ as follows:

$$\mathbf{B} = [1\ 1\ 1\ 1]. \tag{12.22}$$

Based on Eqs. (12.21) and (12.22), the first stage and the second stage of the quantum encoder $\mathcal{V}$ of the QSBC $\mathcal{C}[6, 4, 2]$ is denoted by $\mathcal{V}_B$ and $\mathcal{V}_A$, respectively, in Figure 12.4. To elaborate a little further, the CNOT connections between the logical qubits in the state of $|\psi\rangle$ and the first auxiliary qubits are defined by the matrix $\mathbf{B}$. More specifically, given the element $b_{i,j}$ of the matrix $\mathbf{B}$, if the value of $b_{i,j} = 1$, it means that the $j$th logical qubit controls the CNOT connection of the $i$th auxiliary target qubit. As an example, based on the matrix $\mathbf{B}$ in Eq. (12.22), we can see that at the first stage $\mathcal{V}_B$ of the quantum encoder $\mathcal{V}$ the first auxiliary qubit is controlled by all four logical qubits in the state of $|\psi\rangle$, since the matrix $\mathbf{B}$ contains all 1 elements.

Consequently, the first stage $\mathcal{V}_B$ of the quantum encoder $\mathcal{V}$ transforms the first $m$ auxiliary qubits, which are initialized to the state of $|0\rangle$, according to the logical qubits $|\psi\rangle$. Explicitly, given that $|\psi\rangle = |\mathbf{c}\rangle$, where $\mathbf{c}$ is a $k$-bit binary string, the first stage $\mathcal{V}_B$ of the quantum encoder $\mathcal{V}$ transforms the auxiliary qubits into the state of $|\mathbf{Bc}\rangle$. Therefore, the state of physical qubits at the output of the first stage $\mathcal{V}_B$, namely $|\psi_B\rangle$, created by the action of the first stage $\mathcal{V}_B$ of quantum encoder $\mathcal{V}$ of Figure 12.4 can be expressed as follows:

$$|\psi_B\rangle = \mathcal{V}_B\left(|\mathbf{c}\rangle^k|\mathbf{0}\rangle^{\otimes m}|\mathbf{0}\rangle^{\otimes m}\right) = |\mathbf{c}\rangle^k|\mathbf{Bc}\rangle^m|\mathbf{0}\rangle^{\otimes m}, \tag{12.23}$$

where $m = n - k$. Hence, as mentioned earlier, the first stage $\mathcal{V}_B$ of the quantum encoder $\mathcal{V}$ creates a set of codewords $\mathcal{C}$, which must not have a difference exactly corresponding to a specific legitimate codeword in $\mathcal{C}^{\perp}$.

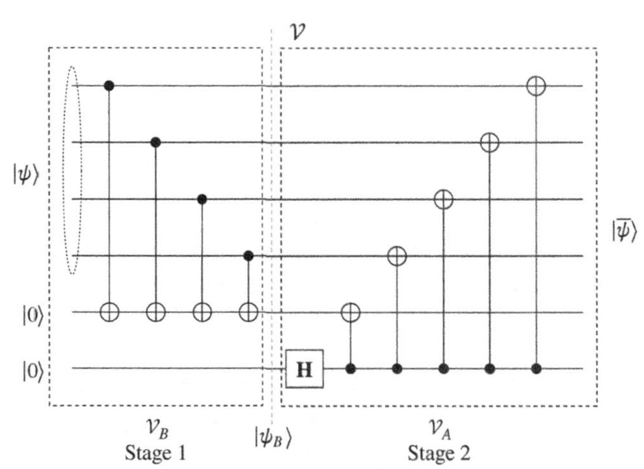


**Figure 12.4** The quantum encoder $\mathcal{V}$ can be described as a two-stage encoder. For the QSBCs, the CNOT connections of the first stage $\mathcal{V}_B$ are defined by matrix **B** of Eq. (12.22), while those of the second stage $\mathcal{V}_A$ are defined by matrix **A** of Eq. (12.21). *Source*: [279]/IEEE/CC BY 4.0.

For example, based on the PCM $\mathbf{H}$ of a classical code $\mathcal{C}(6,5,2)$ given in Eq. (12.20), we can construct the code space of the dual code $\mathcal{C}^{\perp}$ as follows:

$$\mathcal{C}^{\perp} = \{000000, 111111\}. \quad (12.24)$$

For a given $k$-bit binary string of $\mathbf{c}$, the $n$-bit binary string of $[\mathbf{c}, \mathbf{Bc}, \mathbf{0}]$ is indeed a codeword in $\mathcal{C}$. Let us denote the set of all the $n$-bit binary strings of $[\mathbf{c}, \mathbf{Bc}, \mathbf{0}]$ as $\mathcal{B}$, which basically creates a subspace of $\mathcal{C}$, i.e. $\mathcal{B} \subseteq \mathcal{C}$. More explicitly, the code space of $\mathcal{B}$ has 16 codewords, each associated with a minimum distance of $d$=2. Based on the matrix $\mathbf{B}$ of Eq. (12.22) these are given as follows:

$$\begin{aligned}\mathcal{B} = \{&000000, 000110, 001010, 001100, 010010, 010100, 011000, 011110,\\ &100010, 100100, 101000, 101110, 110000, 110110, 111010, 111100\}.\end{aligned} \quad (12.25)$$

It may be readily observed that none of the codewords in $\mathcal{B}$ differs from each other by a legitimate element in $\mathcal{C}^{\perp}$. This may be verified by adding any nonzero codeword in $\mathcal{C}^{\perp}$ to one of the codeword in $\mathcal{B}$ and checking that this action does not yield another codeword in $\mathcal{B}$. This is because the last $m$ bits of $\mathcal{B}$ are all 0 elements, while the nonzero codeword of $\mathcal{C}^{\perp}$ has 1s in the last $m$ bits. Hence, each $k$-bit binary string of $\mathbf{c}$ creates a unique coset in $\mathcal{C}$ relative to $\mathcal{C}^{\perp}$.

The second stage $\mathcal{V}_A$ of the quantum encoder $\mathcal{V}$ relies on initializing the remaining $m = n - k$ auxiliary qubits to the $|+\rangle$ states by using $m$ Hadamard gates, which can be expressed mathematically as follows:

$$\mathbf{H}^{\otimes m}|\mathbf{0}\rangle^{\otimes m} = |+\rangle^{\otimes m} = \left(\frac{|0\rangle + |1\rangle}{\sqrt{2}}\right)^{\otimes m} = \frac{1}{2^{m/2}} \sum_{i}^{2^m-1} |\mathbf{i}\rangle. \quad (12.26)$$

Explicitly, Eq. (12.26) basically represents a sum of the equal superposition of all possible states defined by all $2^m$ binary strings of length $m$. Next, we combine the initialized equiprobable superposition of Eq. (12.26) with the output of the first stage $|\psi_B\rangle$. Let us assume that string $\mathbf{t}$ denotes the string of $[\mathbf{c}, \mathbf{Bc}]$. The effect of this operation is to add rows of the PCM $\widetilde{\mathbf{H}} = [\mathbf{I}_{n-k}|\mathbf{A}_{n-k,k}]$ to the binary string $\mathbf{t}$. Hence, for a given $k$-bit binary input string of $\mathbf{c}$, the final state of the physical qubits after the first and the second stage of the quantum encoder $\mathcal{V}$ can be expressed as

$$|\overline{\psi}\rangle = \frac{1}{2^{m/2}} \sum_{\mathbf{r}\in\mathcal{C}^{\perp}(\mathbf{H})} |\mathbf{r} + \mathbf{t}\rangle^{n}. \quad (12.27)$$

Finally, if the state of the $k$ logical qubits is expressed in the form of the superposition of the binary strings $\mathbf{c}_i$ as follows:

$$|\psi\rangle^{k} = \sum_{i}^{2^k-1} p_i |\mathbf{c}_i\rangle^{k}, \quad (12.28)$$

then the output state of the physical qubits $|\overline{\psi}\rangle$ can be formulated as

$$|\overline{\psi}\rangle^{n} = \sum_{\mathbf{y}\in\mathcal{C}(\mathbf{H})} p_{\mathbf{y}} \sum_{\mathbf{r}\in\mathcal{C}^{\perp}(\mathbf{H})} |\mathbf{r} + \mathbf{y}\rangle^{n}. \quad (12.29)$$

Readers who might be interested in different examples of creating encoders for various dual-containing CSS codes exemplified by Steane's $\mathcal{C}[7,1,3]$ code of [92] and by the quantum Bose–Chaudhuri–Hocquenghem (QBCH) code $\mathcal{C}[15,7,3]$ of [61], please refer to [163].

The resultant quantum encoders $\mathcal{V}$ conceived for the QSBCs $\mathcal{C}[4,2,2]$, $\mathcal{C}[6,4,2]$, and $\mathcal{C}[8,6,2]$ can be seen in Figure 12.5. The figure demonstrates that the resultant QSBC encoders $\mathcal{V}$ exhibit natural design flexibility. Figure 12.5a depicts the quantum encoder $\mathcal{V}$ of the QSBC $\mathcal{C}[4,2,2]$. By incorporating additional gates and connections denoted by the dashed lines in Figure 12.5b into the quantum encoder of Figure 12.5a, we obtain the quantum encoder $\mathcal{V}$ of the QSBC $\mathcal{C}[6,4,2]$. Similarly, by adding more gates and connections denoted by the dashed-dotted lines to the quantum encoder of Figure 12.5b, we can readily create the quantum encoder $\mathcal{V}$ of the QSBC $\mathcal{C}[8,6,2]$ of Figure 12.5c. In other words, we can construct the quantum encoder $\mathcal{V}$ of QSBCs for a high quantum coding rate, which will simultaneously contain the quantum encoder $\mathcal{V}$ of the lower quantum coding rate. Therefore, it

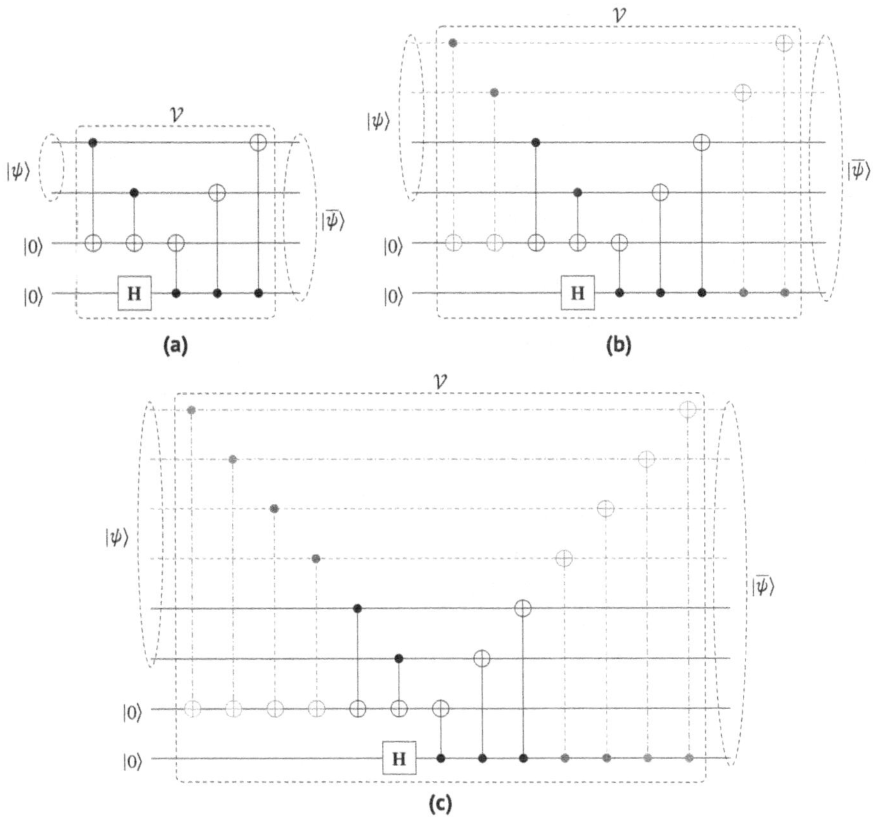


**Figure 12.5** The quantum encoder $\mathcal{V}$ of QSBSc for various quantum coding rates: (a) $\mathcal{C}[4,2,2]$, $r_Q = 1/2$, (b) $\mathcal{C}[6,4,2]$, $r_Q = 2/3$, (c) $\mathcal{C}[8,6,2]$, $r_Q = 3/4$. *Source*: [279]/IEEE/CC BY 4.0.

is no longer necessary to build more than one quantum encoder $\mathcal{V}$ for various quantum coding rates of QSBCs because the quantum encoder $\mathcal{V}$ of QSBCs exhibits a self-contained structure. This is reminiscent of the classical rate-compatible punctured codes proposed in [307].

### 12.2.3 Stabilizer Measurement for QSBCs

The QSCs are capable of predicting both the number and the position of errors without actually observing the states of the physical qubits. In order to achieve this, a syndrome-decoding-like method was introduced in [59]. Instead of observing the information within the physical qubits, which would collapse the superposition state to a classical state, a set of auxiliary qubits are prepared for observing the syndrome of the physical qubits using the so-called stabilizer operators. A stabilizer operator $S_i$ belonging to the stabilizer group $\mathcal{S} \in \mathcal{P}_n$ is an $n$-tuple Pauli operator, which stabilizes the state of the encoded physical qubits $|\overline{\psi}\rangle$ may be formulated as follows:

$$S_i|\overline{\psi}\rangle = |\overline{\psi}\rangle. \tag{12.30}$$

An error operator $P \in \mathcal{P}_n$ represented by the quantum channel corrupting the encoded state of physical qubits transforms the legitimate state $|\overline{\psi}\rangle$ into the contaminated received state $|\widetilde{\psi}\rangle$, which can be expressed as follows:

$$|\widetilde{\psi}\rangle = P|\overline{\psi}\rangle. \tag{12.31}$$

The syndrome values can be obtained by performing eigenvalue-based measurement of the received state $|\widehat{\psi}\rangle$ assisted by the auxiliary qubits, which can be defined as follows:

$$S_i|\widetilde{\psi}\rangle = \begin{cases} |\widetilde{\psi}\rangle, & S_iP = PS_i \\ -|\widetilde{\psi}\rangle, & S_iP = -PS_i. \end{cases} \tag{12.32}$$

The ±1 eigenvalues attained from the stabilizer measurement act similarly to the $\{0, 1\}$ values of the classical syndrome measurements. Hence, they can also be used for inferring both the number and the position of errors without actually observing the state of the physical qubits.

As we briefly discussed, the eigenvalue measurements require an extra auxiliary qubit for each stabilizer measurement. As for QSBCs, the stabilizer measurement can be implemented using the circuits seen in Figure 12.6. More specifically, Figure 12.6a depicts the **Z**-stabilizer measurement, while Figure 12.6b portrays the **X**-stabilizer measurement. It can be observed that for both **X** and **Z** stabilizer measurements, the circuit constructed for realizing the stabilizer measurements of a QSBC having a higher quantum coding rate inherently contains the stabilizer measurements required for a QSBC having a lower quantum coding rate. To elaborate a little further, in Figure 12.6, the circuit implementation of the stabilizer measurements of a 1/2-rate QSBC is highlighted using black solid lines. In case we want to employ another QSBC having a higher quantum coding rate, for example, a 2/3-rate QSBC, we can simply incorporate the stabilizer measurement from the 1/2-rate scheme and add further gates, which are highlighted using dark gray dashed lines in Figure 12.6 without changing the stabilizer measurement circuit. A similar approach is applicable when we want to employ a 3/4-rate QSBC. We incorporate the stabilizer measurements of the 2/3-rate QSBC and then add more gates, which are highlighted using light gray dashed lines. Ultimately, we have shown that the nature of the PCMs from the QSBCs leads to a very convenient design for their quantum encoders and for their stabilizer measurements, which are capable of supporting multiple quantum coding rates of $r_Q = \frac{k}{k+1}$ using a single quantum circuit implementation.

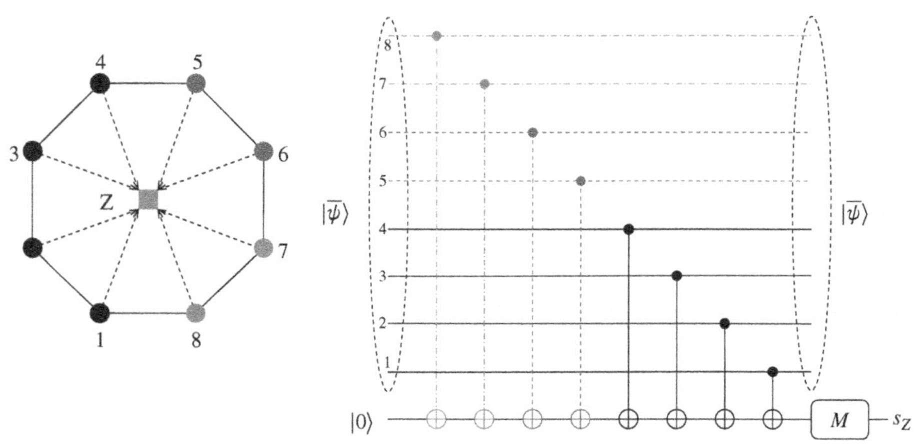


**(a)** **Z**-stabilizer measurement.

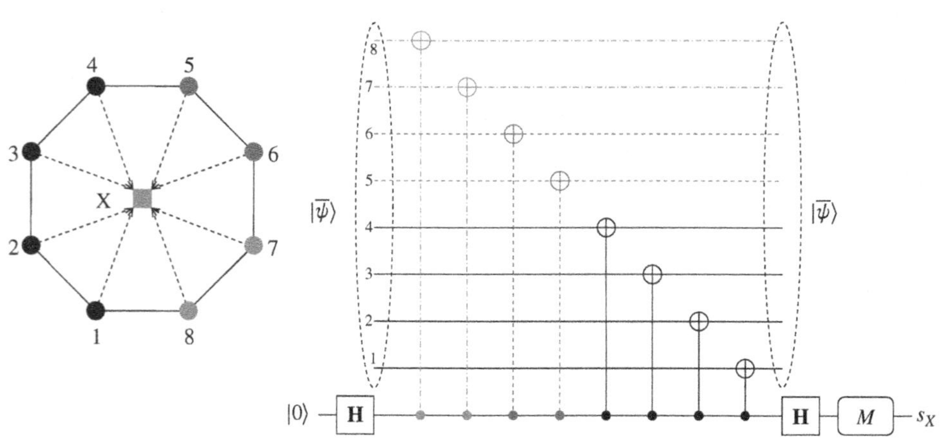


**(b)** **X**-stabilizer measurement.

**Figure 12.6** Stabilizer measurements of QSBCs, which are capable of supporting various quantum coding rates. *Source*: [279]/IEEE/CC BY 4.0.

### 12.2.4 Classical Simulation for QSBCs

The quantum encoder $\mathcal{V}$ of a QSBC and its inverse encoder $\mathcal{V}^{\dagger}$ are composed of quantum Clifford gates. This implies that they can be conveniently simulated using classical computers [161]. An $n$-tuple Pauli operator $P \in \mathcal{P}_n$ can be represented by a $2n$-element binary vector, where each of the $n$-element binary vectors constitutes a Pauli **Z** and a Pauli **X** component. The mapping of the Pauli matrix to the associated binary vector can be formulated as follows:

$$\begin{aligned} \mathbf{I} &\rightarrow \left[0 \middle| 0\right], \\ \mathbf{X} &\rightarrow \left[0 \middle| 1\right], \\ \mathbf{Y} &\rightarrow \left[1 \middle| 1\right], \\ \mathbf{Z} &\rightarrow \left[1 \middle| 0\right]. \end{aligned} \tag{12.33}$$

The evolution of the Pauli operator $P \in \mathcal{P}_n$ over quantum Clifford gates can be described using the conjugation operation. Explicitly, the conjugation of a unitary operator **N** under the unitary transformation **M** is the unitary transformation **V**, which is defined as [161]

$$\mathbf{V} = \mathbf{M} \cdot \mathbf{N} \cdot \mathbf{M}^{\dagger}. \tag{12.34}$$

For instance, based on Eq. (12.34), the conjugation of the Pauli matrix **Z** and **X** over the Hadamard (**H**) gate is given by

$$\begin{aligned} \mathbf{H} \cdot \mathbf{Z} \cdot \mathbf{H}^{\dagger} &= \mathbf{X}, \\ \mathbf{H} \cdot \mathbf{X} \cdot \mathbf{H}^{\dagger} &= \mathbf{Z}. \end{aligned} \tag{12.35}$$

Additionally, we can also describe the conjugation of a Pauli matrix **Z** and **X** over a 2-qubit quantum gate, as exemplified by a CNOT gate, as follows:

$$\begin{aligned} (\mathbf{CNOT}) \cdot (\mathbf{Z} \otimes \mathbf{I}) \cdot (\mathbf{CNOT})^{\dagger} &= \mathbf{Z} \otimes \mathbf{I}, \\ (\mathbf{CNOT}) \cdot (\mathbf{I} \otimes \mathbf{Z}) \cdot (\mathbf{CNOT})^{\dagger} &= \mathbf{Z} \otimes \mathbf{Z}, \\ (\mathbf{CNOT}) \cdot (\mathbf{X} \otimes \mathbf{I}) \cdot (\mathbf{CNOT})^{\dagger} &= \mathbf{X} \otimes \mathbf{X}, \\ (\mathbf{CNOT}) \cdot (\mathbf{I} \otimes \mathbf{X}) \cdot (\mathbf{CNOT})^{\dagger} &= \mathbf{I} \otimes \mathbf{X}, \end{aligned} \tag{12.36}$$

where the first Pauli matrix is applied to the control qubit, while the second Pauli matrix is applied to the target qubit.

Therefore, using the conjugation definition of Eq. (12.34), we can keep track of the evolution of any $n$-tuple Pauli operator $P \in \mathcal{P}_n$ owing to the unitary operations carried out by quantum Clifford gates, such as the QSBC encoders $\mathcal{V}$ and also its inverse encoder $\mathcal{V}^{\dagger}$ illustrated in Figure 12.5. Since the quantum encoders $\mathcal{V}$ of QSBCs are only composed of Hadamard and CNOT gates, we can create a $(2n \times 2n)$-element binary matrix $V$ for classically simulating the evolution of the Pauli operator $P \in \mathcal{P}_n$ over the quantum encoder $\mathcal{V}$. As an example, let us consider the quantum encoder $\mathcal{V}$ of the QSBC $\mathcal{C}[4, 2, 2]$ seen in Figure 12.7.

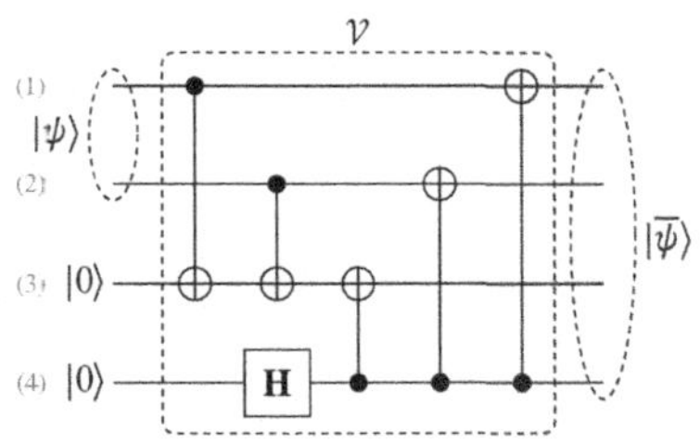


**Figure 12.7** The quantum encoder $\mathcal{V}$ of the QSBC $\mathcal{C}[4, 2, 2]$. *Source:* [279]/IEEE/CC BY 4.0.

We commence by initializing $V^{(0)} = \mathbf{I}_{2n}$, where $\mathbf{I}_{2n}$ is a $2n$-dimensional identity matrix formulated as follows:

$$V^{(0)} = \left[\begin{array}{cccc|cccc} 1 & 0 & 0 & 0 & 0 & 0 & 0 & 0 \\ 0 & 1 & 0 & 0 & 0 & 0 & 0 & 0 \\ 0 & 0 & 1 & 0 & 0 & 0 & 0 & 0 \\ 0 & 0 & 0 & 1 & 0 & 0 & 0 & 0 \\ \hline 0 & 0 & 0 & 0 & 1 & 0 & 0 & 0 \\ 0 & 0 & 0 & 0 & 0 & 1 & 0 & 0 \\ 0 & 0 & 0 & 0 & 0 & 0 & 1 & 0 \\ 0 & 0 & 0 & 0 & 0 & 0 & 0 & 1 \end{array}\right]. \tag{12.37}$$

The $i$th and the $(n+i)$-th column of matrix $V^{(0)}$ are associated with the evolution of the Pauli matrices **Z** and **X**, respectively, on the $i$th qubit.

The first unitary operation in the QSBC encoder $\mathcal{V}$ of Figure 12.7 is the unitary operation CNOT(1, 3), where the notation CNOT($i$, $j$) means that the $i$th qubit controls the $j$th qubit. Now, based on Eq. (12.36), the CNOT unitary transformation propagates the Pauli **X** matrix from the control qubit to the target qubit and by contrast, propagates the Pauli **Z** matrix from the target qubit to the control qubit. Therefore, in the matrix $V$, the unitary transformation CNOT($i$, $j$) can be carried out by replacing the $i$th column with the modulo 2 addition between the $i$th column and the $j$th column. Then we replace the $(n+j)$-th column by the modulo 2 addition between the $(n+i)$-th column and the $(n+j)$-th column. In the case of $V^{(0)}$, the unitary transformation CNOT(1, 3) can simply be viewed as copying the 1 value from the third column to the first column, followed by copying the value 1 from the fifth column to the seventh column. Hence, the unitary transformation CNOT(1, 3) transforms the matrix $V^{(0)}$ into the matrix $V^{(1)}$ as follows:

$$V^{(1)} = \left[\begin{array}{cccc|cccc} 1 & 0 & 0 & 0 & 0 & 0 & 0 & 0 \\ 0 & 1 & 0 & 0 & 0 & 0 & 0 & 0 \\ \mathbf{1} & 0 & \mathbf{1} & 0 & 0 & 0 & 0 & 0 \\ 0 & 0 & 0 & 1 & 0 & 0 & 0 & 0 \\ \hline 0 & 0 & 0 & 0 & \mathbf{1} & 0 & \mathbf{1} & 0 \\ 0 & 0 & 0 & 0 & 0 & 1 & 0 & 0 \\ 0 & 0 & 0 & 0 & 0 & 0 & 1 & 0 \\ 0 & 0 & 0 & 0 & 0 & 0 & 0 & 1 \end{array}\right]. \tag{12.38}$$

We indicate the matrix elements involved in the associated transformation using bold fonts. The unitary transformation CNOT(1, 3) is followed by the second unitary transformation taking place in the QSBC encoder $\mathcal{V}$ of Figure 12.7, namely the CNOT(2, 3). Following the same method as that used for obtaining the matrix $V^{(1)}$, the action of CNOT(2, 3) applied to the matrix $V^{(1)}$ yields the matrix $V^{(2)}$ as follows:

$$V^{(2)} = \left[\begin{array}{cccc|cccc} 1 & 0 & 0 & 0 & 0 & 0 & 0 & 0 \\ 0 & 1 & 0 & 0 & 0 & 0 & 0 & 0 \\ 1 & \mathbf{1} & \mathbf{1} & 0 & 0 & 0 & 0 & 0 \\ 0 & 0 & 0 & 1 & 0 & 0 & 0 & 0 \\ \hline 0 & 0 & 0 & 0 & 1 & 0 & 1 & 0 \\ 0 & 0 & 0 & 0 & 0 & \mathbf{1} & \mathbf{1} & 0 \\ 0 & 0 & 0 & 0 & 0 & 0 & 1 & 0 \\ 0 & 0 & 0 & 0 & 0 & 0 & 0 & 1 \end{array}\right]. \tag{12.39}$$

The third unitary transformation taking place within the QSBC encoder $\mathcal{V}$ of Figure 12.7 is the Hadamard transformation $\mathbf{H}(4)$. Based on Eq. (12.35), the Hadamard transformation modifies the Pauli matrix $\mathbf{Z}$ into $\mathbf{X}$ and vice versa. Therefore, in a matrix $V$, a Hadamard transformation of $\mathbf{H}(i)$ can be interpreted as swapping the value of the $i$th column and the $(n+i)$-th column. In case of the matrix $V^{(2)}$, the action of the unitary transformation $\mathbf{H}(4)$ swaps the value of the fourth column and the eighth column, hence resulting in the matrix $V^{(3)}$ as follows:

$$V^{(3)} = \left[\begin{array}{cccc|cccc} 1 & 0 & 0 & 0 & 0 & 0 & 0 & 0 \\ 0 & 1 & 0 & 0 & 0 & 0 & 0 & 0 \\ 1 & 1 & 1 & 0 & 0 & 0 & 0 & 0 \\ 0 & 0 & 0 & 0 & 0 & 0 & 0 & \mathbf{1} \\ \hline 0 & 0 & 0 & 0 & 1 & 0 & 1 & 0 \\ 0 & 0 & 0 & 0 & 0 & 1 & 1 & 0 \\ 0 & 0 & 0 & 0 & 0 & 0 & 1 & 0 \\ 0 & 0 & 0 & \mathbf{1} & 0 & 0 & 0 & 0 \end{array}\right]. \tag{12.40}$$

These operations are then followed by the unitary transformation CNOT(4, 3), which yields the matrix $V^{(4)}$ as follows:

$$V^{(4)} = \left[\begin{array}{cccc|cccc} 1 & 0 & 0 & 0 & 0 & 0 & 0 & 0 \\ 0 & 1 & 0 & 0 & 0 & 0 & 0 & 0 \\ 1 & 1 & \mathbf{1} & \mathbf{1} & 0 & 0 & 0 & 0 \\ 0 & 0 & 0 & 0 & 0 & 0 & \mathbf{1} & \mathbf{1} \\ \hline 0 & 0 & 0 & 0 & 1 & 0 & 1 & 0 \\ 0 & 0 & 0 & 0 & 0 & 1 & 1 & 0 \\ 0 & 0 & 0 & 0 & 0 & 0 & 1 & 0 \\ 0 & 0 & 0 & 1 & 0 & 0 & 0 & 0 \end{array}\right]. \tag{12.41}$$

The action of CNOT(4, 2) upon the matrix $V^{(4)}$ gives us the matrix $V^{(5)}$ as follows:

$$V^{(5)} = \left[\begin{array}{cccc|cccc} 1 & 0 & 0 & 0 & 0 & 0 & 0 & 0 \\ 0 & \mathbf{1} & 0 & \mathbf{1} & 0 & 0 & 0 & 0 \\ 1 & \mathbf{1} & 1 & \mathbf{0} & 0 & 0 & 0 & 0 \\ 0 & 0 & 0 & 0 & 0 & \mathbf{1} & 1 & \mathbf{1} \\ \hline 0 & 0 & 0 & 0 & 1 & 0 & 1 & 0 \\ 0 & 0 & 0 & 0 & 0 & 1 & 1 & 0 \\ 0 & 0 & 0 & 0 & 0 & 0 & 1 & 0 \\ 0 & 0 & 0 & 1 & 0 & 0 & 0 & 0 \end{array}\right]. \tag{12.42}$$

Finally, applying the CNOT(4, 1) transforms the matrix $V^{(5)}$ into the final matrix $V$ as follows:

$$V = \left[\begin{array}{cccc|cccc} \mathbf{1} & 0 & 0 & \mathbf{1} & 0 & 0 & 0 & 0 \\ 0 & 1 & 0 & 1 & 0 & 0 & 0 & 0 \\ \mathbf{1} & 1 & 1 & \mathbf{1} & 0 & 0 & 0 & 0 \\ 0 & 0 & 0 & 0 & \mathbf{1} & 1 & 1 & \mathbf{1} \\ \hline 0 & 0 & 0 & 0 & 1 & 0 & 1 & 0 \\ 0 & 0 & 0 & 0 & 0 & 1 & 1 & 0 \\ 0 & 0 & 0 & 0 & 0 & 0 & 1 & 0 \\ 0 & 0 & 0 & 1 & 0 & 0 & 0 & 0 \end{array}\right]. \tag{12.43}$$

The resultant matrix $V$ is the classical counterpart of the quantum encoder $\mathcal{V}$ of the QSBC $\mathcal{C}[4, 2, 2]$ seen in Figure 12.7. In order to obtain the matrix $V^{-1}$ of the quantum inverse encoder $\mathcal{V}^{\dagger}$, the same method is invoked. The only difference is that we apply the transformation for each step by reading the quantum circuit from right to the left.

In order to show that the matrix $V$ can be used for classical simulation, let us consider a Pauli operator $P \in \mathcal{P}_4$ as follows:

$$P = \mathbf{Z} \otimes \mathbf{I} \otimes \mathbf{X} \otimes \mathbf{Y}. \tag{12.44}$$

By using the Pauli-to-binary mapping of Eq. (12.33), the Pauli operator $P$ given in Eq. (12.44) can be transformed into its classical analogue as follows:

$$P = \left[\begin{array}{cccc|cccc} 1 & 0 & 0 & 1 & 0 & 0 & 1 & 1 \end{array}\right]. \tag{12.45}$$

The resultant Pauli operator $\hat{P}$ due to the QSBC encoder $V$ can be obtained by modulo-2 multiplication ($*$) of the vector $P$ and the matrix $V$, which gives us

$$\begin{aligned} \hat{P} &= P * V \\ &= \left[\begin{array}{cccc|cccc} 1 & 0 & 0 & 0 & 1 & 1 & 0 & 1 \end{array}\right]. \end{aligned} \tag{12.46}$$

From the resultant vector $\hat{P}$ of Eq. (12.46) and also from the Pauli-to-binary mapping of Eq. (12.33), we can map back the binary vector $\hat{P}$ into its corresponding Pauli operator, which gives us $\hat{P} \in \mathcal{P}_4$ as follows:

$$\hat{P} = \mathbf{Y} \otimes \mathbf{X} \otimes \mathbf{I} \otimes \mathbf{X}. \tag{12.47}$$

**Table 12.1** The seed transformation $\mathcal{U}$ associated with QSBCs having various quantum coding rates $r_Q$.

| Quantum coding rate ($r_Q$) | Seed transformation $\mathcal{U}$ |
|---|---|
| 1/2 | $\{144, 80, 240, 15, 10, 6, 2, 16\}_{10}$ |
| 2/3 | $\{2112, 1088, 576, 320, 4032, 63, 34, 18, 10, 6, 2, 64\}_{10}$ |
| 3/4 | $\{33024, 16640, 8448, 4352, 2304, 1280, 65280, 255, 130, 66, 34, 18, 10, 6, 2, 256\}_{10}$ |

In order to simplify the expression of the matrix $V$, often the seed transformation $\mathcal{U}$ representation is used. The element $U_i$ of the seed transformation $\mathcal{U}=\{U_1, U_2, \ldots, U_{2n}\}$ is the decimal representation of the $i$th row of the binary matrix $V$. Therefore, based on the matrix $V$ of Eq. (12.43), the associated seed transformation $\mathcal{U}$ is given by

$$\mathcal{U}=\{144, 80, 240, 15, 10, 6, 2, 16\}_{10}. \tag{12.48}$$

Finally, the seed transformations $\mathcal{U}$ for all the QSBC encoders of Figure 12.5 are provided in Table 12.1.

## 12.3 Quantum Turbo Code Design Using QSBCs

QSBCs on their own are only capable of detecting the presence of errors in the state of physical qubits, but not correcting them. This limited capability is due to the minimum distance of $d=2$ inherited from the classical SBCs. In this chapter, we invoke the QTC scheme utilized in [68, 83] as the foundation of developing QSBC-based QTCs. The QSBCs are invoked as the outer codes, while a non-catastrophic and non-recursive QURC is used as the inner code. We will refer to this arrangement as the QSBC-QURC scheme for the rest of this chapter.

The QTC scheme was first introduced by Poulin *et. al* in [68]. The proposed QTC utilized two QCCs, which were concatenated serially. Each of the QCC components exhibits a 1/3 quantum coding rate and hence, the final quantum coding rate $r_Q$ is 1/9. To the best of our knowledge, the QTCs operating closest to the quantum hashing bound rely on the construction presented in [83, 290] in the open literature. The near-hashing-bound performance was attained by utilizing QIrCCs both as the outer and the inner codes. Furthermore, the weighting factors of the QIrCC component codes were optimized by invoking EXIT chart-based heuristic search [219, 290]. Readers who are interested to delve deeper into QTCs and near-hashing-bound constructions, please refer to [83].

### 12.3.1 Encoding Process

In this section, we will describe the proposed QSBC-QURC scheme, whose general schematic can be seen in Figure 12.8. The outer encoder $\mathcal{V}_1$ in Figure 12.8 is a QSBC encoder, which was already shown in Figure 12.5a for the instance of a half-rate QSBC. It maps $k_1$ logical qubits into $n_1$ physical qubits with the aid of $(n_1 - k_1)$ auxiliary qubits according to the following transformation:

$$\mathcal{V}_1\left(|\psi\rangle^{k_1} \otimes |0\rangle^{\otimes(n_1-k_1)}\right) = |\overline{\psi}_1\rangle^{n_1}. \tag{12.49}$$

The output of $\mathcal{V}_1$ is fed to the interleaver $\Pi$, which can be represented mathematically as a permutation matrix and can be realized physically as a series of quantum SWAP gates. The interleaving process can be formally written as

$$\Pi\left(|\overline{\psi}_1\rangle^{n_1}\right) = |\psi_2\rangle^{k_2}, \tag{12.50}$$

where we have $k_2 = n_1$, since the interleaver does not alter the number of physical qubits, only rearranges the position of the qubit indices in the quantum state. Hence, the Hamming weight of the state of physical qubits is not changed after this process. Next, the output of the interleaver $\Pi$ is fed into the inner encoder $\mathcal{V}_2$, which carries out the following transformation:

$$\mathcal{V}_2\left(|\psi\rangle^{k_2} \otimes |0\rangle^{\otimes(n_2-k_2)}\right) = |\overline{\psi}_2\rangle^{n_2}. \tag{12.51}$$

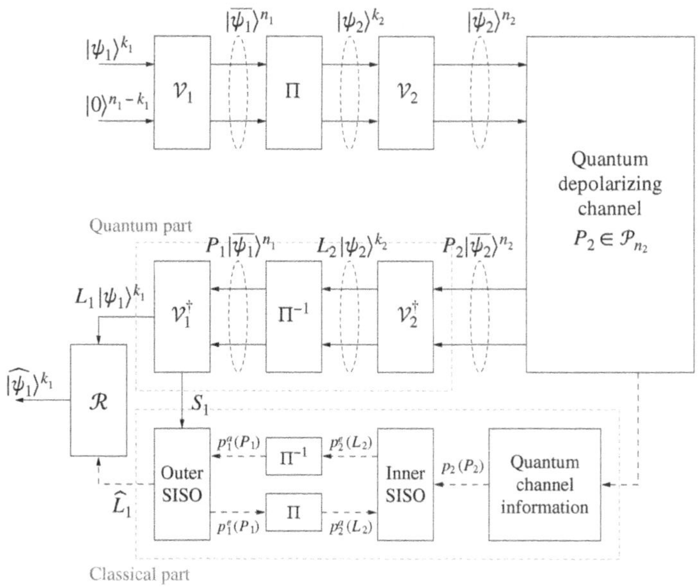


**Figure 12.8** The general schematic of serial QTCs utilizing QURC as the inner code. The decoding process, in general, can be separated into two parallel processes, namely the quantum processing part and the classical processing part. The quantum part is represented by the dashed lines, while the classical part is represented by the dashed lines. *Source*: [279]/IEEE/CC BY 4.0.

The encoder $\mathcal{V}_2$ maps the state of $k_2$ logical qubits into the state of $n_2$ physical qubits with the aid of $(n_2 - k_2)$ auxiliary qubits. Since, we are employing the QURCs as the inner codes, the transformation in Eq. (12.51) can be further simplified as

$$\mathcal{V}_2\left(|\psi\rangle^{k_2}\right) = |\overline{\psi}_2\rangle^{n2}. \tag{12.52}$$

The main difference between the interleaver and the QURC is that the state of physical qubits after the QURC may experience Hamming weight changes.

### 12.3.2 Quantum Depolarizing Channel

After the encoding process, the encoded state of physical qubits may experience quantum decoherence. In this study, we use the quantum depolarizing channel [160]. This depolarizing channel models the imperfection of quantum gates, as well as the decoherence taking place in the quantum memory, and even the actual quantum transmission channel through free space or optical fiber channels. The quantum decoherence is represented by the $n$-tuple Pauli operator $P_2 \in \mathcal{P}_n$ and its action imposed upon the encoded state of physical qubits $|\overline{\psi}_2\rangle^{n2}$ can be expressed as

$$|\widetilde{\psi}\rangle = P_2\left(|\overline{\psi}_2\rangle^{n2}\right). \tag{12.53}$$

The error operator $P_2$ is characterized by the depolarizing probability $p$. To elaborate a little further, the error operator $P \in \mathcal{P}_n$ is an $n$-tuple Pauli operator, where each qubit may independently experience a bit-flip (**X**) error, a phase-flip (**Z**) error as well as a simultaneous bit-flip and phase flip (**Y**) error. The probability of each qubit experiencing an **X**, **Z**, and **Y** error is denoted by $p_X$, $p_Z$, and $p_Y$, respectively. Under the assumption that $p_X + p_Y + p_Z = p$ and $p_X = p_Y = p_Z = p/3$, this quantum channel is classed as a *symmetric quantum depolarizing channel* [160]. Needless to say, it is always possible to create a model where we have the assumption that $p_X \neq p_Y \neq p_Z$, which can be deemed to be more realistic [146]. However, opting for $p_X = p_Y = p_Z$ will provide us with the worst-case scenario, because we have to provide the same level of protection for different types of errors without favoring only one specific type of error, which can result in quantum coding rate or QBER improvements. For a more detailed discourse on QSC design for asymmetric quantum depolarizing channels, enthusiastic readers might like to refer to [146, 176, 308, 309].

### 12.3.3 Decoding Process

Generally speaking, the decoding process of any QSC relies on the conjunction of two parts, namely the quantum information processing part and the classical information processing part. In Figure 12.8, the quantum processing part is marked by the components bounded by the dark gray dashed lines, while the classical processing part is represented by the components bounded by the light gray dashed lines. First, let us describe the quantum processing part. The corrupted state of physical qubits $|\overline{\psi_2}\rangle^{n_2}$ is fed to the inverse encoder $\mathcal{V}_2^{\dagger}$ of Figure 12.8, which represents the conjugate transpose of encoder $\mathcal{V}_2$. Physically, they can be implemented identically, but the input and output of the inverse encoder $\mathcal{V}^{\dagger}$ is in the reverse position compared to the encoder $\mathcal{V}$. Since the quantum encoder $\mathcal{V}$ and its inverse encoder $\mathcal{V}^{\dagger}$ are composed by the quantum Clifford gates and the error operator $P$ is an $n$-tuple Pauli operator $P \in \mathcal{P}_n$, the inverse encoders $\mathcal{V}_2^{\dagger}$ will decompose the error operator $P_2$ into two error components as follows:

$$\mathcal{V}_2^{\dagger}\left(P_2\left(|\overline{\psi_2}\rangle^{n_2}\right)\right) = L_2|\overline{\psi_2}\rangle^{k_2} \otimes S_2|0\rangle^{n_2-k_2}, \tag{12.54}$$

where $L_2$ is the error operator on $k_2$ logical qubits and $S_2$ is the error operator on $(n_2 - k_2)$ auxiliary qubits. The auxiliary qubits are then measured in the relevant computational basis, where the value $S_2$ can be treated as a syndrome in classical error correction codes, which is forwarded to the classical processing part. However, since the inverse encoder of $\mathcal{V}_2^{\dagger}$ is constituted by an inverse encoder of a QURC, Eq. (12.54) can be further simplified to

$$\mathcal{V}_2^{\dagger}\left(P_2\left(|\psi_2\rangle^{n_2}\right)\right) = L_2|\psi_2\rangle^{k_2}, \tag{12.55}$$

since we have $k_2 = n_2$. Next, the output of the inverse encoder $\mathcal{V}_2^{\dagger}$ is passed trough the deinterleaver $\Pi^{-1}$. This transformation can be formally expressed as

$$\Pi^{-1}\left(L_2|\overline{\psi_2}\rangle^{k_2}\right) = P_1|\overline{\psi_1}\rangle^{n_1}. \tag{12.56}$$

The output of the deinterleaver is then processed as the input of $\mathcal{V}_1^{\dagger}$, which is subjected to an identical transformation as $\mathcal{V}_2^{\dagger}$. This can be expressed as follows:

$$\mathcal{V}_1^{\dagger}\left(P_1\left(|\overline{\psi_1}\rangle^{n_1}\right)\right) = L_1|\psi_1\rangle^{k_1} \otimes S_1|0\rangle^{n_1-k_1}. \tag{12.57}$$

In this QSBC-QURC scheme, the inverse encoder of $\mathcal{V}_1^{\dagger}$ is constituted by the quantum inverse encoder $\mathcal{V}^{\dagger}$ of the QSBC, which is implemented by flipping the input and output of the quantum encoder $\mathcal{V}$ seen in Figure 12.5a for an instance of a half-rate QSBC.

Finally, based on the information obtained from the classical information processing part, the error recovery operator $\mathcal{R}$ is applied to the output of the inverse encoder $\mathcal{V}_1^{\dagger}$ in order to obtain the predicted logical qubit state as follows:

$$\mathcal{R}\left(L_1|\psi_1\rangle^{k_1}\right) = |\widehat{\psi_1}\rangle^{k_1}. \tag{12.58}$$

If $\mathcal{R} = L_1$, we obtain $|\widehat{\psi_1}\rangle^{k_1} = |\psi_1\rangle^{k_1}$, which completes our decoding process.

Let us now take a step back to elaborate a little further on the classical processing part of the decoding process. The classical decoder part for a QTC is very similar to that of classical turbo codes. It consists of two soft-input soft-output (SISO) decoders, an interleaver, and a deinterleaver.

As seen in Figure 12.8, the classical processing hinges on the knowledge of the quantum depolarizing probability $p$ of the quantum channel associated with the error operator $P_2$. As an idealized simplifying assumption, we exploit the perfect knowledge of the quantum depolarizing probability $p$. The depolarizing probability value $p$ and the *a-priori* information $p_2^a(L_2)$ obtained from the outer SISO decoder are used by the inner SISO decoder for calculating the extrinsic information $p_2^e(L_2)$. For the first iteration, the depolarizing probability $p$ is the only input value used by the inner SISO decoder. Hence, the value of $p_2^a(L_2)$ is initialized to be equiprobable. Next, the extrinsic information $p_2^e(L_2)$ is interleaved in order to obtain the *a-priori* information $p_1^a(P_1)$ for the outer SISO decoder. By combining the *a-priori* information $p_1^a(P_1)$ and the syndrome value $S_1$, the outer SISO decoder calculates the extrinsic information $p_1^e(P_1)$. The extrinsic value is then deinterleaved to yield $p_2^a(L_2)$ which is fed into the inner SISO decoder. This process is performed iteratively until one of the following conditions is satisfied: the converged mutual information is attained or the maximum affordable number of iterations is reached. On the final iteration, the outer SISO decoder will produce $\hat{L}_1$, which is the most likely error pattern, given the value of $p$ and $S_1$ provided by the quantum processing part. The value of $\hat{L}_1$ is obtained for performing error recovery, as detailed in Eq. (12.58). A more rigorous treatment of the classical processing part of QTCs can be found in [82, 83]

## 12.4 Results and Analysis

In this section, first, we analyze the performance of the QSBC-QURC scheme conceived using EXIT charts [216, 218, 219]. In the classical domain, EXIT charts constitute a powerful tool, which is often used for guiding the design of near-capacity iterative error correction and for predicting their performance. An initial encouraging effort conducted in [290] invoked EXIT charts for predicting the performance of iterative QTCs demonstrating that EXIT charts can be indeed extended to the quantum domain. Second, we proceed by characterizing the performance of the QSBC-QURC scheme in terms of its quantum bit error ratio (QBER), which we obtained from our Monte-Carlo simulations. Third, we translate the QBER performance to the distance from the quantum hashing bound, which is also related to the goodput representing the error-free throughput. Finally, we use the goodput metric for determining the specific depolarizing probability at which switching to different quantum coding rate becomes beneficial in the context of a sophisticated multi-rate QSBC-QURC scheme.

### 12.4.1 EXIT Chart Analysis

In the classical domain, the encoders exhibiting recursive and non-catastrophic properties are highly desirable for conceiving near-capacity turbo codes. Unfortunately, in the quantum domain, the QCCs cannot be simultaneously recursive and non-catastrophic [142]. The recursive structure of QCCs is required for ensuring the convergence of iterative decoding to a vanishingly low QBER. Additionally, the QCCs exhibiting catastrophic structure require a doping mechanism or entanglement-assisted solution to substantially benefit from iterative decoding, since catastrophic QCCs provide zero *a-priori* information [82, 310]. These two solutions are beyond the scope of our discussions in this chapter. Fortunately, a non-recursive and non-catastrophic QCCs can still be designed for striking an attractive compromise, since they can achieve beneficial iteration gains even if the inner decoder EXIT curve terminates at the $(1, y)$ point for $y < 1$, provided that it only intersects with the outer decoder EXIT curves near $x = 1$ [302]. Based on these conditions, an exhaustive EXIT chart-based heuristic search has been conducted to find a "good" QURC.[2] For further details please refer to [125, 219]. The resultant seed transformation for such a QURC is given by

$$\mathcal{U} = \{21, 56, 5, 46, 44, 38\}_{10}. \tag{12.59}$$

In this chapter, our QSBC-QURC scheme utilized a specific a QURC whose seed transformation is given in Eq. (12.59) and the QSBCs of $\mathcal{C}[4, 2, 2]$, $\mathcal{C}[6, 4, 2]$ and $\mathcal{C}[8, 6, 2]$ were used as the outer codes. The seed transformations of the QSBCs are given in Table 12.1. As a benchmark, we use the QIrCC-QURC scheme presented in [302], where the QIrCCs are optimized using the EXIT chart-aided design method specified in [83, 290]. The seed transformation of the QIrCC component codes is given in Table 12.2. As we have described briefly in subsection 12.2.4, the seed transformation is the decimal representation used for describing the quantum gate connections amongst the physical qubits within the quantum encoder $\mathcal{V}$. Also, it can be used for simulating the QSCs classically.

The QURC we chose, which is defined by the seed transformation in Eq. (12.59), has a non-recursive and non-catastrophic structure. Therefore, the inner decoder's EXIT curve will terminate at the $(1, y)$ point, where $y < 1$. In Figure 12.9, we have plotted the inner decoder EXIT curves for QURCs in the face of various depolarizing probabilities of $p = \{0.06, 0.05, 0.04, 0.03, 0.02, 0.01\}$. Superficially it might appear that the inner decoder EXIT curves of the QURC scheme are capable of reaching the $(1, 1)$ point. However, a closer inspection in the vicinity of the $(1, 1)$ point reveals that the inner decoder EXIT curves actually terminate at a point of $(1, y)$, where we have $y < 1$. Hence the decoder might not be able to attain an infinitesimally low QBER, because the intersection of the inner and outer decoder EXIT curves occurs before the $(1, 1)$ point of perfect convergence is reached.

Therefore, in Figure 12.9, we have also plotted the outer decoder EXIT curves for the set of QSBCs having the quantum coding rates of $r_Q = \{1/2, 2/3, 3/4\}$. We can observe that the intersections of the inner and outer decoder

2 In this chapter familiarity with EXIT charts is assumed, but a rudimentary conceptual introduction was provided in Section 12.1

**Table 12.2** The seed transformation $\mathcal{U}$ associated with QCCs exhibiting various quantum coding rates $r_Q$ for constructing the QIrCC of. All of the QCCs exhibiting a memory of $m = 3$.

| Quantum coding rate ($r_Q$) | Seed transformation $\mathcal{U}$ |
|---|---|
| 1/4 | $\{9600, 691, 11713, 4863, 1013, 6907, 1125, 828, 10372, 6337, 5590, 11024, 12339, 3439\}_{10}$ |
| 1/3 | $\{3968, 1463, 2596, 3451, 1134, 3474, 657, 686, 3113, 1866, 2608, 2570\}_{10}$ |
| 1/2 | $\{848, 1000, 930, 278, 611, 263, 744, 260, 356, 880\}_{10}$ |
| 2/3 | $\{529, 807, 253, 1950, 3979, 2794, 956, 1892, 3359, 2127, 3812, 1580\}_{10}$ |
| 3/4 | $\{62, 6173, 4409, 12688, 7654, 10804, 1763, 15590, 6304, 3120, 2349, 1470, 9063, 4020\}_{10}$ |

*Source*: Adapted from [302].

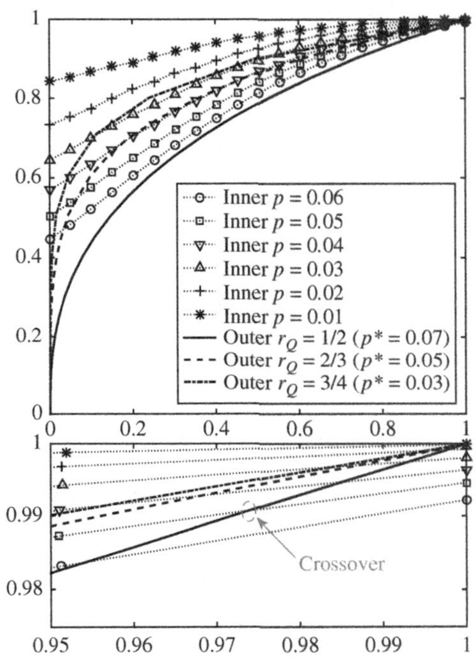


**Figure 12.9** Outer decoder EXIT curves for the QSBCs used as the outer codes and the inner decoder EXIT curves for the QURC as the inner code. We can take a closer look at the vicinity of the (1, 1) point and observe that despite having been carefully selected, the inner decoder EXIT curve does not reach the (1, 1) point due to the nature of the non-recursive structure. *Source*: [279]/IEEE/CC BY 4.0.

EXIT curves seen for the various quantum coding rates $r_Q$ are in the proximity of the $(1, 1)$ point, as desired. Furthermore, a marginally open EXIT tunnel emerges between the inner decoder EXIT curve for $p = 0.05$ and the outer decoder EXIT curve for a 1/2-rate QSBC. This marginally open tunnel indicates that iterative decoding convergence is attained at $p \leq 0.05$, which exhibits itself as a waterfall-shaped QBER curve.

Additionally, in Figure 12.10, we have plotted the stair-case-shaped Monte-Carlo simulation-based decoding trajectory of mutual information exchange between the inner and outer SISO decoders. As expected, the decoding trajectory got stuck after approximately 10 iterations between the inner and outer SISO decoder in the vicinity of the $(1, 1)$ point. Given that the iterative decoding of the QSBC-QURC scheme technically does not achieve full convergence, we expected an error-floor to be present in the QBER curves, which we will discuss in the next subsection.

### 12.4.2 Quantum Bit Error Rate

Let us now evaluate the error correction performance of the QSBC-QURC schemes conceived based both on their QBER and on the QBER curves' distance from the quantum hashing bound. The QBER curves of the half-rate QSBC-QURC scheme having $n = \{500, 1000, 2000\}$ physical qubits after 16 decoding iterations using Monte-Carlo

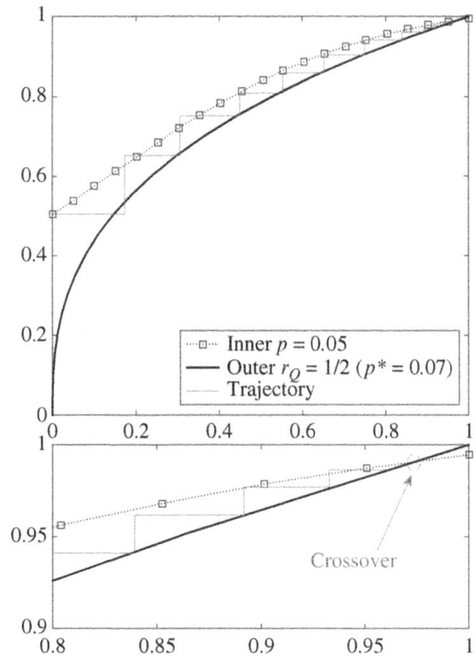


**Figure 12.10** The Monte-Carlo simulation-based decoding trajectory of mutual information exchange between the classical inner and outer SISO decoders. It can be observed that the decoding trajectory is stuck at the vicinity of (1, 1)-point after approximately 10 decoding iterations. *Source*: [279]/IEEE/CC BY 4.0.

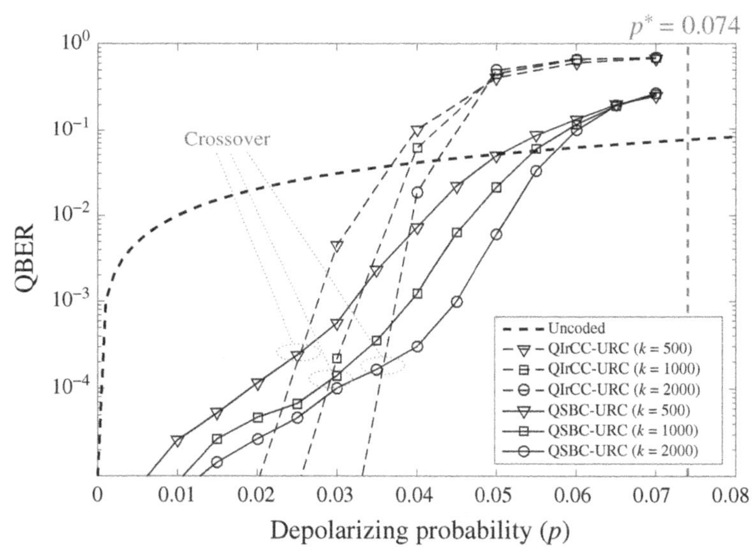


**Figure 12.11** QBER versus quantum depolarizing probability curves for the half-rate QSBC-QURC and the half-rate QIrCC-QURC scheme exhibiting various numbers of logical qubits after 16 decoding iterations. For a half-rate QSC, the quantum hashing bound is $p^* = 0.074$. *Source*: [279]/IEEE/CC BY 4.0.

simulations is portrayed in Figure 12.11. For the sake of benchmarking, we also simulated the QIrCC-QURC scheme of [302] and we added the QBER curves to Figure 12.11. Beneficial performance improvements can be observed for both the QSBC-QURC and the QIrCC-QURC arrangements upon increasing the number of physical qubits.

Let us now compare the QBER performance of the QSBC-QURC and the QIrCC-QURC schemes, where the latter is the most powerful half-rate QTC scheme at the time of writing exhibiting the best QBER performance. It can be observed from Figure 12.11 that for $n = 2000$ physical qubits, the proposed QSBC-QURC scheme offers a substantial performance improvement in the depolarizing probability region of $0.035 < p < 0.055$. However, as we reduce the depolarizing probability of the quantum channel to the region of $p < 0.035$, the QIrCC-QURC scheme outperforms the QSBC-QURC, where the latter has a relatively high error floor. There are two possible explanations for this specific phenomenon exhibited by our design.

First, based on our EXIT chart analysis, we already expected the emergence of an error floor since the stair-case-shaped decoding trajectory of the QSBC-QURC scheme got stuck before reaching the (1, 1)-point of perfect convergence. However, based on this argument, the QIrCC-QURC should also have an error floor. Indeed, in reality, the QIrCC-QURC scheme is also expected to have an error floor, but at a very low QBER, which is unobservable in Figure 12.11.

This brings us to the second reason, which also explains why the QSBC-QURC scheme has a significantly higher error floor than the QIrCC-QURC scheme. The answer is related to the characteristics of the outer codes. Explicitly, as for the QIrCC-QURC scheme, the outer code is constituted by a set of QCCs exhibiting strong error correction performance, despite failing to converge fully. The seed transformation of the QCCs that assembles the QIrCC is given in Table 12.2 [302]. For more detailed discussions on QIrCCs, we refer the motivated reader to [83]. By contrast, the outer codes for our QSBC-QURC schemes are constituted by QSBCs having a minimum distance of $d = 2$. Compared to QIrCCs, QSBCs are the weaker codes. Consequently, they result in residual qubit errors even in the region of a low depolarizing probability $p$. Our QBER performance comparison between the QIrCC-QURC and QSBC-QURC schemes is summarized in Table 12.3. Once again, we want to highlight that the QSBC-QURC outperforms the QIrCC-QURC scheme for the scenarios of $\text{QBER} < \text{QBER}_{\text{uncoded}}$ and $\text{QBER} < 10^{-3}$. However, due to the relatively high error floor of the QSBC-QURC scheme, for a scenario where $\text{QBER} < 10^{-4}$ is required, the QIrCC-QURC scheme succeeds in meeting this requirement at a higher depolarizing probability $p$.

However, the main problem with using QIrCCs as the outer codes is that for each quantum coding rate $r_Q$, it requires another exhaustive search for finding the best code and the resultant codes may not share the same quantum encoder structure. By contrast, the QSBCs having various quantum coding rates $r_Q$ share the same quantum encoder structure, as illustrated in Figure 12.5. Therefore, in terms of flexibility and adaptivity, the QIrCCs-QURC schemes may not be favorable. Since the QSBC-QURC schemes can be configured for various $r_Q$ values using the same quantum encoder, we have to further investigate the performance of the QSBC-QURC scheme exhibiting various $r_Q$ values. In Figure 12.12, we have plotted the QBER performance of the QSBC-QURC scheme having quantum coding rates of $r_Q = \{1/2, 2/3, 3/4\}$. Naturally, we can go beyond $r_Q = 3/4$, however, our QTC simulations are limited by the computational power of our classical computers. Figure 12.12 shows that we can reduce the error floor by increasing the number of physical qubits. It also shows that the QSBC-QURC scheme exhibiting a higher quantum coding rate can only cope with a lower quantum depolarizing probability $p$. However, by increasing the quantum coding rate $r_Q$, the effective throughput of the quantum depolarizing channel can be improved, since it requires a lower number of auxiliary qubits, which will be discussed further in the next subsection. The performance results of QSBC-QURC schemes exhibiting various quantum coding rates are summarized in Table 12.4.

**Table 12.3** Performance comparison of half-rate QIrCC-QURC to half-rate QSBC-QURC for $k = \{500, 1000, 2000\}$ logical qubits. The performance is described using the maximum tolerable depolarizing probability $p$ given various requirements, below which the code improves the QBER. For any half-rate QSC, the quantum hashing bound is $p^* = 0.074$.

| **Requirement** | $k = 500$ | | $k = 1000$ | | $k = 2000$ | |
|---|---|---|---|---|---|---|
| | $p$ **QIrCC** | $p$ **QSBC** | $p$ **QIrCC** | $p$ **QSBC** | $p$ **QIrCC** | $p$ **QSBC** |
| QBER < uncoded QBER | 0.037 | **0.050** | 0.039 | **0.055** | 0.043 | **0.058** |
| $\text{QBER} = 10^{-3}$ | 0.028 | **0.032** | 0.033 | **0.039** | 0.037 | **0.045** |
| $\text{QBER} = 10^{-4}$ | **0.024** | 0.019 | **0.029** | 0.028 | **0.035** | 0.030 |

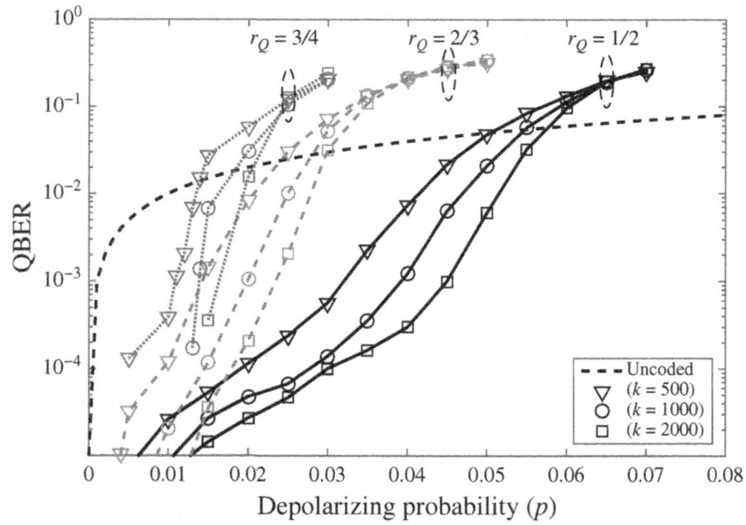


**Figure 12.12** QBER versus quantum depolarizing probability curves for QSBC-QURC schemes exhibiting quantum coding rates of $r_Q = \{1/2, 2/3, 3/4\}$ having $k = \{500, 1000, 2000\}$ logical qubits after 16 decoding iterations. *Source*: [279]/IEEE/CC BY 4.0.

**Table 12.4** Performance comparison of QSBC-QURC schemes having $k = \{500, 1000, 2000\}$ logical qubits and quantum coding rates of $r_Q = \{1/2, 2/3, 3/4\}$. The performance is described using the maximum tolerable depolarizing probability $p$ given various requirements, below which the code improves the QBER performance. The quantum hashing bound for QSCs having $r_Q = \{1/2, 2/3, 3/4\}$ is given by $p^* = \{0.074, 0.044, 0.031\}$.

| **Requirement** | **QBER < uncoded QBER** | | | **QBER = $10^{-3}$** | | |
|---|---|---|---|---|---|---|
| | $r_Q = 1/2$ | $r_Q = 2/3$ | $r_Q = 3/4$ | $r_Q = 1/2$ | $r_Q = 2/3$ | $r_Q = 3/4$ |
| $k = 500$ | 0.051 | 0.024 | 0.014 | 0.032 | 0.014 | 0.011 |
| $k = 1000$ | 0.055 | 0.028 | 0.018 | 0.039 | 0.020 | 0.014 |
| $k = 2000$ | **0.058** | **0.030** | **0.021** | **0.045** | **0.023** | **0.016** |

### 12.4.3 Goodput

When the quality of the quantum channel starts degrading, a QSC having a certain quantum coding rate $r_Q$, which was previously capable of correcting all the quantum errors flawlessly, may no longer succeed in error-free decoding. In a condition where a QSC operates in the face of the quantum channel having the depolarizing probability beyond its error correction capability, the QSC may in fact inflict more quantum errors by correcting them in the wrong positions. Hence, the quantum coding rate of a QSC should be adjusted according to the quality of the quantum channel. The most intuitive way of improving the error correction capability of a QSC is to reduce its quantum coding rate, which means imposing more redundancy. Similarly, when the quality of the quantum channel starts improving, one can increase the quantum coding rate accordingly to reduce the overhead imposed by the QSC and hence, improve the effective throughput.

To elaborate a little further, for a random QSC $\mathcal{C}$ exhibiting a quantum coding rate of $r_Q$ having a sufficiently high number of physical qubits, there exists a limit $p^*$ below which it can operate perfectly, yielding an infinitesimally low QBER. Hence, the goal of designing a QSC is to ensure that it can operate as close as possible to the limit of $p^*$. Similarly, for a given depolarizing probability $p$, we can find a random QSC $\mathcal{C}$ exhibiting a quantum coding rate of $r_Q \leq C_Q(p)$ and having a sufficiently high number of physical qubits that is capable of yielding an infinitesimally low QBER. This specific limit is referred to as the quantum hashing bound, which is defined as follows [67, 82, 242]:

$$\mathcal{C}_Q = 1 - H(p) - p \cdot \log_2(3), \tag{12.60}$$

where $H(p)$ is the binary entropy of $p$ defined by $H(p) = -p\log_2 p - (1-p)\log_2(1-p)$. Given a value of $p$, then $C_Q$ is the quantum hashing bound for $p$. Conversely, given a value of $r_Q$, the value of $p^* = p(r_Q)$ represents the quantum hashing bound for $r_Q$. For instance, for a QSC having a quantum coding rate of $r_Q = 1/2$, the quantum hashing bound is given by $p^* = 0.074$. In Figure 12.11, the quantum hashing bound is represented by dashed line. It can be observed that for QBER $= 10^{-3}$, the QSBC-QURC scheme operates closer to the quantum hashing bound. Quantitatively, the distance from the quantum hashing bound can be formally defined as

$$D \triangleq p^* - p, \tag{12.61}$$

where $p$ is the achievable depolarizing probability, below which the QSC yields an infinitesimally low QBER. For example, in this chapter, we set the QBER $= 10^{-3}$. Therefore, based on the results in Table 12.3, the half-rate QIrCC-QURC scheme having $n = 2000$ physical qubits operates at $D = 0.074 - 0.037 = 0.0037$ from the quantum hashing bound, while the half-rate QSBC-QURC scheme also having $n = 2000$ physical qubits operates at $D = 0.074 - 0.045 = 0.029$ from the quantum hashing bound, provided that we have QBER $= 10^{-3}$. The distance from the quantum hashing bound constitutes a fair metric of comparing the efficiency of QSCs exhibiting various quantum coding rates. Hence, it has a direct relationship with the goodput, which represents the effective number of logical qubits after the decoding step. The achievable goodput taking the quantum coding rate $r_Q$ into account for normalization can be formally defined as

$$\text{Goodput} = r_Q \cdot (1 - \text{QBER}). \tag{12.62}$$

By applying Eq. (12.62), we can transform the QBER performance seen in Figure 12.12 into the goodput performance of Figure 12.13. We have also plotted the quantum hashing bound formula of Eq. (12.60) to show the visual representation of the relationship between the quantum hashing bound and the goodput performance. In Figure 12.13, the distance from the quantum hashing bound is shown by the dashed lines for various quantum coding rates $r_Q$ at QBER $= 10^{-3}$. Quantitatively, given that $r_Q = \{1/2, 2/3, 3/4\}$, the resultant quantum hashing bound is given by $p^* = \{0.074, 0.044, 0.031\}$, while the distance from the quantum hashing bound is given by $D = \{0.029, 0.021, 0.015\}$.

### 12.4.4 Reconfigurable Scheme

Given a range of various requirements and quantum coding rates, the maximum tolerable depolarizing probability value, below which the QSBC-QURC schemes improve the QBER performance is portrayed in Table 12.4. As we have described earlier, for a certain requirement, there is a quantum coding scheme $\mathcal{C}$ that will satisfy it

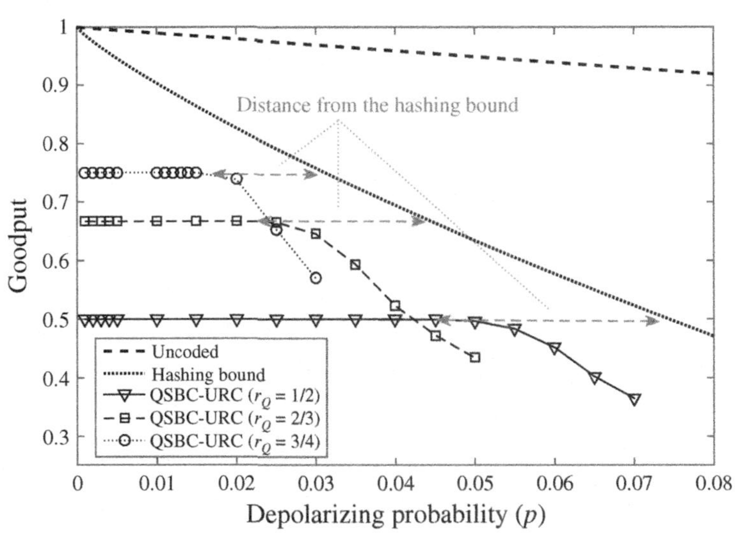


**Figure 12.13** Goodput curves versus depolarizing probability for QSBC-URC exhibiting various quantum coding rates having logical qubits $k = 2000$ after 16 decoding iterations. The dashed lines represent the distance to the quantum hashing bound for each quantum coding rate. *Source*: [279]/IEEE/CC BY 4.0.

with the highest quantum coding rate. Again, for instance, given that the depolarizing probability of the quantum channel is $p = 0.01$ and the QBER requirement of QBER $< 10^{-3}$ is good enough for the quantum computation or communication considered, we do not necessarily invoke a half-rate QSBC-QURC scheme for this purpose, since a 3/4-rate QSBC-QURC scheme is already capable of satisfying the aforementioned conditions. By utilizing a 3/4-rate QSBC-QURC scheme, we can have 50% less auxiliary qubits. Based on our QSBC-QURC scheme, a multi-rate scheme can be readily constructed, since a single QSBC-QURC encoder is capable of providing multiple quantum coding rates, as described in Section 12.2.

Consequently, based on the goodput results of Figure 12.13, we can determine the quantum coding rate switching point for our QSBC-QURC scheme in order to adjust the quantum coding rate based on the depolarizing probability experienced. For instance, the switching depolarizing probability for the requirement of QBER $<$ QBER$_{\text{uncoded}}$ is given by $p = \{0.058, 0.030, 0.021\}$ for the three QSBC-QURC schemes considered, which can be seen in Table 12.4. The effective goodput after applying the switching probability is represented by the bold line in Figure 12.14a. We can also infer from Figure 12.14a that for a depolarizing probability of $0.030 \leq p \leq 0.058$ we

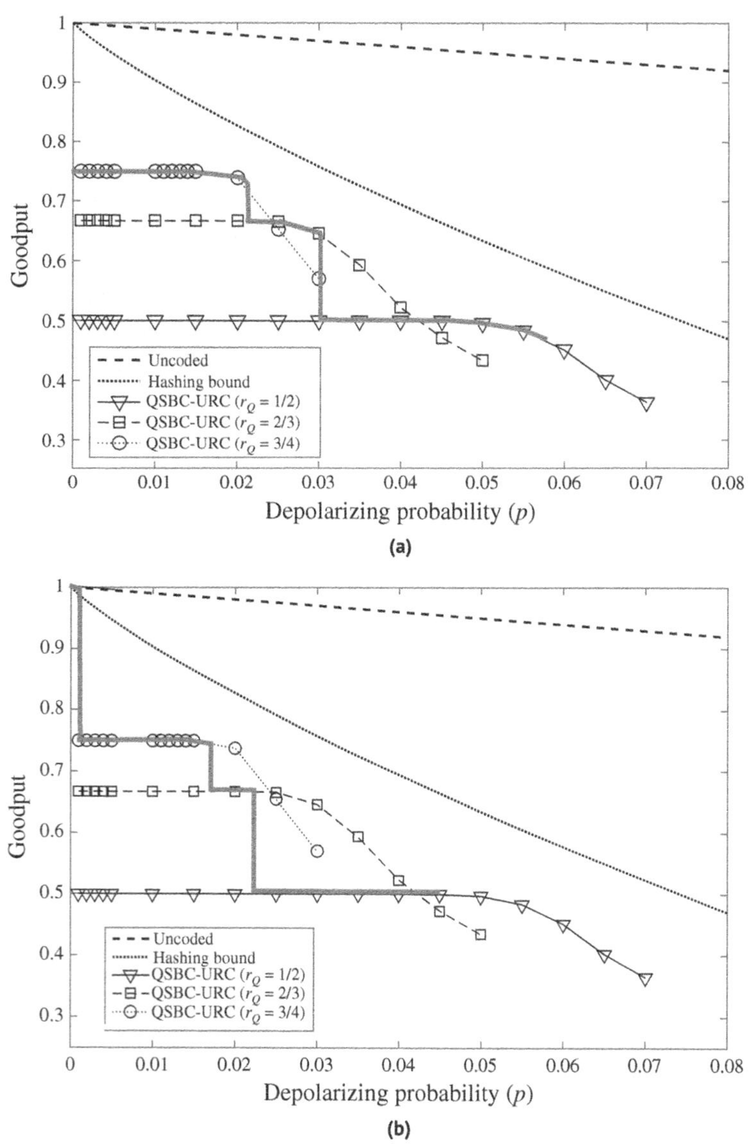


**Figure 12.14** Goodput versus depolarizing probability curves for QSBC-QURC schemes exhibiting various quantum coding rates having $k = 2000$ logical qubits after 16 decoding iterations. The bold line represents the achievable goodput using our multi-rate scheme given the minimum requirement: (a) QBER $\leq$ QBER$_{\text{uncoded}}$, (b) QBER $= 10^{-3}$. *Source:* [279]/IEEE/CC BY 4.0.

can utilize the QSBC-QURC having $r_Q = 1/2$ in order to maintain the requirement of $\text{QBER} < \text{QBER}_{\text{uncoded}}$, while the QSBC-QURC having $r_Q = 2/3$ is invoked for $0.021 \leq p \leq 0.030$, and finally a QSBC-QURC having $r_Q = 3/4$ is invoked for $p < 0.021$.

Similarly, the effective goodput attained upon applying the switching regime specified in Table 12.4 for maintaining $\text{QBER} < 10^{-3}$ is portrayed in Figure 12.14b. Based on Table 12.4 and Figure 12.14a, the QSBC-QURC schemes may be configured for operating at $r_Q = 1/2$ for $0.023 \leq p \leq 0.045$, operating at $r_Q = 2/3$ for $0.016 \leq p \leq 0.023$, operating at $r_Q = 2/3$ for $10^{-3} \leq p \leq 0.016$ and finally, the system may switch to the uncoded mode when the quantum channel reaches the condition of $p < 10^{-3}$.

## 12.5 Conclusions and Future Research

We have conceived a QTC scheme exhibiting multiple quantum coding rates using a single quantum encoder. This construction was created by exploiting the inherent properties of our QSBC encoders. We have amalgamated the QSBCs and QURC schemes to transform the error detection capability of QSBCs into an error correction capability without sacrificing the quantum coding rate. We predicted and analyzed the performance of our QSBC-QURC schemes both by EXIT charts and by Monte-Carlo simulations. Despite their moderate complexity, the QSBC-QURC schemes are capable of operating relatively close to the quantum hashing bound at $\text{QBER} = 10^{-3}$. Furthermore, we have compared our half-rate QSBC-QURC to the best-performing half-rate QTC scheme, namely the QIrCC-QURC of [302]. The QSBC-QURC outperforms the QIrCC-QURC in terms of operating closer to the quantum hashing bound at $\text{QBER} = 10^{-3}$. By contrast, observe in Figure 12.11 that the QIrCC-QURC has the edge over the QSBC-QURC arrangements for low values of $p$. This trend is a consequence of the relatively high error floor of our QSBC-QURC scheme, which was indeed expected based on its EXIT chart analysis.

We have also extended our discussions to the option of creating a multi-rate scheme for our QSBC-QURC. By using the distance from the quantum hashing bound and the goodput, we quantified the normalized performance of our QSBC-QURC scheme by taking into account its quantum coding rate. Furthermore, we have also determined the quantum coding rate switching point based on the depolarizing probability for two specific requirements, $\text{QBER} < \text{QBER}_{\text{uncoded}}$ and $\text{QBER} < 10^{-3}$. Finally, we quantified the goodput achieved by appropriately adapting the coding rate in response to the specific quantum depolarizing probability experienced.

As an initial study and first instantiation of QTCs exhibiting multiple quantum coding rates in a single quantum encoder, we present several potential research directions as an extension of this result. Firstly, it is indeed possible to have a higher quantum coding rate than $r_Q = 3/4$ as we have demonstrated in this chapter. However, the simulations will become more time consuming, since the simulation time of each block of the quantum encoder is roughly doubled each time we add one more qubit into the block. Our powerful parallel computer is only capable of simulating the QSBC-QURC exhibiting quantum coding rates up to $r_Q = 3/4$. Ultimately, the QSBCs can be combined with QURC arrangements for creating a QSBC-QURC scheme exhibiting an arbitrary quantum coding rate, similar to the QIrCCs. An EXIT chart-based heuristic search can also be carried out for constructing the best combination of the subcomponent QSBCs. Consequently, this would result in a very smooth goodput performance curve.

However, one of the requirements for the multi-rate scheme for QSCs to work flawlessly is having perfect channel estimation for predicting the depolarizing probability. Our simulation results are based on the assumption that we have perfect knowledge of the depolarizing probability at the decoder. However, it is worth mentioning that it has been demonstrated in classical settings that classical parallel turbo codes are generally rather insensitive to inaccurate signal-to-noise ratio estimation [311–313]. Having said that, for QTCs, the effect of inaccurate depolarizing probability knowledge on the QBER performance is still unknown at the time of writing. Some investigations of this problem have been conducted for QLDPC codes in [314, 315]. These results give an early indication that there is no significant QBER performance difference variation between having a perfect and imperfect quantum channel knowledge [316].

Hence, the next step is to find the most appropriate depolarizing probability estimator for QSBCs. A plausible option is using some known pilot qubits or pre-shared entanglement for estimating the depolarizing probability. However, we have to rely on the idealistic assumption that the quantum depolarizing channel is a static channel implying that the value of depolarizing probability does not vary rapidly over time [317–319]. An alternative approach is invoking syndrome-based depolarizing probability estimation, which can be derived from the classical realm [316, 320–322]. The syndrome-based estimator may be deemed to be more efficient because it eliminates the need for pilot qubits or pre-shared entanglement and also the necessity of measuring the quantum information. However, a syndrome-based channel estimator would require a high number of physical qubits work accurately whereas currently, we are working on a QSC scheme having a relatively short block ($k < 2000$). Needless to say, a joint study of the effect of the inaccuracy depolarizing probability on the QBER performance of our QSBC-QURC scheme and the design of online depolarizing probability estimation is a promising subject.

# 13

# EXIT-chart-aided Design of Irregular Multiple-rate Quantum Turbo Block Codes

## 13.1 Introduction

As detailed in Chapter 12, QSBs constitute a potent technique of mitigating the deleterious effects of quantum decoherence that is prevalent in quantum systems [323, 324]. The conception of quantum stabilizer codes (QSCs) [59] has triggered a massive redesign of classical correction codes for their application in the quantum realm. Consequently, the "quantumization" of powerful classical error correction codes [325–328] leads to the emergence of novel classes of QSCs, such as quantum polar codes (QPCs) [69, 278], quantum low-density parity-check (QLDPC) codes [67, 80], as well as quantum turbo codes (QTCs) [68, 83]. However, classical error-correction codes cannot be directly transplanted into the quantum domain, since they have to satisfy the stringent requirement of the so-called symplectic criterion [60, 170]. This challenge becomes particularly pronounced when attempting to design a broad class of QSCs capable of adapting their error correction capability to the quality of quantum channels. Explicitly, when the quality of the quantum channel starts degrading, a QSC operating beyond its quantum error correction capability may actually introduce more errors instead of correcting them. Thus, we may reduce the quantum coding rate of the QSC by incorporating more redundancy qubits. Similarly, when the quality of the quantum channel starts improving, we may increase the quantum coding rate accordingly to reduce the number of redundancy qubits for the sake of improving the effective throughput of the QSC. However, the well-established classical methods such as puncturing and extending the mother code often do not satisfy the stringent symplectic criterion imposed in quantum domain [300, 329]. Therefore, a novel design paradigm has to be conceived for designing adaptive and rate-compatible QSCs.

The seminal family of rate-compatible QTCs was conceived in [83, 290] by employing quantum irregular convolutional codes (QIrCCs) as the inner and outer codes. However, unfortunately, the subcomponent QIrCCs proposed in [83, 290] cannot be created from a single mother code. Hence, the implementation of QIrCCs requires a different quantum encoder for each subcomponent code. Furthermore, since they rely on fractional encoding of the input stream by each subcomponent code, several subcomponent quantum encoders have to be prepared. Subsequently, another design was proposed in [302], namely the QIrCC-QURC, where the inner codes previously constituted by QIrCCs were replaced by a quantum unity-rate code (QURC). The QURC was employed as the inner code, iteratively exchanging information with the QIrCCs serving as the outer codes. The benefit of this QURC-based design was that it did not reduce the quantum coding rate. Furthermore, since the irregular encoding operations carried out by each different subcomponent that applied to a fraction of the input stream were only performed by the outer codes, the number of quantum encoders required for the entire scheme was moderate. More recently, an alternative QTC scheme was proposed in [279], where the outer codes were constructed by quantum short-block codes (QSBC). While the QSBCs conceived successfully accommodate a wide range of quantum coding rates as the outer codes, the proposed design only covered the quantum coding rates of $r_Q \geq 0.5$. Additionally, the outer codes were not optimized. Nonetheless, they had the potential of performing fractional encoding using single-encode for constructing multiple-rate quantum short-block codes (MR-QSBCs). These codes were detailed in Chapter 12. Hence it is beneficial for readers to consult the previous chapter before delving into this chapter, but expert readers might like to explore this chapter directly, because sufficient introductory material is included here.

The design of near-capacity QTCs based on optimal fractional subcomponent codes may be achieved by invoking extrinsic information transfer (EXIT)-chart-based heuristic optimization [83, 216, 218, 219, 221, 290, 302, 330, 331]. Explicitly, a near-capacity operation may be attained for any arbitrary coding rate by optimizing the weighting factors of the subcomponent codes, where this weighting factor determines the specific fraction of the input stream to be encoded by each of the subcomponents. In the conventional near-capacity QTCs, the subcomponent codes having various quantum coding rates will be represented by different dedicated quantum encoders. However, in this chapter we conceive an attractive solution, where a carefully designed single quantum encoder can be used for accommodating a set of component codes having a wide range of quantum coding rates. Therefore, the benefit of EXIT-chart-based optimization can be conveniently exploited when the subcomponent codes can be represented by a single encoder.

To elaborate a little further, we detail how to conceive *a single encoder that fits all* types of QECCs. More specifically, the contributions of this chapter may be summarized as follows:

- We formulate and characterize the family of single-encoder-based MR-QSBCs, where only a single quantum encoder is required for supporting a wide range of quantum coding rates suitable for different quantum depolarizing probabilities.
- We design single-encoder-based multiple-rate quantum turbo short-block codes by concatenating single-encoder-based MR-QSBCs with a QURC. We refer to this design as a MR-QSBC-QURC scheme.
- We perform heuristic EXIT-chart-based optimization for designing optimal MR-QSBC-QURC arrangements. Despite the low complexity of MR-QSBCs harnessed as the outer codes, they attain a near-hashing bound performance. Specifically, the quantum bit error ratio (QBER) of the half-rate MR-QSBC-QURC designed is comparable to that of the best-performing half-rate QTCs found in the open literature, namely the QIrCC-QURC of [302].
- Finally, we demonstrate that the schemes designed are capable of approaching the quantum hashing bound for a wide range of quantum coding rates, while maintaining a QBER of $10^{-3}$.

The rest of this chapter is organized as follows. In Section 13.2, we present the proposed MR-QSBCs and demonstrate that they can be constructed using only a single quantum encoder for a wide range of quantum coding rates. In Section 13.3, we amalgamate MR-QSBCs and a QURC for constructing multiple-rate QTCs, which we refer to as MR-QSBC-QURC. The step-by-step optimization of the MR-QSBCs using the EXIT-chart-based heuristic search is given in Section 13.4. We evaluate the performance of the optimized MR-QSBC-QURCs in terms of their QBER, performance gaps with respect to the quantum hashing bound as well as goodput for various quantum coding rates in Section 13.5. Finally, we conclude and formulate a range of design guidelines in Section 13.6, while highlighting some potential future research directions.

## 13.2 Quantum Short-block Codes

The classical short-block codes (SBCs) are binary systematic linear block codes $\mathcal{C}(n, k, d)$, whose generator matrix $\boldsymbol{G}$ is defined by

$$\boldsymbol{G} = [\boldsymbol{I}_k | \boldsymbol{P}_{k,(n-k)}] = [\boldsymbol{I}_k | \mathbf{1}_{k,1}], \tag{13.1}$$

for $k < n$, where $k$ is the length of the original information word, $n$ is the length of the encoded codeword, $\boldsymbol{I}_k$ is a $k$-dimension identity matrix, $\boldsymbol{P}_{k,(n-k)}$ is a $[k \times (n-k)]$-element binary matrix, and $\mathbf{1}_{m,n}$ is a $(m \times n)$-element all-one matrix. The parity-check matrix (PCM) $\boldsymbol{H}$ of a systematic linear block code is formulated as $\boldsymbol{H} = [\boldsymbol{P}^T | \boldsymbol{I}_{n-k}]$. Therefore, the PCM $\boldsymbol{H}$ of the classical SBCs is given by

$$\boldsymbol{H} = \mathbf{1}_{1,n}, \tag{13.2}$$

which is an all-one $(1 \times n)$-element matrix. Finally, the resultant classical coding rate $r_C$ is given by

$$r_C = \frac{k}{n} = \frac{n-1}{n}, \tag{13.3}$$

for $n \geq 2$. The minimum distance of the SBCs conceived is $d = 2$, which implies that classical SBCs constitute a family of single-error detection codes. Having said that, the minimum distance $d = 2$ guarantees the convergence of iterative decoding to a vanishingly low BER, when they are employed as the outer code within a concatenated coding scheme [303, 304].

By exploiting the classical-to-quantum isomorphism [179], the classical SBCs whose PCM is specified in Eq. (13.2) can be readily transformed into their quantum counterparts. Given a pair of classical codes $\mathcal{C}_1(n, k_1, d_1)$ and $\mathcal{C}_2(n, k_2, d_2)$ having PCMs of $\boldsymbol{H}_1$ and $\boldsymbol{H}_2$, respectively, a quantum stabilizer code (QSC) $\mathcal{C}[N, K, D]$[1] having a binary PCM $\boldsymbol{H}$ can be constructed by having $\boldsymbol{H}_x = \boldsymbol{H}_1$ and $\boldsymbol{H}_z = \boldsymbol{H}_2$, where $\boldsymbol{H}_x$ is used for mitigating the bit-flip ($\boldsymbol{X}$) errors and $\boldsymbol{H}_z$ is used for mitigating the phase-flip errors ($\boldsymbol{Z}$) of quantum Pauli channels. Given a pair of PCMs $\boldsymbol{H}_x$ and $\boldsymbol{H}_z$, we may construct a Calderbank-Shor-Steane (CSS)-type QSC, whose binary PCM $\boldsymbol{H}$ is defined as follows [55, 86]:

$$\boldsymbol{H} = \left[\begin{array}{c|c} \boldsymbol{H}_z & \boldsymbol{0} \\ \boldsymbol{0} & \boldsymbol{H}_x \end{array}\right]. \tag{13.4}$$

Thus, the code parameters of the resultant CSS-type QSC are constrained by the parameters of the classical constituent codes. More specifically, we have $N = n$, $K = k_1 + k_2 - n$, and $D = \min(d_1, d_2)$. In order to conceive a valid PCM $\boldsymbol{H}$ for a CSS-type QSC, a pair of PCMs $\boldsymbol{H}_x$ and $\boldsymbol{H}_z$ has to satisfy the following symplectic criterion [60, 94]:

$$\boldsymbol{H}_z \boldsymbol{H}_x^T = 0. \tag{13.5}$$

A specific case of CSS-type QSCs associated with $\boldsymbol{H}_x = \boldsymbol{H}_z$ may be referred to as a dual-containing CSS-type QSC. Therefore, the PCM $\boldsymbol{H}$ of dual-containing CSS-type QSCs derived from the classical SBCs of Eq. (13.2) is given by the following definition.

**Definition 13.1:** *QSBCs Type-I* [279]. QSBCs obtained from the classical PCM of Eq. (13.2) resulting in the following PCM of dual-containing CSS-type QSCs:

$$\boldsymbol{H} = \left[\begin{array}{c|c} \boldsymbol{1}_{1,n} & \boldsymbol{0} \\ \boldsymbol{0} & \boldsymbol{1}_{1,n} \end{array}\right], \tag{13.6}$$

where $n \geq 2$ is an even number – which automatically satisfies the symplectic criterion of Eq. (13.5) – are referred to as quantum short-block codes (QSBCs) Type-I [279].

For a dual-containing CSS-type QSC, the relationship between the classical coding rate of $r_C = k/n$ and its quantum coding rate counterpart of $r_Q = K/N$ can be described explicitly as follows [83, 153, 170]:

$$r_Q = 2r_C - 1. \tag{13.7}$$

Since the quantum coding rate $r_Q$ has to be positive ($r_Q > 0$), the classical mother codes must exhibit a classical coding rate of $r_C > 1/2$. Consequently, the quantum coding rate $r_Q$ of the QSBCs Type-I can be directly expressed as

$$r_Q = \frac{N-2}{N}, \tag{13.8}$$

for any even number of $N > 2$.

**Remark:** *The classical SBCs of* $\mathcal{C}(n, k, d) = \mathcal{C}(n, n-1, 2)$ *can be readily transformed into QSBCs Type-I of* $\mathcal{C}[N, K, D] = \mathcal{C}[n, n-2, 2]$ *for any even number* of $n > 2$.

1 Recall that to avoid confusion, we use the notation of $\mathcal{C}(n, k, d)$ for representing classical error-correction codes and $\mathcal{C}[N, K, D]$ for quantum error-correction codes. For classical error-correction codes, $n$ is the length of the codeword, $k$ is the length of the information word, and the $d$ is the minimum distance of the classical code. By contrast, for quantum error correction codes, $N$ is the number of physical/encoded qubits, $K$ is the number of logical/information qubits, and $D$ is the minimum distance of the quantum code.

**Example 13.1:** *For $n = 6$, we obtain a QSBC Type-I of $\mathcal{C}[N, K, D] = [6, 4, 2]$ having the stabilizer generators of $S = \{XXXXXX, ZZZZZZ\}$. The syndrome value evaluation for a single bit-flip ($X$) error is given in Table 13.1. The syndrome value evaluation for a single phase-flip error ($Z$) is identical to that of a single bit-flip error, since QSBCs of Type-I belong to the family of dual-containing CSS-type QSCs.*

We employed the method of constructing dual-containing CSS-type QSC encoders $\mathcal{V}$ presented in [67, 163, 279] to design the QSBC Type-I encoder $\mathcal{V}$ of Figure 13.1.[2] The quantum encoder of any QSC may be constructed using the quantum gates constituted by quantum Clifford gates. Furthermore, the quantum encoder of the MR-QSBCs advocated in this chapter can be constructed using only Hadamard ($H$)[3] and controlled-NOT (CNOT) gates. Specifically, Figure 13.1a depicts the QSBC $\mathcal{C}[4, 2, 2]$ encoder $\mathcal{V}$, which is identical to that presented in [167]. By incorporating additional quantum gates and connections marked by the dashed lines in the encoder $\mathcal{V}$ of Figure 13.1b into the encoder $\mathcal{V}$ of Figure 13.1a, we obtain the QSBC $\mathcal{C}[6, 4, 2]$ encoder $\mathcal{V}$. Similarly, by adding the quantum gates and connections marked by dashed-dotted lines to the encoder $\mathcal{V}$ of Figure 13.1c, we can readily create the QSBC $\mathcal{C}[8, 6, 2]$ encoder $\mathcal{V}$. This way we can construct a QSBC Type-I encoder $\mathcal{V}$ having a high quantum coding rate that simultaneously contains the quantum encoder $\mathcal{V}$ exhibiting lower quantum coding rates. Consequently, it is not necessary to construct more than a single encoder $\mathcal{V}$ for the various quantum coding rates of a QSBC Type-I, since the QSBC's encoder $\mathcal{V}$ exhibits a self-contained structure.

It is important to highlight that this appealing feature is reminiscent of the classical rate-compatible punctured coding philosophy proposed in [307], where the redundant part of the codeword may be flexibly punctured to

**Table 13.1** The syndrome value evaluation of a single bit-flip error using the QSBC Type-I having the stabilizer generators provided in Example 13.1.

| Error ($e$) | Syndrome ($s$) | Error Detection |
|---|---|---|
| $IIIIIX$ | 1 | Yes |
| $IIIIXI$ | 1 | Yes |
| $IIIXII$ | 1 | Yes |
| $IIXIII$ | 1 | Yes |
| $IXIIII$ | 1 | Yes |
| $XIIIII$ | 1 | Yes |

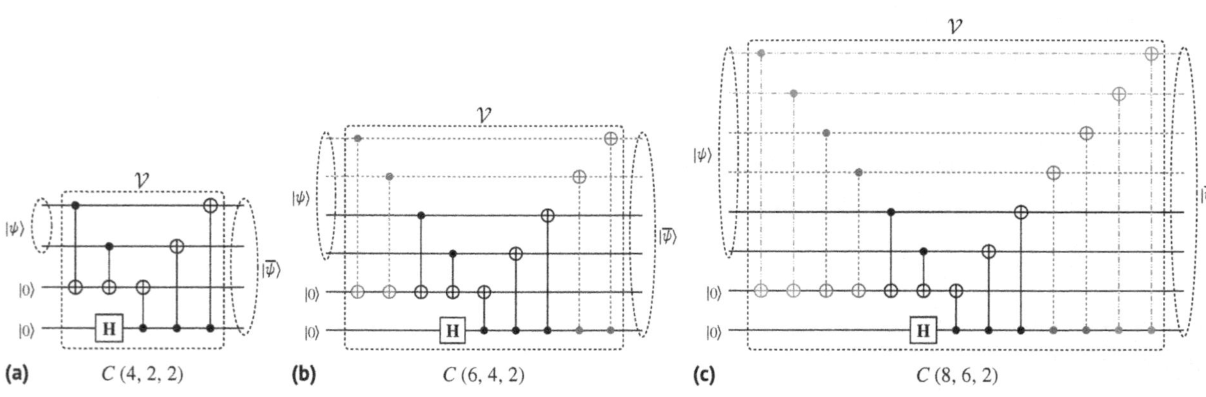


**Figure 13.1** The QSBCs Type-I encoder $\mathcal{V}$ for quantum coding rates of $r_Q = \{1/2, 2/3, 3/4\}$ illustrating the flexibility and scalability of the code constructions. *Source*: [332]/IEEE/CC BY 4.0.

2 Again, in this chapter our emphasis is on designing the quantum encoder $\mathcal{V}$ of dual-containing CSS-type QSCs. For readers who might like to delve deeper into the general construction of the quantum encoder $\mathcal{V}$, including non-CSS QSCs, we recommend the paper by Cleve and Gottesman [180].

3 In Figure 13.1, the notation $H$ represents a Hadamard gate, rather than a parity-check matrix.

obtain a higher-rate classical code. Therefore, the mother code should be designed very carefully so that the punctured version of the code will inherit the desired error correction properties.

As we can observe, the multiple-rate QSBC Type-I encoder $\mathcal{V}$ of Figure 13.1 is only scalable for $r_Q \geq 0.5$. Therefore, in addition to the QSBC Type-I, we propose a novel family of QSBCs, whose quantum encoder is capable of accommodating multiple quantum coding rates of $r_Q \leq 0.5$. The proposed QSBCs are obtained based on classical SBCs having the systematic generator matrix $\boldsymbol{G} = [\boldsymbol{I}_k | \boldsymbol{P}_{k,(n-k)}]$, where the matrix $\boldsymbol{P}^T$ is given by $\boldsymbol{P}^T = [\mathbf{1}_{(n-k),(2k-n)} | \boldsymbol{I}_{n-k}]$ for $2k > n$. Therefore, the PCM $\boldsymbol{H}$ of this particular family of classical SBCs assumes a systematic form given by

$$\boldsymbol{H} = [\mathbf{1}_{(n-k),(2k-n)} | \boldsymbol{I}_{n-k} | \boldsymbol{I}_{n-k}]. \tag{13.9}$$

The PCM of the classical SBCs in Eq. (13.9) automatically satisfies the symplectic criterion for even numbers $n$. The resultant classical SBCs also exhibit the minimum distance of $d \geq 2$, which is lower-bounded by the row-weight of the generator matrix $\boldsymbol{G}$. Finally, the PCM $\boldsymbol{H}$ of dual-containing CSS-type QSCs derived from the classical SBCs of Eq. (13.9) is given by the following definition.

**Definition 13.2:** *QSBCs Type-II.* The QSBCs obtained from the classical PCM of Eq. (13.9) result in the following PCM of dual-containing CSS-type QSCs:

$$\boldsymbol{H} = \left[\begin{array}{c|c} \mathbf{1}_{(n-k),(2k-n)} | \boldsymbol{I}_{n-k} | \boldsymbol{I}_{n-k} & \mathbf{0} \\ \mathbf{0} & \mathbf{1}_{(n-k),(2k-n)} | \boldsymbol{I}_{n-k} | \boldsymbol{I}_{n-k} \end{array}\right], \tag{13.10}$$

where $n \geq 2$ is an even number and $k = \frac{1}{2}(n+2)$ automatically satisfy the symplectic criterion of Eq. (13.5). These are referred to as quantum short-block codes (QSBCs) Type-II.

Therefore, the quantum coding rate $r_Q$ of the resultant QSBC Type-II can be explicitly expressed as

$$r_Q = \frac{2}{N}, \tag{13.11}$$

for any even number of $N > 2$.

**Remark:** *The classical SBCs of* $\mathcal{C}(n, k, d) = \mathcal{C}(n, \frac{1}{2}(n+2), 2)$ *can be readily transformed into QSBCs Type-II of* $\mathcal{C}[N, K, D] = \mathcal{C}[n, 2, 2]$ *for any even number of* $n > 2$.

**Example 13.2:** *For* $n = 6$, *we obtain a QSBC Type-II of* $\mathcal{C}[N, K, D] = [6, 2, 2]$ *having the stabilizer generators of* $\boldsymbol{S} = \{\boldsymbol{XXIXIX}, \boldsymbol{XXXIXI}, \boldsymbol{ZZIZIZ}, \boldsymbol{ZZZIZI}\}$. *The syndrome vector evaluation for a single bit-flip* ($\boldsymbol{X}$) *error is given in Table 13.2. The syndrome vector evaluation for a single phase-flip error* ($\boldsymbol{Z}$) *is identical to that of a single bit-flip error, since QSBCs Type-II belong to the family of dual-containing CSS-type QSCs.*

**Table 13.2** The syndrome vector evaluation of a single bit-flip error using the QSBC Type-II having the stabilizer generators provided in Example 13.2.

| Error $e$ | Syndrome $(s_1, s_2)$ | Error detection |
|---|---|---|
| $\boldsymbol{IIIIIX}$ | (0 1) | Yes |
| $\boldsymbol{IIIIXI}$ | (1 0) | Yes |
| $\boldsymbol{IIIXII}$ | (0 1) | Yes |
| $\boldsymbol{IIXIII}$ | (1 0) | Yes |
| $\boldsymbol{IXIIII}$ | (1 1) | Yes |
| $\boldsymbol{XIIIII}$ | (1 1) | Yes |

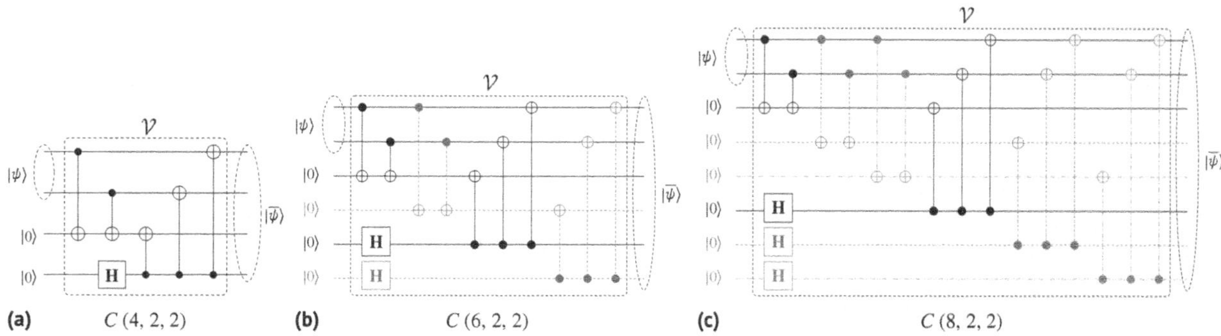

**Figure 13.2** The quantum encoders $\mathcal{V}$ of QSBC type-II for quantum coding rates of $r_Q = \{1/2, 1/3, 1/4\}$ illustrating the flexibility and scalability of the code constructions. *Source*: [332]/IEEE/CC BY 4.0.

Similarly, by following the method of constructing encoder $\mathcal{V}$ presented in [67, 163, 279] and based on the PCM $\boldsymbol{H}$ of Eq. (13.9), we obtain the multiple-rate QSBC Type-II encoder $\mathcal{V}$ having $N = \{4, 6, 8\}$ number of physical qubits, as shown in Figure 13.2. More explicitly, Figure 13.2a depicts the QSBC $\mathcal{C}[4, 2, 2]$ encoder $\mathcal{V}$, which is identical to the encoder $\mathcal{V}$ of Figure 13.1a. Similar to Figure 13.1, the encoder $\mathcal{V}$ of Figure 13.2a can be transformed into the QSBC $\mathcal{C}[6, 2, 2]$ encoder $\mathcal{V}$ of Figure 13.2b by adding the quantum gates and connections marked by dashed lines and into the QSBC $\mathcal{C}[8, 2, 2]$ encoder $\mathcal{V}$ of Figure 13.2c by incorporating the quantum gates and connections marked by dashed-dotted lines.

**Remark:** *The quantum encoders $\mathcal{V}$ portrayed in Figures 13.1 and 13.2 can be combined into a single encoder $\mathcal{V}$. Ultimately, we have successfully amalgamated QSBCs exhibiting a wide range of quantum coding rates $r_Q$ into a single quantum encoder $\mathcal{V}$. We refer to this joint code construction as a multiple-rate quantum short-block code (MR-QSBC).*

## 13.3 Quantum Turbo Short-block Codes

### 13.3.1 Concatenated Code Design

The resultant MR-QSBCs exhibit the minimum distance of $d = 2$, which means that they only have an error-detection capability, but no error-correction capability. To upgrade this error-detection capability, so that the scheme can also correct errors, we may serially concatenate the set of MR-QSBCs with a quantum unity-rate code (QURC). This serial concatenation scheme provides us with two main benefits. Firstly, this allows us to employ iterative turbo decoding iteratively exchanging information between the MR-QSBCs employed as the outer codes and a QURC used as the inner code. Secondly, this is achieved without reducing the quantum coding rate of the MR-QSBCs harnessed as the outer codes, since the QURC does not reduce the throughput [279, 302]. In the following subsections, we will elaborate on the detailed operation of the resultant multiple-rate quantum turbo short-block codes (MR-QSBC-QURC). We commence with the encoding process, followed by the quantum depolarizing channel model, and finally, the decoding process. The general schematic of the proposed MR-QSBC-QURC scheme is portrayed in Figure 13.3.

### 13.3.2 Encoding Process

The encoding process is initiated by the outer quantum encoder $\mathcal{V}_1$ of Figure 13.3, which is constituted by MR-QSBC encoders. This first step maps $K_1$ logical qubits into $N_1$ encoded physical qubits with the aid of $(N_1 - K_1)$ auxiliary qubits, which can be formally expressed as

$$\mathcal{V}_1 \left( |\psi\rangle^{K_1} \otimes |0\rangle^{\otimes(N_1 - K_1)} \right) = |\overline{\psi}_1\rangle^{N_1}. \tag{13.12}$$

The output of $\mathcal{V}_1$ is then fed into the interleaver $\Pi$ of Figure 13.3, which can be represented as a permutation matrix formulated as

$$\Pi \left( |\overline{\psi}_1\rangle^{N_1} \right) = |\psi_2\rangle^{K_2}, \tag{13.13}$$

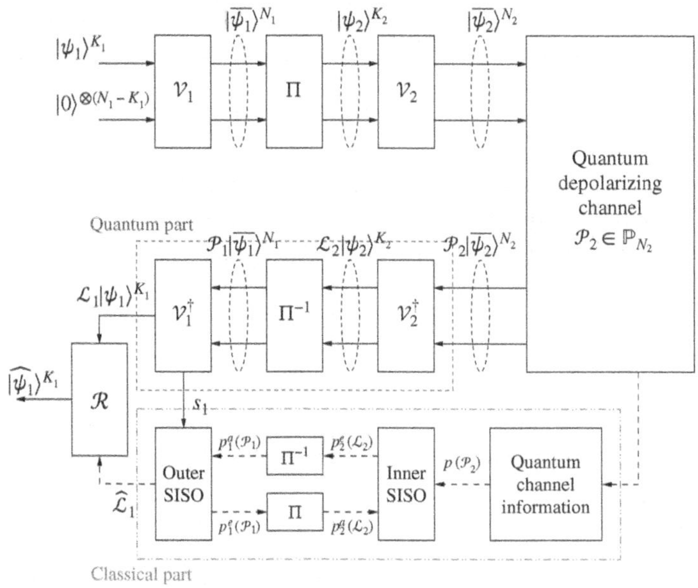


**Figure 13.3** The general schematic of the proposed MR-QSBC-QURC scheme. *Source*: [332]/IEEE/CC BY 4.0.

where we have $K_2 = N_1$. The interleaver does not modify the number of physical qubits, since it only rearranges the qubit indices within the encoded state of the physical qubits. In this chapter, we utilize simple pseudo-random interleavers, but there are different interleaver types available in the literature [333].

Next, the output of the interleaver $\Pi$ is fed into the inner encoder $\mathcal{V}_2$, which carries out the following transformation:

$$\mathcal{V}_2\left(|\psi\rangle^{K_2} \otimes |0\rangle^{\otimes(N_2-K_2)}\right) = |\overline{\psi_2}\rangle^{N_2}. \tag{13.14}$$

The encoder $\mathcal{V}_2$ of Figure 13.3 maps the state of $K_2$ logical qubits into the state of $N_2$ physical qubits with the aid of $(N_2 - K_2)$ auxiliary qubits. Here, we employ the QURC as the inner code. Therefore, the transformation in Eq. (13.14) can be simplified as follows:

$$\mathcal{V}_2\left(|\psi\rangle^{K_2}\right) = |\overline{\psi_2}\rangle^{N_2}, \tag{13.15}$$

where $K_2 = N_2$. Finally, the physical qubits exhibiting the quantum state $|\overline{\psi_2}\rangle^{N_2}$ are sent through the quantum channel.

### 13.3.3 Quantum Depolarizing Channel

In this chapter, we rely on the quantum depolarizing channel [160], which is a special type of quantum Pauli channels popularly used for modeling the bit-flips and phase-flips inflicted by quantum decoherence. Accordingly, the quantum channel is modeled by a quantum error operator $\mathcal{P}_2$, which is represented by the $N_2$-tuple Pauli operator ($\mathcal{P}_2 \in \mathbb{P}_{N_2}$). The action of the error operator $\mathcal{P}_2$ on the encoded state of physical qubits $|\overline{\psi_2}\rangle^{N_2}$ can be formulated as

$$|\widetilde{\psi}\rangle^{N_2} = \mathcal{P}_2\left(|\overline{\psi_2}\rangle^{N_2}\right), \tag{13.16}$$

where the error operator $\mathcal{P}_2$ is characterized by the depolarizing probability $p$. More specifically, each qubit may independently experience a bit-flip (***X***) error, a phase-flip (***Z***) error as well as a simultaneous bit-flip and phase-flip (***Y***) error. The probability that each qubit is experiencing an ***X***, ***Z***, and ***Y*** error is denoted by $p_x$, $p_z$, and $p_y$, respectively. Here, we assume that $p_x + p_z + p_y = p$ and $p_x = p_z = p_y = p/3$ [160]. Nonetheless, we can extend the assumption to the asymmetric scenario of $p_x \neq p_z \neq p_y$, which can be deemed to be more realistic based on the particular physical implementation [146]. However, choosing the values of $p_x = p_z = p_y$ provides us with an identical level of protection for different types of errors without favoring only one specific type of error. For a more detailed discourse on QTCs designed for asymmetric quantum Pauli channels, we refer the enthusiastic readers to [146].

### 13.3.4 Decoding Process

The decoding of MR-QSBC-QURC schemes relies on the same iterative processing principles as the conventional QTCs. Specifically, it can be separated into two main parts, namely the classical part and the quantum part. As shown in Figure 13.3, the quantum part is marked by all the components bounded by the dashed lines and the classical part is represented by all the components bounded by the dashed-dotted lines. Let us first commence by describing the quantum part of MR-QSBC-QURC decoding.

#### 13.3.4.1 Quantum Part

For MR-QSBC-QURC, the quantum-domain operations of Figure 13.3 are commenced by the inverse encoder $\mathcal{V}_2^\dagger$ that applies the following transformation to the corrupted quantum state of the physical qubits:

$$\mathcal{V}_2^\dagger(|\widehat{\psi}\rangle^{N_2}) = \mathcal{V}_2^\dagger\left(\mathcal{P}_2|\overline{\psi_2}\rangle^{N_2}\right) = \mathcal{L}_2|\psi_2\rangle^{K_2} \otimes \mathcal{S}_2|0\rangle^{\otimes(N_2-K_2)}. \tag{13.17}$$

The inverse encoder $\mathcal{V}_2^\dagger$ has a strong resemblance to the quantum encoder $\mathcal{V}_2$, since they are constituted by an identical quantum circuit, but it relies on a reversed processing order between the input and output. Observe in Eq. (13.17) that the effect of the inverse encoder $\mathcal{V}_2^\dagger$ on the Pauli error operator $\mathcal{P}_2$ is the decomposition of $\mathcal{P}_2$ into two Pauli operator components. The first component is $\mathcal{L}_2$, which is the logical error operator potentially corrupting the $K_2$ logical qubits, while the second component is $\mathcal{S}_2$, which is the error operator applied to the $(N_2 - K_2)$ auxiliary qubits. The measurement of the erroneous auxiliary qubits $\mathcal{S}_2|0\rangle^{N_2-K_2}$ results in the classical bits $\boldsymbol{s}_2$, which are fed into the classical part of the iterative decoder. For any MR-QSBC-QURC, the outer inverse encoder $\mathcal{V}_2^\dagger$ is constituted by the inverse encoder of QURC, and therefore we have $N_2 = K_2$. Consequently, the expression of Eq. (13.17) can be further simplified to

$$\mathcal{V}_2^\dagger\left(\mathcal{P}_2|\overline{\psi_2}\rangle^{N_2}\right) = \mathcal{L}_2|\psi_2\rangle^{K_2}. \tag{13.18}$$

Next, the output of the inverse encoder $\mathcal{V}_2^\dagger$ is passed through the deinterleaver $\Pi^{-1}$, which performs the following operation:

$$\Pi^{-1}(\mathcal{L}_2|\psi_2\rangle^{K_2}) = \mathcal{P}_1|\overline{\psi_1}\rangle^{N_1}. \tag{13.19}$$

The output of the deinterleaver is then fed into the quantum inverse encoder $\mathcal{V}_1^\dagger$, which carries out the following transformation:

$$\mathcal{V}_1^\dagger(\mathcal{P}_1|\overline{\psi_1}\rangle^{N_1}) = \mathcal{L}_1|\psi_1\rangle^{K_1} \otimes \mathcal{S}_1|0\rangle^{\otimes(N_1-K_1)}. \tag{13.20}$$

Similar to the action of the inverse encoder $\mathcal{V}_2^\dagger$, the inverse encoder $\mathcal{V}_1^\dagger$ also performs a decomposition of the Pauli error operator $\mathcal{P}_1$ into two components, namely $\mathcal{L}_1$ and $\mathcal{S}_1$. More specifically, $\mathcal{L}_1$ is the logical error operator potentially corrupting the $K_1$ logical qubits and $\mathcal{S}_1$ is the error operator applied to the $(N_1 - K_1)$ auxiliary qubits.

In MR-QSBC-QURC, the inverse encoder $\mathcal{V}_1^\dagger$ is constituted by the inverse encoders of the MR-QSBCs, which are described by the conjugate transpose of the encoder $\mathcal{V}_1$. The measurement of the erroneous auxiliary qubits $\mathcal{S}_1|0\rangle^{N_1-K_1}$ results in the classical bits of $\boldsymbol{s}_1$, which are equivalent to the classical syndrome values. These syndrome values are then fed into the classical part of the iterative decoder. Finally, based on the result obtained from the classical part of the iterative decoder, an error recovery operator $\mathcal{R}$ is applied to the output of the inverse encoder $\mathcal{V}_1^\dagger$, which can be described as follows:

$$\mathcal{R}\left(\mathcal{L}_1|\psi_1\rangle^{K_1}\right) = |\widehat{\psi_1}\rangle^{K_1}. \tag{13.21}$$

If $\mathcal{R} = \mathcal{L}_1$, we obtain $|\widehat{\psi_1}\rangle^{K_1} = |\psi_1\rangle^{K_1}$, which completes the decoding process.

#### 13.3.4.2 Classical Part

For MR-QSBC-QURC, the classical-domain operations of Figure 13.3 are started by obtaining the information about the depolarizing probability $p$ of the quantum depolarizing channel associated with the error operator $\mathcal{P}_2$. We assume that the MR-QSBC-QURC decoder has perfect knowledge of the depolarizing probability $p$, which is acceptable since an online depolarizing probability estimator based on syndrome measurements tailored for QTC has been proposed recently in [334]. Additionally, the QBER performance of QTCs in the range of low depolarizing probability values is rather insensitive to the depolarizing probability estimation [335].

In summary, based on the classical syndrome $\boldsymbol{s}_1$ and on the depolarizing probability $p$, the pair of classical soft-input and soft-output (SISO) decoders of Figure 13.3 aim for determining the most likely error coset $\widehat{\mathcal{L}_1}$ imposed on the logical qubits $|\psi_1\rangle^{K_1}$. Formally, this can be written as a maximum *a posteriori* (MAP) decoding process formulated as follows [83, 290]:

$$\widehat{\mathcal{L}_1}(\boldsymbol{s}_1, p) = \arg\max_{\mathcal{L}} P(\mathcal{L}|\boldsymbol{s}_1, p). \tag{13.22}$$

The depolarizing probability value $p$ and the *a priori* information $\boldsymbol{p}_2^a(\mathcal{L}_2)$ gleaned from the outer soft-input soft-output (SISO) decoder of Figure 13.3 are utilized by the inner SISO decoder for calculating the *extrinsic* information $\boldsymbol{p}_2^e(\mathcal{L}_2)$. For the first iteration, the inner SISO decoder only has the depolarizing probability $p$ as the input. Thus, the value of *a priori* information $\boldsymbol{p}_2^a(\mathcal{L}_2)$ is initialized to be equiprobable. Next, an interleaver is utilized to transform the output of the inner SISO decoder, namely the *extrinsic* information $\boldsymbol{p}_2^e(\mathcal{L}_2)$ to *a priori* information $\boldsymbol{p}_1^a(\mathcal{P}_1)$ as the input of the outer SISO decoder. By combining the *a priori* information $\boldsymbol{p}_1^a(\mathcal{P}_1)$ and the syndrome value $\boldsymbol{s}_1$, the outer SISO decoder of Figure 13.3 calculates the *extrinsic* information $\boldsymbol{p}_1^e(\mathcal{P}_1)$. The *extrinsic* information $\boldsymbol{p}_1^e(\mathcal{P}_1)$ is then deinterleaved to yield the *a priori* information $\boldsymbol{p}_2^a(\mathcal{L}_2)$, which is fed into the inner SISO decoder. This whole process is performed iteratively until one of the following conditions is satisfied: 1) the converged mutual information is attained; 2) the maximum affordable number of iterations $l$ is reached. At the final iteration, the outer SISO decoder produces $\widehat{\mathcal{L}_1}$, which is the most likely error pattern, given the value of $p$ and $\boldsymbol{s}_1$ provided by the quantum part of Figure 13.3. Finally, the recovery operator $\mathcal{R} = \widehat{\mathcal{L}_1}$ is applied to complete the error correction.

## 13.4 EXIT-chart Analysis

### 13.4.1 The Fundamentals

In the classical domain, EXIT charts are utilized for visualizing the convergence behavior of iterative decoding schemes, which is based on the average mutual information (MI) at the input and the output of the constituent decoders. The EXIT chart was originally proposed by ten Brink [218, 330] for dispensing with the exhaustive Monte–Carlo simulations of classical error-correction codes. However, as the research progressed, EXIT charts have also been shown to be a very powerful tool for designing near-capacity error-correction codes without resorting to tedious distance spectrum analysis.[4] Therefore, EXIT charts have been extensively exploited for designing near-capacity classical [216, 219] as well as quantum error-correction codes [83, 290].

The main differences between the EXIT chart used for classical error-correction codes and their quantum counterparts have been extensively discussed in [83, 290]. In summary, quantum stabilizer codes only infer information about the quantum errors through syndrome measurements, while classical error-correction codes allow the measurement of the input bits of the inner encoder (and output bits of the outer encoder). As a result, the main difference of the EXIT chart for quantum error-correction codes is that it models the a priori information related to the error-sequence corresponding to the input qubits of the inner quantum encoder, instead of the input bits of the inner encoder themselves, which is in contrast to classical codes.

4 To elaborate briefly, classical codes used to be designed on the basis of finding the specific generator polynomials, which were capable of maximizing the minimum distance between any pair of legitimate codewords. For a linear code the all-zero codeword is always a legitimate one. Hence the legitimate codeword having the lowest nonzero Hamming weight directly determined the minimum distance of the code. More sophisticated designs went further and evaluated the so-called distance spectrum of the code, which – by definition – represented the number of legitimate codewords of any specific Hamming weight. However, for powerful long codes the number of codewords became excessive even for the most powerful classical computers. This was particularly so for turbo codes having long turbo interleavers.

Let us revisit the iterative decoder of the MR-QSBC-QURC arrangement depicted in Figure 13.3. In this scenario, the EXIT chart is utilized for visualizing the exchange of four MI terms, namely the average *a priori* MI $I_{A,\mathcal{L}_2}$ of the inner decoder, the average *a priori* MI $I_{A,\mathcal{P}_1}$ of the outer decoder, the average extrinsic MI $I_{E,\mathcal{L}_2}$ of the inner decoder, and finally, the average extrinsic MI $I_{E,\mathcal{P}_1}$ of the outer decoder. The input-output relation between $I_{A,\mathcal{L}_2}$ and $I_{E,\mathcal{L}_2}$ constitutes the EXIT curve of the inner decoder, which can be simply referred to as the *inner decoder's EXIT curve*, while that of $I_{A,\mathcal{P}_1}$ and $I_{E,\mathcal{P}_1}$ represents the EXIT curve of the outer decoder, which can be simply referred to as the *outer decoder's EXIT curve*. For a full discourse on how to calculate the MI terms for the inner and outer decoders, we refer the enthusiastic readers to [83, 290].

A pivotal metric required for understanding the process of EXIT-chart-aided QTC design is the quantum domain counterpart of the classical communication capacity, namely the quantum hashing bound. To elaborate a little further, for a QSC $\mathcal{C}$ having a sufficiently high number of physical qubits exhibiting a quantum coding rate of $r_Q$, there exists a limit $p^* = p(r_Q)$ below which it can operate at an infinitesimally low QBER. Conversely, for a given depolarizing probability $p$, we can find a QSC $\mathcal{C}$ exhibiting a quantum coding rate of $r_Q \leq C_Q(p)$ and having a sufficiently high number of physical qubits that is capable of yielding an infinitesimally low QBER. This specific limit is referred to as the quantum hashing bound, which is based on the following definition.

**Definition 13.3:** *Quantum hashing bound* [67, 82, 83, 242]. Given a quantum depolarizing channel having a depolarizing probability $p$, the quantum hashing bound is defined as

$$C_Q(p) = 1 - H(p) - p\ \log_2 3, \tag{13.23}$$

where $H(p)$ is the binary entropy of $p$ defined as $H(p) = -p \log_2 p - (1-p)\log_2(1-p)$. Given a value of $p$, then $C_Q(p)$ is the quantum hashing bound for $p$. Conversely, given a value of $r_Q$, the value of $p^* = p(r_Q)$ represents the quantum hashing bound for $r_Q$.

Hence, the goal of designing a QSC exhibiting a quantum coding rate $r_Q$ is to ensure that it can operate as close as possible to the limit of $p^* = p(r_Q)$. Similarly, given the depolarizing probability $p$, we may design a QSC exhibiting $r_Q$ very close to $C_Q(p)$, yielding an infinitesimally low QBER. For instance, a QSC having a quantum coding rate of $r_Q = 1/2$, the quantum hashing bound is given by $p^* = 0.074$. Conversely, for a quantum depolarizing channel having a depolarizing probability $p = 0.050$, the quantum hashing bound is given by $C_Q(p) = 0.634$.

### 13.4.2 Inner EXIT Curves

The QTC design advocated in this chapter relies on the concatenation of MR-QSBCs as the outer codes and a QURC as the inner code. As the terminology suggested, a QURC is a quantum convolutional code (QCC) having a quantum coding rate of unity ($r_Q = 1$). To conceive a QTC design having a near-capacity error correction performance, it is highly desirable that QCC encoders exhibit recursive and non-catastrophic properties as defined in [68]. The recursive structure of QCCs is required for ensuring the convergence of iterative decoding to a vanishingly low QBER. Meanwhile, the QCCs that exhibit catastrophic structure require a doping mechanism or entanglement-assisted solution in order to substantially benefit from iterative decoding, since catastrophic QCCs provide zero *a priori* information [82, 310]. Unfortunately, the QCCs cannot be simultaneously recursive and non-catastrophic [142].

To circumvent these impediments of constructing a *good* QCC, a non-recursive and non-catastrophic QURC can be very carefully designed for striking this delicate compromise, since it still can benefit from the iteration gains even if the inner EXIT curve terminates at the $(1, y)$ point for $y < 1$, as long as it only intersects with the outer EXIT curve very close to $(x, y) = (1, 1)$ point. Obeying these stringent constraints, an exhaustive EXIT-chart-based heuristic search has been conducted to find a *good* non-recursive and non-catastrophic QURC. The resultant memory-2 QURC has the following seed transformation [302]:[5]

$$\mathcal{U} = \{21, 56, 5, 46, 44, 38\}_{10}. \tag{13.24}$$

---

5 A quantum encoder $\mathcal{V}$ can be represented using a binary matrix $\boldsymbol{V}$, and seed transformation $\mathcal{U}$ is used for simplifying the representation of binary matrix $\boldsymbol{V}$. A complete tutorial of transforming a quantum encoder $\mathcal{V}$ to its seed transformation $\mathcal{U}$ can be found in [279].

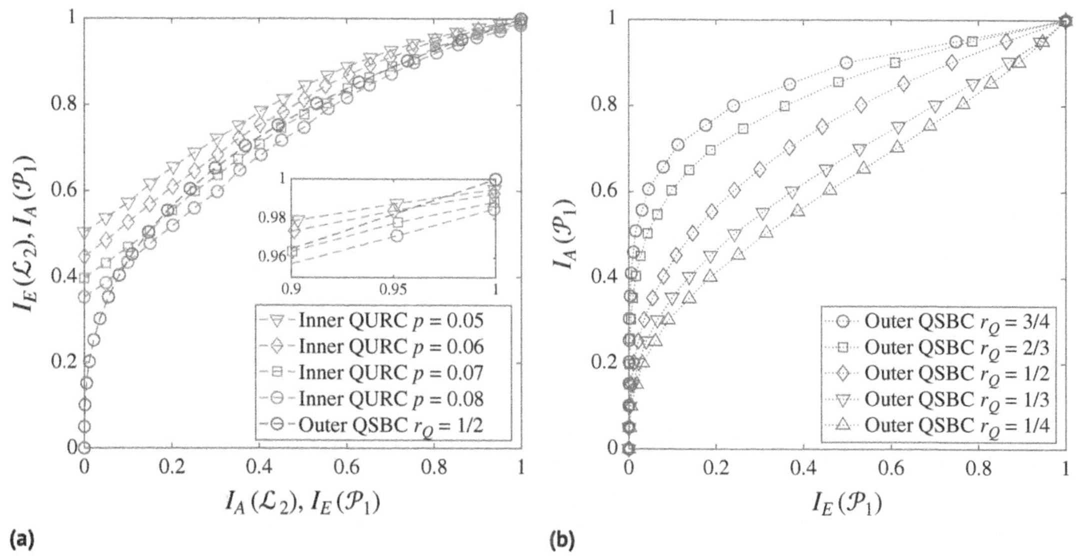


**Figure 13.4** (a) The inner decoder EXIT curves for non-recursive and non-catastrophic QURC and the outer decoder EXIT curve of a half-rate QSBC. The quantum hashing bound is $p^* = 0.074$. (b) Outer decoder EXIT curves for MR-QSBCs. *Source*: [332]/IEEE/CC BY 4.0.

For the rest of this chapter the QURC specified in (13.24) will be employed as the inner code in the MR-QSBC-QURC scheme advocated.

Figure 13.4a portrays the inner EXIT curves of the selected QURC in (13.24) for depolarizing probability values of $p = \{0.08, 0.07, 0.06, 0.05\}$. We also depict the outer EXIT curve of the half-rate QSBC given in Figure 13.1a. For a half-rate QSBC ($r_Q = 1/2$), the quantum hashing bound is given by $p^* = 0.074$ based on (13.23). Therefore, the $p$ values used for generating the inner EXIT curves are selected around $p^*$. In Figure 13.4a, we can observe that for $p = 0.07$, the inner and outer EXIT curves intersect very early. As we decrease the depolarizing probability to $p = 0.06$, a marginally open tunnel between the inner and outer EXIT curves can be seen, which means that at this $p$ value the concatenation between half-rate QSBCs and a QURC will start to glean iterative decoding gains. However, we can also see in the inset of Figure 13.4a that the inner and outer EXIT curves intersect before they reach the $(x, y) = (1, 1)$ point, albeit it is very close. As the depolarizing probability value decreases ($p = 0.05$), the inner EXIT curve shifts higher and the intersection point is getting closer to the $(x, y) = (1, 1)$ point. Consequently, based on the observation with regard to the inner and outer EXIT curves in Figure 13.4a, we may predict the QBER curve obtained by the Monte–Carlo simulations: a waterfall-like QBER curve is expected for the $p$ values close to $p^*$, $(0.05 \leq p \leq 0.6)$ followed by an error floor, as the $p$ value decreases ($p < 0.05$). In fact, this simple concatenation of half-rate QSBCs and a QURC has been demonstrated to provide an excellent error correction performance near the quantum hashing bound in [279], as predicted accurately by the EXIT curves presented in Figure 13.4a.

### 13.4.3 Outer Decoder EXIT Curves

In contrast to the inner decoder's EXIT curve, the outer decoder's EXIT curve is independent of the depolarizing probability value of the quantum depolarizing channel, since the *a priori* information obtained by the outer code is provided by the inner code, not by the quantum channel. Therefore, the outer EXIT curve of the QSBCs only depends on its quantum coding rate. Based on the quantum encoders of MR-QSBCs illustrated in Figures 13.1 and 13.2, the seed transformations of the MR-QSBCs are given in Table 13.3. Figure 13.4b portrays the outer EXIT curves of the proposed MR-QSBCs exhibiting the quantum coding rates of $r_Q = \{3/4, 2/3, 1/2, 1/3, 1/4\}$. We can observe from Figure 13.4b that as the quantum coding rate increases, the outer EXIT curve shifts higher. Consequently, the inner code has to operate at a lower depolarizing probability to appropriately attain a marginally open tunnel between the inner and outer EXIT curves, which is a trend we also learned from Figure 13.4a. Similarly, we can also infer approximately the $p$ values required by the QURC as the inner code based on the quantum

**Table 13.3** The seed transformation $\mathcal{U}$ associated with the subcomponent MR-QSBCs exhibiting various quantum coding rates $r_q$.

| $r_q$ | $\mathcal{U}$ |
|---|---|
| 1/4 | $\{34560, 18176, 58368, 53760, 51456, 228, 210, 201, 184, 120, 32, 16, 8, 1024, 512, 256\}_{10}$ |
| 1/3 | $\{2240, 1216, 3712, 3392, 58, 53, 44, 28, 8, 4, 128, 64\}_{10}$ |
| 1/2 | $\{144, 80, 240, 15, 10, 6, 2, 16\}_{10}$ |
| 2/3 | $\{2112, 1088, 576, 320, 4032, 63, 34, 18, 10, 6, 2, 64\}_{10}$ |
| 3/4 | $\{33024, 16640, 8448, 4352, 2304, 1280, 65280, 255, 130, 66, 34, 18, 10, 6, 2, 256\}_{10}$ |

hashing bound $p^*$ to produce a marginally open tunnel. Explicitly, given the quantum coding rate of the QSBCs $r_Q = \{3/4, 2/3, 1/2, 1/3, 1/4\}$, we obtain $p^* = \{0.116, 0.094, 0.074, 0.056, 0.039\}$.

We will utilize the results in Figure 13.4b for optimizing the MR-QSBCs as the outer codes of the proposed MR-QSBC-QURC scheme in the following subsection. Each of the MR-QSBCs having a different quantum coding rate will serve as a subcomponent code. It is important to note that although we only consider five subcomponent codes in this chapter, the range of MR-QSBC quantum coding rates can be readily extended to the higher as well as lower quantum coding rates to increase the number of subcomponent codes by directly following the discussions of Section 13.2.

### 13.4.4 EXIT-chart-aided Design

The primary objective of the EXIT-chart-aided QTC design is to obtain the best possible inner and outer code combination by evaluating their inner and outer EXIT curves. Assuming we have many copies of the MR-QSBCs encoders, our design objective here is to find the optimal configuration of the outer codes constituted by MR-QSBCs, which provides the best match to the given inner code – in this case to the QURC. The optimization is performed by utilizing the EXIT-chart-based heuristic search by finding the optimal outer EXIT curve having a marginally open tunnel with regard to the inner EXIT curve at a depolarizing probability close to the quantum hashing bound of the quantum coding rate required. More specifically, due to the inherent flexibility of the proposed MR-QSBCs encoders, we may design a QTC that exploits not only the quantum encoder that exhibits a single quantum coding rate. More precisely, we may configure the MR-QSBCs as the outer codes so that they encode a specifically designed fraction of the $K$ logical qubits. The fraction of the logical qubits is determined by the weighting coefficient satisfying the following constraints [221, 331]:

$$r_Q = \sum_{q=1}^{Q} r_q w_q, \text{ s.t. } \sum_i w_i = 1, \tag{13.25}$$

where $r_Q$ is the target of quantum coding rate, $Q$ is the number of subcomponent codes, $r_q$ is the subcomponent quantum coding rate, and $w_q$ is the weighting coefficient of the subcomponent code subjected to the normalization. Since we employ multiple-rate QSBCs as the outer codes of the MR-QSBC-QURC scheme advocated, we have $r_q = \{1/4, 1/3, 1/2, 2/3, 3/4\}$. Therefore, our design objective can be reformulated as that of finding the weighting coefficient $w_q$ to produce the optimal MR-QSBC-QURC design.

Let us now formally define the inner and outer EXIT curves presented in Sections 13.4.2 and 13.4.3. Firstly, the inner EXIT curve can be formally described as a transfer function $T_1$ mapping the average MI $I_{A,\mathcal{L}_2}$ of the *a priori* information to the average MI $I_{E,\mathcal{L}_2}$ of the *extrinsic* information by taking into account the depolarizing probability $p$ as follows:

$$I_{E,\mathcal{L}_2} = T_1[I_{A,\mathcal{L}_2}, p]. \tag{13.26}$$

Secondly, similar to the inner EXIT curve, the outer EXIT curve can be formally described as a transfer function $T_2$ mapping the average MI $I_{A\mathcal{P}_1}$ of the *a priori* information to the average MI $I_{E,\mathcal{P}_1}$ of the *extrinsic* information as follows:

$$I_{E,\mathcal{P}_1} = T_2[I_{A,\mathcal{P}_1}]. \tag{13.27}$$

Notice that in Figure 13.4b, we inverted the plot of the outer EXIT curves, since the *extrinsic* information provided by the outer code is utilized as the *a priori* information of the inner code. Therefore, the outer EXIT curves portrayed in Figure 13.4b are more accurately described as

$$I_{A,\mathcal{P}_1} = T_2^{-1}[I_{E,\mathcal{P}_1}]. \tag{13.28}$$

Let $Q$ be the number of MR-QSBCs subcomponent codes. In this chapter, we have $Q = 5$, and $T_{2,q}^{-1}$ is the outer EXIT curve of the $q$th subcomponent code for $q = \{1, \ldots, Q\}$. Therefore, the resultant outer EXIT curve $I_{E,Q,\mathcal{P}_1}$ of the MR-QSBCs after fractional encoding using the weighting coefficients of Eq. (13.25) can be determined as

$$I_{E,Q,\mathcal{P}_1} = T_{2,Q}^{-1}[I_{A,\mathcal{P}_1}] = \sum_{q=1}^{Q} w_q T_{2,q}^{-1}[I_{A,\mathcal{P}_1}]. \tag{13.29}$$

To find the optimal weighting coefficient for the MR-QSBCs subcomponent codes, we have to perform a curve matching optimization by minimizing area represented by the the square of errors between the inner and outer EXIT curves. For simplifying the notation, let $T_1[I_{A,\mathcal{L}_2}, p] = T_1[j, p]$, $T_{2,Q}^{-1}[I_{A,\mathcal{P}_1}] = T_2^{-1}[j]$, and $T_{2,q}^{-1}[I_{A,\mathcal{P}_1}] = T_{2,q}^{-1}[j]$ for $j = \{1, \ldots, J\}$, where $J$ is the number of sample points displayed in the inner and outer decoder EXIT curves. Therefore, the error can be directly calculated as

$$e[j] = T_1[j, p] - T_2^{-1}[j], \tag{13.30}$$

where we have $p = p^* - \epsilon$, given that $\epsilon$ is chosen to be arbitrarily small. Therefore, the corresponding matrix-based representation can be written as

$$\boldsymbol{e} = \boldsymbol{a} - \boldsymbol{B}\boldsymbol{w}, \tag{13.31}$$

where we have

$$\boldsymbol{e} = \begin{pmatrix} e[1] \\ e[2] \\ \vdots \\ e[J] \end{pmatrix}, \quad \boldsymbol{a} = \begin{pmatrix} T_1[1, p] \\ T_1[2, p] \\ \vdots \\ T_1[J, p] \end{pmatrix}, \quad \boldsymbol{w} = \begin{pmatrix} w_1 \\ w_2 \\ \vdots \\ w_Q \end{pmatrix},$$

$$\boldsymbol{B} = \begin{pmatrix} T_{2,1}^{-1}[1] & T_{2,2}^{-1}[1] & \cdots & T_{2,Q}^{-1}[1] \\ T_{2,1}^{-1}[2] & T_{2,2}^{-1}[2] & \cdots & T_{2,Q}^{-1}[2] \\ \vdots & \vdots & \ddots & \vdots \\ T_{2,1}^{-1}[J] & T_{2,2}^{-1}[J] & \cdots & T_{2,Q}^{-1}[J] \end{pmatrix}. \tag{13.32}$$

Since we do not want the inner and outer EXIT curves to crossover far from the (1, 1) point, we have to impose an additional constraint that guarantees a marginally open tunnel between the inner and outer EXIT curves, which can be explicitly expressed as

$$e[j] > 0 \text{ for } j = \{1, \ldots, J\}. \tag{13.33}$$

Thus, the cost function used for finding the weighting coefficients $\boldsymbol{w}$ is given by

$$E(\boldsymbol{w}) = \sum_{j=1}^{J} e[j]^2 = \boldsymbol{e}^T \boldsymbol{e}. \tag{13.34}$$

Finally, the overall EXIT-chart-based curve matching required for finding the optimal weighting coefficient $\hat{\boldsymbol{w}}$ can be summarized as

$$\hat{\boldsymbol{w}} = \arg\min_{\boldsymbol{w}} E(\boldsymbol{w}), \tag{13.35}$$

which is subject to Eqs. (13.25) and (13.33). The unconstrained optimization of Eq. (13.35) can be iteratively solved using the gradient descent method, where we have

$$\frac{\partial E(\boldsymbol{w})}{\partial \boldsymbol{w}} = 2\boldsymbol{e}. \tag{13.36}$$

The solutions are then reevaluated according to the constraints of Eqs. (13.25) and (13.33). For a full discourse on the EXIT-chart-based optimization algorithm of finding the optimal weighting coefficient $\hat{\boldsymbol{w}}$, we refer the enthusiastic readers to [221, 331].

We now present the results of the aforementioned optimization algorithm after optimizing the MR-QSBCs as the outer codes for the proposed MR-QSBC-QURC. Figure 13.5 depicts the iterative decoding trajectory of the MR-QSBC-QURC, where the inner code is constituted by the QURC of Eq. (13.24) and the outer code is constituted by the optimized MR-QSBCs having $r_Q = 0.5$. Explicitly, by implementing the optimization algorithm we just described, we found that the optimal weighting coefficient $\hat{\boldsymbol{w}}$ of half-rate MR-QSBCs matching the inner EXIT curve of the QURC at $p = 0.05$ is given by $\hat{\boldsymbol{w}} = \{0, 0.60, 0, 0, 0, 40\}$. It can be immediately verified that the constraints in Eqs. (13.25) and (13.33) are satisfied. The decoding trajectory represents the iterative MI improvements based on the information exchange between the inner and outer decoders, which is illustrated by the staircase-like curve in Figure 13.5. We can observe a marginally open tunnel between the inner and outer EXIT curves that guarantees the convergence of the iterative decoding to vanishingly low QBER. In the inset of Figure 13.5, the decoding trajectory terminates before reaching the $(x, y) = (1, 1)$ point due to the non-recursive and non-catastrophic nature of the QURC encoder. Therefore, we expect to witness an error floor in its QBER curve. To demonstrate that the proposed MR-QSBC-QURC scheme can be designed to cater for a wide range of quantum coding rate requirements, we have also performed EXIT-chart-aided optimization for the MR-QSBCs covering quantum coding rates of $r_Q = \{0.3, 0.4, 0.6, 0.7\}$ and the results are presented in Figure 13.6. Similarly, each of the MR-QSBCs have been optimized to match the inner EXIT curve at a depolarizing probability $p$ close to their respective quantum hashing bounds $p^*$. The resultant optimal weighting coefficient $\hat{\boldsymbol{w}}$ obtained for all the target quantum coding rates evaluated is summarized in Table 13.4. We can observe in Figure 13.6 that all the inner and outer EXIT curves of the MR-QSBC-QURC designed provide a marginally open tunnel for the $p$ values close to the quantum hashing bound $p^*$ and the decoding trajectories terminate really close to the $(x, y) = (1, 1)$ point. We note that the decoding

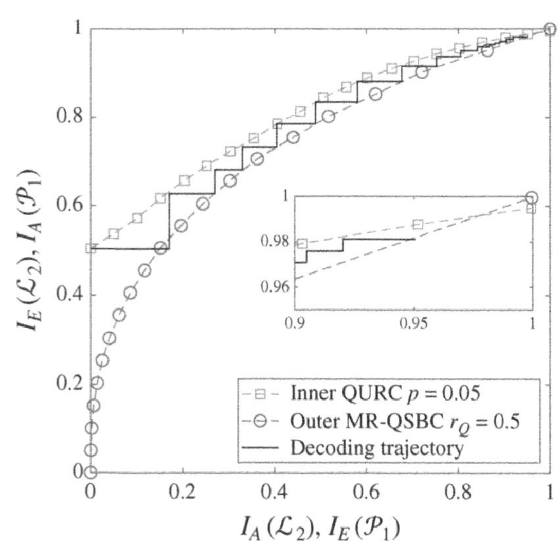


**Figure 13.5** Decoding trajectory of MR-QSBC-QURC at the depolarizing probability of $p = 0.05$. The inner code is a non-recursive and non-catastrophic QURC and the outer code is the optimized MR-QSBCs having $r_Q = 0.5$. The quantum hashing bound is $p^* = 0.074$. *Source*: [332]/IEEE/CC BY 4.0.

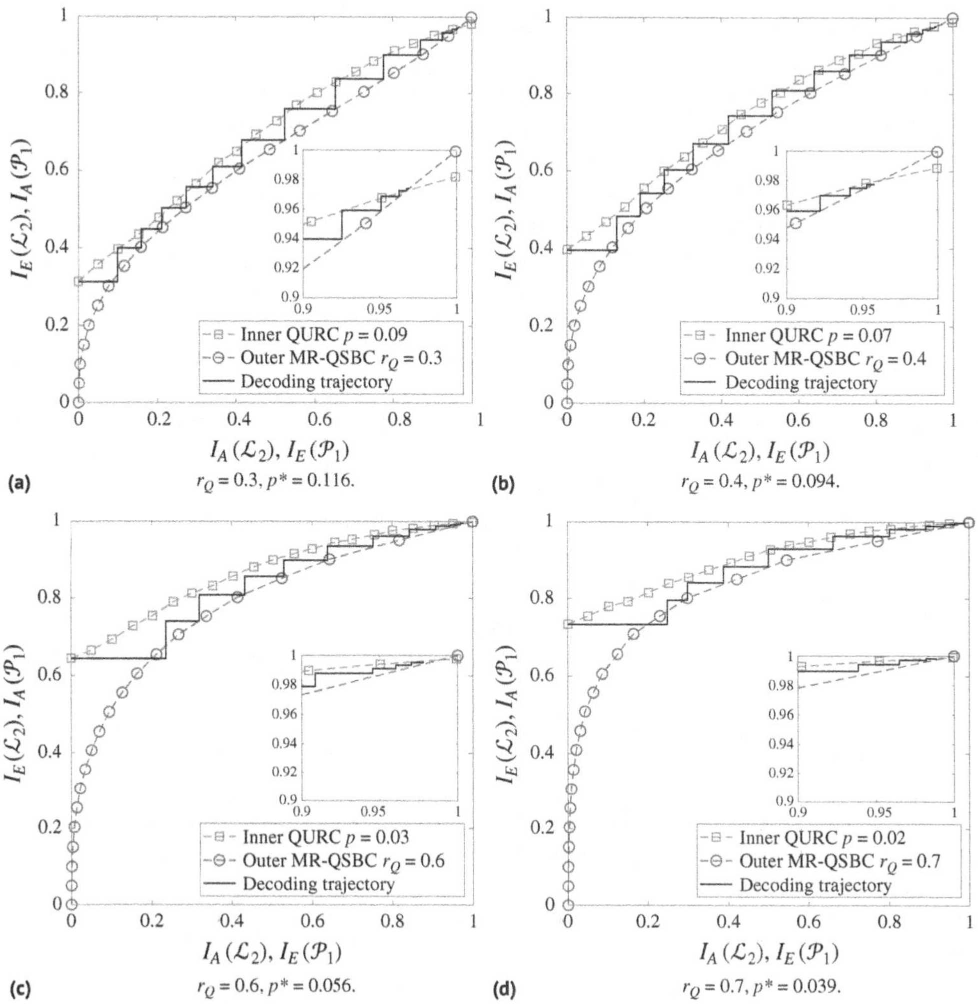


**Figure 13.6** The decoding trajectories of MR-QSBC-QURC exhibiting various quantum coding rates. *Source*: [332]/IEEE/CC BY 4.0.

**Table 13.4** The result of subcomponent codes optimal weighting coefficient $\hat{w}_i$ obtained from EXIT-chart-based exhaustive curve matching for various target of quantum coding rates $r_Q$. The subcomponent quantum coding rates are $r_q = \{1/4, 1/3, 1/2, 2/3, 3/4\}$.

| $r_Q$ | $\hat{w}_i$ |
|---|---|
| 0.3 | {0.44 0.54 0.02 0 0} |
| 0.4 | {0.11 0.44 0.46 0 0} |
| 0.5 | {0 0.60 0 0 0.40} |
| 0.6 | {0 0 0.60 0 0.40} |
| 0.7 | {0 0 0.20 0 0.80} |

trajectory terminates earlier for MR-QSBCs exhibiting lower $r_Q$. Consequently, we predict that the QBER curve of MR-QSBC-QURC having $r_Q = 0.3$ will have a higher error floor than the MR-QSBC-QURC having $r_Q = 0.7$. We have to reiterate once again that the proposed MR-QSBC-QURC scheme may be designed and be optimized for arbitrary values of $0 < r_Q < 1$.

## 13.5 Multiple-rate Quantum Turbo Short-block Codes

This section is dedicated to validating the EXIT-chart-aided design presented in Section 13.4. We evaluate the performance of the proposed MR-QSBC-QURC scheme in terms of its QBER, its distance to the quantum hashing bound, and finally, the achievable goodput through Monte–Carlo simulations. For this purpose, we consider the MR-QSBC-QURC having the target quantum coding rates of $r_Q = \{0.3, 0.4, 0.5, 0.6, 0.7\}$, with their quantum hashing bounds given by $p^* = \{0.116, 0.094, 0.074, 0.056, 0.039\}$. To produce simulation results having significant appeal for near-future implementation, we consider a moderate number of logical qubits, namely, $K = \{500, 1000, 2000\}$ for all the schemes considered during the simulations.

### 13.5.1 Qubit Error Ratio

In this chapter, we define the qubit error ratio (QBER) as the ratio between the number of errors imposed on the logical qubits $|\widehat{\psi_1}\rangle^{K_1}$ after applying the recovery $\mathcal{R}$ at the end of the decoding of MR-QSBC-QURC to the total number of logical qubits simulated. First, we compare the QBER of the proposed half-rate MR-QSBC-QURC scheme to that of half-rate QTCs using QIrCCs as the outer codes and a QURC as the inner code, which we refer to as QIrCC-QURC. Similar to the proposed scheme, the outer code of QIrCC-QURC is also optimized using the EXIT-chart-based heuristic search presented in Section 13.4. The main difference is that the outer codes of the QIrCC-QURC are composed of QCC subcomponent codes. More specifically, the seed transformation $\mathcal{U}$ of the QCC subcomponent codes utilized as the outer codes is described in Table 13.5. The EXIT-chart-based optimal weighting coefficients of half-rate QIrCC-QURC scheme are given by $\hat{\varpi} = \{0.1316, 0.1869, 0.2962, 0.3852, 0\}$. The outer codes of QIrCC-QURC exhibit a stronger error-correction capability than the outer codes of MR-QSBC-QURC, which are constituted by MR-QSBC that exhibit a minimum distance of $d = 2$. Additionally, the QIrCC-QURC also represents the best-performing half-rate QCC-based QTC in the open literature. However, as we have elaborated on earlier, the MR-QSBC-QURC scheme advocated has the advantage that it can be designed to accommodate arbitrary quantum coding rates using only a single quantum encoder. By contrast, puncturing QCCs may result in QCCs that do not satisfy the symplectic criterion.

Figure 13.7 depicts the QBER comparison between the half-rate MR-QSBC-QURC and half-rate QIrCC-QURC schemes. The quantum hashing bound of half-rate QSCs is given by $p^* = 0.074$, marked by the dashed line. The maximal number of iterations invoked for both schemes is $l = 16$. The QBER curves of the QIrCC-QURC scheme are represented by the black dashed lines, while those of the MR-QSBC-QURC scheme are depicted using solid lines.

We observe from Figure 13.7 that both schemes provide QBER improvements as the number of physical qubits increases, which is the expected trend based on the pertinent quantum coding trade-offs [179]. Furthermore, as we have predicted using the EXIT chart analysis of Section 13.4, that the QBER waterfall region of MR-QSBC-QURC can be seen in the region of $0.04 < p < 0.06$. However, as the depolarizing probability decreases, an error floor emerges, which is expected, since we have witnessed in the EXIT chart analysis that the decoding trajectory terminates before reaching the $(x, y) = (1, 1)$ point due to the crossover between the inner and outer EXIT curves. Having said that, the waterfall region of the QBER curve appears near to the quantum hashing bound.

**Table 13.5** The seed transformation $\mathcal{U}$ associated with QCC subcomponent codes exhibiting various quantum coding rates $r_q$ for constructing the QIrCC-QURC. All of the QCCs exhibiting a memory of $m = 3$.

| $r_q$ | $\mathcal{U}$ |
|---|---|
| 1/4 | $\{9600, 691, 11713, 4863, 1013, 6907, 1125, 828, 10372, 6337, 5590, 11024, 12339, 3439\}_{10}$ |
| 1/3 | $\{3968, 1463, 2596, 3451, 1134, 3474, 657, 686, 3113, 1866, 2608, 2570\}_{10}$ |
| 1/2 | $\{848, 1000, 930, 278, 611, 263, 744, 260, 356, 880\}_{10}$ |
| 2/3 | $\{529, 807, 253, 1950, 3979, 2794, 956, 1892, 3359, 2127, 3812, 1580\}_{10}$ |
| 3/4 | $\{62, 6173, 4409, 12688, 7654, 10804, 1763, 15590, 6304, 3120, 2349, 1470, 9063, 4020\}_{10}$ |

*Source*: Adapted from [302].

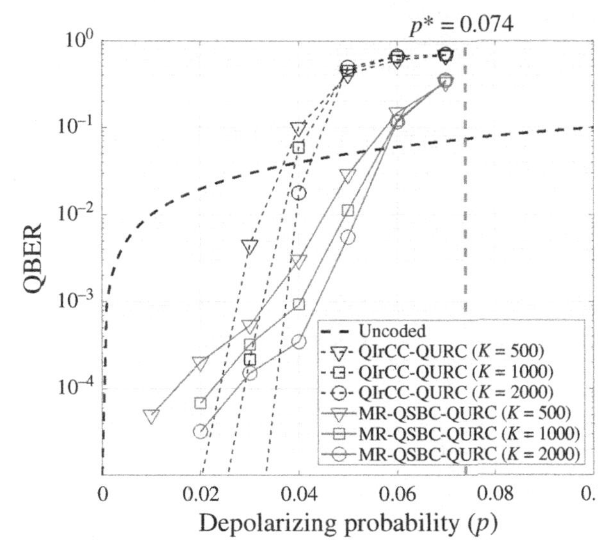


**Figure 13.7** The QBER comparison between half-rate QIrCC-QURC and MR-QSBC-QURC. *Source*: [332]/IEEE/ CC BY 4.0.

Compared to the QIrCC-QURC, the QBER curve of the MR-QSBC-QURC intersects with the uncoded QBER curve at a higher depolarizing probability value in Figure 13.7. For instance, let us observe the scenario of $K = 2000$. In Figure 13.7, we locate the cross-over point between the uncoded QBER curve and the QBER curve of the MR-QSBC-QURC at $p = 0.058$. Meanwhile, the QBER curve of the QIrCC-QURCC intersects at $p = 0.043$. Thus, the proposed scheme provides a higher coding gain when we consider a scenario having the requirement of QBER $\leq$ uncoded QBER.

Let us now consider in Figure 13.3 a case where the requirement is QBER $\leq 10^{-3}$. We obtain the maximum tolerable depolarizing probability of $p = 0.044$, below which the MR-QSBC-QURC satisfies the QBER requirement, while for the QIrCC-QURC, we find the maximum tolerable depolarizing probability of $p = 0.037$. In this scenario, the advocated MR-QSBC-QURC still outperforms the QIrCC-QURC. However, when we consider the case where the requirement is QBER $\leq 10^{-4}$, we find that the depolarizing probability threshold must be lower for MR-QSBC-QURC than for QIrCC-QURC to avoid the emergence of an error floor. More specifically, for the MR-QSBC-QURC, we have $p = 0.027$, while for QIrCC-QURC, we have $p = 0.035$ in Figure 13.3. Since the outer code of the QIrCC-QURC is based on an ensemble of QCC subcomponent codes having stronger error correction capabilities than the MR-QSBCs, the QIrCC-QURC tends to further degrade the QBER by imposing additional errors when it tries to perform error correction beyond its capability, instead of correcting them. However, once the QIrCC-QURC operates within its convergence region, it starts correcting more errors than the MR-QSBC-QURC. Therefore, the QBER curve of the QIrCC-QURC intersects with the uncoded QBER at a slightly higher QBER value than the MR-QSBC-QURC, but the former has a steeper QBER curve and lower error floor. Thus, the advocated scheme performs well at relatively high quantum depolarizing probabilities, providing reasonably low QBER. However, once the MR-QSBC-QURC operates at lower depolarizing probabilities within its convergence region, we may switch the MR-QSBC-QURC to a higher quantum coding rate for meeting the QBER requirement. The summary of our QBER comparisons between QIrCC-QURC and MR-QSBC-QURC is provided in Table 13.6.

To provide a complete picture of the MR-QSBC-QURC performance, Figure 13.8 portrays the QBER of the MR-QSBC-QURC having various quantum coding rates. Recall that all the outer codes of MR-QSBC-QURC can be represented by a single quantum encoder, along with the optimal weighting coefficient $\hat{\boldsymbol{\omega}}$ required for performing fractional encoding. In Figure 13.8, we indicate the quantum hashing bound for each quantum coding rate with dashed line. Since the outer codes have been specifically designed using EXIT-chart-based optimization, as expected, the waterfall region of their QBER curves appears near to their respective quantum hashing bound $p^*$. Additionally, the error floor of the MR-QSBC-QURC having a higher quantum coding rate is lower than that of its counterparts having lower quantum coding rate, since during the EXIT chart analysis the inner and outer EXIT curves of the higher quantum coding rate intersects closer to the $(x, y) = (1, 1)$ point. However, for a high quantum coding rate, the error floor is low enough to become invisible, since it would require excessive time to capture the qubit errors by simulations involving limited numbers of physical qubits. We summarize the maximum tolerable depolarizing probability for meeting the requirement of QBER $\leq$ uncoded QBER as well as QBER $\leq 10^{-3}$ in Table 13.7.

**Table 13.6** Performance comparison of half-rate QIrCC-QURC to half-rate MR-QSBC-QURC for logical qubits of $k = \{500, 1000, 2000\}$. The performance is described using the maximum tolerable depolarizing probability $p$ given various requirements, below which the code improves the QBER. The quantum hashing bound is $p^* = 0.074$.

| Requirement | $k = 500$ | | $k = 1000$ | | $k = 2000$ | |
|---|---|---|---|---|---|---|
| | $p$ QIrCC | $p$ QSBC | $p$ QIrCC | $p$ QSBC | $p$ QIrCC | $p$ QSBC |
| QBER ≤ Uncoded | 0.037 | **0.054** | 0.039 | **0.057** | 0.043 | **0.058** |
| QBER ≤ $10^{-3}$ | 0.028 | **0.034** | 0.033 | **0.040** | 0.037 | **0.044** |
| QBER ≤ $10^{-4}$ | **0.024** | 0.015 | **0.029** | 0.022 | **0.035** | 0.027 |

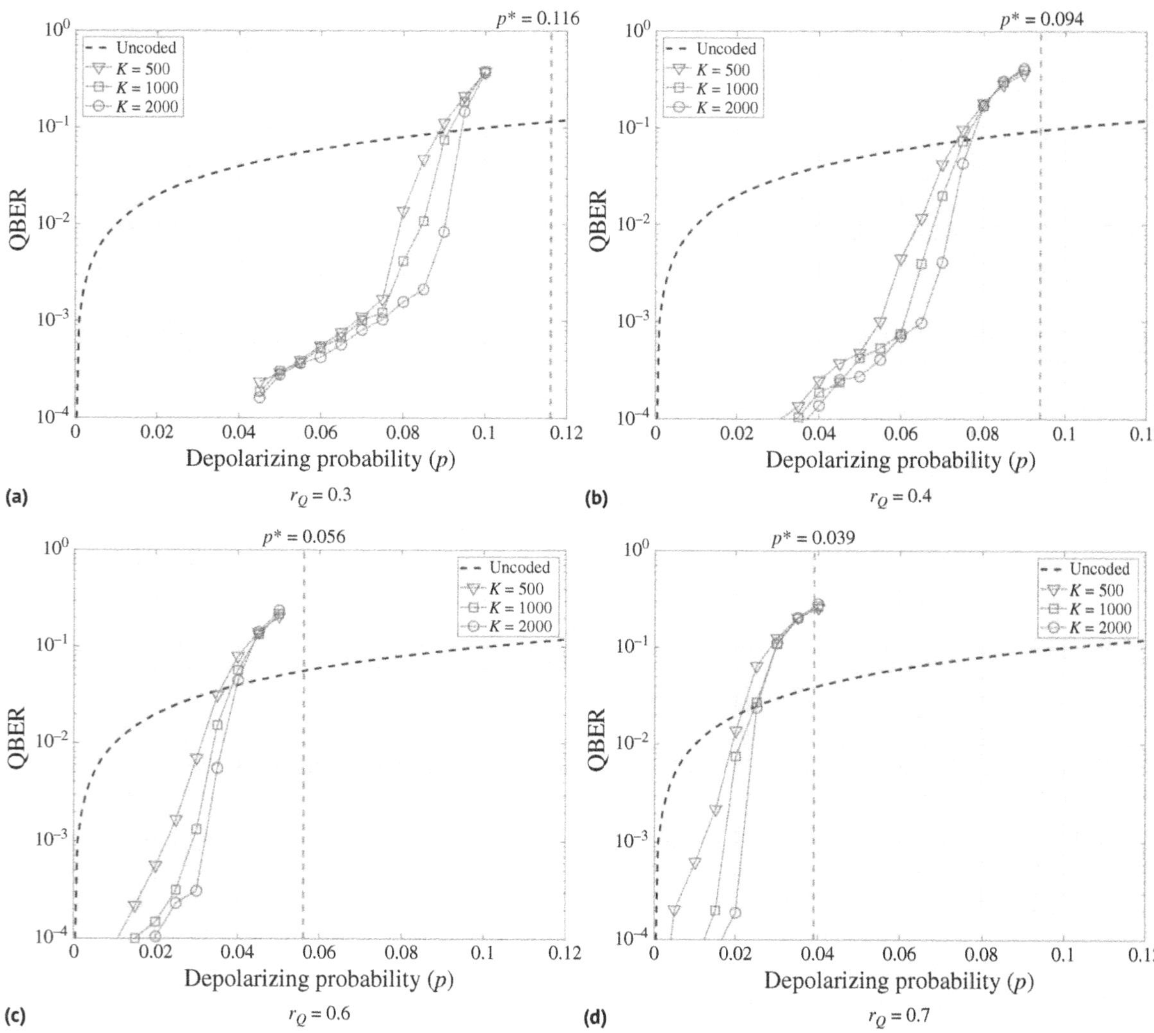


**Figure 13.8** The QBER performance of MR-QSBC-QURC exhibiting various quantum coding rates $r_Q$. The dashed line represents the quantum hashing bound of the associated quantum coding rate $r_Q$. *Source:* [332]/IEEE/CC BY 4.0.

It is worth emphasizing that the cost of achieving a lower QBER is an increase in the depth of the quantum encoder and quantum inverse encoder, as well as an increase in the complexity of the classical decoder. Explicitly, the QBER performance of MR-QSBC-QURC exhibiting different quantum coding rates was evaluated while keeping both the number of logical qubits ($K$) and the number of decoding iterations fixed ($I = 16$). Therefore, the main factor affecting the encoding and decoding complexity of the MR-QSBC-QURC is the number of physical

**Table 13.7** The maximum tolerable depolarizing probability $p$ given various QBER requirements and different numbers of logical qubits $K$, below which the code improves the QBER of MR-QSBC-QURC.

| Requirement | QBER ≤ Uncoded | | | | |
|---|---|---|---|---|---|
| | $r_Q = 0.3$ | $r_Q = 0.4$ | $r_Q = 0.5$ | $r_Q = 0.6$ | $r_Q = 0.7$ |
| $K = 500$ | 0.089 | 0.073 | 0.054 | 0.036 | 0.021 |
| $K = 1000$ | 0.091 | 0.075 | 0.057 | 0.039 | 0.024 |
| $K = 2000$ | **0.094** | **0.077** | **0.058** | **0.040** | **0.025** |
| **Requirement** | **QBER ≤ $10^{-3}$** | | | | |
| | $r_Q = 0.3$ | $r_Q = 0.4$ | $r_Q = 0.5$ | $r_Q = 0.6$ | $r_Q = 0.7$ |
| $K = 500$ | 0.069 | 0.055 | 0.034 | 0.023 | 0.012 |
| $K = 1000$ | 0.070 | 0.061 | 0.040 | 0.029 | 0.017 |
| $K = 2000$ | **0.074** | **0.065** | **0.044** | **0.032** | **0.022** |

qubits. More specifically, for QSBCs used as outer codes, the depth of the quantum encoder is independent of the number of physical qubits ($N$). By contrast, for the QURC used as inner code – which belongs to the family of quantum convolutional codes – the depth of the quantum encoder is linearly proportional to the number of auxiliary qubits ($N - K$). Since the quantum inverse encoder is the reversed version of the quantum encoder, its depth is also identical to that of the quantum encoder. On the other hand, the complexity of the classical decoder is linearly proportional to the length of the classical syndrome vector constituted by the ($N - K$) classical bits inferred from the measurements of the erroneous auxiliary qubits. For example, for a quantum coding rate of $r_Q = 1/2$ and $K = 1000$ logical qubits the length of the syndrome vector is $(N - K) = 1000$ bits. By comparison, for an MR-QSBC-QURC having the same quantum coding rate of $r_Q = 1/2$, but encoding $K = 2000$ logical qubits, the length of the syndrome vector is $(N - K) = 2000$ bits. Similarly, when fixing the number of logical qubits to $K = 1000$, but reducing the quantum coding rate to $r_Q = 1/4$, the length of the syndrome vector becomes $(N - K) = 3000$ bits. In both examples, we observe that a QBER performance improvement is attained by increasing the complexity of the classical decoder.

### 13.5.2 Distance from the Quantum Hashing Bound

It is clear from the results presented in Figure 13.8 that by reducing the quantum coding rate of MR-QSBC-QURC, we are capable of correcting the errors imposed by the quantum depolarizing channels having higher depolarizing probability. We summarize the results of Figure 13.8 in Figure 13.9a by considering the QBER results for $K = 2000$. Indeed, the results follow the expected trends – the lower the quantum coding rate, the higher its tolerable depolarizing probability. However, in contrast to classical communication systems, we do not have a quantitative metric that directly takes into account the quantum coding rate differences of the QSCs having different quantum coding rates. Since the QBER is plotted versus the depolarizing probability rather than the classical energy per bit to noise power spectral density ratio ($E_b/N_0$), having an appropriate normalization metric may be beneficial for a fair comparison. Explicitly, it is essential to provide such a normalization, since the most intuitive step to be taken for improving the QBER of any QSC is to reduce its quantum coding rate, which results in encoding fewer logical qubits and/or incorporating more auxiliary qubits. While indeed this improves the QBER, as demonstrated in Figure 13.8, it reduces the effective throughput. Therefore, in this chapter, we introduce a pair of additional metrics for transforming the QBER of Figure 13.8 by accounting for the different quantum coding rates $r_Q$, namely, the distance from the quantum hashing bound and the goodput.

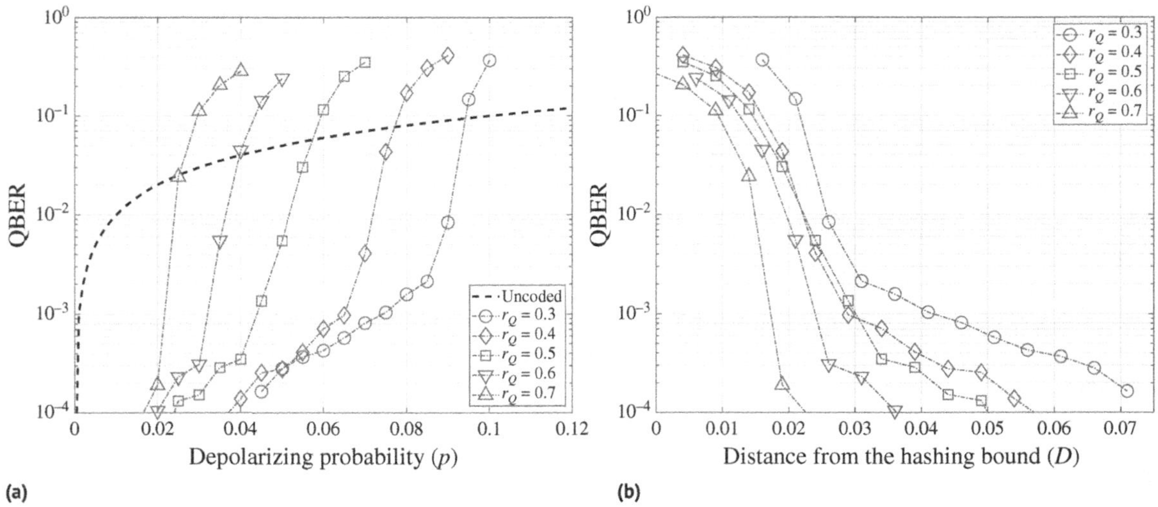


**Figure 13.9** The QBER of the MR-QSBC-QURCs exhibiting various quantum coding rates $r_Q = \{0.3, 0.4, 0.5, 0.6, 0.7\}$ versus: (a) depolarizing probability $p$; (b) the distances to the quantum hashing bound $D$. The MR-QSBC-QURCs are used for protecting $K = 2000$ logical qubits. *Source*: [332]/IEEE/CC BY 4.0.

**Definition 13.4:** *Distance from the quantum hashing bound* [153, 279]. Given a quantum coding rate $r_Q$, $p^*$ represents the quantum hashing bound for $r_Q$. Therefore, the distance $D$ from the quantum hashing bound is defined by

$$D = p - p^*, \tag{13.37}$$

where $p$ is the depolarizing probability.

Figure 13.9b explicitly portrays the appropriately shifted version of the QBER curves in Figure 13.9a according to each of the quantum hashing bounds $p^*$. More precisely, the quantum hashing bound of QSCs having $r_Q = \{0.3, 0.4, 0.5, 0.6, 0.7\}$ is given by $p^* = \{0.116, 0.094, 0.074, 0.056, 0.039\}$. If we consider QBER $= 10^{-3}$, we attain the distances of $D = \{0.042, 0.029, 0.030, 0.024, 0.017\}$ from the quantum hashing bound. It is important to highlight that these near-hashing-bound results are achieved for protecting $K = 2000$ logical qubits using practical nonzero quantum coding rates.

A closer inspection of Figure 13.8 reveals that as we reduce the quantum coding rate $r_Q$, the QBER curve shifts further away from the quantum hashing bound. However, we also have to point out that at higher quantum coding rates, for instance st $r_Q = 0.7$, the quantum hashing bound is as low as at $p^* = 0.039$, which only results in a modest shift of QBER curve. Consequently, the aforementioned absolute distance $D$ from the quantum hashing bound may still require further normalization by the quantum hashing bound $p^*$ for defining the normalized distance from it.

**Definition 13.5:** *Normalized distance from the hashing bound.* Given a quantum coding rate $r_Q$, $p^*$ represents the quantum hashing bound and $D$ is the absolute distance from the quantum hashing bound. The normalized distance $R$ from the quantum hashing bound is then defined by

$$R = \frac{D}{p^*}. \tag{13.38}$$

Using Eq. (13.38), we obtain the normalized distance from the quantum hashing bound for the proposed MR-QSBC-QURC scheme having $r_Q = \{0.3, 0.4, 0.5, 0.6, 0.7\}$ as follows: $R = \{0.362, 0.309, 0.405, 0.429, 0.436\}$. Now, we observe that the higher quantum coding rates exhibit a slightly larger normalized distance from the quantum hashing bound. Since we have individually optimized the MR-QSBC-QURC for different quantum coding rates, the resultant normalized distances from the quantum hashing bound do not exhibit large variations. We argue that the absolute and the normalized distances from the quantum hashing bound provide a balanced view when it comes to comparing the QBER of QSCs having different quantum coding rates.

### 13.5.3 Goodput

The final metric that we consider for comparing the QBER results of Figure 13.8 is goodput, which is based on the following definition.

**Definition 13.6:** *Goodput* [279]. Goodput represents the effective number of logical qubits obtained after error correction, which is defined as the fraction of error-free logical qubits normalized by the quantum coding rate $r_Q$ formulated as follows:

$$G = r_Q(1 - \text{QBER}). \tag{13.39}$$

We portray the goodput of MR-QSBC-QURC in Figure 13.10 for two different QBER requirements. Explicitly, in Figure 13.10a, we show the achievable goodput for QBER $\leq$ uncoded QBER, while in Figure 13.10b, for QBER $\leq 10^{-3}$. The MR-QSBC-QURC scheme may commence its operation at a lower quantum coding rate for coping with a high depolarizing probability, but once the QBER requirement is met it may switch to higher quantum coding rates for increasing the goodput. For instance, let us observe Figure 13.10a, where the requirement is QBER $\leq$ uncoded QBER. Assume that we initially operate at $p = 0.06$, implying that the MR-QSBC-QURC runs at $r_Q = 0.4$. As the quality of the quantum channel improves, the depolarizing probability may reduce to $p = 0.05$. Hence, the MR-QSBC-QURC switches its quantum coding rate to $r_Q = 0.5$, since we can still satisfy the QBER requirement, while yielding a higher goodput. Similarly, consider Figure 13.10b, where the requirement is QBER $\leq 10^{-3}$. The MR-QSBC-QURC may start operating at $r_Q = 0.4$ when $p = 0.05$. Then, it may switch to $r_Q = 0.5$ once the quantum channel improves to $p = 0.04$ for meeting the QBER requirement, while increasing the goodput. These switching points indicated in Figure 13.10 are based on the results summarized in Table 13.7.

In Figure 13.10, we also include the quantum hashing bound as a benchmark. This is because goodput and quantum hashing bound are intimately linked. Explicitly, quantum hashing bound may be viewed as the maximum achievable goodput, when the mandatory requirement is QBER = 0. Let us now imagine that we have infinitely many quantum coding rates to cover all the quantum coding rates of $0 < r_Q < 1$, which is actually plausible for the MR-QSBC-QURC considered. In that case, the resultant goodput curve will be a perfectly smooth line near-parallel to the quantum hashing bound. Finally, the distance of goodput curve from the quantum hashing bound depends on the codeword length, the higher it is the lower its distance from the quantum hashing bound. Therefore, we suggest that this characteristic curve should be used more prevalently as a fair metric of rate-compatible QSC designs in the future.

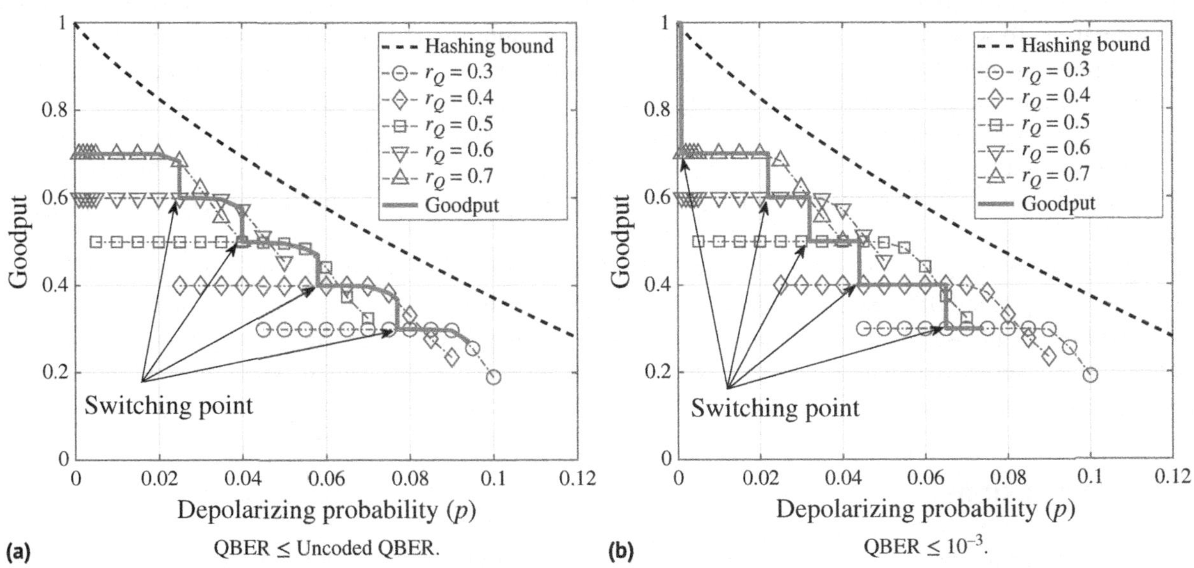


**Figure 13.10** The achievable goodput for different QBER requirements: (a) QBER $\leq$ Uncoded QBER; (b) QBER $\leq 10^{-3}$. The number of logical qubits $K = 2000$. The switching points are based on the results summarized in Table 13.7. *Source:* [332]/IEEE/CC BY 4.0.

**Remark:** *The future development of rate-compatible QSCs should aim for achieving the highest goodput possible given the specific QBER requirement and codeword length. Additionally, for attaining a low QBER, the achievable goodput is expected to be close from the quantum hashing bound.*

### 13.5.4 Comparison with State-of-the-art

Most of the quantum stabilizer codes found in the literature suffer from low quantum coding rates. Moreover, it has proven to be challenging to find a family of quantum stabilizer codes that offers the same level of flexibility as the MR-QSBC-QURC advocated. Recent advances in the field have introduced two novel QLDPC codes that exhibit relatively high quantum coding rates: multiple-rate (MR) QLDPC codes [336] and spatially coupled QLDPC codes [337].

In [336], a family of QLDPC codes is proposed, which utilizes a single stabilizer measurement circuit across a wide range of quantum coding rates. This is in contrast to the MR-QSBC-QURC scheme advocated, which employs a single encoder and inverse decoder circuit. The multiple-rate nature of the proposed QLDPC codes is achieved by utilizing row-circulant matrices within the parity-check matrix. Some of the resulting QLDPC codes achieve quantum coding rates of $r_Q \approx 0.75$ and $r_Q \approx 0.87$, with a convergence region $p \approx 0.0185$ and $p \approx 0.0128$, respectively. The smallest reported number of logical qubits in [336] is $K \approx 3900$. In comparison, the MR-QSBC-QURC scheme having a quantum coding rate of $r_Q = 0.7$ and $K = 2000$ achieves a convergence region of $p = 0.0250$.

Inspired by the powerful classical spatially coupled (SC) LDPC codes, the quantum version of SC-LDPC codes, known as spatially coupled QLDPC codes, is proposed in [337]. This novel QLDPC codes family demonstrates an impressive error-correction performance, achieving a convergence region around $p = 0.065$ for a quantum coding rate of $r_Q \approx 0.34$ with $K = 1600$ logical qubits and a convergence region around $p = 0.080$ for a quantum coding rate of $r_Q \approx 0.28$ with $K = 1600$ logical qubits. This remarkable performance is largely attributed to an effective algorithm that eliminates all four-cycle and six-cycle configurations in the parity-check matrix. As a comparison, the MR-QSBC-QURC scheme achieves a convergence region of $p = 0.094$ for a quantum coding rate of $r_Q = 0.3$ with $K = 2000$ logical qubits.

### 13.5.5 Practical Aspects

We can see that the MR-QSBC-QURC has immediate potential for applications in quantum-secure direct classical [338, 339] and quantum communications [340]. As quantum communication channels exhibit time-varying characteristics, it becomes essential to have a set of quantum error-correction codes that can efficiently adapt to this dynamic nature. To achieve this, an accurate estimation of the quantum depolarizing channels is crucial in assigning the appropriate quantum coding rate based on the channel quality. One approach for assessing the quality of quantum communication channels involves using known pilot qubits or pre-shared entanglement to estimate the depolarizing probability. However, this method assumes that the quantum depolarizing channel remains static or quasi-static, implying that the depolarizing probability does not vary significantly over time. An alternative approach is to employ syndrome-based depolarizing probability estimation, which draws on classical principles [334, 335].

The potential application of MR-QSBC-QURC in the field of quantum computation is highly intriguing. One notable advantage of multiple-rate quantum turbo codes, compared to other quantum stabilizer codes, is their ability to offer flexible quantum coding rates and accommodate varying numbers of logical qubits, all while ensuring a guaranteed convergence region. However, more research is needed to investigate the feasibility and implementation of error-corrected quantum gates using quantum turbo codes.

## 13.6 Conclusions

We have conceived near-hashing-bound single-encoder-based multiple-rate MR-QSBC-QURC using EXIT-chart-based heuristic search. The main advantage of the proposed design is that it can be tailored for any arbitrary quantum coding rate $r_Q$. This may be achieved by performing fractional encoding of the input stream by harnessing MR-QSBCs as the outer codes. This is plausible in the light of trends in classical error-correction codes design.

Despite the low complexity of the outer codes, our Monte–Carlo simulation results show that the MR-QSBC-QURC advocated is capable of approaching the quantum hashing bound at QBER $= 10^{-3}$ for the specific quantum coding rates considered. More precisely, the MR-QSBC-QURC design advocated is capable of operating at the distance of $D = \{0.042, 0.029, 0.030, 0.024, 0.017\}$ from the quantum hashing bound for quantum coding rates of $r_Q = \{0.3, 0.4, 0.5, 0.6, 0.7\}$. Despite its low-complexity code construction, the MR-QSBC-QURC scheme advocated offers a competitive QBER performance even against the best-performing QCC-based QTC in the literature. These solutions may be expected to open the pathway for the future development of rate-compatible QSCs capable of adapting to diverse QBER requirements and quantum channel qualities without relying on different quantum encoders.

### 13.6.1 Design Guidelines

Based on the discussions throughout this chapter, we provide the following design guidelines for MR-QSBC-QURC capable of operating at various quantum coding rates in line with different quantum channel qualities.

- Determine the MR-QSBC-QURC parameters based on the uncoded QBER, including the expected quantum coding rates $r_Q$ for the given depolarizing probabilities $p$ or vice versa, using the quantum hashing bound of (13.23).
- Determine the number of MR-QSBC subcomponent codes according to the desired $r_Q$. In this chapter, we consider only five MR-QSBC subcomponent codes. However, the number of subcomponent codes can be readily extended to both higher and lower quantum coding rates by Section 13.2.
- For each quantum coding rate, optimize the outer code constituted by MR-QSBCs by choosing the optimal weighting coefficient using the EXIT-chart-based heuristic search. The optimization objective is to obtain a marginally open tunnel at the associated depolarizing probability value $p$ between the inner and the outer decoder's EXIT curves, as described in Section 13.4.
- Perform Monte–Carlo simulations for each MR-QSBC-QURC having different quantum coding rates to determine the switching points for meeting the QBER requirements. These switching points may be utilized for quantifying the achievable goodput of the MR-QSBC-QURC scheme according to the specific QBER requirements, as exemplified in Section 13.5.

### 13.6.2 Future Research

The development of quantum error-correction codes that possess a small number of physical qubits, high quantum coding rates, and demonstrate robust error correction performance has posed a significant challenge in the field of quantum information. However, recent progress in the field has brought forth notable advancements, particularly in the area of decoding techniques adapted from classical noise-guessing decoding for the quantum domain [275, 341]. One such approach, known as quantum-aided GRAND, has emerged as a versatile and promising method that exhibits universality across various quantum stabilizer decoding paradigms. This innovative decoding technique has demonstrated exceptional error-correction performance, particularly for quantum stabilizer codes with a modest number of physical qubits. Given these exciting developments, it becomes highly intriguing to explore the potential of applying the quantum-aided GRAND approach to decode MR-QSBC-QURC codes.

# 14

# Quantum Low-density Parity Check Codes

## 14.1 Introduction

In Chapter 11, we conceived hashing bound approaching designs for concatenated quantum codes. Pursuing further the quest for designing iterative code structures, in this chapter we focus on the family of quantum low density parity check (QLDPC) codes. In particular, the outstanding near-capacity performance of the classical low density parity check (LDPC) codes [126, 342–345] attained at an affordable decoding complexity has inspired the community to design QLDPC codes. The sparseness of the QLDPC matrix is of particular interest in the quantum domain, because it requires only a small number of interactions per qubit during the error correction procedure. More specifically, each qubit is only involved in a small fraction of the stabilizer generators (or the rows of the QLDPC matrix). Consequently, the sparse nature of the QLDPC matrix inherently limits the propagation of errors, hence facilitating "fault tolerant" decoding.

QLDPC codes belong to the family of quantum stabilizer codes (QSCs) [57, 59], which is a generalized formalism for designing quantum codes from any arbitrary classical binary and quaternary codes, as discussed in Chapter 10. However, this transfiguration from the classical to the quantum domain imposes the stringent symplectic criterion on the classical "mother" codes, which brings with it various design challenges. Against this backdrop, in this chapter we survey the evolution of QLDPC code is portrayed in Figure 14.5 designs, focusing on the various code constructions to conceive powerful QLDPC codes from the known families of classical LDPC codes. We also review the syndrome-based iterative decoding algorithms invoked for QLDPC codes. Finally, we contribute to these developments by conceiving a new code design and an improved decoding algorithm. More specifically, our novel contributions in this chapter are as follows [80, 346]:

- We have proposed a radically new class of high-rate row-circulant quasi cyclic (QC) QLDPC codes. More specifically, our proposed unassisted non-dual-containing CSS QLDPC codes can be constructed from arbitrary row-circulant classical QC-LDPC matrices, which are known to generate efficient short and moderate length high-rate classical QC-LDPC codes.
- We have conceived a modified non-binary decoding algorithm for homogeneous CSS type QLDPC codes, which is capable of mitigating the impact of the unavoidable length-4 cycles.
- We demonstrate that the uniformly reweighted belief propagation (URW-BP) technique of [347, 348] may also be invoked for further improving the attainable performance.

The rest of the chapter is organized as follows. We commence with a review of QLDPC code designs in Section 14.2, while a range of powerful decoding techniques are discussed in Section 14.3. We next propose our new code design in Section 14.4, whose performance is evaluated in Section 14.5. Finally, we present our proposed decoding algorithm in Section 14.6, while in Section 14.7 we detail the reweighted belief propagation. The corresponding simulation results are presented in Section 14.8, while Section 14.9 concludes our discourse.

## 14.2 Quantum LDPC Code Designs

Analogous to classical LDPC codes, which belong to the family of linear block codes discussed in Section 10.2, QLDPC codes are inherently stabilizer codes, which may be characterized using an equivalent classical parity check matrix (PCM) $H$ of Eq. (10.30). More specifically, an $[n, k]$ QLDPC code having a coding rate of $R_Q = k/n$ is equivalent to a $(2n, n+k)$ binary LDPC code having a coding rate of $R_c = (n+k)/2n$. We may divide the QLDPC codes into three main categories on the basis of the general global structure of the associated PCM $H$, namely CSS codes, non-CSS codes and entanglement-assisted (EA) codes, as summarized in Figure 14.1. The CSS-type constructions may also be classified as dual-containing and as non-dual-containing codes. Let us now take a look at each of these categories individually.

### 14.2.1 Calderbank–Shor–Steane Codes

Ideally, any pair of classical binary LDPC codes, which meet the symplectic criterion, may be used for constructing a CSS-based QLDPC code. However, randomly choosing the constituent pair of classical codes is not feasible, because finding two sparse codes, which satisfy the stringent symplectic constraint, is highly unlikely. This motivated Postol [76] to conceive the first example of a CSS-based non-dual-containing QLDPC code from a small (15, 7) finite geometry based classical LDPC code in 2001. More specifically, in Postol's code, the PCM of a finite geometry based cyclic classical LDPC code constitutes the $H'_z$ of Eq. (10.35), while $H'_x$ is derived from $H'_z$, so that the symplectic criterion is satisfied, i.e. we have $H'_z H_x'^T = 0$. Since both the constituent PCMs, i.e. $H'_z$ and $H'_x$, are cyclic, this facilitates the implementation of the encoder. However, Postol did not develop a generalized method for his proposed design, which could facilitate the construction of QLDPC codes from any arbitrary finite geometry based classical LDPC codes. This gap was filled by MacKay *et al.* in [67], where several systematic constructions were developed for the CSS-based QLDPC codes by restricting the designs to the dual-containing structure.

Before proceeding with the constructions of [67], let us take a look at the symplectic condition of Eq. (10.34) in the context of the dual-containing QLDPC codes. Recall from Section 10.3.2.1 that the symplectic criterion of Eq. (10.34) reduces to $H'_z H_z'^T = 0$ for the dual-containing QLDPC codes, which have $H'_x = H_z'^T$. This in turn implies that the PCM of a classical LDPC code may only be used for constructing a dual-containing QLDPC code if:

**a.** it has an even row weight;
**b.** every pair of rows has an even number of overlapping 1's, which we may term as an "even overlap."

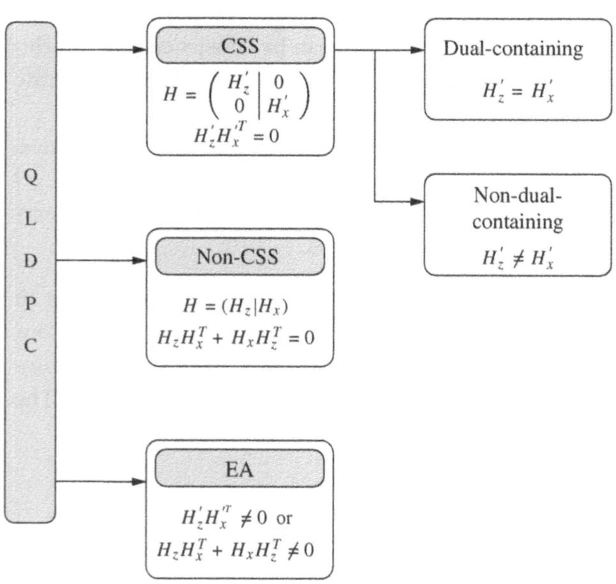


**Figure 14.1** Classification of QLDPC codes. *Source*: [80]/IEEE.

By contrast, good classical LDPC codes must have at most a single overlapping 1 between every pair of rows for the sake of avoiding length-4 cycles because short cycles of length-4 impair the performance of the associated decoding algorithm. Consequently, the "even overlap" condition results in unavoidable cycles of length 4 in the resultant PCM, as depicted in Figure 14.2 for a random binary PCM $H'_z$ given by:[1]

$$H'_z = \begin{pmatrix} 1 & 0 & 1 & 1 \\ 1 & 1 & 1 & 0 \end{pmatrix}. \tag{14.1}$$

Furthermore, the constraint $H'_z H'^T_z = 0$ also implies that the code-space of the underlying classical code must contain its dual. Hence, the resultant code contains codewords having a weight equal to the row weight $\rho$. Therefore, the minimum distance of the classical dual-containing code is upper-bounded by $\rho$. Surprisingly, this upper-bound does not exist for quantum codes due to the degenerate nature of quantum errors. Recall from Section 10.3.3 that the $n$-tuple channel error pattern acting on the codewords of a QSC, may be classified as:

a. **Detected Error Patterns:** These error patterns anti-commute with the stabilizers of the code, yielding a nontrivial syndrome.
b. **Harmful Undetected Error Patterns:** This class of error patterns commutes with the stabilizers. Consequently, these error patterns are harmful, because they map one valid codeword onto another; thus, corrupting the codeword without triggering a nontrivial syndrome. Harmful undetected error patterns are attributed to the small minimum distance of the code.
c. **Harmless Undetected Error Patterns:** This is a unique class of error patterns, which do not have a classical analogue. Similar to the "harmful undetected error patterns," these error patterns also commute with the stabilizers, but they are harmless in the context of quantum codes. This is because these are the degenerate errors, which belong to the stabilizer group, and therefore do not corrupt the state of the valid codewords. More explicitly, for dual-containing CSS codes, the harmless undetected error patterns lie in the code-space of the dual code $C_1^{\perp}$, as depicted in Figure 14.3. It must be mentioned here that although the harmless undetected errors do not affect the minimum distance of the resultant quantum code, they lead to the "symmetric degeneracy error" in the iterative decoding procedure of QLDPC codes, which will be discussed in Section 14.3.3.

Bicycle codes, which were proposed by MacKay *et al.* in [67], marked the first major breakthrough toward the realization of CSS-based dual-containing quantum LDPC codes. The proposed code design relies on a semi-random/semi-structured construction, which satisfies the dual-containing constraint by deliberately imposing a global structure on the constituent PCM. A bicycle code having a row weight of $\rho$, a block length of $n$ and $(n-k)$ stabilizers is constructed using a random sparse $n/2 \times n/2$ cyclic matrix $C_m$, which has a row weight of $\rho/2$. The nonzero entries in $C_m$ can be chosen either randomly or using a difference set satisfying the property that every

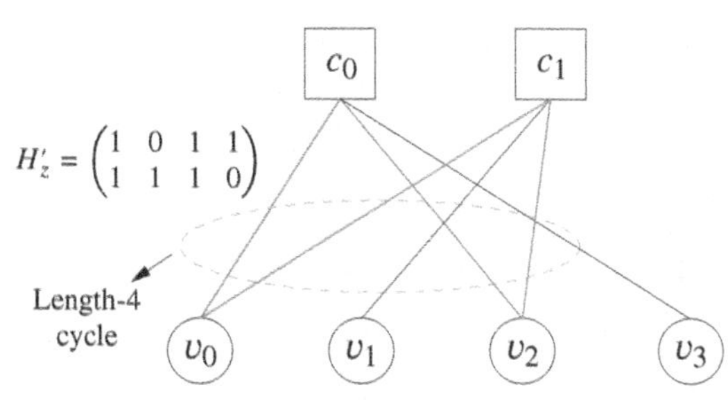


**Figure 14.2** Tanner graph of $H'_z$. An "even overlap" between the rows of $H'_z$ results in a length-4 cycle.

1 This is a random example for illustrating the impact of an even number of overlaps. The row weight must be even. Furthermore, the $H'_z$ of Eq. (14.1) may not be a good classical code.

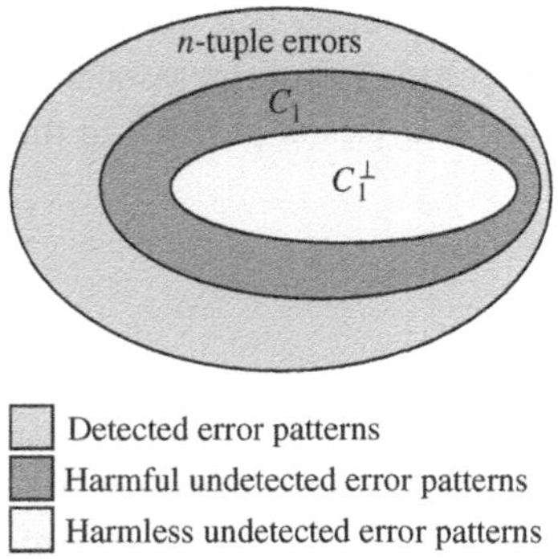


**Figure 14.3** Error pattern classification for dual-containing CSS codes. *Source:* [80]/IEEE.

difference (modulo $n/2$) occurs at most once in the set. This matrix $C_m$ is then used for constructing a base matrix $H_0$, which is a concatenation of $C_m$ and its transpose, i.e. we have:

$$H_0 = (C_m, C_m^T). \tag{14.2}$$

Consequently, $H_0$ is a dual-containing code satisfying the "even overlap" constraint, because every overlap that occurs in $C_m$ may also be found in $C_m^T$. Furthermore, since $H_0$ is an $n/2 \times n$ matrix, the resultant dual-containing quantum LDPC code has a coding rate $R_Q = 0$ (or equivalently $R_c = 1/2$). To achieve a nonzero coding rate, $k$ rows of $H_0$ are discarded, so that the column weights of the resultant $(n-k) \times n$ PCM $H_z'$ are as uniform as possible. This code design offers flexibility in choosing the code parameters, i.e. $\rho$, $n$, and $k$. However, the minimum distance of the resultant code is upper-bounded by $\rho$. This is because the discarded rows of $H_0$ are all codewords of weight $\rho$, which are not contained in the dual, and therefore contribute to the harmful undetected error patterns.

MacKay *et al.* also proposed unicycle codes in [67], which are derived from perfect difference sets.[2] The perfect difference set property implies that all pairs of rows of the PCM must have a single overlapping 1. Since we need an "even overlap" to achieve a dual-containing structure, the PCM is extended by adding an extra column having all logical ones. Hence, every pair of rows in the resultant PCM have two overlapping 1's, which result in a single length-4 cycle between every pair of rows. Thus, an $(n, k)$ PCM is transformed into a dual-containing $(n+1, k+1)$ PCM, which has a row weight of $(\rho+1)$ (where $\rho$ is the row weight of the initial matrix and must be odd) and whose column weights are all $\rho$, except for the last 'all-one' column. MacKay *et al.* also suggested that the unique structure of unicycle codes may be exploited for avoiding the length-4 cycles during the decoding procedure [67]. More explicitly, a unicycle code may be viewed as a superposition of two codes, i.e. one having an "all-zero" column at the end and the other having an "all-one" column. For the sake of avoiding the short cycles, each of the two codes is decoded separately using the sum product algorithm [67]. If both decoders return a valid codeword, the codeword which has the maximum likelihood is chosen. Hence, an improved decoding procedure is conceived at the cost of an increased decoding complexity. Furthermore, the minimum distance of the unicycle codes constructed using difference sets is upper-bounded by the row weight, because the resultant code has codewords of weight $\rho$, which do not lie in the dual. Since the choice of $n$, $k$, and $\rho$ for perfect difference sets is limited, this design does not offer much flexibility in choosing the code parameters. By contrast, bicycle codes can be constructed from any arbitrary cyclic classical LDPC.

To extend the application of MacKay's unicycle codes to a wider range of code parameters, Aly [129] exploited the classical type-II Euclidean geometry (EG) LDPC codes of [349]. Similar to the perfect difference sets, a classical

---

2 A perfect difference set characterized on the additive group of size $n$ has the unique property that every integer from 1 to $n-1$ may be expressed as a difference of two integers in the set (modulo $n$) in exactly one way. By contrast, in the plain difference sets, every difference occurs at most once, i.e. either it may not occur or will occur only once. For example, the set $\{1, 2, 4\}$ forms a perfect difference set for the group of size 7 because every integer from 1 to 6 can be expressed as the difference of two elements in the difference set, i.e. we have:

$$(1-2) \bmod 7 = 6, \quad (1-4) \bmod 7 = 4, \quad (2-1) \bmod 7 = 1,$$

$$(2-4) \bmod 7 = 5, \quad (4-1) \bmod 7 = 3, \quad (4-2) \bmod 7 = 2.$$

type-II EG LDPC code having a PCM $H_{\text{EG-II}}$ has the unique characteristic that all pairs of rows have a single overlapping value of 1. Consequently, Aly suggested that the code characterized by an $(n-k)\times n$ matrix $H_{\text{EG-II}}$ may be converted into a dual-containing code in the following two ways:

**a.** If the row weight of $H_{\text{EG-II}}$ is odd, then similar to the unicycle codes, an "all-one" column **1** is appended to $H_{\text{EG-II}}$, i.e. we have:

$$H'_z = (H_{\text{EG-II}}|\mathbf{1}). \tag{14.3}$$

**b.** If the row weight of $H_{\text{EG-II}}$ is even, then **1** is appended to $H_{\text{EG-II}}$ for the sake of ensuring an "even overlap," while an identity matrix **I** of size $(n-k)\times(n-k)$ is appended to make the row weight even, i.e. we have:

$$H'_z = (H_{\text{EG-II}}|\mathbf{1}|\mathbf{I}). \tag{14.4}$$

The resultant codes offer beneficial high coding rates. However, they have an upper-bounded minimum distance of at least $(\gamma+1)$, where $\gamma$ denotes the column weight.

Unicycle code construction was further explored by Djordjevic [130] for designing quasi-cyclic (QC) high-rate dual-containing QLDPC codes from the balanced incomplete block design (BIBD) based classical LDPC codes [350, 351], which have a minimum distance of at least $(\gamma+1)$, where $\gamma$ denotes the column weight. More specifically, the BIBD[3] is characterized by the parameter $\lambda$. A BIBD-based LDPC code has exactly $\lambda$ overlaps between every pair of rows. Since good classical LDPC codes must have at most a single row overlap, $\lambda$ is set to 1 for designing classical LDPC codes with a girth of at least 6. Consequently, analogous to the perfect difference set based classical LDPC codes, each pair of rows has a single overlapping value of 1, which can be made even by imposing the unicycle code structure on the PCM. Djordjevic also designed dual-containing LDPC codes by using BIBDs associated with an even $\lambda$. Unfortunately, the even $\lambda$ based QLDPC codes failed to outperform the unicycle based BIBD constructions [130].

Since all the aforementioned dual-containing constructions resulted in an upper-bounded minimum distance, the quest for the construction of unbounded QLDPC codes continued. Pursuing this objective, another nontrivial class of dual-containing QLDPC codes was proposed by MacKay *et al.* in [127], which was derived from Cayley graphs. These codes were further investigated by Couvreur *et al.* in [103, 128], where it was formally shown that the lower bound on the minimum distance of the resultant code is a logarithmic function of the code length, thus the minimum distance can be improved by extending the codeword (or block) length, albeit again, only logarithmically. However, this is achieved at the cost of an increased decoding complexity imposed by the escalating row weight, which also increases logarithmically with the block length. Furthermore, Cayley graph based designs may be viewed as a special class of the topological codes [96, 100, 238],[4] which are already known to have growing minimum distances.

Let us recall that the dual-containing QLDPC codes have unavoidable short cycles, which impair the performance of the decoding algorithm. Hence, even if dual-containing QLDPC codes having an unbounded minimum distance are designed, they are unlikely to surpass the performance of their non-dual-containing counterparts. Therefore, in the midst of these activities, Lou *et al.* [131, 132] rekindled the interest in CSS-based non-dual-containing QLDPC codes by invoking the classical low density generator matrix (LDGM) codes for code construction. More specifically, since both the generator matrix and the PCM of an LDGM code are sparse, they

---

3 BIBD($v, b, r, k, \lambda$) distributes all the $v$ elements (or points) of a set $V$ into $b$ subsets (or blocks) of size $k$ such that,

- each pair of elements occurs in exactly $\lambda$ of the blocks,
- every element occurs in exactly $r$ blocks, and
- the number of elements in each block $k$ is small as compared to the size $v$ of set $V$; thus, giving it the name "incomplete."

Let us consider a set $V$ of seven numbers, which is given by $V=\{1,2,3,4,5,6,7\}$. Then, the blocks $\{1,2,4\}$, $\{2,6,5\}$, $\{3,4,6\}$, $\{4,5,7\}$, $\{1,5,6\}$, $\{2,6,7\}$, and $\{1,3,7\}$ constitute the BIBD(7,7,3,3,1) since there are seven elements ($v$) in the set $V$ which are distributed among seven blocks ($b$), each element appears in three blocks ($r$), each block has 3 elements ($k$), and each pair of elements occur in one block ($\lambda$).

4 Topological constructions are beyond the scope of this work.

can be used as the components of a CSS code. Let $\tilde{G}$ and $\tilde{H}$ be the generator matrix and PCM, respectively, of an $(n,k)$ LDGM code. Then the resultant CSS code may be formulated as follows:

$$H=\begin{pmatrix} \tilde{H} & \mathbf{0} \\ \mathbf{0} & \tilde{G} \end{pmatrix}. \tag{14.5}$$

Since $\tilde{H}$ is an $(n-k)\times n$ matrix, while $\tilde{G}$ is a $k\times n$ matrix, the resultant PCM $H$ is an $n\times 2n$ matrix. Consequently, the corresponding QLDPC code has a coding rate of zero. Lou *et al.* [131, 132] suggested that this may be avoided by applying linear row operations both to $\tilde{G}$ as well as to $\tilde{H}$ for the sake of reducing their number of rows. Unfortunately, this row-reduction may in turn create short cycles in the resultant PCM. For the sake of avoiding the adverse impact of these short cycles, Lou *et al.* [131, 132] also conceived a modified Tanner graph, which requires code doping [352] for pushing the iterative decoding process toward convergence. Hence, an improved performance is achieved at the cost of an increased decoding complexity.

Unfortunately, the constituent codes of all the aforementioned CSS constructions, both those of the dual-containing as well as of the non-dual-containing codes, suffer from the presence of length-4 cycles. To dispense with these short cycles, Hagiwara *et al.* [133, 353] conceived a unique class of non-dual containing QC-QLDPC codes, which have a girth of at least 6. More specifically, let us consider a circulant matrix $T$ having a size of $LP/2\times LP/2$, $\rho=L/2$ and $\gamma=L$, which is given by [353]:

$$T=\begin{pmatrix} t_0 & t_1 & \dots & t_{L/2-1} \\ t_{L/2-1} & t_0 & \dots & t_{L/2-2} \\ \vdots & & & \vdots \\ t_1 & t_2 & \dots & t_0 \end{pmatrix}, \tag{14.6}$$

where $t_i$ denotes the index of the circulant permutation matrix[5] of size $P$ and $t_i\in[P_\infty]:=\{0,1,\dots,P-1\}\cup\{\infty\}$. Hagiwara *et al.* have shown that $H_z'$ and $H_x'$ derived from the matrix $T$ of Eq. (14.6) satisfy the symplectic criterion, if they have the form:

$$H_z'=(T_1,T_2) \quad \text{and} \quad H_x'=\left(-T_2^T,-T_1^T\right). \tag{14.7}$$

Furthermore, since row deletion does not perturb the symplectic criterion, rows may be deleted from $H_z'$ and $H_x'$ in order to achieve the desired coding rate. For the sake of ensuring a girth of 6, Hagiwara *et al.* relied upon algebraic combinatorics for designing the constituent circulant matrices $T_1$ and $T_2$, so that all the rows of $H_z'$ as well as of $H_x'$ have at most a single overlap. The bicycle codes of [67] may be viewed as a special case of this construction, i.e. when $P=1$ and $T_2=T_1^T$. Unfortunately, the resultant codes failed to outperform MacKay's bicycle codes [67] and their minimum distance is upper-bounded by the row weight.

---

5 A circulant permutation matrix $I(1)$ of size $P$ is given by:

$$I(1)=\begin{pmatrix} 0 & 1 & 0 & \dots & 0 \\ 0 & 0 & 1 & \dots & 0 \\ 0 & 0 & 0 & \dots & 0 \\ \vdots & & & & \vdots \\ 1 & 0 & 0 & \dots & 0 \end{pmatrix}.$$

More explicitly, $I(1)$ is a $P\times P$ identity matrix shifted to the right by one position. Therefore, $I(x)$ may be defined as a $P\times P$ identity matrix shifted to the right by $x$ positions, where $x$ is known as the index of the permutation matrix. Moreover, $x=0$ defines an unshifted identity matrix, while $x=\infty$ is specially used to denote a zero matrix of size $P\times P$.

Among all the dual-containing codes discussed earlier, MacKay's bicycle construction [67] offers the best performance at an affordable decoding complexity. However, the resultant performance is still not on par with that of the classical LDPC codes. For example, the rate-1/4 bicycle code of [67], having $n = 19{,}014$, operates within about 5.5 dB of the Hashing limit at a Word Error Rate (WER) of $10^{-3}$. Furthermore, all the aforementioned codes have an upper-bounded minimum distance except for the Cayley graph based designs. In the quest for increasing the minimum distance and hence to approach the capacity, Hagiwara *et al.* extended the QC design of [133, 153] to spatially coupled (SC) codes in [136], which outperformed their corresponding "non-coupled" counterparts at the cost of a small coding rate loss. However, the performance still remained relatively far from the capacity. More specifically, the SC QC-QLDPC of [136], having a coding rate of 0.49 and a length of $n = 1{,}81{,}000$, operates within about 3.8 dB of the Hashing limit at a WER of $10^{-3}$. Kasai *et al.* further contributed to these developments by deriving non-binary QC-QLDPC codes in [134, 135] from the design of [133, 353]. The resultant codes outperformed their binary counterparts at the cost of an increased decoding complexity.

A rate-1/2 code, having a length of $n = 20{,}560$ and a Galois field of $GF(2^{10})$, was shown to operate within about 1.9 dB of the Hashing limit at a WER of $10^{-3}$. The SC codes were further investigated by Andriyanova *et al.* in [354], where the constituent codes were derived from the classical LDGM codes as in [131, 132]. Analogous to the EA quantum codes, Andriyanova *et al.* assumed that some qubits are transmitted over a noiseless channel. Consequently, the resultant rate-1/4 LDGM-based SC-QLDPC codes, having a length of $n = 76{,}800$, succeeded in operating within about 1.7 dB of the Hashing limit at a WER of $10^{-3}$. The assumption of having noiseless qubits was later eliminated in [355], whereby these qubits were protected by the error reducing quantum turbo code (QTC) of [355], which resulted in a modest coding rate loss and in a moderately increased complexity for the overall code. It was shown that the performance of the resultant rate-1/2 QTC-assisted LDGM-based SC-QLDPC code, having a length of $n = 8, 21, 760$, is within about 0.7 dB of the hashing limit at a WER of $10^{-3}$. Figure 14.4 compares the achievable performance of the aforementioned codes, namely "bicycle" code of [67], "SC QC-QLDPC" code of [136], "non-binary QC-QLDPC" code of [134, 135], "LDGM-based SC-QLDPC" code of [354] and the "QTC-assist DGM-based SC-QLDPC" code of [355], at a WER of $10^{-3}$, which is benchmarked against the hashing bound. All the main contributions pertaining to CSS-based QLDPC codes are summarized in Figure 1.4.

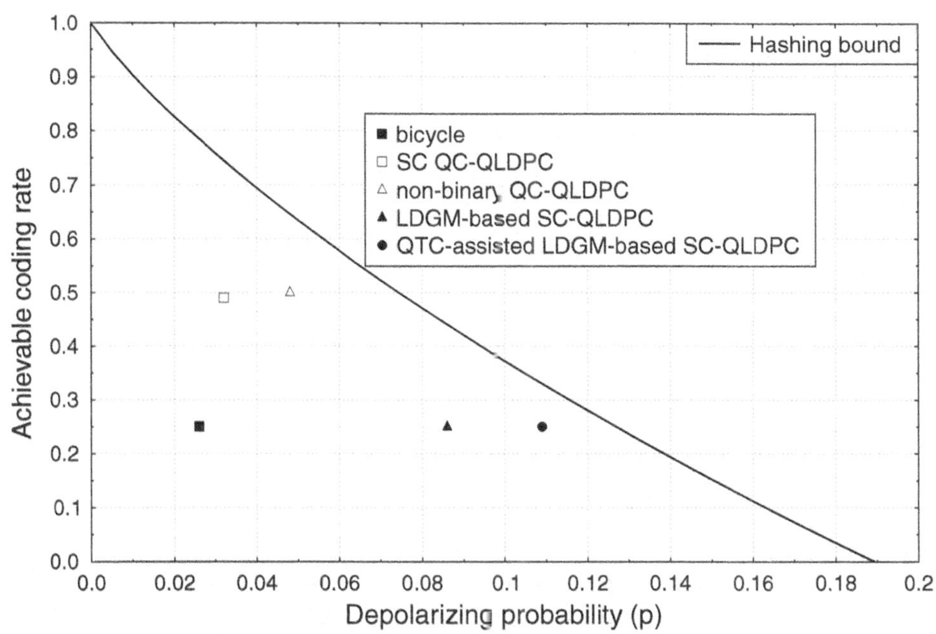


**Figure 14.4** Achievable performance at a WER of $10^{-3}$ benchmarked against the Hashing bound for the "bicycle" code ($R = 0.25$, $n = 19{,}014$), "SC QC-QLDPC" code ($R = 0.49$, $n = 1{,}81{,}000$), "non-binary QC-QLDPC" code ($R = 0.5$, $n = 20{,}560$, $GF(2^{10})$), "LDGM-based SC-QLDPC" code ($R = 0.25$ $n = 76{,}800$) and the "QTC-assisted LDGM-based SC-QLDPC" code ($R = 0.25$, $n = 8{,}21{,}760$). *Source*: Adapted from [67, 130, 134, 135, 354, 355], Babar et al. [80].

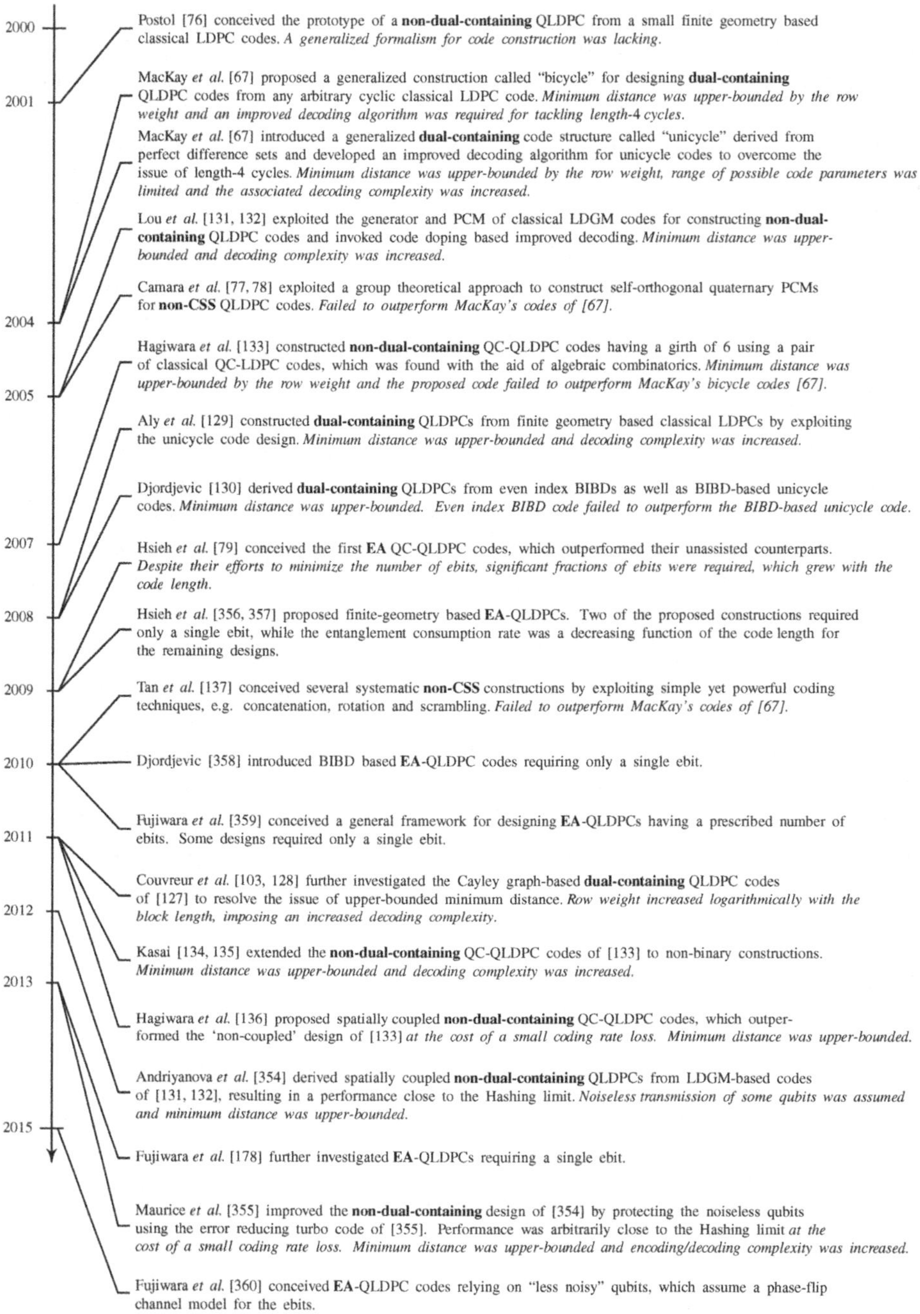


**Figure 14.5** The evolution of QLDPC codes. The "code type" is in **bold**, while the associated "cons" are in *italics*. *Source*: [80]/IEEE.

### 14.2.2 Non-CSS Codes

Non-CSS stabilizer codes have the potential of exploiting any redundancy more efficiently than their CSS-based counterparts. For example, a CSS-based block code requires a block length of 7 qubits to correct a single bit-flip or phase-flip [92], while only five qubits are required for a non-CSS block code [56]. Consequently, Camara *et al.* [77, 78] proposed the construction of non-CSS (also called unrestricted) QLDPC codes (Figure 14.5). In contrast to most of the aforementioned dual-containing constructions, which satisfy the symplectic criterion in their global code structure, the design conceived by Camara *et al.* aims at building the symplectic constraint into the local code structure. More specifically, since the PCM of a classical quaternary LDPC code can be mapped onto the generators of a QSC based on Eq. (10.39), Camara *et al.* developed a group theoretical approach for constructing self-orthogonal quaternary LDPC codes satisfying the symplectic criterion of Eq. (10.41). It was found that the Tanner graph of the resultant self-orthogonal quaternary PCM has cycles of length 4. However, these short cycles are imposed by the commutativity constraint. More specifically, every column of a quaternary PCM must contain at least two different nonzero entries, i.e Pauli-**X**, Pauli-**Z**, or Pauli-**Y**, so that it can correct both phase-flips as well as bit-flips occurring on that qubit. On the other hand, any two rows of the PCM must have an even number of positions with different nonzero elements (or non-identity Pauli operators). For example, let us consider a weight-2 column of a PCM, which is involved in two rows with a value of 1 and $\omega$, respectively. Now to meet the commutativity constraint, these two rows must have another overlapping column having different nonzero entries; thus, creating cycles of length-4. Intuitively, these short cycles are also present in the PCM $H$ of the CSS codes, when they are viewed in the quaternary domain. In fact, these cycles are excessive in the dual-containing CSS codes, which also have the additional cycles resulting from the dual-containing constraint[6]. The proposed non-CSS QLDPC codes of [77, 78] outperformed the bicycle codes in the waterfall region of their performance curve, while yielding a higher error floor due to their small minimum distance. It is expected that this non-CSS construction may have an unbounded minimum distance, thus yielding lower error floors, when the block length is sufficiently large. However, this was not explicitly proven in [77, 78].

Pursuing the same line of research, Tan *et al.* [137] were the first researchers to design the constituent PCMs $H_z$ and $H_x$ of a non-CSS code by invoking classical binary codes. More specifically, they conceived several systematic constructions for non-CSS QLDPC codes, which imposed both global as well as local structures on the underlying binary codes for the sake of satisfying the symplectic criterion. This is achieved by exploiting simple yet powerful coding techniques, which include concatenation, rotation and scrambling. The designed codes exhibit a better performance than the non-CSS codes of [77, 78]. However, they still failed to outperform MacKay's codes of [67]. In conclusion, the major milestones achieved in the domain of non-CSS QLDPC codes are summarized in Figure 1.4.

### 14.2.3 Entanglement-assisted QLDPC Codes

Efficient classical LDPC codes exist, which are known to approach the Shannon capacity for a large block size. For example, the optimized 1/2-rate classical LDPC code of [361] operates within 0.13 dB of the capacity limit for transmission over an additive white Gaussian noise (AWGN) channel at a bit error rate (BER) of $10^{-6}$ using a code length of $10^6$. More specifically, the turbo cliff of this LDPC code is merely 0.06 dB away from the Shannon capacity. This inspired researchers to achieve a comparable performance for QLDPCs. Unfortunately, the symplectic criterion, or more specifically the commutativity requirement of the stabilizers, limits the direct application of such efficient classical codes in the quantum domain. As discussed in Sections 14.2.1 and 14.2.2, only a limited class of classical codes, which conform to stringent local or global structural constraints, may be used as the constituents of a quantum code. This obstacle may be overcome by exploiting the EA quantum code designs of [74, 143, 144], which assist us in importing any classical code into the quantum domain. However, the pre-shared noiseless entangled qubits (ebits) of an EA code constitute a valuable resource, because maintaining a noiseless entangled state is not a trivial task. Consequently, a practically realizable code design should aim for minimizing the number of pre-shared noiseless ebits.

The first EA-QLDPC codes were conceived by Hsieh *et al.* in [79], whereby EA CSS-based QC-QLDPC codes were designed from their classical counterparts. Hsieh *et al.* chose the constituent circulant matrices of the classical QC code by ensuring that the number of ebits required is minimized. Despite their efforts, a significant number of these ebits was required, which grew with the code length. More importantly, these designs supported the conjecture that the high efficiency of EA codes should be attributed to the large fractions of pre-shared ebits. On a positive note, since the EA quantum codes of [79] shared the same attributes as the classical parent code, especially in terms of the girth and the minimum distance, these EA-QLDPC codes outperformed the state-of-the-art unassisted QLDPC codes. Working further in the direction of minimizing the number of pre-shared ebits, in [356, 357] Hsieh *et al.* conceived finite-geometry based EA-QLDPCs, whose "entanglement consumption rate" decreases with the code length. Furthermore, two of these constructions required only a single ebit regardless of the code length; thus dispensing with the then prevailing apprehensions surrounding the family of EA-codes. It must be emphasized

6 This is further discussed in Section 14.3.3.

here that the proposed design does not impose any restrictions on the underlying finite geometry based classical LDPC codes of [349]. A more general framework conceived for designing the EA-QLDPCs, having a prescribed number of ebits, was presented in [359], which was derived from combinatorial design theory. Some of these designs required only a single ebit, despite having a high performance, a high coding rate and a low complexity. The necessary and sufficient conditions for designing single-ebit based EA-QLDPCs were further investigated in [178]. Moreover, BIBD based EA-QLDPC codes requiring only a single ebit were also identified in [358]. Recently, Fujiwara [362] introduced the notion of quantum codes relying on "less noisy" (or "reliable") qubits. More explicitly, unlike the EA formalism, which requires completely noiseless ebits, the framework of [362] assumes that these auxiliary qubits are subjected to a phase-flip channel, which is a more realistic noise model. In this spirit, Fujiwara *et al.* [360] conceived QLDPC codes relying on "less noisy" qubits. The major contributions made in the domain of EA-QLDPC codes are summarized in Figure 1.4.

## 14.3 Iterative Decoding of Quantum LDPC Codes

Analogous to the classical LDPC codes, QLDPC codes invoke the classic belief propagation (BP) based decoding, also referred to as the sum-product algorithm (SPA), which operates over the Tanner graph of the corresponding PCM. However, let us recall that qubits collapse upon measurement. Therefore, the syndrome-based version [363] of the classic codeword decoding has to be used for QLDPC codes. The underlying BP can be implemented both in the binary as well as in the quaternary domain, which are discussed in Sections 14.3.1 and 14.3.2, respectively.

### 14.3.1 Binary Decoding

A quantum depolarizing channel characterized by the depolarizing probability $p$ is isomorphic to two independent binary symmetric channels (BSCs) [67], i.e. one for phase-flips and the other for bit-flips, each having a crossover probability of $2p/3$. More explicitly, based on the Pauli-to-binary isomorphism encapsulated in Eq. (10.29), a Pauli error $\mathcal{P} \in \mathcal{G}_n$ experienced by an $n$-qubit block transmitted over a depolarizing channel can be modeled by an effective error-vector $P$, which is a binary vector of length $2n$. The effective error $P$ may be represented as $P = (P_z, P_x)$, where both $P_z$ and $P_x$ are $n$-bit long and represent **Z** and **X** errors, respectively. This implies that an **X** error imposed on the $t$th qubit will yield a 0 and a 1 at the $t$th and $(n+t)$th index of $P$, respectively. Similarly, a **Z** error imposed on the $t$th qubit will give a 1 and a 0 at the $t$th and $(n+t)$th index of $P$, respectively, while a **Y** error on the $t$th qubit will result in a 1 at both the $t$th as well as $(n+t)$th index of $P$. Since a depolarizing channel characterized by the probability $p$ incurs **X**, **Y** and **Z** errors with an equal probability of $p/3$, the effective error-vector $P$ reduces to two BSCs having a crossover probability of $2p/3$, where we have one channel for the **Z** errors and the other for the **X** errors.

Based on the aforementioned simplified notion, which ignores the correlation between the **X** and **Z** errors, QLDPC codes can be decoded by running the syndrome-based BP over the Tanner graph of the equivalent binary code having $H = (H_z|H_x)$ [137]. More explicitly, let $S$ be the observed syndrome sequence, which is given by the symplectic product of $H$ and $P$, as formulated here:

$$S = H \star P^T = H_z P_x^T + H_x P_z^T. \tag{14.8}$$

The observed syndrome $S$ of Eq. (14.8) is fed to a classical syndrome-based LDPC decoder to estimate the most likely inflicted channel error $\tilde{P}$, as depicted in Figure 14.6. For an $H$ of size $m \times 2n$, where we have $m = (n-k)$, the resultant estimated error vector $\tilde{P}$ is of length $2n$, whose first $n$ bits are for the estimated phase errors $\tilde{P}_z$, while the other $n$ bits indicate the estimated bit errors $\tilde{P}_x$. Finally, the $2n$-bit binary vector is mapped onto the $n$-qubit Pauli error $\tilde{\mathcal{P}}$ based on the mapping encapsulated in Eq. (10.29). More explicitly, the $t$th and $(n+t)$th value of $\tilde{P}$ are combined based on Eq. (10.29) to estimate the error inflicted on the $t$th qubit.

For CSS codes, we have $H_z = \begin{pmatrix} H'_z \\ \mathbf{0} \end{pmatrix}$ and $H_x = \begin{pmatrix} \mathbf{0} \\ H'_x \end{pmatrix}$. Consequently, the Tanner graph of the matrix $H$ consists of two independent Tanner graphs corresponding to the matrices $H'_z$ and $H'_x$. This in turn implies that **X** and **Z** errors can be decoded independently using the matrices $H'_z$ and $H'_x$, respectively [67]. Hence, the quBit error rate (QBER)

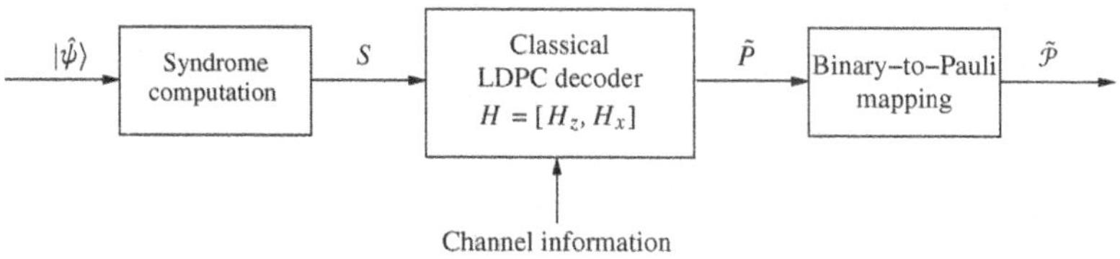


**Figure 14.6** General schematic of a syndrome-based decoder for QLDPC codes. *Source*: [80]/IEEE.

of a CSS QLDPC code may be approximated by the sum of the BER of the two constituent classical codes. More explicitly, if $p_e^x$ and $p_e^z$ are the classical BERs for $H_z'$ and $H_x'$, respectively, then the overall QBER is equivalent to $(p_e^x + p_e^z - p_e^x p_e^z) \approx (p_e^x + p_e^z)$, which reduces to $2p_e^z$ for a dual-containing CSS code having $H_x' = H_z'$.

For a binary $m \times 2n$ LDPC matrix $H$, the classical LDPC decoder of Figure 14.6 aims for finding the most likely error $P$ of length $2n$ given the observed syndrome $S$, i.e. we have:

$$\tilde{P} = \arg \max_{P \in (\mathbb{F}_2)^{2n}} \mathrm{P}(P|S), \tag{14.9}$$

where $\mathrm{P}(P|S)$ is the probability of experiencing the error $P \in (\mathbb{F}_2)^{2n}$ imposed on the transmitted codewords, given that the syndrome of the received qubits $|\hat{\psi}\rangle$ is $S \in (\mathbb{F}_2)^m$. Unfortunately, Eq. (14.9) defines an NP-complete problem [364]. A sub-optimal algorithm for solving Eq. (14.9) is constituted by the classic BP, which finds the element-wise optimum value rather than the global optimum. More explicitly, for $P = (P_0, P_1, \ldots, P_t, \ldots, P_{2n-1})$, BP finds $P_t$ such that:

$$\tilde{P}_t = \arg \max_{P_t \in \mathbb{F}_2} \mathrm{P}(P_t|S), \tag{14.10}$$

where $\mathrm{P}(P_t|S)$ is the marginalized probability of the $t$th bit. The BP operates by exchanging messages over the Tanner graph of $H$ having check nodes $c_i$ for $i \in \{0, m-1\}$ and variable nodes $v_t$ for $t \in \{0, 2n-1\}$. The messages sent by the $i$th check node $c_i$ to the $t$th variable node are denoted by $m_{c_i \to v_t}^{P_t}$, while the messages directed from the $t$th variable node to the $i$th check node are given by $m_{v_t \to c_i}^{P_t}$, where $P_t$ is the error imposed on the $t$th variable node. The overall syndrome-based message exchange procedure is summarized in Algorithm 14.1, which proceeds as follows [363]:

- **Initialization:** The algorithm begins by initializing the messages $m_{v_t \to c_i}^{P_t}$ according to the channel model $\mathrm{P_{ch}}(P_t)$. For a BSC having a crossover probability of $2p/3$, we have:

$$\begin{aligned} m_{v_t \to c_i}^{0} &= 1 - 2p/3, \\ m_{v_t \to c_i}^{1} &= 2p/3. \end{aligned} \tag{14.11}$$

- **Horizontal Message Exchange:** Let $V(c_i)$ be the set of variable nodes connected to the check node $c_i$, i.e. $V(c_i) \equiv \{v_t : H_{it} = 1\}$, and $V(c_i) \setminus v_t$ be the set $V(c_i)$ excluding the variable node $v_t$. As depicted in Figure 14.7a, in this step the algorithm runs through the rows of $H$ (checks) and computes the message $m_{c_i \to v_t}^{P_t}$ for each $v_t \in V(c_i)$ and $P_t \in \mathbb{F}_2$. The message $m_{c_i \to v_t}^{a}$ represents the probability that the syndrome value observed for the check $c_i$ is $S_i$ given that the $t$th variable node has the error $(P_t = a)$, where $a \in \{0, 1\}$. This can be mathematically formulated as:

$$m_{c_i \to v_t}^{a} = K \sum_{P : P_t = a} \mathrm{P}(S_i|P) \prod_{v_{t'} \in V(c_i) \setminus v_t} m_{v_{t'} \to c_i}^{P_{t'}}, \tag{14.12}$$

where $K$ is the normalization constant invoked for ensuring $\sum_{a \in \{0,1\}} m_{c_i \to v_t}^{a} = 1$, while $\mathrm{P}(S_i|P)$ is a binary function, which is equal to 1 only when the check $c_i$ is satisfied, i.e. when the value of the check node $c_i$ computed using the error vector $P$ matches the measured syndrome value $S_i$, otherwise it is 0. Furthermore, according to Eq. (14.12), the messages $m_{c_i \to v_t}^{a}$ destined for the $t$th variable node do not take into account the messages flowing in the opposite direction along the same edge, i.e. $m_{v_t \to c_i}^{a}$. Consequently, $m_{c_i \to v_t}^{a}$ only contains the new information gleaned from the messages sent by the other variable nodes and it is therefore termed as being "*extrinsic*." This ensures that the successive iterations of this iterative algorithm are independent.

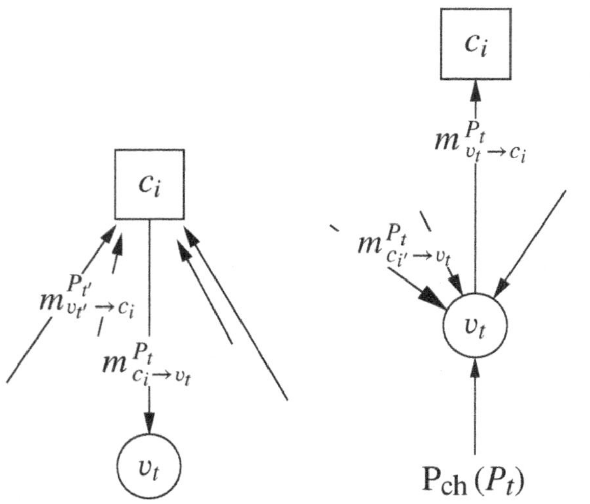


(a) Horizontal message exchange (b) Vertical message exchange

**Figure 14.7** Belief propagation (BP) algorithm. Check nodes and variable nodes are denoted by $c_i$ and $v_t$, respectively.

- **Vertical Message Exchange:** Let $C(v_t)$ be the set of check nodes connected to the variable node $v_t$, i.e. $C(v_t) \equiv \{c_i : H_{it} = 1\}$, and $C(v_t) \setminus c_i$ be the set $C(v_t)$ excluding the check node $c_i$. As shown in Figure 14.7b, for each column of $H$ (hence called "vertical"), the BP computes the message $m^{P_t}_{v_t \to c_i}$ for all $c_i \in V(v_t)$ and $P_t \in \mathbb{F}_2$. More explicitly, the messages $m^a_{v_t \to c_i}$ are computed by evaluating the product of the channel information $\mathrm{P_{ch}}(P_t = a)$ and the messages $m^a_{c_{i'} \to v_t}$ flowing into the variable node $v_t$ along all the edges connected to it, but excluding $m^a_{c_i \to v_t}$, which is received along the same edge. Hence, the *extrinsic* message is computed as:

$$m^a_{v_t \to c_i} = K\, \mathrm{P_{ch}}(P_t = a) \prod_{c_{i'} \in C(v_t) \setminus c_i} m^a_{c_{i'} \to v_t}, \tag{14.13}$$

  where $K$ is the normalization constant, which ensures that $\sum_{a \in \{0,1\}} m^a_{v_t \to c_i} = 1$.
- **Element-wise Marginal Probability:** Finally, the element-wise marginal probability $\mathrm{P}(P_t|S)$ for $P_t \in \mathbb{F}_2$ is calculated as follows:

$$\mathrm{P}(P_t = a|S) = K\, \mathrm{P_{ch}}(P_t = a) \prod_{c_i \in C(v_t)} m^a_{c_i \to v_t}, \tag{14.14}$$

  which takes into account all the messages flowing into the variable node $v_t$.
- **Hard Decision and Syndrome Check:** As previously portrayed in Eq. (14.10), a hard decision is made by finding the most likely error $\tilde{P}_t$, which maximizes the marginal probability computed in Eq. (14.14). Based on the estimated error vector $\tilde{P}$, the syndrome $\tilde{S} = H(\tilde{P}_x : \tilde{P}_z)^T$ is computed. If the syndrome $\tilde{S}$ of the estimated error $\tilde{P}$ is the same as the observed syndrome $S$, the process halts, indicating that the correct solution is found. Otherwise, the algorithm repeats itself from the horizontal message exchange step onwards. This iterative procedure continues, until either $\tilde{S} = S$ or the maximum number of iterations $\mathtt{I}_{\max}$ is reached.

### 14.3.2 Non-binary Decoding

Based on the Pauli-to-GF(4) formalism of Eq. (10.39), QLDPC codes can be decoded by invoking the non-binary BP, which takes into account the correlation between the phase-flips and bit-flips. The syndrome-based non-binary BP is similar to the binary BP of Algorithm 14.1, with the following two major modifications:

- Non-binary BP exploits the depolarizing channel model, which does not ignore the correlation between the bit and phase errors. The equivalent 4-ary channel model has the following probability distribution:

$$\mathbf{P}_{\mathrm{ch}}\left(\hat{P}_t = \hat{a}\right) = \begin{cases} 1 - p, & \text{if } \hat{a} = 0 \\ p/3, & \text{if } \hat{a} \in \{1, \omega, \overline{\omega}\}, \end{cases} \tag{14.15}$$

**Algorithm 14.1** Syndrome-based BP Babar *et al.* [80]

```
Set $P_{ch}(0) \leftarrow (1-2p/3)$ and $P_{ch}(1) \leftarrow 2p/3$.
Initialize $m^a_{v_t \to c_i} \leftarrow P_{ch}(a), \forall v_t, c_i \in C(v_t)$ and $a \in \{0,1\}$.
for iter ← 1 to $I_{max}$ do
    for all $i \in \{0,(m-1)\}, v_t \in V(c_i)$ and $a \in \{0,1\}$ do
        $m^a_{c_i \to v_t} \leftarrow k \sum_{P:P_t=a} P(S_i|P) \prod_{v_{t'} \in V(c_i) \setminus v_t} m^{P_{t'}}_{v_{t'} \to c_i}$.
    end for
    for $t \leftarrow 0$ to $(2n-1)$ do
        for all $c_i \in C(v_t)$ and $a \in \{0,1\}$ do
            $m^a_{v_t \to c_i} \leftarrow k\, P_{ch}(P_t = a) \prod_{c_{i'} \in C(v_t) \setminus c_i} m^a_{c_{i'} \to v_t}$.
        end for
        for all $a \in \{0,1\}$ do
            $P(P_t = a|S) \leftarrow k\, P_{ch}(P_t = a) \prod_{c_i \in C(v_t)} m^a_{c_i \to v_t}$.
        end for
        $\tilde{P}_t \leftarrow \arg\max_{P_t \in \mathbb{F}_2} P(P_t|S)$.
    end for
    $\tilde{S} \leftarrow H(\tilde{P}_x : \tilde{P}_z)^T$.
    if $(\tilde{S} = S)$ then
        return $\tilde{P}$.
    end if
end for
```

where we have $\hat{P} = (\hat{P}_0, \hat{P}_1, \dots, \hat{P}_t, \dots, \hat{P}_{n-1})$ and $\hat{P}_t$ denotes the error inflicted on the $t$th qubit.

- The syndrome $S_i$, which was computed as $H_i(P_x : P_z)^T$ in the binary scenario, is now given by the trace inner product of $\hat{H}_i$ and $\hat{P}$ (see Eq. [10.41]):

$$S_i = \mathrm{Tr}(\hat{H}_i \cdot \hat{P}), \tag{14.16}$$

where $\hat{H}_i$ is the $i$th row of $H$ in GF(4) and $i \in \{0, m-1\}$.

As compared to the binary BP, non-binary decoding imposes an increased complexity, specifically on the horizontal message exchange step. More explicitly, since the summation in Eq. (14.12) runs for all possible error sequences $\{\hat{P} : \hat{P}_t = \hat{a}\}$, which yield the syndrome $S_i$ for the $i$th check node, the complexity increases both with the row weight as well as with the dimensionality of the Galois field. For classical non-binary LDPC codes, this increased complexity is alleviated by invoking the Fast Fourier Transform (FFT) based decoding of [365], which can be conveniently adapted to the syndrome-based decoding of QLDPC codes.

Based on the notion of the trace inner product of Eq. (10.41), Eq. (14.16) can be expanded as:

$$S_i = \mathrm{Tr}(\hat{S}_i) = \mathrm{Tr}\left(\sum_{t \in V(c_i)} \hat{H}_{it} \times \overline{\hat{P}}_t\right), \tag{14.17}$$

where we have $\hat{S}_i \in \{0, 1, \omega, \overline{\omega}\}$, which can also be expressed as:

$$\hat{S}_i = \hat{H}_{it} \times \overline{\hat{P}}_t + \sum_{t' \in V(c_i) \setminus v_t} \hat{H}_{it'} \times \overline{\hat{P}}_{t'}. \tag{14.18}$$

Unlike in the binary scenario, where we have $H_{it} \in \{0,1\}$, here we have $\hat{H}_{it} \in \{1, \omega, \overline{\omega}\}$ in Eq. (14.18). Therefore, given the messages $m^{\hat{a}}_{c_i \to v_t}$ and $m^{\hat{a}}_{v_t \to c_i}$ exchanged between the check node $c_i$ and the variable node $v_t$ for $\hat{P} = \hat{a}$, we denote the equivalent messages for $(\hat{H}_{it} \times \overline{\hat{P}}_t)$ as $\check{m}^{\hat{a}_s}_{c_i \to v_t}$ and $\check{m}^{\hat{a}_s}_{v_t \to c_i}$, respectively, where we have $(\hat{H}_{it} \times \overline{\hat{a}}) = \hat{a}_s$. Based on this notation, we may infer from Eqs. (14.17) and (14.18) that the Probability Density Function (PDF) of the horizontal message $\check{m}^{\hat{a}_s}_{c_i \to v_t}$ can be obtained by convolving the PDFs of the messages $\check{m}^{\hat{a}_s + \hat{S}_i}_{v_{t'} \to c_i}$ for $v_{t'} \in V(c_i) \setminus v_t$.

We may further notice in Eq. (14.17) that for a given $S_i$, $\hat{S}_i$ can have two possible values. More explicitly, for GF(4), we have $\mathrm{Tr}(0) = \mathrm{Tr}(1) = 0$, while $\mathrm{Tr}(\omega) = \mathrm{Tr}(\overline{\omega}) = 1$. Consequently, for $S_i = \mathrm{Tr}(\hat{S}_i = 0) = \mathrm{Tr}(\hat{S}_i = 1) = 0$, we have:

$$\begin{aligned} PDF\{\check{m}^{0}_{c_i \to v_t}\} &= PDF\{\check{m}^{1}_{c_i \to v_t}\} \\ &= \frac{1}{2}\left(\bigotimes_{v_{t'}} PDF\{\check{m}^{0}_{v_{t'} \to c_i}\} + \bigotimes_{v_{t'}} PDF\{\check{m}^{1}_{v_{t'} \to c_i}\}\right), \\ PDF\{\check{m}^{\omega}_{c_i \to v_t}\} &= PDF\{\check{m}^{\overline{\omega}}_{c_i \to v_t}\} \\ &= \frac{1}{2}\left(\bigotimes_{v_{t'}} PDF\{\check{m}^{\omega}_{v_{t'} \to c_i}\} + \bigotimes_{v_{t'}} PDF\{\check{m}^{\overline{\omega}}_{v_{t'} \to c_i}\}\right), \end{aligned} \tag{14.19}$$

where $\otimes$ represents the convolution process and $v_{t'} \in V(c_i) \setminus v_t$. Similarly, for $S_i = \mathrm{Tr}(\hat{S}_i = \omega) = \mathrm{Tr}(\hat{S}_i = \overline{\omega}) = 1$, we have:

$$\begin{aligned} PDF\{\check{m}^{0}_{c_i \to v_t}\} &= PDF\{\check{m}^{1}_{c_i \to v_t}\} \\ &= \frac{1}{2}\left(\bigotimes_{v_{t'}} PDF\{\check{m}^{\omega}_{v_{t'} \to c_i}\} + \bigotimes_{v_{t'}} PDF\{\check{m}^{\overline{\omega}}_{v_{t'} \to c_i}\}\right), \\ PDF\{\check{m}^{\omega}_{c_i \to v_t}\} &= PDF\{\check{m}^{\overline{\omega}}_{c_i \to v_t}\} \\ &= \frac{1}{2}\left(\bigotimes_{v_{t'}} PDF\{\check{m}^{0}_{v_{t'} \to c_i}\} + \bigotimes_{v_{t'}} PDF\{\check{m}^{1}_{v_{t'} \to c_i}\}\right). \end{aligned} \tag{14.20}$$

The complex convolution operation required in Eqs. (14.19) and (14.20) can be efficiently implemented by multiplying the corresponding PDFs in the frequency domain with the aid of the FFT-based algorithm of [365].

### 14.3.3 Decoding Issues and Heuristic Methods for Improvement

Belief propagation invoked for decoding LDPC codes gives the exact solution only when the underlying Tanner graph is a tree. Nonetheless, it yields reasonably good approximations even in the presence of cycles, provided that the girth of the associated LDPC matrix is sufficiently large, at least 6. This has been proven by the capacity approaching classical LDPC codes, for example in [342, 343]. Unfortunately, short cycles of length 4 are unavoidable in the construction of QLDPC codes, which in turn impair the iterative decoding procedure.

The unavoidable cycles of length 4 found in QLDPC codes are the result of the commutativity property of the stabilizers. More explicitly, the constituent stabilizer generators of a stabilizer code must commute, i.e. they should have even number of places with different non-identity Pauli operators. In other words, if an anti-commuting pair of Pauli operators acts on the $t$th variable node in a pair of stabilizer generators, then there should be another anti-commuting pair of Pauli operators acting on the $t'$th variable node in the same pair of generators for the sake of ensuring that the generators commute with each other. For example, the generators:

$$\begin{aligned} g_0 &= \mathbf{XIYZ}, \\ g_1 &= \mathbf{ZYXI}, \end{aligned} \tag{14.21}$$

commute[7] because there are two pairs of anti-commuting Pauli operators acting on the first and third qubits, respectively. This in turn implies that the corresponding rows in the resultant PCM have even number of overlaps, which give rise to short cycles in the Tanner graph, as illustrated in Figure 14.8. Since here the key point is to have "different non-identity operators," a possible option could be to assign only a single type of non-identity operator to each variable node of the Tanner graph. If we only assign Pauli-**X** to the variable node $v_t$ so that it does not anti-commute in any pair of generators, then we will be unable to detect both Pauli-**X** as well as Pauli-**Y** errors acting on $v_t$. This would yield an undesirable code, which has a minimum distance of one. We may conclude that:

a. each column of a QLDPC matrix must have at least two different non-identity Pauli operators, and
b. every pair of rows must an have even number of places with different non-identity Pauli operators.

7 This is just a random example to illustrate the concept of commutativity and the resulting short cycles. The generators $g_0$ and $g_1$ of this example may not constitute a good stabilizer code.

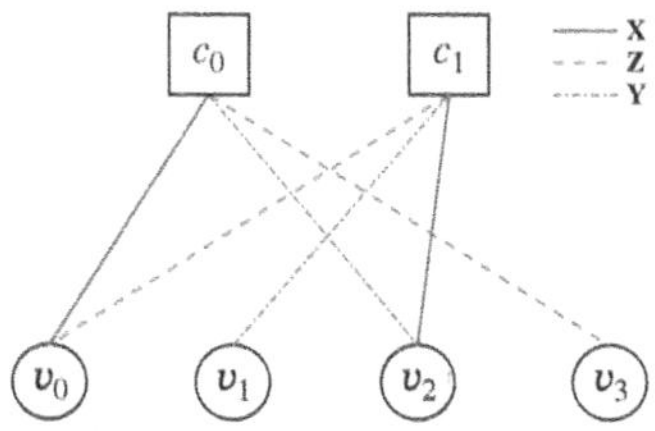


**Figure 14.8** Tanner graph of a commuting pair of stabilizer generators, where $c_0$ and $c_1$ are the check nodes for the generators $g_0 = \mathbf{XIYZ}$ and $g_1 = \mathbf{ZYXI}$, respectively. The edges connected to the variable nodes $v_0$ and $v_2$ constitute a cycle of length 4.

Consequently, all CSS as well as non-CSS QLDPC constructions have a Tanner graph of girth-4. It is interesting to observe here that these short cycles may be avoided in the corresponding binary formalism. Let us consider the example given in Eq. (14.21), which can be expressed in the binary form as follows:

$$\begin{aligned} g_0 &\rightarrow \left(1\,0\,1\;\;0 \,\middle|\, 0\;\;0\;\;1\;\;1\right), \\ g_1 &\rightarrow \left(0\,1\,1\;\;0 \,\middle|\, 1\;\;1\;\;0\;\;0\right). \end{aligned} \tag{14.22}$$

Since these binary generators only have a single overlapping 1, the length 4 cycle no longer exits. However, let us recall from Section 14.3.2 that binary decoding ignores the correlation between the **X** and **Z** errors, which degrades the performance. Hence, a compromise must be struck between these two conflicting aspects.

The issue of short cycles is more pronounced in both the dual-containing QLDPC codes as well as in the EA CSS QLDPC codes having $H'_x = H'_z$. We may call them homogeneous CSS codes, since identical PCMs are used for correcting bit-flips and phase-flips. Let the resultant $m \times n$ PCM in GF(4) be $\hat{H}$ as follows:

$$\hat{H} = \begin{pmatrix} \omega H'_z \\ H'_z \end{pmatrix}. \tag{14.23}$$

Consequently, the $i$th and $(i + m/2)$th rows completely overlap, resulting in numerous cycles of length 4. Furthermore, the dual-containing code construction also has the additional short cycles within the matrix $H'_z$, as discussed in Section 14.2.1, which exist even in the binary formalism. Table 14.1 summarizes the presence of unavoidable short cycles in various code structures, while Figure 14.9 captures the merits and demerits of GF(4) decoding as compared to its binary counterpart.

Degeneracy is another unique aspect, which distinguishes a quantum code from a classical one. Let us recall from Section 10.3.3 that errors, which differ only by the stabilizer group, have the same impact on the transmitted codewords and can therefore be corrected by the same recovery operation. This in turn improves the performance of quantum codes. Unfortunately, the iterative decoding invoked for QLDPC codes does not take into account this degeneracy. More explicitly, rather than finding the most likely error, as in Eq. (14.9), the decoding algorithm should find the most likely error coset by summing the probabilities of all degenerate errors [72, 139]. Furthermore, QLDPC codes are highly degenerate as compared to the other families of quantum codes. This is because the generators of a QLDPC code are sparse in nature. Consequently, it has many low-weight degenerate errors, which dominate the probability of the error coset. It is therefore more likely that the most probable error $\tilde{P}$ of Eq. (14.9) may not coincide with the most probable error coset for QLDPC codes. However, rather than exploiting the benefits of high degeneracy associated with sparse codes, the marginalized iterative decoding invoked for QLDPC codes is impaired by degeneracy [72, 139]. This is because degenerate errors of equal weight have the same marginalized probability distribution, which can be attributed to the symmetry of the probability distribution of the channel depicted in Eq. (14.15).

Let us review the case study given in [139]. Consider a 2-qubit stabilizer code having the generators **XX** and **ZZ**. Assume furthermore that **IX** is the channel error encountered during transmission over a depolarizing channel, whose PDF is given in Eq. (14.15). The resultant syndrome is $S = (0\ 1)$ and the corresponding set of degenerate

**Table 14.1** Unavoidable short cycles in various code structures (✓= present, ✗ = absent, ✓= numerous cycles present).

| Code Type | Unavoidable short cycles | |
|---|---|---|
| | **Binary formalism** | **GF(4) formalism** |
| Dual-containing CSS (Homogeneous) | ✓ | ✓ |
| Non-dual-containing CSS | ✗ | ✓ |
| Non-CSS | ✗ | ✓ |
| Homogeneous CSS EA | ✗ | ✓ |
| All other EA | ✗ | ✗ |

*Source:* [316]/IEEE.

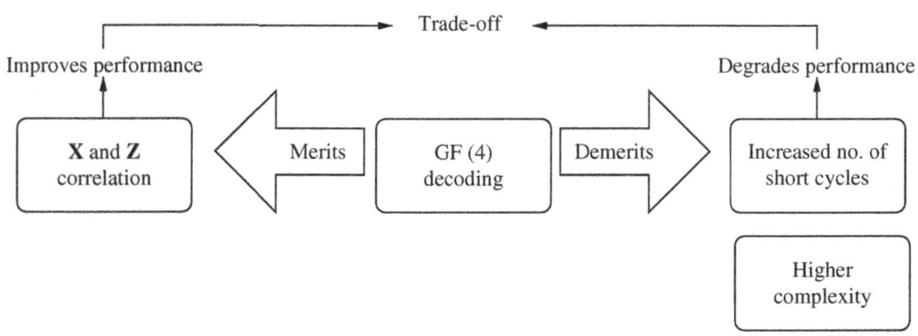


**Figure 14.9** Merits and demerits of GF(4) decoding as compared to binary decoding. *Source:* [80]/IEEE.

errors is $\{\mathbf{XI}, \mathbf{IX}, \mathbf{YZ}, \mathbf{ZY}\}$. Consequently, the marginalized conditional probability of the error on each of the two qubits is given by:

$$\mathrm{P}\left(\hat{P}_t = \hat{a}|S\right) = \begin{cases} 1-p, & \text{if } \hat{a}=0 \\ p/3, & \text{if } \hat{a} \in \{1, \omega, \overline{\omega}\}, \end{cases} \tag{14.24}$$

where $t = \{0, 1\}$. Hence, the marginalized probability is identical for both the qubits. This symmetry forces the decoder to detect the same error on both the qubits. However, none of the associated errors, i.e. $\{\mathbf{XI}, \mathbf{IX}, \mathbf{YZ}, \mathbf{ZY}\}$, exhibit this symmetry, hence leading to the "symmetric degeneracy error" concept of [139]. Moreover, since the channel profile of Eq. (14.15) is biased toward the Identity operator, the probability of "no-error" dominates at low noise levels.

Poulin and Chung investigated various heuristic methods in [139] to break the symmetry exhibited by the marginalized probabilities of Eq. (14.24). Among the investigated methods, "random perturbation" provides the best performance. It aims for breaking the degenerate symmetry by randomly perturbing the channel PDF of Eq. (14.15) for the qubits involved in the frustrated checks,[8] thus putting an end to the decoding impasse. Random perturbation begins with the standard nonbinary BP, which gives the estimated channel error $\tilde{\hat{P}}$. If the syndrome computed for $\tilde{\hat{P}}$ is not the same as the observed channel syndrome $S$, the channel probabilities of all variable nodes $v_t$ connected to a randomly chosen frustrated check $c_i$ are perturbed (up to a normalization) as follows:

$$\begin{aligned} \mathbf{P}_{\text{ch}}(\hat{P}_t = 0) &\rightarrow \mathbf{P}_{\text{ch}}(\hat{P}_t = 0), \\ \mathbf{P}_{\text{ch}}(\hat{P}_t = 1) &\rightarrow (1+\delta_1)\mathbf{P}_{\text{ch}}(\hat{P}_t = 1), \\ \mathbf{P}_{\text{ch}}(\hat{P}_t = \omega) &\rightarrow (1+\delta_\omega)\mathbf{P}_{\text{ch}}(\hat{P}_t = \omega), \\ \mathbf{P}_{\text{ch}}(\hat{P}_t = \overline{\omega}) &\rightarrow (1+\delta_{\overline{\omega}})\mathbf{P}_{\text{ch}}(\hat{P}_t = \overline{\omega}), \end{aligned} \tag{14.25}$$

8 Check nodes for which the computed syndrome does not match the observed syndrome are known as frustrated checks [139].

where $\delta_1$, $\delta_\omega$, and $\delta_{\overline{\omega}}$ are random variables in the range $[0, \delta]$. Non-binary BP is re-run with these modified channel probabilities for $T_{\text{pert}}$ iterations and $\tilde{P}$ is estimated again. If all the check nodes are satisfied now, the process terminates. Otherwise, the channel probabilities perturbed in Eq. (14.25) are restored and the process is repeated with another randomly chosen frustrated check.

Another heuristic method of alleviating the symmetric degeneracy problem was conceived in [140], which exploits an enhanced feedback procedure. More specifically, Wang *et al.* [140] proposed an "enhanced feedback" strategy for perturbing the channel probabilities similar to the random perturbation, but this perturbation is based both on the stabilizer generators involved in the frustrated checks as well as on the channel model. Similar to the random perturbation method, the enhanced feedback algorithm randomly selects a frustrated check $c_i$. It also selects a variable node $v_t$ connected to $c_i$. Let $\tilde{S}_i$ be the value of the $i$th check node for the estimated error $\tilde{P}$, while $S_i$ be the $i$th observed channel syndrome. The channel probability for $v_t$ is then perturbed as follows:

- If $\tilde{S}_i = 0$ and $S_i = 1$, then:

$$\mathbf{P}_{\text{ch}}\left(\hat{P}_t = \hat{a}\right) = \begin{cases} p/2, & \text{if } \hat{a} = 0 \text{ or } \hat{H}_{it}, \\ (1-p)/2, & \text{otherwise.} \end{cases} \tag{14.26}$$

- If $\tilde{S}_i = 1$ and $S_i = 0$, then:

$$\mathbf{P}_{\text{ch}}\left(\hat{P}_t = \hat{a}\right) = \begin{cases} (1-p)/2, & \text{if } \hat{a} = 0 \text{ or } \hat{H}_{it}, \\ p/2, & \text{otherwise.} \end{cases} \tag{14.27}$$

The perturbed values are fed to the standard non-binary BP decoder, which provides a new estimate of the channel error. The perturbation process is repeated, until all the checks are satisfied or the maximum number of feedbacks $n_a$ is reached. Since these perturbations are more reliable than random perturbations, this method outperforms the random perturbation based heuristic method of [67].

## 14.4 High-rate QLDPC Codes from Row-circulant Classical LDPCs

Classical row-circulant QC-LDPC matrices are known to generate efficient short and moderate length high-rate QC-LDPC codes, which outperform the corresponding randomly constructed codes. More specifically, short and moderate length random (unstructured) LDPC matrices with a high coding rate have numerous cycles of length 4, which may be avoided in the structured configurations. The BIBD and cyclic difference family (CDF) based code structures of [350, 351, 366–368] are particularly significant in this respect, which have at least a girth of 6.

Let us have a look at the BIBD constructions proposed by Bose [369], which constitute the row-circulant classical QC-LDPCs. Recall that a BIBD, having the parameters $(v, b, r, k, \lambda)$, divides all the $v$ elements of a set $V$ into $b$ blocks of size $k$ such that, each pair of elements occurs in exactly $\lambda$ of the blocks, every element occurs in exactly $r$ blocks, and the number of elements in each block $k$ is small as compared to the size $v$ of set $V$. These parameters are summarized in Table 14.2. Based on this notation, Bose proposed the following BIBD [369] constructions, which are suitable for the row-circulant QC-LDPCs [351, 370].

**Table 14.2** BIBD parameters.

| Variable | Description |
|---|---|
| $V$ | Finite set |
| $v$ | Number of elements of $V$ |
| $b$ | Number of blocks |
| $r$ | Number of blocks containing a given element |
| $k$ | Number of elements of a block |
| $\lambda$ | Number of blocks containing a given pair of elements |

a. **Type-I Bose BIBDs:** Given that t is a positive integer such that (12t + 1) is a power of a prime, then there exists a prime Galois field GF(12t + 1) having elements from 0 to 12t. The elements of GF(12t + 1) constitute the finite set $V$ of the BIBD. Furthermore, let $\alpha$ be the primitive element of GF(12t + 1), which satisfies the following condition:

$$\alpha^{4t} - 1 = \alpha^{c}, \tag{14.28}$$

where c is an integer in the range $0 < c < 12t + 1$. The legitimate values of t along with the corresponding primitive elements are listed in Table 14.3 [370, p. 526]. For these values of t and $\alpha$, Bose [369] proposed that there exists a BIBD having the parameters $v = (12t + 1)$, $b = t(12t + 1)$, $r = 4t$, $k = 4$ and $\lambda = 1$, whose t base blocks are given by:

$$B_i = \{0, \alpha^{2i}, \alpha^{2i+4t}, \alpha^{2i+8t}\}, \tag{14.29}$$

for $0 \leq i < t$. We can further create (12t + 1) blocks for block $B_i$ by adding each element of the Galois field to each element of the base block, hence resulting in a total of t(12t + 1) blocks. The incidence matrix of this BIBD is a $(12t + 1) \times t(12t + 1)$ matrix, which is formed by t submatrices as follows:

$$H_{\text{BIBD}} = (H_0, H_1, \ldots, H_{t-1}), \tag{14.30}$$

where the $i$th submatrix $H_i$ is a $(12t + 1) \times (12t + 1)$ circulant matrix. More specifically, $H_i$ is the incidence matrix corresponding to the $i$th base block constructed by adding each element of the GF(12t + 1) to the elements of the $i$th base block. Furthermore, the row weight and column weight of each submatrix is 4. Therefore, the matrix $H_{\text{BIBD}}$ has a row weight of 4t and a column weight of 4. Since the incidence matrix of Eq. (14.30) has the required properties of a QC-LDPC matrix, a subarray of $H_{\text{BIBD}}$ can be used for constructing a classical QC-LDPC code. For $0 < m < t$, the PCM of the resulting code is given by [351]:

$$H = (H_0, H_1, \ldots, H_{m-1}), \tag{14.31}$$

which is a $(12t + 1) \times m(12t + 1)$ QC matrix having a row weight of $4m$ and a column weight of 4. The minimum distance of the resulting LDPC code is at least 5 and the coding rate is approximately $(m - 1)/m$ [351].

**Table 14.3** Legitimate values of t for GF(12t + 1) along with the corresponding primitive elements satisfying Eq. (14.28).

| t | GF($q$) | ($\alpha$, c) |
|---|---|---|
| 1 | GF(13) | (2, 1) |
| 6 | GF(73) | (5, 33) |
| 8 | GF(97) | (5, 27) |
| 9 | GF(109) | (6, 71) |
| 15 | GF(181) | (2, 13) |
| 19 | GF(229) | (6, 199) |
| 20 | GF(241) | (7, 191) |
| 23 | GF(277) | (5, 209) |
| 28 | GF(337) | (10, 129) |
| 34 | GF(409) | (21, 9) |
| 35 | GF(421) | (2, 167) |
| 38 | GF(457) | (13, 387) |
| 45 | GF(541) | (2, 7) |
| 59 | GF(709) | (2, 381) |
| 61 | GF(733) | (6, 145) |

*Source:* [424]/Cambridge University Press.

**b. Type-II Bose BIBDs:** Let $\mathtt{t}$ be a positive integer such that $(20\mathtt{t}+1)$ is a power of a prime, then there exists a prime Galois field GF$(20\mathtt{t}+1)$ having elements from 0 to $20\mathtt{t}$. Analogous to the type-I design, the elements of GF$(20\mathtt{t}+1)$ constitute the finite set $V$ of the BIBD. However, in contrast to Eq. (14.28), the primitive element $\alpha$ of GF$(20\mathtt{t}+1)$ has to satisfy the condition:

$$\alpha^{4\mathtt{t}}+1=\alpha^{\mathtt{c}}, \tag{14.32}$$

where $\mathtt{c}$ is an integer in the range $0<\mathtt{c}<20\mathtt{t}+1$. The legitimate values of $\mathtt{t}$ along with the corresponding primitive elements are listed in Table 14.4 [424, p. 532]. For these values of $\mathtt{t}$ and $\alpha$, Bose [423] proposed that we can construct a BIBD having the parameters $v=(20\mathtt{t}+1)$, $b=\mathtt{t}(20\mathtt{t}+1)$, $r=5\mathtt{t}$, $k=5$ and $\lambda=1$, whose $\mathtt{t}$ base blocks are given by:

$$B_i=\{\alpha^{2i},\alpha^{2i+4\mathtt{t}},\alpha^{2i+8\mathtt{t}},\alpha^{2i+12\mathtt{t}},\alpha^{2i+16\mathtt{t}}\}, \tag{14.33}$$

for $0\leq i<\mathtt{t}$. Similar to the type-I design, $(12\mathtt{t}+1)$ blocks can be constructed for each base block $B_i$ by adding each element of the Galois field to each element of the base block. Hence, there is a total of $\mathtt{t}(20\mathtt{t}+1)$ blocks. The incidence matrix of the resulting BIBD is a $(20\mathtt{t}+1)\times\mathtt{t}(20\mathtt{t}+1)$ matrix, which is formed by $\mathtt{t}$ submatrices as previously shown in Eq. (14.30). For the type-II design, the row weight and column weight of each submatrix $H_i$ is 5. Therefore, the matrix $H_{\text{BIBD}}$ has a row weight of $5\mathtt{t}$ and a column weight of 5. Again, according to Eq. (14.31), we can construct a QC-LDPC of size $(20\mathtt{t}+1)\times m(20\mathtt{t}+1)$, which has a row weight of $5m$ and a column weight of 5 [351].

In [130], Djordjevic proposed that BIBDs having an odd row weight and $\lambda=1$ can be transformed into a dual-containing QLDPC code by appending an all-ones column to the original PCM, while in [358] Djordjevic conceived the EA BIBD-based QLDPC codes, which required a single e-bit.

In contrast to these developments, we conceive a radically new class of codes for constructing unassisted non-dual-containing CSS QLDPC codes from arbitrary row-circulant classical QC-LDPC matrices. This construction brings with it the following obvious benefits:

- Pre-shared ebits are not required.
- Since the constructed codes are non-dual-containing, they do not suffer from the excessive short cycles, which are a characteristic of the dual-containing designs as well as the homogeneous CSS EA codes (Table 14.1).

Particularly, we apply our proposed construction to the family of BIBD-based classical codes for evaluating the resulting performance.

**Table 14.4** Legitimate values of $\mathtt{t}$ for $(20\mathtt{t}+1)$ along with the corresponding primitive elements satisfying Eq. (14.32).

| $\mathtt{t}$ | GF($q$) | $(\alpha, \mathtt{c})$ |
|---|---|---|
| 2 | GF(41) | (6, 3) |
| 3 | GF(61) | (2, 23) |
| 12 | GF(241) | (7, 197) |
| 14 | GF(281) | (3, 173) |
| 21 | GF(421) | (2, 227) |
| 30 | GF(601) | (7, 79) |
| 32 | GF(641) | (3, 631) |
| 33 | GF(661) | (2, 657) |
| 35 | GF(701) | (2, 533) |
| 41 | GF(821) | (2, 713) |

*Source*: [424]/Cambridge University Press.

Let us consider the row-circulant QC-LDPC matrix of Eq. (14.31), assuming that it consists of an even number of square circulant submatrices. Inspired by the QC-QLDPC codes of [133, 353], we propose that if we formulate $H'_z$ and $H'_x$ as follows:

$$H'_z = H,$$
$$H'_x = \left(H^T_{\frac{m}{2}}, H^T_{\frac{m}{2}+1}, \ldots, H^T_{m-1}, H^T_0, H^T_1, \ldots, H^T_{\frac{m}{2}-1}\right), \tag{14.34}$$

where when $m$ is even, the resulting CSS code satisfies the symplectic criterion $H'_z H'^T_x = 0$. This may be readily proved as shown here:

$$H'_z H'^T_x = \left(H_0, H_1, \ldots, H_{\frac{m}{2}-1}, H_{\frac{m}{2}}, H_{\frac{m}{2}+1}, \ldots, H_{m-1}\right)\begin{pmatrix} H_{\frac{m}{2}} \\ H_{\frac{m}{2}+1} \\ \vdots \\ H_{m-1} \\ H_0 \\ H_1 \\ \vdots \\ H_{\frac{m}{2}-1} \end{pmatrix} \tag{14.35}$$
$$= H_0 H_{\frac{m}{2}} + H_1 H_{\frac{m}{2}+1} + \cdots + H_{\frac{m}{2}-1} H_{m-1}$$
$$+ H_{\frac{m}{2}} H_0 + H_{\frac{m}{2}+1} H_1 + \cdots + H_{m-1} H_{\frac{m}{2}-1}\,.$$

Since the multiplication of circulant matrices is commutative, the two parts of Eq. (14.35), i.e. $(H_0 H_{\frac{m}{2}} + H_1 H_{\frac{m}{2}+1} + \cdots + H_{\frac{m}{2}} H_m)$ and $(H_{\frac{m}{2}} H_0 + H_{\frac{m}{2}+1} H_1 + \cdots + H_{m-1} H_{\frac{m}{2}-1})$ are equal. Hence, the modulo 2 addition of Eq. (14.35) yields 0; thus, satisfying the symplectic criterion. Furthermore, the resulting quantum coding rate is $(m-2)/2$. We may also notice here that our proposed code structure may be viewed as a special case of Eq. (14.7) for $m=2$, given further that $T_1$ and $T_2$ of Eq. (14.7) are binary circulant matrices, i.e. $t_i \in \{0, 1\}$ in Eq. (14.6).

Let us now have a look at the girth of the resulting QC-QLDPC code. The constituent $l \times l$ circulant submatrix $H_i$ of Eq. (14.31), which has a row weight and a column weight of $\gamma$, is completely characterized by the polynomial $h_i(x) = x^{d_{i,0}} + x^{d_{i,1}} + \cdots + x^{d_{i,\gamma-1}}$, where $d_{i,j}$ denotes the column index of the $j$th nonzero entry in the first row of $H_i$. For example, if the first row of $H_i$ has a 1 at index 0, 5, and 8, then the polynomial is given by $1 + x^5 + x^8$. The PCM $H$ has a girth of at least 6 if every difference $(d_{i,j_1} - d_{i,j_2})$ modulo $l$, for $0 \leq i \leq (m-1)$ and $0 \leq j_1, j_2 \leq (\gamma - 1)$ is a unique integer between 0 and $(l-1)$. Furthermore, the polynomial transpose is defined as $h_i(x)^T = x^{l-d_{i,1}} + x^{l-d_{i,2}} + \cdots + x^{l-d_{i,\gamma-1}}$, which would yield the same differences as $h_i(x)$. Hence, since in Eq. (14.34) we are taking the transpose of all the sub-matrices $H_i$ and just permuting their location, the differences $(d_{i,j_1} - d_{i,j_2})$ for $H'_z$ and $H'_x$ are the same and both have the same girth.

## 14.5 Results and Discussions I

To evaluate the performance of our proposed design, we considered BIBD$(12\mathtt{t}+1, \mathtt{t}(12\mathtt{t}+1), 4\mathtt{t}, 4, 1)$. We further arbitrarily chose $\mathtt{t} = 15$ from Table 14.3, whose primitive root is $\alpha = 2$. Consequently, the resulting $\mathtt{t}$ base blocks are give by:

$$B_i = \{0, 2^{2i}, 2^{2i+4\mathtt{t}}, 2^{2i+8\mathtt{t}}\}, \tag{14.36}$$

for $0 \leq i < \mathtt{t}$. Since our design requires $m$ to be even, we chose $m = 14$, which would yield a [2534, 2172] QLDPC code having a coding rate of 0.857. Furthermore, the row weight of the resulting QLDPC code is 56, while its

**Table 14.5** Simulation parameters.

| **BIBD parameters** | |
|---|---|
| Galois field | GF(12t + 1) |
| t | 15 |
| $\alpha$ | 2 |
| $B_i$ | $\{0, 2^{2i}, 2^{2i+4t}, 2^{2i+8t}\}$ |
| $m$ | 14 |
| **LDPC parameters** | |
| Coded qubits | $n = 2534$ |
| Information qubits | $k = 2172$ |
| E-bits | $c = 0$ |
| Row weight | 56 |
| Column weight | 4 |
| **QLDPC decoder** | |
| Standard decoding iterations | $I_{max} = 100$ |

column weight is 4. These parameters are summarized in Table 14.5. We further compare our design with an equivalent bicycle QLDPC code, whose PCM is given by:

$$H'_x = H'_z = [H_0, H_1, \ldots, H_{\frac{m}{2}-1}, H_0^T, H_1^T, \ldots, H_{\frac{m}{2}-1}^T], \tag{14.37}$$

and a comparable EA-QLDPC, which requires a single e-bit and has:

$$H'_x = H'_z = [H_0, H_1, \ldots, H_{m-1}]. \tag{14.38}$$

Figure 14.10 compares the performance of our designed QLDPC code (labeled "Proposed"), the bicycle code of Eq. (14.37) (labeled "BiC") and the EA-QLDPC code of Eq. (14.38) (labeled "EA") for both the binary as well as the non-binary decoding. We invoked a maximum of 100 iterations. Each decoding algorithm iterates until either a valid error is found or the maximum number of iterations is reached. Furthermore, the WER metric here counts the detected as well as the undetected block errors. We may observe in Figure 14.10 that the performance of our designed QLDPC is exactly the same as that of the EA-QLDPC code for binary decoding, while that of the bicycle QLDPC code is slightly worse, which is due to the presence of length-4 cycles. By contrast, when non-binary decoding is invoked, then the performance of our proposed design improves significantly as compared to both the bicycle code as well as the EA-QLDPC. More specifically, the bicycle code achieves a WER of $10^{-4}$ at $p = 0.00055$, which increases to $p = 0.0007$ when EA-QLDPC is used. By contrast, our construction exhibits a WER of $10^{-4}$ at $p = 0.00215$, which is almost a three times increase as compared to EA-QLDPC. As mentioned in Section 14.4, unlike the bicycle codes and EA-QLDPC, which have numerous short cycles in the GF(4) formalism, our design has only a few short cycles in the GF(4) formalism. Consequently, it outperforms the comparable bicycle and EA counterparts. It is also pertinent to notice in Figure 14.10 that the performance of the non-binary decoder is not always better than that of the binary decoder. As previously discussed in Figure 14.9, a non-binary decoder tends to improve the performance because it takes into account the correlation between the bit and phase errors. However, the GF(4) formalism increases the number of short cycles, which degrades the performance. Due to these conflicting attributes, a non-binary decoder may not always outperform its binary counterpart, as observed Figure 14.10 in the low-noise regime.

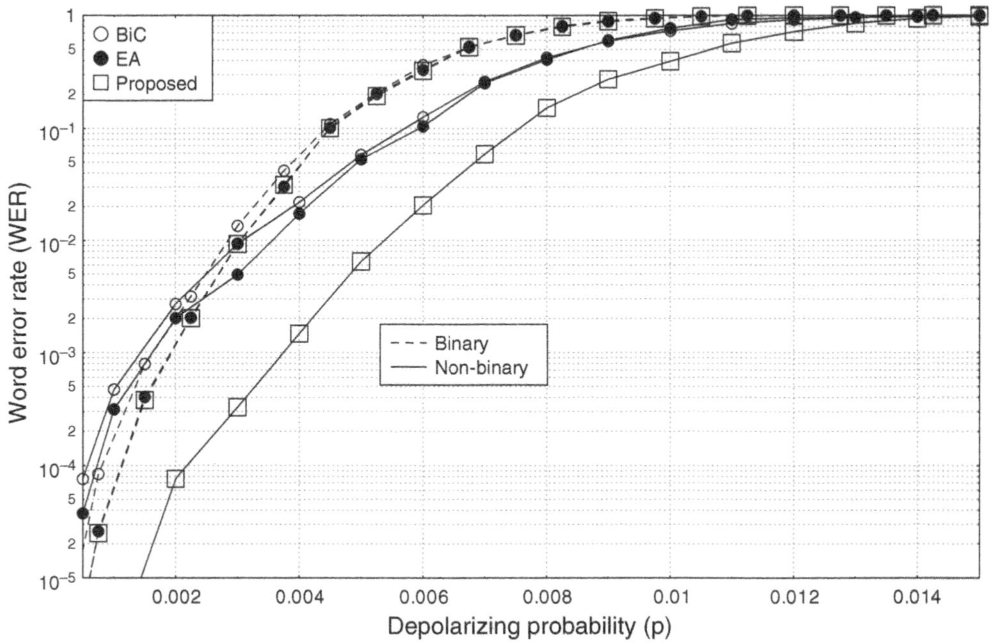


**Figure 14.10** Comparison of the achievable WER performance of our proposed [2534, 2172] QLDPC code (labeled "Proposed") with the bicycle code of Eq. (14.37) (labeled "BiC") and the EA-QLDPC code of Eq. (14.38) (labeled "EA"), using the simulation parameters of Table 14.5. *Source*: [346]/IEEE.

## 14.6 Modified Non-binary Decoding

Let us recall from Section 14.3.3 that homogeneous CSS-type QLDPC codes, which include both the dual-containing construction as well as the EA-QLDPC codes, have an excessive number of short cycles. The $i$th and $(i+m/2)$th rows of the associated PCM $\hat{H}$ are related by a multiple of $\omega$, i.e. we have $\hat{H}_i = \omega\hat{H}_{i+m/2}$, as seen in Eq. (14.23). For example, consider the 7-qubit Steane code [55], which is derived from the (7, 4) Hamming code. The PCM of a classical (7, 4) Hamming code is given by:

$$H_z' = \begin{pmatrix} 1 & 0 & 0 & 1 & 0 & 1 & 1 \\ 0 & 1 & 0 & 1 & 1 & 0 & 1 \\ 0 & 0 & 1 & 0 & 1 & 1 & 1 \end{pmatrix}. \tag{14.39}$$

Consequently, according to Eq. (14.23), the corresponding PCM of the 7-qubit Steane code is:

$$\hat{H} = \begin{pmatrix} \omega & 0 & 0 & \omega & 0 & \omega & \omega \\ 0 & \omega & 0 & \omega & \omega & 0 & \omega \\ 0 & 0 & \omega & 0 & \omega & \omega & \omega \\ 1 & 0 & 0 & 1 & 0 & 1 & 1 \\ 0 & 1 & 0 & 1 & 1 & 0 & 1 \\ 0 & 0 & 1 & 0 & 1 & 1 & 1 \end{pmatrix}, \tag{14.40}$$

whose Tanner graph is plotted in Figure 14.11. As gleaned from Figure 14.11, cycles of length 4 exist between all the variable nodes connected to the checks $c_i$ and $c_{i+3}$. The dual-containing nature of Steane code also results in some additional short cycles. However, here we focus our attention only on the cycles resulting from the homogeneous

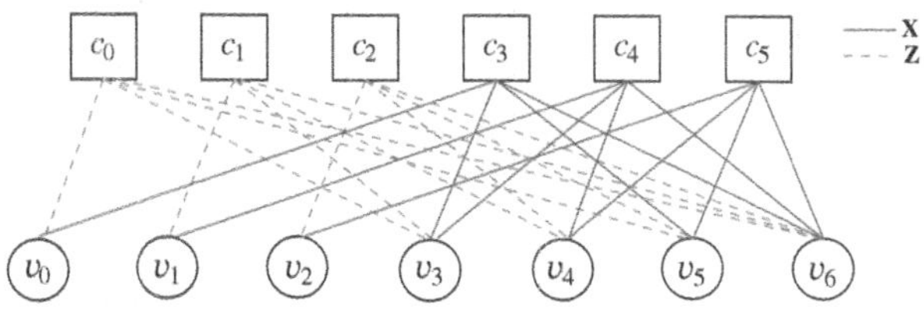


**Figure 14.11** Tanner graph of the 7-qubit Steane code.

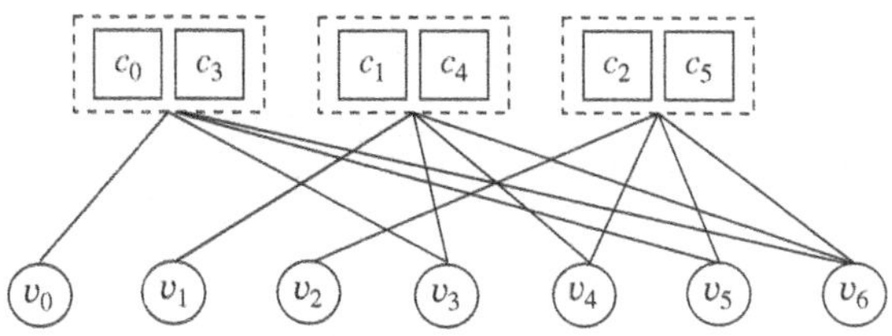


**Figure 14.12** Modified Tanner graph of 7-qubit Steane code. Check nodes $c_i$ and $c_{i+m/2}$ are combined to form a supernode.

**Table 14.6** List of all possible values of $\hat{S}_i$ and the corresponding values of $\hat{S}_{i+m/2}$ and the binary syndromes $S_i = \text{Tr}(\hat{S}_i)$ and $S_{i+m/2} = \text{Tr}(\hat{S}_{i+m/2})$.

| $\hat{S}_i$ | $\hat{S}_{i+m/2}$ | $S_i$ | $S_{i+m/2}$ |
|---|---|---|---|
| 0 | 0 | 0 | 0 |
| 1 | $\overline{\omega}$ | 0 | 1 |
| $\omega$ | 1 | 1 | 0 |
| $\overline{\omega}$ | $\omega$ | 1 | 1 |

CSS structure. To alleviate the impact of these short cycles, we propose a modified Tanner graph, which amalgamates the check nodes $c_i$ and $c_{i+m/2}$ into a supernode, thereby eliminating the cycles. The resultant modified Tanner graph is given in Figure 14.12. Based on the modified Tanner graph of Figure 14.12, the horizontal messages exchanged between the supernodes $(c_i, c_{i+m/2})$ and the variable nodes $v_t$ aim for satisfying both the checks $c_i$ and $c_{i+m/2}$ simultaneously. Therefore, we have to modify Eqs. (14.19) and (14.20) of the non-binary BP accordingly.

Since we have $\hat{H}_i = \omega\hat{H}_{i+m/2}$, the non-binary syndromes $\hat{S}_i$ and $\hat{S}_{i+m/2}$ are also related similarly, i.e. we have $\hat{S}_i = \omega\hat{S}_{i+m/2}$. Based on this relation, Table 14.6 enlists the possible values of $\hat{S}_{i+m/2}$ for all the possible values of $\hat{S}_i$ along with the corresponding binary syndromes $S_i = \text{Tr}(\hat{S}_i)$ and $S_{i+m/2} = \text{Tr}(\hat{S}_{i+m/2})$. As gleaned from Table 14.6, for each value of $S_i$ (or $S_{i+m/2}$), there are two possible values of $\hat{S}_i$ (or $\hat{S}_{i+m/2}$). Recall from Section 14.3.2 that this is because $\text{Tr}(0) = \text{Tr}(1) = 0$, while $\text{Tr}(\omega) = \text{Tr}(\overline{\omega}) = 1$. On the other hand, for every pair of $(S_i, S_{i+m/2})$, there is a unique value of $\hat{S}_i$ and $\hat{S}_{i+m/2}$. Consequently, for the supernode $C_i = (c_i, c_{i+m/2})$, the PDFs of Eqs. (14.19) and (14.20) may be modified as follows:

- If the observed channel syndromes are $(S_i, S_{i+m/2}) = (0, 0)$, then:

$$PDF\{\check{m}^{\hat{a}_s}_{C_i \to v_t}\} = \bigotimes_{v_{t'}} PDF\{\check{m}^{\hat{a}_s}_{v_{t'} \to C_i}\}. \tag{14.41}$$

- If the observed channel syndromes obey $(S_i, S_{i+m/2}) = (0, 1)$, then we have:

$$PDF\{\check{m}^{\hat{a}_s}_{C_i \to v_t}\} = \bigotimes_{v_{t'}} PDF\{\check{m}^{\hat{a}_s+1}_{v_{t'} \to C_i}\}. \tag{14.42}$$

- If the observed channel syndromes satisfy $(S_i, S_{i+m/2}) = (1, 0)$, then we arrive at:

$$PDF\{\check{m}^{\hat{a}_s}_{C_i \to v_t}\} = \bigotimes_{v_{t'}} PDF\{\check{m}^{\hat{a}_s+\omega}_{v_{t'} \to C_i}\}. \tag{14.43}$$

- If the observed channel syndromes are $(S_i, S_{i+m/2}) = (1, 1)$, then:

$$PDF\{\check{m}^{\hat{a}_s}_{C_i \to v_t}\} = \bigotimes_{v_{t'}} PDF\{\check{m}^{\hat{a}_s+\overline{\omega}}_{v_{t'} \to C_i}\}. \tag{14.44}$$

Here $\hat{a}_s = (\hat{H}_{it} \times \overline{\hat{a}})$ for $\hat{a} \in \{0, 1, \omega, \overline{\omega}\}$.

Hence, Eqs. (14.41) to (14.44) ensure that both the constituent check nodes $c_i$ and $c_{i+m/2}$ of the supernode $C_i$ are satisfied simultaneously. This is achieved without any additional complexity overhead. In fact, our proposed method requires less computations than the standard non-binary BP, because the number of check nodes is reduced to half.

Let us consider the Steane code of Eq. (14.40) for explaining the decoding procedure. Assume that when the 7-qubit codeword is transmitted over a quantum depolarizing channel having a depolarizing probability of $p = 0.26$, an **X** error is inflicted on the first qubit, i.e. we have $\mathcal{P} = \mathbf{XIIIIII}$. Using Eq. (14.16), the observed syndrome may be computed as:

$$S = \mathrm{Tr}\left(\begin{pmatrix} \omega & 0 & 0 & \omega & 0 & \omega & \omega \\ 0 & \omega & 0 & \omega & \omega & 0 & \omega \\ 0 & 0 & \omega & 0 & \omega & \omega & \omega \\ 1 & 0 & 0 & 1 & 0 & 1 & 1 \\ 0 & 1 & 0 & 1 & 1 & 0 & 1 \\ 0 & 0 & 1 & 0 & 1 & 1 & 1 \end{pmatrix} \cdot \begin{pmatrix} 1 \\ 0 \\ 0 \\ 0 \\ 0 \\ 0 \\ 0 \end{pmatrix}\right) = \mathrm{Tr}\begin{pmatrix} \omega \\ 0 \\ 0 \\ 1 \\ 0 \\ 0 \end{pmatrix} = \begin{pmatrix} 1 \\ 0 \\ 0 \\ 0 \\ 0 \\ 0 \end{pmatrix}. \tag{14.45}$$

We first run the standard non-binary BP on the Tanner graph of Figure 14.11 for estimating the channel error. The non-binary BP algorithm proceeds as follows:

- **Initialization:** The messages $m^{\hat{a}}_{v_t \to c_i}$, which are sent from the variable nodes $v_t \in \{v_0, v_1, \ldots, v_6\}$ to the check nodes $c_i \in \{c_0, c_1, \ldots, c_5\}$ for $\hat{a} \in \{0, 1, \omega, \overline{\omega}\}$, are initialized according to the channel depolarizing probability of $p = 0.26$, i.e. we have:

$$m^{\hat{a}}_{v_t \to c_i} = \begin{cases} 0.74, & \text{if } \hat{a} = 0 \\ 0.0867, & \text{if } \hat{a} \in \{1, \omega, \overline{\omega}\}. \end{cases} \tag{14.46}$$

- **Horizontal Message Exchange:** The horizontal messages $m^{\hat{a}}_{c_i \to v_t}$ equivalent to Eq. (14.12), which are sent from the check nodes $c_i$ to the variable nodes $v_t$, may be computed using the FFT-based algorithm of [365]. The algorithm is briefly outlined as follows:

  a. **PDF of $\check{m}^{\hat{a}_s}_{v_t \to c_i}$:** Recall from Section 14.3.2 that we have:

$$\hat{a}_s = \hat{H}_{it} \times \overline{\hat{a}}. \tag{14.47}$$

Consequently, the PDF of $\check{m}^{\hat{a}_s}_{v_t \to c_i}$ can be obtained by permuting the corresponding PDF of $m^{\hat{a}}_{v_t \to c_i}$ according to the value of $\hat{H}_{it}$ using Eq. (14.47). Let us consider the PDF of the message $m^{\hat{a}}_{v_0 \to c_0}$, which is equivalent to $(m^0_{v_0 \to c_0}, m^1_{v_0 \to c_0}, m^{\omega}_{v_0 \to c_0}, m^{\overline{\omega}}_{v_0 \to c_0})$. The corresponding entry in $\hat{H}$ is $\hat{H}_{00} = \omega$. Hence, using Eq. (14.47) and Table 10.7, we get $\hat{a}_s = (0, \omega, 1, \overline{\omega})$ for $\hat{a} = (0, 1, \omega, \overline{\omega})$. This implies that the PDF of $\check{m}^{\hat{a}_s}_{v_0 \to c_0}$ is equivalent to $(m^0_{v_0 \to c_0}, m^{\omega}_{v_0 \to c_0}, m^1_{v_0 \to c_0}, m^{\overline{\omega}}_{v_0 \to c_0})$. For the $\hat{H}$ of Eq. (14.40), we may generalize the computation of $\check{m}^{\hat{a}_s}_{v_t \to c_i}$ as follows:

$$PDF\{\check{m}^{\hat{a}_s}_{v_t \to c_i}\} = \begin{cases} (m^0_{v_t \to c_i}, m^{\omega}_{v_t \to c_i}, m^1_{v_t \to c_i}, m^{\overline{\omega}}_{v_t \to c_i}), & \text{if } c_i \in \{c_0, c_1, c_2\} \\ (m^0_{v_t \to c_i}, m^1_{v_t \to c_i}, m^{\omega}_{v_t \to c_i}, m^{\overline{\omega}}_{v_t \to c_i}), & \text{if } c_i \in \{c_3, c_4, c_5\}. \end{cases} \tag{14.48}$$

Furthermore, for the initial PDF of Eq. (14.46), Eq. (14.48) reduces to:

$$\check{m}_{v_t \to c_i}^{\hat{a}_s} = \begin{cases} 0.74, & \text{if } \hat{a}_s = 0 \\ 0.0867, & \text{if } \hat{a}_s \in \{1, \omega, \overline{\omega}\}, \end{cases} \tag{14.49}$$

for $c_i \in \{c_0, c_1, \ldots, c_5\}$.

b. **FFT of the PDF of $\check{m}_{v_t \to c_i}^{\hat{a}_s}$:** Recall from Section 14.3.2 that the convolution operation required in Eqs. (14.19) and (14.20) is equivalent to the multiplication of the corresponding PDFs in the frequency domain. The FFT of the PDF of Eq. (14.49) can be computed using the FFT matrix as follows:

$$\mathcal{F}\{\check{m}_{v_t \to c_i}^{\hat{a}_s}\} = \begin{pmatrix} 1 & 1 & 1 & 1 \\ 1 & -1 & 1 & -1 \\ 1 & 1 & -1 & -1 \\ 1 & -1 & -1 & 1 \end{pmatrix} \cdot \begin{pmatrix} \check{m}_{v_t \to c_i}^{0} \\ \check{m}_{v_t \to c_i}^{1} \\ \check{m}_{v_t \to c_i}^{\omega} \\ \check{m}_{v_t \to c_i}^{\overline{\omega}} \end{pmatrix}, \tag{14.50}$$

where $\mathcal{F}$ denotes the FFT operation. Hence, the FFT of the PDF of Eq. (14.49) is equivalent to

$$\mathcal{F}\{\check{m}_{v_t \to c_i}^{\hat{a}_s}\} = \begin{pmatrix} 1 \\ 0.6533 \\ 0.6533 \\ 0.6533 \end{pmatrix}. \tag{14.51}$$

c. **Convolution of PDFs:** The convolution operations of Eqs. (14.19) and (14.20), which are invoked for computing the horizontal messages related to the variable node $v_t$, can be carried out using FFT as follows:

$$\bigotimes_{v_{t'}} PDF\{\check{m}_{v_{t'} \to c_i}^{\hat{a}_s}\} \equiv \mathcal{F}^{-1}\left\{\prod_{v_{t'}} \mathcal{F}\{\check{m}_{v_{t'} \to c_i}^{\hat{a}_s}\}\right\}, \tag{14.52}$$

where $\mathcal{F}^{-1}$ denotes the Inverse FFT (IFFT) operation and $v_{t'} \in V(c_i) \setminus v_t$. Given the $\hat{H}$ of Eq. (14.40) and the FFT of Eq. (14.51), we get:

$$\prod_{v_{t'}} \mathcal{F}\{\check{m}_{v_{t'} \to c_i}^{\hat{a}_s}\} \equiv \begin{pmatrix} 1 \\ 0.2788 \\ 0.2788 \\ 0.2788 \end{pmatrix}. \tag{14.53}$$

Then, the inverse FFT of Eq. (14.53) is computed by multiplying with the FFT matrix, which is the same as that in Eq. (14.50). More explicitly, we have:

$$\mathcal{F}^{-1}\left\{\prod_{v_{t'}} \mathcal{F}\{\check{m}_{v_{t'} \to c_i}^{\hat{a}_s}\}\right\} = \begin{pmatrix} 1 & 1 & 1 & 1 \\ 1 & -1 & 1 & -1 \\ 1 & 1 & -1 & -1 \\ 1 & -1 & -1 & 1 \end{pmatrix} \cdot \begin{pmatrix} 1 \\ 0.2788 \\ 0.2788 \\ 0.2788 \end{pmatrix} = \begin{pmatrix} 1.8364 \\ 0.7212 \\ 0.7212 \\ 0.7212 \end{pmatrix}. \tag{14.54}$$

Finally, the PDF of Eq. (14.54) is normalized to yield the output of Eq. (14.52), i.e. we get:

$$\bigotimes_{v_{t'}} PDF\{\check{m}^{\hat{a}_s}_{v_{t'}\to c_i}\} \equiv \begin{pmatrix} 0.4591 \\ 0.1803 \\ 0.1803 \\ 0.1803 \end{pmatrix}. \tag{14.55}$$

**d. PDF of $\check{m}^{\hat{a}_s}_{c_i\to v_t}$:** The PDF of the messages $\check{m}^{\hat{a}_s}_{c_i\to v_t}$ may be computed using Eqs. (14.19) or (14.20) depending on the value of the syndrome observed, which was computed in Eq. (14.45). Since the syndrome of Eq. (14.45) is 1 for the first check node $c_0$, we use Eq. (14.20) for computing the PDF of the messages emerging from the check node $c_0$. Therefore, we get:

$$\check{m}^{\hat{a}_s}_{c_0\to v_t} = \begin{pmatrix} 0.1803 \\ 0.1803 \\ 0.3197 \\ 0.3197 \end{pmatrix}. \tag{14.56}$$

Furthermore, the syndrome of Eq. (14.45) has a value of 0 for all other check nodes. Therefore, we use Eq. (14.19) for $c_i \neq c_0$, which yields the following PDF:

$$\check{m}^{\hat{a}_s}_{c_i\to v_t} = \begin{pmatrix} 0.3197 \\ 0.3197 \\ 0.1803 \\ 0.1803 \end{pmatrix}. \tag{14.57}$$

**e. PDF of $m^{\hat{a}}_{c_i\to v_t}$:** For the sake of retrieving the messages $m^{\hat{a}}_{c_i\to v_t}$ from the PDF of $\check{m}^{\hat{a}_s}_{c_i\to v_t}$, the resultant PDFs of Eqs. (14.56) and (14.57) have to permuted as we did in Step 1. More specifically, the permutation operation, which is required for this step, is the reverse of the permutation operation carried out in Step 1. Let us consider the check nodes $c_i \in \{c_0, c_1, c_2\}$, for which the non-zero values of $\hat{H}_{it}$ are always equal to $\omega$ (or equivalently all the branches emerging from these check nodes in the Tanner graph of Figure 14.11 are labeled with the Pauli-**Z** operator). Furthermore, recall from Step 1 that $\hat{a}_s = (0, \omega, 1, \overline{\omega})$ for $\hat{a} = (0, 1, \omega, \overline{\omega})$, when $\hat{H}_{it} = \omega$. This implies that the PDF of $m^{\hat{a}}_{c_i\to v_t}$ is equivalent to $(\check{m}^{0}_{c_i\to v_t}, \check{m}^{\omega}_{c_i\to v_t}, \check{m}^{1}_{c_i\to v_t}, \check{m}^{\overline{\omega}}_{c_i\to v_t})$, for $c_i \in \{c_0, c_1, c_2\}$. For all other check nodes, the PDF of $m^{\hat{a}}_{c_i\to v_t}$ is same as that of $\check{m}^{\hat{a}_s}_{c_i\to v_t}$, because $\hat{H}_{it} = 1$. Therefore, the resultant PDFs are as follows:

$$m^{\hat{a}}_{c_i\to v_t} = \begin{pmatrix} 0.1803 \\ 0.3197 \\ 0.1803 \\ 0.3197 \end{pmatrix}, \tag{14.58}$$

for $c_i = c_0$, while we have:

$$m^{\hat{a}}_{c_i\to v_t} = \begin{pmatrix} 0.3197 \\ 0.1803 \\ 0.3197 \\ 0.1803 \end{pmatrix}, \tag{14.59}$$

for $c_i \in \{c_1, c_2\}$, and we have:

$$m^{\hat{a}}_{c_i \to v_t} = \begin{pmatrix} 0.3197 \\ 0.3197 \\ 0.1803 \\ 0.1803 \end{pmatrix}, \tag{14.60}$$

for the remaining check nodes $c_i \in \{c_3, c_4, c_5\}$.

- **Vertical Message Exchange:** We next compute the vertical messages $m^{\hat{a}}_{v_t \to c_i}$ using Eq. (14.13). For example, consider the message $m^{\hat{a}}_{v_0 \to c_0}$, which is destined from the variable node $v_0$ to the check node $c_0$. Since the variable node $v_0$ is only connected to $c_0$ and $c_3$ in the Tanner graph of Figure 14.11, the message $m^{\hat{a}}_{v_0 \to c_0}$ may be computed as:

$$m^{\hat{a}}_{v_0 \to c_0} = K\, \mathrm{P}_{\mathrm{ch}}(P_0 = \hat{a}) \times m^{\hat{a}}_{c_3 \to v_0} = \begin{pmatrix} 0.8005 \\ 0.0937 \\ 0.0529 \\ 0.0529 \end{pmatrix}. \tag{14.61}$$

- **Element-wise Marginal Probability:** The element-wise marginal probabilities of the error on the variable node $v_t$, given the observed syndrome $S$, may be computed using Eq. (14.14). Let us consider again the variable node $v_0$, which is connected to check nodes $c_0$ and $c_3$. Consequently, the resultant marginal distribution of the error $P_t$ inflicted on the variable node $v_t$ may be computed as:

$$\mathrm{P}(P_0 = \hat{a}|S) = K\, \mathrm{P}_{\mathrm{ch}}(P_0 = \hat{a}) \times m^{\hat{a}}_{c_0 \to v_0} \times m^{\hat{a}}_{c_3 \to v_0} = \begin{pmatrix} 0.7189 \\ 0.1493 \\ 0.0475 \\ 0.0842 \end{pmatrix}. \tag{14.62}$$

The process is repeated for all the variable nodes and the resultant marginalized probabilities are tabulated in Table 14.7.

**Table 14.7** Marginal probability $\mathrm{P}(P_t = \hat{a}|S)$ after the first iteration, when the standard non-binary BP decoding algorithm is invoked over the Tanner graph of the 7-qubit Steane code for transmission through a depolarizing channel having $p = 0.26$, which inflicts an **X** error on the first qubit, i.e. we have $\mathcal{P} = $ **XIIIIII**.

| $t$ | $\hat{a} = 0$ | $\hat{a} = 1$ | $\hat{a} = \omega$ | $\hat{a} = \overline{\omega}$ | $\tilde{P}_t$ |
|---|---|---|---|---|---|
| 0 | 0.7189 | 0.1493 | 0.0475 | 0.0842 | 0 |
| 1 | 0.8552 | 0.0565 | 0.0565 | 0.03185 | 0 |
| 2 | 0.8552 | 0.0565 | 0.0565 | 0.03185 | 0 |
| 3 | 0.8392 | 0.0983 | 0.0313 | 0.0313 | 0 |
| 4 | 0.9205 | 0.0343 | 0.0343 | 0.0109 | 0 |
| 5 | 0.8392 | 0.0983 | 0.0313 | 0.0313 | 0 |
| 6 | 0.9100 | 0.0601 | 0.0191 | 0.0108 | 0 |

- **Hard Decision and Syndrome Check:** Finally, a hard decision is made for the sake of finding the most likely error $\tilde{P}_t$, which maximizes the marginal probability computed in the previous step. The resultant values of $\tilde{P}_t$ are listed in the last column of Table 14.7. More specifically, the probability of "no-error" dominates for all the variable nodes. The syndrome corresponding to the resultant estimated error $\tilde{P}_t$ does not match the observed syndrome $S$ of Eq. (14.45). Hence, the algorithm repeats itself from the horizontal message exchange step.

Figure 14.13a plots the resultant marginal probability $\text{P}(P_t = \hat{a}|S)$ for the first qubit, as the iterations proceed. As gleaned from Figure 14.13a, the standard decoding algorithm fails to converge. We next invoke our modified non-binary BP algorithm for the sake of analyzing the impact of our proposed algorithm. Recall from Figure 14.12 that the check nodes $c_i$ and $c_{i+3}$ are amalgamated into a single supernode $C_i$. The corresponding observed syndrome values of Eq. (14.45) are also amalgamated, which yields $(S_0, S_3) = (1, 0)$, $(S_1, S_4) = (0, 0)$, and $(S_2, S_5) = (0, 0)$. Consequently, the modified BP differs from the standard non-binary in the Step 4 of the "horizontal message exchange," since it takes into account the amalgamated supernodes, rather than the individual check nodes. Using Eqs. (14.41) to (14.44), Step 4 of the "horizontal message exchange" may be carried out as follows:

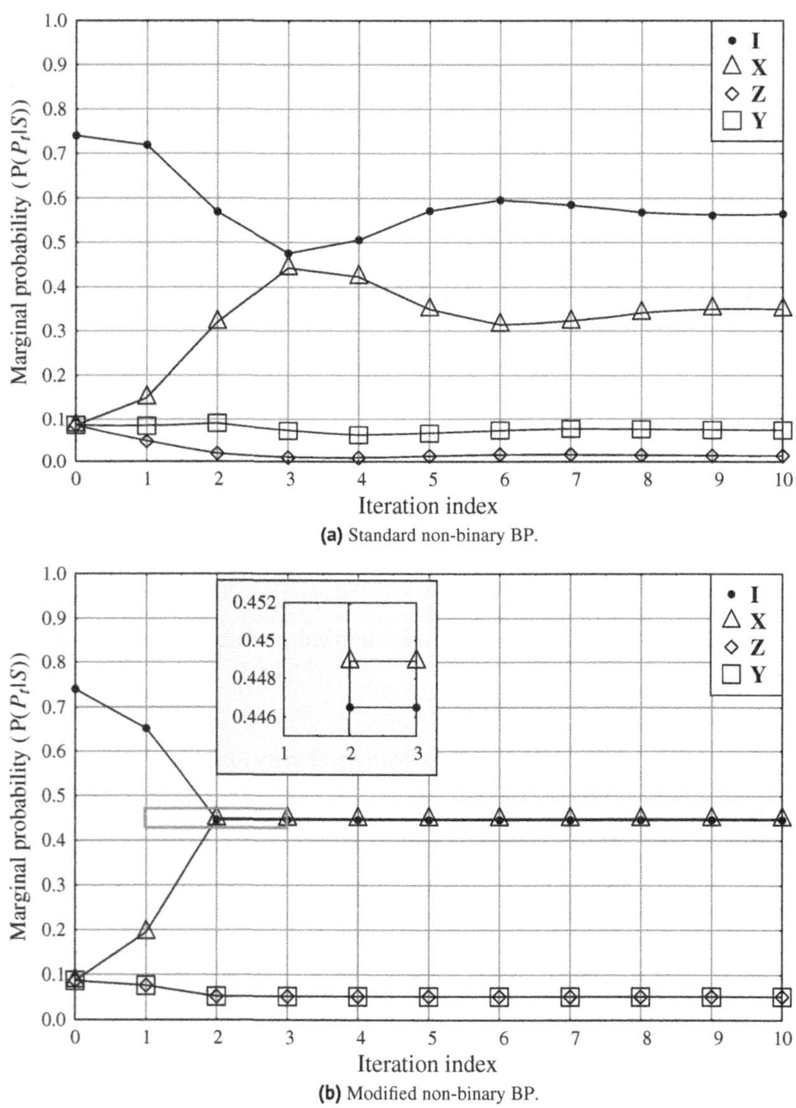


**Figure 14.13** Evolution of the marginal probability for the first qubit of the 7-qubit Steane code for transmission through a depolarizing channel having $p = 0.26$, which inflicts an **X** error on the first qubit, i.e. we have $\mathcal{P} =$ **XIIIIII**. Standard BP fails to converge, while our modified BP converges to the correct solution in two iterations. *Source*: [80]/IEEE.

**Table 14.8** Marginal probability $P(P_t = \hat{a}|S)$ after the first iteration, when the modified non-binary BP decoding algorithm is invoked over the Tanner graph of the 7-qubit Steane code for transmission through a depolarizing channel having $p = 0.26$, which inflicts an **X** error on the first qubit, i.e. we have $\mathcal{P} = \mathbf{XIIIIII}$.

| $t$ | $\hat{a} = 0$ | $\hat{a} = 1$ | $\hat{a} = \omega$ | $\hat{a} = \overline{\omega}$ | $\tilde{P}_t$ |
|---|---|---|---|---|---|
| 0 | 0.1946 | 0.6525 | 0.0764 | 0.0764 | 0 |
| 1 | 0.8788 | 0.0404 | 0.0404 | 0.0404 | 0 |
| 2 | 0.8788 | 0.0404 | 0.0404 | 0.0404 | 0 |
| 3 | 0.8271 | 0.0969 | 0.0380 | 0.0380 | 0 |
| 4 | 0.9486 | 0.0171 | 0.0171 | 0.0171 | 0 |
| 5 | 0.8271 | 0.0969 | 0.0380 | 0.0380 | 0 |
| 6 | 0.9241 | 0.0425 | 0.0167 | 0.0167 | 0 |

- **PDF of $\check{m}^{\hat{a}_s}_{C_i \to v_t}$:** Since the syndrome observed for the supernode $C_0$ is $(S_0, S_3) = (1, 0)$, we use Eq. (14.43) for computing the PDF of the messages emerging from this supernode. Consequently, we arrive at:

$$\check{m}^{\hat{a}_s}_{C_0 \to v_t} = \bigotimes_{v_{t'}} PDF\{\check{m}^{\hat{a}_s+\omega}_{v_{t'} \to C_0}\} = \begin{pmatrix} 0.1803 \\ 0.1803 \\ 0.4591 \\ 0.1803 \end{pmatrix}. \tag{14.63}$$

Furthermore, since the syndrome is $(S_i, S_{i+3}) = (0, 0)$ for all other supernodes, we use Eq. (14.41) for computing the corresponding PDFs. Hence, we get:

$$\check{m}^{\hat{a}_s}_{C_i \to v_t} = \bigotimes_{v_{t'}} PDF\{\check{m}^{\hat{a}_s}_{v_{t'} \to C_i}\} = \begin{pmatrix} 0.4591 \\ 0.1803 \\ 0.1803 \\ 0.1803 \end{pmatrix}, \tag{14.64}$$

for $C_i \in \{C_1, C_2\}$.

The rest of the decoding algorithm is same as the standard non-binary BP, except that we only have three supernodes in the modified Tanner graph of Figure 14.12 in contrast to the six check nodes of Figure 14.11. The resultant marginalized probabilities are tabulated in Table 14.8, while Figure 14.13b plots the marginal probability for the first qubit, as the iterations proceed. We may observe in Figure 14.13b that our modified BP algorithm converges to the correct estimate in two iterations. On the other hand, the standard non-binary decoder initially tends to converge toward the correct solution. However, it starts diverging from the correct estimate after the third iteration, because the probability values become highly correlated (or over-confident) due to the presence of numerous short cycles.

## 14.7 Reweighted BP for Graphs Exhibiting Cycles

Belief propagation is capable of providing a reasonably good approximation to the optimization problem of Eq. (14.10), provided that the underlying Tanner graph has a sufficiently high girth. However, it is not guaranteed to converge or may converge onto an incorrect solution in the presence of cycles [371, 372]. Furthermore, it may require a large number of iterations for achieving convergence, especially in the high noise regime, thereby imposing a higher complexity. These shortcomings of the classic BP algorithm are primarily due to the fact that the BP messages become dependent with time when short cycles exist in the Tanner graph. Alternatively, we may refer to the messages as being "over-confident" or "over-estimated." To alleviate the impact of this over-confidence, Wainwright *et al.* [371] conceived the tree-reweighted belief propagation (TRW-BP) method for pair-wise interactions, which improves the convergence of the classic BP by reweighting the edges of the underlying graph with their edge appearance probabilities (EAP).[9] The TRW-BP algorithm was extended to higher-order interactions in [347, 348], whereby EAPs were replaced by the factor appearance probabilities (FAPs) of the nodes.[10] Based on this extended TRW-BP, Wymeersch *et al.* reformulated the vertical message exchange step of the classic BP (Eq. (14.13)) as [347, 348]:

$$m^a_{v_t\to c_i} = K\,\mathrm{P_{ch}}(P_t=a)\left(m^a_{c_i\to v_t}\right)^{\rho_i-1}\prod_{c_{i'}\in C(v_t)\setminus c_i}\left(m^a_{c_{i'}\to v_t}\right)^{\rho_{i'}}, \tag{14.65}$$

where $\rho_i$ is the FAP of the $i$th check node. Similarly, the computation of the element-wise marginal probability (Eq. (14.14)) was modified as:

$$\mathrm{P}(P_t=a|S) = K\,\mathrm{P_{ch}}(P_t=a)\prod_{c_i\in C(v_t)}\left(m^a_{c_i\to v_t}\right)^{\rho_i}. \tag{14.66}$$

Both Eqs. (14.65) and (14.66) reduces to the classic BP for $\rho_i = 1\,\forall i$.

The TRW-BP technique requires the optimization of $\rho_i$ for all nodes. To reduce this optimization task, Wymeersch *et al.* [347, 348] also proposed the URW-BP, which invokes a uniform FAP value for all the nodes, where we have $\rho_i = \rho\,\forall i$. Various other variations of TRW-BP have been investigated in [373–376] for classical binary LDPC codes, which demonstrate that the TRW-BP effectively improves the convergence of binary LDPC codes, when the number of iterations is not too high. Inspired by these results, in Section 14.8 we also analyze the impact of URW-BP on the non-binary decoding of quantum LDPC codes, which are known to have unavoidable short cycles.

## 14.8 Results and Discussions II

### 14.8.1 Modified Non-binary Decoding

For the sake of quantifying the attainable performance gain of our modified non-binary BP of Section 14.6, in this section we compare its performance in conjunction with the decoding algorithms of Section 14.3. Our first system of Table 14.9 relies on MacKay's 1/2-rate [800, 400] bicycle code having a row weight of 30. The corresponding WER performance recorded for varying channel depolarizing probabilities is plotted in Figure 14.14, where we have considered the following decoders:

a. **Binary:** the binary BP decoding algorithm of Section 14.3.1,
b. **Standard Non-binary:** the non-binary BP decoding algorithm of Section 14.3.2,
c. **Random Perturbation:** the random perturbation technique [139] of Section 14.3.3,
d. **Enhanced Feedback:** the enhanced feedback method [140] of Section 14.3.3,
e. **Modified Non-binary:** our modified non-binary BP of Section 14.6,
f. **Modified and Enhanced Feedback:** our modified non-binary BP of Section 14.6 amalgamated with the enhanced feedback method [140] of Section 14.3.3.

For all the decoding schemes, we have used a maximum of $I_{\max} = 90$ iterations. Furthermore, for both the "random perturbation" as well as for the "enhanced feedback," we set $T_{\text{pert}} = 40$, while the random perturbation strength was set to $\delta = 0.1$ and the maximum number of feedbacks to $n_a = 40$ for the "enhanced feedback".[11] These simulation parameters are tabulated in Table 14.9. Each decoding algorithm iterates until either a valid error is found or the maximum number of iterations is reached. Furthermore, the WER metric here counts both the detected as well as the undetected block errors.

9 EAP of an edge represents the probability of appearance of that edge in a randomly chosen spanning tree.
10 FAP denotes the appearance probability of a node in the collection of trees [347, 348].
11 We have used the decoding parameters of [140].

**Table 14.9** System I – Simulation parameters.

| **QLDPC matrix** | |
|---|---|
| Code construction | MacKay's bicycle code |
| Coded qubits | $n = 800$ |
| Information qubits | $k = 400$ |
| E-bits | $c = 0$ |
| Row weight | 30 |
| **QLDPC decoder** | |
| Standard decoding iterations | $I_{max} = 90$ |
| Perturbation iterations | $T_{pert=40}$ |
| Random perturbation strength | $\delta = 0.1$ |
| Maximum no. of feedbacks | $n_a = 40$ |

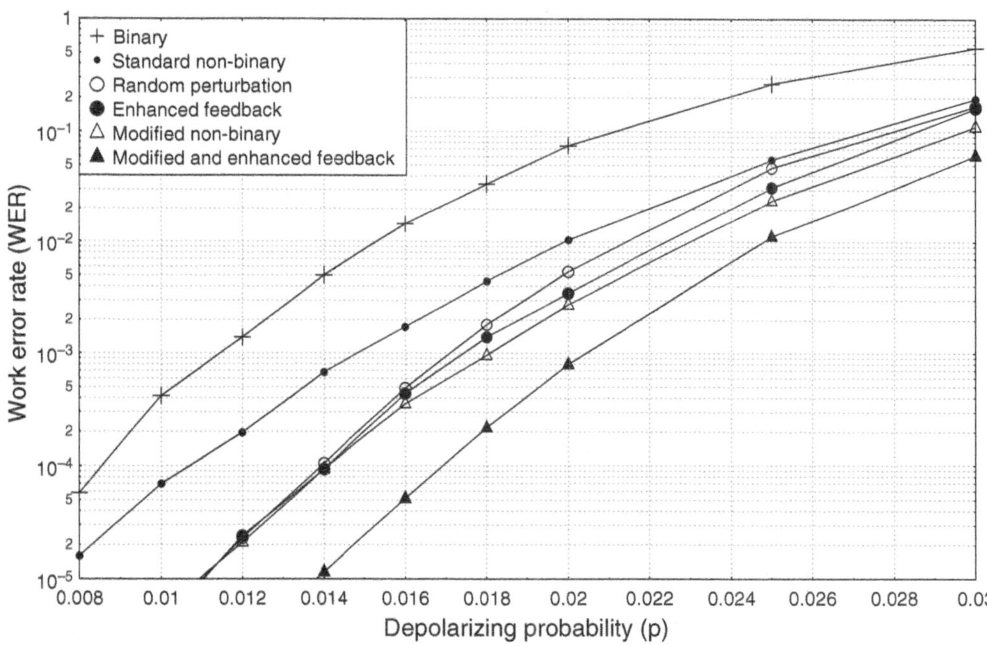


**Figure 14.14** Achievable WER performance comparison of the modified BP with the existing decoding schemes, using the simulation parameters of Table 14.9. *Source*: [80]/IEEE.

We may observe in Figure 14.14 that the "binary" decoder exhibits the worse performance. Using the "binary" decoder, we achieve a WER of $10^{-4}$ at a channel depolarizing probability of $p = 0.0085$, which increases to $p = 0.01075$ with the "standard non-binary" decoder. This is equivalent to a $(\frac{(0.01075-0.0085)}{0.0085} \times 100) = 26\%$ depolarizing probability increase that the decoder can cope with. Furthermore, the "random perturbation," the "enhanced feedback" and the "modified non-binary" decoders have a similar performance at low noise levels, increasing the tolerable depolarizing probability to $p = 0.014$ at a WER of $10^{-4}$, which corresponds to a $(\frac{(0.014-0.01075)}{0.01075} \times 100) = 30\%$ increase of $p$ at WER $= 10^{-4}$ with respect to the "standard non-binary" decoder. Furthermore, with the "modified and enhanced feedback" configuration, the tolerable depolarizing probability increases to $p = 0.017$ at a WER of $10^{-4}$, which is equivalent to about $(\frac{(0.017-0.014)}{0.014} \times 100) = 21\%$ increase with respect to $p = 0.014$. Table 14.10[12] summarizes these results.

12 "With respect to" is abbreviated as "w.r.t." in Table 14.10.

**Table 14.10** Achievable depolarizing probability (p) at a WER of $10^{-4}$, based on Figure 14.14.

| Dec. No. | Decoding method | *p* | Improvement |
|---|---|---|---|
| 1 | Binary | 0.0085 | - |
| 2 | Standard non-binary | 0.01075 | 26% w.r.t. Dec. 1 |
| 3 | Random perturbation | 0.014 | 30% w.r.t. Dec. 2 |
| 4 | Enhanced feedback | 0.014 | 30% w.r.t. Dec. 2 |
| 5 | Modified non-binary | 0.014 | 30% w.r.t. Dec. 2 |
| 6 | Modified and enhanced feedback | 0.017 | 21% w.r.t. Dec. 5 |

*Source*: [316]/IEEE.

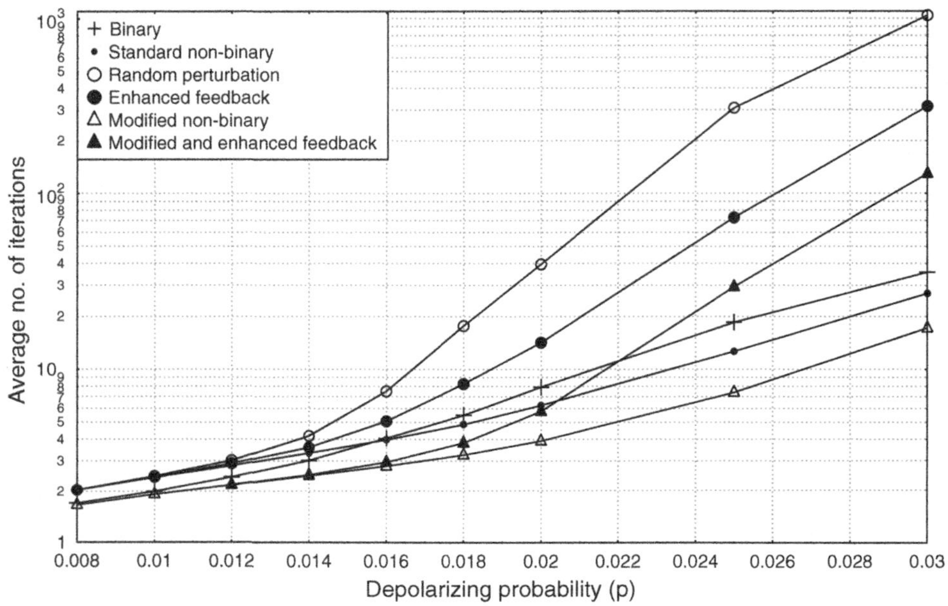


**Figure 14.15** Comparison of the average number of decoding iterations invoked by the modified BP and the existing decoding schemes using the simulation parameters of Table 14.9. *Source*: [80]/IEEE.

The performance of our "modified non-binary" BP at a WER of $10^{-4}$ is similar to that of the heuristic methods, namely "random perturbation" and "enhanced feedback." However, the "modified non-binary" technique imposes a lower decoding complexity in terms of the average number of decoding iterations, which is evidenced in Figure 14.15. Consequently, our "modified non-binary" BP converges faster than the existing decoding schemes. In particular, in the high-noise regime, our "modified non-binary" decoder outperforms both the "random perturbation" and the "enhanced feedback" in terms of its WER performance recorded in Figure 14.14 as well as in terms of the average number of iterations seen in Figure 14.15. As compared to the "standard non-binary" decoder, the "modified non-binary" algorithm always yields a lower WER and invokes on average less decoding iterations.

We may observe furthermore in Figure 14.15 that the amalgamated "modified and enhanced feedback" invokes less iterations as compared to the "enhanced feedback," while the performance of the former is also superior in terms of the WER curve of Figure 14.14. This is again due to the fact that the modified BP of Section 14.6 facilitates faster convergence as compared to the standard non-binary decoding. More specifically, in the region of interest, i.e. for $p \leq 0.017$ corresponding to the desired WER of $\leq 10^{-4}$, the combination of the enhanced feedback method with our modified BP, namely "modified and enhanced feedback," imposes almost the same complexity as that imposed by the "modified non-binary" BP, when used on its own. However, the former exhibits a much lower WER than the latter. We compare furthermore the performance of all the decoding schemes at a depolarizing probability of $p = 0.016$ in Table 14.11.

**Table 14.11** Performance comparison in terms of the achievable WER and the average number of decoding iterations ($I_{avg}$) invoked at a depolarizing probability of $p = 0.016$, based on Figures 14.14 and 14.15.

| Dec. No. | Decoding method | WER | $I_{avg}$ |
|---|---|---|---|
| 1 | Binary | $1.57 \times 10^{-2}$ | 3.98 |
| 2 | Standard non-binary | $1.47 \times 10^{-3}$ | 4.28 |
| 3 | Random perturbation | $4.57 \times 10^{-4}$ | 7.52 |
| 4 | Enhanced feedback | $4.47 \times 10^{-4}$ | 5.08 |
| 5 | Modified non-binary | $3.67 \times 10^{-4}$ | 2.81 |
| 6 | Modified and enhanced feedback | $5.27 \times 10^{-5}$ | 2.96 |

*Source*: [316]/IEEE.

**Table 14.12** System II – Simulation parameters.

| | |
|---|---|
| **QLDPC matrix** | |
| Code construction | Homogeneous EA-QLDPC |
| Coded qubits | $n = 816$ |
| Information qubits | $k = 404$ |
| E-bits | $c = 404$ |
| Row weight | 6 |
| Column weight | 3 |
| **QLDPC decoder** | |
| Standard decoding iterations | $I_{max} = 90$ |
| Perturbation iterations | $T_{pert} = 40$ |
| Random perturbation strength | $\delta = 0.1$ |
| Maximum no. of feedbacks | $n_a = 81$ |

Let us now compare the performance of the different decoding schemes in the context of our second system of Table 14.12, relying on the homogeneous EA-QLDPC code of [140] having $n = 816$, $k = 404$ and $e = 404$, which is derived from the MacKay's classical $(816, 408)$ LDPC, having a row weight of 6 and a column weight of 3. For all the decoding schemes, we have used a maximum of $I_{max} = 90$ iterations. Furthermore, for both the the "random perturbation" as well as for the "enhanced feedback" methods, we set $T_{pert} = 40$, while the random perturbation strength was set to $\delta = 0.1$ and the maximum number of feedbacks $n_a = 81$ was used for the "enhanced feedback" decoder. These simulation parameters are summarized in Table 14.12. The resultant WER performance curves are compared in Figure 14.16, while the average number of decoding iterations invoked for varying channel depolarizing probabilities are compared in Figure 14.17. As observed from Figure 14.16, the "binary" decoder achieves a WER of $10^{-4}$ at $p = 0.057$, which increases to $p = 0.069$ when the "standard non-binary" decoder is invoked. Consequently, the "standard non-binary" increases the tolerable depolarizing probability by $(\frac{(0.069-0.057)}{0.057} \times 100) = 21\%$ as compared to the "binary" decoder. This is further increased to $p = 0.076$ in conjunction with the "random perturbation," which corresponds to about $(\frac{(0.076-0.069)}{0.069} \times 100) = 10\%$ increase and to $p = 0.082$ for the "enhanced feedback," which represents a $(\frac{(0.082-0.069)}{0.069} \times 100) = 19\%$ increase. By contrast, our "modified non-binary" BP exhibits a WER of $10^{-4}$ around $p = 0.085$, which corresponds to a $(\frac{(0.085-0.069)}{0.069} \times 100) = 23\%$ increase as compared to the "standard non-binary" decoder. Using the heuristic enhanced feedback approach with our modified BP, namely "modified and enhanced feedback" provides a further increase to $p = 0.0945$, which represents a $(\frac{(0.0945-0.085)}{0.085} \times 100) = 11\%$ increase. These results are tabulated in Table 14.13.

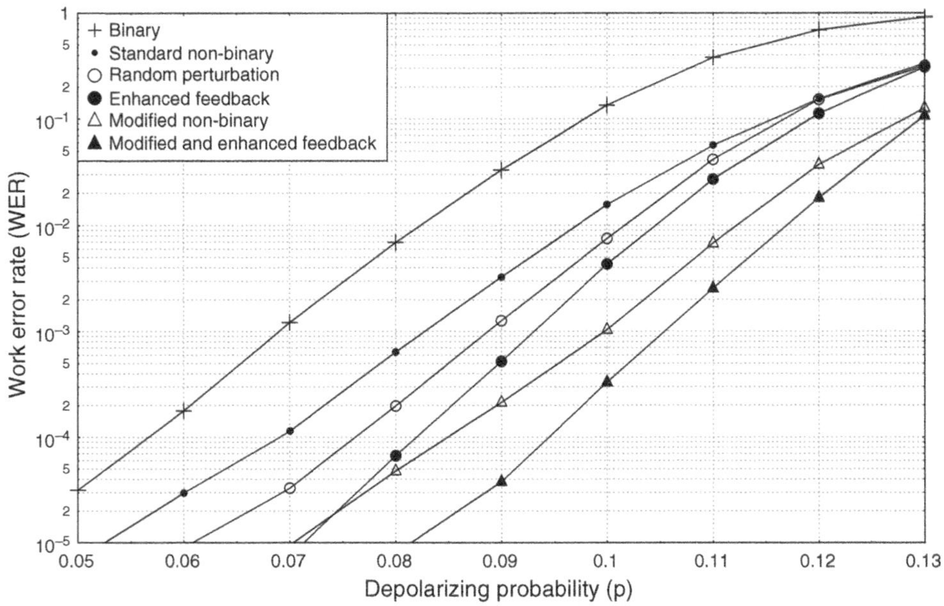


**Figure 14.16** Achievable WER performance comparison of the modified BP with the existing decoding schemes, using the simulation parameters of Table 14.12. *Source*: [80]/IEEE.

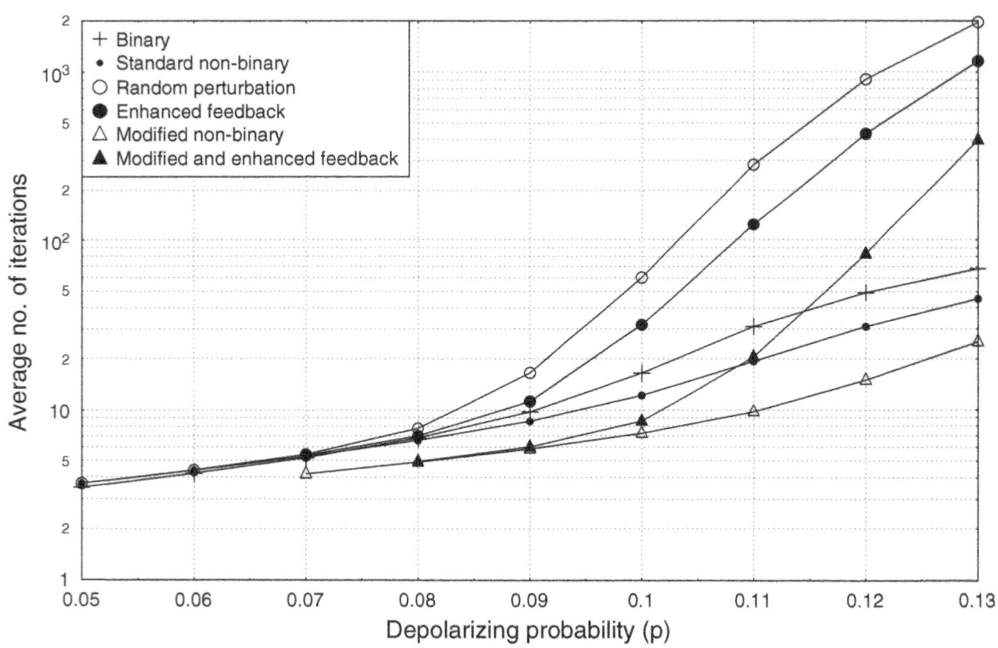


**Figure 14.17** Comparison of the average number of decoding iterations invoked by the modified BP and the existing decoding schemes using the simulation parameters of Table 14.12. *Source*: [80]/IEEE.

In terms of the average number of decoding iterations, our "modified non-binary" BP always outperforms both the "standard non-binary" decoder as well as the "random perturbation" and the "enhanced feedback" solutions, as depicted in Figure 14.17.

### 14.8.2 Uniformly Reweighted BP

Since bicycle codes exhibit numerous short cycles, we use our first system of Table 14.9 for the analysis of the URW-BP of Section 14.7, which is combined with our modified non-binary decoder of Section 14.6. More precisely,

**Table 14.13** Achievable depolarizing probability (p) at a WER of $10^{-4}$, based on Figure 14.16.

| Dec. No. | Decoding method | $p$ | Improvement |
|---|---|---|---|
| 1 | Binary | 0.057 | — |
| 2 | Standard non-binary | 0.069 | 21% w.r.t. Dec. 1 |
| 3 | Random perturbation | 0.076 | 10% w.r.t. Dec. 2 |
| 4 | Enhanced feedback | 0.082 | 19% w.r.t. Dec. 2 |
| 5 | Modified non-binary | 0.085 | 23% w.r.t. Dec. 2 |
| 6 | Modified and enhanced feedback | 0.0945 | 11% w.r.t. Dec. 5 |

*Source*: [316]/IEEE.

we amalgamate the horizontal exchange step of our modified non-binary BP with the vertical exchange step of the URW-BP.

We commence by heuristically determining the optimum value $\rho$ of the FAP, which varies with both the channel depolarizing probability as well as with the maximum number of decoding iterations. Figure 14.18 shows the impact of $\rho$ on the WER performance at varying channel depolarizing probabilities $p$ for $I_{max} = 10$, 20 and 90 iterations. We may observe in Figure 14.18 that the WER varies with the value of $\rho$, attaining a minimum value at the optimum $\rho$. This optimum $\rho$ is different for each $p$ value, tending to move toward $\rho = 1$ as the value of $p$ increases or as the maximum affordable number of iterations increases. The resultant values of $\rho$ optimized for different channel depolarizing probabilities $p$ and for different maximum number of iterations are summarized in Table 14.14.

To quantify the performance gain achieved with the aid of the URW-BP, we compare the performance of the optimized URW-BP to our modified non-binary BP in Figure 14.19 for $I_{max} = 10$, 20, and 90 iteration. Here the optimized URW-BP is based on the best values of $\rho$ listed in Table 14.14. The performance curves of Figure 14.19 reveal that the improvement in WER is lower for higher values of $p$ as well as for larger values of the maximum number of affordable iterations. For example, when a maximum of $I_{max} = 10$ decoding iterations are invoked at a WER of $10^{-3}$, the URW-BP scheme increases $p = 0.0125$ to $p = 0.0155$, which is around a $(\frac{(0.0155-0.0125)}{0.0125} \times 100) = 24\%$ increase. By contrast, for a maximum of $I_{max} = 20$ iterations, URW-BP increases from $p = 0.015$ to $p = 0.017$ at a WER of $10^{-3}$. This is equivalent to an increase of $(\frac{(0.017-0.015)}{0.015} \times 100) = 13\%$. Furthermore, at an even higher maximum number of iterations of $I_{max} = 90$, URW-BP achieves a WER of $10^{-3}$ at $p = 0.0185$, which is only a $(\frac{(0.0185-0.018)}{0.018} \times 100) = 3\%$ increase as compared to the modified non-binary algorithm. These values are summarized in Table 14.15. Hence, the notion of reweighting the message probabilities is more beneficial at low depolarizing probabilities and for smaller values of the maximum affordable number of iterations. This is because at higher depolarizing probabilities (and similarly larger values of the maximum number of iterations), the messages are highly correlated.

## 14.9 Summary and Conclusions

Classical LDPC codes are known to exhibit a near-capacity performance at an affordable decoding complexity. This has spurred considerable interest in the design of QLDPC codes over the recent years. The sparseness of LDPC matrix is also particularly important for quantum codes because it facilitates fault tolerant decoding.

QLDPC codes may be constructed from the classical binary as well as quaternary codes, as discussed in the review of QLDPC construction methods in Section 14.2. The design guidelines for constructing QLDPC codes may be summarized as follows:

- An $[n, k]$ QLDPC code, having a coding rate of $R_Q = k/n$, may be constructed from a classical $(2n, n + k)$ binary LDPC code, having a coding rate of $R_c = (n + k)/2n$, if the associated PCM $H$ satisfies the stringent symplectic criterion.

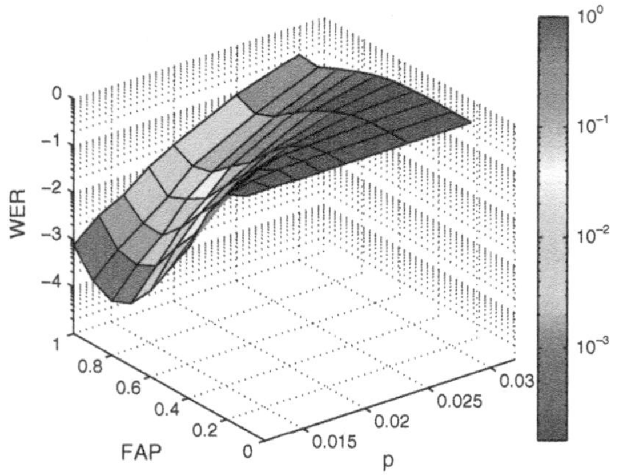


**(a)** $I_{max}$ = 10 iterations.

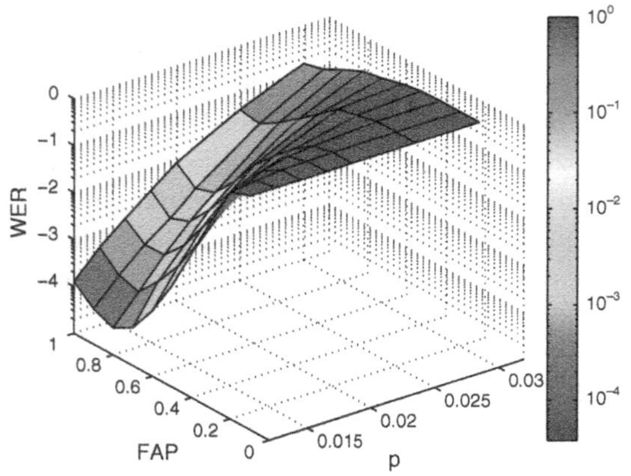


**(b)** $I_{max}$ = 20 iterations.

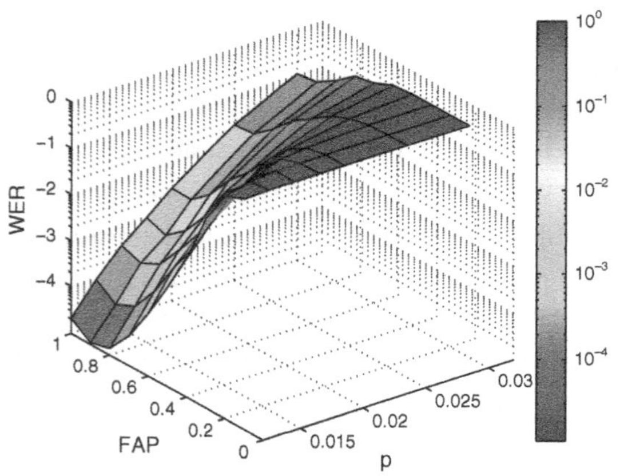


**(c)** $I_{max}$ = 90 iterations.

**Figure 14.18** URW-BP optimization: impact of varying FAP values on the WER performance at various channel depolarizing probabilities *p*. URW-BP is amalgamated with the modified non-binary decoder and the performance is analyzed for the System I of Table 14.9. *Source:* [80]/IEEE.

- Ideally, the rows of the PCM $H$ should have at most a single overlapping value of 1 (or nonzero value in the GF(4) formalism)) for the sake of avoiding length-4 cycles in the Tanner graph, which degrade the performance of the iterative decoding algorithm. Unfortunately, the symplectic criterion requires "even overlaps" between the rows of $H$, thus resulting in unavoidable length-4 cycles. A major design challenge is therefore to construct good QLDPC codes in the wake of the unavoidable length-4 cycles.

**Table 14.14** Optimized $\rho$ for different values of $p$ and maximum number of iterations $I_{max}$ for System I of Table 14.9, based on the performance curves of Figure 14.18.

| | **Optimized $\rho$ for different values of $p$** | | | | | | |
|---|---|---|---|---|---|---|---|
| $I_{max}$ | **0.012** | **0.014** | **0.016** | **0.018** | **0.02** | **0.025** | **0.03** |
| 10 | 0.8 | 0.8 | 0.8 | 0.9 | 0.9 | 0.9 | 0.9 |
| 20 | 0.8 | 0.8 | 0.9 | 0.9 | 0.9 | 0.9 | 1 |
| 90 | 0.9 | 0.9 | 0.9 | 0.9 | 0.9 | 1 | 1 |

*Source:* [316]/IEEE.

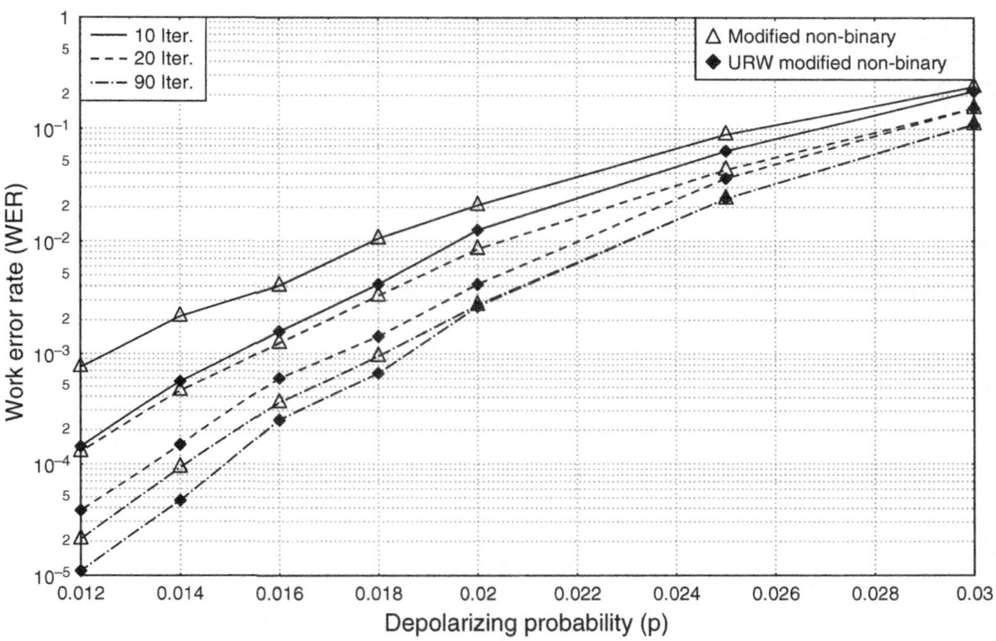


**Figure 14.19** Achievable WER performance of the URW-BP, having the best values of $\rho$ listed in Table 14.14, compared with the "modified non-binary," when used on its own. Performance is evaluated for the System I of Table 14.9 using $I_{max} = 10$, 20 and 90 iterations. *Source*: [80]/IEEE.

**Table 14.15** Performance comparison of URW-BP with the modified BP for System I of Table 14.9, based on Figure 14.19.

| | ***p* at a WER of $10^{-3}$** | | |
|---|---|---|---|
| $I_{max}$ | **Modified BP** | **URW-BP** | **Increase** |
| 10 | 0.0125 | 0.0155 | 24% |
| 20 | 0.015 | 0.017 | 13% |
| 90 | 0.018 | 00185 | 3% |

*Source*: [316]/IEEE.

- We may exploit four main global structures of the PCM $H$ for designing QLDPC codes, namely dual-containing CSS, non-dual-containing CSS, non-CSS and entanglement-assisted solutions of Figure 14.1. The design challenges associated with each of these structures are summarized as follows:
  - **Dual-containing CSS (Section 14.2.1):** MacKay's bicycle codes are so far the best amongst the dual-containing CSS codes, but their performance is not on par with the classical LDPC codes. This is because

  this construction suffers the most from having short cycles, which exist both in the binary as well as in the GF(4) formalism.
  - **Non-dual-containing CSS Codes (Section 14.2.1):** It is difficult to find a pair of sparse binary PCMs satisfying the symplectic criterion, which constitute good QLDPC codes. At the time of writing, only the SC QC-LDPC codes and the non-binary QC-QLDPC codes are known to perform close to the Hashing bound. But this comes either at the cost of pre-shared noiseless ebits or at an increased complexity.
  - **Non-CSS Codes (Section 14.2.2):** Ideally, non-CSS constructions are preferred over the CSS codes because they exploit the redundant qubits more efficiently. However, finding good non-CSS QLDPC codes remains an open challenge at the time of writing.
  - **EA Codes (Section 14.2.3):** Entanglement-assistance may aid in achieving a performance comparable to that of the classical LDPC codes. However again, this requires pre-shared ebits, which constitute a valuable resource gleaned at the cost of a transmission overhead. Therefore, efforts must be made to minimize the number of required ebits.
- Additionally, it is desirable that the resulting QLDPC code has the following attributes:
  - A structured PCM, for example a cyclic or quasi-cyclic structure, for facilitating its implementation; and
  - An unbounded minimum distance or at least a sufficiently high minimum distance for long block lengths.

We further discussed in Section 14.3 that QLDPC codes may be decoded using syndrome-based BP either in the binary domain or in the non-binary domain. Besides the obvious lower complexity of the binary decoding, the two main differences between these decoding regimes are:

- In contrast to the binary decoding of Section 14.3.1, which assumes that the bit-flips and phase-flips are independent, non-binary decoding of Section 14.3.2 takes into account the correlation between them, which improves their performance.
- The number of length-4 cycles is higher in the non-binary formalism of the PCM as compared to the binary one. This tends to degrade the performance of the non-binary decoder.

Hence, we have a pair of conflicting attributes.

From the perspective of decoding, the challenges discussed in Section 14.3.3 may be summarized as follows:

- **Degeneracy:** Quantum codes are inherently degenerate in nature. This may improve the associated decoding performance if the decoder takes this degeneracy into account. Unfortunately, the BP algorithm does not exploit this degeneracy. In fact, since BP is based on marginalized probabilities, the presence of degenerate errors impairs its performance.
- **Short Cycles:** Unavoidable length-4 cycles found in QLDPC codes degrade the performance of BP. This gets even worse for the homogeneous CSS codes, when they are decoded in the non-binary domain.

Heuristic methods, namely random perturbation and enhanced feedback, are known to mitigate both these issues to some extent. However, this is achieved at the cost of an increased decoding complexity.

In the spirit to construct non-dual-containing CSS QLDPC codes, we conceived a formalism in Section 14.4 for constructing high-rate row-circulant QC-QLDPC codes from arbitrary row-circulant classical LDPC matrices. Since our design is merely based on the transpose and column permutation operations, the characteristics of the underlying classical LDPC matrix are not compromised. In particular, we applied our formalism to the BIBD-based classical LDPCs for evaluating its performance in Section 14.5. It was demonstrated in Figure 14.10 that our designed [2534, 2172] QLDPC code is capable of tolerating three times higher depolarizing probability at a WER of $10^{-4}$ as compared to its EA (homogeneous) counterpart and about four times higher depolarizing probability, when compared to an equivalent dual-containing bicycle code in the GF(4) formalism. This is because both the homogeneous EA-QLDPC codes as well as the dual-containing QLDPCs have numerous short cycles in the GF(4) formalism, which impair the performance of the decoding algorithm.

In Section 14.6, we conceived a modified non-binary decoding algorithm for homogeneous CSS-type QLDPC codes, which successfully mitigated the problems imposed by unavoidable length-4 cycles. In Section 14.8.1, we demonstrated in Figures 14.14–Figure 14.17 that our modified decoder exhibits a superior WER performance,

**Table 14.16** Summary of the simulation results of Section 14.8.1 at a WER of $10^{-4}$.

| Dec. No. | Decoding method | $p$ at WER $= 10^{-4}$ | Improvement in $p$ | $I_{avg}$ |
|---|---|---|---|---|
| System I of Table 14.9 (Figures 14.14 and 14.15) | | | | |
| 1 | Binary | 0.0085 | — | 1.7 |
| 2 | Standard non-binary | 0.01075 | 26% w.r.t. Dec. 1 | 2.6 |
| 3 | Random perturbation | 0.014 | 30% w.r.t. Dec. 2 | 4.19 |
| 4 | Enhanced feedback | 0.014 | 30% w.r.t. Dec. 2 | 3.6 |
| 5 | Modified non-binary | 0.014 | 30% w.r.t. Dec. 2 | 2.47 |
| 6 | Modified and enhanced feedback | 0.017 | 21% w.r.t. Dec. 5 | 3.4 |
| System II of Table 14.12 (Figures 14.16 and 14.17) | | | | |
| 1 | Binary | 0.057 | — | 4 |
| 2 | Standard non-binary | 0.069 | 21% w.r.t. Dec. 1 | 5 |
| 3 | Random perturbation | 0.076 | 10% w.r.t. Dec. 2 | 7.5 |
| 4 | Enhanced feedback | 0.082 | 19% w.r.t. Dec. 2 | 7 |
| 5 | Modified non-binary | 0.085 | 23% w.r.t. Dec. 2 | 5.5 |
| 6 | Modified and enhanced feedback | 0.0945 | 11% w.r.t. Dec. 5 | 7 |

despite its lower decoding complexity, when compared to the state-of-the-art decoding techniques. We also amalgamated our improved decoding algorithm with the heuristic methods for attaining additional performance gains. Results are summarized in Table 14.16.

In Section 14.7, we laid out the reweighted BP algorithm, which is known to alleviate the issue of short cycles in classical LDPC codes. In Section 14.8.2, we amalgamated our modified algorithm of Section 14.6 with the URW-BP of Section 14.7 for evaluating the performance. It was demonstrated in Figure 14.19 that URW-BP can be exploited for counteracting the issues of short-cycles, particularly when the maximum number of decoding iterations is small. More specifically, the results summarized in Table 14.15 reveal that URW-BP improves the tolerable depolarizing probability by 24% at a WER of $10^{-3}$, when $I_{max} = 10$ decoding iterations are invoked, while the improvement decreases to 13% at $I_{max} = 20$. Increasing the maximum number of affordable decoding iterations to $I_{max} = 90$ reduces the performance gain to 3%.

# 15

# Summary and Future Research

## 15.1 Summary

The employment of QECCs for mitigating the deleterious effects of quantum decoherence is one of the promising techniques of realizing large-scale high-reliability quantum computers. The proposal of QSCs, which can be viewed as syndrome-based QECCs, has opened up the opportunity of transforming any powerful classical error correction codes into the quantum domain. In the field of classical error correction code, the main goal is to protect the transmission of classical information over classical channels. However, in the quantum domain, the quantum transmission channel is not the only source of quantum decoherence that may erode the integrity of quantum information. The imperfect quantum gates may also impose additional deleterious effects on quantum information. Against this background, this research monograph has aimed for

- **a.** Exploiting the classical-to-quantum isomorphism to characterize the performance of QSCs;
- **b.** Finding the appropriate mechanism for utilizing QSCs not only for protecting the transmission of fragile quantum information over quantum channels but also for improving the reliability of imperfect quantum gates.

In light of these goals, the results of the research portrayed in the book can be summarized as follows:

- **a. Chapter 1:** In Section 1.1, we presented the motivation of quantum computation as well as quantum communication and argued that using QECCs is vital for realizing reliable quantum computers. In Section 1.2, we proceeded with a historical perspective on the important milestones in the field of QSCs and QTECCs.
- **b. Chapter 2 Preliminaries on Quantum Information**
  In this chapter, we provided a rudimentary introduction to quantum information processing. In Section 2.2, we introduced the elementary unit of quantum information, namely quantum bit (qubit). This was followed by Section 2.3, where we described the basics of quantum information processing widely used for manipulating the quantum state of the qubits, which cover the unitary transformations and quantum measurements. In Section 2.4, we elaborated on the different quantum channel models used throughout this part of the book, while in Section 2.5, we presented one of the challenges imposed in designing QSCs, namely the no-cloning theorem. Finally, in Section 2.6, we portrayed the quantum entanglement as one of the distinct properties inherited by quantum information, which does not have a classical counterpart.
- **c. Chapter 3 From Classical to Quantum Coding**
  In this chapter, we presented the classical-to-quantum isomorphism and used it for constructing QSCs by highlighting their similarity with classical linear block codes. The general concept of syndrome-based decoding conceived for classical linear block codes was introduced in Section 3.2. By exploiting the classical-to-quantum Pauli mapping in Section 3.3, we demonstrated that any QSC can be treated as a classical linear block code having two separate PCMs. Furthermore in Section 3.4, we described three pioneering contributions on QSCs, namely, the 9-qubit Shor's code, the 7-qubit Steane's code, and the 5-qubit Laflamme's code. The code parameters and the description of the aforementioned codes are given in Table 15.1. In Figure 3.8, we have demonstrated that the three codes performed similarly in the face of quantum depolarizing channels despite their different code parameters while exhibiting different types of QSCs.

**Table 15.1** Code parameters for Shor's, Steane's, and Laflamme's code. All the QSCs presented here are capable of correcting a single-qubit error.

| Codes | $n$ | $k$ | $d$ | $r_Q$ | Type |
|---|---|---|---|---|---|
| Shor's code | 9 | 1 | 3 | 1/9 | non-dual-containing CSS |
| Steane's code | 7 | 1 | 3 | 1/7 | dual-containing CSS |
| Laflamme's code | 5 | 1 | 3 | 1/5 | non-CSS |

**d. Chapter 4: Revisiting Classical Syndrome Decoding**

The stabilizer codes discussed relied on classical syndrome decoding applied to the equivalent classical code derived on the basis of the underlying quantum-to-binary or quantum-to-quaternary isomorphism. In this chapter we further detailed our discussions on the family of classical syndrome decoding techniques.

Recall that the notion of syndrome decoding derives its essence from the look-up table (LUT)-based syndrome decoding of classical linear block codes, which was discussed in Section 4.2. More explicitly, in contrast to the conventionally used codeword decoding, which aims for finding the most likely codeword, syndrome decoding aims for identifying the most likely channel error vector. It was demonstrated in Section 4.2 that in the context of linear block codes, LUT-based syndrome decoding substantially reduces the storage requirements of the standard array-based codeword decoding. In Section 4.3, the concept of syndrome decoding was extended to trellis-based decoding. In particular, Section 4.3.1 discussed the construction of syndrome-based trellis of linear block codes, while Section 4.3.2 presented the syndrome-based trellis of convolutional codes. It was pointed out that since every path in the error trellis of Figure 4.6 corresponds to a path in the codeword trellis of Figure 4.7, these representations are exactly equivalent. Furthermore, each path of the error trellis is a legitimate error sequence for a given observed syndrome, while each path in the codeword trellis is a valid codeword. Consequently, the former is used for syndrome decoding, while the latter is exploited for codeword decoding.

The error trellis-based syndrome decoding is of particular significance, because the state probabilities of an error trellis depend on the channel errors, rather than on the coded sequence. Consequently, in the low noise regime, the syndrome decoder is more likely to encounter a zero-state due to having predominantly error-free transmissions. This unique feature of error trellis-based syndrome decoding led to the discussion on block syndrome decoding (BSD) in Section 4.4. Section 4.4.1 presented the general BSD formalism, while Section 4.4.2 conceived a reduced-complexity BSD for turbo trellis coded modulation (TTCM), hence referred to as "BSD-TTCM," whose schematic was given in Figure 4.10. The proposed BSD-TTCM divides the received frame into error-free and erroneous sub-blocks based on the syndrome of the received frame. Only the erroneous blocks are subsequently decoded, thereby reducing the decoding complexity. This yields a reduction in the decoding complexity in the higher signal-to-noise ratio (SNR) region as well as for higher-indexed decoding iterations. Furthermore, the performance of BSD-TTCM of Figure 4.10 depends on the design parameter $L_{\min}$, which is the minimum number of consecutive zero syndromes after which the sub-block is deemed to be error-free. Section 4.5 evaluated the performance of the BSD-TTCM of Figure 4.10 for transmission over a classical additive white Gaussian noise (AWGN) channel as well as an uncorrelated Rayleigh fading channel. The results of Figures 4.12 to 4.17 obtained for the TTCM of Table 4.1 are summarized in Table 15.2. Here, the design parameter $L_{\min}$ was heuristically optimized for ensuring that BSD-TTCM yields the same BER performance as the conventional full-complexity decoder TTCM decoder, as evidenced in Figures 4.12 and 4.15 for transmission over an AWGN and a Rayleigh fading channel, respectively. Section 4.5.3 further evaluated the performance of BSD-TTCM for a short frame of only 500 symbols. The BSD-TTCM scheme was found to outperform the frequently used high-SNR early termination technique shown in Figure 4.20, despite the short frame length.

**e. Chapter 5 Near-capacity Code Designs for Entanglement-assisted Classical Communication**

In this chapter, extrinsic information transfer (EXIT) chart-aided near-capacity classical code designs were presented for reliable transmission of classical information over a secure quantum channel. In particular, we focused our attention on the entanglement-assisted transmission of classical information over a depolarizing channel, which was achieved with the aid of the SuperDense (SD) coding protocol.

**Table 15.2** Decoding complexity reduction of BSD-TTCM (summarized from the simulation results of Figures 4.12 to 4.17, which were obtained for the TTCM of Table 4.1). Decoding complexity is quantified in terms of the percentage of no-decoding (second column) and the equivalent number of iterations (third column). Complexity reduction is further compared with high-SNR early termination technique (fourth column).

| Channel | Percentage of no-decoding | Equivalent no. of iterations | Comparison with early termination |
|---|---|---|---|
| AWGN | At least 20% and 45% reduction in the 5th and 6th iterations, respectively. | At least 17% deduction. | At least a reduction of 0.5 iteration. |
| Rayleigh | At least 20% and 30% reduction in the 5th and 6th iterations, respectively. | At least 12% deduction. | At least a reduction of 0.5 iteration. |

Explicitly, in Section 5.2, we briefly reviewed the SD protocol, which maps the classical bits onto qubits for transmission over a quantum channel. More specifically, the 2-qubit SD (2SD) protocol was presented in Section 5.2.1, which transmits two classical bits per channel use (cbits/use) with the aid of a single pre-shared entangled qubit. The 2SD protocol of Section 5.2.1 was further generalized to its $N$-qubit SD (NSD) counterpart in Section 5.2.2, which facilitates the transmission of $N$ classical bits by sending only $(N-1)$ qubits over the noisy quantum channel, while one qubit is pre-shared with the receiver before actual transmission takes place. More explicitly, we considered the $N=3$ scenario, resulting in a transmission rate of 1.5 cbits/use. The corresponding quantum circuits designed for the 2SD and 3SD protocols were given in Figures 5.2 and 5.3, respectively. The associated Entanglement-Assisted Classical Capacity (EACC) was derived for the generalized NSD transmission in Section 5.3, which was specifically characterized for the 2SD and 3SD schemes in Eqs. (5.17) and (5.19), respectively.

Section 5.4 proposed a radically new amalgamated classical-quantum code structure, where a classical Irregular convolutional code (IRCC) was concatenated with a classical symbol-based recursive unity rate code (URC) and a quantum-based SD mapper through a bit interleaver. More explicitly, an IRCC constitutes the outer code of the proposed code design, while the URC and SD scheme were combined to form a single inner component. The resultant system was referred to as a "bit-based IRCC-URC-SD" arrangement, whose schematic was given in Figure 5.4. Furthermore, iterative decoding was invoked for exchanging *extrinsic* information between the inner (URC-SD) and outer (IRCC) decoders. We next presented our EXIT-chart-aided near-capacity design criterion in Section 5.5 for optimizing the weighting coefficients of the IRCC. The design guidelines conceived for our IRCC-URC-SD structure are summarized as follows:

- Using the bit-based capacity curves of Figure 5.5, the noise limit $p^*$, which may be defined as the maximum tolerable channel depolarizing probability, is determined for the desired classical information transmission rate in cbits/use and for the required SD protocol.
- The inner decoder EXIT curve of the amalgamated twin-component inner (URC-SD) decoder is computed at a channel depolarizing probability of $p=(p^*-\epsilon)$ using the binary EXIT chart generation approach of Section 5.5.1. Here $\epsilon$ is a small number, which characterizes the distance from the capacity $p^*$.
- Finally, as discussed in Section 5.5.2, the weighting coefficients of the IRCC subcodes, having an overall coding rate of $R_o$, are optimized for the sake of ensuring that a marginally open tunnel exists between the EXIT curves of the outer and inner decoder at the highest possible depolarizing probability, i.e at the lowest value of $\epsilon$. This in turn guarantees that the system has a near-capacity performance.

The performance of the bit-based IRCC-URC-SD design invoked for our 2SD and 3SD schemes was evaluated in Sections 5.6.1 and 5.6.2, respectively, which was benchmarked against the bit-based EACC of Figure 5.5. It was demonstrated that the actual convergence threshold determined using the bit error rate (BER) performance curves of Figures 5.8 and 5.12 was the same as the EXIT chart predictions of Figures 5.7 and 5.11, respectively. Furthermore, the BER performance improved upon increasing the number of iterations, as long as the depolarizing probability was lower than the convergence threshold, which was quantified in Figures 5.9 and 5.13 in terms of the distance from capacity (dB) at BER of $10^{-4}$. However, the performance only improved with diminishing returns at a higher number of iterations. In particular, the convergence threshold of the designed systems of Figures 5.7 and 5.11 was within 0.4 dB of the achievable noise limit for both 2SD as well as for 3SD schemes. More specifically, the normalized capacity loss was only

**Table 15.3** Comparison of the decoding complexity and the achievable performance of the TC-SD and IRCC-URC-SD schemes. Decoding complexity is quantified in terms of the number of iterations required for achieving a near-perfect convergence, which is denoted as $I_\infty$, while the achievable performance is measured in terms of the distance from the bit-based capacity at a BER of $10^{-4}$.

| Code structure | $I_\infty$ | Distance from capacity at BER = $10^{-4}$ | Reference figures |
|---|---|---|---|
| IRCC-URC-2SD | 32 | 0.6 dB | Figures 5.8 and 5.9 |
| IRCC-URC-3SD | 32 | 0.7 dB | Figures 5.12 and 5.13 |
| TC-2SD | 16 | 1.9 dB | Figure 5.14 |
| TC-3SD | 16 | 2.2 dB | Figure 5.14 |

**Table 15.4** Comparison of the decoding complexity and the achievable performance of the bit-based IRCC-URC-2SD and the symbol-based CC-URC-2SD schemes. The decoding complexity is quantified in terms of the number of iterations required for achieving a near-perfect convergence, which is denoted as $I_\infty$, while the achievable performance is measured in terms of the distance from the symbol-based capacity at a BER of $10^{-4}$.

| Code structure | $I_\infty$ | Distance from capacity at BER = $10^{-4}$ | Reference figures |
|---|---|---|---|
| IRCC-URC-2SD | 32 | 1.2 dB | Figures 5.8 and 5.9 |
| CC(2, 1, 2)-URC-2SD | 20 | 1 dB | Figures 5.17 and 5.18 |
| CC(2, 1, 3)-URC-2SD | 20 | 1 dB | Figure 5.21 |
| CC(2, 1, 4)-URC-2SD | 20 | 1 dB | Figure 5.21 |

0.062 and 0.031 cbits/use from the corresponding 2-qubit and 3-qubit noise limits, respectively. The attainable performance was also benchmarked against that of classical turbo codes in Figure 5.14. These results are summarized in Table 15.3.

The bit-based IRCC-URC-SD code structure of Figure 5.4 incurred a capacity loss due to the symbol-to-bit conversion, which was quantified in Figure 5.5. To alleviate this issue, a symbol-based CC-URC-SD scheme was conceived in Section 5.7, where a symbol-based classical convolutional code (CC) was concatenated with an integrated URC-SD through a symbol interleaver. The proposed CC-URC-SD scheme was optimized with the aid of nonbinary EXIT charts. More specifically, we optimized the system in Section 5.8 by exhaustively searching through all the possible generator polynomials in Figure 5.16 for finding the specific CC whose EXIT curve yields a marginally open tunnel at the highest possible depolarizing probability. The resultant optimal memory-2, memory-3, and memory-4 CCs of Figure 5.20 were found to have the octally represented generator polynomials of $(g_1, g_2) = (7, 5)_8$, $(g_1, g_2) = (17, 15)_8$ and $(g_1, g_2) = (31, 36)_8$, respectively. The simulation results of Figure 5.19 demonstrated that the symbol-based CC-URC-2SD provides a significant BER performance improvement, despite its lower encoding/decoding complexity than that of the bit-based IRCC-URC-2SD. Quantitatively, we observed in Figure 5.19 that after two iterations our proposed symbol-based CC-URC-2SD design incorporating a memory-4 CC outperformed the bit-based IRCC-URC-2SD scheme of Figure 5.4 by 3.7 dB at a BER of $10^{-4}$. Even the memory-2 and memory-3 designs were found to outperform the bit-based IRCC-URC-2SD in Figure 5.21. Furthermore, the performance of the bit-based IRCC-URC-2SD and the symbol-based CC-URC-2SD were comparable, once perfect convergence was achieved. Nonetheless, the symbol-based designs imposed a lower decoding complexity, because they require less iterations, as quantified in Table 15.4.

**f. Chapter 6 Quantum Coding Bounds**

In this chapter, we discussed the natural trade-off between the conflicting parameters of QSC design, which were described with the aid of quantum coding bound formulations. By exploiting the classical to quantum isomorphism in Section 6.2, we have derived the quantum coding bounds from their classical counterparts. More explicitly, we derived the quantum-domain version of Singleton, Hamming, and Gilbert-Varshamov bounds. Next, we conducted a comprehensive survey of quantum coding bounds along with

**Table 15.5** The realistically achievable minimum distance $d$ for QSCs exhibiting various quantum coding rates and various numbers of physical qubits. Additionally, when the number of physical qubits is sufficiently large ($n \to \infty$), the scaling of the minimum distance $d$ is linear with constant factor $\delta$. The values portrayed here were obtained using the approximation presented in Section 6.5 and have been illustrated in Figure 6.8.

| $r_Q$ | $d(n=32)$ | $n=64$ | $n=128$ | $n=256$ | $n=512$ | $n=1024$ | $n \to \infty$ |
|---|---|---|---|---|---|---|---|
| 3/4 | 4 | 5 | 9 | 15 | 26 | 47 | $\delta = 0.048$ |
| 2/3 | 5 | 7 | 11 | 19 | 35 | 67 | $\delta = 0.065$ |
| 1/2 | 6 | 10 | 17 | 29 | 54 | 99 | $\delta = 0.100$ |
| 1/3 | 8 | 13 | 22 | 40 | 75 | 139 | $\delta = 0.137$ |
| 1/4 | 8 | 14 | 25 | 46 | 87 | 163 | $\delta = 0.157$ |
| $1/n \approx 0$ | 10 | 18 | 34 | 66 | 130 | 258 | $\delta = 0.219$ |

**Table 15.6** The normalized minimum distance $\delta$ for EA-QSCs having a sufficiently large number of physical qubits ($n \to \infty$) for various entanglement ratios $\theta$. The values portrayed here were calculated using the approximation described in Section 6.4 and have been illustrated in Figure 6.4.

| $r_Q$ | $\delta(\theta = 0.10)$ | $\theta = 0.25$ | $\theta = 0.50$ | $\theta = 0.75$ | $\theta = 1$ |
|---|---|---|---|---|---|
| 3/4 | 0.053 | 0.061 | 0.073 | 0.087 | 0.100 |
| 2/3 | 0.072 | 0.082 | 0.100 | 0.118 | 0.137 |
| 1/2 | 0.111 | 0.128 | 0.157 | 0.187 | 0.219 |
| 1/3 | 0.153 | 0.177 | 0.219 | 0.265 | 0.316 |
| 1/4 | 0.175 | 0.203 | 0.253 | 0.310 | 0.375 |
| $1/n \approx 0$ | 0.246 | 0.290 | 0.374 | 0.484 | **0.750** |

the proposal of a simple closed-form approximation for determining the realistically achievable minimum distance given, a specific the codeword length and quantum coding rate as a promising toolkit for designing the QSCs. Our proposed formula is applicable for both the idealized asymptotical case as detailed in Section 6.3, as well as for practical finite-length codeword length as described in Section 6.4. Finally in Section 6.5, we derived the quantum coding bounds for arbitrarily entangled QSCs to unify the bounds for entanglement-assisted and the unassisted QSCs.

More explicitly, we constructed Table 15.5 portraying the realistically achievable minimum distance for finite-length QSCs exhibiting various quantum coding rates and numbers of physical qubits based on the approximation formula provided in Section 6.4. Furthermore, provided that we have obtained the realistically achievable minimum distance value, we can directly approximate the QBER performance using the formula in Eq. (6.30). It is pertinent to mention that for a QSC having a very large number of physical qubits ($n \to \infty$), the minimum distance of the QSC is linearly proportional to the number of physical qubits as defined by the constant factor $\delta$. For instance, the $\delta$ value obtained is equal to 0.100 for a half-rate QSC at the asymptotical limit, as shown in Table 15.5. Furthermore, we constructed Table 15.6, where we describe the value of normalized minimum distance $\delta$ for various EA-QSCs having entanglement ratios of $\theta = \{0.1, 0.25, 0.50, 0.75, 1\}$. Additionally, when $\theta$ is equal to 0, we arrive at the relevant approximation for the unassisted QSCs. By contrast, when $\theta = 1$ and $r_Q = 0$, we achieve the ultimate limit of QSCs, where we have $\delta = 0.750$.

g. **Chapter 7 Quantum Topological Error Correction Codes**

In this chapter, we extended our parametric study of the minimum distance versus quantum coding rate to QTECCs. In Section 7.2, we commenced by presenting the explicit construction of classical TECCs based on the underlying lattice structure. We found that the resultant TECCs constitute a class of LDPC codes for long codewords. The properties of the classical TECC-based LDPC codes are summarized in Table 15.7. We can observe that the resultant LDPC codes inherit some beneficial properties, such as low row-weight ($\rho$) and low column-weight ($\gamma$). However, the TECC-based LDPC codes have a moderate advantage, since the growth of

**Table 15.7** The code parameters of TECC-based LDPC codes obtained from Section 7.2.

| Parameter | Square | Triangular | Rotated-square |
|---|---|---|---|
| $r$ | $\approx \frac{1}{2}$ | $\approx \frac{1}{2}$ | $\approx \frac{1}{2}$ |
| $d$ | $\mathcal{O}(\sqrt{n})$ | $\mathcal{O}(\sqrt{n})$ | $\mathcal{O}(\sqrt{n})$ |
| $\delta$ | $\frac{d}{2d^2-2d+1}$ | $\frac{4d}{3d^2+1}$ | $\frac{1}{d}$ |
| $\rho_{max}$ | 4 | 6 | 4 |
| $\gamma_{max}$ | 2 | 3 | 2 |
| Girth | 6 | 4 | 8 |

**Table 15.8** The code parameters of QTECC viewed as QLDPC codes obtained from Section 7.3.

| Parameter | Square | Triangular | Rotated-square |
|---|---|---|---|
| $r$ | $\approx 0$ | $\approx 0$ | $\approx 0$ |
| $d$ | $\mathcal{O}(\sqrt{n})$ | $\mathcal{O}(\sqrt{n})$ | $\mathcal{O}(\sqrt{n})$ |
| $\delta$ | $\frac{d}{2d^2-2d+1}$ | $\frac{4d}{3d^2+1}$ | $\frac{1}{d}$ |
| $\rho_{max}$ | 4 | 6 | 4 |
| $\gamma_{max}$ | 2 | 3 | 2 |
| Girth | 6 | 4 | 8 |

the minimum distance is proportional to the square-root of the codeword length. Additionally, we can find numerous short cycles in the Tanner graph representation of the TECC-based LDPC codes.

Next in Section 7.3, we extended the code construction of the classical domain to create the associated quantum dual pairs, namely the QTECCs. In contrast to the classical TECCs, the QTECCs suffer from a low quantum coding rate, because in order to create the stabilizer formalism of the QTECCs, we need a pair of classical PCM of the TECCs. Consequently, the quantum coding rate of QTECCs tends to zero, when the number of physical qubits is high. Therefore, we believe that the QTECCs are preferable for short to moderate codeword lengths. We summarized the properties of QTECCs as QLDPC codes in Table 15.8. Once again, the properties of the QTECCs are practically identical to those of the classical TECCs, except for having low quantum coding rates. In addition, based on the QBER formula of Eq. (7.31), we found the values of the quantum depolarizing probability threshold ($p_{th}$) for four different QTECCs, namely the color, rotated-surface, surface, and toric codes. These $p_{th}$ values ultimately characterize the QBER performance of the QTECCs on asymptotical limit, namely when $n \rightarrow \infty$ and $r_Q \approx 0$. However, this QBER formula, unfortunately, does not capture the benefit of the degeneracy property, which is inherent in the QTECCs construction. Nonetheless, the $p_{th}$ values obtained from Eq. (7.31) can be used for estimating the upper bound which is the worst-case scenario of the attainable QTECCs performance. The $p_{th}$ value of each type of the QTECC is presented in Table 15.9.

**h. Chapter 8 Protecting Quantum Gates Using Quantum Topological Error Correction Codes**

The benefits of QSCs are more far-reaching than simply protecting quantum information from the effects of quantum decoherence imposed by the quantum channel. They are also eminently suitable for improving the reliability of imperfect quantum gates. In this chapter, we presented the general framework of protecting quantum gates by utilizing QSCs. In Section 8.2, we commenced by demonstrating how to transform the formulation of QSCs conceived for correcting quantum bits into the QSCs formulation suitable for improving the reliability of imperfect quantum gates. More specifically, we introduced the notion of effective stabilizer formalism and effective inverse encoder in the context of accommodating imperfect unitary transformations. More specifically, we represented the unitary transformations by the transversal configuration of quantum Clifford gates. In Section 8.3, we provided an elaborate example of the scheme advocated by using 1/3-rate quantum repetition codes for protecting transversal Hadamard gates and transversal CNOT gates. Moving one step further, by exploiting the attractive properties of QTECCs such as the limited number of

**Table 15.9** The upper bound and the lower bound of the depolarizing probability threshold ($p_{th}$) values for different QTECCs. The upper bound values are obtained using Eq. (7.31) in Section 7.4, while the lower bound values are obtained using Eq. (8.82) in Section 8.5.2.

| Codes | Upper bound $p_{th}$ | Lower bound $p_{th}$ |
|---|---|---|
| Color codes | 1.83% | 10.78% |
| Rotated-surface codes | 1.36% | 10.20% |
| Surface codes | 0.63% | 10.63% |
| Toric codes | 0.68% | 10.85% |

**Table 15.10** The upper bound and the lower bound of the depolarizing fidelity threshold ($F_{th}$) values for Hadamard gates protected by different types of QTECCs. These values are obtained from Section 8.5.2 using Eqs. (8.81) and (8.82) for the upper bound and the lower bound, respectively.

| Codes | Upper bound $F_{th}$ | Lower bound $F_{th}$ |
|---|---|---|
| Color codes | 99.74% | 98.46% |
| Rotated-surface codes | 99.73% | 97.96% |
| Surface codes | 97.87% | 97.87% |
| Toric codes | 99.86% | 97.83% |

interactions amongst the qubits and the localized stabilizer measurements, we invoked QTECCs as our prime examples for this scheme in Section 8.5.

The main results of this chapter can be summarized as follows. Firstly, in order to gain a better insight into the true QBER performance of QTECCs, we derived an analytical lower bound formula for a given number of logical and physical qubits in Eq. (8.82). This lower bound QBER performance of Eq. (8.82) is obtained by using the sphere-packing bound for CSS-type QSCs. When $n$ is very large, this lower bound is equivalent to the quantum hashing limit for CSS-type QSCs. This formula can be used as the lower bound of the QBER performance since, at the time of writing, there are no QSCs that can perform beyond the hashing limit, not even when the degeneracy property can be successfully exploited. Based on Eq. (8.82), we also obtained the lower bound of the depolarizing probability threshold ($p_{th}$) values for various QTECCs, which we have summarized in Table 15.9.

Secondly, by assuming that we can provide a perfectly encoded quantum state and that the effects of quantum decoherence imposed on the qubits are uncorrelated, we obtained the minimum fidelity threshold values required by the physical implementation of quantum gates. In other words, we can significantly improve the performance of imperfect quantum Clifford gates, provided that a set of quantum gates exhibiting fidelity values better than $F_{th}$ are available. Otherwise, instead of beneficially improving the reliability of the quantum gates, the QSCs will actually further aggravate the error effects imposed by the imperfection of the quantum gates. The summary of the fidelity threshold $F_{th}$ values obtained for Hadamard and CNOT gates protected by various QTECCs is depicted in Tables 15.10 and 15.11, respectively.

i. **Chapter 9 Universal Decoding of Quantum BCH and Polar Codes via Classical Guesswork**
In this chapter a universal decoding scheme was designed for QSCs by further evolving the GRAND decoding philosophy–which was originally conceived for classical codes–for employment in the quantum domain. We demonstrated that the decoding scheme conceived may be adopted for two different QSC decoding paradigms, namely for both stabilizer-measurement-based and the inverse-encoder-based decoding. We then applied the resultant decoder for both quantum BCH codes and quantum polar codes and quantified their QBLER, QBLER per logical qubits as well as their decoding complexity. We concluded the chapter by a parametric study of the associated design trade-offs and provided design guidelines for the implementation of quantum-GRAND-aided QSC decoders. Based on our QBLER simulations, we demonstrated that when a

**Table 15.11** The upper bound and the lower bound of the depolarizing fidelity threshold ($F_{th}$) values for CNOT gates protected by different types of QTECCs. These values are obtained from Section 8.5.3 using Eqs. (8.90) and (8.91) for the upper bound and the lower bound, respectively.

| Codes | Upper bound $F_{th}$ | Lower bound $F_{th}$ |
|---|---|---|
| Color codes | 99.48% | 96.92% |
| Rotated-surface codes | 99.46% | 95.92% |
| Surface codes | 99.74% | 95.74% |
| Toric codes | 99.72% | 95.66% |

fixed number of $N$ physical qubits is considered, the higher the minimum distance $D$, the better the performance becomes.

According to the list of quantum BCH codes considered in Table 9.3, our simulations showed that the quantum BCH $[[63, 27, 7]]$ is much preferred for practical systems upon applying the Quantum-GRAND-aided stabilizer-measurement-based decoder. On the other hand, for quantum polar codes relying on the Quantum-GRAND-aided inverse-encoder-based decoder, the best overall QBLER performance is achieved by the $[[16, 2, D]]$ having quantum coding rate of $r_Q = 0.125$. Furthermore, based on our simulations, the Quantum-GRAND-aided decoder complexity of quantum BCH codes and quantum polar codes was shown to be dominated by $N$, because a lower $N$ requires a lower number of guesses to find the correct decoded codeword. Our future research might also explore the employment of soft-information-aided GRAND [271, 280, 281], which can also be done efficiently from the complexity point of view.

j. **Chapter 10 Revisiting the Classical to Quantum Coding Evolution**

As we stated repeatedly, quantum codes may be designed from the known classical codes by exploiting the underlying quantum-to-classical isomorphism. This transition from the classical to the quantum domain was introduced in Section 10.2, where the family of classical linear block codes was reviewed with a particular emphasis on the simple 3-bit repetition code. The stabilizer formalism, which facilitates the design of quantum codes from the classical ones, was then discussed in Section 10.3. It was demonstrated with the aid of the 3-qubit bit-flip repetition code and 3-qubit phase-flip repetition code that:

- The copying operation of classical codes is equivalent to copying the basis states of the qubit, which can be achieved via quantum entanglement;
- Measurement of a qubit may be circumvented by observing the channel errors without observing the actual quantum information by invoking the classical syndrome decoding techniques;
- Phase-flips may be corrected by copying in the Hadamard basis.

This quantum to classical transition was summarized in Figure 10.6.

Section 10.3.2 detailed the equivalence between the quantum and classical parity-check matrices (PCMs), focusing specifically on the Pauli-to-binary isomorphism in Section 10.3.2.1, while the Pauli-to-quaternary isomorphism was discussed in Section 10.3.2.2. The underlying mapping was also summarized in Table 10.11, which facilitates the design of quantum codes from arbitrary classical binary codes, if they meet the symplectic criterion, and from arbitrary classical quaternary codes, if they satisfy the Hermitian inner product. This in turn led to various structures of quantum stabilizer codes (QSCs), namely to the dual-containing Calderbank–Shor–Steane (CSS) as well as to the non-dual-containing CSS and non-CSS structures, which are summarized in Table 15.12. Furthermore, it was discussed in Section 10.3.3 that QSCs are degenerate in nature. Consequently, errors, which only differ by the generator of the stabilizer group have the same impact on the transmitted qubit and can be corrected by the same recovery operation. This further leads to the class of harmless undetected error patterns in Figure 10.9, which only exist in the quantum domain.

Section 10.4 extended the discussion of Section 10.3.2 to the family of convolutional codes, where both CSS-type and non-CSS-type quantum convolutional codes (QCCs) were designed from the known classical CCs. Section 10.5 then presented the entanglement-assisted (EA) stabilizer formalism. This formalism allows any classical code to be used as a quantum code, even if it does not meet the symplectic or Hermitian inner product

**Table 15.12** Summary of the stabilizer code structures.

| Code type | Parity-check matrix | Criteria | Design Examples |
|---|---|---|---|
| Dual-containing CSS | $\begin{pmatrix} H'_z & \mathbf{0} \\ \mathbf{0} & H'_z \end{pmatrix}$ | $H'_z H'^T_z = 0$ | Steane code of Eq. (10.36) and QCC of Eq. (10.65) |
| Non-dual-containing CSS | $\begin{pmatrix} H'_z & \mathbf{0} \\ \mathbf{0} & H'_x \end{pmatrix}$ | $H'_z \neq H'_x$ and $H'_z H'^T_x = 0$ | - |
| Non-CSS | $(H_z \vert H_x)$ | $H_z H_x^T + H_x H_z^T = 0$ | Hamming code of Eq. (10.51) and QCC of Eq. (10.68) |
| EA | $\begin{pmatrix} H'_z & \mathbf{0} \\ \mathbf{0} & H'_z \end{pmatrix}$ and $(H_z \vert H_x)$ | None | EA-QSC of Eq. (10.77) |

criterion. However, this is achieved with the aid of pre-shared entanglement, which is indeed a valuable resource gleaned at the cost of a transmission overhead. Therefore, efforts must be made to minimize the number of required entangled qubits.

The various stabilizer code structures discussed in this chapter are summarized in Table 15.12.

**k. Chapter 11 Near-hashing-bound Concatenated Quantum Codes**

Based on the insights developed in Chapter 10 as well as Chapter 4 and inspired by the EXIT-chart-aided near-capacity classical code designs of Chapter 5, we conceived a whole suite of near-hashing-bound concatenated QECCs using EXIT charts.

Section 11.2 presented our code design objectives, where the achievable capacity region, or more precisely the hashing region, was characterized in Figure 11.1, which depends on the coding rate, on the channel depolarizing probability as well as on the entanglement consumption rate. We then proceeded with the circuit-based representation of QCCs in Section 11.3, which facilitates the degenerate iterative decoding of concatenated quantum codes. We also discussed the construction of the Clifford unitary encoder, which is completely specified by the Hadamard as well as by the phase and the controlled-NOT gates of Eq. (11.12). This was further explained by constructing the equivalent binary Clifford encoder for a 3-qubit bit-flip repetition code using the encoding circuit of Figure 11.4. Finally, Section 11.4 detailed the structure and decoding of concatenated quantum codes, which may also be referred to as Quantum Turbo Codes (QTCs). More specifically, the schematic of a quantum communication system relying on a pair of concatenated QSCs was presented in Section 11.4.1, while the associated degenerate iterative decoding was detailed in Section 11.4.2. In particular, it was highlighted in Section 11.4.2 that unlike the conventional Maximum *A-Posteriori* (MAP) decoder, which yields the most likely error for a given syndrome, a degenerate MAP decoder aims for finding the most likely error coset by summing the probabilities over the set of degenerate errors (Eq. [11.49]).

Section 11.5 conceived the EXIT charts of the concatenated quantum code structure of Figure 11.6. More specifically, the classical nonbinary EXIT chart generation technique was extended to the circuit-based syndrome decoder of QTCs in Figures 11.9 and 11.10 for the inner and outer decoders, respectively. While the classical EXIT charts aim for modeling the *a-priori* information concerning the input bits of the inner encoder (and similarly the output bits of the outer encoder), the EXIT chart conceived for quantum codes models the *a-priori* information concerning the corresponding error-sequence, i.e. the error-sequence related to the input qubits of the inner encoder (and similarly the error-sequence related to the output qubits of the outer encoder). Section 11.6 then evaluated the accuracy of the EXIT charts of Section 11.5. It was demonstrated in Section 11.6.1 that the convergence threshold predicted by the EXIT-chart of Figure 11.12 is the same as the one determined using the Monte–Carlo simulation results of Figure 11.13. In Section 11.6.2, we analyzed the inner decoder EXIT curves of recursive (unassisted) and non-recursive (entanglement-assisted) QCCs in Figure 11.14 for demonstrating that the EXIT curve of a recursive inner QCC reaches the $(1, 1)$-point of perfect convergence. This in turn facilitates the design of families of QTCs having an unbounded minimum distance. Section 11.6.3 presented the inner and outer components of our optimized QTC in Figure 11.15, which were found using an EXIT-chart-aided exhaustive search. Our design guidelines for achieving a hashing-bound-approaching performance may be summarized as follows:

- **Design Criterion:** Determine the noise limit $p^*$ for the desired code parameters, i.e the coding rate and the entanglement consumption rate of the resultant QTC.
- **Selection of Inner Component:** Select a recursive and non-catastrophic inner EA-QCC, which can be either derived from the family of known classical codes, as discussed in Chapter 10, or it can be constructed using random Clifford operations, which were discussed in Section 11.3. At this point, the EXIT-chart technique investigated in Section 11.5 is invoked for the sake of finding that specific QCC, which yields the largest area under its inner decoder EXIT-curve at the noise limit $p^*$.
- **Selection of Outer Component:** Find a non-catastrophic outer QCC, whose EXIT curve gives the best EXIT-curve match with the inner decoder EXIT curve of the chosen inner code. Our EXIT-chart-aided design of Section 11.5 aims for creating a narrow, but marginally open tunnel between the EXIT curves of the inner and outer decoders at the highest possible depolarizing probability, as demonstrated in Figure 11.15. The narrower the tunnel area, the lower is the deviation from the hashing bound, which is quantified using Eq. (11.2).

Based on the EXIT chart of Figure 11.15 and the achievable performance of Figure 11.16, it was demonstrated in Section 11.6.3 that the convergence threshold of our optimized QTC is 0.6 dB closer to the hashing limit as compared to the distance-spectra-based QTCs of [82]. However, this is achieved at the cost of a higher word error rate (WER) floor, which may be reduced upon increasing the interleaver length, as evidenced in Figure 11.16, hence imposing a longer delay.

Section 11.7 proposed the structure of a 10-subcode quantum irregular convolutional code (QIRCC) for further facilitating the hashing-bound-approaching code design. The proposed QIRCC may be dynamically adapted to match any given inner code using EXIT charts, hence allowing us to dispense with the exhaustive code search. Section 11.8 quantified the impact of using QIRCC as the outer component in Figure 11.6, which was recorded in Figure 11.21. As evidenced in Figure 11.22, the QIRCC-based optimized design, when used in conjunction with the same inner code as that of the QTC in [82], outperformed the QTC of [82] both in terms of the convergence threshold as well as the achievable WER performance. The results are also summarized in Table 15.13. However, this was achieved at the cost of an increased decoding complexity, because the former invoked a maximum of $\mathtt{I}_{max} = 15$ iterations in contrast to the $\mathtt{I}_{max} = 8$ iterations invoked by the latter. The QIRCC-based optimized design of Figure 11.20 also had a lower WER than the exhaustive-search-based optimized design of Section 11.6.3, as demonstrated in Figure 11.22.

l. **Chapter 12 Near-hashing-bound Quantum Turbo Short-block Codes**
Throughout the book we have repeatedly emphasized that QSCs suffer from a low quantum coding rate since they have to recover the qubits in the face of both bit-flip and phase-flip errors. In this chapter, we conceived a low-complexity concatenated QTC design exhibiting a high quantum coding rate. This high quantum coding rate was achieved by combining the quantum-domain version of SBCs as the outer codes and QURCs as the inner codes. In Section 12.2, we commenced by providing the explicit description of QSBCs in terms of the PCM formulations, quantum encoders, stabilizer measurements, as well as their classical simulation. In Section 12.3, we detailed our novel QTC design, which is utilizing QSBCs as the outer codes and QURCs as

**Table 15.13** Comparison of the performance of the QTC of [82] with our QIRCC-based QTC, when the same inner code was used.

| | Distance from capacity | |
|---|---|---|
| **Code structure** | **Convergence threshold** | **Performance at WER = $10^{-3}$** |
| QTC of [82] | 0.9 dB | 1.15 dB |
| QIRCC-based QTC | 0.4 dB | 0.7 dB |

*Source:* Adapted from [82].

**Table 15.14** The minimum depolarizing probability ($p$) values required for QIrCC-QURC and QSBC-QURC for achieving various QBER targets as seen in Figure 12.11. The number of logical qubits is $k = 2000$.

| Target | $p$ QIrCC-QURC | $p$ QSBC-QURC |
|---|---|---|
| QBER < $QBER_{uncoded}$ | 0.043 | **0.058** |
| QBER < $10^{-3}$ | 0.037 | **0.045** |
| QBER < $10^{-4}$ | **0.035** | 0.030 |

**Table 15.15** The minimum depolarizing probability ($p$) values required QSBC-QURC having quantum coding rates of $r_Q = \{1/2, 2/3, 3/4\}$ for achieving various QBER targets as seen in Figure 12.12. The number of logical qubits is $k = 2000$.

| Target | $r_Q = 1/2$ | $r_Q = 2/3$ | $r_Q = 3/4$ |
|---|---|---|---|
| QBER < $QBER_{uncoded}$ | 0.058 | 0.030 | 0.021 |
| QBER < $10^{-3}$ | 0.045 | 0.023 | 0.016 |

the inner codes referred to as QSBC-QURC scheme. Then in Section 12.4, we presented the simulation results of the proposed QTCs in the face of the quantum depolarizing channels.

Despite its design simplicity, the proposed QTC yields a near-hashing-bound error-correction performance. For instance, compared to the best half-rate QTC known in the literature, namely the QIrCC-QURC scheme of [302], which operates at the distance of $D = 0.037$ from the quantum hashing bound, our novel QSBC-QURC scheme can operate at the distance of $D = 0.029$ at the depolarizing probability value of $p = 10^{-3}$. Table 15.14 portrays the partial results we have presented in Chapter 12. We can observe in Figure 12.11 that our QSBC-QURC scheme has an advantage over QIrCC-QURC of [302] in the range of QBER > $10^{-4}$. However, as we reduced the target depolarizing probability values, an error floor started to emerge for our QSBC-QURC and the above trend was reversed. Also, it is worth mentioning that this is the first instantiation of QTCs that are capable of adjusting the quantum encoders according to the quantum coding rate required for mitigating the Pauli errors, given the different depolarizing probabilities of the quantum channel. A single reconfigurable quantum encoder of the proposed QSBC-QURC scheme is capable of accommodating a range of quantum coding rates, specifically $r_Q = \frac{k}{k+1}$. The depolarizing probability values at which quantum coding rate switching is recommended for different QBER targets are summarized in Table 15.15.

m. **Chapter 13 EXIT-chart-aided Design of Irregular Multiple-rate Quantum Turbo Block Codes**
In this chapter we designed near-hashing-bound single-encoder-based MR-QSBC-QURC schemes by harnessing an EXIT-chart-aided procedure. The salient benefit of the design conceived is that it is eminently suitable for any arbitrary quantum coding rate $r_Q$. Recall that this is achieved by applying a number of different-rate codes of the MR-QSBCs scheme to carefully optimized fractions of the input stream as the outer codes. This was made plausible in the light of our experience with classical error-correction code design. Despite the low-complexity of the outer codes, our Monte–Carlo simulation results show that the resultant MR-QSBC-QURC arrangement is capable of operating near to the quantum hashing bound at QBER = $10^{-3}$ for the specific quantum coding rates considered. More precisely, our MR-QSBC-QURC is capable of operating at the distance of $D = \{0.042, 0.029, 0.030, 0.024, 0.017\}$ from the quantum hashing bound for quantum coding rates of $r_Q = \{0.3, 0.4, 0.5, 0.6, 0.7\}$. Despite its low-complexity code constructions, the advocated MR-QSBC-QURC scheme offers a competitive QBER performance even against the best-performing QCC-based QTC in the literature. We believe our solutions will open the pathway for the future development of rate-compatible QSCs capable of adapting to diverse QBER requirements and quantum channel qualities without relying on different quantum encoders.

n. **Chapter 14 Quantum Low-density Parity-check Codes**
Pursuing further the design of iterative code structures, Chapter 14 was focused on quantum low-density parity-check (QLDPC) codes, providing insights into various QLDPC structures as well as into their associated decoding.

**Table 15.16** Summary of the QLDPC constructions considered.

| Code Type | Merits | Demerits |
|---|---|---|
| Dual-containing CSS | MacKay's bicycle codes are so far the best among the QLDPC codes. | Numerous short cycles. |
| Non-dual-containing CSS | Few short cycles in GF(4) formalism and none in the binary formalism. | Difficult to find good non-dual-containing CSS QLDC codes. |
| Non-CSS | Efficiently exploit redundant qubits. | Difficult to find good non-CSS QLDC codes. |
| EA | Performance comparable to the classical LDPC codes. | Pre-shared entangled qubits required. |

In line with the categorization of Table 15.12, Section 14.2 reviewed the QLDPC code construction methods, focusing in particular on the related design issues. A major design challenge highlighted in this discussion was the presence of unavoidable length-4 cycles, resulting from the commutativity requirement of the stabilizers. More explicitly, an arbitrary binary or quaternary code may be used for constructing a QLDPC matrix, if it meets the symplectic product or the Hermitian inner product criterion, as also summarized in Table 15.12. This in turn results in short (length-4) cycles. We summarize the design challenges of Section 14.2 in Table 15.16. Section 14.3 discussed the syndrome decoding of QLDPC codes. In particular, binary decoding was presented in Section 14.3.1, while its nonbinary counterpart was the subject of Section 14.3.2. The differences highlighted between the two decoding schemes may be summarized as follows:

- In contrast to the binary decoding of Section 14.3.1, which assumes that bit and phase errors are independent, the nonbinary decoding of Section 14.3.2 takes into account the correlation between them, which improves their performance.
- The number of length-4 cycles is higher in the nonbinary formalism of the PCM as compared to the binary formalism. This tends to degrade the performance of the nonbinary decoder.

Section 14.3.3 presented the decoding issues associated with QLDPC codes, which may be summarized as:

- **Degeneracy:** Quantum codes are inherently degenerate in nature. This may improve the associated decoding performance, provided that the decoder takes this degeneracy into account. Unfortunately, the belief propagation (BP) algorithm does not exploit this degeneracy. In fact, since BP is based on marginalized probabilities, the presence of degenerate errors impairs its performance.
- **Short cycles:** Unavoidable length-4 cycles found in QLDPC codes deteriorate the performance of BP. This gets even worse for the homogeneous CSS codes, when they are decoded in the nonbinary domain.

Heuristic methods, namely random perturbation and enhanced feedback, were then invoked for alleviating these issues at the cost of an increased decoding complexity.

Section 14.4 conceived a formalism for constructing high-rate row-circulant QC-QLDPC codes from arbitrary row-circulant classical LDPC matrices. Since the proposed design is merely based on the transpose and column permutation operations, the characteristics of the underlying classical LDPC matrix are not compromised. In particular, the new formalism was applied to the family of BIBD-based classical LDPCs for evaluating their performance in Section 14.5. It was demonstrated in Figure 14.10 that the proposed construction outperforms the comparable bicycle code as well as the EA-QLDPC code. Quantitatively, our designed [2534, 2172] QLDPC code of Table 14.5 is capable of tolerating three times higher depolarizing probability at a WER of $10^{-4}$ as compared to its EA counterpart and about four times higher depolarizing probability, when compared to an equivalent dual-containing bicycle code.

Section 14.6, we proposed a modified non-binary decoding algorithm for homogeneous CSS-type QLDPC codes, which successfully mitigated the issue of unavoidable length-4 cycles. In Section 14.8.1, it was demonstrated in Figures 14.14 to 14.17 that the modified decoder exhibits a superior WER performance as well as a lower decoding complexity than the state-of-the-art benchmark decoding techniques. The improved decoding algorithm of Section 14.6 was also amalgamated with heuristic methods for attaining additional performance gains. The simulation results of Figures 14.14 to 14.17 are summarized in Table 15.17.

**Table 15.17** Summary of the simulation results of Section 14.8.1, where performance is quantified for the dual-containing QLDPC (System I) and the homogeneous EA-QLDPC (System II) in terms of the achievable channel depolarizing probability $p$ at a WER of $10^{-4}$ and the corresponding average number of decoding iterations $I_{avg}$.

| System | Dec. No. | Decoding method | Improvement in $p$ | $I_{avg}$ | Reference |
|---|---|---|---|---|---|
| System I | 1 | Binary | - | 1.7 | Table 14.9, Figure 14.14, Figure 14.15 |
| | 2 | Standard nonbinary | 26% w.r.t. Dec. 1 | 2.6 | |
| | 3 | Random perturbation | 30% w.r.t. Dec. 2 | 4.19 | |
| | 4 | Enhanced feedback | 30% w.r.t. Dec. 2 | 3.6 | |
| | 5 | Modified nonbinary | 30% w.r.t. Dec. 2 | 2.47 | |
| | 6 | Modified and enhanced feedback | 21% w.r.t. Dec. 5 | 3.4 | |
| System II | 1 | Binary | - | 4 | Table 14.12, Figure 14.16, Figure 14.17 |
| | 2 | Standard Nonbinary | 21% w.r.t. Dec. 1 | 5 | |
| | 3 | Random perturbation | 10% w.r.t. Dec. 2 | 7.5 | |
| | 4 | Enhanced feedback | 19% w.r.t. Dec. 2 | 7 | |
| | 5 | Modified nonbinary | 23% w.r.t. Dec. 2 | 5.5 | |
| | 6 | Modified and enhanced feedback | 11% w.r.t. Dec. 5 | 7 | |

Section 14.7 presented the Uniform ReWeighted BP (URW-BP) algorithm, which is known to alleviate the issue of short cycles in classical LDPC codes. In Section 14.8.2, we also amalgamated our modified algorithm of Section 14.6 with the URW-BP of Section 14.7. It was demonstrated in Figure 14.19 that the URW-BP can be exploited for counteracting the problems imposed by short cycles, particularly when the maximum number of decoding iterations is small.

## 15.2 Future Research

In this section, we will briefly discuss a range of potential future research directions.

a. **Conceiving QSCs for protecting a complex quantum circuit.**
   We have relied on a general formalism of protecting quantum gates, which is denoted by unitary transformation $U_f$, and we exemplified the employment of our protocol by utilizing transversal Hadamard gates and CNOT gates as the unitary transformation $U_f$. Choosing transversal Hadamard and CNOT gates has the advantages of preserving the stabilizer group $\mathcal{S}$ and simplified construction of effective inverse encoder $\widehat{\mathcal{V}}^{\dagger}$. As we observe from Figure 15.1, the effective inverse encoder $\widehat{\mathcal{V}}^{\dagger}$ is identical to the initial inverse encoder $\widehat{\mathcal{V}}^{\dagger}$, if we consider protecting the transversal CNOT gates. However, as we try to involve more quantum gates, for instance, by simply concatenating transversal Hadamard gates with the transversal CNOT gates, the advantage of having a preserved effective inverse encoder $\widehat{\mathcal{V}}^{\dagger}$ no longer exists, as illustrated in Figure 15.2. Therefore, finding a way of transforming the complex effective inverse encoder into a simpler circuit can be an interesting research direction. Another technique that can be considered is the stabilizer measurement-based quantum encoder and the employment of repeated stabilizer measurements for the inverse encoder, as presented in [254, 263].

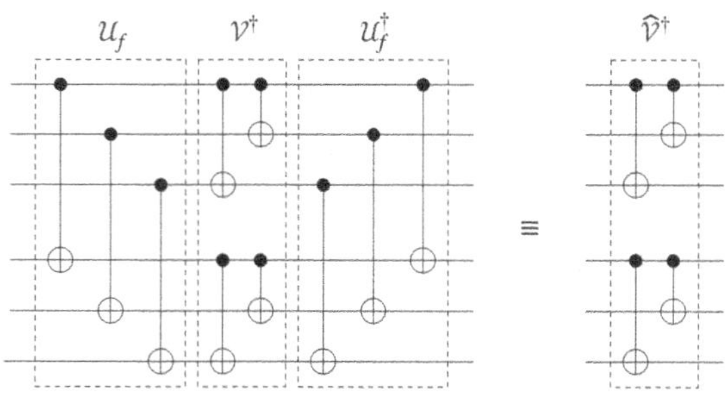


**Figure 15.1** Given that the unitary transformation $U_f$ is represented by the transversal CNOT gates, the quantum circuit for inverse encoder $\mathcal{V}^\dagger$ and effective inverse encoder $\widehat{\mathcal{V}}^\dagger$ can be realized identically.

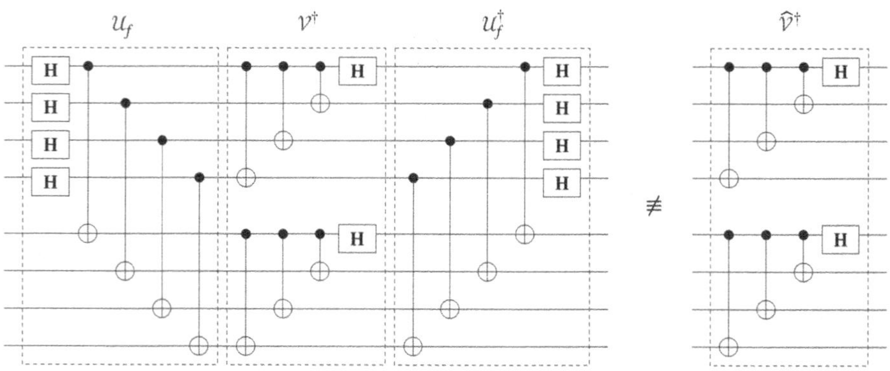


**Figure 15.2** For a more complex quantum circuit, the effective inverse encoder $\widehat{\mathcal{V}}^\dagger$ is not always identical to the inverse encoder $\mathcal{V}^\dagger$. In fact, if we follow explicitly the formulation of effective inverse encoder in Eq. (8.16), the resultant effective inverse encoder can be deemed to be more complex. Finding a way to simplify the circuit is an interesting research avenue to pursue.

b. **Symbol-based IRCC-URC-SD for Entanglement-Assisted Classical Communication**
In Chapter 5 we conceived bit-based IRCC-URC-SD schemes for approaching the bit-based EACC, while a CC-URC-SD arrangement was proposed for the sake of approaching the symbol-based EACC. More specifically, the symbol-based CC-URC-SD scheme outperformed the bit-based IRCC-URC-SD because the symbol-to-bit conversion invoked in the bit-based arrangement incurs an irrecoverable capacity loss. However, we exhaustively searched through all the possible convolutional codes for designing a near-capacity CC-URC-SD code. To dispense with the exhaustive search, it may be helpful to conceive a symbol-based IRCC, whose weighting coefficients can be dynamically adapted to provide the best EXIT-curve match with a given inner code.

c. **Near-capacity Code Designs for Classical Communication Assisted by Less Noisy Qubits or by Noisy Qubits**
In Chapter 5 we focused our attention on the code designs conceived for EA classical communication over a quantum depolarizing channel, assuming that the pre-shared entangled qubits are transmitted over a noiseless channel. Alternatively, we may assume that:

- the ebits are *less* noisy [362], i.e. they only experience phase errors, which generally dominate the bit errors in realistic scenarios; or alternatively
- the ebits are also shared over a noisy channel [215].

From an implementational perspective, it might be useful to extend our proposed code designs to these two scenarios.

d. **Reduced-complexity Block Syndrome Decoding for Quantum Turbo Codes**
In Chapter 4 we conceived a reduced-complexity BSD for the classical TTCM, whose performance was analyzed for transmission over the classical AWGN and Rayleigh fading channels. Furthermore, we proposed

hashing-bound-approaching concatenated quantum codes, or more precisely QTCs. It will be beneficial to apply the concept of BSD to the decoding of QTCs (BSD-QTC). In TTCM decoding, the trellis of erroneous sub-blocks emerges from and terminates at the all-zero state. By contrast, a QTC is decoded over the equivalent circuit-based representation. Hence, in the context of the BSD-QTC, it will also be important to investigate how to initialize and terminate the memory states of the circuit-based representation.

e. **EXIT-chart-aided Design of Classically Enhanced EA Quantum Turbo Codes**
The hashing-bound-approaching QTCs considered only encode qubits. By contrast, classically enhanced EA-QTCs [82, 377] support the simultaneous transmission of both classical as well as quantum information. In this context, it may be important to invoke the EXIT-chart-aided design methodology for optimizing the constituent components of a classically enhanced EA-QTC, which aim for approaching the corresponding capacity limits/bounds of [378, 379].

f. **Union Bounds for Quantum Turbo Codes**
The convergence threshold of our optimized QTC design of Section 11.6.3 is only 0.3 dB away from the achievable noise limit. However, it exhibits a high error floor in Figure 11.16. We managed to reduce the error floor by employing QIRCC as the outer component, as seen in Figure 11.17. Alternatively, it may be helpful to derive the QuBit error rate (QBER) union bound of the QTC based on its distance spectrum. We may then optimize the design with the aid of EXIT charts as well as the union bounds, where EXIT charts would ensure a hashing-bound-approaching performance, while considering the union bounds would ensure a low error floor [217].

g. **Unity Rate Code or Short Block Code Aided Concatenated Quantum Codes**
In Chapter 5 we demonstrated the beneficial impact of classical URCs in achieving a near-capacity performance, when used as the inner code. By contrast, in Chapter 11, we used EA-QCCs as the inner components, which in turn yielded low-rate concatenated quantum codes. Alternatively, we may replace the inner EA-QCC by a quantum unity rate code (QURC), which would merely act as a scrambler. In this context, the design of a QURC is a promising research area. Since unassisted QCCs cannot be simultaneously recursive and non-catastrophic, the design of a QURC seems to be a formidable task. As an alternative option, we conjecture that if quantum short block codes (QSBCs) are conceived analogous to the classical short block codes (SBCs) of [305, 306], which have a minimum distance of at least two, then they can be used as the inner component for reaching the $(1, 1)$ point of perfect convergence.

h. **Hashing-bound-approaching Quantum Low-density Parity-check Codes**
The domain of QLDPC codes has a lot of research potential, both from the perspective of code design as well as decoder design. As discussed in Chapter 14, only the spatially coupled QLDPC codes have managed to approach the hashing bound, which is achieved at the cost of an increased complexity or pre-shared noiseless qubits. Therefore, designing hashing-bound-approaching QLDPC codes is still an open challenge. Furthermore, unlike the degenerate iterative decoding of QTCs, the decoding of QLDPC codes does not take into account the degeneracy issue. It is worth conceiving a degenerate decoding algorithm for QLDPC codes, or at least conceiving deterministic methods for improving the QLDPC decoding, rather than the heuristic methods of Section 14.3.3.

# A

# Construction of Syndrome Former

In this appendix, we detail the construction of the syndrome former, which was invoked in Chapter 4 for constructing the syndrome-based trellis. More specifically, in Section A.1, we derive the syndrome former of the convolutional code (CC) of Section 10.4, while in Section A.2 we construct the syndrome former of the turbo trellis coded modulation (TTCM) of Section 4.4.2.

## A.1 Convolutional Codes

Recall from Section 10.4 that convolutional codes are equivalent to linear block codes having a semi-infinite length. Therefore, the generator polynomials of a convolutional code CC$(n, k, m)$ may be arranged to construct the corresponding generator matrix $G$, as depicted in Eq. (10.60). For the special class of systematic CCs, whose $n$-bit codewords consist of $k$ information bits followed by $(n-k)$ parity bits, the matrix $G$ of Eq. (10.60) may also be represented as follows[1]:

$$G = \begin{pmatrix} \mathbf{IP}_0 & \mathbf{0P}_1 & \mathbf{0P}_2 & \dots & \mathbf{0P}_m & & & \\ & \mathbf{IP}_0 & \mathbf{0P}_1 & \mathbf{0P}_2 & \dots & \mathbf{0P}_m & & \\ & & \mathbf{IP}_0 & \mathbf{0P}_1 & \mathbf{0P}_2 & \dots & \mathbf{0P}_m & \\ & & \ddots & & \dots & & \ddots & \end{pmatrix}, \tag{A.1}$$

where $\mathbf{I}$ is a $(k \times k)$-element identity matrix, $\mathbf{0}$ is a $(k \times k)$-element all-zero matrix and $\mathbf{P}_l$ is a $k \times (n-k)$-element matrix with entries:

$$\mathbf{P}_l = \begin{pmatrix} g_{1,l}^{(k)} & g_{1,l}^{(k+1)} & \dots & g_{1,l}^{(n-1)} \\ g_{2,l}^{(k)} & g_{2,l}^{(k+1)} & \dots & g_{2,l}^{(n-1)} \\ \vdots & & & \vdots \\ g_{k,l}^{(k)} & g_{k,l}^{(k+1)} & \dots & g_{k,l}^{(n-1)} \end{pmatrix}. \tag{A.2}$$

1 Blank spaces in the matrix indicate zeros.

If $\mathbf{g}_i^{(j)} = (g_{i,0}^{(j)}, g_{i,1}^{(j)}, \ldots, g_{i,m}^{(j)})$ represents the generator polynomial for the $i$th input (information) bit and the $j$th output (coded) bit, then the resultant $(k \times n)$-element transform-domain matrix $G(D)$ is given by:

$$G(D) = \begin{pmatrix} 1 & 0 & \ldots & 0 & \mathbf{g}_1^{(k)}(D) & \mathbf{g}_1^{(k+1)}(D) & \ldots & \mathbf{g}_1^{(n-1)}(D) \\ 0 & 1 & \ldots & 0 & \mathbf{g}_2^{(k)}(D) & \mathbf{g}_2^{(k+1)}(D) & \ldots & \mathbf{g}_2^{(n-1)}(D) \\ \vdots & \vdots & & \vdots & \vdots & \vdots & & \vdots \\ 0 & 0 & \ldots & 1 & \mathbf{g}_k^{(k)}(D) & \mathbf{g}_k^{(k+1)}(D) & \ldots & \mathbf{g}_k^{(n-1)}(D) \end{pmatrix}, \tag{A.3}$$

where $\mathbf{g}_i^{(j)}(D) = g_{i,0}^{(j)} + g_{i,1}^{(j)} D + g_{i,2}^{(j)} D^2 + \cdots + g_{i,m}^{(j)} D^m$, given that $D$ represents the delay of a single memory element (or register). Furthermore, the associated parity check matrix (PCM) $H$ of Eq. (10.62) takes the following form:

$$H = \begin{bmatrix} \mathbf{P}_0^T & \mathbf{I} & & & & & & & & & \\ \mathbf{P}_1^T & \mathbf{0} & \mathbf{P}_0^T & \mathbf{I} & & & & & & & \\ \mathbf{P}_2^T & \mathbf{0} & \mathbf{P}_1^T & \mathbf{0} & \mathbf{P}_0^T & \mathbf{I} & & & & & \\ \vdots & \vdots & \vdots & \vdots & \vdots & \vdots & & & & & \\ \mathbf{P}_m^T & \mathbf{0} & \mathbf{P}_{m-1}^T & \mathbf{0} & \mathbf{P}_{m-2}^T & \mathbf{0} & \ldots & \mathbf{P}_0^T & \mathbf{I} & & \\ & & \mathbf{P}_m^T & \mathbf{0} & \mathbf{P}_{m-1}^T & \mathbf{0} & \mathbf{P}_{m-2}^T & \mathbf{0} & \ldots & \mathbf{P}_0^T & \mathbf{I} \\ & & \vdots & \vdots & \vdots & \vdots & \vdots & \vdots & & \vdots & \vdots \end{bmatrix}, \tag{A.4}$$

where $\mathbf{I}$ is an $(n-k) \times (n-k)$-element identity matrix, while $\mathbf{0}$ is an $(n-k) \times (n-k)$-element all-zero matrix. The corresponding $(n-k) \times n$ transform-domain PCM $H(D)$ is given by:

$$H(D) = \begin{pmatrix} \mathbf{g}_1^{(k)}(D) & \mathbf{g}_2^{(k)}(D) & \ldots & \mathbf{g}_k^{(k)}(D) & 1 & 0 & \ldots & 0 \\ \mathbf{g}_1^{(k+1)}(D) & \mathbf{g}_2^{(k+1)}(D) & \ldots & \mathbf{g}_k^{(k+1)}(D) & 0 & 1 & \ldots & 0 \\ \vdots & \vdots & & \vdots & \vdots & \vdots & & \vdots \\ \mathbf{g}_1^{(n-1)}(D) & \mathbf{g}_2^{(n-1)}(D) & \ldots & \mathbf{g}_k^{(n-1)}(D) & 0 & 0 & \ldots & 1 \end{pmatrix}. \tag{A.5}$$

Based on the preceding discussion, we next construct the syndrome former given in Eq. (4.14) for the generator matrix of Eq. (4.13), i.e. we have:

$$G(D) = \begin{pmatrix} 1+D & D & 1+D \\ D & 1 & 1 \end{pmatrix}. \tag{A.6}$$

We first find the equivalent systematic form analogous to Eq. (A.3) by applying elementary row operations to Eq. (A.6) as follows:

- **Divide row 1 by** $(1+D)$

$$G(D) = \begin{pmatrix} 1 & D/(1+D) & 1 \\ D & 1 & 1 \end{pmatrix}. \tag{A.7}$$

- **Add** $(D\times$ **row 1) to row 2**

$$G(D) = \begin{pmatrix} 1 & D/(1+D) & 1 \\ 0 & (1+D+D^2)/(1+D) & (1+D) \end{pmatrix}. \tag{A.8}$$

- **Multiply row 2 by** $(1+D)/(1+D+D^2)$

$$G(D)=\begin{pmatrix}1 & D/(1+D) & 1\\ 0 & 1 & (1+D^2)/(1+D+D^2)\end{pmatrix}. \tag{A.9}$$

- **Add** $(D/1+D\times$ **row 2) to row 1**

$$G(D)=\begin{pmatrix}1 & 0 & 1/(1+D+D^2)\\ 0 & 1 & (1+D^2)/(1+D+D^2)\end{pmatrix}. \tag{A.10}$$

Hence, Eq. (A.10) is the systematic form of the generator matrix given in Eq. (A.6). Based on this systematic matrix, we may deduce from Eq. (A.5) that the corresponding PCM $H(D)$ is as follows:

$$H(D)=\begin{pmatrix}1/(1+D+D^2) & (1+D^2)/(1+D+D^2) & 1\end{pmatrix}. \tag{A.11}$$

The equivalent non-systematic form of Eq. (A.11) can be derived by applying elementary row operations to Eq. (A.11). More specifically, multiply $H(D)$ with $1/(1+D+D^2)$, which yields:

$$H(D)=\begin{pmatrix}1 & 1+D^2 & 1+D+D^2\end{pmatrix}. \tag{A.12}$$

## A.2 Turbo Trellis Coded Modulation

In Section 4.4.2, we have employed Ungerboeck's 8-state TCM-8PSK [205], given in Figure A.1, for evaluating the performance of our proposed reduced-complexity decoder. The associated generator matrix is given by:

$$G(D)=\begin{pmatrix}1 & 0 & D^2/(1+D^3)\\ 0 & 1 & D/(1+D^3)\end{pmatrix}. \tag{A.13}$$

The corresponding PCM is:

$$H(D)=\begin{pmatrix}D^2/(1+D^3) & D/(1+D^3) & 1\end{pmatrix}. \tag{A.14}$$

according to Eq. (A.5). We may further simplify Eq. (A.14) by multiplying it with $(1+D^3)$, which yields:

$$H(D)=\begin{pmatrix}D^2 & D & 1+D^3\end{pmatrix}. \tag{A.15}$$

The syndrome former circuit of the PCM of Eq. (A.15) is given in Figure A.2.

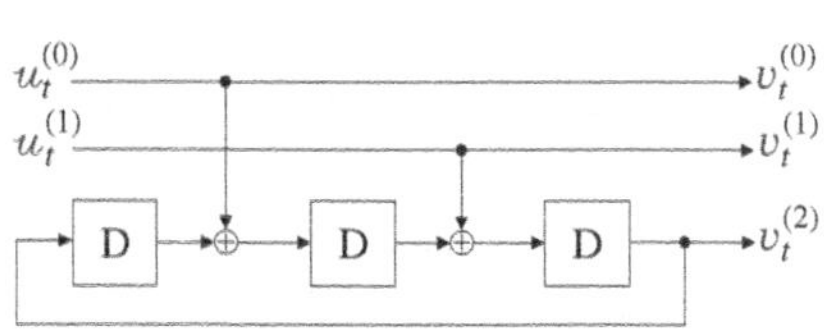


**Figure A.1** Encoder of Ungerboeck's 8-state TCM-8PSK.

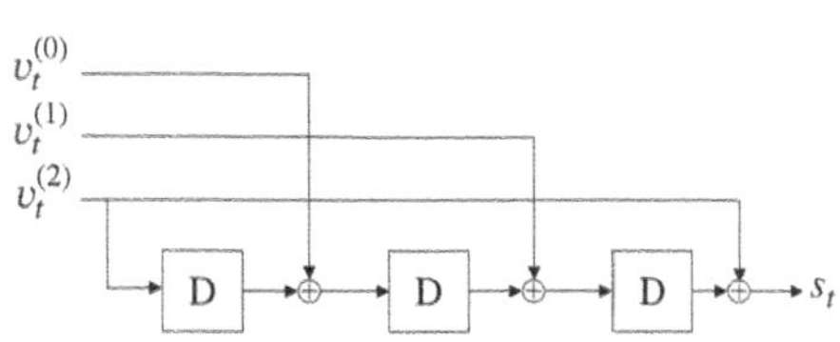


**Figure A.2** Syndrome former of Ungerboeck's 8-state TCM-8PSK.

# B

## Simulation of QLDPC Decoding

The syndrome-based quantum low density parity check (QLDPC) decoding algorithms of Chapter 14 may be simulated by invoking the conventional codeword decoding approach in conjunction with the equivalent classical binary or quaternary parity check matrix (PCM). Recall from Chapter 4 that syndrome decoding aims for finding the most likely error pattern inflicted by the channel given the observed syndrome, while the classic codeword decoding aims for finding the most likely transmitted codeword, given the received codeword. If $y = (y_0, y_1, \ldots, y_t, \ldots, y_{n-1})$ is the received sequence, then the transmitted code sequence $v = (v_0, v_1, \ldots, v_t, \ldots, v_{n-1})$ and the channel error $e = (e_0, e_1, \ldots, e_t, \ldots, e_{n-1})$ are related as follows:

$$y_t = v_t \oplus e_t, \tag{B.1}$$

where $\oplus$ denotes the modulo 2 addition. The most likely codeword estimated by the codeword decoding and the most likely error pattern estimated by the syndrome decoding are also related through Eq. (B.1). Hence, these approaches are equivalent.

The codeword-based counterpart of the non-binary QLDPC decoding of Section 14.3.2 may be implemented by:

- initializing the messages according to the received code sequence as well as the channel model;
- only considering the zero-syndrome scenario of Eq. (14.19).

We assume furthermore the transmission of all-zero codewords for facilitating simulations. Let us consider the decoding example detailed in Section 14.6, where the channel error inflicted is $\mathcal{P} = \mathbf{XIIIIII}$, which is equivalent to (1 0 0 0 0 0 0) according to the Pauli-to-quaternary mapping. Since we are transmitting an all-zero codeword, i.e. $v = (0\ 0\ 0\ 0\ 0\ 0\ 0)$, the received codeword is $y = (1\ 0\ 0\ 0\ 0\ 0\ 0)$. For codeword decoding, the initialization step of Eq. (14.46) takes into account the received sequence $y$, as follows:

$$m^{\hat{a}}_{v_t \to c_i} = \begin{cases} 0.74, & \text{if } \hat{a} = y_t \\ 0.0867, & \text{otherwise,} \end{cases} \tag{B.2}$$

where $\hat{a} \in \{0, 1, \omega, \overline{\omega}\}$ is the $t$th hypothetically transmitted bit. Furthermore, the probability density function (PDF) of $\check{m}^{\hat{a}_s}_{c_i \to v_t}$, which is computed in Step 4 of the horizontal message exchange (Eqs. [14.56] and [14.57]), is calculated by only using Eq. (14.19).

Analogous to the codeword-based counterpart of the non-binary QLDPC decoding, the codeword-based counterpart of our modified non-binary decoding of Section 14.6 also considers only the zero-syndrome scenario of Eq. (14.41). The resultant decoding algorithm is equivalent to running the conventional (codeword) classical GF(4) decoding over the first $m/2$ rows of the equivalent PCM of Eq. (14.40). However, in the conventional classical GF(4) decoding we have $\hat{a}_s = \hat{H}_{it} \times \hat{a}$, while for QLDPC decoding we use $\hat{a}_s = \hat{H}_{it} \times \overline{\hat{a}}$.

## Glossary

**Abelian group** A multiplicative group $G$ is Abelian iff $\forall a, b \in G, a \times b = b \times a$.

**basis** Basis of a vector space $V$ is a set of linearly independent vectors $\{|v_1\rangle, \ldots, |v_n\rangle\}$ such that any vector $|v\rangle$ in the vector space $V$ can be written as a linear combination of the basis vectors $\{|v_1\rangle, \ldots, |v_n\rangle\}$, i.e. $|v\rangle = \sum_i a_i |v_i\rangle$.

**Bell-basis measurement** Bell-basis measurement is a joint measurement on a 2-qubit composite system for the sake of detecting the orthonormal Bell states.

**Bell states** The orthonormal 2-qubit states given by:

$$\frac{1}{\sqrt{2}}(|00\rangle + |11\rangle), \qquad \frac{1}{\sqrt{2}}(|00\rangle - |11\rangle),$$
$$\frac{1}{\sqrt{2}}(|01\rangle + |10\rangle), \qquad \frac{1}{\sqrt{2}}(|01\rangle - |10\rangle),$$

are known as the Bell state, named after John S. Bell, which are also referred to as the Einstein–Podolsky–Rosen (EPR) pairs.

**centralizer** The centralizer of a stabilizer code is a set of elements which commute with the stabilizer generators. It is denoted as $C(\mathcal{H})$, where $\mathcal{H}$ is the stabilizer group of the stabilizer code.

**Clifford operator** An $n$-qubit Clifford operator $\mathcal{V}$ preserves the elements of the Pauli group under conjugation such that for $\mathcal{P} \in \mathcal{G}_n$, $\mathcal{V}\mathcal{P}\mathcal{V}^\dagger \in \mathcal{G}_n$.

**Clifford transformation** An $n$-qubit Clifford transformation $\mathcal{V}$ maps an $n$-qubit Pauli group $\mathcal{G}_n$ onto itself under conjugation such that $\mathcal{V}\mathcal{G}_n\mathcal{V}^\dagger = \mathcal{G}_n$.

**coherence time** Coherence time may be defined as the time duration over which a qubit retains its coherent quantum state.

**commute** Two operators $A$ and $B$ commute if and only if $A \times B = B \times A$.

**coset** If $G$ is a group, and $H$ is a subgroup of $G$, and $g \in G$, then $gH = \{gh : h \in H\}$ is a left coset of $H$ in $G$, and $Hg = \{hg : h \in H\}$ is a right coset of $H$ in $G$.

**decoherence** Decoherence is the undesirable entanglement of qubits with the environment, which perturbs the fragile superposition of quantum states, thus leading to the detrimental effects of noise. The overall decoherence process may be characterized either by bit-flips or phase-flips or in fact possibly both, inflicted on the qubits.

**degeneracy** Pauli errors which differ only by the stabilizer group have the same impact on all the codewords and therefore can be corrected by the same recovery operations. This is known as degeneracy.

**depolarizing channel** The depolarizing channel characterized by the probability $p$ inflicts an $n$-tuple error $\mathcal{P} \in \mathcal{G}_n$ on $n$ qubits, where the $i^{th}$ qubit may experience either a bit flip (**X**), a phase flip (**Z**) or both (**Y**) with a probability of $p/3$.

**dimension of vector space** The number of elements in the basis set of the vector space $V$ is defined to be the dimension of $V$.

**dual code** If $G$ and $H$ are the generator and parity-check matrices for any linear block code $C$, then its dual code $C^{\perp}$ is a unique code with $H^T$ and $G^T$ as the generator and parity-check matrices respectively.

**dual-containing code** Code $C$ with parity check matrix $H$ is said to be dual-containing if it contains its dual code $C^{\perp}$, i.e. $C^{\perp} \subset C$ and $HH^T = 0$.

**eigenvector** An eigenvector of a linear operator $A$ is a nonzero vector $|v\rangle$ such that $Av = v\,|v\rangle$, where $v$ is a complex number known as the eigenvalue of $A$.

**entanglement-assisted classical capacity** The entanglement-assisted classical capacity (EACC) of a quantum channel quantifies the capacity limit of reliable transmission of classical information over a noisy quantum channel, when an unlimited amount of noiseless entanglement is shared between the transmitter and the receiver.

**fidelity** Fidelity is a measure of closeness of two quantum states.

**Greenberger–Horne–Zeilinger (GHZ)** Greenberger–Horne–Zeilinger (GHZ) state is an $N$-qubit entangled state for $N > 2$ given by:

$$|GHZ\rangle = \frac{1}{\sqrt{2}}\left(|0\rangle^{\otimes N} + |1\rangle^{\otimes N}\right).$$

**hashing bound** Hashing bound determines the code rate at which a random quantum code facilitates reliable transmission for a particular depolarizing probability $p$.

**Hermitian matrix** Hermitian matrix (also called self-adjoint) is a square matrix, which is equivalent to its conjugate transpose, i.e. $A = A^{\dagger}$.

**Hilbert space** A $d$-dimensional Hilbert space is a $d$-dimensional complex vector space with an inner product, and hence a norm. It is denoted as $\mathbb{C}^d$.

**inner product** Inner product is a function, which takes two complex-valued vectors $|a\rangle$ and $|b\rangle$ as input and yields a complex number as the output. More explicitly, we have:

$$(|a\rangle, |b\rangle) = [a_1^*, \ldots, a_n^*]\begin{pmatrix} b_1 \\ \vdots \\ b_n \end{pmatrix} = \sum_i a_i^* b_i.$$

Inner product $(|a\rangle, |b\rangle)$ is conventionally written as $\langle a|b\rangle$, where the bra notation $\langle v|$ represents the dual (adjoint or Hermitian conjugate) of $|v\rangle$.

**noise limit** The noise limit of a quantum depolarizing channel is the maximum tolerable channel depolarizing probability.

**normalizer** Normalizer of a stabilizer code is a set of elements which commute with the stabilizer generators. It is denoted as $N(\mathcal{H})$, where $\mathcal{H}$ is the stabilizer group of the stabilizer code.

**outer product** The outer product of a ket and a bra vector $|a\rangle\langle b|$ is a linear operator, whose action on a vector $|v\rangle$ is defined as follows:

$$(|a\rangle\langle b|)(|v\rangle) = |a\rangle\langle b|v\rangle.$$

More specifically, $|a\rangle\langle b|$ maps all input vectors $|v\rangle$ to $|a\rangle$ multiplied by the scalar product $\langle b|v\rangle$. The corresponding matrix for the linear operator $|a\rangle\langle b|$ may be computed in $\mathbb{C}^2$ as follows:

$$|a\rangle\langle b| = \begin{pmatrix} a_1 \\ a_2 \end{pmatrix}\begin{pmatrix} b_1^* & b_2^* \end{pmatrix} = \begin{pmatrix} a_1 b_1^* & a_1 b_2^* \\ a_2 b_1^* & a_2 b_2^* \end{pmatrix}.$$

**Pauli group** A single qubit Pauli group $\mathcal{G}_1$ consists of all the Pauli matrices together with the multiplicative factors $\pm 1$ and $\pm i$, i.e. we have:

$$\mathcal{G}_1 \equiv \{\pm\mathbf{I}, \pm i\mathbf{I}, \pm\mathbf{X}, \pm i\mathbf{X}, \pm\mathbf{Y}, \pm i\mathbf{Y}, \pm\mathbf{Z}, \pm i\mathbf{Z}\}.$$

**Pauli operators** The **I**, **X**, **Y**, and **Z** Pauli operators are defined by the following matrices:

$$\mathbf{I} = \begin{pmatrix} 1 & 0 \\ 0 & 1 \end{pmatrix}, \ \mathbf{X} = \begin{pmatrix} 0 & 1 \\ 1 & 0 \end{pmatrix},$$

$$\mathbf{Y} = \begin{pmatrix} 0 & -i \\ i & 0 \end{pmatrix}, \ \mathbf{Z} = \begin{pmatrix} 1 & 0 \\ 0 & -1 \end{pmatrix},$$

where the **X**, **Y**, and **Z** operators anti-commute with each other.

**positive operator** A positive operator $A$ is defined to be an operator such that for any vector $|v\rangle$, the inner product $(|v\rangle, A\,|v\rangle)$ is a real and nonnegative number. If $(|v\rangle, A\,|v\rangle) > 0$ for all $|v\rangle \neq 0$, then $A$ is said to be positive definite.

**projector** The outer product of a unit vector $|a\rangle$ with itself, i.e. $\mathbf{P}_a = |a\rangle\langle a|$, is said to be a project on to the state $|a\rangle$, as shown in Figure B.1.

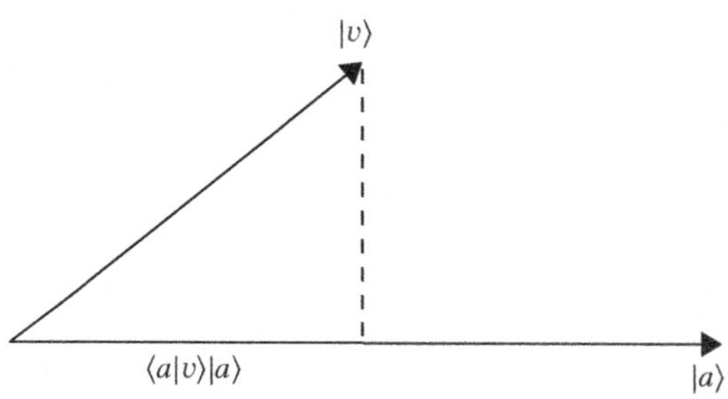


**Figure B.1** Geometric interpretation of the projector operator.

Furthermore, $\mathbf{P}_a^2 = \mathbf{P}_a$ and a complete set of orthogonal projectors in $n$-dimensional Hilbert space is a set $\{\mathbf{P}_1, \ldots \mathbf{P}_m\}$ such that $\sum_{i=1}^{m} \mathbf{P}_i = 1$.

**quantum interleaver** An $N$-qubit quantum interleaver is an $N$-qubit symplectic transformation, which randomly permutes the $N$ qubits and also applies single-qubit symplectic transformations to the individual qubits.

**stabilizer code** An $[n, k]$ quantum stabilizer code, constructed over a code space $\mathcal{C}$, which maps the information word (logical qubits) $|\psi\rangle \in \mathbb{C}^{2^k}$ onto the codeword (physical qubits) $|\overline{\psi}\rangle \in \mathbb{C}^{2^n}$, where $\mathbb{C}^d$ denotes the $d$-dimensional Hilbert space, is defined by a set of $(n-k)$ independent commuting $n$-tuple Pauli operators $g_i$, for $1 \leq i \leq (n-k)$. More specifically, the corresponding stabilizer group $\mathcal{H}$ contains both $g_i$ and all the products of $g_i$ for $1 \leq i \leq (n-k)$ and forms an Abelian subgroup of $\mathcal{G}_n$. A unique feature of these operators is that they do not change the state of valid codewords, while yielding an eigenvalue of $-1$ for corrupted states.

**stabilizer group** see stabilizer code.

**symplectic condition** If $\mathbf{a} = (a_1, \ldots, a_n)$, $\mathbf{b} = (b_1, \ldots, b_n)$, $\mathbf{a}' = (a_1', \ldots, a_n')$ and $\mathbf{b}' = (b_1', \ldots, b_n')$, then the symplectic condition between $(\mathbf{a}'|\mathbf{b}')$ and $(\mathbf{a}|\mathbf{b})$[1] is defined as:

$$\langle(\mathbf{a}'|\mathbf{b}'), (\mathbf{a}|\mathbf{b})\rangle_S = \mathbf{a}'\mathbf{b}^{\mathrm{T}} - \mathbf{b}'\mathbf{a}^{\mathrm{T}} = 0. \tag{B.3}$$

**symplectic inner product** If $\mathbf{a} = (a_1, \ldots, a_n)$, $\mathbf{b} = (b_1, \ldots, b_n)$, $\mathbf{a}' = (a_1', \ldots, a_n')$ and $\mathbf{b}' = (b_1', \ldots, b_n')$, then the symplectic inner product (also called twisted product or symplectic product) between $(\mathbf{a}'|\mathbf{b}')$ and $(\mathbf{a}|\mathbf{b})$ is defined as:

$$\langle(\mathbf{a}'|\mathbf{b}'), (\mathbf{a}|\mathbf{b})\rangle_S = \mathbf{a}'\mathbf{b}^{\mathrm{T}} - \mathbf{b}'\mathbf{a}^{\mathrm{T}}. \tag{B.4}$$

It can also be represented as $(\mathbf{a}'|\mathbf{b}') \star (\mathbf{a}|\mathbf{b})$.

---

1 Solid vertical bar, i.e. |, denotes the concatenation operation, e.g. concatenation of **a** and **b** is given by $(\mathbf{a}|\mathbf{b})$.

**tensor product** Given two vector subspaces $A$ and $B$ with dimensions $m$ and $n$ respectively, then the tensor product $A \otimes B$ yields an $mn$ dimensional vector space, whose elements are linear combinations of the tensor products $|a\rangle \otimes |b\rangle$ of elements $|a\rangle$ of $A$ and $|b\rangle$ of $B$. More explicitly, let $|a\rangle = a_1 |0\rangle + a_2 |1\rangle$ and $|b\rangle = b_1 |0\rangle + b_2 |1\rangle$, then we have:

$$\begin{pmatrix} a_1 \\ a_2 \end{pmatrix} \otimes \begin{pmatrix} b_1 \\ b_2 \end{pmatrix} = \begin{pmatrix} a_1 b_1 \\ a_1 b_2 \\ a_2 b_1 \\ a_2 b_2 \end{pmatrix}.$$

Tensor product $|a\rangle \otimes |b\rangle$ may also be abbreviated as $|a\rangle |b\rangle$, $|a, b\rangle$ or $|ab\rangle$.

**trace** Trace of a square matrix $A$ is the sum of its diagonal elements, i.e. $\mathrm{tr}(A) = \sum_i A_{ii}$.

**trace distance** Trace distance between two operators $A$ and $B$ is given by:

$$||A - B||_1 = \mathrm{tr}\left\{\sqrt{(A - B)^{\dagger}(A - B)}\right\}$$

Trace distance is a measure of separation between two quantum states with density operators $\rho$ and $\sigma$. Equivalent quantum states have $||\rho - \sigma||_1 = 0$, while orthogonal states have $||\rho - \sigma||_1 = 2$.

**twisted product** see symplectic inner product.

**unbounded minimum distance** The unbounded minimum distance of a code implies that its minimum distance increases almost linearly with the interleaver length.

**unitary operator** An operator $U$ is unitary if $UU^{\dagger} = \mathbf{I}$, where $U^{\dagger}$ is the adjoint (Hermitian conjugate) of $U$ and $\mathbf{I}$ is identity matrix. Unitary operator preserves the inner product.

## References


**1** E. Schrödinger, "Die gegenwärtige Situation in der Quantenmechanik," *Naturwissenschaften*, vol. 23, no. 49, pp. 823–828, 1935.

**2** J. D. Trimmer, "The present situation in quantum mechanics: A translation of Schrödinger's 'Cat Paradox' paper," *Proceedings of the American Philosophical Society*, vol. 124, no. 5, pp. 323–338, 1980.

**3** S. Imre and F. Balazs, *Quantum Computing and Communications: An Engineering Approach*. John Wiley & Sons, 2005.

**4** P. Botsinis, S. X. Ng, and L. Hanzo, "Quantum search algorithms, quantum wireless, and a low-complexity maximum likelihood iterative quantum multi-user detector design," *IEEE Access*, vol. 1, pp. 94–122, 2013. [Online]. Available: http://ieeexplore.ieee.org/xpl/articleDetails.jsp?arnumber=6515077

**5** D. Deutsch, "Quantum theory, the Church-Turing principle and the universal quantum computer," *Proceedings of the Royal Society of London. Series A, Mathematical and Physical Sciences*, vol. 400, pp. 97–117, 1985.

**6** D. Deutsch and R. Jozsa, "Rapid solution of problems by quantum computation," *Proceedings of the Royal Society of London A: Mathematical, Physical and Engineering Sciences*, vol. 439, no. 1907, pp. 553–558, 1992.

**7** P. W. Shor, "Algorithms for quantum computation: discrete logarithms and factoring," in *Proceedings of the 35th Annual Symposium on Foundations of Computer Science*. Washington, DC, USA: IEEE Computer Society, 1994, pp. 124–134. [Online]. Available: http://portal.acm.org/citation.cfm?id=1398518.1399018

**8** L. K. Grover, "A fast quantum mechanical algorithm for database search," in *Proceedings of the Twenty-eighth Annual ACM Symposium on Theory of Computing*, ser. STOC '96. New York, NY, USA: ACM, 1996, pp. 212–219. [Online]. Available: http://doi.acm.org/10.1145/237814.237866

**9** "Moore's Law - The Number of transistors on integrated circuit chips (1971-2018)," https://ourworldindata.org/technological-progress, accessed: 2019-08-21.

**10** G. E. Moore, "Cramming more components onto integrated circuits," *Electronics Magazine*, pp. 114–117, 1965.

**11** M. M. Waldrop, "The chips are down for Moore's law," *Nature News*, vol. 530, pp. 144–147, 2016.

**12** L. Hanzo, H. Haas, S. Imre, D. O'Brien, M. Rupp, and L. Gyongyosi, "Wireless myths, realities, and futures: from 3G/4G to optical and quantum wireless," *Proceedings of the IEEE (Special Centennial Issue)*, vol. 100, pp. 1853–1888, 2012.

**13** R. P. Feynman, "Simulating physics with computers," *International Journal of Theoretical Physics*, vol. 21, no. 6, pp. 467–488, 1982.

**14** P. W. Shor, "Polynomial-time algorithms for prime factorization and discrete logarithms on a quantum computer," *SIAM Review*, vol. 41, no. 2, pp. 303–332, 1999.

**15** M. Boyer, G. Brassard, P. HØyer, and A. Tapp, "Tight bounds on quantum searching," *arXiv preprint quant-ph/9605034*, 1996.

**16** C. Durr and P. HØyer, "A quantum algorithm for finding the minimum," *arXiv preprint quant-ph/9607014*, 1996.

**17** L. K. Grover, "Quantum mechanics helps in searching for a needle in a haystack," *Physical Review Letters*, vol. 79, no. 2, 1997.

**18** C. Zalka, "Grover's quantum searching algorithm is optimal," *Physical Review A*, vol. 60, no. 4, 1999.

**19** G. Brassard, F. Dupuis, S. Gambs, and A. Tapp, "An optimal quantum algorithm to approximate the mean and its application for approximating the median of a set of points over an arbitrary distance," *arXiv preprint arXiv:1106.4267*, 2011.

**20** P. Botsinis, S. X. Ng, and L. Hanzo, "Fixed-complexity quantum-assisted multi-user detection for CDMA and SDMA," *IEEE Transactions on Communications*, vol. 62, no. 3, pp. 990–1000, 2014.

**21** P. Botsinis, D. Alanis, S. X. Ng, and L. Hanzo, "Low-complexity soft-output quantum-assisted multiuser detection for direct-sequence spreading and slow subcarrier-hopping aided SDMA-OFDM systems," *IEEE Access*, vol. 2, pp. 451–472, 2014.

**22** D. Alanis, P. Botsinis, S. X. Ng, and L. Hanzo, "Quantum-assisted routing optimization for self-organizing networks," *IEEE Access*, vol. 2, pp. 614–632, 2014.

**23** P. Botsinis, D. Alanis, Z. Babar, S. X. Ng, and L. Hanzo, "Noncoherent quantum multiple symbol differential detection for wireless systems," *IEEE Access*, vol. 3, pp. 569–598, 2015.

**24** P. Botsinis, D. Alanis, Z. Babar, S. X. Ng, and L. Hanzo, "Iterative quantum-assisted multi-user detection for multi-carrier interleave division multiple access systems," *IEEE Transactions on Communications*, vol. 63, no. 10, pp. 3713–3727, 2015.

**25** D. Alanis, P. Botsinis, Z. Babar, S. X. Ng, and L. Hanzo, "Non-dominated quantum iterative routing optimization for wireless multihop networks," *IEEE Access*, vol. 3, pp. 1704–1728, 2015.

**26** P. Botsinis, D. Alanis, Z. Babar, H. V. Nguyen, D. Chandra, S. X. Ng, and L. Hanzo, "Quantum search algorithms for wireless communications," *IEEE Communications Surveys & Tutorials*, vol. 21, no. 2, pp. 1209–1242, 2018.

**27** C. H. Bennett, "Quantum cryptography: Public key distribution and coin tossing," in *Proceedings on IEEE International Conference on Computer System and Signal Processing*, 1984, pp. 175–179.

**28** A. K. Ekert, "Quantum cryptography based on Bell's theorem," *Physical Review Letters*, vol. 67, no. 6, 1991.

**29** C. H. Bennett and S. J. Wiesner, "Communication via one-and two-particle operators on Einstein–Podolsky–Rosen states," *Physical Review Letters*, vol. 69, no. 20, 1992.

**30** C. H. Bennett, G. Brassard, C. Crépeau, R. Jozsa, A. Peres, and W. K. Wootters, "Teleporting an unknown quantum state via dual classical and Einstein–Podolsky–Rosen channels," *Physical Review Letters*, vol. 70, no. 13, 1993.

**31** F.-G. Deng, G. L. Long, and X.-S. Liu, "Two-step quantum direct communication protocol using the Einstein–Podolsky–Rosen pair block," *Physical Review A*, vol. 68, no. 4, 2003.

**32** F.-G. Deng and G. L. Long, "Secure direct communication with a quantum one-time pad," *Physical Review A*, vol. 69, no. 5, 2004.

**33** N. L. Piparo and M. Razavi, "Long-distance trust-free quantum key distribution," *IEEE Journal of Selected Topics in Quantum Electronics*, vol. 21, no. 3, pp. 123–130, 2014.

**34** C. Panayi, M. Razavi, X. Ma, and N. Lütkenhaus, "Memory-assisted measurement-device-independent quantum key distribution," *New Journal of Physics*, vol. 16, no. 4, 2014.

**35** M. Razavi, "Multiple-access quantum key distribution networks," *IEEE Transactions on communications*, vol. 60, no. 10, pp. 3071–3079, 2012.

**36** A. S. Cacciapuoti, M. Caleffi, R. Van Meter, and L. Hanzo, "When entanglement meets classical communications: Quantum teleportation for the quantum internet," *arXiv preprint arXiv:1907.06197*, 2019.

**37** G. De Lange, Z. Wang, D. Riste, V. Dobrovitski, and R. Hanson, "Universal dynamical decoupling of a single solid-state spin from a spin bath," *Science*, vol. 330, no. 6000, pp. 60–63, 2010.

**38** T. Van der Sar, Z. Wang, M. Blok, H. Bernien, T. Taminiau, D. Toyli, D. A. Lidar, D. Awschalom, R. Hanson, and V. Dobrovitski, "Decoherence-protected quantum gates for a hybrid solid-state spin register," *Nature*, vol. 484, no. 7392, pp. 82–86, 2012.

**39** J. L. O'Brien, G. Pryde, A. Gilchrist, D. James, N. Langford, T. Ralph, and A. White, "Quantum process tomography of a controlled-NOT gate," *Physical Review Letters*, vol. 93, no. 8, 2004.

**40** A. Politi, M. J. Cryan, J. G. Rarity, S. Yu, and J. L. O'Brien, "Silica-on-silicon waveguide quantum circuits," *Science*, vol. 320, no. 5876, pp. 646–649, 2008.

**41** A. Politi, J. C. Matthews, and J. L. O'brien, "Shor's quantum factoring algorithm on a photonic chip," *Science*, vol. 325, no. 5945, pp. 1221–1221, 2009.

**42** L. DiCarlo, J. M. Chow, J. M. Gambetta, L. Bishop, B. Johnson, D. Schuster, J. Majer, A. Blais, L. Frunzio, S. Girvin, et al., "Demonstration of two-qubit algorithms with a superconducting quantum processor," *Nature*, vol. 460, no. 7252, p. 240, 2009.

**43** E. Martín-López, A. Laing, T. Lawson, R. Alvarez, X.-Q. Zhou, and J. L. O'Brien, "Experimental realization of Shor's quantum factoring algorithm using qubit recycling," *Nature Photonics*, vol. 6, no. 11, pp. 773–776, 2012.

**44** J. M. Chow, J. M. Gambetta, A. Córcoles, S. T. Merkel, J. A. Smolin, C. Rigetti, S. Poletto, G. A. Keefe, M. B. Rothwell, J. Rozen, et al., "Universal quantum gate set approaching fault-tolerant thresholds with superconducting qubits," *Physical Review Letters*, vol. 109, no. 6, 2012.

**45** M. Veldhorst, J. Hwang, C. Yang, A. Leenstra, B. De Ronde, J. Dehollain, J. Muhonen, F. Hudson, K. M. Itoh, A. Morello, et al., "An addressable quantum dot qubit with fault-tolerant control-fidelity," *Nature Nanotechnology*, vol. 9, no. 12, pp. 981–985, 2014.

**46** M. Veldhorst, C. Yang, J. Hwang, W. Huang, J. Dehollain, J. Muhonen, S. Simmons, A. Laucht, F. Hudson, K. M. Itoh, et al., "A two-qubit logic gate in silicon," *Nature*, vol. 526, no. 7573, pp. 410–414, 2015.

**47** S. Weidt, J. Randall, S. Webster, K. Lake, A. Webb, I. Cohen, T. Navickas, B. Lekitsch, A. Retzker, and W. K. Hensinger, "Trapped-ion quantum logic with global radiation fields," *Physical review letters*, vol. 117, no. 22, 2016.

**48** B. Lekitsch, S. Weidt, A. G. Fowler, K. MØlmer, S. J. Devitt, C. Wunderlich, and W. K. Hensinger, "Blueprint for a microwave trapped ion quantum computer," *Science Advances*, vol. 3, no. 2, 2017.

**49** D. P. DiVincenzo, "The physical implementation of quantum computation," *Fortschritte der Physik*, vol. 48, no. 9-11, pp. 771–783, 2000.

**50** P. A. Dirac, "A new notation for quantum mechanics," *Proceedings of the Cambridge Philosophical Society*, vol. 35, pp. 416–418, 1939.

**51** S. Aaronson and D. Gottesman, "Improved simulation of stabilizer circuits," *Physical Review A*, vol. 70, no. 5, 2004.

**52** J. Preskill, "Reliable quantum computers," *Proceedings of the Royal Society of London A: Mathematical, Physical and Engineering Sciences*, vol. 454, no. 1969, pp. 385–410, 1998.

**53** C. E. Shannon, "A mathematical theory of communication," *Bell System Technical Journal*, vol. 27, no. 3, pp. 379–423, 1948.

**54** P. W. Shor, "Scheme for reducing decoherence in quantum computer memory," *Physical Review A*, vol. 52, no. 4, 1995.

**55** A. M. Steane, "Error correcting codes in quantum theory," *Physical Review Letters*, vol. 77, no. 5, 1996.

**56** R. Laflamme, C. Miquel, J. P. Paz, and W. H. Zurek, "Perfect quantum error correcting code," *Physical Review Letters*, vol. 77, no. 1, 1996.

**57** D. Gottesman, "Class of quantum error-correcting codes saturating the quantum Hamming bound," *Physical Review A*, vol. 54, no. 3, 1996.

**58** A. K. Ekert and C. Macchiavello, "Quantum error correction for communication," *Physical Review Letters*, vol. 77, no. 12, 1996.

**59** D. Gottesman, "Stabilizer codes and quantum error correction," Ph.D. dissertation, California Institute of Technology, 1997.

**60** A. R. Calderbank, E. M. Rains, P. W. Shor, and N. J. A. Sloane, "Quantum error correction via codes over GF(4)," *IEEE Transactions on Information Theory*, vol. 44, no. 4, pp. 1369–1387, 1998.

**61** M. Grassl and T. Beth, "Quantum BCH codes," in *Proceedings of International Symposium Theoretical Electrical Engineering*, 1999, pp. 207–212.

**62** M. Grassl, W. Geiselmann, and T. Beth, "Quantum Reed-Solomon codes," in *Applied Algebra, Algebraic Algorithms and Error-correcting Codes*. Springer Berlin Heidelberg, 1999, pp. 231–244.

**63** A. M. Steane, "Quantum Reed-Muller codes," *IEEE Transactions on Information Theory*, vol. 45, no. 5, pp. 1701–1703, 1999.

**64** G. Bowen, "Entanglement required in achieving entanglement-assisted channel capacities," *Physical Review A*, vol. 66, no. 5, 2002.

**65** T. A. Brun, I. Devetak, and M.-H. Hsieh, "Correcting quantum errors with entanglement," *Science*, vol. 314, no. 5798, pp. 436–439, 2006.

**66** H. Ollivier and J.-P. Tillich, "Description of a quantum convolutional code," *Physical Review Letters*, vol. 91, no. 17, 2003.

**67** M. M. Wilde and T. A. Brun, "Entanglement-assisted quantum convolutional coding," *Physical Review A*, vol. 81, no. 4, 2010.

**68** M. S. Postol, "A proposed quantum low density parity check code," *arXiv preprint quant-ph/0108131*, 2001.

69 D. J. MacKay, G. Mitchison, and P. L. McFadden, "Sparse-graph codes for quantum error correction," *IEEE Transactions on Information Theory*, vol. 50, no. 10, pp. 2315–2330, 2004.

70 T. Camara, H. Ollivier, and J.-P. Tillich, "Constructions and performance of classes of quantum LDPC codes," *arXiv preprint quant-ph/0502086*, 2005.

71 T. Camara, H. Ollivier, and J.-P. Tillich, "A class of quantum LDPC codes: Construction and performances under iterative decoding," in *Proceedings of IEEE International Symposium on Information Theory (ISIT)*, 2007, pp. 811–815.

72 M.-H. Hsieh, T. A. Brun, and I. Devetak, "Entanglement-assisted quantum quasicyclic low-density parity-check codes," *Physical Review A*, vol. 79, no. 3, 2009.

73 Z. Babar, P. Botsinis, D. Alanis, S. X. Ng, and L. Hanzo, "Fifteen years of quantum LDPC coding and improved decoding strategies," *Access, IEEE*, vol. 3, pp. 2492–2519, 2015.

74 D. Poulin, J.-P. Tillich, and H. Ollivier, "Quantum serial turbo codes," *IEEE Transactions on Information Theory*, vol. 55, no. 6, pp. 2776–2798, 2009.

75 M. M. Wilde and M.-H. Hsieh, "Entanglement boosts quantum turbo codes," in *Proceedings of IEEE International Symposium on Information Theory (ISIT)*, 2011, pp. 445–449.

76 M. M. Wilde, M.-H. Hsieh, and Z. Babar, "Entanglement-assisted quantum turbo codes," *IEEE Transactions on Information Theory*, vol. 60, no. 2, pp. 1203–1222, 2014.

77 Z. Babar, P. Botsinis, D. Alanis, S. X. Ng, and L. Hanzo, "The road from classical to quantum codes: A hashing bound approaching design procedure," *IEEE Access*, vol. 3, pp. 146–176, 2015.

78 J. M. Renes, F. Dupuis, and R. Renner, "Efficient polar coding of quantum information," *Physical Review Letters*, vol. 109, no. 5, 2012.

79 M. M. Wilde and J. M. Renes, "Quantum polar codes for arbitrary channels," in *Proceedings of IEEE International Symposium on Information Theory (ISIT)*, 2012, pp. 334–338.

80 M. Grassl, T. Beth, and T. Pellizzari, "Codes for the quantum erasure channel," *Physical Review A*, vol. 56, no. 1, 1997.

81 H. F. Chau, "Quantum convolutional error-correcting codes," *Physical Review A*, vol. 58, no. 2, 1998.

82 D. A. Lidar and K. B. Whaley, "Decoherence-free subspaces and subsystems," in *Irreversible Quantum Dynamics*. Springer, 2003, pp. 83–120.

83 A. Shabani and D. A. Lidar, "Theory of initialization-free decoherence-free subspaces and subsystems," *Physical Review A*, vol. 72, no. 4, 2005.

84 D. Lidar and T. Brun, *Quantum Error Correction*. Cambridge University Press, 2013. [Online]. Available: http://books.google.co.uk/books?id=XV9sAAAAQBAJ

85 E. Knill and R. Laflamme, "Theory of quantum error-correcting codes," *Physical Review A*, vol. 55, no. 2, 1997.

86 A. R. Calderbank and P. W. Shor, "Good quantum error-correcting codes exist," *Physical Review A*, vol. 54, no. 2, 1996.

87 D. Gottesman, "Theory of fault-tolerant quantum computation," *Physical Review A*, vol. 57, no. 1, 1998.

88 E. Knill, R. Laflamme, and W. H. Zurek, "Resilient quantum computation," *Science*, vol. 279, no. 5349, pp. 342–345, 1998.

89 E. Knill, R. Laflamme, and W. H. Zurek, "Resilient quantum computation: Error models and thresholds," *Proceedings of the Royal Society of London A: Mathematical, Physical and Engineering Sciences*, vol. 454, no. 1969, pp. 365–384, 1998.

90 D. Gottesman, "Fault-tolerant quantum computation with constant overhead," *Quantum Information & Computation*, vol. 14, no. 15-16, pp. 1338–1372, 2014.

91 J. Akhtman, R. Maunder, N. Bonello, and L. Hanzo, "Closed-form approximation of maximum free distance for binary block codes," in *Proceedings of IEEE 70th Vehicular Technology Conference Fall (VTC-Fall)*, 2009, pp. 1–3.

92 A. M. Steane, "Multiple-particle interference and quantum error correction," *Proceedings of the Royal Society of London A: Mathematical, Physical and Engineering Sciences*, vol. 452, no. 1954, pp. 2551–2577, 1996.

93 P. W. Shor, "Fault-tolerant quantum computation," in *Proceedings of 37th Annual Symposium on Foundations of Computer Science (FOCS)*, 1996, pp. 56–65.

94 A. R. Calderbank, E. M. Rains, P. W. Shor, and N. J. A. Sloane, "Quantum error correction and orthogonal geometry," *Physical Review Letters*, vol. 78, no. 3, 1997.

95 "IBM Quantum Experience," https://www.research.ibm.com/ibm-q, accessed: 2017-10-01.

**96** A. Y. Kitaev, "Quantum computations: Algorithms and error correction," *Russian Mathematical Surveys*, vol. 52, no. 6, pp. 1191–1249, 1997.

**97** A. Y. Kitaev, "Fault-tolerant quantum computation by anyons," *Annals of Physics*, vol. 303, no. 1, pp. 2–30, 2003.

**98** M. H. Freedman, D. A. Meyer, and F. Luo, "Z2-systolic freedom and quantum codes," *Mathematics of Quantum Computation*, pp. 287–320, 2002.

**99** S. Bravyi and A. Y. Kitaev, "Quantum codes on a lattice with boundary," *arXiv preprint quant-ph/9811052*, 1998.

**100** C. Horsman, A. G. Fowler, S. J. Devitt, and R. Van Meter, "Surface code quantum computing by lattice surgery," *New Journal of Physics*, vol. 14, no. 12, 2012.

**101** H. Bombin and M. A. Martin-Delgado, "Topological quantum distillation," *Physical Review Letters*, vol. 97, no. 18, 2006.

**102** J. Haah, "Local stabilizer codes in three dimensions without string logical operators," *Physical Review A*, vol. 83, no. 4, 2011.

**103** G. Zémor, "On Cayley graphs, surface codes, and the limits of homological coding for quantum error correction," in *Coding and Cryptology*. Springer, 2009, pp. 259–273.

**104** A. Couvreur, N. Delfosse, and G. Zemor, "A construction of quantum LDPC codes from Cayley graphs," *IEEE Transactions on Information Theory*, vol. 59, no. 9, pp. 6087–6098, 2013.

**105** N. Delfosse, "Tradeoffs for reliable quantum information storage in surface codes and color codes," in *Proceedings of IEEE International Symposium on Information Theory (ISIT)*, 2013, pp. 917–921.

**106** J.-P. Tillich and G. Zémor, "Quantum LDPC codes with positive rate and minimum distance proportional to the square root of the blocklength," in *Proceedings of IEEE International Symposium on Information Theory (ISIT)*, 2009, pp. 799–803.

**107** A. A. Kovalev and L. P. Pryadko, "Improved quantum hypergraph-product LDPC codes," in *Proceedings of IEEE International Symposium on Information Theory (ISIT)*, 2012, pp. 348–352.

**108** J.-P. Tillich and G. Zémor, "Quantum LDPC codes with positive rate and minimum distance proportional to the square root of the blocklength," *IEEE Transactions on Information Theory*, vol. 60, no. 2, pp. 1193–1202, 2014.

**109** S. Bravyi and M. B. Hastings, "Homological product codes," in *Proceedings of the 46th Annual ACM Symposium on Theory of Computing*, 2014, pp. 273–282.

**110** S. Bravyi and J. Haah, "Quantum self-correction in the 3D cubic code model," *Physical Review Letters*, vol. 111, no. 20, 2013.

**111** L. Guth and A. Lubotzky, "Quantum error correcting codes and 4-dimensional arithmetic hyperbolic manifolds," *Journal of Mathematical Physics*, vol. 55, no. 8, 2014.

**112** H. Bombín, "Dimensional jump in quantum error correction," *New Journal of Physics*, vol. 18, no. 4, 2016.

**113** W. Zeng and L. P. Pryadko, "Higher-dimensional quantum hypergraph-product codes with finite rates," *Physical Review Letters*, vol. 122, no. 23, 2019.

**114** P. Piret, *Convolutional Codes: An Algebraic Approach*. MIT Press, Cambridge, MA, 1988.

**115** H. F. Chau, "Good quantum-convolutional error-correction codes and their decoding algorithm exist," *Phys. Rev. A*, vol. 60, pp. 1966–1974, Sep 1999. [Online]. Available: http://link.aps.org/doi/10.1103/PhysRevA.60.1966

**116** H. Ollivier and J.-P. Tillich, "Quantum convolutional codes: fundamentals," *quant-ph/0401134*, 2004.

**117** A. Aido De Almeida and J. Palazzo, R., "A concatenated [(4, 1, 3)] quantum convolutional code," in *IEEE Information Theory Workshop*, Oct. 2004, pp. 28–33.

**118** G. Forney and S. Guha, "Simple rate-1/3 convolutional and tail-biting quantum error-correcting codes," in *International Symposium on Information Theory*, Sep. 2005, pp. 1028–1032.

**119** G. D. Forney, M. Grassl, and S. Guha, "Convolutional and tail-biting quantum error-correcting codes," *IEEE Transactions on Information Theory*, vol. 53, no. 3, pp. 865–880, Mar. 2007.

**120** M. Grassl and M. Rotteler, "Quantum block and convolutional codes from self-orthogonal product codes," in *International Symposium on Information Theory*, Sep. 2005, pp. 1018–1022.

**121** M. Grassl and M. Rotteler, "Constructions of quantum convolutional codes," in *IEEE International Symposium on Information Theory*, Jun. 2007, pp. 816–820.

**122** S. Aly, M. Grassl, A. Klappenecker, M. Rotteler, and P. Sarvepalli, "Quantum convolutional BCH codes," in *10th Canadian Workshop on Information Theory*, Jun. 2007, pp. 180–183.

**123** S. A. Aly, A. Klappenecker, and P. K. Sarvepalli, "Quantum convolutional codes derived from generalized Reed-Solomon codes," in *IEEE International Symposium on Information Theory*, Jun. 2007, pp. 821–825.

**124** E. Pelchat and D. Poulin, "Degenerate Viterbi decoding," *IEEE Transactions on Information Theory*, vol. 59, no. 6, pp. 3915–3921, 2013.

**125** L. Hanzo, T. H. Liew, B. L. Yeap, R. Y. S. Tee and S. X. Ng, *Turbo Coding, Turbo Equalisation and Space-Time Coding: EXIT-Chart-Aided Near-Capacity Designs for Wireless Channels, 2nd Edition*. New York, USA: John Wiley IEEE Press, Mar. 2011.

**126** R. Gallager, "Low-density parity-check codes," *IRE Transactions on Information Theory*, vol. 8, no. 1, pp. 21–28, Jan. 1962.

**127** D. MacKay, G. Mitchison, and A. Shokrollahi, "More sparse-graph codes for quantum error-correction," *www.inference.phy.cam.ac.uk/mackay/cayley.pdf* , 2007.

**128** A. Couvreur, N. Delfosse, and G. Zemor, "A construction of quantum LDPC codes from Cayley graphs," in *IEEE International Symposium on Information Theory Proceedings*, 31 2011-Aug. 5 2011, pp. 643–647.

**129** S. Aly, "A class of quantum LDPC codes constructed from finite geometries," in *IEEE Global Telecommunications Conference*, 30 2008-Dec. 4 2008, pp. 1–5.

**130** I. Djordjevic, "Quantum LDPC codes from balanced incomplete block designs," *IEEE Communications Letters*, vol. 12, no. 5, pp. 389–391, May 2008.

**131** H. Lou and J. Garcia-Frias, "Quantum error-correction using codes with low-density generator matrix," in *IEEE 6th Workshop on Signal Processing Advances in Wireless Communications*, Jun. 2005, pp. 1043–1047.

**132** H. Lou and J. Garcia-Frias, "On the application of error-correcting codes with low-density generator matrix over different quantum channels," *International ITG-Conference on Source and Channel Coding*, pp. 1–6, Apr. 2006.

**133** M. Hagiwara and H. Imai, "Quantum quasi-cyclic LDPC codes," in *IEEE International Symposium on Information Theory*, Jun. 2007, pp. 806–810.

**134** K. Kasai, M. Hagiwara, H. Imai, and K. Sakaniwa, "Non-binary quasi-cyclic quantum LDPC codes," in *IEEE International Symposium on Information Theory Proceedings*, 31 2011-Aug. 5 2011, pp. 653–657.

**135** K. Kasai, M. Hagiwara, H. Imai, and K. Sakaniwa, "Quantum error correction beyond the bounded distance decoding limit," *IEEE Transactions on Information Theory*, vol. 58, no. 2, pp. 1223–1230, Feb. 2012.

**136** M. Hagiwara, K. Kasai, H. Imai, and K. Sakaniwa, "Spatially coupled quasi-cyclic quantum LDPC codes," in *IEEE International Symposium on Information Theory Proceedings*, 31 2011-Aug. 5 2011, pp. 638–642.

**137** P. Tan and J. Li, "Efficient quantum stabilizer codes: LDPC and LDPC-convolutional constructions," *IEEE Transactions on Information Theory*, vol. 56, no. 1, pp. 476–491, Jan. 2010.

**138** A. A. Kovalev and L. P. Pryadko, "Quantum Kronecker sum-product low-density parity-check codes with finite rate," *Phys. Rev. A*, vol. 88, p. 012311, Jul 2013. [Online]. Available: http://link.aps.org/doi/10.1103/PhysRevA.88.012311

**139** D. Poulin and Y. Chung, "On the iterative decoding of sparse quantum codes," *Quantum Info. Comput.*, vol. 8, no. 10, pp. 987–1000, Nov. 2008. [Online]. Available: http://dl.acm.org/citation.cfm?id=2016985.2016993

**140** Y.-J. Wang, B. Sanders, B.-M. Bai, and X.-M. Wang, "Enhanced feedback iterative decoding of sparse quantum codes," *IEEE Transactions on Information Theory*, vol. 58, no. 2, pp. 1231–1241, Feb. 2012.

**141** D. Poulin, J.-P. Tillich, and H. Ollivier, "Quantum serial turbo-codes," in *IEEE International Symposium on Information Theory*, Jul. 2008, pp. 310–314.

**142** M. Houshmand and M. M. Wilde, "Recursive quantum convolutional encoders are catastrophic: A simple proof," *IEEE Transactions on Information Theory*, vol. 59, no. 10, pp. 6724–6731, 2013.

**143** T. A. Brun, I. Devetak, and M.-H. Hsieh, "General entanglement-assisted quantum error-correcting codes," in *IEEE International Symposium on Information Theory*, June 2007, pp. 2101–2105.

**144** M.-H. Hsieh, I. Devetak, and T. Brun, "General entanglement-assisted quantum error-correcting codes," *Phys. Rev. A*, vol. 76, p. 062313, Dec. 2007. [Online]. Available: http://link.aps.org/doi/10.1103/PhysRevA.76.062313

**145** M.-H. Hsieh, T. A. Brun, and I. Devetak, "Entanglement-assisted quantum quasicyclic low-density parity-check codes," *Phys. Rev. A*, vol. 79, p. 032340, Mar 2009. [Online]. Available: http://link.aps.org/doi/10.1103/PhysRevA.79.032340

**146** M. M. Wilde and T. A. Brun, "Entanglement-assisted quantum convolutional coding," *Phys. Rev. A*, vol. 81, p. 042333, Apr 2010. [Online]. Available: http://link.aps.org/doi/10.1103/PhysRevA.81.042333

**147** C. Ballance, T. Harty, N. Linke, M. Sepiol, and D. Lucas, "High-fidelity quantum logic gates using trapped-ion hyperfine qubits," *Physical review letters*, vol. 117, no. 6, 2016.

**148** H. V. Nguyen, Z. Babar, D. Alanis, P. Botsinis, D. Chandra, S. X. Ng, and L. Hanzo, "EXIT-chart aided quantum code design improves the normalised throughput of realistic quantum devices," *IEEE Access*, vol. 4, pp. 10 194–10 209, 2016.

**149** S. Bravyi and A. Y. Kitaev, "Universal quantum computation with ideal Clifford gates and noisy ancillas," *Physical Review A*, vol. 71, no. 2, 2005.

**150** D. Aharonov and M. Ben-Or, "Fault-tolerant quantum computation with constant error rate," *SIAM Journal on Computing*, vol. 38, no. 4, pp. 1207–1282, 2008.

**151** H. Bombín, "Single-shot fault-tolerant quantum error correction," *Physical Review X*, vol. 5, no. 3, 2015.

**152** O. Fawzi, A. Grospellier, and A. Leverrier, "Constant overhead quantum fault-tolerance with quantum expander codes," in *Proceedings of 59th IEEE Annual Symposium on Foundations of Computer Science (FOCS)*, 2018, pp. 743–754.

**153** E. Campbell, "A theory of single-shot error correction for adversarial noise," *Quantum Science and Technology*, vol. 4, no. 2, 2019.

**154** T. Jochym-O'Connor, "Fault-tolerant gates via homological product codes," *Quantum*, vol. 3, 2019.

**155** D. Chandra, Z. Babar, H. V. Nguyen, D. Alanis, P. Botsinis, S. X. Ng, and L. Hanzo, "Quantum topological error correction codes: The classical-to-quantum isomorphism perspective," *IEEE Access*, vol. 6, pp. 13 729–13 757, 2018.

**156** S. Bravyi and B. Terhal, "A no-go theorem for a two-dimensional self-correcting quantum memory based on stabilizer codes," *New Journal of Physics*, vol. 11, no. 4, 2009.

**157** S. Bravyi, D. Poulin, and B. Terhal, "Tradeoffs for reliable quantum information storage in 2D systems," *Physical Review Letters*, vol. 104, no. 5, 2010.

**158** Y. Fujiwara, "Ability of stabilizer quantum error correction to protect itself from its own imperfection," *Physical Review A*, vol. 90, no. 6, 2014.

**159** A. Ashikhmin, C.-Y. Lai, and T. A. Brun, "Robust quantum error syndrome extraction by classical coding," in *Proceedings of IEEE International Symposium on Information Theory (ISIT)*, 2014, pp. 546–550.

**160** A. Ashikhmin, C.-Y. Lai, and T. A. Brun, "Correction of data and syndrome errors by stabilizer codes," in *Proceedings of IEEE International Symposium on Information Theory (ISIT)*, 2016, pp. 2274–2278.

**161** W. Zeng, A. Ashikhmin, M. Woolls, and L. P. Pryadko, "Quantum convolutional data-syndrome codes," *arXiv preprint arXiv:1902.07395*, 2019.

**162** M. A. Nielsen and I. L. Chuang, *Quantum Computation and Quantum Information*. Cambridge University Press, 2000.

**163** D. Gottesman, "The Heisenberg representation of quantum computers," *arXiv preprint quant-ph/9807006*, 1998.

**164** T. Toffoli, "Reversible computing," in *International Colloquium on Automata, Languages, and Programming*. Springer, 1980, pp. 632–644.

**165** P. Botsinis, Z. Babar, D. Alanis, D. Chandra, H. V. Nguyen, S. X. Ng, and L. Hanzo, "Quantum error correction protects quantum search algorithms against decoherence," *Scientific Reports*, vol. 6, 2016.

**166** A. Barenco, C. H. Bennett, R. Cleve, D. P. DiVincenzo, N. Margolus, P. W. Shor, T. Sleator, J. A. Smolin, and H. Weinfurter, "Elementary gates for quantum computation," *Physical Review A*, vol. 52, no. 5, 1995.

**167** U. Fano, "Description of states in quantum mechanics by density matrix and operator techniques," *Reviews of Modern Physics*, vol. 29, no. 1, 1957.

**168** G. M. D'Ariano, M. G. Paris, and M. F. Sacchi, "Quantum tomography," *Advances in Imaging and Electron Physics*, vol. 128, pp. 206–309, 2003.

**169** J. Roffe, "Quantum error correction: An introductory guide," *arXiv preprint arXiv:1907.11157*, 2019.

**170** A. Ashikhmin, "Remarks on bounds for quantum codes," *arXiv preprint quant-ph/9705037*, 1997.

**171** P. K. Sarvepalli and A. Klappenecker, "Degenerate quantum codes and the quantum Hamming bound," *Physical Review A*, vol. 81, no. 3, 2010.

**172** Z. Babar, D. Chandra, H. V. Nguyen, P. Botsinis, D. Alanis, S. X. Ng, and L. Hanzo, "Duality of Quantum and Classical Error Correction Codes: Design Principles and Examples," *IEEE Communications Surveys & Tutorials*, vol. 21, no. 1, pp. 970–1010, 2018.

**173** F. Schmidt-Kaler, S. Gulde, M. Riebe, T. Deuschle, A. Kreuter, G. Lancaster, C. Becher, J. Eschner, H. Häffner, and R. Blatt, "The coherence of qubits based on single Ca+ ions," *Journal of Physics B: Atomic, Molecular and Optical Physics*, vol. 36, no. 3, p. 623, 2003.

**174** L. M. Vandersypen, M. Steffen, G. Breyta, C. S. Yannoni, M. H. Sherwood, and I. L. Chuang, "Experimental realization of Shor's quantum factoring algorithm using nuclear magnetic resonance," *Nature*, vol. 414, no. 6866, pp. 883–887, 2001.

**175** A. Tyryshkin, J. Morton, S. Benjamin, A. Ardavan, G. Briggs, J. Ager, and S. Lyon, "Coherence of spin qubits in silicon," *Journal of Physics: Condensed Matter*, vol. 18, no. 21, p. S783, 2006.

**176** J. Petta, A. C. Johnson, J. Taylor, E. Laird, A. Yacoby, M. D. Lukin, C. Marcus, M. Hanson, and A. Gossard, "Coherent manipulation of coupled electron spins in semiconductor quantum dots," *Science*, vol. 309, no. 5744, pp. 2180–2184, 2005.

**177** P. Bertet, I. Chiorescu, G. Burkard, K. Semba, C. Harmans, D. P. DiVincenzo, and J. Mooij, "Dephasing of a superconducting qubit induced by photon noise," *Physical Review Letters*, vol. 95, no. 25, 2005.

**178** L. Ioffe and M. Mézard, "Asymmetric quantum error-correcting codes," *Physical Review A*, vol. 75, no. 3, 2007.

**179** P. Sarvepalli, A. Klappenecker, and M. Rotteler, "Asymmetric quantum LDPC codes," in *IEEE International Symposium on Information Theory*, July 2008, pp. 305–309.

**180** Y. Fujiwara and V. Tonchev, "A characterization of entanglement-assisted quantum low-density parity-check codes," *IEEE Transactions on Information Theory*, vol. 59, no. 6, pp. 3347–3353, Jun. 2013.

**181** D. Chandra, Z. Babar, H. V. Nguyen, D. Alanis, P. Botsinis, S. X. Ng, and L. Hanzo, "Quantum coding bounds and a closed-form approximation of the minimum distance versus quantum coding rate," *IEEE Access*, vol. 5, pp. 11 557–11 581, 2017.

**182** R. Cleve and D. Gottesman, "Efficient computations of encodings for quantum error correction," *Physical Review A*, vol. 56, no. 1, 1997.

**183** I. Djordjevic, *Quantum Information Processing and Quantum Error Correction: An Engineering Approach*. Academic press, 2012.

**184** S. Lin and D. J. Costello, *Error Control Coding*. Pearson Education India. [Online]. Available: http://books.google.co.uk/books?id=BG08Zylo_7gC

**185** L. Bahl, J. Cocke, F. Jelinek, and J. Raviv, "Optimal decoding of linear codes for minimizing symbol error rate (corresp.)," *IEEE Transactions on Information Theory*, vol. 20, no. 2, pp. 284–287, Mar. 1974.

**186** J. Wolf, "Efficient maximum likelihood decoding of linear block codes using a trellis," *IEEE Transactions on Information Theory*, vol. 24, no. 1, pp. 76–80, Jan. 1978.

**187** J. Schalkwijk and A. Vinck, "Syndrome decoding of convolutional codes," *IEEE Transactions on Communications*, vol. 23, no. 7, pp. 789–792, Jul. 1975.

**188** J. Schalkwijk and A. Vinck, "Syndrome decoding of binary rate-1/2 convolutional codes," *IEEE Transactions on Communications*, vol. 24, no. 9, pp. 977–985, Sep 1976.

**189** J. Schalkwijk, A. Vinck, and K. Post, "Syndrome decoding of binary-rate k/n convolutional codes," *IEEE Transactions on Information Theory*, vol. 24, no. 5, pp. 553–562, Sep 1978.

**190** M. Ariel and J. Snyders, "Soft syndrome decoding of binary convolutional codes," *IEEE Transactions on Communications*, vol. 43, no. 234, pp. 288–297, Feb./Mar./Apr. 1995.

**191** V. Sidorenko and V. Zyablov, "Decoding of convolutional codes using a syndrome trellis," *IEEE Transactions on Information Theory*, vol. 40, no. 5, pp. 1663–1666, Sep. 1994.

**192** T. Minowa and H. Imai, "Decoding of high-rate turbo codes using a syndrome trellis," *IEEE International Conference on Communications*, vol. 1, pp. 74–78, Jun. 2001.

**193** J. Geldmacher, K. Hueske, and J. Götze, "Syndrome based block decoding of convolutional codes," *IEEE International Symposium on Wireless Communication Systems*, pp. 542–546, Oct. 2008.

**194** K. Hueske, J. Geldmacher, and J. Götze, "Adaptive decoding of convolutional codes," *Advances in Radio Science*, vol. 5, pp. 209–214, 2007. [Online]. Available: http://www.adv-radio-sci.net/5/209/2007/

**195** K. Hueske, J. Geldmacher, and J. Götze, "Multi core implementation of a trellis based syndrome decoder with adaptive complexity," in *International Symposium on Wireless Communication Systems*, Sept. 2010, pp. 859–863.

**196** J. Geldmacher, K. Hueske, J. Götze, and M. Kosakowski, "Low complexity syndrome based decoding of turbo codes," *IEEE International Symposium on Information Theory Proceedings*, pp. 2371–2375, Jul. 2012.

**197** J. Geldmacher, K. Hueske, J. Götze, and S. Bialas, "Adaptive low complexity MAP decoding for turbo equalization," *International Symposium on Turbo Codes and Iterative Information Processing*, pp. 63–67, Sept. 2010.

**198** J. Geldmacher, K. Hueske, and J. Götze, "An adaptive and complexity reduced decoding algorithm for convolutional codes and its application to digital broadcasting systems" in *International Conference on Ultra Modern Telecommunications Workshops*, Oct. 2009, pp. 1–7.

**199** K. Hueske, J. Geldmacher, and J. Götze, “Syndrome based adaptive complexity channel decoding and turbo equalization for atsc dtv,” in *Conference Record of the Forty Fourth Asilomar Conference on Signals, Systems and Computers*, Nov. 2010, pp. 155–159.

**200** J. Geldmacher, K. Hueske, J. Götze, and M. Kosakowski, “Hard decision based low SNR early termination for LTE turbo decoding,” in *International Symposium on Wireless Communication Systems*, Nov. 2011, pp. 26–30.

**201** Z. Babar, S. X. Ng, and L. Hanzo, “Reduced-complexity syndrome-based TTCM decoding,” *IEEE Communications Letters*, vol. 17, no. 6, pp. 1220–1223, Jun. 2013.

**202** A. Viterbi, “Error bounds for convolutional codes and an asymptotically optimum decoding algorithm,” *IEEE Transactions on Information Theory*, vol. 13, no. 2, pp. 260–269, Apr. 1967.

**203** M. Tajima, K. Shibata, and Z. Kawasaki, “Relation between encoder and syndrome former variables and symbol reliability estimation using a syndrome trellis,” *IEEE Transactions on Communications*, vol. 51, no. 9, pp. 1474 – 1484, Sep. 2003.

**204** T. Filler, J. Judas, and J. Fridrich, “Minimizing additive distortion in steganography using syndrome-trellis codes,” *IEEE Transactions on Information Forensics and Security*, vol. 6, no. 3, pp. 920–935, Sep. 2011.

**205** M. Tajima, K. Shibata, and Z. Kawasaki, “Modification of syndrome trellises for high-rate convolutional codes,” *IEICE Technical Report*, vol. 102, no. 66, pp. 7–12, May 2002.

**206** P. Robertson and T. Worz, “Bandwidth-efficient turbo trellis-coded modulation using punctured component codes,” *IEEE Journal on Selected Areas in Communications*, vol. 16, no. 2, pp. 206–218, Feb. 1998.

**207** G. Ungerboeck, “Channel coding with multilevel/phase signals,” *IEEE Transactions on Information Theory*, vol. 28, no. 1, pp. 55–67, Jan. 1982.

**208** H. Chen and A. Haimovich, “Exit charts for turbo trellis-coded modulation,” *IEEE Communications Letters*, vol. 8, no. 11, pp. 668–670, Nov. 2004.

**209** C. H. Bennett, P. W. Shor, J. A. Smolin, and A. V. Thapliyal, “Entanglement-assisted classical capacity of noisy quantum channels,” *Phys. Rev. Lett.*, vol. 83, pp. 3081–3084, Oct 1999. [Online]. Available: http://link.aps.org/doi/10.1103/PhysRevLett.83.3081

**210** A. Holevo, “On entanglement-assisted classical capacity,” *J. Math. Phys.*, vol. 43, no. 9, pp. 4326–4333, 2002.

**211** Z. Babar, S. X. Ng, and L. Hanzo, “Near-capacity code design for entanglement-assisted classical communication over quantum depolarizing channels,” *IEEE Transactions on Communications*, vol. 61, no. 12, pp. 4801–4807, Dec. 2013.

**212** Z. Babar, S. X. Ng, and L. Hanzo, “EXIT-chart aided code design for symbol-based entanglement-assisted classical communication over quantum channels,” in *IEEE Vehicular Technology Conference (VTC Fall)*, Sept 2014, pp. 1–5.

**213** S. Bose, V. Vedral, and P. L. Knight, “A multiparticle generalization of entanglement swapping,” *Phys. Rev. A*, vol. 57, no. quant-ph/9708004. 2, pp. 822–829, 1998.

**214** A. Chiuri, S. Giacomini, C. Macchiavello, and P. Mataloni, “Experimental achievement of the entanglement-assisted capacity for the depolarizing channel,” *Phys. Rev. A*, vol. 87, p. 022333, Feb 2013. [Online]. Available: http://link.aps.org/doi/10.1103/PhysRevA.87.022333

**215** P. Kaye, R. Laflamme, and M. Mosca, *An introduction to quantum computing*. Oxford University Press, 2007. [Online]. Available: http://books.google.com/books?id=gLFQAAAAMAAJ

**216** D. M. Greenberger, M. A. Horne, A. Shimony, and A. Zeilinger, “Bell’s theorem without inequalities,” *American Journal of Physics*, vol. 58, pp. 1131–1143, Dec. 1990.

**217** Z. Shadman, H. Kampermann, C. Macchiavello, and D. Bruss, “Optimal super dense coding over noisy quantum channels,” *New Journal of Physics*, vol. 12, Jul. 2010.

**218** C. E. Shannon, “A Mathematical Theory of Communication,” *The Bell system Technical Journal*, vol. 27, no. 3, pp. 379–656, July 1948.

**219** J. Kliewer, S. X. Ng, and L. Hanzo, “Efficient computation of EXIT functions for non-binary iterative decoding,” *IEEE Transactions on Communications*, vol. 54, no. 12, pp. 2133–2136, Dec. 2006.

**220** S. X. Ng, O. Alamri, Y. Li, J. Kliewer, and L. Hanzo, “Near-capacity turbo trellis coded modulation design based on EXIT charts and union bounds,” *IEEE Transactions on Communications*, vol. 56, no. 12, pp. 2030 –2039, Dec. 2008.

**221** S. ten Brink, “Convergence behaviour of iteratively decoded parallel concatenated codes,” *IEEE Transactions on Communications*, vol. 49, no. 10, pp. 1727–1737, Oct. 2001.

**222** M. El-Hajjar and L. Hanzo, “EXIT charts for system design and analysis,” *IEEE Communications Surveys Tutorials*, pp. 1–27, 2013.

**223** M. Tüchler and J. Hagenauer, "EXIT charts of irregular codes," in *Proceedings of Conference on Information Science and Systems*, Princeton University, 20-22 Mar. 2002, pp. 465–490.

**224** M. Tüchler, "Design of serially concatenated systems depending on the block length," *IEEE Transactions on Communications*, vol. 52, no. 2, pp. 209–218, Feb. 2004.

**225** K. R. Narayanan, "Effect of precoding on the convergence of turbo equalization for partial response channels," *IEEE Journal on Selected Areas in Communications*, vol. 19, no. 4, pp. 686–698, Apr. 2001.

**226** A. Ashikhmin, G. Kramer, and S. ten Brink, "Extrinsic information transfer functions: model and erasure channel properties," *IEEE Transactions on Information Theory*, vol. 50, no. 11, pp. 2657–2673, Nov. 2004.

**227** C. Weidmann and G. Lechner, "A fresh look at coding for q-ary symmetric channels," *IEEE Transactions on Information Theory*, vol. 58, no. 11, pp. 6959–6967, Nov 2012.

**228** R. C. Singleton, "Maximum distance Q-nary codes," *IEEE Transactions on Information Theory*, vol. 10, no. 2, pp. 116–118, 1964.

**229** R. W. Hamming, "Error detecting and error correcting codes," *Bell System Technical Journal*, vol. 29, no. 2, pp. 147–160, 1950.

**230** E. N. Gilbert, "A comparison of signalling alphabets," *Bell System Technical Journal*, vol. 31, no. 3, pp. 504–522, 1952.

**231** R. J. McEliece, E. R. Rodemich, H. Rumsey Jr, and L. R. Welch, "New upper bounds on the rate of a code via the Delsarte-MacWilliams inequalities," *IEEE Transactions on Information Theory*, vol. 23, no. 2, pp. 157–166, 1977.

**232** M. Plotkin, "Binary codes with specified minimum distance," *IRE Transactions on Information Theory*, vol. 6, no. 4, pp. 445–450, 1960.

**233** E. M. Rains, "Quantum shadow enumerators," *IEEE Transactions on Information Theory*, vol. 45, no. 7, pp. 2361–2366, 1999.

**234** A. Ashikhmin and S. Litsyu, "Upper bounds on the size of quantum codes," *IEEE Transactions on Information Theory*, vol. 45, no. 4, pp. 1206–1215, 1999.

**235** C.-Y. Lai and C.-C. Lu, "A construction of quantum stabilizer codes based on syndrome assignment by classical parity-check matrices," *IEEE Transactions on Information Theory*, vol. 57, no. 10, pp. 7163–7179, 2011.

**236** Y. Xie, J. Yuan, et al., "Design of quantum stabilizer codes from quadratic residues sets," *arXiv preprint arXiv:1407.8249*, 2014.

**237** M. Grassl, "Bounds on the minimum distance of linear codes and quantum codes," Online available at http://www.codetables.de, 2007, accessed on 2016-05-14.

**238** C.-Y. Lai, "Linear programming bounds for entanglement-assisted quantum error-correcting codes by split weight enumerators," *arXiv preprint arXiv:1602.00413*, 2016.

**239** L. Guo and R. Li, "Linear Plotkin bound for entanglement-assisted quantum codes," *Physical Review A*, vol. 87, no. 3, 2013.

**240** C.-Y. Lai, T. A. Brun, and M. M. Wilde, "Dualities and identities for entanglement-assisted quantum codes," *Quantum Information Processing*, vol. 13, no. 4, pp. 957–990, 2014.

**241** H. Bombin and M. A. Martin-Delgado, "Homological error correction: Classical and quantum codes," *Journal of Mathematical Physics*, vol. 48, no. 5, 2007.

**242** R. Tanner, "A recursive approach to low complexity codes," *IEEE Transactions on Information Theory*, vol. 27, no. 5, pp. 533–547, 1981.

**243** F. R. Kschischang, B. J. Frey, and H.-A. Loeliger, "Factor graphs and the sum-product algorithm," *IEEE Transactions on Information Theory*, vol. 47, no. 2, pp. 498–519, 2001.

**244** R. Steele and L. Hanzo, *Mobile Radio Communications: Second and Third Generation Cellular and WATM Systems.* IEEE Press-John Wiley, 1999.

**245** C. H. Bennett, D. P. DiVincenzo, J. A. Smolin, and W. K. Wootters, "Mixed-state entanglement and quantum error correction," *Physical Review A*, vol. 54, no. 5, 1996.

**246** R. Jozsa, "Fidelity for mixed quantum states," *Journal of Modern Optics*, vol. 41, no. 12, pp. 2315–2323, 1994.

**247** B. Schumacher, "Quantum coding," *Physical Review A*, vol. 51, no. 4, 1995.

**248** J. Von Neumann, "Probabilistic logics and the synthesis of reliable organisms from unreliable components," *Automata Studies*, vol. 34, pp. 43–98, 1956.

**249** A. M. Steane, "Space, time, parallelism and noise requirements for reliable quantum computing," *Fortschritte der Physik*, vol. 46, no. 4-5, pp. 443–457, 1998.

**250** D. E. Deutsch, "Quantum computational networks," *Proceedings of the Royal Society of London A: Mathematical, Physical and Engineering Sciences*, vol. 425, no. 1868, pp. 73–90, 1989.

**251** R. Raussendorf, D. E. Browne, and H. J. Briegel, "Measurement-based quantum computation on cluster states," *Physical Review A*, vol. 68, no. 2, 2003.

**252** G. Grössing and A. Zeilinger, "Quantum cellular automata," *Complex Systems*, vol. 2, no. 2, pp. 197–208, 1988.

**253** M. H. Freedman, A. Y. Kitaev, M. Larsen, and Z. Wang, "Topological quantum computation," *Bulletin of the American Mathematical Society*, vol. 40, no. 1, pp. 31–38, 2003.

**254** E. Farhi, J. Goldstone, S. Gutmann, and M. Sipser, "Quantum computation by adiabatic evolution," *arXiv preprint quant-ph/0001106*, 2000.

**255** M. Grassl, "Variations on encoding circuits for stabilizer quantum codes," in *Proceedings of International Conference on Coding and Cryptology*. Springer, 2011, pp. 142–158.

**256** S. J. Devitt, W. J. Munro, and K. Nemoto, "Quantum error correction for beginners," *Reports on Progress in Physics*, vol. 76, no. 7, 2013.

**257** J. Łodyga, P. Mazurek, A. Grudka, and M. Horodecki, "Simple scheme for encoding and decoding a qubit in unknown state for various topological codes," *Scientific Reports*, vol. 5, 2015.

**258** D. Chandra, Z. Babar, H. V. Nguyen, D. Alanis, P. Botsinis, S. X. Ng, and L. Hanzo, "Quantum topological error correction codes are capable of improving the performance of Clifford gates," *IEEE Access*, vol. 7, pp. 121 501–121 529, 2019.

**259** A. M. Steane, "Overhead and noise threshold of fault-tolerant quantum error correction," *Physical Review A*, vol. 68, no. 4, 2003.

**260** H. Bombin and M. A. Martin-Delgado, "Quantum measurements and gates by code deformation," *Journal of Physics A: Mathematical and Theoretical*, vol. 42, no. 9, 2009.

**261** H. Bombin, "Clifford gates by code deformation," *New Journal of Physics*, vol. 13, no. 4, 2011.

**262** J. T., Anderson, G. Duclos-Cianci, and D. Poulin, "Fault-tolerant conversion between the Steane and Reed-Muller quantum codes," *Physical review letters*, vol. 113, no. 8, 2014.

**263** C. Vuillot, L. Lao, B. Criger, C. G. Almudever, K. Bertels, and B. Terhal, "Code deformation and lattice surgery are gauge fixing," *New Journal of Physics*, vol. 21, no. 3, 2019.

**264** A. G. Fowler, A. M. Stephens, and P. Groszkowski, "High-threshold universal quantum computation on the surface code," *Physical Review A*, vol. 80, no. 5, 2009.

**265** D. S. Wang, A. G. Fowler, and L. C. Hollenberg, "Surface code quantum computing with error rates over 1%," *Physical Review A*, vol. 83, no. 2, 2011.

**266** A. G. Fowler, M. Mariantoni, J. M. Martinis, and A. N. Cleland, "Surface codes: Towards practical large-scale quantum computation," *Physical Review A*, vol. 86, no. 3, 2012.

**267** T. A. Brun, Y.-C. Zheng, K.-C. Hsu, J. Job, and C.-Y. Lai, "Teleportation-based fault-tolerant quantum computation in multi-qubit large block codes," *arXiv preprint arXiv:1504.03913*, 2015.

**268** A. J. Landahl, J. T., Anderson, and P. R. Rice, "Fault-tolerant quantum computing with color codes," *arXiv preprint arXiv:1108.5738*, 2011.

**269** F. J. MacWilliams and N. J. A. Sloane, *The theory of error-correcting codes*. Elsevier, 1977.

**270** J. I. Hall, *Notes on coding theory*. FreeTechBooks, 2003.

**271** M. M. Christiansen, K. R. Duffy, F. du Pin Calmon, and M. Médard, "Multi-user guesswork and brute force security," *IEEE Transactions on Information Theory*, vol. 61, no. 12, pp. 6876–6886, 2015.

**272** M. M. Christiansen and K. R. Duffy, "Guesswork, large deviations, and Shannon entropy," *IEEE Transactions on Information Theory*, vol. 59, no. 2, pp. 796–802, 2012.

**273** K. R. Duffy, J. Li, and M. Médard, "Capacity-achieving guessing random additive noise decoding," *IEEE Transactions on Information Theory*, vol. 65, no. 7, pp. 4023–4040, 2019.

**274** K. R. Duffy, M. Médard, and W. An, "Guessing random additive noise decoding with symbol reliability information (SRGRAND)," *IEEE Transactions on Communications*, vol. 70, no. 1, pp. 3–18, 2021.

**275** K. R. Duffy, E. P. Gabhart, and M. Médard, "Quantized guessing random additive noise decoding," *arXiv preprint arXiv:2203.13552*, 2022.

**276** A. Rényi, "On measures of entropy and information," in *Proceedings of the Fourth Berkeley Symposium on Mathematical Statistics and Probability: Contributions to the Theory of Statistics*, vol. 4. University of California Press, 1961, pp. 547–562.

**277** A. Riaz, V. Bansal, A. Solomon, W. An, Q. Liu, K. Galligan, K. R. Duffy, M. Medard, and R. T. Yazicigil, "Multi-code multi-rate universal maximum likelihood decoder using GRAND," in *Proceedings of IEEE 47th European Solid-State Circuits Conference (ESSCIRC)*. IEEE, 2021, pp. 239–246.

**278** D. Chandra, Z. B. K. Egilmez, Y. Xiong, S. X. Ng, R. G. Maunder, and L. Hanzo, "Universal decoding of quantum stabilizer codes via classical guesswork," *IEEE Access*, vol. 11, pp. 19 059–19 072, 2023.

**279** A. M. Steane, "Simple quantum error-correcting codes," *Physical Review A*, vol. 54, no. 6, 1996.

**280** M. Grassl and T. Beth, "Quantum BCH codes," *arXiv preprint quant-ph/9910060*, 1999.

**281** Z. Babar, Z. B. K. Egilmez, L. Xiang, D. Chandra, R. G. Maunder, S. X. Ng, and L. Hanzo, "Polar codes and their quantum-domain counterparts," *IEEE Communications Surveys & Tutorials*, vol. 22, no. 1, pp. 123–155, 2019.

**282** D. Chandra, Z. Babar, S. X. Ng, and L. Hanzo, "Near-hashing-bound multiple-rate quantum turbo short-block codes," *IEEE Access*, vol. 7, pp. 52 712–52 730, 2019.

**283** A. Solomon, K. R. Duffy, and M. Médard, "Soft maximum likelihood decoding using GRAND," in *Proceedings of IEEE International Conference on Communications (ICC)*. IEEE, 2020, pp. 1–6.

**284** K. R. Duffy, W. An, and M. Médard, "Ordered reliability bits guessing random additive noise decoding," *IEEE Transactions on Signal Processing*, vol. 70, pp. 4528–4542, 2022.

**285** D. M. Nguyen and S. Kim, "Quantum stabilizer codes construction from Hermitian self-orthogonal codes over GF (4)," *Journal of Communications and Networks*, vol. 20, no. 3, pp. 309–315, 2018.

**286** Z. Yi, Z. Liang, and X. Wang, "Quantum polar stabilizer codes based on polarization of pure quantum channel are bad stabilizer codes for quantum computing," *arXiv preprint arXiv:2204.11655*, 2022.

**287** W. K. Wootters and W. H. Zurek, "A single quantum cannot be cloned," *Nature*, vol. 299, no. 5886, pp. 802–803, Oct. 1982. [Online]. Available: http://dx.doi.org/10.1038/299802a0

**288** R. Cleve, "Quantum stabilizer codes and classical linear codes," *Phys. Rev. A*, vol. 55, pp. 4054–4059, Jun 1997. [Online]. Available: http://link.aps.org/doi/10.1103/PhysRevA.55.4054

**289** S. Lloyd, "Capacity of the noisy quantum channel," *Phys. Rev. A*, vol. 55, pp. 1613–1622, Mar 1997. [Online]. Available: http://link.aps.org/doi/10.1103/PhysRevA.55.1613

**290** P. W. Shor, "The quantum channel capacity and coherent information," *Lecture Notes, MSRI Workshop on Quantum Computation*, 2002.

**291** I. Devetak, "The private classical capacity and quantum capacity of a quantum channel," *IEEE Transactions on Information Theory*, vol. 51, no. 1, pp. 44–55, Jan 2005.

**292** C. Berrou, A. Glavieux, and P. Thitimajshima, "Near Shannon limit error-correcting coding and decoding: Turbo-codes. 1," in *IEEE International Conference on Communications*, vol. 2, May 1993, pp. 1064–1070.

**293** Z. Babar, S. X. Ng, and L. Hanzo, "EXIT-chart-aided near-capacity quantum turbo code design," *IEEE Transactions on Vehicular Technology*, vol. 64, no. 3, pp. 866–875, Mar. 2015.

**294** D. P. DiVincenzo, P. W. Shor, and J. A. Smolin, "Quantum-channel capacity of very noisy channels," *Phys. Rev. A*, vol. 57, pp. 830–839, Feb 1998. [Online]. Available: http://link.aps.org/doi/10.1103/PhysRevA.57.830

**295** G. Smith and J. A. Smolin, "Degenerate quantum codes for Pauli channels," *Phys. Rev. Lett.*, vol. 98, p. 030501, Jan 2007. [Online]. Available: http://link.aps.org/doi/10.1103/PhysRevLett.98.030501

**296** J. Dehaene and B. De Moor, "Clifford group, stabilizer states, and linear and quadratic operations over GF(2)," *Phys. Rev. A*, vol. 68, p. 042318, Oct 2003. [Online]. Available: http://link.aps.org/doi/10.1103/PhysRevA.68.042318

**297** S. Ten Brink, "Rate one-half code for approaching the Shannon limit by 0.1 dB," *Electronics Letters*, vol. 36, no. 15, pp. 1293–1294, 2000.

**298** L. Kong, S. X. Ng, R. Maunder, and L. Hanzo, "Maximum-throughput irregular distributed space-time code for near-capacity cooperative communications," *IEEE Transactions on Vehicular Technology*, vol. 59, no. 3, pp. 1511–1517, 2010.

**299** S. Ibi, T. Matsumoto, R. Thoma, S. Sampei, and N. Morinaga, "EXIT chart-aided adaptive coding for multilevel BICM with turbo equalization in frequency-selective MIMO channels," *IEEE Transactions on Vehicular Technology*, vol. 56, no. 6, pp. 3757–3769, 2007.

**300** A. Grant, "Convergence of non-binary iterative decoding," in *IEEE Global Telecommunications Conference*, vol. 2, 2001, pp. 1058–1062 vol. 2.

**301** M. M. Wilde, *Quantum Information Theory*. Cambridge University Press, May 2013. [Online]. Available: http://arxiv.org/abs/1106.1445

**302** D. P. Divincenzo, D. Leung, and B. Terhal, "Quantum data hiding," *IEEE Transactions on Information Theory*, vol. 48, no. 3, pp. 580–598, Mar 2002.

303 E. Rains, "Nonbinary quantum codes," *IEEE Transactions on Information Theory*, vol. 45, no. 6, pp. 1827–1832, 1999.

304 M. Abbara and J.-P. Tillich, "Quantum turbo codes with unbounded minimum distance and excellent error-reducing performance," in *Proceedings of IEEE Information Theory Workshop (ITW)*, 2011, pp. 252–256.

305 Z. Babar, H. V. Nguyen, P. Botsinis, D. Alanis, D. Chandra, S. X. Ng, and L. Hanzo, "Serially concatenated unity-rate codes improve quantum codes without coding-rate reduction," *IEEE Communications Letters*, vol. 20, no. 10, pp. 1916–1919, 2016.

306 S. Benedetto, D. Divsalar, G. Montorsi, and F. Pollara, "Serial concatenation of interleaved codes: Performance analysis, design, and iterative decoding," *IEEE Transactions on Information Theory*, vol. 44, no. 3, pp. 909–926, 1998.

307 I. Land, "Reliability information in channel decoding," Ph.D. dissertation, Christian-Albrechts-University of Kiel, 2005.

308 L. Hanzo and Nasruminallah, "Short block codes for guaranteed convergence in soft-bit assisted iterative joint source and channel decoding," *Electronics Letters*, vol. 44, no. 22, pp. 1315–1316, 2008.

309 L. Hanzo and Nasruminallah, "EXIT-chart optimized short block codes for iterative joint source and channel decoding in H. 264 video telephony," *IEEE Transactions on Vehicular Technology*, vol. 58, no. 8, pp. 4306–4315, 2009.

310 J. Hagenauer, "Rate-compatible punctured convolutional codes (RCPC codes) and their applications," *IEEE Transactions on Communications*, vol. 36, no. 4, pp. 389–400, 1988.

311 P. K. Sarvepalli, A. Klappenecker, and M. Rötteler, "Asymmetric quantum codes: constructions, bounds and performance," *Proceedings of the Royal Society of London A: Mathematical, Physical and Engineering Sciences*, vol. 465, no. 2105, pp. 1645–1672, 2009.

312 L. Wang, K. Feng, S. Ling, and C. Xing, "Asymmetric quantum codes: Characterization and constructions," *IEEE Transactions on Information Theory*, vol. 56, no. 6, pp. 2938–2945, 2010.

313 A. Banerjee, F. Vatta, B. Scanavino, and D. J. Costello, "Nonsystematic turbo codes," *IEEE Transactions on Communications*, vol. 53, no. 11, pp. 1841–1849, 2005.

314 T. A. Summers and S. G. Wilson, "SNR mismatch and on-line estimation in turbo decoding," *IEEE Transactions on Communications*, vol. 46, pp. 421–423, 1998.

315 A. Worm, P. Hoeher, and N. Wehn, "Turbo-decoding without SNR estimation," *IEEE Communications Letters*, vol. 4, no. 6, pp. 193–195, 2000.

316 M. A. Khalighi, "Effect of mismatched SNR on the performance of log-MAP turbo detector," *IEEE Transactions on Vehicular Technology*, vol. 52, no. 5, pp. 1386–1397, 2003.

317 Y. Xie, J. Li, R. Malaney, and J. Yuan, "Channel identification and its impact on quantum LDPC code performance," in *Proceedings of the Australian Communications Theory Workshop (AusCTW)*, 2012, pp. 140–144.

318 Y. Xie, J. Li, R. Malaney, and J. Yuan, "Improved quantum LDPC decoding strategies for the misidentified quantum depolarization channel," in *Proceedings of the 24th European Signal Processing Conference (EUSIPCO)*, 2016, pp. 493–497.

319 Y. Fujiwara, "Instantaneous quantum channel estimation during quantum information processing," *arXiv preprint arXiv:1405.6267*, 2014.

320 T. C. Bschorr, D. G. Fischer, and M. Freyberger, "Channel estimation with noisy entanglement," *Physics Letters A*, vol. 292, no. 1, pp. 15–22, 2001.

321 D. Collins and J. Stephens, "Depolarizing-channel parameter estimation using noisy initial states," *Physical Review A*, vol. 92, no. 3, 2015.

322 E. Dumitrescu and T. S. Humble, "Direct characterization of quantum dynamics with noisy ancilla," *Physical Review A*, vol. 92, no. 5, 2015.

323 V. Toto-Zarasoa, A. Roumy, and C. Guillemot, "Maximum likelihood BSC parameter estimation for the Slepian-Wolf problem," *IEEE Communications Letters*, vol. 15, no. 2, pp. 232–234, 2011.

324 G. Lechner and C. Pacher, "Estimating channel parameters from the syndrome of a linear code," *IEEE Communications Letters*, vol. 17, no. 11, pp. 2148–2151, 2013.

325 J. Combes, C. Ferrie, C. Cesare, M. Tiersch, G. Milburn, H. J. Briegel, and C. M. Caves, "In-situ characterization of quantum devices with error correction," *arXiv preprint arXiv:1405.5656*, 2014.

326 G. Cariolaro and G. Pierobon, "Performance of quantum data transmission systems in the presence of thermal noise," *IEEE Transactions on Communications*, vol. 58, no. 2, pp. 623–630, 2010.

**327** A. S. Cacciapuoti, M. Caleffi, R. Van Meter, and L. Hanzo, "When entanglement meets classical communications: Quantum teleportation for the Quantum Internet," *IEEE Transactions on Communications (Invited Paper)*, vol. 68, no. 6, pp. 3808–3833, 2020.

**328** S. Shao, P. Hailes, T.-Y. Wang, J.-Y. Wu, R. G. Maunder, B. M. Al-Hashimi, and L. Hanzo, "Survey of turbo, LDPC, and polar decoder ASIC implementations," *IEEE Communications Surveys & Tutorials*, vol. 21, no. 3, pp. 2309–2333, 2019.

**329** Z. B. K. Egilmez, L. Xiang, R. G. Maunder, and L. Hanzo, "The development, operation and performance of the 5G polar codes," *IEEE Communications Surveys & Tutorials*, vol. 22, no. 1, pp. 96–122, 2019.

**330** V. Bioglio, C. Condo, and I. Land, "Design of polar codes in 5G new radio," *IEEE Communications Surveys & Tutorials*, vol. 23, no. 1, pp. 29–40, 2020.

**331** Y. Fang, Y. Bu, P. Chen, F. C. Lau, and S. Al Otaibi, "Irregular-mapped protograph LDPC-coded modulation: A bandwidth-efficient solution for 6G-enabled mobile networks," *IEEE Transactions on Intelligent Transportation Systems*, vol. Early Access, pp. 1–14, 2021.

**332** F. R. F. Pereira, G. G. La Guardia, and F. M. de Assis, "Classical and quantum convolutional codes derived from algebraic geometry codes," *IEEE Transactions on Communications*, vol. 67, no. 1, pp. 73–82, 2018.

**333** S. Ten Brink, "Convergence of iterative decoding," *Electronics Letters*, vol. 35, no. 10, pp. 806–808, 1999.

**334** M. Tüchler, "EXIT charts of irregular codes," in *Proceedings of the Conference on Information Sciences and Systems*, 2002, pp. 748–753.

**335** D. Chandra, S. X. Ng, and L. Hanzo, "EXIT-chart aided design of irregular multiple-rate quantum turbo block codes," *IEEE Access*, vol. 11, pp. 96 177–96 195, 2023.

**336** J. Etxezarreta Martinez, P. M. Crespo, and J. Garcia-Frías, "On the performance of interleavers for quantum turbo codes," *Entropy*, vol. 21, no. 7, pp. 1–9, 2019.

**337** J. E. Martinez, P. Fuentes, P. M. Crespo, and J. Garcia-Frías, "Pauli channel online estimation protocol for quantum turbo codes," in *Proceedings of IEEE International Conference on Quantum Computing and Engineering (QCE)*. IEEE, 2020, pp. 102–108.

**338** J. E. Martinez, P. M. Crespo, and J. Garcia-Frías, "Depolarizing channel mismatch and estimation protocols for quantum turbo codes," *Entropy*, vol. 21, no. 12, pp. 1133–1147, 2019.

**339** Y.-J. Wang, Z.-Y. Xiao, Y. Zhang, X.-Y. Xiong, and S. Shi, "Construction of multiple-rate quantum LDPC codes sharing one scalable stabilizer circuit," *IEEE Transactions on Communications*, vol. 71, no. 2, pp. 1071–1082, 2023.

**340** S. Yang and R. Calderbank, "Quantum spatially-coupled codes," *arXiv preprint arXiv:2305.00137*, 2023.

**341** X.-J. Li, D. Pan, G.-L. Long, and L. Hanzo, "Single-photon-memory measurement-device-independent quantum secure direct communication — Part I: Its fundamentals and evolution," *IEEE Communications Letters*, vol. 27, no. 4, pp. 1055–1059, 2023.

**342** X.-J. Li, D. Pan, G.-L. Long, and L. Hanzo, "Single-photon-memory measurement-device-independent quantum secure direct communication — Part II: A practical protocol and its secrecy capacity," *IEEE Communications Letters*, vol. 27, no. 4, pp. 1060–1064, 2023.

**343** D. Chandra, A. S. Cacciapuoti, M. Caleffi, and L. Hanzo, "Direct quantum communications in the presence of realistic noisy entanglement," *IEEE Transactions on Communications*, vol. 70, no. 1, pp. 469–484, 2021.

**344** D. Cruz, F. A. Monteiro, and B. C. Coutinho, "Quantum error correction via noise guessing decoding," *arXiv preprint arXiv:2208.02744*, 2022.

**345** D. MacKay, "Good error-correcting codes based on very sparse matrices," *IEEE Transactions on Information Theory*, vol. 45, no. 2, pp. 399–431, Mar 1999.

**346** S.-Y. Chung, J. Forney, G.D., T. Richardson, and R. Urbanke, "On the design of low-density parity-check codes within 0.0045 dB of the Shannon limit," *IEEE Communications Letters*, vol. 5, no. 2, pp. 58–60, Feb 2001.

**347** N. Bonello, S. Chen, and L. Hanzo, "Low-density parity-check codes and their rateless relatives," *IEEE Communications Surveys Tutorials*, vol. 13, no. 1, pp. 3–26, First 2011.

**348** N. Bonello, S. Chen, and L. Hanzo, "Design of low-density parity-check codes," *IEEE Vehicular Technology Magazine*, vol. 6, no. 4, pp. 16–23, Dec 2011.

**349** Z. Babar, P. Botsinis, D. Alanis, S. X. Ng, and L. Hanzo, "High-rate QLDPC codes from row-circulant classical LDPCs," *IEEE Communications Letters (to be submitted)*.

**350** H. Wymeersch, F. Penna, and V. Savic, "Uniformly reweighted belief propagation: A factor graph approach," in *IEEE International Symposium on Information Theory Proceedings*, Jul. 2011, pp. 2000–2004.

**351** H. Wymeersch, F. Penna, and V. Savic, "Uniformly reweighted belief propagation for estimation and detection in wireless networks," *IEEE Transactions on Wireless Communications*, vol. 11, no. 4, pp. 1587–1595, Apr. 2012.

**352** Y. Kou, S. Lin, and M. Fossorier, "Low-density parity-check codes based on finite geometries: a rediscovery and new results," *IEEE Transactions on Information Theory*, vol. 47, no. 7, pp. 2711–2736, Nov. 2001.

**353** B. Vasic and O. Milenkovic, "Combinatorial constructions of low-density parity-check codes for iterative decoding," *IEEE Transactions on Information Theory*, vol. 50, no. 6, pp. 1156–1176, jun. 2004.

**354** B. Ammar, B. Honary, Y. Kou, J. Xu, and S. Lin, "Construction of low-density parity-check codes based on balanced incomplete block designs," *IEEE Transactions on Information Theory*, vol. 50, no. 6, pp. 1257–1269, jun. 2004.

**355** S. ten Brink, "Code doping for triggering iterative decoding convergence," in *IEEE International Symposium on Information Theory*, 2001, pp. 235–.

**356** M. Hagiwara and H. Imai, "Quantum quasi-cyclic LDPC codes," in *arXiv:quant-ph/0701020v4*, Aug 2010.

**357** I. Andriyanova, D. Maurice, and J.-P. Tillich, "Spatially coupled quantum LDPC codes," in *IEEE Information Theory Workshop*, Sept 2012, pp. 327–331.

**358** D. Maurice, J.-P. Tillich, and I. Andriyanova, "A family of quantum codes with performances close to the hashing bound under iterative decoding," in *IEEE International Symposium on Information Theory Proceedings*, Jul. 2013, pp. 907–911.

**359** T. Camara, H. Ollivier, and J.-P. Tillich, "Constructions and performance of classes of quantum LDPC codes," *arXiv:quant-ph/0502086v2*, 2005.

**360** M.-H. Hsieh, W.-T. Yen, and L.-Y. Hsu, "Performance of entanglement-assisted quantum LDPC codes constructed from finite geometries," *http://arxiv-web3.library.cornell.edu/abs/0906.5532v1*, 2009.

**361** M.-H. Hsieh, W.-T. Yen, and L.-Y. Hsu, "High performance entanglement-assisted quantum LDPC codes need little entanglement," *Information Theory, IEEE Transactions on*, vol. 57, no. 3, pp. 1761–1769, Mar. 2011.

**362** I. B. Djordjevic, "Photonic entanglement-assisted quantum low-density parity-check encoders and decoders," *Opt. Lett.*, vol. 35, no. 9, pp. 1464–1466, May 2010. [Online]. Available: http://ol.osa.org/abstract.cfm?URI=ol-35-9-1464

**363** Y. Fujiwara, D. Clark, P. Vandendriessche, M. De Boeck, and V. Tonchev, "Entanglement-assisted quantum low-density parity-check codes," *Phys. Rev. A*, vol. 82, p. 042338, Oct 2010. [Online]. Available: http://link.aps.org/doi/10.1103/PhysRevA.82.042338

**364** Y. Fujiwara, A. Gruner, and P. Vandendriessche, "High-rate quantum low-density parity-check codes assisted by reliable qubits," *IEEE Transactions on Information Theory*, vol. 61, no. 4, pp. 1860–1878, Apr. 2015.

**365** T. Richardson, M. Shokrollahi, and R. Urbanke, "Design of capacity-approaching irregular low-density parity-check codes," *IEEE Transactions on Information Theory*, vol. 47, no. 2, pp. 619–637, Feb 2001.

**366** Y. Fujiwara, "Quantum error correction via less noisy qubits," *Phys. Rev. Lett.*, vol. 110, p. 170501, Apr 2013. [Online]. Available: http://link.aps.org/doi/10.1103/PhysRevLett.110.170501

**367** D. J. MacKay, *Information Theory, Inference, and Learning Algorithms*. Cambridge University Press, 2003.

**368** E. Berlekamp, R. McEliece, and H. Van Tilborg, "On the inherent intractability of certain coding problems (corresp.)," *IEEE Transactions on Information Theory*, vol. 24, no. 3, pp. 384–386, May 1978.

**369** T. Richardson and R. Urbanke, "The capacity of low-density parity-check codes under message-passing decoding," *IEEE Transactions on Information Theory*, vol. 47, no. 2, pp. 599–618, Feb 2001.

**370** S. Johnson and S. R. Weller, "Regular low-density parity-check codes from combinatorial designs," in *IEEE Information Theory Workshop*, 2001, pp. 90–92.

**371** S. Johnson and S. R. Weller, "A family of irregular LDPC codes with low encoding complexity," *IEEE Communications Letters*, vol. 7, no. 2, pp. 79–81, Feb 2003.

**372** H. Park, S. Hong, J.-S. No, and D.-J. Shin, "Construction of high-rate regular quasi-cyclic LDPC codes based on cyclic difference families," *IEEE Transactions on Communications*, vol. 61, no. 8, pp. 3108–3113, Aug. 2013.

**373** R. Bose, "On the construction of balanced incomplete block designs," *Ann. Eugen*, vol. 9, pp. 353–399, 1939.

**374** W. Ryan and S. Lin, *Channel Codes: Classical and Modern*. Cambridge University Press, 2009. [Online]. Available: http://books.google.co.uk/books?id=n9BNngEACAAJ

**375** M. Wainwright, T. Jaakkola, and A. Willsky, "A new class of upper bounds on the log partition function," *IEEE Transactions on Information Theory*, vol. 51, no. 7, pp. 2313–2335, Jul. 2005.

**376** T. Roosta, M. Wainwright, and S. Sastry, "Convergence analysis of reweighted sum-product algorithms," *IEEE Transactions on Signal Processing*, vol. 56, no. 9, pp. 4293–4305, Sept 2008.

**377** J. Liu and R. de Lamare, "Knowledge-aided reweighted belief propagation decoding for regular and irregular LDPC codes with short blocks," in *International Symposium on Wireless Communication Systems*, Aug 2012, pp. 984–988.

**378** J. Liu and R. de Lamare, "Low-latency reweighted belief propagation decoding for LDPC codes," *IEEE Communications Letters*, vol. 16, no. 10, pp. 1660–1663, Oct. 2012.

**379** J. Liu, R. de Lamare, and H. Wymeersch, "Locally-optimized reweighted belief propagation for decoding finite-length LDPC codes," in *IEEE Wireless Communications and Networking Conference*, Apr. 2013, pp. 4311–4316.

**380** H. Wymeersch, F. Penna, V. Savic, and J. Zhao, "Comparison of reweighted message passing algorithms for LDPC decoding," in *IEEE International Conference on Communications*, Jun. 2013, pp. 3264–3269.

**381** I. Kremsky, M.-H. Hsieh, and T. A. Brun, "Classical enhancement of quantum-error-correcting codes," *Phys. Rev. A*, vol. 78, p. 012341, Jul 2008. [Online]. Available: http://link.aps.org/doi/10.1103/PhysRevA.78.012341

**382** M.-H. Hsieh and M. M. Wilde, "Entanglement-assisted communication of classical and quantum information," *IEEE Transactions on Information Theory*, vol. 56, no. 9, pp. 4682–4704, Sep. 2010.

**383** M.-H. Hsieh and M. M. Wilde, "Trading classical communication, quantum communication, and entanglement in quantum Shannon theory," *IEEE Transactions on Information Theory*, vol. 56, no. 9, pp. 4705–4730, Sep. 2010.

# Subject Index

# Author Index

## a



## b

## c



## d



## e



## f



## g

## m



## n



## o



## p